The Emergence of Ukraine

Self-Determination, Occupation, and War in Ukraine, 1917–1922

The Emergence of Ukraine

Self-Determination, Occupation, and War in Ukraine, 1917–1922

Wolfram Dornik, Georgiy Kasianov, Hannes Leidinger, Peter Lieb, Alexei Miller, Bogdan Musial, Vasyl Rasevych

Translated from the German
by Gus Fagan

KIYC CIUS
Canadian Institute of Ukrainian Studies Press
Edmonton 2015 Toronto

Canadian Institute of Ukrainian Studies Press

University of Alberta
Edmonton, Alberta
Canada T6G 2H8

University of Toronto
Toronto, Ontario
Canada M5T 1W5

ISBN 978-1-894865-40-1 (pbk.)

Library and Archives Canada Cataloguing in Publication

Dornik, Wolfram, 1978-, author
The emergence of Ukraine : self-determination, occupation, and war in Ukraine, 1917-1922 / Wolfram Dornik, Georgiy Kasianov, Hannes Leidinger, Peter Lieb, Alexei Miller, Bogdan Musial, Vasyl Rasevych ; translated from the German by Gus Fagan.

Partial translation of: Die Ukraine : zwischen selbstbestimmung und fremdherrschaft
1917-1922.
Includes bibliographical references and index.
ISBN 978-1-894865-40-1 (pbk.)

1. Ukraine--History--Revolution, 1917-1921. 2. Ukraine--History--Autonomy and independence movements. 3. Ukraine--History--1917-. I. Kasianov, H. V. (Heorhii Volodymyrovych), 1961-, author II. Lieb, Peter, 1974-, author III. Fagan, Gus, translator IV. Title.

DK508.832.D6713 2015 947.7′0841 C2015-900103-X

The translation and publication of this book has been funded by a generous grant from the Austrian Science Fund (FWF Der Wissenschafsfonds), Vienna, Austria. A grant for this book has also been provided by the Canadian Foundation of Ukrainian Studies.

Cover photo: Austro-Hungarian and Ukrainian soldiers on the railway, Kryvyi Rih, April 1918. (Reproduced with permission of the Heeresgeschichtliches Museum, Vienna).

Printed in Canada

Contents

List of Maps

[Page numbers following map titles refer to pages in the electronic files]

List of Illustrations

[Page numbers following map titles refer to pages in the electronic files]

Publisher's Preface

The publication of *The Emergence of Ukraine: Self-Determination, Occupation, and War in Ukraine, 1917–1922*, edited by Wolfram Dornik and others, is an important milestone in the long-standing efforts of the Canadian Institute of Ukrainian Studies and CIUS Press to research, publish, and disseminate information pertaining to Ukraine's struggle for independence in the years 1917–21. This was one of the most complex, as well as understudied, periods of twentieth-century European history, when the defeat of the Central Powers in the First World War and the collapse of the Austro-Hungarian and Russian empires made it possible for the "non-historical nations" of Central and Eastern Europe to undertake the creation of independent states.

The first CIUS Press book dedicated to this complex subject, Michael Palij's monograph *The Ukrainian-Polish Defensive Alliance, 1919–1921*, appeared in 1995. This book focused on the joint Ukrainian-Polish military operation against Soviet Russia, the causes of its failure, and the subsequent Soviet offensive in Poland and its defeat. Against the background of these developments, the book presented a much broader picture of the political situation in Ukraine at that momentous time and of the difficult Polish-Ukrainian relations that then prevailed. The book presented the biographies of two national leaders, Symon Petliura and Józef Piłsudski, and recounted the war of 1918–19 in Galicia between Poland and the Western Ukrainian People's Republic. It went on to discuss in detail the Polish-Ukrainian Treaty of Warsaw (1920) and the Polish-Soviet Treaty of Riga (1921), which ended the Polish-Soviet war. The book also included a discussion of the fate of the Ukrainian Army after the end of the conflict, as well as Symon Petliura's exile and assassination in Paris in 1926.

This book was soon followed by Anna Procyk's monograph *Russian Nationalism and Ukraine: The Nationality Policy of the Volunteer Army during the Civil War*, published later in 1995. It focused on the nationality policy of the Russian Volunteer Army and the Russian liberals who dominated its policy-making. Challenging the generally accepted view that the character and aims of the White movement were mainly anti-Bolshevik or even restorationist, Procyk showed that the concept of "One, Indivisible Russia" was central to the Volunteer Army's ideology and contributed to its failure. She persuasively demonstrated that the political program of the liberal Russian intellectuals who dominated the Volunteer Army's Political Center reinforced General Anton Denikin's refusal to deal with the independent Ukrainian governments of 1918–19 and his hostility to the idea of a Russo-Ukrainian federation and/or anti-Bolshevik alliance. In essence, the book argued that the Volunteer Army failed to defeat the Bolsheviks because it was unwilling and unable to come to terms with the Ukrainian question and because, at critical junctures during the war, its struggle against an independent Ukraine overshadowed its struggle against the Bolsheviks.

In 2009, CIUS Press published an English translation of the monograph *Western Ukraine in Conflict with Poland and Bolshevism, 1918–1923* by a participant in the events analyzed, Vasyl Kuchabsky, whom a renowned specialist on modern Ukraine, Ivan Lysiak-Rudnytsky, called "the most interesting historian of the Ukrainian revolution." Originally published in German in Berlin in 1934, this monograph remains one of the most comprehensive accounts of the political, military, and diplomatic aspects of the Western Ukrainian struggle for independence. Although the central issues of this study were Polish-Ukrainian relations and the Ukrainian-Polish War in Galicia (1918–19), Kuchabsky also examined state-building in the Western Ukrainian People's Republic and, to some extent, in the Ukrainian People's Republic, as well as relations between the two republics. Making extensive use of the historical materials available at the time, he analyzed the Ukrainian-Polish conflict within the broader context of European politics, the Paris Peace Conference, the interests of the Allied powers, and the Russian attitude toward Ukrainian independence.

Apart from book-length studies of the revolutionary period of 1917–21 in Ukraine, CIUS Press published several important essays on the subject in its collections on Russian-Ukrainian, Polish-Ukrainian, German-Ukrainian, and Jewish-Ukrainian relations. Other articles devoted to the period appeared over the years in the *Journal of Ukrainian Studies* published by CIUS. Moreover, various CIUS centres and programs cosponsored several conferences on the revolutionary period (such as the conference on "The First World War: The Ukrainian Dimension" held in Lviv on 12–14 September 2014, cosponsored by the Petro Jacyk Program for the Study of Modern Ukrainian History and Society at CIUS), as well as on related subjects (such as the conference on "Canada, the Great War and the Internment of Enemy Aliens, 1914–1920," held in Banff, Alberta, on 17–18 October 2014 and cosponsored by the Kule Centre for Ukrainian Canadian Studies at CIUS).

Currently, the Peter Jacyk Centre for Ukrainian Historical Research at CIUS and CIUS Press are preparing for publication Pavlo

Khrystiuk's *Comments and Materials on the History of the Ukrainian Revolution, 1917–1920*, edited by a prominent specialist in the field, Professor Mark von Hagen. This will be another important study of the collapse of the Russian Empire, Ukrainian state-building, and the Ukrainian-Soviet War to appear in English.

The present volume, a slightly condensed version of the German-language *Die Ukraine zwischen Selbstbestimmung und Fremdherrschaft 1917–1922* (Graz, 2011), marks an important new stage of our work in this area. It initiates a promising cooperative endeavor between CIUS and several prominent historians from Austria, Germany, Ukraine, and Russia, making available to English-speaking readers a wealth of hitherto unknown historical information based on the thorough research and evaluation of documents from military archives in Vienna, Freiburg, Berlin, Munich, and Stuttgart. While I appreciate the high scholarly quality of all the contributions to this book and commend their authors, I am particularly grateful to Wolfram Dornik for organizing this project and approaching CIUS Press with an offer of cooperation. All texts were very competently translated from the German by Gus Fagan and carefully edited by Myroslav Yurkevich. Last but not least, I would like to express my gratitude to the Austrian Science Fund (*Fonds für Wissenschaft und Forschung*, FWF), whose generous financial support made this publication possible, and to the Canadian Foundation for Ukrainian Studies for providing additional funding. It is thanks to the contributions of these individuals and institutions that we are now able to present English-speaking readers with this new perspective on the historical context of Ukraine's struggle for independence during and after the First World War.

Marko Robert Stech

Editor's Preface

Since 2011, when the German-language edition of this book was published, historians have actively pursued research on the period under discussion here. Innumerable publications have appeared in conjunction with the centennial of the First World War, presenting new interpretations of the subject. In countries where the Great War had been a neglected topic, the centennial has stimulated considerable scholarly output. This also applies to Ukraine: many new sources have been uncovered and new questions raised. We are thus witnesses to a re-examination of the "great seminal catastrophe" (George F. Kennan) and the "new time of troubles" (Manfred Hildermeier) in Ukraine and Eastern Europe.

The integration of all this recent research into our volume would have required a new book, delaying its publication in English. The present English translation is a slightly condensed version of the German original; a Ukrainian translation is also in preparation and will be published soon.

The project that produced this book has led to broader study of the subject. A new research project was undertaken to investigate the experience of warfare on the Eastern Front in the course of the First World War. This project, conducted at the Ludwig Boltzmann Institute for Research on the Consequences of War from 2011 to 2014, was funded (like its predecessor) by the Austrian Science Fund (*Fonds für Wissenschaft und Forschung*, FWF; P-23070). It also involved research on Ukraine, and we benefited from the methodological and organizational experience of the previous project. A further result of the project was broader coverage of the subject. Although historical research on Ukraine is still underdeveloped, especially in German-speaking countries, and there is still too little cooperation with Ukrainian scholars and institutions, we hope to have improved this to a modest extent.

Translation is a lengthy process requiring the assistance and goodwill of many people and institutions. As the scholarly supervisor of the research project that produced the German version of this book, I wish to express my deepest gratitude to them. The FWF funded the translation and printing of the English version (PUB 46-V18). I also want to highlight the contribution of our partners at the Canadian Institute of Ukrainian Studies at the University of Alberta. Without their willingness to integrate this translation into their publications program and their great commitment to the volume, it would not have been possible to produce it with such extraordinary scholarly diligence. I also wish to thank Marko Robert Stech for managing the project on behalf of CIUS, Gus Fagan for translating the book, and Myroslav Yurkevich for his editing of the text. I am grateful to Bernhard Bachinger for his editorial assistance in Austria. Finally, I want to express my thanks to the authors, who reviewed the translated texts of their contributions and supported us throughout the process. Their enthusiasm has been indispensable to the success of this enterprise, offering a fine example of how transnational projects can succeed, not only in the field of scholarly research but beyond.

Wolfram Dornik
Graz, October 2014

Introduction

Wolfram Dornik

It is still the case, especially in the German-speaking world, that the First World War, in both public and academic perception, is overshadowed by the events of the Second World War and the Holocaust. The events of 1914 to 1918 appear marginal when compared with the incredible scope of the murder and persecution of the European Jews, the crimes against humanity perpetrated by the National Socialists, and their responsibility for the Second World War and its destructive consequences. The Stalinist crimes committed between the 1920s and the early 1950s, as yet inadequately analyzed, also overshadow those that had gone before. The view is gaining ground in academic research that the fundamental preconditions for fascism, Nazism, and Stalinism are to be found in the events of the First World War.[1] This includes not just the postwar order established in Paris. Many states considered that order unjust and demanded its revision. Recent research suggests that the events following the war were influenced much more decisively by soldiers' experience of extreme violence on the front, the total mobilization of society in the warring states, radical nationalism, the removal of restrictions on violence against the civilian population, hunger, and increasing social inequality in the traumatized societies. In addition, research into the Eastern Front in the First World War was and still is overshadowed internationally by research into the war on the Western Front. The same applies to other theaters of war, such as Italy, Southeastern Europe, the Caucasus, the Near East, Africa, and the war at sea.

We thought it especially important, therefore, to undertake a detailed study of one as yet inadequately researched occupation from the final year of the First World War—the occupation of Ukraine by the Central Powers in 1918. It would allow us to study all the issues mentioned over a longer period, such as nationalist pressure in East European societies and its effects on political discourse, the cohesion of social groups influenced by the experience or practice of massive violence, the treatment of the civilian population by indigenous or

---

1 Alan Kramer, *Dynamic of Destruction: Culture and Mass Killing in the First World War* (Oxford and New York, 2007); Vejas Gabriel Liulevicius, *War Land on the Eastern Front: Culture, National Identity, and German Occupation in World War I* (Cambridge, 2000).

foreign troops and by irregular armed groups, and the international state system of Eastern Europe, which was shaken by the upheavals of 1917–18 and the accompanying border changes.

Another central theme in recent research on the First World War is the questioning of traditional chronologies. Chronological divisions are particularly difficult in the case of East European conflicts.[2] The declarations of war in July/August 1914 obviously mark the beginning. The end of the war, however, is fluid. Did it end with the exit from the war of one of the main players on the Eurasian continent, the Russian Empire, or with the February Revolution of 1917, the December 1917 truce of Brest-Litovsk, or the Brest-Litovsk peace treaties of February and March 1918? Or did the First World War end with the truce treaties signed by the Entente with Austria-Hungary and Germany in November 1918? Throughout that whole year there were battles and occupations in Eastern Europe that went on well after 1918 and continued into the 1920s, such as the *Freikorps* (Free Corps) battles in the Baltics, the Ukrainian-Soviet war, and the Polish-Russian war.[3] Of course, most of the soldiers who had done the fighting found themselves "at home" from the turn of the year 1918–19. But in the following months "peace" did not mean "the absence of war." War and armed conflict still dominated those areas for a long time.[4] The usual periodization of the twentieth century also needs to be questioned, and other well-established concepts need to be looked at, such as Eric Hobsbawm's "short twentieth century"[5] (1914/17–1989/91) or Dan Diner's "thirty-year world civil war."[6]

We need to interpret developments after the First World War not so much as a break but as a continuity (George F. Kennan: "the great seminal catastrophe of this century").[7] The February Revolution of

---

2 Cf. Hannes Leidinger, "Knotenpunkte—Der historische Moment oder eine Geschichte der kurzen Dauer," in Verena Moritz and Hannes Leidinger, *Die Nacht des Kirpitschnikow. Eine andere Geschichte des Ersten Weltkriegs* (Vienna, 2006), 244–70; *The Eastern Front, 1914–1920: From Tannenberg to the Russo-Polish War,* ed. Michael Neiberg and David Jordan (London, 2008).

3 Neiberg and Jordan have made a significant contribution here: see *The Eastern Front, 1914–1920*, cited in the preceding footnote.

4 As Timothy Snyder also found with regard to 1939–40: see his *Bloodlands: Europe between Hitler and Stalin* (London, 2010).

5 Eric Hobsbawm, *Age of Extremes: The Short Twentieth Century* (London, 1994).

6 Dan Diner, *Das Jahrhundert verstehen: Eine universalhistorische Deutung* (Munich, 1999).

7 "Original catastrophe" (*Urkatastrophe*) is one of the metaphors used most frequently in connection with the First World War, although there are many who consider this term problematic: Wolfgang J. Mommsen, *Die Urkatastrophe Deutschlands. Der Erste Weltkrieg 1914–1918* (Stuttgart, 2002); see also the articles by Gerhard Hirschfeld and Aribert Reimann in *Aus Politik und Zeitgeschichte*, nos. 29–30 (2004).

1917 not only shattered the institutions and borders of the Russian Empire but also set in motion a social upheaval that would stamp the entire twentieth century with its conflict between communism and the "free Western world." The year 1918 was already clearly marked by this incipient dichotomy. The overwhelming majority of the states involved in the war opposed the stabilization and expansion of Bolshevik power. But the old lines of conflict were still in place, which meant that unity against the revolutionaries was not possible. The Whites, the Entente, the Central Powers, and the newly emerging states of Eastern Europe (Poland, Czechoslovakia, Ukraine, the Baltic states) were all anti-Bolshevik but for different reasons. For many, it was because they feared the restoration of Russian power, now under the guise of the red flag. For others, it was because, as bourgeois democratic or conservative military leaders, they felt threatened by the radical "left-wing" politics of the Bolsheviks. All of them also reacted differently to the perceived threat. The result, as the present volume makes clear, was a variety of realpolitik responses to the phenomenon of revolutionary Bolshevism, which was difficult to understand fully at the time.

The present study also makes it clear that traditional concepts and periodizations need to be rethought. Severe doubt is cast, for instance, on the concept of the "Russian Civil War." This conflict had many elements that went far beyond civil war, as Hannes Leidinger shows in the first section of this book. Many of the decisive interveners in this Russian "Civil" War, such as the Czechoslovak Legion, the armies of the Central Powers in the western parts of the Russian Empire, or the Entente troops in eastern Asia, Murmansk, or the Caucasus, were not citizens of the Russian Empire. Similarly, the conflicts over autonomy and secession in the peripheral regions of the old tsarist empire were centered around issues not typical of civil wars (even when secessionist movements are central factors in a civil war, as was the case in the American Civil War). These influences were so decisive that they cannot be treated as side effects but have to be part of the conceptualization.

What these considerations have in common is the need to confront the narrowness of traditional perspectives and chronologies. The present study cannot offer a resolution of this dilemma but is presented as a contribution to the debate. We attempt to offer a new approach to the chronology of the First World War that integrates European perspectives more strongly and takes transitional phases into account.

The Planning and Implementation of the Project

The present study is the product of a two-year project at the Ludwig Boltzmann Institute for Research on the Consequences of War under the title "The 1918 Occupation of Ukraine by the Central Powers" (P 21505-G18). It was financed by the Austrian Science Fund (FWF) and led by Stefan Karner. It was based on another project also led by Karner, entitled "The Economic and Social Consequences of the First World War for East Central Europe," financed by the Jubilee Fund of the Austrian National Bank. This earlier project had already encountered the 1918 occupation of Ukraine by the Central Powers and its consequences. With this topic in mind, we organized a workshop in April 2008, the contributions to which we published in German that same year in the institute's *Blaue Reihe* series.[8] The following year, in cooperation with the Bukovyna Center in Chernivtsi, we published the collection in Ukrainian. At the same time, we set up a successor project to deal with this subject in greater depth and place it in the general context of Eastern Europe between the outbreak of the First World War in 1914 and the founding of the Soviet Union in 1922. It was accepted by the FWF and begun in June 2009. From the very beginning, we saw the present study as a continuation of the earlier projects.

In view of the many overlaps between the different subjects and the close cooperation among the members of the project team, we decided to present the final study as a multi-author monograph. An arrangement according to subjects, in individually or collaboratively written chapters, seemed more compelling and informative because, with such an approach, the expertise of different individual participants, though with slightly different emphases, could then contribute to those subjects. We also opted for a collaborative project in order to strengthen the consistency of the work. Nevertheless, such an approach will still entail different styles, opinions, and responsibilities, which we wanted to acknowledge in the eventual format of the book.

As originally conceived, the central theme of the FWF project was the military occupation of Ukraine by German and Austro-Hungarian troops between February and November 1918. This section is the core of the present study. Wolfram Dornik and Peter Lieb deal with the concrete military events of the conquest, the suppression of uprisings,

---

8 *Die Besatzung der Ukraine 1918. Historischer Kontext – Forschungsstand – wirtschaftliche und soziale Folgen*, ed. Wolfram Dornik and Stefan Karner (Graz, 2008).

and the retreat. They also deal with the administration of what was not officially occupied territory, as well as the economic utilization of the country. They undertake an evaluation and reevaluation of the documents in military archives in Vienna, Freiburg, Berlin, Munich, and Stuttgart, as well as the memoir and heritage literature and existing academic publications. This is complemented by Vasyl Rasevych's contribution dealing with the internal Ukrainian perspective on the occupation, based on Ukrainian discourse. This core is then flanked by three chapters that place the occupation in a broader context. In the first chapter, Hannes Leidinger examines the Russian Revolution of 1917 and its military consequences until the beginning of the 1920s. Then Wolfram Dornik and Peter Lieb give an account of the eastern and Ukrainian policy of the Central Powers, which forms the basis for the chapters on the occupation in section 3.[9]

In the second section of the book, Georgiy Kasianov gives a concise account of internal developments in Ukraine between 1917 and 1922. He examines the numerous simplifications in the German and English academic literature, for instance, with regard to the Central Rada and the Hetmanate. Vasyl Rasevych closes this section with a chapter on Western Ukraine, a short-lived political experiment of central importance with regard to the successor states of the Habsburg Monarchy and the Polish-Ukrainian conflict.

The fourth and final section of this book is an analysis of the international context that formed the background to Ukraine's attempts to establish a state between 1914 and 1922. As we shall see, the central players in the Ukrainian question between 1914 and 1922 were Tsarist Russia, its Bolshevik/Soviet Russian successor, the Central Powers, France, Great Britain, the United States, and Poland. There was a significant difference in the methodological approach of Tsarist and Bolshevik Russia to the national question, but not in the fundamental claim to Russian power made by both regimes. The articles by Alexei Miller and Bogdan Musial seek to analyze these differences. Finally, the article by Hannes Leidinger and Wolfram Dornik is devoted to the Ukrainian policies of France, Great Britain, and the United States. Of course, both the United States and Great Britain pursued their own interests in Eastern Europe, which in both cases were predominantly economic and strategic. But it was France that saw itself here as the key player, with a central economic interest

9 In the English translation, Wolfram Dornik's survey of developments on the Eastern Front has been omitted for lack of space.

in Ukraine. It was fears of a German advance in Central Asia that prompted the Entente powers to become involved in the Russian and Ukrainian question.[10] We pay very little attention to Italy's Ukrainian policy because Rome, confronted by difficulties on its own front, was never able to develop the presence here that it might have hoped for.[11]

We thought it exceptionally important to examine not just the positions of the most important Central Powers and Entente states with regard to Ukraine but also those of other central actors. Among these, Poland was especially important because it had to fight, in the truest sense of the word, on its southern and southeastern borders with both new Ukrainian states at the end of 1918. Bogdan Musial demonstrates the dilemma of Polish politics, caught between the battle for Polish territory and the search for an ally in the struggle against the expansion of Russian power.[12]

This final section portrays the international network in which Ukrainian politics attempted to operate in order to approach the question of why Ukraine failed to win international support for its independence. What seems to emerge from this is that Ukraine found no allies because an independent Ukrainian state did not correspond to the interests of any of the great powers, and it was unable to achieve that goal alone.

The study ends with a comparison of the First and Second World Wars, a frequent topic in German and English academic debate. This comparison emerged and was recognized as a topic for research during the very first meetings of the project group. We therefore decided to integrate into our work a critical comparison of the occupations of 1918 and 1941–44. In this chapter, Wolfram Dornik, Georgiy Kasianov, and Peter Lieb identify ten factors that point to parallels and differences between the occupations and thereby make a contribution to the critical debate about continuity.

Of course, the themes addressed and outlined here do not illuminate all outstanding questions. In the present volume, we have not managed adequately to address such issues as the response of the Ukrainian population to the occupation during and after 1918, the attitude of the occupiers to Ukraine and to the East in general, the growth of Ukrainian national discourse, and the long-term economic

---

10 For the English translation, we have combined three chapters of the German edition here. Because the Entente states seldom shared a common position on the governments in St. Petersburg/Moscow and Kyiv, they were treated in separate chapters in that edition..

11 David Stevenson, *The First World War and International Politics* (Oxford and New York, 1991), 186–90.

12 The chapter on Switzerland's Ukrainian policy has been omitted from the English translation.

consequences of war, occupation, and revolution in Ukraine. The book frequently refers to but, because of its limited frame of reference, does not adequately discuss such issues as the biographical continuity of individuals or even social groups, the change in nationality discourses between 1914 and 1922, or the response to the experience of violence. Other important aspects would be illuminated by a study of the Ukrainian policies of the newly emerging states in the Caucasus, the Crimea, Belarus, the Baltic region, Finland, the Nordic states, Romania, Bulgaria, Italy, and Turkey. We hope that, with the present work, we have taken a first step toward encouraging a new and more lively academic encounter with Ukrainian history in the German- and English-speaking world and provoking further discussion. The unanswered political, economic, and social questions that have emerged in the Black Sea region in the past two decades need to be more strongly anchored in European research and public awareness. The states of this region are the bridge from Europe to Asia and are, for that reason, particularly sensitive regions for the future, regardless of whether this has to do with the preservation of political autonomy or the transit of people, culture, goods, services, and energy.

Sociopolitical Dimensions of East European History

A study dealing with cultural identity, even if it is based on political, military, and diplomatic history, always has sociopolitical relevance. Simply by opening up questions, by treating (or not treating) subjects, we are taking positions in the present. This is particularly clear today if we follow the political and historiographic discourses in Ukraine. Intense debates about cultural identity are going on, and the boundaries between what is and what is not Ukrainian are a central aspect of that discourse. This rigid deindividualized attribution of identities to groups on the basis of preestablished parameters goes back to the nationality discourse that has been current since the nineteenth century.[13] Nationalism offers political legitimation, which has become increasingly important since the end of the eighteenth century owing to the erosion of the identity-forming and power-stabilizing function of religion in the aftermath of the Enlightenment and the French Revolution. In these politically motivated processes of

---

13 This has been discussed in great detail since the late 1970s: see Benedict Anderson, *Imagined Communities: Reflections on the Origin and Spread of Nationalism* (1983); Ernest Gellner, *Nations and Nationalism* (1983); Eric Hobsbawm, *Nations and Nationalism since 1780: Programme, Myth, Reality* (1991); Hugh Seton-Watson, *Nations and States: An Inquiry into the Origins of Nations and the Politics of Nationalism* (London, 1977).

homogenization, large social groups with a common language, culture, and tradition were defined. Quite by chance, certain elements were assigned to a nation and others excluded. As part of these processes, certain cultural elements or whole social groups were excluded.

In the present volume we neither wish to nor indeed can we offer a definition of what is Ukrainian or who is a Ukrainian. In the course of our work, however, we were repeatedly confronted by questions of definition, for instance, deciding to what national historiography and language group to assign an individual involved in a number of different cultural circles. This question has particular relevance for the present work. Is a Soviet politician who was born and grew up in Ukraine, who then worked his way up through local and republican institutions to Moscow and finally oriented himself on the supranational Soviet *nomenklatura* a Ukrainian or a Russian? Especially when he himself defines himself as neither one nor the other? Is the use of Russian for a Ukrainian individual a hegemonic action? Should we impose a national identity on someone who, in his lifetime, rejected it out of profound conviction? Or is this conviction handed down from him just propaganda?

These questions are all research subjects in themselves and cannot be part of the present volume. This work is based on an individualist concept of identity; it assumes the possibility of multiple identities and gives central significance to the individual's self-identification. Which religion, which mother tongue, which state one belongs to either by birth or passport are all irrelevant. The question is rather to which identities an individual feels that he or she belongs. But that is often difficult for us to verify retroactively. Since we regard this volume as a contribution to Ukrainian historiography, we have decided to use Ukrainian orthography and the corresponding transliteration of personal names in dubious cases to facilitate readability. In general, we follow the approach of "transnational history," an approach that has been widely discussed in academic research in recent years and that Georgiy Kasianov and Philipp Ther define in their book on Ukrainian historiography: "Problems of Ukrainian history can usefully be presented from a transnational perspective, involving cultural transfers and processes of intercultural exchange.... [I]n our view transnational history concentrates on the relations between cultures and societies, deliberately eschewing concentration on any one culture or country. It compares sending and receiving cultures, highlighting agents of cultural exchange, and is thus oriented toward agency. Transnational history challenges simple models of diffusion.

It studies the ways in which cultures use and appropriate cultural goods of distant or foreign origin."[14]

The present book, although its theme is primarily political, military, and economic history, should therefore also be understood as a cultural project, one presented as transnational history. We thus subscribe to the deconstruction of large national narratives, the demise of which was announced by Jean-François Lyotard as early as 1979.[15] We confront archival materials with the historiographic traditions of different states in order to overcome the national perspective. The close collaboration of international project teams makes it easier to overcome one's own national boundaries without thereby either creating a new hegemonic hierarchy or dissolving one's own cultural ties. This method does not "press" history into a uniform narration but rather lets in different viewpoints, as becomes evident especially in the third and fourth sections of the present book. What has emerged here is a trend toward the transnational negotiation of history. These processes increasingly escape appropriation by national political discourses. Without completely losing individual cultural backgrounds, these narrations are becoming increasingly natural in the era of digital "collective intelligence" in the Internet (for instance, Wikipedia or Twitter).[16] Nation still matters, even now, more than two decades after the introduction of the World Wide Web and the alleged "end of history"[17] that followed the collapse of the Eastern Bloc and the Soviet Union. But it is clear both from the work method we have chosen in this collaborative book and from the results of our work that "nation" is being increasingly deconstructed and is losing its unique position. Since the linguistic turn it has become impossible to write history that is unaware of the fact that language reflects power.[18] In a

---

14 Georgiy Kasianov and Philipp Ther, "Introduction," in *A Laboratory of Transnational History: Ukraine and Recent Ukrainian Historiography,* ed. Georgiy Kasianov and Philipp Ther (Budapest and New York, 2009), 2–3.

15 Jean-François Lyotard, *La Condition postmoderne: Rapport sur le savoir* (Paris, 1979).

16 Wolfram Dornik, "Internet: Maschine des Vergessens oder globaler Gedächtnisspeicher? Der Holocaust in den digitalen Erinnerungskulturen zwischen 1990 und 2010," in *Öffentliche Erinnerung und Medialisierung des Nationalsozialismus. Eine Bilanz der letzten dreißig Jahre,* ed. Gerhard Paul and Bernhard Schoßig (Göttingen, 2010), 79–97.

17 The concept first appeared in an article in *The National Interest* in the summer of 1989, then three years later in Francis Fukuyama, *The End of History and the Last Man* (New York, 1992).

18 Doris Bachmann-Medick, *Cultural Turns: Neuorientierungen in den Kulturwissenschaften* (Hamburg, 2009); *Geschichte schreiben in der Postmoderne: Beiträge zur aktuellen Diskussion,* ed. Christoph Conrad and Martin Kessel (Stuttgart, 1994); Hayden White, "Das Problem der Erzählung in der modernen Geschichtstheorie," in *Theorie der modernen Geschichtsschreibung,* ed. Pietro Rossi (Frankfurt am Main, 1987), 57–106.

scholarly publication, this is relevant not only to the analysis. In the case of multicultural Central and Eastern Europe, it is relevant to the choice of place-names. Since the end of the First World War, borders have been redrawn here without the involvement of local populations. Borders frequently do not reflect cultural realities but the balance of power at the time the borders were drawn. One of the consequences of this process is the renaming of places to fit new circumstances. Discussions about toponyms still continue today in the nationality discourses of regions previously belonging to the Habsburg and Romanov empires. In this translation, place-names are given in the language of the country in which they are now located, with variants in other languages supplied parenthetically on first mention in the text and in the index at the end of the volume.

The Current State of Research

The results brought together in this book, even when partly based on comprehensive archival research, are part of a long historiographical tradition. Since we treat a great number of subjects in the chapters that follow, all of which have their own historiographies, it is not possible for us to acknowledge all of them here. We shall make reference only to the English, German, and most important East European studies on the First World War and Ukraine in 1918.[19]

Although, in the German-speaking sphere, there has been little research on the First World War in general and the Eastern Front specifically, the number of relevant publications has grown in recent years. For German scholars, the main reference for many years was Norman Stone's *The Eastern Front* (1975). In the meantime, Timothy Dowling, William C. Fuller, Gerhard P. Gross, Michael Neiberg, and David Jordan have produced important works on the German Empire, Austria-Hungary, and Russia in the war in Eastern Europe between 1914 and 1917. They have revised conclusions in many areas and, through their research in the East European and especially the Russian archives since 1989–91, have managed to open up many issues for deeper and more comprehensive study.[20] German publications on

---

19 Since this is a translation of the German-language volume published in 2011, we have not revised it to integrate the scholarly discourse of subsequent years (2011–14).

20 Timothy C. Dowling, *The Brusilov Offensive* (Indianapolis, 2008); G. P. Groß, ed., *Die vergessene Front. Der Osten 1914/15: Ereignis, Wirkung, Nachwirkung* (Paderborn, 2006); William C. Fuller, *The Foe Within: Fantasies of Treason and the End of Imperial Russia* (Ithaca, 2006); Mark von Hagen, *War in a European Borderland: Occupations and Occupation Plans in Galicia and Ukraine, 1914–1918* (Seattle and London, 2007); Geoffrey Jukes, *The First World War: The*

the Eastern Front are still lacking, but particular aspects of that front have been convincingly studied in a number of dissertations. These include Rudolf Jeřábek's work on the Brusilov offensive and Richard Lein's dissertation on the attitude of the Czechs to the Eastern Front.[21] Verena Moritz, Hannes Leidinger, Reinhard Nachtigal, Jochen Oltmer, Alon Rachamimov, and Georg Wurzer have aroused special interest in recent years with their work on prisoners of war on the Eastern Front, and that subject can now be considered well researched.[22]

Up to now, works on the war in Eastern Europe have tended to emphasize military events between 1914 and 1917. There are significantly fewer studies of the occupations by Russian troops (Galicia and Bukovyna, as well as East Prussia in 1914–15) or troops of the Central Powers (Poland from 1915, the Baltic states from 1915, Belarus and Ukraine in 1918, as well as their troops stationed in Eastern Europe until 1919). So far there have been a few works on Poland and Vejas Liulevicius's comprehensive work on the Baltic states.[23] Abba Strazhas and Winfried Baumgart have written works on Germany's

---

Eastern Front, 1914–1918 (Oxford, 2002); Vejas Gabriel Liulevicius, *War Land on the Eastern Front: Culture, National Identity, and German Occupation in World War I* (Cambridge, 2000); *The Eastern Front, 1914–1920,* ed. Michael Neiberg and David Jordan; G. Irving Root, *Battles East: A History of the Eastern Front of the First World War* (Baltimore, 2007); Norman Stone, *The Eastern Front, 1914–1917* (London, 1998).

21 Rudolf Jeřábek, "Die Brussilowoffensive 1916. Ein Wendepunkt der Koalitionskriegführung der Mit-telmächte" (Ph.D. diss., Vienna, 1982); Richard Lein, "Das militärische Verhalten der Tschechen im Ersten Weltkrieg" (Ph.D.. diss., Vienna, 2009). Also Christian Reiter, "Der Untergang des IR 36. Der 'Verrat' der tschechischen Soldaten im Gefecht bei Sieniewa 1915" (Ph.D. diss., Vienna, 2008); Gabriel Zupcan, "Der Tschechoslowakische Legionär in Russland, 1914–1920" (Ph.D. diss., Vienna, 2008).

22 Hannes Leidinger and Verena Moritz, *Gefangenschaft, Revolution, Heimkehr. Die Bedeutung der Kriegs-gefangenenproblematik für die Geschichte des Kommunismus in Mittel- und Osteuropa 1917–1920* (Vienna, Cologne, and Weimar, 2003); Reinhard Nachtigal, *Russland und seine österreichisch-ungarischen Kriegsgefangenen (1914–1918)* (Remshalden, 2003); *Kriegsgefangene im Europa des Ersten Weltkrieges,* ed. Jochen Oltmer (Paderborn, 2006); Alon Rachamimov, *POWs and the Great War: Captivity on the Eastern Front* (Oxford and New York, 2002); Georg Wurzer, *Die Kriegsgefangenen der Mittelmächte in Russland im Ersten Weltkrieg* (Göttingen, 2005). See also the special issue of the journal *Zeitgeschichte. Kriegsgefangenschaft 1914–1920. Am Beispiel Österreichs und Rußlands* 25, nos. 11/12 (1998).

23 Jerzy Gaul, "The Austro-Hungarian Empire and Its Political Allies in the Polish Kingdom, 1914–1918," in *Karl I. (IV.), der Erste Weltkrieg und das Ende der Donaumonarchie,* ed. Andreas Gottsmann (Vienna, 2007), 203–21; Eugeniusz Cezary Król, "Besatzungsherrschaft in Polen im Ersten und Zweiten Weltkrieg. Charakteristik und Wahrnehmung," in *Erster Weltkrieg – Zweiter Weltkrieg. Ein Vergleich. Krieg, Kriegserlebnis, Kriegserfahrung in Deutschland,* ed. Bruno Thoß and Hans-Erich Volkmann (Paderborn, Munich, Vienna, and Zurich, 2002), 577–91; Liulevicius, *War Land on the Eastern Front.* Stephan Lehnstaedt is currently writing a Habilitation thesis for the German Historical Institute in Warsaw on the economics of the occupation of Poland in the First and Second World Wars. We await the results of his research with interest.

eastern policy in which they contextualize the military aspects for the first time.[24] In the present volume, we acknowledge Baumgart's work throughout. But we still lack more comprehensive research on Austro-Hungarian occupations in Eastern and Southeastern Europe.[25] Although Serbia was not part of the Eastern Front, Jonathan Gumz's integrated work on the occupation by Austro-Hungarian troops is exemplary.[26]

A number of studies have appeared in the German-speaking world on the occupation that is the subject of the present work. Wolfdieter Bihl was one of the pioneers here. He collaborated on the four-volume edition of documents about events in Ukraine from 1914 to 1922 (*Ereignisse in der Ukraine 1914–1922*) edited in the 1960s by Theophil Hornykiewicz. In the years that followed, he published a series of articles on various aspects of Austria-Hungary's Ukrainian policy.[27] Peter Borowsky's study of Germany's Ukrainian policy appeared in 1970, and in 2005 Frank Grelka published a comparative study on the Ukrainian national movement under German occupation in 1918 and in 1941/42.[28] Frank Golczewski has recently published a comprehensive study of German-Ukrainian relations in the First World War and in the interwar period that also integrates the Austro-Hungarian perspective.[29] Peter Lieb had already written about the military aspects of the occupation with reference to the German

---

24 Winfried Baumgart, *Deutsche Ostpolitik 1918. Von Brest-Litowsk bis zum Ende des Ersten Weltkrieges* (Vienna and Munich, 1966); Abba Strazhas, *Deutsche Ostpolitik im Ersten Weltkrieg. Der Fall Ober Ost 1915–1917* (Wiesbaden, 1993).

25 One of the studies in this area is the work on Austro-Hungarian military administration by military figures involved: Hugo Kerchnawe et al., *Die Militärverwaltung in den von den österreichisch-ungarischen Truppen besetzten Gebieten* (Vienna, 1928). Tamara Scheer has written a patchy and not very analytical work: Tamara Scheer, *Zwischen Front und Heimat. Österreich-Ungarns Militärverwaltungen im Ersten Weltkrieg* (Frankfurt am Main, 2009).

26 Jonathan E. Gumz, *The Resurrection and Collapse of Empire in Habsburg Serbia, 1914–1918* (New York, 2009).

27 *Ereignisse in der Ukraine 1914–1922. Deren Bedeutung und historische Hintergründe*, ed. Theophil Hornykiewicz, 4 vols. (Philadelphia, 1966); Wolfdieter Bihl, "Beiträge zur Ukraine-Politik Österreich-Ungarns 1918," *Jahrbücher für Geschichte Osteuropas*, n.s. 14 (1966): 51–62; idem, "Die österreichisch-ungarischen Dienststellen in der Ukraine 1918," *Mitteilungen des Österreichischen Staatsarchivs*, no. 20 (1967): 379–88; idem, "Zur Tätigkeit des ukrainophilen Erzherzogs Wilhelm nach dem Ersten Weltkrieg," *Jahrbücher für Geschichte Osteuropas*, n.s. 19 (1971): 538–40. In 2007 there was a thesis by a Viennese historian (supervised by Lothar Höbelt) on aspects of Austria-Hungary's Ukrainian policy: Richard Oskar Friedrich Pucher, "Ukraine 1918 in offiziellen österreichischen Dokumenten" (Ph.D. diss., Vienna, 2007).

28 Peter Borowsky, *Deutsche Ukrainepolitik 1918 unter besonderer Berücksichtigung der Wirtschaftsfragen* (Lübeck and Hamburg, 1970); Frank Grelka, *Die ukrainische Nationalbewegung unter deutscher Besatzungsherrschaft 1918 und 1941/42* (Wiesbaden, 2005).

29 Frank Golczewski, *Deutsche und Ukrainer 1914–1939* (Paderborn, 2010).

troops in Ukraine before the start of the present project, and Reinhard Nachtigal wrote an article in which he examined the battle of the Mius Firth during the German advance.[30] The work of two American experts on Eastern Europe, Mark von Hagen and Timothy Snyder, deserves mention here. Von Hagen is the author of a brief work on the Ukrainian policy of the Central Powers based on American, Canadian, and Russian sources, and Snyder has contributed a study of Archduke Wilhelm.[31] What all these publications have in common is that they each cover only a partial area and are based on a small national body of sources. In that work, however, the Ukrainian and Russian perspective was under-represented, as compared with the richly documented perspective of the Central Powers. We have attempted, in the present work, to ensure very broad access with documents from as many countries as possible and working jointly with historians from most of the countries involved.

We are obviously aware that other emphases would have been possible in a study of Ukraine in 1918. In the present study, for instance, we pay very little attention to cultural history. We are unable to offer a history of the reception of the occupation, nor have we done a detailed study of nation-building processes, of gender-specific aspects, of cultural or know-how transfers, or of how the occupied population perceived the occupiers. On the one hand, this had to do with our limited time and resources and. on the other hand, with the poorly developed level of research and the extremely difficult situation with regard to access to sources. Following the Soviet takeover, Ukrainian sources were filtered out to marginalize the anti-Bolshevik opposition and to prevent it from finding an appropriate place in communicative and cultural memory.[32] Further research from Lviv, Budapest, Zagreb, Prague, and Warsaw on the military units of the Habsburg Monarchy

---

30 Peter Lieb, "A Precursor of Modern Counter-Insurgency Operations? The German Occupation of the Ukraine in 1918," in University of Salford, European Studies Research Institute, *Working Papers in Military History and International History,* no. 4 (Salford, 2007); Peter Lieb, "Deutsche Herrschaft in der Ukraine 1918/19: Wegweiser zum Vernichtungskrieg?" *Militärgeschichte. Zeitschrift für historische Bildung*, no. 4 (2008): 10–13; Reinhard Nachtigal, "Krasnyj Desant: Das Gefecht an der Mius-Bucht. Ein unbeachtetes Kapitel der deutschen Besetzung Südrußlands 1918," *Jahrbücher für Geschichte Osteuropas,* n.s. 53 (2005): 221–46.

31 Von Hagen makes no use of German or Austrian documents: Mark von Hagen, *War in a European Borderland: Occupations and Occupation Plans in Galicia and Ukraine, 1914–1918* (Seattle and London, 2007); Timothy Snyder, *The Red Prince: The Secret Lives of a Habsburg Archduke* (New York, 2008).

32 Here we follow the definition of Jan and Aleida Assmann: Aleida Assmann, *Erinnerungsräume. Formen und Wandlungen des kulturellen Gedächtnisses* (Munich, 1999); Jan Assmann, *Das kulturelle Gedächtnis. Schrift, Erinnerung und politische Identität in frühen Hochkulturen* (Munich, 1992).

could complement the theses developed in the third section of this book. Likewise, research in Turkish and Bulgarian sources on those countries' economic and political interests, as well as their collaboration with their German and Austro-Hungarian allies, would be very valuable.

Acknowledgments

From the beginning, our efforts were supported by a number of people whom I would like to thank at this point. Our thanks go first to Stefan Karner, head of the Ludwig Boltzmann Institute for Research on the Consequences of War and deputy director of the Institute for Economic, Social, and Enterprise History at the Karl Franz University in Graz. He assumed the scholarly and organizational leadership of the project and was always ready with advice and assistance from the inception of the project to its conclusion. The staff at the Boltzmann Institute, with their long years of experience, have made this study possible through their active help with research, language problems, and conceptual issues: Dieter Bacher, Christoph Benedikter, Alexander Fritz, Peter Fritz, Walter M. Iber, Harald Knoll, Armin Laussegger, Sigrid Lazar, Philipp Lesiak, Peter Ruggenthaler, Peter Sixl, Barbara Stelzl-Marx, Silke Stern, and Arno Wonisch. Our special thanks go to Juliane Nitsch for her editorial support in finalizing the present volume and to Martin Florian for arranging the maps.

A big thanks to all the coworkers on this project for their wide-ranging and disciplined work! Special mention here goes to Peter Lieb, who has worked on the German occupation of Ukraine for some time and was a decisive influence in the planning of this project. His work has helped us in many respects as an essential starting point for a new look at Ukraine. His almost boundless enthusiasm for research helped me not only with his own contributions to the book but also with advice on a variety of technical and organizational matters and with assistance in my research in London. For a similar length of time we have had the support of Hannes Leidinger and Verena Moritz, whose knowledge and expertise on Central and Eastern Europe made a decisive contribution to the birth of this project and the theses developed in the study. Alexei Miller of the Central European University in Budapest and the Russian Academy of Sciences, with his long international academic experience, has added the Russian perspective. Georgiy Kasianov of the National Academy of Sciences of Ukraine in Kyiv and Vasyl Rasevych from its partner institute in Lviv provided valuable support in bringing into the project a stronger Ukrainian focus, of which few German-speaking academics were previously aware. Bogdan Musial, a long-time partner of our institute, strengthened our project team with his expertise in the history of the Soviet Union and Soviet communism. Heartfelt thanks to all for their collegial cooperation in this project. It was the attitude of all those involved that enabled us to meet the challenges of a multi-authored study.

But it was not just the authors who produced this book; it was a whole series of helpers who worked in the background, out of sight. Elisabeth Klöckl-Stadler and Cornelia Stiegler edited the manuscripts. Harald Fleischmann of the Institute of Theoretical and Applied Translation Science at the University of Graz took on the translation of the Ukrainian and Russian contributions. Anna Yeromina kept the Ukrainian-Austrian information streams flowing during the project. Benjamin Grilj and Serhii Osadchuk of the Bukovyna Center and the Austrian Library in Chernivtsi; Andreas Wenninger, head of the Austro-Ukrainian Cooperation Bureau for Science, Education, and Culture; and Michael Dippelreiter of the Center for International Cooperation and Mobility of the Austrian Exchange Service were helpful with communication and organizational issues. Heartfelt thanks for assistance in organizing the preliminary workshop goes to Ewald Stadler, member of the Cultural Council of Austria and, in 2009, deputy director of the Cultural Forum of the Austrian Embassy in Budapest; also to Ambassador Michael Zimmermann and to Elisabeth Kornfeind, director of the Cultural Forum. In the fertile atmosphere of this event, we were able to lay the foundations of the present work. Last but not least, we are indebted to Gerald Schöpfer, the director of the Institute for Economic, Social, and Enterprise History of the University of Graz, and to his colleagues: Michaela Hohenwarter, Sabine List, Doris Mauthner, and Peter Teibenbacher have always been helpful with expert advice and with the organization of the final conference. Finally, our thanks to Wolfgang Hölzl of Leykam-Verlag and Helmut Lenhart for their fantastic cooperation in finalizing the German-language book for publication.

As is clear from the list of sources, this book is the result of comprehensive research carried out by those involved in the project. Many people from archive staff have helped us in our work. Among these are the staff of the War Archive of the Austrian State Archives, especially Christoph Tepperberg, Otto Kellner, Andrea Hackel, Robert Rill, Klaus Pillmayer, Mirijana Josipovic, and Bernhard Wenninger. The director of the Military History Museum in Vienna, Mario Christian

Ortner, made possible our research in the museum's picture archive and the reproduction of some of these for the book. Our gratitude for hospitality and support in our archival research in the United States goes to the staff of the Harvard Ukrainian Research Institute; also to Mark Kramer of the Davis Center at Harvard University and the staff of the Austrian Cultural Forum in Washington, especially Andrea Schrammel and Thomas Brandhuber. The staff of the Cultural Forum of the Austrian Embassy in London were similarly helpful, especially Melita Essenko and the director, Peter Mikl. Nicole-Melanie Goll and Éva Kosa assisted us in our research in the Budapest War Archives. We would also like to thank the Military History Research Bureau in Potsdam, especially Rolf-Dieter Müller, for logistical help in the Federal Archives/Military Archives. Martin Schmitz of Augsburg put very valuable documents at our disposal.

Besides the funding for the German edition supplied by the FWF, others also contributed, especially the Styrian provincial governor, Franz Voves, the mayor of Graz, Siegfried Nagl, and the Research Service of the University of Graz. They made possible the organization of the final conference in June 2011. For support in the printing of the book, we want to thank the city of Vienna, the Federal Ministry for Science and Research, and the provincial government of Carinthia (Contemporary Historical Documents/Ethnic Groups Bureau).

1a. A Time of Troubles: Revolutionary Upheavals and Armed Conflicts in the Former Tsarist Empire, 1917–1922

Hannes Leidinger

The Decayed System

The knowledge that later generations have about individual events and historical processes can lead them to see developments more clearly than they really were or were seen at the time. Historians need to be aware of the temptation to become "prophets after the event." They might otherwise tend to create an account suggesting "fateful" preconditions, "determinants" of a particular chain of events, or "fatal" turning points.[1] From this vantage point, the fall of the Romanov Empire had been inevitable for some time. Its decline and fall is then seen as unavoidable. It is certainly the case that the events of 1905 and the conflicts of the following years had shaken the foundations of the tsarist regime of Nicholas II. Following the war with Japan in 1904, Russia slid into its first revolution, which then ended with half-hearted and questionable concessions. Uprisings were brutally suppressed, and a restriction of voting rights limited the possibilities of restructuring within the constitutional monarchy to a narrow social stratum, with the result that there was no decisive impulse to overcome the obstacles to reform. Industrialization measures and efforts to improve agricultural production did nothing to overcome the gulf between government and opposition or between privileged layers of society and the poor.[2]

The collapse of the fragile state structure, however, was not inevitable, although its existence was soon threatened by additional challenges and especially by military conflicts with competing great powers. The years 1904 and 1905, the defeat in the war against Japan, with its enormous domestic consequences, should have served as a lesson. But when, in the summer of 1914, Nicholas sent his army against Germany and Austria-Hungary, he had overdrawn his bow.

1 Verena Moritz and Hannes Leidinger, *Die Nacht des Kirpitschnikow. Eine andere Geschichte des Ersten Weltkriegs* (Vienna, 2006), 121ff.

2 Verena Moritz and Hannes Leidinger, *Die Russische Revolution* (Vienna, Cologne, and Weimar, 2011), 23–35.

The jingoism of the early days of the war, though limited to part of the urban population, as well as the "patriotic sentiment" of the Duma, though the latter was usually viewed critically and barely tolerated by the ruler and his advisers, served to draw a temporary veil over the country's problems.[3]

The crisis soon deepened beyond the problems that were already evident. The civil and military leadership of the fragile empire rapidly lost ground both strategically and economically. Criticism of the incompetence of the autocracy and of its bureaucratic apparatus led to the creation of special committees with which the local self-governing bodies, the zemstvos in particular, attempted to overcome the lack of materials and supply bottlenecks. It was said, in this context, that the higher social circles should have stepped in earlier to rescue the empire. But actually these new bodies worked more often against than with one another. The fragmentation of economic life created problems of coordination. Consumers waited in vain for necessary supplies, a problem exacerbated by the desolate transport system.[4]

To economic and organizational deficits were added social and political protests, the articulation of special interests, and a creeping dissolution of state structures. By 1916–17 the tsar, the army, and government ministers were largely discredited. The sacrifices of the soldiers and of the population lost all meaning in the context of organizational deficits, defeats on the front, rising living costs, poor distribution of goods, and inadequate food supplies. Disillusionment increased with reports of wrong decisions, corruption, and war profiteering, as well as with rumors of arrests of "troublemakers" who had dared to express their outrage at all of this. Dissatisfaction grew, as well as a willingness to engage in opposition, particularly in urban centers. Strikes and street demonstrations increased, as did sharper criticism of the system.[5]

At protest demonstrations in the capital, St. Petersburg, renamed Petrograd in 1914, the chain of command broke at its most important points: the garrisons were reluctant to shoot at their "rebellious brothers and sisters." The Duma resisted the orders of Nicholas II and, without his agreement, set up an independent committee to take control of the difficult situation. "Peasant soldiers" got rid of commanders they

3 Moritz and Leidinger, *Die Nacht des Kirpitschnikow*, 122.

4 Hannes Leidinger and Verena Moritz, *Der Erste Weltkrieg* (Vienna, Cologne, and Weimar, 2011), 56, 65ff.

5 Ibid.

disliked and fraternized with the "people." Soviets (councils), which had first appeared in the events of 1905, reappeared. When leading organs of the soviets made contact with parliamentarians and coordinated their activities with those of the parliamentary committee, the tsar resigned. When potential pretenders to the throne failed to come forward, the Romanovs' three centuries of rule came to an end.[6]

Decentralization

The February Revolution of 1917 appeared, on the whole, as an elementary uprising against the monarchy, the symbols and functionaries of which disappeared immediately. Monarchic collapse provoked an accelerated disintegration that transformed a creeping into a galloping collapse of the state. The new Provisional Government, under the liberal Prince Georgii Lvov, was therefore confronted with numerous centrifugal forces that, taken together, led gradually to an almost complete atomization of society.[7]

It is also significant that the number of strikes did not decline following the events of that spring of 1917. On the contrary, as the claims and expectations of the factory workers grew, so also did the self-confidence of the "proletariat." The creation of factory committees indicated a significant shift in power. Employee committees in the enterprises scrutinized the activities of management. At the same time, they took charge of the supply of raw materials, of hiring and firing, as well as the maintenance of production and discipline. A "neutral ministerial council," whose task it was to arbitrate disputes but that aimed mainly at maintaining production in the service of the war economy, was unable, under these circumstances, to maintain a durable prohibition of the "class struggle." The Lvov cabinet was considered partial by factory directors and workers alike. It was challenged by a proletarian militancy that, with the Red Guards, in existence since February, was undermining the authority of the urban militia. This proletariat, engaged now in an unending series of meetings, was being increasingly politicized.[8]

---

6 Ibid.; cf. Moritz and Leidinger, *Die Russische Revolution*, 36–41.

7 For observations on the increasing destabilization of Russia during the period of the Lvov government, see GARF, f. 1791, op. 2, d. 144, 82.

8 S. A. Smith, *Red Petrograd: Revolution in the Factories, 1917–1918* (Cambridge, 1983), 80–98, 139–67; Rex Wade, *Red Guards and Workers' Militias in the Russian Revolution* (Stanford, 1984), 80–114, 173–82; Konstantin Paustovskij, *Der Beginn eines verschwundenen Zeitalters* (Frankfurt am Main, 2002), 481.

Developments in the countryside were now dominated by the desire on the part of the population to leave fundamental decisions to nobody else and to take charge of important matters themselves. Unlike the autarchic small units promoted by the tsarist prime minister Petr Stolypin, it was the *obshchina*, the village community responsible for the redistribution of land and the collective payment of communal taxes, that experienced a revival in 1917. It was the *obshchina* that undertook the initiative to demand lower rents from the well-off estate owners, as well as fair prices for grain, tools, and animals. There was then a significant radicalization from mid-1917. Following the appointment of Viktor Chernov from the Party of Socialist Revolutionaries as agriculture minister, the peasantry began a massive confiscation of estate land, spurred on at times by returnees from the front and by deserters. The villagers not only took action on their own initiative but also frequently used force. The plundering and destruction of estate homes was a manifestation of brutal vandalism that sometimes cost the nobility their lives. Murders and acts of revenge for the execution of peasant rebels in 1905 increased.[9] Incidents of lynch law were reported from the provinces, from Tambov, Penza, Voronezh, Saratov, Orel, Tula, and Kazan. In September and October alone, peasants burned down 250 estate houses, about a fifth of all estate houses in the region.[10] According to later publications in the USSR, the Provisional Government's militia, in July 1917, reported an increase in "deforestation, damage to land, and arbitrariness" while, from June to September, the statistics recorded almost a threefold increase in the "destruction and occupation of estate houses."[11]

Parallel to this settling of scores with the aristocracy, the local population created soviets, which, as a "revolutionary form of *obshchina*," incorporated the ideals of village self-government. These local councils paid little attention to orders from the central government. Sometimes they declared their own village republics, with their own emblems and flags. Many established their own police forces and elected their own judges, as well as creating volunteer militias or Red Guards.[12]

---

9 See GARF, f. 398, op. 2, d. 144, 158.

10 Orlando Figes, *A People's Tragedy: Russian Revolution 1891–1924* (London, 1996), 464. On the general topic of disintegration, see also *Revoliutsiia i grazhdanskaia voina v Rossii, 1917–1923. Ėntsiklopediia*, 4 vols. (Moscow, 2008), 1: 364–81.

11 *Geschichte des Bürgerkrieges in der UdSSR*, vol. 1, *Die Vorbereitung der Oktoberrevolution* (Offenbach, 1999), 381 (first published in 1936).

12 Figes, *A People's Tragedy*, 464ff.

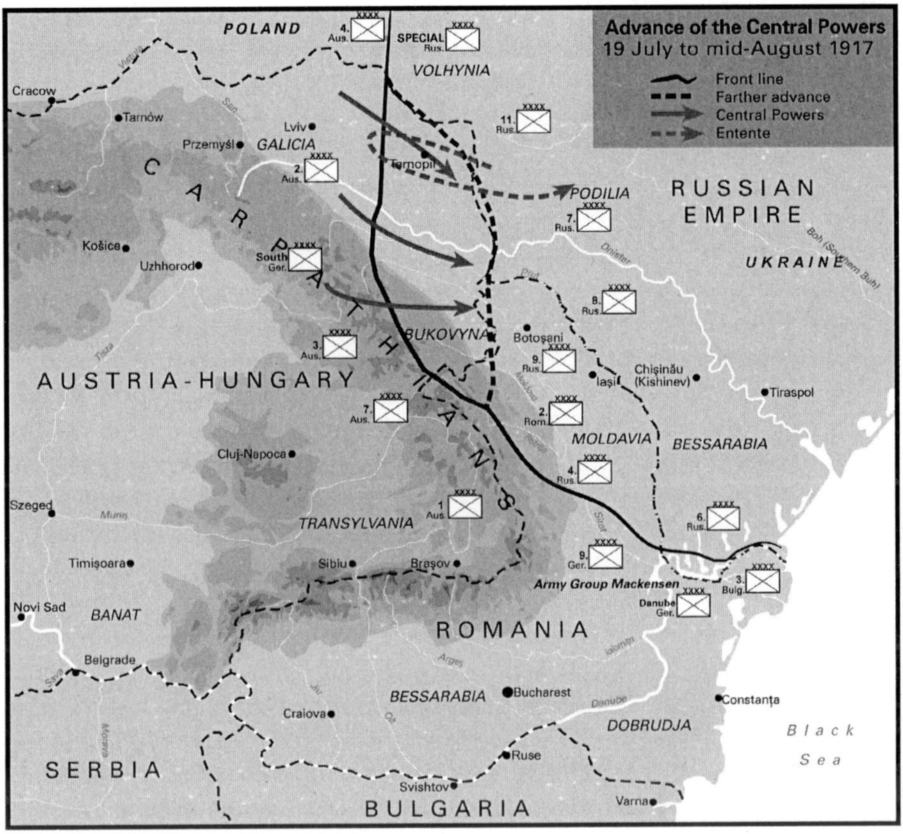

Map 1: The Kerensky Offensive and the "Response" of the Central Powers, Summer 1917 (Banks, *A Military Atlas of the First World War*, 176; Ellis and Cox, *The World War I Databook*, 36ff.)

Loss of Authority

In this situation, one can hardly speak of dual power existing between soviet deputies and government officials.[13] Apart from the fact that the various institutions and social forces in the provincial centers tended to want cooperation, the Workers' and Soldiers' Soviet in the capital could have seized power at any time. The masses saw the Soviet as having the highest authority, all the more so as the government, in spite of the pacifist mood of the population, was continuing to pursue the war. The last straw was the attitude of the prominent Constitutional Democrat and foreign minister, Pavel Miliukov,[14] who not only stood

13 In academic accounts of the revolution, "dual power" was and still is a central dogma.

14 On the Constitutional Democrats (Cadets) and Miliukov, see P. N. Miliukov, *Istoriia vtoroi*

by Russia's obligations to its allies but also talked of winning new territories from the war.[15]

A storm of indignation swept Miliukov from office. With him went the minister of war, Aleksandr Guchkov, who was replaced by Aleksandr Kerensky. Until then, Kerensky had been the minister of justice and was seen as the only representative of the left in the Lvov cabinet. A number of socialist politicians now entered the government. The Socialist Revolutionaries and Mensheviks, whose base was in the soviets, thereby gave their assistance to a weak government, not least because they themselves had been unprepared for the upheavals and for taking power.[16]

In Marxist circles there was talk of the need for a "bourgeois" phase of the revolution. Among the divided Social Democrats, it was Vladimir Lenin alone who, on returning from exile, set his Bolsheviks on a new course. With his demands for peace and all power to the soviets, he spoke for the popular mood and offered an alternative to the government course supported by the other socialists, a course leading to the Kerensky offensive, which ended in disaster. The offensive on the front was a failure. Whole regiments mutinied, and the army was disintegrating.[17]

Some units, such as the machine-gun regiment in St. Petersburg and the sailors at the Kronstadt naval base, were determined to get rid of the Provisional Government. In July 1917 they were joined by an increasing number of demonstrators who opposed the government. The level of violence increased. It seemed that the February events were about to be repeated. A large number of lives were lost, but eventually the protest ended without a change of government. The intervention of a number of army units that remained loyal to the government was decisive for the Bolsheviks. They hesitated to call for an armed uprising because, as Lenin warned, a premature uprising could end in defeat.[18] Kerensky, who had replaced Prince Lvov as prime minister, nonetheless denounced him and his party as "putschists" and "agents of the Germans." Representatives of the government

russkoi revoliutsii. Izdanie snabzheno nauchnymi kommentariiami (Moscow, 2001); also *Revoliutsiia i grazhdanskaia voina v Rosii*, 2: 208–10.

15 Rex Wade, *The Russian Search for Peace, February–October 1917* (Stanford, 1969), 26–38.

16 Nikolaj Suchanow, *1917, Tagebuch der Russischen Revolution* (Munich, 1967), 28; N. K. Krupskaya, *Memories of Lenin* (London, 1942).

17 Allan K. Wildman, *The End of the Russian Imperial Army*, 2 vols. (Princeton, 1980–87).

18 Alexander Rabinowitch, *Prelude to Bolshevism: The Petrograd Bolsheviks and the July Uprising* (Bloomington, 1968), 117ff., 121ff.

declared that the Bolsheviks were carrying out the orders of Berlin and wanted to create chaos in Russia. About eight hundred Bolsheviks were arrested.[19] Lenin himself went underground and fled to Finland, where he planned and demanded a transfer of power that would ultimately favor his own party more than the soviets. Lenin's followers were divided about the way ahead, but the increasing destabilization of the country worked in his favor. "The state," remarked the writer Konstantin Paustovsky, "fell apart like a lump of wet clay," and "the army at the front melted away."[20]

The general situation also threatened to destroy the leading bodies of the socialist parties in the government. The Kerensky government continued to lose support because it offered no energetic solutions to the problems of foreign policy, war, social policy, or agriculture. Indeed, the prime minister and the new commander in chief of the army, Lavr Kornilov, fought over which role each of them should play in the restoration of "order." Kerensky took advantage of disputes and misunderstandings to get rid of rivals.[21] His success in the so-called "Kornilov putsch" turned out to be a Pyrrhic victory. The "united socialist front" that he constructed against the military only helped the Bolsheviks, who soon were the dominant voices in the urban soviets. Lenin's most important ally at this time, Lev Trotsky, was elected chair of the Petrograd Soviet. In October, Trotsky created the Military Revolutionary Committee for the defense of Petrograd against advancing German troops and against counterrevolutionaries. Trotsky thereby acquired a general staff that had the allegiance of the Petrograd garrison.[22]

The October Revolution happened as a *coup d'état*. In an unspectacular manner, power shifted to the Bolsheviks. The modest resistance of a few units that had remained loyal to Kerensky was defeated in the few days that followed. The supporters of Kornilov, whom the right had celebrated as the man of discipline who would rescue Russia, found themselves imprisoned in fairly comfortable quarters in the Bykhov Monastery. Having fallen out with Kerensky, whom they blamed for the chaos, they did not lift a finger to defend him against the attack by the extreme left.

---

19 Figes, *A People's Tragedy*, 434.

20 Paustovsky, *Der Beginn eines verschwundenen Zeitalters*, 11.

21 See George Katkov, *The Kornilov Affair: Kerensky and the Break-up of the Russian Army* (London, 1980); Alexander Rabinowitch, *The Bolsheviks Come to Power: The Revolution of 1917 in Petrograd* (New York, 1978), 132–44.

22 Leon Trotsky, *History of the Russian Revolution*, vol. 3 (London, 1967), 87–119.

Since no one believed that the radical socialists would hold on to power for long, they just let them be. There were indeed reasons to believe that they were just temporary beneficiaries of the collapse of authority and the decentralization of the state.[23]

The fact that Lenin took power in the name of the soviets, but only to establish a Bolshevik monopoly of power, gave domestic politics the character of a "war of all against all." But inside the workers' movement there was a desire to have a sharing of power. This was the view of the railworkers' union, which threatened to bring the transport system to a halt if that did not happen.[24] Since armed conflict between supporters and opponents of the Bolsheviks was taking place in Moscow, the Bolshevik leadership agreed to negotiate with the Mensheviks and Socialist Revolutionaries. But then the tide turned, and Kerensky came out the loser. The new government, the Council of People's Commissars (*Sovnarkom*), under the leadership of Lenin, prevailed, and Lenin withdrew from the talks.[25] He demanded instead the arrest of the railway unionists and criticized his opponents inside the party for their willingness to compromise with socialist "traitors." The individuals attacked by Lenin withdrew in protest from the party's Central Committee. Five people's commissars resigned their posts. Disunity and discord prevailed from the periphery to the highest organs of the center. Russia was never closer to anarchy than in those days of the "Great Socialist October Revolution" and in the months that followed.[26]

Particularism and Autonomism, Federalism and Separatism

Following his arrest, Aleksei Nikitin, Kerensky's minister of the interior, is alleged to have said to Volodymyr Antonov-Ovsiienko, "That's your problem now." It was Antonov-Ovsiienko's task, with the units under his command, to storm the Winter Palace and arrest the heads of state. In the SS. Peter and Paul Fortress, Nikitin pulled from his pocket a telegram from the Central Rada in Kyiv. According to this telegram, the leading representatives of the Ukrainian people were more inclined to separate from Russia than ever before.[27]

---

23 Moritz and Leidinger, *Die Russische Revolution*, 55–57.

24 On opinions among the soldiers, see GARF, f. 1236, op. 1, d. 1, 28.

25 RGASPI, f. 17, op. 1, d. 39.

26 Karsten Brüggemann, *Die Gründung der Republik Estland und das Ende des "Einen und unteilbaren Russland." Die Petrograder Front des Russischen Bürgerkriegs 1918–1920* (Wiesbaden, 2002), 17ff.

27 GARF, f. 3348, op. 1, d. 149, 2ff.; Georg von Rauch, *Geschichte der Sowjetunion* (Stuttgart,

The nationality problem also reflected the disintegration of the old imperial structures. Representatives of the minorities had been meeting since the spring of 1917 and expressing their desire for autonomy. What they envisaged was a concept of federalism as proposed by the socialists and especially by the Socialist Revolutionaries that would reconstitute the republic proclaimed in September as a federal state. They had expected more information from Kerensky about this, but in vain.[28] It would have been better if the Provisional Government had made a statement on this issue, as there were already instances of confrontation between St. Petersburg and the "peripheral nations." A change in the unitary centralized nature of the Russian state was already an issue in the 1905 revolution. Regional and national consciousness had been on the rise since the late nineteenth century in the culturally and religiously diverse empire, in which more than half the population did not consist of ethnic Russians and was better described by the state/territorial term *rossiiskii* than the ethnic term *russkii*.[29]

Opposed only by a privileged elite at the beginning, Russification soon found its opponents among the lower urban and rural classes. Also not to be overlooked was the fact that the growth of national sentiment in 1917 was having its effect in the tsarist army. Units were being formed along ethnic lines. The creation of Ukrainian formations was particularly important. However, plans for the long-term reorganization of the army came to grief on developments in the territories of the old Romanov Empire. Most "peasant soldiers," like the majority of the civilian population, opposed any continuation of the war. Many soldiers wanted to return to their local village in order not to lose out in the redistribution of land.[30] The majority of the population, well over 80 percent, lived in the countryside, with a world view that was narrowly focused on the field and the village. They were nonetheless influenced by the social and national policies of local leaders. The Socialist Revolutionaries in particular were very successful in linking

---

1987), 94.

28 Geoffrey Swain, *Russia's Civil War* (Stroud and Charleston, 2000), 133; Nikolaus Katzer, *Die weisse Bewegung in Russland. Herrschaftsbildung, praktische Politik und politische Programmatik im Bürgerkrieg* (Cologne, Weimar, and Vienna, 1999), 401; Rauch, *Geschichte der Sowjetunion*, 92ff.

29 Katzer, *Die weisse Bewegung in Russland*, 399ff.

30 Mark von Hagen, "War and the Transformation of Loyalties and Identities in the Russian Empire, 1914–1918," in *Russia in the Age of Wars, 1914–1945*, ed. Silvio Pons and Andrea Romano (Milan, 2000), 1–35, esp. 2ff., 23–30, 34ff.

the interests of the village with demands for ethnic autonomy and for the recognition of regional languages and cultures.[31]

These developments created difficulties for the Constitutional Democrats (Cadets) in the Provisional Government. In their view, the "nations" were not ready for self-administration. In the course of 1917, practically the entire leadership of the Cadets moved toward a Russian nationalist position.[32] Lvov's cabinet was prepared to allow independence only to Poland. Even the soviets, in the first months after the tsar's abdication, impressed on the Finns that they should undertake no unilateral steps toward self-determination. When Rada representatives arrived in St. Petersburg with relatively moderate demands, the Russians reacted initially by ignoring them. It was only under pressure from the Ukrainians, who interpreted their freedom with reference to the privileges of the seventeenth-century Cossack hetmans and confronted the Lvov government as sovereign representatives, that a three-man committee was formed, including Kerensky, to negotiate a compromise.[33]

Recognition of the Rada and of national autonomy provoked a government crisis in St. Petersburg. The rightward-drifting Cadets were outraged. Three of the party's spokespersons resigned. They had assumed a rather weak national feeling among the peasantry. For them, it was petty-bourgeois groups that obviously identified themselves more strongly with movements for independence, and the rise of those movements was seen as having to do with the collapse of the empire. What these Russian centralists overlooked was that their own insistence on unity actually boosted the trend from autonomy to separation and that those forces in the "periphery" pushing for self-determination had broad mass support. When the repeatedly postponed elections to the Constituent Assembly took place after the October Revolution, socialist parties with national demands won majorities in Ukraine, Estonia, Georgia, Finland, and Armenia.[34]

Under these conditions, the Council of People's Commissars, in its declaration of November 1917, offered the "nations" "complete

31 Figes, *A People's Tragedy*, 374ff.

32 Katzer, *Die weisse Bewegung in Russland*, 401ff.

33 Anthony F. Upton, *The Finnish Revolution, 1917–1918* (Minneapolis, 1980); *The Ukraine, 1917–1921: A Study in Revolution*, ed. Taras Hunczak (Cambridge, Mass., 1977); John Reshetar, *The Ukrainian Revolution, 1917–1920* (Princeton, N.J., 1950).

34 Ronald Grigor Suny, *The Revenge of the Past: Nationalism, Revolution, and the Collapse of the Soviet Union* (Stanford, 1993), 29ff., 45, 54, 63, 75; Steven L. Guthier, "The Popular Base of Ukrainian Nationalism in 1917," *Slavic Review* 38 (1979): 40.

independence from Russia," thereby recognizing the strength of the prevailing particularist sentiment in the regions of the old Romanov Empire. With decrees enacted immediately after the overthrow of Kerensky, Lenin endorsed not only the national aspirations of the people and their desire for peace but also the redistribution of land. Behind this propagandistically utilized alliance with "the people" was an ideologically colored calculation of power. "Bourgeois nationalism," in the view of leading Bolsheviks, would be overcome by a class solidarity that transcended national boundaries. At meetings of the Council of People's Commissars, faith in the "world proletariat" was no longer separate from Great Russian chauvinism. Peripheral regions were regarded as belonging to them, even though Stalin, as people's commissar for nationalities, defended the independence of Finland, and Lenin added his signature to the independence declarations of the Scandinavians. In reality, the October regime stoked conflict in the regions in order to maintain its own and thus Russian dominance.[35]

In Kyiv, the Rada declared Ukraine a sovereign state,[36] and representatives of Estonia, Livonia, and Georgia declared their intentions of establishing their own states. Although most ethnic minorities, up to then, would have accepted a federation within the borders of the defunct Romanov Empire, the situation changed fundamentally in January 1918. The Constituent Assembly, which had been seen as the platform for the restructuring of the whole empire, was dissolved by the Bolsheviks. Because they did not have a majority in that largely freely elected assembly, they decided to stop this democratic development in good time.[37] Counterdemonstrations in St. Petersburg were violently suppressed. The Socialist Revolutionaries, the winners in the election, had to recognize that the peasants who had voted for them cared little about what happened in the capital and agreed in principle with the decrees of the people's commissars. The opposition was also weak, mainly as a result of the conflicts that followed the February Revolution. The Socialist Revolutionaries were divided. Their Ukrainian members were sympathetic to national programs. One faction broke away from

---

35 For related debates and agendas of sessions of the Council of People's Commissars, see RGASPI, f. 2, op. 1, d. 5133; ibid., f. 19, op. 1, d. 66; cf. Rauch, *Geschichte der Sowjetunion*, 93ff.

36 See chapter 2a in the present volume.

37 V. D. Bonch-Bruevich, *Na boevykh postakh fevral'skoi i oktiabr'skoi revoliutsii* (Moscow, 1930), 250; *The Bolshevik Revolution, 1917–1918: Documents and Materials,* ed. James Bunyan and Harold H. Fisher (Stanford, 1961), 369ff.; Pitirim Sorokin, *Leaves from a Russian Diary* (New York, 1924), 125.

the mother party to enter into a coalition with the Bolsheviks.[38] These left Socialist Revolutionaries took over the agricultural portfolio. The solidarity between the "village"[39] and the "industrial proletariat," especially now that the workers', soldiers', and peasants' soviets had fused, seemed to be manifesting itself both at the government level and in the soviet organizations.[40]

The right-wing Socialist Revolutionaries were also drawn into this battle and faced challenges from the Cadets as well as from right-wing and more far-right forces, including authoritarian circles among military officers. The splits in the party spectrum reflected rivalries among anti-Bolshevik governments that had been formed in Siberia and in the Volga and Ural regions in 1918. Programmatic differences, as well as conflicts over the substantial political and economic interests of bodies that aimed at regional autonomy rather than separation, led to "wars" between the authorities in Omsk, Samara, and Ekaterinburg.[41] The disagreements took on the character of confrontations between "foreigners." At the same time, antagonism between territories controlled by the Bolsheviks and those in which their opponents were dominant increased particularly. A few days after the Constituent Assembly was dissolved, a Don Republic was declared, led by Ataman Aleksei Kaledin. Although this did not mean that all hope for a future Russian federation had been abandoned, the decision of Kaledin and his Cossack supporters meant separation from the Russian center.[42]

Lenin's opponents believed that defection from the "fatherland" was a result of the "despotic power and destructive policy of the Bolshevik dictators," but other observers thought this explanation inadequate.[43]

---

38 Oliver H. Radkey, *Russia Goes to the Polls: The Election to the All-Russian Constituent Assembly, 1917* (Ithaca, N.Y., and London, 1989), 18ff., 23.

39 Recent scholars are quite right to criticize the tendency of existing literature to overstate the unity of the Russian peasantry. For reasons of space, we are unable to go into social and regional differences in this article. However, the existing literature does hint at these differences, as well as acknowledging the fact that the behavior of large parts of rural society was sometimes similar. Cf. Aaron Retish, *Peasants in Revolution and Civil War: Citizenship, Identity and the Creation of the Soviet State, 1914–22* (Cambridge, 2008); cf. Geoffrey Swain, review of Retish's book in *Revolutionary Russia* 22, no. 2 (December 2009): 234–36.

40 Manfred Hildermeier, *Geschichte der Sowjetunion 1917–1991. Entstehen und Niedergang des ersten sozialistischen Staates* (Munich, 1998), 124.

41 E. P. Sichinskii, "Iz istorii Vremennogo oblastnogo pravitel'stva Urala," *Istoria SSSR*, 1992, no.1: 167; G. Z. Ioffe, *Kolchakovskaia avantiura i ee krakh* (Moscow, 1983), 76ff.

42 Peter Kenez, *Civil War in South Russia, 1918: The First Year of the Volunteer Army* (Berkeley, Los Angeles, and London, 1971), 61.

43 Katzer, *Die weisse Bewegung in Russland*, 518.

The opinion of the British Foreign Office, in early May 1919, was that Bolshevism had facilitated the disintegration of the tsarist empire. But on the issue of a federal structure for the empire, there were numerous views and tendencies. The Ukrainians, for instance, were not united on this. The leaders in Ukraine, as in Belarus, the Don, and the Kuban, were occupied with building their own independent states. Reuniting these in a new union would prove difficult. Apart from their stronger national identities, these nations would be unequally represented in a new constituent assembly chosen on the basis of population size. London commentators were critical of the fact that conflict between minorities and majorities would favor the Great Russian majority and would be difficult to reconcile with the principle of self-determination promoted by the Western powers.[44]

Ethnic minorities demanded guarantees of their rights. The task of a new constituent assembly would only be to give these a stamp of approval. The desire to send a common delegation of south Russian governments to the Paris Peace Conference ran up against the problem of how to find common agreement between, on the one hand, the Great Russian group and, on the other hand, the Ukrainians, Cossacks from the Don, the Kuban, and the Terek, as well as the Azerbaijanis and Georgians.[45] Many therefore rejected the idea of a federal state and pursued their own separatist goals. The government in the Kuban broke with the other south Russian forces and sent its own delegation to Paris with the aim of seeking membership in the League of Nations. At the same time, it intended to sign a treaty with the Caucasian Mountain Republic regarding mutual support and recognition of independence.[46] In Paris in October 1919, the representatives of Azerbaijan, Georgia, Estonia, Latvia, Lithuania, and Ukraine requested recognition as "independent states" and members of the League of Nations.[47] Even without such declarations of sovereignty, many Cossacks, long seen as patriotic defenders of the tsarist empire and its borders, distanced themselves from Russia.[48] At any rate, their concerns were not focused on the power struggles in St. Petersburg and Moscow but on the self-determined development of

---

44 TNA, FO 608/206, pp. 261–63.

45 Katzer, *Die weisse Bewegung in Russland*, 266.

46 Ibid., 267.

47 TNA, FO 608/201, 30–35.

48 Hannes Leidinger and Verena Moritz, *Gefangenschaft, Revolution, Heimkehr. Die Bedeutung der Kriegsgefangenenproblematik für die Geschichte des Kommunismus in Mittel- und Osteuropa 1917–1920* (Vienna, Cologne, and Weimar, 2003), 324.

their own regions, in which, however, they brutally persecuted non-native populations and pursued a policy of "ethnic cleansing."[49]

The Russian population inside those "peripheral areas," in the Cossack regions or in the urban centers and industrial areas, where they made up a considerable part of the general population, tended, especially among the less privileged social groups, to support socialist and pro-Bolshevik forces.[50] The thin bourgeois and aristocratic stratum, whose leading groups were divided among themselves, was marginalized in the wake of the revolutionary upheavals. This section of society in the periphery experienced the rise of ethnic movements for self-determination. Gradually, they formed their own autonomous administrative and national bureaucratic structures. Initially, these offered little protection against the October regime, although that regime was by no means yet firmly in place. The future would also be determined by other forces.

Intervention

Following Lenin's seizure of power, it was the actions of the Central Powers, the Germans with their Austro-Hungarian, Bulgarian, and Ottoman allies, that most influenced developments on the territory of the old tsarist empire. The Bolsheviks, renamed communists in the spring of 1918, had begun negotiations with the Central Powers. These collapsed initially because of demands from Berlin. The Communist Party and the Soviet leaders were divided on this. Some called for revolutionary war. Trotsky, however, as people's commissar for foreign affairs, wanted an end to the war without formal negotiations.[51] Trotsky's tactic, which was intended to gain time, did little to alter the balance of forces. When the troops of the Hohenzollerns and Habsburgs began their march eastward, Trotsky joined Lenin who, for practical political reasons, preferred to sign a treaty with the Germans that would be disadvantageous to the Soviet government but would give the newly established Russian Socialist Federal Republic a breathing space.[52] The Council of People's Commissars withdrew from St. Petersburg, which was now under threat, and moved to the new capital, Moscow.[53] The Russian government signed a peace treaty with

49 Figes, *A People's Tragedy*, 570, 581–83.

50 Andreas Kappeler, *Kleine Geschichte der Ukraine* (Munich, 2000), 181ff.

51 Leon Trotsky, *My Life* (New York, 1960), 379–94.

52 On the debates in the state and party leadership of the October regime, see RGASPI, f. 17, op. 1, d. 405, 1–13; ibid., d. 410, 3–17; ibid., d. 412, 9.

53 Helmut Altrichter, *Staat und Revolution in Sowjetrussland 1917–1922/23* (Darmstadt, 1996), 53.

the Central Powers in Brest-Litovsk on 3 March 1918, relinquishing thereby 34 percent of its population, 30 percent of its rail network, 32 percent of its agricultural land, 54 percent of its industrial area, and 89 percent of its coal mines.[54] In the relinquished areas, it was now German and Austro-Hungarian troops that determined events. Under their protection and dependent on them, Ukraine, the Don region, Georgia, Azerbaijan, and Armenia declared themselves independent states. England and Turkey wielded influence in the Caucasus.[55]

In Kyiv, during this period, the Rada lost power to the conservative Hetman Pavlo Skoropadsky. At almost the same time, troops of the Central Powers advanced to Rostov on the Don. In return for supplies, they provided the Cossacks, led by Petr Krasnov, with cannons, machine guns, more than 10,000 weapons, and 12 million shells.[56] This was what Krasnov wanted from the German troops. He, in turn, presented himself vis-à-vis Kaiser Wilhelm as "sovereign ruler" of an independent state.[57] These declarations of independence, dependent on Berlin, contradicted what, since the turn of the year 1917–18, had been the goal of the White Volunteer Army. This army was in the process of being formed and had chosen the Don region as a base of operations in the struggle against the Bolsheviks. Led by previous commanders of the Russian army, Mikhail Alekseev and Lavr Kornilov and, following their early death, by Anton Denikin, this army could not survive without foreign support. It was also anything but sympathetic to the autonomist and separatist tendencies in these peripheral regions of the Romanov Empire. Moreover, the Whites sought an alliance with the states of the Entente, the enemies of the Central Powers. In spite of his own personal inclinations, toward Great Britain in particular, Denikin's Volunteer Army profited from the relation of forces in the west and south of the old tsarist empire. Krasnov, whose own inclinations favored Germany, allied himself with Denikin. Denikin sought recruits for his small force in Ukraine. Germany tolerated these activities at first and showed sympathy for Lenin's opponents. This was followed by negotiations with the Cadets and assistance for monarchist forces.[58]

---

54 *Revoliutsiia i grazhdanskaia voina v Rossii*, 1: 202ff.; John Wheeler-Bennett, *Brest-Litovsk: The Forgotten Peace* (New York, 1938), 269; Rauch, *Geschichte der Sowjetunion*, 89.

55 Rauch, *Geschichte der Sowjetunion*, 99ff.

56 Kenez, *Civil War in South Russia*, 145.

57 David Golinkow, *Fiasko einer Konterrevolution: Das Scheitern antisowjetischer Verschwörungen in der UdSSR (1917–1925)* (Berlin, 1982), 152ff.

58 Kenez, *Civil War in South Russia*, 127ff.; Oleg Fediushin, *Ukrainskaia Revoliutsiia 1917–1918* (Moscow, 2007), 275.

At the official and diplomatic level, however, the Germans and Austro-Hungarians were attempting to approach the Soviet government. Apart from strategic considerations, it was economic interests that brought together these unequal partners in Moscow, Berlin, and Vienna. This situation put pressure on the pro-Entente Volunteer Army. The Central Powers now opposed its recruitment efforts in Ukraine and were also hostile to Krasnov's support for Denikin. He continued to offer the Whites money and arms but, among the anti-Bolshevik leaders, mistrust and discord now ruled. Denikin feared German influence on the Don Cossacks and did not think highly of Krasnov. The latter, in turn, became involved in a border dispute with Skoropadsky. If the heterogeneous resistance to the communists survived under these conditions, it was mainly due to the presence of the German and Austro-Hungarian armies.[59]

Within the territory under his control, Lenin considered the domestic Russian conflict settled. His opponents remained weak. The left-wing Socialist Revolutionaries had also failed when, in protest against the Brest-Litovsk peace, they left the Council of People's Commissars and sought to change government policy by attempted uprisings and by murdering the German ambassador in Moscow, Wilhelm von Mirbach-Harff. In this way, the Russian Soviet Federative Socialist Republic (RSFSR) became a one-party dictatorship under the Communist Party. The Mensheviks and Socialist Revolutionaries were forced out of the soviets. Rebellions were suppressed by Lenin's security forces, by units of the secret police, the Cheka, as well as by the Red Army being created by Trotsky.[60]

In spite of these acts of violence, external instruments were needed to help the anti-Bolshevik forces get off the ground in territories controlled by the communists. The Czechoslovak Legion, the *Druzhina*, played a key role in this. Formed from soldiers of the Austro-Hungarian army who had defected to the Russians or were in Russian prisoner-of-war camps during the First World War, the *Druzhina* had fought against the Central Powers and had been involved in the Kerensky offensive. Following the Treaty of Brest-Litovsk, these soldiers were to be sent along the only open route—through Siberia to Vladivostok—to strengthen Allied forces on the Western Front. But the transport of this well-armed force, numbering some tens of thousands of men during the period of the Provisional Government,

59 Kenez, *Civil War in South Russia*, 127, 148, 157, 163.

60 Figes, *A People's Tragedy*, 642–47.

posed a high security risk in those regions where Soviet power was still very fragile.[61]

Mistrust also played a role. The Kremlin rulers were seen as instruments of German war policy. When the people's commissars attempted to recruit "internationalists," especially prisoners of war from the ranks of the Austro-Hungarian troops,[62] to the Red Army, the legionnaires saw this as a strategy of the Central Powers and a direct threat. For various reasons, there were delays in the transport to Vladivostok. As a result of conflicts between the Czechoslovak units and local Soviet representatives, Trotsky decided to disarm the Legion, by force if necessary.[63] The crisis escalated in May and June 1918. The Legion resisted and occupied the rail line in Siberia and in the area west of the Urals.[64] The resulting power vacuum was filled by Russian oppositionists with the direct support of the Czechoslovaks. A Committee of Members of the Constituent Assembly (*Komuch*) was established in Samara, consisting overwhelmingly of Socialist Revolutionary delegates. However, obtaining little support from the local population and viewed critically by both left and right, the new rulers in Samara had little to put up against the approaching Red Army. At a conference in Ufa initiated by the Allies, the Socialist Revolutionaries were prepared to compromise with the national-conservative government in Omsk that had also emerged in the course of the "Czech uprising." As a result of this compromise, a "Directory" of the different power centers was established.[65]

This body, claiming "all-Russian" authority and consisting mainly of Socialist Revolutionaries, was short-lived. There was increasing criticism and intervention from the right. When the Czechs refused to help, the days of the Directory were numbered. With the full knowledge of the Allies, the onetime commander of the Black Sea Fleet, Admiral Aleksandr Kolchak, established his rule, arresting and persecuting socialist groups. The proclamation of Admiral Kolchak as supreme commander (*verkhovnyi pravitel'*), almost exactly one year

---

61 On the Czechoslovak Legion, see GARF, f. r-393, op. 3, d. 591; RGASPI, f. 17, op. 109, d. 117.

62 RGASPI, f. 17, op. 109, d. 10.

63 Gerbung Thunig-Nittner, *Die Tschechoslowakische Legion in Russland. Ihre Geschichte und Bedeutung als politisch-geistiger Faktor bei der Entstehung der tschechoslowakischen Republik* (Wiesbaden, 1970), 55ff.

64 Leidinger and Moritz, *Gefangenschaft, Revolution, Heimkehr*, 387ff.

65 David Footman, *Civil War in Russia* (New York and London, 1961), 96–103; Richard Luckett, *The White Generals: An Account of the White Movement and the Russian Civil War* (London, 1971), 164; Manfred Hildermeier, *Die Russische Revolution 1905–1921* (Frankfurt, 1989), 271.

after the October Revolution, marked the defeat of the non-Bolshevik left. In the "revolutionary turmoil," notions of regional government and federalism disappeared in the face of demands from the White officers that Russia be treated as one indivisible whole.[66]

Kolchak's power, however, was without any firm base. Lacking popular support, he engaged in conflicts with local warlords and Cossack atamans who had the backing of the Japanese and the Western powers. During 1918, resistance to the Reds depended principally on the effective Czechoslovak Legion. Without its constant support, in the opinion of those who were familiar with the situation, the rule of the *verkhovnyi pravitel'* would have required greater engagement on the part of Western powers. Margarete Klante, an official in the department dealing with protection of detainees in the Prussian war ministry between 1914 and 1918, expressed publicly what many believed to be the case. Although she herself was anti-Czech, in the interwar period she carried out very fundamental research into the history of the Czechoslovak Legion, emphasizing its military prowess, and arrived at the conclusion that "it was when the Czechs began to withdraw that the White Russian front began to falter, and it never recovered."[67] A further factor, of course, was the lack of unity among the Allies. To protect the supplies they had delivered to the tsarist army in their struggle against the Central Powers, they landed troops in Murmansk, Arkhangelsk, and Vladivostok. The action in northern Russia was justified by the presence of German troops in Finland, and it proceeded with the initial agreement of the Bolsheviks. Before the Treaty of Brest-Litovsk, Moscow saw itself threatened by the German army and therefore did not oppose the continued alliance with the Entente. But when British and Japanese naval contingents landed in Vladivostok in early April 1918, the people's commissars judged this to be the beginning of "hostile action against the Soviets."[68]

Rumors circulated in Allied capitals about plans of the German emperor and his generals to bring the entire territory of the ex-tsarist empire under Berlin's control, mainly by mobilizing hundreds of thousands of German and Austro-Hungarian prisoners of war.[69]

66 On the policies of the White generals, see GARF, f. 6817, op. 1, d. 14; cf. Swain, *Russia's Civil War*, 61–63.

67 ÖSTA, KA, Nachlass Raabl-Werner, B 141/4, Part II; See HGM, Plennyarchiv, Harald Halls to Joachim Givens, 26 January 1932.

68 RGASPI, f. 17, op. 109, d. 10.

69 James William Morley, *The Japanese Thrust into Siberia, 1918* (New York, 1957), 343; cf. Leo Trotzki, *Die Geburt der Roten Armee* (Vienna, 1924).

These reports were used by the Allies, in addition to their hostility to the Bolsheviks, to justify Allied intervention. More important still were Entente efforts, by "reestablishing the Eastern Front,"[70] to keep German troops away from the Western Front.[71] But Paris and London disagreed on how concretely to do this. For a long time the French prime minister, Georges Clemenceau, could not be persuaded about any "Russian engagement" of the Czechoslovaks. Clemenceau wanted to see them in action on the French battlefield.[72] The American president, Woodrow Wilson, wanted to use his troops to defend the legionnaires "against German and Austrian prisoners of war." Whether innocently or hypocritically, he linked the American presence in Siberia to the principle of maintaining neutrality with regard to internal developments in Russia.[73] Another motive could not easily be rejected out of hand: Washington saw its small force, in alliance with the Czechoslovak Legion, as a counterweight to Japanese troops. Japanese expansionist aims in the Far East also divided leaders in Tokyo. The civilian and military elite warned against any unilateral move against Russia, as well as a possible confrontation with the American competitors in the Pacific. There were powerful opponents of any intervention that had not been adequately discussed and approved by all involved.[74]

It was a similar situation with the leaders in Britain and France. They agreed that their policy toward Russia was part of their world war strategy.[75] David Lloyd George, the British prime minister, impressed on his collaborators that everything had to be done to counteract reinforcement of the Germans and Austro-Hungarians by the Soviets. "Seen in this light," said Lloyd George, "a civil war or even the continuation of chaos would be advantageous for us."[76]

The situation changed, however, with the armistice on the Western Front, the end of the First World War, and the annulment of the Brest-

---

70 See chapter 4c-e in the present volume.

71 David Bullock, *The Russian Civil War, 1918–22* (Oxford and New York, 2008), 90ff.

72 George Kennan, *The Decision to Intervene* (Princeton, 1958), 144ff.; John Bradley, *Allied Intervention in Russia* (London, 1968), 77.

73 TNA, FO 379/3332, 85–91; George Kennan, *Russia and the West under Lenin and Stalin* (New York, 1961), 143; cf. chapter 4c-e in the present volume.

74 Morley, *The Japanese Thrust into Siberia,* 55–57; Betty Miller Unterberger, *The United States, Revolutionary Russia and the Rise of Czechoslovakia* (Chapel Hill, N.C., and London, 1989), 146–48.

75 Bullock, *The Russian Civil War, 1918–22*, 90.

76 A. M. Gollin, *Proconsul in Politics: A Study of Lord Milner in Opposition and Power* (London, 1964), 557; see also the relevant sections of chapter 4c-e in the present volume.

Litovsk treaty. Anti-Bolshevik motives then came to the forefront. The Allied victors even agreed to German troops remaining temporarily in the western regions of the ex-tsarist empire. The spread of "October ideas" and the offensive of the Red Army spurred the leaders in Paris and London to take "defensive measures." Uncompromising anticommunists such as the British war minister, Winston Churchill, and the French general Ferdinand Foch were decisively in favor of an intervention to support the Whites.[77] Impressive "plans for a crusade" which, as envisaged by Foch, would see large forces marching on Moscow, did not gain the support of civilian governments. When Woodrow Wilson's proposal to bring the Bolsheviks and their opponents to the negotiating table had fallen through, Clemenceau, who had little sympathy for Wilson's initiative, drew back from any "Russian adventure."[78] French troops, mostly stationed on the Black Sea coast, were withdrawn. Paris now supported the creation of a *cordon sanitaire* of Central European states against Soviet rule, a plan that gradually won acceptance, at the end of 1919, among the victorious powers of the First World War.[79]

Winston Churchill, who in May of that year had reinforced the British contingent in Arkhangelsk, eventually had to draw back from an active policy of intervention. Most British troops left the Caucasus and northern Russia in the autumn of 1919. They held on for a few more months in Batumi. Meanwhile, the evacuation of Siberia was in full swing. The Japanese were the last to leave their region around Vladivostok in October 1922.[80]

A vague recognition of the Kolchak government in June 1919 had no effect. The Whites received less and less assistance. In view of the desire for peace among their own populations and occasional mutinies among their forces, the Western powers decided to normalize relations with the Russian Soviet Republic.[81] In this context, it proved to be an advantage that the Entente states had never succeeded in agreeing on a united approach to the Kremlin leadership. Even during the phase of confrontation, negotiating channels had been kept open. Talks were

---

77 Leidinger and Moritz, *Gefangenschaft, Revolution, Heimkehr*, 630–32; Figes, *A People's Tragedy*, 573ff.

78 Alex P. Schmid, *Churchills privater Krieg. Intervention und Konterrevolution im russischen Bürgerkrieg, November 1918–März 1920* (Zurich, 1974), 76–78.

79 Evan Mawdsley, *The Russian Civil War* (Edinburgh, 2008), 179.

80 Rauch, *Geschichte der Sowjetunion*, 123, 142ff.

81 Schmid, *Churchills privater Krieg*, 249.

begun, compromises were sought, bilateral treaties were desired and finally achieved in the early 1920s.[82]

The Weakness of the Whites

Although the foreign intervention may appear contradictory, largely uncoordinated and half-hearted,[83] the anti-Bolshevik forces would not have been viable without the influence of the Central Powers and their wartime opponents. With their occupied territories and bases in the hinterland and in the coastal towns of the "peripheral regions," they offered the national movements and White forces secure zones and areas for retreat. Even though Bolshevik propaganda about an elaborate plan of the "world bourgeoisie" and large-scale assaults on "proletarian people's power" may have had little to do with reality, the Czechoslovak forces under French command, estimated by Paris to be sixty thousand men, were a vital military factor on the Siberian front as well as in the Ural and Volga regions. In northern Russia there were more than ten thousand Entente soldiers engaged in battle against Soviet forces.[84]

Apart from this, however, the Allies played a subordinate role everywhere. Their assistance concentrated on providing funds. But this had little effect in view of the economic crisis in the ex-tsarist empire, with high inflation, devaluation of the ruble following the February Revolution, Bolshevik nationalization of the banks, the large-scale collapse of the financial system, and the transition to a natural and subsistence economy. The tactic of the British secret service, which was to get the big financial institutions under British control and, by this means, under the pretext of fighting German influence, to support London's "capitalist imperialist" aims, was at work again from the beginning of 1918.[85]

The sending of armaments, weapons, and munitions had a more substantial effect. The Entente arsenal, bulging at the end of the First World War, was largely placed at the disposal of the anti-Bolshevik forces, especially in 1919. But as the Western powers gradually moved toward relations with the Kremlin leadership and deliveries

82 See GARF, f. 7506, op. 1, d. 12, 6–8; ibid., d. 15, 28–36; TNA, FO 371/390, pp. 304–6.

83 For a complaint about this from the British Foreign Office, see TNA, FO 608/206, p. 390–401.

84 Mawdsley, *The Russian Civil War*, 219.

85 TNA, WO 32 5697 and 33 967, also FO 608/247, 442–44; cf. Michael Occleshaw, *Dances in Deep Shadows: Britain's Clandestine War in Russia, 1917–20* (London, 2006), 45–48, 60–65. On French strategy, see chapter 4c-e in the present volume.

to Kolchak, Denikin, and the anti-Bolshevik *Atamanshchina*[86] were reduced or halted altogether, the shortages had an immediate effect on the enemies of the October regime.[87]

The defeat of the Whites revealed their dependence on foreign powers. In spite of this, it cannot be seen as the only reason for their failure. The tsarist officers had not, at the time, responded adequately to the revolutionary turmoil. With a nostalgic vision of the past, they carried out their operations against the Soviets, the *Sovdepiia*,[88] as they had previously against the representatives of the February revolt, the *Kerenshchina*,[89] solely by military means, without paying adequate attention to their political program. Plans for later regulations from a constituent assembly gave their decrees a purely provisional character.[90]

There was also some doubt about whether the Constitutional Democrats, the conservatives or the right-wing parties would be willing to give their approval to an as yet immature Russian parliamentarism. In any case, the Constituent Assembly of January 1918 was dominated by the Socialist Revolutionaries who, by that time, were being ostracized and persecuted by the White generals. Among the Cadets who had joined the anti-Bolshevik military, efforts were made to respond to the social unrest in the country, but their proposals were heeded by very few. Moreover, liberal plans lagged behind developments in the cities and villages.[91]

For the workers and peasants, the Whites represented reaction, the return of entrepreneurs and estate holders. Baron Petr Wrangel, the successor to Denikin, also had to combat this broad front from his Crimean base in 1920, when he attempted to "liberate a piece of Russian territory" from the Bolsheviks. Promises to implement a progressive agrarian law ended up as complex and badly propagated regulations that gave considerable powers to the erstwhile rulers.[92] The old elite's sentiments of revenge were dominant even in Wrangel's

86 Cossack ataman rulers and their followers.

87 There are contradictory views on this: Figes, *A People's Tragedy*, 574ff., 680; Mawdsley, *The Russian Civil War*, 369, 394. On British deliveries to various anti-Bolshevik forces until the end of 1918/beginning of 1919, see TNA, FO 608/177, 193. On the supply of English planes to Denikin, see TNA, FO 608/207, 78–80. On London's criticism of the poor distribution of war materials in territories controlled by the Whites, see TNA, WO 158/752, 79ff.

88 A derogatory term used by anti-Bolshevik forces to refer to Soviet Russia.

89 The rule of Kerensky and his supporters.

90 See Katzer, *Die weisse Bewegung in Russland*, 134ff., 457–75, 483–93.

91 GARF, f. 439, op. 1, d. 51.

92 P. N. Wrangel, *The Memoirs of General Wrangel* (London, 1929), 171–75.

own entourage. This led frequently to excessive acts of violence that only confirmed the population in its already existing hostility. Against this background, the Whites, even more infuriated, turned against the "underprivileged classes," especially against the Jews, vilified as the "stirrups of Bolshevism." According to various estimates, between fifty and two hundred thousand died in pogroms. Ethnic independence movements such as the Ukrainian national movement were also responsible for pogroms. At least thirty thousand Jews were murdered in Ukraine.[93] Moreover, Red Army units were not immune to widespread anti-Semitism.[94]

For a variety of reasons, the Red Army had the advantage. The skirmishes and then the all-out war between Poland and Soviet Russia ended in a truce and, eventually, a peace treaty after the failure of the Soviet offensive on the Vistula. The Red Army was therefore able to strengthen its forces in the Crimea and defeat Wrangel at the end of 1920. Here we have a final example of how the interaction between different national and regional goals had its effect on the White offensive.[95]

The White defense of "Russia, one and indivisible" had already created problems, especially in 1919. In his advance on Kyiv, Denikin ignored the language, culture, and institutions of the local population, to which, in the centralist tradition, rejecting Ukrainian national feelings, he referred as "Little Russians." The Whites ruled out the Ukrainian Directory, led by Symon Petliura, as a partner. Petliura, following a controversial alliance with Poland, eventually had to give way to the Bolsheviks, as did the Russian anti-Bolsheviks, who had neglected to create a functioning administrative system in the territories they had conquered.[96] At the same time, morale declined among Denikin's most important partners. The Cossacks lacked any

---

93 Scholars are skeptical of claims exceeding one hundred thousand: Kappeler, *Kleine Geschichte der Ukraine*, 182. See also Ulrich Herbeck, *Das Feindbild vom "jüdischen Bolschewiken." Zur Geschichte des russischen Antisemitismus vor und während der Russischen Revolution* (Berlin, 2009), 234–314; A. F. Maleev, *Tridtsat' dnei evreiskogo pogroma v mestechke Krivoe Ozero* (Moscow, 1921); I. E. Tscherikover, *Antisemitizm i pogromy na Ukraine, 1917–1918* (Berlin, 1923); Iu. Larin, *Evrei i antisemitizm v SSSR* (Moscow and Leningrad, 1929); I. B. Shechtman, *Pogromy dobrovol'cheskoi armii na Ukraine* (Berlin, 1932).

94 Herbeck, *Das Feindbild vom "jüdischen Bolschewiken,"* 373–98; *Lenin on the Jewish Question*, ed. Hyman Lumer (New York, 1974); Sonja Margolina, *Das Ende der Lügen. Russland und die Juden im 20. Jahrhundert* (Berlin, 1992); Louis Rapoport, *Hammer, Sichel, Davidstern. Judenverfolgung in der Sowjetunion* (Berlin, 1992).

95 Bullock, *The Russian Civil War*, 116–22.

96 A. I. Denikin, *Ocherki russkoi smuty*, vol. 4 (Paris, 1925), 86–88.

enthusiasm for an offensive against Moscow.[97] Outside their own areas of settlement, they achieved less by their military ability than by their tendency to go on forays in search of booty. Especially when retreating, they engaged in plundering and acts of violence. These also featured in the defeat of Kolchak in his failed attempt to overthrow Soviet power from Siberia. In this battle sector as well, the population was not won over to the side of the Whites, although there were hardly any noble estates east of the Urals, and the peasants of the region, engaged in the dairy industry and in a mixed economy, were comparatively well off.[98] In some areas, resistance to the anti-Bolshevik military was not restricted to the villages. In the struggle against Denikin, especially in Ukraine, whole areas placed themselves under rival gangs and particularly under partisan leaders such as Nykyfor Hryhoriiv and the anarchist leader Nestor Makhno.[99]

Under such circumstances, the Whites did not have enough time to stabilize their rule in the territories they occupied. It was also a general disadvantage for them that they operated separately from one another, in peripheral regions of the old tsarist empire, while the Soviet government ruled over the central area, with access to weapons stores, industrial enterprises, and dense transport networks. The situation for the anticommunists was also worsened by internal conflicts. Denikin, with his relatively liberal views, was surrounded by conservatives and monarchists. Kolchak was encircled by Siberian and Far Eastern atamans, "schemers," and "ambitious egotists," a following that, in his own estimation, largely hung around behind the front and contributed little to the support of the troops.[100] At the same time, Kolchak and his supporters were reluctant to give other military leaders too much scope for action. Denikin, for his part, unwillingly accepted the claim of the *verkhovnyi pravitel'* and his government in Omsk to sole representation. This government had also for some time regarded Nikolai Yudenich, who had risen to commander of a pro-Allied army in northwestern Russia, as a competitor.[101]

In an action that must have displeased the supporters of an "indivisible fatherland," Yudenich, who himself rejected separatist

97 K. N. Sokolov, *Pravlenie generala Denikina* (Sofia, 1921), 191.

98 Figes, *A People's Tragedy*, 671.

99 See, for example: Nestor Makhno, *Krest'ianskoe dvizhenie na Ukraine 1918–1921. Dokumenty i materialy* (Moscow, 2006).

100 TNA, FO 608/177, 133–35; Peter Fleming, *The Fate of Admiral Kolchak* (Edinburgh, 2001), 136.

101 GARF, f. 6817, op. 1, d. 14. See also Christopher Lazarski, *The Lost Opportunity: Attempts at Unification of the Anti-Bolsheviks, 1917–1919* (Lanham, Md., 2008).

tendencies, was forced to come to a compromise with Estonia.[102] But the willingness of Estonians to support the Whites had its limits. Like the British units on the territory, their attitude was a more defensive one. Yudenich's attempt to capture St. Petersburg in the autumn of 1919 failed.[103] Similarly unsuccessful were the operations of Prince Pavel Bermondt-Avalov. He attempted, with German assistance, to establish a foothold in Latvia in order to march eastward from there and capture Moscow before Kolchak or Denikin. The victors in the First World War viewed the possible expansion of Berlin's influence with suspicion. In Riga, English naval units put an end to Bermondt-Avalov's adventure. Latvia, Estonia, and Lithuania seceded from the empire, as Finland had already done in practice in May 1918. In 1920 they signed peace treaties with Lenin's Soviet government, which thereby recognized the sovereignty of these neighboring western states.[104]

The Kremlin leadership, in the meantime, had succeeded in tightening up the militarized state apparatus. The Red Army functioned as the main support of the regime. Numerically it was far larger than the White forces. In fact, in what was militarily the most difficult period for Council of People's Commissars, in 1919, Trotsky's forces had twice as many infantrymen and machine guns as Denikin's troops.[105] It was only his cavalry that was weaker. As a result, Trotsky pushed forward his "proletarian" offensive on horseback. At the same time, in all weapons categories, he recruited officers from the old tsarist army in order to provide the leadership of his troops with experts. Although this policy was criticized in party circles, it proved successful militarily and was not simply the result of pressure applied to the potential "class enemy" and its supporters. Even such individuals as the former commander in chief of the army, Aleksei Brusilov, did not see the Whites as a genuine alternative to the October regime. In spite of ideological reservations, there were many who thought like Brusilov. To them, the Bolsheviks seemed to be the only possible representatives of the "Russian fatherland."[106]

The Red Army grew steadily. Between December 1918 and mid-1919, it increased from around 400,000 to 1.5 million and, by 1920, to 5

---

102 GARF, f. 6817, op. 1, d. 14.

103 Figes, *A People's Tragedy*, 679–81; Brüggemann, *Die Gründung der Republik Estland*, 448.

104 Leidinger and Moritz, *Gefangenschaft, Revolution, Heimkehr*, 631; Rauch, *Geschichte der Sowjetunion*, 140.

105 Swain, *Russia's Civil War*, 154.

106 GARF, f. 5972, op. 1, d. 101; ibid., op. 3, d. 170.

million.[107] The overall character of the battles and campaigns changed. Until then, small units had ruled the terrain with "rapid movements." What now emerged were stable front lines with larger fighting units ranging in size from ten thousand to one hundred thousand men. This form of war was made possible by conscription, which, in turn, led to many desertions and refusals to serve.[108]

But here also, if we look more closely, we can see that the people's commissars acted more wisely than their opponents. On the Soviet side, there were many attempts to reeducate insubordinate soldiers, while the Whites, without exception, had them killed. Against this background, when, for instance, Denikin's units advanced on the army and weapons base at Tula, south of Moscow, deserters rejoined the Soviet troops. The Mensheviks, in addition, mobilized those workers who were still "on strike" against Lenin's government to come to the defense against the Whites. Band leaders such as Makhno declared that it was essential first to eliminate the Whites in order then to get rid of the Reds. This temporary alliance between the communists and the "green" peasant revolution, the latter partly supportive of the Socialist Revolutionaries, gave Lenin's government a temporary advantage.[109] But behind this limited alliance, an internal front was apparent in the Soviet power base.[110]

Internal Conflict

The struggle between supporters and opponents of the October regime was accompanied by a radicalization that manifested itself in acts of repression against the population. Most of the population kept its distance from the warring parties and, for that very reason, was affected by these coercive measures—attacks from the Whites and an increasingly systematic Red terror. The special instrument of this terror was the Cheka, which had 37,000 men in January 1919 and about 137,000 in the late summer of 1921. Tens of thousands were arrested, held as hostages, or executed. The system of camps for control and economic exploitation of the "class enemy" was already making its appearance.[111]

---

107 Swain, *Russia's Civil War*, 154; Hildermeier, *Geschichte der Sowjetunion*, 142.

108 GARF, f. 130, op. 2, d. 120; ibid., d. 277.

109 Peter Kenez, review of Christopher Lazarski, *The Lost Opportunity: Attempts at Unification of the Anti-Bolsheviks, 1917–1919*, in *Revolutionary Russia* 23, no. 1 (June 2010): 129ff.

110 Swain, *Russia's Civil War*, 127; cf. GARF, f. 130, op. 3, d. 198; ibid., d. 363.

111 See George Leggett, *The Cheka: Lenin's Political Police: The All-Russian Extraordinary Commission for Combatting Counter-Revolution and Sabotage (December 1917 to February 1922)* (Oxford, 1981).

The Bolsheviks carried on a social campaign that, as a conflict among "Russian brothers," was rejected not least by the village, although it took place in an already violent society.[112] Conscription in the "modern state" and the First World War as a "total" war, involving all personal and material resources, changed whole regions, even those distant from the front. The return of soldiers from the ranks of the fallen tsarist army brought aggressive forces into the community (*obshchina*) that traditionally had attempted to enforce their code of ethics with frightful methods of torture and death.[113]

These various sources of brutality often served as a justification for the brutality of the Kremlin leadership's rule. The Communist Party's followers also made use of ideological weapons that served to further sharpen the conflict. This allowed them to claim, for instance, that nationalization decrees had transferred the management of factories from the workers to communist officials. The dissatisfaction of the proletariat, intensified by the shortage of supplies in the cities and industrial areas, expressed itself in an almost permanent readiness to strike. Among Bolshevik cadres, there was frequent criticism of the way in which workers' needs were ignored and of rule by an increasingly bureaucratic party apparatus.[114]

Moreover, Lenin and his comrades regarded themselves as a "red island" in a "green" ocean of anti-Marxist "peasant masses." The attempt to create a cleavage in agrarian society and the struggle of the newly formed "committees of the village poor" against the "wealthy kulaks" were directed, as a "strategy of socialist restructuring," toward the maintenance of Bolshevik power. These committees, which were to provide assistance in the requisition of supplies by procurement troops and in the expropriation of the "rural bourgeoisie," proved to be a failure.[115] The rural population did not allow itself to be divided and reacted in a much more united fashion against the intrusion from outside. Following the lynching of village committee members, Lenin retreated from this form of class struggle in the village but continued to insist on the destruction of the village elite, still referred to in derogatory fashion as "kulaks." The "grain war," designed to provide

112 On the issue of violence in Russian or Soviet history of the first half of the twentieth century, see Jörg Baberowski, *Der Rote Terror. Die Geschichte des Stalinismus* (Frankfurt am Main, 2007).

113 See Maxim Gorki, "Vom russischen Bauern," in Alexander W. Tschajanow, *Reise ins Land der bäuerlichen Utopie* (Frankfurt am Main, 1984), 97–99.

114 Hildermeier, *Geschichte der Sowjetunion*, 155.

115 *Revoliutsiia i grazhdanskaia voina v Rossii*, 2: 316.

supplies to the urban centers, was continued and intensified.[116] Added to all this were the efforts of War Communism, especially the attempt to hand over estates to state farms and collective farms. The socialist collective economy aroused the anger of the peasants, who regarded their ownership of "God's earth" as an achievement of the 1917 revolution.[117] The alliance between the people and the Bolsheviks appeared to have ended. The crisis reached its height when famine claimed the lives of millions. Peasant rebellions spread, and half the agrarian collectives were destroyed. Often as a result of activities encouraged by the Socialist Revolutionaries, in 1920–21 the Council of People's Commissars lost control of western Siberia, as well as territories in Ukraine and in the province of Tambov. Practically all the local population here joined the uprising led by Aleksandr Antonov.[118]

Following the defeat of the Whites, these uprisings represented an existential threat to the Communist Party leadership. This was evident in the anti-Bolshevik activities of Makhno after the collapse of the Wrangel front. Makhno upheld ideals of "soviet democracy," a slogan that also appeared among the demands of the Kronstadt sailors for a Soviet with more parties. The sailors who, until then, had been reliable supporters of the Lenin group confronted the Council of People's Commissars in a way similar to the striking workers, except that the workers were also demanding a recall of the Constituent Assembly.[119]

St. Petersburg, the city of the October Revolution, was in turmoil. Lenin and Trotsky reacted decisively to the challenge: disputes inside the Communist Party were dealt with by a "banning of factions." Kronstadt was captured by the Kremlin's elite force. Makhno was pursued for so long that he finally fled abroad in August 1921. Antonov was killed in a skirmish the following year. In June 1921 the revolt in Tambov was put down. Thousands died in these confrontations. An even larger number, including children, were imprisoned and later deported or shot.[120]

Antonov's resistance had achieved a relatively high level of organization. The cooperation of regional peasant groups resembled

---

116 See, e.g., GARF, f. 130, op. 2, d. 277; ibid., f. 393, op. 3, d. 336.

117 V. V. Kabanov, *Krest'ianskoe khoziaistvo v usloviiakh voennogo kommunizma* (Moscow, 1988), 240–73.

118 See Eric C. Landis, *Bandits and Partisans: The Antonov Movement in the Russian Civil War* (Pittsburgh, 2008); Swain, *Russia's Civil War*, 142–47.

119 Figes, *A People's Tragedy*, 767.

120 Swain, *Russia's Civil War*, 145–47; RGASPI, f. 76, op. 3, d. 137.

soviet rule without the communists. The victory of Lenin's government was due, in no small measure, to the military means available to the Bolsheviks. To a certain extent, it was a collision of two different epochs. The Council of People's Commissars had very reliable troops and security organizations with tanks, heavy weapons, bombers, and poison gas. The initially spontaneous peasant revolt was armed with hay forks, axes, pikes, and hoes.[121] The Communist Party was also successful because it succeeded in uniting very loyal supporters behind it. By the end of 1920, the Red Army had built almost three thousand schools that, following the "ideals of the Enlightenment," contributed to mass literacy but, first and foremost, carried out ideological indoctrination.[122] As a result, half a million soldiers joined the communists. They spread Lenin's ideas and stabilized and militarized Soviet institutions, which were being led by younger officials in the meantime. The communists' "youth work" bore fruit. The attempt to undermine the old order of agrarian society through class struggle had failed, but the generational conflict was effective. It was the adolescents from the village who swelled the ranks of the Young Communist League (*Komsomol*), and it was these members who participated to a significant extent in putting down the peasant revolts and the Kronstadt uprising.[123]

The Moscow party leadership and people's commissars had created a new "guard" for future conflicts. For the moment, they pulled back from the fight against their own population. Parallel to the violent suppression of the revolts, Lenin signaled a course correction and a willingness to compromise. His New Economic Policy (NEP) replaced the forced collection of food with levies; it also liberalized trade and small industry.[124]

At almost the same time as it won the struggle against the Whites and the Allied intervention, Moscow changed its attitude toward the peripheral regions of the old tsarist empire that it had conquered between 1920 and 1922. The final takeover of power in Ukraine, the occupation of nation-states in the Caucasus, the possession of Siberia and the Far East, the elimination of Muslim princedoms, and the union with Soviet Turkestan, until then territorially separate from the

121 On the Antonov revolt, see also G. M. Mikhalev and I. Ia. Trifonov, "Antonovschina," in *Sovetskaia istoricheskaia ėntsiklopediia*, vol. 1 (Moscow, 1961), 635–37. See also RGASPI, f. 17, op. 3, d. 128.

122 GARF, f. 2313, op. 3, d. 26; ibid., f. 2314, op. 9, d. 2.

123 Figes, *A People's Tragedy*, 767ff.

124 *Historisches Lexikon der Sowjetunion 1917/22 bis 1991*, ed. Hans-Joachim Torke (Munich, 1993), 216–18.

Russian Federation, not only created the preconditions for the founding of the Union of Soviet Socialist Republics (USSR) in 1922–23. From the viewpoint of the Soviet leadership, it was now time to openly oppose the Great Russian chauvinism that the Whites, to their disadvantage, had inscribed on their banner, and which had often been concealed beneath the Red slogans of proletarian internationalism.[125]

Although the one-party dictatorship of the communists was not in doubt, and their leaders held the "commanding heights" in the emerging Soviet Union, the New Economic Policy also signaled a change in nationality policy. At the same time as the NEP came into force, the Tenth Bolshevik Party Congress passed a resolution on the promotion of national cultures and the opening of the administration to local forces. This "taking root" (*korenizatsiia*) also had its effect in Ukraine, where the independence movement, following constant changes of regime, had collapsed. Communist policy now favored local elites and allowed the use of national languages in the local press, schools, and state administration.[126]

Review and Definitions

Any attempt to summarize what is already a rather summary account of events from the eve of the February Revolution to the founding of the USSR runs into difficulties if one attempts to subsume the many conflicts under the heading of "Russian civil war." Considering that the territory of the Russian Empire was involved and that communist "Soviet power" extended, in many cases, to the borders of that empire, we are dealing with a multi-ethnic area of action that should be denoted by the state/territorial term *rossiiskii*, as distinct from the ethnic term *russkii*. But can we legitimately use the term "civil war" here? Similarly, these events cannot be described simply as a crisis of the state in which the Red party dictatorship replaced the monarchy.

The collapse of the system in February 1917 created a particularism that called the existing polity into question. Disintegrative tendencies made their appearance, effectively an "atomization of the empire." Regions and even individual areas presented themselves as "miniature republics." The mass of the agrarian population, whose political thinking had long been restricted to its own villages and fields, regarded the mostly spontaneous takeover of aristocratic estates and

125 See Hannes Leidinger, "Nationale Kräfte," in Barry McLoughlin, Hannes Leidinger, and Verena Moritz, *Kommunismus in Österreich* (Innsbruck, Vienna, and Bozen, 2009), 203–7.

126 Kappeler, *Kleine Geschichte der Ukraine*, 188–91.

the establishment of local self-determination as the realization of old ideals and goals. Redistribution had begun before the "Red October." Lenin's land decree had merely given its blessing to this development. Decisions of any constituent assembly were therefore irrelevant.

Previous to their seizure of power, the Bolsheviks had generally profited from these processes of disintegration and from the initiatives of the peasants and workers. Their temporary alliance with the masses was further strengthened by their agreement with the desire for peace articulated by both the civil population and the soldiers, likewise by their apparent support for the movements for ethnic autonomy and independence. In this respect, it was not just the Russian Revolution but also the First World War that acted as an accelerating factor. The downfall of the Romanov Empire, the Habsburg Monarchy, and the Ottoman Empire, as well as the principle of self-determination formulated by both Lenin and Woodrow Wilson, particularly the interpretation of that principle following the end of the long global mass slaughter, contributed to the establishment of the nation-state as the norm of political order. Among the "nations" hitherto united under the rule of the tsar, the movement toward sovereignty, which so far had been weak, was strengthened. The demands that arose in this situation frequently went beyond autonomy. Separatist movements appeared, and regional governments, including those hostile to the Bolsheviks, saw Lenin's coming to power as an opportunity to break away from Russia.

However, on Russia's western borders, national movements aiming at sovereignty found themselves dependent on foreign powers. This was most clearly the case in Finland, the Baltic states, Ukraine, and the Caucasus. The most powerful intervention on the territory of the fallen Romanov Empire was that of the Central Powers. As was also the case with the Allies, their strategies were basically limited to meeting their military, economic, and political goals in the First World War. In the power vacuum created by the February Revolution, it became possible to produce a large effect with relatively small means. The half-hearted and flawed intervention of the disunited Allies managed, under such circumstances, to put their mark on events and strengthen the opponents of the communists.

The people's commissars in Moscow, who, in spite of their initially weak rule, proved themselves more capable than their "internal enemies," described this as a large-scale conspiracy planned by foreign "imperialists" and "capitalists." But in reality there was no "general plan." These conflicts were exacerbated by, among other things, the "imponderables of history," such as the appearance of the Czechoslovak Legion which, with its revolt against the October regime, took control of more territory than any other force during the First World War.

Russia's opponents established anti-Bolshevik governments and armies behind the lines of foreign troops and in the regions where they operated, as well as on the territories of the "peripheral nations" that had, on a number of occasions, struggled for independence in the past. The intervention of the Allies, frequently researched and partly exaggerated, was only one of a number of external factors. The impression was thus created, including among the decision-makers of the Entente governments, that an "artificial civil war" was being fomented and sustained from outside. After all, the fronts against Soviet units almost always collapsed as soon as the support of their foreign allies was removed. In Paris and London, in particular, there was the vain hope that Lenin's enemies, after some initial assistance, would stand on their own two feet.[127]

The relatively large military forces that confronted each other in the old Romanov Empire, especially in 1919, should not distract our attention from the real balance of forces. Both sides conscripted local populations. The result was mass desertion. In the decisive moments, however, the local populations supported the October regime because its slogans corresponded more closely to their wishes. The White officers, on the contrary, were badly equipped for a civil war. They lacked relevant programs. In addition, existing programs were often subordinated to the requirements of military operations. Many of their decrees appeared to have a purely provisional character, inasmuch as no one really believed that any definitive solutions were to be found by recalling the Constituent Assembly. In the meantime, their battles against the communists appeared as acts of revenge and punishment directed against workers and peasants who saw, in the tsarist generals and their advisers, only their previous exploiters. Divided among themselves or at least not well coordinated, the Whites, with their support for an "undivided Russia," ran up against the various national movements. They thus alienated potential partners in the peripheral regions, and it was precisely from those regions, under initially difficult conditions, that the military campaigns against the Red central area, with its larger population and greater resources, would have to be led.

It became clear, once again, that most of the population had little

127 See TNA, FO 608/177, 156ff.

interest in the power struggles going on in St. Petersburg and Moscow. Particularist forces continued to dominate. The conflict between the October regime and its opponents appeared, in many areas, as an import of external conflict. The Cossacks, for this and other reasons, were difficult allies for Denikin, as was confirmed by the Socialist Revolutionaries: "The peasants are indifferent; they simply want to be left in peace." They "are hesitant to support a war between the different political parties" and would not "fight against their own brothers."[128] Thus, many village communities declared themselves "neutral republics." They created their own forces to protect themselves against foreign armies and appealed to both the Reds and the Whites to end their conflict by negotiation. The protests in many regions against the "willful unleashing of civil war" came not only from the peasantry but also from within the proletariat itself.[129]

In many cases, the Bolsheviks were considered responsible for the armed confrontations. More than any other politician or party leader, Lenin had expected civil war,[130] thought in those terms, pushed for it, and, following his relatively rapid triumph over the internal opposition in the spring of 1918, declared it ended.[131] But then came the campaign of the people's commissars against the village, the "grain war" and the "class struggle" against the so-called kulaks. The result was a strengthening of the "green front," which, according to Lenin, constituted a greater threat to the Kremlin leadership than the armies of Denikin, Yudenich, and Kolchak put together.[132] These uprisings attained an unprecedented scale and also underwent a qualitative change. "Peasant wars," combined with workers' strike actions and the uprising of the Kronstadt sailors, took on the character of a new

---

128 Quoted in Figes, *A People's Tragedy*, 581.

129 Martin Krispin, "Bolschewiki und bäuerliche Opposition im russischen Bürgerkrieg. Der Bauernaufstand im Gouvernement Tambov 1920–21," in *Volksaufstände in Rußland. Von der Zeit der Wirren bis zur "Grünen Revolution" gegen die Sowjetherrschaft*, ed. Heinz-Dietrich Löwe (Wiesbaden, 2006), 528.

130 Contemporary witnesses and historians have seen the revolution and the civil war as a unity, on the model of the French Revolution. For the Duma president, Mikhail Rodzianko, the overthrow of the tsar in the spring of 1917 was the beginning of a bloody civil war. Socialists as well, such as Georgii Plekhanov, made Lenin and his April Theses responsible for the intensification of the conflict. See Moritz and Leidinger, *Die Russische Revolution*, 40, 45.

131 It is worth noting, in this respect, the differences in the periodization of the Russian civil war by supporters and opponents of the Communist Party regime. For Rodzianko, among others, it began with the February Revolution. Many others place it at the time of the Kornilov putsch or during and after the October Revolution. See Moritz and Leidinger, *Die Nacht des Kirpitschnikow*, 185.

132 Figes, *A People's Tragedy*, 766; Ronald Kowalski, *The Russian Revolution 1917–1921* (London and New York, 1997), 146.

revolution. Influenced to some extent by the Socialist Revolutionaries, demands in the countryside for a "genuine soviet democracy" were now combined with calls for the rule of law and an increasing interest in the state as a whole.[133]

The civil revolution (*grazhdanskaia revoliutsiia*), which aimed at representing the whole "working people" and was seen as the great new revolution after 1917,[134] came to grief on the consolidated and militarized October regime. In spite of the many attempts to establish contact among the "rebels," the poorly equipped insurgents were largely isolated in the regions. Following the brutal suppression of the uprisings, Lenin ordered a period of compromise and relaxation. It was not until the forced collectivization under Stalin in the late 1920s and early 1930s that the Communist Party again went to war against an even more defenseless rural population.

Under such conditions, tensions and confrontations in the Soviet domain were limited to local revolts. In the regions of the old Romanov Empire that were sovereign for shorter or longer periods, conflicts were mostly internal. These internal rivalries were always dependent on the actions of foreign interventionist forces, as the cases of Finland and Ukraine make clear. Great-power strategies and border-transcending conflicts of interest mixed with social unrest, particularist concerns, and separatist aspirations.

Recent Russian publications give a similar account of the *Makhnovshchina*,[135] in which the self-determination of the villages did not correspond to the anarchist ideas of the insurgent leader. It was rather a "peasant revolution" shaped by the land shortage of serfdom and provoked by the German occupation, the threat of White restoration, and Red war communism.[136] Many scholars see the period from the fall of Nicholas II to the formation of the USSR as a new "Time of Troubles," with reference to the crisis of the Muscovite empire at the beginning of the seventeenth century.[137] Although this description is

---

133 On the "national concerns" of peasant communities and indications of an interest in the state on the part of the peasantry in 1918 and 1919, see, among others, Retish, *Peasants in Revolution and Civil War*, 166, 212, 265.

134 It was, in other words, a "bourgeois revolution" (*bürgerliche revolution*) or a "citizens' revolution" (*Bürgerrevolution*), equivalent to the fundamental changes that had taken place following the overthrow of the tsar, i.e., the events of 1917, transcending partial interests in many ways and directed toward a restructuring of the entire polity.

135 The movement associated with Nestor Makhno.

136 Makhno, *Krest'ianskoe dvizhenie na Ukraine*, 5–7.

137 See Hildermeier, *Geschichte der Sowjetunion*, 134.

imprecise, it does capture the complexity of the problematic. Liberal and conservative contemporaries saw the period from 1917 to 1922 as a second *smuta*.[138] But this period of "chaos" and "troubles" was not followed by a monarchy, by another ruling dynasty on the throne. Likewise, the social upheavals could not be contained but led rather to the Bolshevik dictatorship. The analogy thus has its limits. The emphasis here must be on the novelty of the "troubles."[139]

Notwithstanding such attempts at definition, this complex conflict is presented in the literature in a mostly unreflective manner simply as the "Russian civil war."[140] This term refers to a split in the polity, within which rival groups attempt to establish, by force of arms, their right to rule and their model of rule. After the February Revolution, however, there was neither an uncontested conception of a single state and duties of citizenship, nor did the Whites, in particular, have a chance of survival without foreign assistance. Nor was there much scope for "civil war" in regions with a large agrarian population that were able to achieve many of their goals independently in 1917–18. The "civil war" was created artificially not just by external factors but also by the ideology of the communist leaders in the Kremlin. It was typical that Trotsky should see the actions of the Czechoslovak Legion as part of a gigantic struggle between the capitalist "stock market" and the Soviet "people's power."[141] Lenin and his supporters prepared for a great class struggle that would transcend national borders and secure their power base in Russia. Lenin's "internationalism," which included recruiting foreign Red Army and communist cadres as the nucleus of the later Comintern, operated ultimately within a scenario of global civil war.[142]

Outside the Marxist-Leninist framework, however, it does seem doubtful whether one could integrate the antagonism between revolution and counterrevolution, Bolshevism and anti-Bolshevism, freedom and equality, universalism and particularism into an imposing interpretative model of European and global "civil wars."

138 Russian term for the "Time of Troubles."

139 Katzer, *Die weisse Bewegung in Russland*, 1.

140 For example: Kruglyi stol, "Grazhdanskaia voina v Rossii," *Otechestvennaia istoriia*, 1993, no. 3: 102–15; Iu. A. Poliakov, "Grazhdanskaia voina v Rossii: vozniknovenie i ėskalatsiia," *Otechestvennaia istoriia*, 1992, no. 6: 32–41. For a more complete bibliography on the "civil war," see Jonathan D. Smele, *The Russian Revolution and Civil War, 1917–1921: An Annotated Bibliography* (London and New York, 2003).

141 Trotzki, *Die Geburt der Roten Armee*, 65.

142 Leidinger and Moritz, *Gefangenschaft, Revolution, Heimkehr*, 287–322, 409–39, 533–646.

Imperial endeavors and models of the polity based on the nation-state have been central to our understanding of "late modernity" and the "short twentieth century." In addition and beyond this, there is no reason why we should not conceptualize border-transcending conflicts as transnational or supranational crises.[143]

To describe these events as a "Russian civil war" would be not only to marginalize important phenomena at the end of the First World War but also to accept the perspective of the October regime, whose terminology has entered the thinking and language of its opponents and neutral observers.[144] Taking a critical distance from this, one has to give due weight to the aspirations for self-determination of the "peoples" of the old tsarist empire, as well as the concerns of the Russian workers and peasants. Considered in this way, the events of 1917 to 1922 constitute a phase of efforts to achieve independence at the moment of the Bolshevik seizure and assertion of power. These developments also assume the tragic character of a futile attempt by most of the population to prevent a violent conflict "between brothers" and to defend the gains of 1917 less against the hapless Whites than against the victorious Bolsheviks. The new "Time of Troubles" is not, in this view, a period of civil war. In its totality, it should be understood rather as an era of revolution shaped by intervention and secession, as a phase of systemic collapse and far-reaching reorganization that offered alternatives to communist dictatorship until the founding of the USSR.[145]

143 For a different view concerning the use of the concept of "civil war," see Enzo Traverso, *Im Bann der Gewalt. Der europäische Bürgerkrieg 1914–1945* (Munich, 2008); Dan Diner, *Das Jahrhundert verstehen. Eine universalhistorische Deutung* (Munich, 1999); Ernst Nolte, *Der europäische Bürgerkrieg 1917–1945. Nationalsozialismus und Bolschewismus* (Frankfurt am Main, 1987). There is a lack of comparative research into civil wars, for which a number of reasons have been advanced. Among them is the fact that it is a very challenging task for scholars to find a common basis for processes that are complex and difficult to grasp empirically and are determined by an interplay of internal and external factors. See Peter Waldmann, "Bürgerkriege," in *Internationales Handbuch der Gewaltforschung,* ed. Wilhelm Heitmeyer and John Hagan (Wiesbaden, 2002), 371ff.

144 Hannes Leidinger, "'Rot' gegen 'Weiß.' Die Ukraine und der 'Russische Bürgerkrieg,'" in *Die Besatzung der Ukraine 1918. Historischer Kontext – Forschungsstand – wirtschaftliche und soziale Folgen,* ed. Wolfram Dornik and Stefan Karner (Graz, 2008), 93.

145 Ibid.

1b. The Ukrainian Policy of the Central Powers during the First World War

Peter Lieb and Wolfram Dornik

The Central Powers did not really have a coherent Ukrainian policy. In the German Empire, this question was given no priority before 1914. It was quite a different matter, however, for their Austro-Hungarian allies. The Ukrainian question was not only a foreign-policy issue for Austria-Hungary but also a virulent internal problem, given that in 1910, roughly 3.5 million "Ruthenians" lived in the Austrian crownlands (Cisleithania), and almost half a million on the Hungarian side (Transleithania). They were settled in Galicia and Bukovyna, as well as in the Hungarian regions of Máramaros, Bereg, Ugosca, and Ung, where they made up about 40 percent of the population. Thus it was not merely symbolic that the chancelleries of Vienna and Budapest insisted on using the terms "Ruthenian" and "Ruthenia" to emphasize their difference from the "Ukrainians" of tsarist Russia.[1] They were aware of the risk that the Ukrainian national movement in Austria-Hungary would demand unification with Ukrainians in the Russian Empire. Within the Ukrainian national movement in the Habsburg Empire, however, there were three different approaches to this problem. Those belonging to the first group emphasized their identity with the Ukrainian nation, considered to be distinct from Russia, and described themselves as Ukrainians. They were also known as "Young Ruthenians." The second group were the "Old Ruthenians," who emphasized their affiliation to Russian culture. This may, to some extent, have been an expression of religious orientation, as many of those who belonged to the Russian Orthodox Church felt themselves to be "Ruthenians," especially in Bukovyna. The third group were the Russophile "Old Ruthenians," who rejected not only any confession that was not Russian Orthodox but also the Habsburg monarchy itself.

---

1 Wolfdieter Bihl, "Einige Aspekte der österreich-ungarischen Ruthenenpolitik 1914–1918," *Jahrbücher für Geschichte Osturopas* (Wiesbaden), n.s. 14 (1966): 540–42; Wolfdieter Bihl, "Die Ruthenen," in *Die Habsburgermonarchie 1848–1918*, vol. 3, *Die Völker des Reiches*, pt. 1, ed. Adam Wandruszka and Peter Urbanitsch (Vienna, 1980), 555–84; Jaroslav Hrycak, "Die Formierung der modernen ukrainischen Nation," in *Ukraine. Geographie, Ethnische Struktur, Geschichte, Sprache und Literatur, Kultur, Politik, Bildung, Wirtschaft, Recht,* ed. Peter Jordan et al. (Vienna, 2000), 189–210.

Austro-Hungarian officials did not make a clear distinction between these two latter groups and suspected both of being Russophile.[2]

The Polish and Hungarian national movements felt particularly threatened by the Ukrainians and adopted a strongly anti-Ukrainian attitude well before 1914, as evidenced by the numerous polemical brochures that circulated in Vienna.[3] However, the government attempted to keep the Ukrainian national movement on side by tolerating Ukrainian religious and cultural practices in Galicia.[4] The Polish and Hungarian opposition had the effect of producing a certain amount of Russophilism in the Ukrainian movement. The hope here was that Ukraine would have more national autonomy in an alliance with Russia than in the Habsburg Monarchy, where the Poles had been the "ruling class" since the granting of autonomy to Galicia in 1873.[5]

Ukrainian activities in Galicia that aimed at achieving an independent Ukrainian nation led to frequent tensions between Russia and Austria-Hungary in the years before the war. At this time Vienna had not yet begun to exploit the Ukrainian independence movement in Galicia for its own political ends. Some small concessions were made to the Ruthenians, but only insofar as they did not antagonize the Poles. For Russia, however, even this indicated a "hotbed of hostility to Russia," as Klaus Bachmann so aptly described it in his work on Austro-Hungarian and Russian relations before 1914.[6]

When war broke out in 1914, the dominant expression from the Ukrainians was one of solidarity with the Habsburg throne, and the Ruthenians were seen in Vienna as "the Tyroleans of the east."[7] The Supreme Ukrainian Council (*Holovna Ukraïns'ka Rada*), formed on

2 Klaus Bachmann, *Ein Herd der Feindschaft gegen Russland. Galizien als Krisenherd in den Beziehungen der Donaumonarchie mit Russland (1907–1914)* (Vienna, 2001), 24–28.

3 On the anti-Ukrainian attitudes of the Poles in Galicia, see Oleh S. Fedyshyn, "The Germans and the Union for the Liberation of Ukraine, 1914–1917," in *The Ukraine, 1917–1921: A Study in Revolution,* ed. Taras Hunczak (Cambridge, Mass., 1977), 305–22; Antoni Podraza, "Polen und die nationalen Bestrebungen der Ukrainer, Weissrussland und Litauen," in *Entwicklung der Nationalbewegungen in Europa 1850–1914,* ed. Heiner Timmermann (Berlin, 1998), 205.

4 Heinz Lemke, *Allianz und Rivalität. Die Mittelmächte und Polen im Ersten Weltkrieg (bis zum Februarrevolution)* (Vienna, Graz, and Cologne, 1977), 104.

5 Paul R. Magocsi, *A History of Ukraine* (Seattle, 1996), 397–457; Taïsija Sydorčuk, "Die Ukrainer in Wien," in *Ukraine. Geographie*, 457–82; Anna Veronika Wendland, "Galizien: Westend des Ostens, Ostend des Westens. Annäherung an eine ukrainische Grenzlandschaft," in *Ukraine. Geographie*, 389–422.

6 Bachmann, *Ein Herd der Feindschaft gegen Russland.*

7 Magocsi, *A History of Ukraine*, 397–457; Sydorčuk, "Die Ukrainer in Wien," 457–82; Wendland, "Galizien: Westend des Ostens, Ostend des Westens," 389–422.

1 August 1914 by National Democrats, Radicals, and Social Democrats,[8] began immediate negotiations with the authorities over the formation of a Ukrainian Legion. This Legion would also act as a positive signal for the Ukrainians in Russia. A Union for the Liberation of Ukraine (*Soiuz vyzvolennia Ukraïny*) was formed at the same time, mainly by emigrants from central and eastern Ukraine.[9]

Eastern Europe and Ukraine in the Discussion of German War Aims until the End of 1917

Before 1914, the German Empire had no political interest in Ukraine, much less a plan for an independent Ukrainian state. A few German intellectuals concerned themselves with this subject in the nineteenth century and saw in Ukraine a separatist potential to weaken tsarist Russia. These ideas were then taken up again during the First World War.[10] To understand Germany's Ukrainian policy between 1914 and 1918, it is essential to study the attitudes of German historiography on this issue. The question of imperial Germany's war aims was one of the great historical debates after 1945. In the so-called "Fischer controversy" of the 1960s, there was a lively and sometimes polemical debate among experts about the continuity of German war aims during the First World War, which included a debate about Germany's eastern policy. In his influential book *Griff nach der Weltmacht* (translated as *Germany's Aims in the First World War*),[11] Fritz Fischer argued that the military and political elite of the German Empire had had a kind of master plan. The contours of the policy of large-scale annexation that emerged in 1918 had already crystallized during the euphoria following the rapid victories in the West in August and September 1914. It was Fischer's view that the harsh conditions of the Treaty of Brest-Litovsk stood in a long tradition of Germany's "reach for world power."[12] Although Fischer dealt with Germany's Ukrainian policy only marginally, he saw it in the same light.

---

8 On the party system of the Austro-Hungarian Ukrainians, see Harald Binder, "Parteiwesen und Parteibegriffe bei den Ruthenen der Habsburgermonarchie," in *Ukraine. Geographie*, 211–40.

9 Frank Golczewski, *Deutsche und Ukrainer 1914–1939* (Paderborn, 2010), 86–102; Torsten Wehrhahn, *Die Westukrainische Volksrepublik. Zu den polnisch-ukrainischen Beziehungen und dem Problem der ukrainischen Staatlichkeit in den Jahren 1918 bis 1923* (Berlin, 2004), 29–56.

10 Fedyshyn, "The Germans and the Union for the Liberation of Ukraine," 307ff.; Golczewski, *Deutsche und Ukrainer*, 246.

11 See Fritz Fischer, *Griff nach der Weltmacht. Die Kriegsziele des kaiserlichen Deutschland 1914/18* (Düsseldorf, 1961).

12 Fischer sharpened his theses later, claiming that this world power policy already existed before 1914. See Fritz Fischer, *Krieg der Illusionen. Die deutsche Politik von 1911 bis 1914* (Düsseldorf, 1969).

These claims about Germany's eastern policy met very rapidly with opposition.[13] Winfried Baumgart was the first to publish a large and detailed study of the final year of the war and rejected Fischer's principal claims. According to Baumgart, Germany's eastern policy, including its policy on Ukraine, was not the product of planned long-term war aims but represented an adaptation to particular military situations. He emphasized, in addition, the different attitudes of the military high command and the Foreign Office. A few years later, Oleh Fedyshyn came to the conclusion that Fischer's theses were "simply not borne out by the available documentation."[14] He stressed the lack of planning in Germany's eastern policy throughout the war.

Fischer's claims were supported, however, by his onetime student Peter Borowsky, who saw his own work explicitly as a "special study that continues the contribution made by Fritz Fischer."[15] According to Borowsky, there was indeed a planned long-term German policy on Ukraine in which political, economic, and public-relations interests dovetailed and reinforced one another.[16] He claimed that the economic and political elite were even more "imperialist" than the military high command because the aim of the former was more long-term.[17] A later study by Claus Remer went even further.[18] He saw a continuity in German policy even from the period before the outbreak of the First World War. Brest-Litovsk and the German invasion were a logical consequence of previous policy. Since then, historical research has moved between these two poles of a purposeful and directionless Ukrainian policy.

What can be said today, more than forty years after the Fischer controversy, about Germany's Ukrainian policy between 1914 and 1917? Some German politicians were taking an interest in Ukraine as early as August 1914 in connection with so-called "attempts to instigate insurgency" in the Russian Empire. According to this plan,

---

13 See *Aus Politik und Zeitgeschichte*, supplement to the weekly *Das Parlament*, 17 May, 14 June, and 21 June 1961.

14 Winfried Baumgart, *Deutsche Ostpolitik 1918. Von Brest-Litowsk bis zum Ende des Ersten Weltkrieges* (Vienna and Munich, 1966); Oleh Fedyshyn, *Germany's Drive to the East and the Ukrainian Revolution, 1917–1918* (New Brunswick, N.J., 1971), 256.

15 Peter Borowsky, *Deutsche Ukrainepolitik 1918 unter besonderer Berücksichtigung der Wirtschaftsfragen* (Lübeck and Hamburg, 1970), 17.

16 Borowsky described Baumgart's foundational study as "undoubtedly...a backward step" because of its "loaded politics": Borowsky, *Deutsche Ukrainepolitik*, 15.

17 Borowsky, *Deutsche Ukrainepolitik,* 298.

18 Claus Remer, *Die Ukraine im Blickfeld deutscher Interessen. Ende des 19. Jahrhunderts bis 1917/18* (Frankfurt am Main, 1997). Remer's work is based on a thesis submitted to the University of Jena in the period of the German Democratic Republic and makes use of no new documents.

the non-Russian "peoples on the periphery" were to be incited to rebel against the central government and bring down the Russian colossus from within.[19] Poland, the Baltic states, Finland, the Caucasus, and even Ukraine were seen by Germany as potential areas for insurgency. Some thoughts about insurgency in Ukraine are already evident in August 1914 and, on 8 August, Kaiser Wilhelm himself expressed an interest. A strong supporter of this project was the undersecretary of state in the Foreign Office, Arthur Zimmermann, who spoke of inciting revolution from Finland to the Caucasus.[20] Following these mind games, the first official government exploration took place. On 11 August 1914 the foreign minister, Gottlieb von Jagow, informed the German ambassador in Vienna, Heinrich von Tschirschky: "We see insurgency as very important, not just in Poland but also in Ukraine."[21] The driving force behind these ideas was the very active German consul general in Lviv, Karl Heinze, who, in these weeks, was sending almost daily memoranda to Tschirschky or directly to the Foreign Office and the government. Heinze stressed the alleged anti-Russian sentiment among the Ukrainians in Lviv, a sentiment supposedly shared by many Ukrainians in the Russian Empire. He emphasized the existence of Ukrainian national sentiment and a separatist mood among the Russian-ruled Ukrainians. He also made frequent reference in his reports to the economic potential of this very large country.[22]

The Austrian foreign minister, Count Leopold Berchtold, reacted quite sensitively to these "insurgency efforts," as he feared that the German Empire might be aiming to establish new nation-states under its own influence by promoting such insurgencies. On 12 August 1914, in a statement explaining Austria-Hungary's plans for Poland, and as a response to Germany's eastern plans, he expressed the suspicion

---

19 Fischer, *Griff nach der Weltmacht*, 109. There were similar plans against the British Empire, beginning with Ireland and Afghanistan. But all these plans came to nothing in spite of a few daring attempts, such as the well-known expedition of the Bavarian officer Oskar Niedermayer. See his memoirs: Oskar Ritter von Niedermayer, *Meine Rückkehr aus Afghanistan* (Munich, 1918); also Hans-Ulrich Seidt, *Berlin, Kabul, Moskau. Oskar Ritter von Niedermayer und Deutschlands Geopolitik* (Munich, 2002).

20 Mark von Hagen, *War in a European Borderland: Occupations and Occupation Plans in Galicia and Ukraine, 1914–1918* (Seattle and London, 2007), 55, 67. With regard to Wilhelm II, von Hagen makes use of an unpublished dissertation: Jerry Hans Hoffman, "The Ukrainian Adventure of the Central Powers" (Ph.D. diss., Pittsburgh, 1967).

21 Fischer, *Griff nach der Weltmacht*, 117.

22 See the numerous writings of Heinze in the archives: TNA, GFM, 6/107–8.

"that the German government is discussing the idea that, in the event of a victory for our troops against Russia, it would establish an independent Kingdom of Poland and a Ukrainian state as a buffer against Russia."[23] Berchtold concluded that Poland would have to be attached to Austria-Hungary, which would also be advantageous to the German Empire, as it would block any Polish claims on Prussia. Even if Berchtold overreacted, the episode does demonstrate Austro-Hungarian fears that the German Empire wanted to create satellite states in Eastern Europe under its dominance.

Were these fears justified? Some historical research indicates that they were. For Fritz Fischer, Jagow's telegram of 11 August 1914 showed that "as early as the second week of the war, breaking Ukraine away from Russia was declared as a goal of official German policy."[24] However, a more careful study of sources makes this claim look highly questionable. Jagow changed his mind very quickly and reacted negatively to Heinze's proposals. On 31 August he sent a telegraph to Tschirschky saying that there was some interest in a Ukrainian insurgency but that the Germans had no direct links with people in Russia. Therefore it was Austria-Hungary that should take the lead here. If their ally did not warm to this idea, then Jagow would not be able "to promise to follow the plan or to spend a significant amount of money."[25] So the imperial government rejected the insurgency project in Ukraine.[26] On the military side, there were parallel discussions about this with the Turkish and Austro-Hungarian "brothers in arms" until the winter of 1914–15. But when the Turks refused to make any troops available for such an expedition, the plan was finally dropped.[27]

The first kind of war aims program of the imperial government was the so-called September Program of Chancellor Theobald von

---

23 Quoted in Joachim Lilla, "Innen- und Außenpolitische Aspekte der austropolnischen Lösung 1914–1916," *Mitteilungen des Österreichischen Staatsarchivs* (Vienna), no. 30 (1977): 228ff.

24 See Fischer, *Griff nach der Weltmacht*, 118. Fischer's student Borowsky wrote of a "definite role for Ukraine in the new order": Peter Borowsky, "Germany's Ukrainian Policy during World War I and the Revolution of 1918–1919," in *German-Ukrainian Relations in Historical Perspective*, ed. Hans-Joachim Torke and John-Paul Himka (Edmonton and Toronto, 1994), 84; Borowsky, *Deutsche Ukrainepolitik*, 292.

25 TNA, GFM 6/107, Foreign Office A.H. 475/14, 31.8.1914.

26 Fischer and Borowsky simply omitted this central document, although it was in the archive they used. See Fischer, *Griff nach der Weltmacht*, 120; Remer, *Die Ukraine im Blickfeld*, 172. This argument was largely accepted by von Hagen, *War in a European Borderland*, 54ff., but he himself used no primary sources.

27 ÖStA, HHStA, MdÄ, PA 1, Krieg 8b Januar-Juli 1918, Kt. 902, Mappe "Krieg 1914–1918 Insurrektion in Russland, in der Ukraine, Anfang: August-September 1914."

Bethmann Hollweg.[28] This suggested in a vague manner that "Russia's dominance over the non-Russian vassal peoples must be broken."[29] But no matter how significant one considers the September Program, one fact remains: Ukraine plays no role in this document because, shortly before, the insurgency project for this part of Russia was judged to be unrealistic. When, in the following months, tsarist Russia occupied parts of Galicia and Bukovyna, direct intervention in Russian-ruled Ukraine became illusory.

This reticence in the Ukrainian question is also apparent in later war aims programs. Certainly the German Empire wanted to redraw the map in Eastern Europe, but its interest was mainly in the Baltic countries and Poland.[30] While Lithuania and Courland were to be annexed to the empire, Poland was to become a satellite state. These ideas were explicitly stated in the Kreuznach War Aims Program of 23 April 1917, which has become almost a symbol of the excessiveness of the German Supreme Army Command (OHL).[31] At that time, with the establishment of the Central Rada in Kyiv in March 1917, new perspectives should have opened for the German Empire in Ukraine. But there was no change of course. There is no indication, in this period, even of German financial support for the Rada.[32]

---

28 The *Septemberprogramm* is one of the main sources in the great debate about German war aims. Until the appearance of Fischer's *Griff nach der Weltmacht*, this source was unknown to scholars. This document, written at the height of the Battle of the Marne, played a central role in his argument. For him, it was the master plan of German war policy in the First World War and remained valid throughout the war. According to this view, the imperial chancellor, Bethmann Hollweg, had not distanced himself from the demands of the Pan-Germans or the Supreme Army Command, or had done so only gradually. In his later book, *Krieg der Illusionen*, Fischer saw the *Septemberprogramm* as a continuation of ideas developed before the war. Karl-Dietrich Erdmann, however, argued that the *Septemberprogramm* was not the cause but a consequence of the war. Gerhard Ritter thought that the document had a rather defensive character. In his view, the *Septemberprogramm* represented a moderation of the much more extensive demands of influential circles in the frenzy of German victories in the early weeks of the war. A peace program without annexations would have been completely illusory in those weeks. See Fischer, *Griff nach der Weltmacht*; Fischer, *Krieg der Illusionen*; Karl-Dietrich Erdmann, *Der Erste Weltkrieg* (Munich, 1980); Gerhard Ritter, *Staatskunst. Bethmann Hollweg als Kriegskanzler (1914–1917)* (Munich, 1964).

29 Fischer, *Griff nach der Weltmacht*, 93.

30 Immanuel Geiss, *Der polnische Grenzstreifen 1914–1918. Ein Beitrag zur deutschen Kriegszielpolitik im Ersten Weltkrieg* (Hamburg and Lübeck, 1960); Abba Strazhas, *Deutsche Ostpolitik im Ersten Weltkrieg, Der Fall Ober Ost 1915–1917* (Wiesbaden, 1993); Vejas Gabriel Liulevicius, *War Land on the Eastern Front: Culture, National Identity, and German Occupation in World War I* (Cambridge, 2000).

31 On the core content of the *Programm*, see Fischer, *Griff nach der Weltmacht*, 290ff.

32 See Fedyshyn, *Germany's Drive to the East*, 47.

In contrast, the most radical elements in the German war aims discussion advocated very ambitious demands with regard to Ukraine. The Pan-German League defended the "peripheral states plan" as a way of resisting Russian influence. In the autumn of 1914 the head of the League, Heinrich Class, put forward more concrete proposals, suggesting that Ukraine should be an independent state under a German or Austro-Hungarian dynasty.[33] Class was unable to suggest any definite borders for the new state, as the geographic extent of Ukrainian national consciousness was still unclear. The tycoon August Thyssen also had an eye on Ukraine, although for him it was not Russia but the British Empire that was the main enemy of Imperial Germany. In order to strike at the heart of the English lion in its principal colonies, Egypt and India, the German Empire would have to bring southern Russia, the Caucasus, Asia Minor, and Persia into its sphere of influence. Thyssen wrote in this regard of "the Don region and Odesa."[34] This demand not only revealed ignorance of geography but also showed how an irrational hubris can be father to the thought. Other economically liberal circles had similar ideas during the course of the war.[35]

The most ambitious project of German economic liberals was the establishment of an economically united Central Europe under German leadership. This plan for a customs union of the German Empire with Austria-Hungary originated before the war. Emperor Wilhelm spoke to a small circle in 1912 about a United States of Europe as an economic counterweight to the United States of America. Walther Rathenau took up this idea in August 1914 and hoped that "the production of both empires would indissolubly" grow together. As a further step, he wanted France and Italy to be "forced" into the customs union.[36] Rathenau's proposals met no public response, unlike those of Friedrich Naumann and his book, *Mitteleuropa*, published in

---

33 See Remer, *Die Ukraine im Blickfeld*, 172–74; Golczewski, *Deutsche und Ukrainer*, 153.

34 Remer, *Die Ukraine im Blickfeld*, 176.

35 According to the politician Ernst Müller-Meiningen of the Progress Party (*Fortschrittspartei*), "The way to the Mediterranean for Germany does not go through Gibraltar but through the Black Sea and the Dardanelles, i.e., through Ukraine." See Ernst Müller-Meiningen, *Diplomatie und Weltkrieg. Ein Führer durch die Entstehung und Ausbreitung der Weltkrisis auf Grund der amtlichen Materialien*, vol. 2 (Berlin, 1917), 1224. See also the positions of the Prussian war ministry, written by Major Müldner von Mülheim in the summer of 1918 and quoted by Golczewski, *Deutsche und Ukrainer*, 248ff.

36 This text, unpublished to date, is currently being edited by Alexander Jaser of Freiburg on behalf of the Rathenau-Gesellschaft as part of a project to publish material from the Rathenau archive. The authors wish to thank Mr. Jaser for allowing them to have a copy of the text.

1915.[37] With this book, Naumann was able to have direct influence on the public debate about war aims. His ideas had a much more critical reception in Austria-Hungary, where they were tagged with the stigma of imperialism. For Naumann, the world economy consisted of core zones dominated by powerful states. Three of these had existed so far: Great Britain, the United States, and Russia. So-called "satellite states" or "planet states" were to enlarge the core zones. These small states, "in the great thread of history, would no longer follow their own laws" but would serve "to strengthen the leading group to which they belong."[38] Naumann insisted that the German Empire and Austria-Hungary should form a common economic union in order to compete with other powers. Unlike Rathenau, Naumann saw the future of Central Europe, including the German Empire, in the East and not in the West. Naumann deliberately left open the question of Russia's western border.[39]

In addition, a small circle of academics had a relatively large influence with their writings on Ukraine.[40] The principal figures here were Theodor Schiemann and especially Paul Rohrbach. Both were Baltic Germans who had emigrated to Germany at the end of the nineteenth century. Rohrbach succeeded in reaching beyond an academic audience. He was a highly educated, widely traveled and extremely productive writer. In his works he linked the ideas of nationalism with a belief in progress. He saw reactionary Russia as the tormenter of the non-Russian nationalities and, at the same time, as the main enemy of imperial Germany. This fear of Russia and sympathy for the aspirations of the non-Russian peoples to independence made him an enthusiastic promoter of the "peripheral states policy."[41] Rohrbach saw Ukraine as the key to defeating Russia: "Without Ukraine, Russia is not Russia; it has no iron, no coal, no grain, no harbors!... Life in Russia will peter out if an enemy takes Ukraine.... Whoever possesses

---

37 Friedrich Naumann, *Mitteleuropa* (Berlin, 1915). The book was reissued many times.

38 Ibid., 165.

39 Ibid., 99–101, 193.

40 Golczewski, *Deutsche und Ukrainer*, 218–39; Frank Grelka, *Die ukrainische Nationalbewegung unter deutscher Besatzungsherrschaft 1918 und 1941/42* (Wiesbaden, 2005), 84–92.

41 See Peter Borowsky, "Paul Rohrbach und die Ukraine. Ein Beitrag zum Kontinuitätsproblem," in *Deutschland in der Weltpolitik des 19. und 20. Jahrhunderts,* ed. Immanuel Geiss and Bernd Jürgen Wendt (Düsseldorf, 1972), 437–62. On Rohrbach's influence up to 1912, see Walter Mogk, *Paul Rohrbach und das "Größere Deutschland." Ethischer Imperialismus im wilhelminischen Zeitalter. Ein Beitrag zur Geschichte des Kulturprotestantismus* (Munich, 1972). See also his memoirs: Paul Rohrbach, *Um des Teufels Handschrift. Zwei Menschenalter erlebter Weltgeschichte* (Hamburg, 1953).

Kyiv can force Russia!"[42] This was how Rohrbach summarized his ideas in his 1916 publication, *Weltpolitisches Wanderbuch*.[43] By 1918, ninety-five thousand copies had been sold, so it can be assumed that his ideas had a certain public outreach. One should not conclude from this, however, that Rohrbach played a key role in Germany's policy on Ukraine.[44] In spite of his publishing success, his influence on German politics was very limited.[45]

So what kind of overall assessment should we make of Germany's Ukrainian policy between 1914 and the end of 1917? That winning Ukraine might be the lever to break the Russian or even the British Empire? That the Pan-German League or German industrialists were engaged in this? Or that the writings of Paul Rohrbach reached a wide audience? In reality, none of this matters, for all these ideas came from different interest groups or individuals without any concrete political influence. The German government may have had vague ideas, but none of them were taken up in the official war aims program. There was no insurgency project and no thought of Ukraine as key to defeating Russia in any of the official or semi-official war aims programs between 1914 and 1917.[46] There is no basis in reality for speaking of continuity in Imperial Germany's Ukrainian policy during the First World War.[47]

Austro-Hungarian Policy on Ukraine, 1914–1917

The war aims debate in Austria-Hungary is difficult to summarize clearly because of the conflicting plans and ideas of so many different

42 Quoted in Borowsky, "Paul Rohrbach und die Ukraine," 437.

43 Paul Rohrbach, *Weltpolitisches Wanderbuch 1897–1915* (Königstein, 1916).

44 This is Borowsky's view: see his "Paul Rohrbach und die Ukraine." For a different opinion, see Fedyshyn, *Germany's Drive to the East*, 24–30.

45 From 1915 he worked in the Central Office for Foreign Services at the Foreign Office, where he assessed the Russian press. But he was eventually removed from his post because his judgments about Russian conditions were considered incorrect. When Ukraine came under German control in 1918, Rohrbach traveled to the Germany embassy in Kyiv for two weeks. He was unable to achieve anything because the concrete political situation made his ideas irrelevant. He made a positive impression, however, on the chief of staff of *Ober Ost*, Major General Max Hoffmann. See Karl Friedrich Nowak, ed., *Die Aufzeichnungen des Genaralmajors Max Hoffmann*, vol. 1 (Berlin, 1929), entries for 7 and 21 May 1918.

46 Hans Beyer, *Die Mittelmächte und die Ukraine 1918* (Munich, 1956). One finds a similar argument in Grelka, *Die ukrainische Nationalbewegung*, 85.

47 Strongly supported by Fedyshyn, *Germany's Drive to the East*, but opposed by Fischer, *Griff nach der Weltmacht*; Remer, *Die Ukraine im Blickfeld*; and Borowsky, *Deutsche Ukrainepolitik*. In the case of Borowsky, reference to Ukraine in the documents he cites is a matter of interpretation, since the word "Ukraine" does not appear there.

groups and interests. The dissolution of the Imperial Council in Cisleithania in 1918 meant that the discussion of war aims was carried on at an informal level among ministries, the general staff, and officials.[48] At this level, the frequent differences between the military and civilian leadership as well as the different positions taken by the governments in Vienna and Budapest played a role.[49] Hungary made its own demands, especially with regard to territories in Southeastern Europe. The Hungarian prime minister, István Tisza, was particularly tenacious and refused to compromise. This led to accusations from all sides of excessive "egoism" on Hungary's part. But Hungary was not alone. The other nationalities in this multinational empire demanded their share of any gains from the war. Although not declared in so many words, from the very beginning the most important aim of this war for the Dual Monarchy was the survival and maintenance of its own integrity as a state. In addition, Austria-Hungary wanted to stabilize itself as a regional power on the basis of territorial gains from Russia. As early as November 1914, in guidelines sent to ambassadors in Constantinople and Berlin, the Ministry of Foreign Affairs wrote that "our main goal in this war is the long-term weakening of Russia, and therefore, in the event of victory, we would welcome the establishment of a Ukrainian state independent of Russia."[50] Territorial acquisitions would balance the different national aspirations in Europe as well as within the Dual Monarchy itself.

One of the most important instruments to achieve this was the "Austro-Polish solution." This was a key aspect of foreign policy and was at the center of the internal debate. Led by the finance minister, the Pole Leon von Biliński, a plan was drawn up to create a third state within the Monarchy by uniting Russian Congress Poland with Galicia. Its inclusion on an equal basis with Cis- and Transleithania

---

48 For a general account of the war aims debate, see Manfried Rauchensteiner, *Der Tod des Doppeladlers. Österreich-Ungarn und der Erste Weltkrieg* (Graz, Vienna, and Cologne, 1994), 189–95, 311–20.

49 The essential references here are Wolfdieter Bihl, "Die österreichisch-ungarischen Kriegsziele 1918," in *Die Auflösung des Habsburgerreiches. Zusammenbruch und Neuorientierung im Donauraum,* ed. Richard Georg Plaschka and Karlheinz Mack (Vienna, 1970), 119–23; Holger Herwig, *The First World War: Germany and Austria-Hungary, 1914–1918* (London and New York, 1997); Rauchensteiner, *Der Tod des Doppeladlers.*

50 ÖStA, HHStA, MdÄ, PA I, Krieg 8b Januar-Juli 1918, Kt. 902, Mappe "Krieg 1914/18 Insurrektion in Russland, in Ukraine, Anfang: August-September 1914," Fol. 407ff., Schreiben des Ministers des Äußern an Pallavicini und Hohenlohe, 20.11.1914.

would create a triple monarchy. Powerful interventions from both Hungary and the German Empire prevented this plan from being realized even though, until the end of 1915, it would have brought some gains for Germany. During the course of the war, however, Germany moved away from the Austro-Polish solution and itself began to exert influence on Poland. Emperor Karl promoted this idea again at the end of 1916.[51] But within the Dual Monarchy, the Ukrainians as well as those who favored a greater German state were opposed to the idea. The Ukrainians were opposed because they feared being placed permanently "under the Polish heel" were Galicia to be joined to Poland within the triple state. Rather different solutions were being proposed within Ukrainian circles, whether in Austria-Hungary, in Russia, or in exile. Among them was the idea put forward by Archduke Wilhelm for the creation of a Habsburg monarchy in Ukraine.

The Ukrainian question was not just a theoretical one in Austria-Hungary, since it was involved in the authorities' practical negotiations with their own Ukrainian (Ruthenian) population in Galicia. On the one side was a radical Polish nationalism that was dominant in the Galician administration and had considerable support in the various ministries in Vienna and in the military. On the other side were firm expressions of support for the Kaiser from the Ukrainians. The Austro-Hungarian Army High Command (AOK) had discovered the Ukrainian question for itself before the summer of 1914.[52] The k.k. Ukrainian Legion in the Austrian army (*Landwehr*) reflected these ambivalences. Sent to the Eastern Front, the legion was composed of volunteers from among Austro-Hungarian citizens "of Ruthenian nationality." Its members were regarded as military personnel and were treated according to guidelines for volunteer defense organizations.[53] But the Legion was poorly armed, its members were

51 Henryk Batowski, "Die Polen," in *Die Habsburgermonarchie 1848–1914*, vol 3, *Die Völker des Reiches*, pt. 1, ed. Adam Wandruszka and Peter Urbanitsch (Vienna, 1980), 550–53; Jerzy Gaul, "The Austro-Hungarian Empire and Its Political Allies in the Polish Kingdom, 1914–1918," in *Karl I. (IV.), der Erste Weltkrieg und das Ende der Donaumonarchie,* ed. Andreas Gottsmann (Vienna, 2007), 205–7; Lemke, *Allianz und Rivalität*, 33ff., 427–29. 467–70; Lilla, "Innen- und Außenpolitische Aspekte," 221–50.

52 Lemke, *Allianz und Rivalität*, 101ff. On the Ukrainian Legion and various other military volunteer organizations and formations of ex-prisoners of war, see Golczewski, *Deutsche und Ukrainer*, 271–91; Sokrates Iwanyc'kyj, "Die Ukrainische Legion und ihre Rolle im Kampf für die Freiheit der Ukraine," in *Arbeits- und Förderungsgemeinschaft der Ukrainischen Wissenschaft e.V., Mitteilungen* 2, pt.1 (1965): 5–13.

53 With just a few exceptions: ÖStA, KA, AdT, 145. IBrig, Kt. 1379, Nr. 420, Bestimmungen für die Freiwilligen Schützenformationen.

either very young or very old, and they were often completely exhausted by reckless actions. Constantly renewed, the Legion played an important role in the plans of Archduke Wilhelm.[54]

There was one chapter that cast a dark shadow across Austro-Hungarian policy toward the Ukrainians in Galicia in the first months of the war.[55] As the Russians advanced with surprising speed toward Galician territory, thousands of Ukrainians were suspected of being "Russophiles" and were either summarily executed by military and civilian officials or deported to a camp at Thalerhof near Graz or to other smaller camps in Lower Austria.[56] Even in the years before the war, exaggerated stories had circulated in Vienna about Russophile infiltration of Eastern Galicia that the authorities now took for real. The suspects transported to Thalerhof in the autumn of 1914 were dumped on a green-field site and had to find their own accommodation. But before some suitable accommodation could be erected, an epidemic broke out in November and raged until April of the following year, costing 1,448 people their lives. A total of 16,400 people were interned at Thalerhof between 1914 and 1918.[57] Only a few months later, the AOK admitted that this sweeping judgment about the "Ruthenian population" had been a mistake: "The misorientation of the troops with regard to the political allegiance and attitude of the population in Eastern Galicia, Bukovyna, and southwestern Russia often led to

54 See chapters 3a and 3b in the present volume. Also: Wolfram Dornik, "Polityka Avstro-Uhorshchyny shchodo Ukraïny v roky Pershoï svitovoï viiny," in *Persha svitova viina ta problemy derzhavotvorennia u Tsentral'nii ta skhidnii Ievropi (do 90-richchia zakinchennia Pershoï svitovoï viiny). Materialy mizhnarodnoï naukovoï konferentsiï, Chernivtsi, 29-30 zhovtnia 2008* (Chernivtsi, 2009), 6–22; Golczewski, *Deutsche und Ukrainer*, 102–6; Ernst Rutkowski, "Die k.u.k. Ukrainische Legion 1914–1918," in *Österreichische militärhistorische Forschungen*, nos. 9–10 (2009); Timothy Snyder, *The Red Prince: The Secret Lives of a Habsburg Archduke* (New York, 2008), 99–120. See also the references in footnote 36 in Wolfram Dornik, "Besatzung der Ukraine durch österreichisch-ungarische Truppen 1918," in *Die Besatzung der Ukraine 1918. Historischer Kontext – Forschungsstand – wirtschaftliche und soziale Folgen*, ed. Wolfram Dornik and Stefan Karner (Graz, 2008), 152ff.

55 On the ethnic situation in Galicia before 1914, see Bachmann, *Ein Herd der Feindschaft gegen Russland.*

56 As well as to smaller camps and stations in Lower Austria: Elizaveta Olentchouk, *Die Ukrainer in der Wiener Politik und Publizität 1914–1918. Ein Beitrag zur Geschichte der Österreichischen Ukrainer (Ruthenen) aus den letzten Jahren des Österreichisch-Ungarischen Monarchie* (Vienna, 1998), 199–214. There were, in addition, thousands of refugees in refugee camps in the Habsburg Monarchy (ibid., 234–74).

57 In the summer of 1917, this became a prisoner-of-war camp. With regard to the figures quoted, see Georg Hoffmann, Nicole-Melanie Goll, and Philipp Lesiak, *Thalerhof 1914–1936. Die Geschichte eines vergessenen Lagers und seiner Opfer* (Herne, 2010), 17–24, 114ff., 177. I would like to thank Katharina Sampler for useful advice and for making available the first results of her dissertation research on this subject. See also Olentchouk, *Die Ukrainer in der Wiener Politik*, 214–33.

serious errors of judgment and improper treatment of citizens." It pointed to the differences between the Russophile "semi-intelligentsia" and the broad mass of Ukrainians. The latter aspired to "a unification of all Ukrainians attached to the Monarchy"; hence the army should not regard all suspects "equally as traitors." It is also notable that the AOK ordered quite firmly that all announcements, warnings, and instructions should be posted in German, Polish, and Ukrainian ("with Cyrillic letters").[58] At the same time, all official statements for the "Ruthenians" were under no circumstances to recognize the notion of "Ukrainian."

While "Russophile Ruthenians" were being hunted in Galicia, the Austrian Foreign Ministry intervened in the discussion under way between the Germans and the Ottoman Turks about sending an expeditionary corps into the Caucasus and Ukraine. The idea of "instigating an insurgency" in Russian-ruled Ukraine was something from which Vienna could benefit.[59] At the outbreak of the war, a number of exile Ukrainians in Vienna had formed the "Union for the Liberation of Ukraine" (SVU; *Bund zur Befreiung der Ukraine,* BBU), which was promoted and financed by the Foreign Ministry. Others were recruited by Austro-Hungarian agents of the Foreign Ministry from various pro-independence organizations such as the "Zalizniak Group"[60] and the "Austrian Ruthenians" (*Österreichische Ruthenen*): these were employed to destabilize tsarist Russia. Tens of thousands of crowns were paid to trusted Ukrainians abroad, especially in Turkey. From the autumn of 1914, the SVU was used for propaganda activities among Russian prisoners of war of Ukrainian nationality being held by Austria-

58 ÖStA, HHStA, MdÄ, PA 1, Krieg 8b/Ukraina August-Dezember 1918, Kt. 903, Nr. 5271, Belehrung über die politische Orientierung der ruthenischen Bevölkerung, Juni 1915.

59 Wolfdieter Bihl, "Das im Herbst 1914 geplante Schwarzmeer-Unternehmen der Mittelmächte," *Jahrbücher für Geschichte Osteuropas* (Wiesbaden), n.s. 14 (1966): 362–66; Helga Grebing, "Österreich-Ungarn und die 'Ukrainische Aktion' 1914–1918. Zur österreichisch-ungarischen Ukraine-Politik im ersten Weltkrieg," *Jahrbücher für Geschichte Osteuropas* (Stuttgart), special edition, n.s. 7, no. 3 (1959): 270–76.

60 Mykola Zalizniak was a founding member of the SVU but broke with it as early as September 1914 and remained an opponent until 1918. From 1914, as part of the effort to instigate insurgency, Zalizniak received money for propaganda activities at home and abroad. He was influential in the Austrian Foreign Ministry until 1918 and advised Czernin during the peace negotiations at Brest-Litovsk. See Wolfdieter Bihl, "Die Tätigkeit des ukrainischen Revolutionärs Mykola Zalizniak in Österreich-Ungarn," *Jahrbücher für Geschichte Osteuropas* (Wiesbaden), n.s. 13 (1965): 226–30; Golczewski, *Deutsche und Ukrainer*, 292; Grebing, "Österreich-Ungarn und die 'Ukrainische Aktion,'" 282–87; Olentchouk, *Die Ukrainer in der Wiener Politik*, 145–74. On Zalizniak, see also ÖstA, HHStA, MdÄ, PA 1, Krieg 8b/Ukraine August-Dezember 1918, Kt. 903, Mappe: "Material zur Beurteilung Zalisniak's (November 14–Februar 15)."

Hungary.[61] This cooperation with the SVU was reassessed at the end of 1914 in view of the changes in the military situation. Any extension of the theatre of war into Russian-ruled Ukraine and a Ukrainian uprising now appeared illusory. Nevertheless, the Austro-Hungarian Foreign Ministry and the German Foreign Office were interested in maintaining the SVU.[62] Until the end of the war, the SVU concentrated on propaganda and cultural activity among Ukrainian prisoners of war in prisoner-of-war camps, especially in Freistadt. Its activity became more intense in 1918, when the task was to provide political instruction for Ukrainians in the various camps for the formation of a Ukrainian (Cossack) Rifle Division (*Schützen-Division*).[63] As far as we know, the SVU was not able to strengthen its ties beyond that either to the German Empire or to the subsequently established Ukrainian state.[64]

After the February Revolution of 1917, Ukrainian exiles increased their pressure on Austria-Hungary. Some held out the prospect of establishing a Ukrainian crownland in the framework of the Habsburg Monarchy. This was not a new idea: it had circulated repeatedly in the Ukrainian movement since 1848.[65] In the course of the war, however, this plan took on greater relevance. In a memorandum from the Ukrainian Parliamentary Representation in the Imperial Council in August 1917, the representative Kost Levytsky called on the Central Powers to recognize Ukraine as rapidly as possible and "strongly support the wishes of the Ukrainian people at the peace conference." Levytsky demanded that Ukrainians replace the Polish civilian and military representatives in the militarily occupied Kholm (Chełm) region. In general, the Ukrainian question would have to be addressed on a completely new basis in Volhynia and Kholm:[66] "The

---

61 Golczewski, *Deutsche und Ukrainer*, 108–28; Grebing, "Österreich-Ungarn und die 'Ukrainische Aktion,'" 276–82; von Hagen, *War in a European Borderland*, 54–71; Lemke, *Allianz und Rivalität*, 102; Olentchouk, *Die Ukrainer in der Wiener Politik*, 98–145.

62 ÖStA, HHStA, MdÄ, PA 1, Krieg 8b Januar-Juli 1918, Kt. 902, Mappe "Krieg 1914/18 Insurrektion in Russland, in der Ukraine, Anfang: August-September 1914." In addition to generous "compensation" for further independent activity, the SVU presented a comprehensive bill for propaganda work among Ukrainians in the prisoner-of-war camps. The Foreign Ministry and the AOK were in conflict about this payment until the end of November 1915. See ÖStA, HHStA, MdÄ, PA1, Krieg 8b/Ukraine August-Dezember 1918, Kt. 903, Nr. 4704, Ministerium des Äußern an AOK, 2.10.1915; ibid., Nr. 5373, Protokoll zwischen Forgach und Hranilovic, 26.11.1915.

63 ÖStA, KA, FA, AOK, Evidenzbüro 1918, Nachrichtenabteilung, Kt. 3671, Nr. 23.750, Ronge an Kriegsministerium/Abt. 10, Oktober 1918. See also chapter 3b in the present volume.

64 Fedyshyn, "The Germans and the Union for the Liberation of Ukraine," 322.

65 Golczewski, *Deutsche und Ukrainer*, 128–36; Lemke, *Allianz und Rivalität*, 106; Wehrhahn, *Die Westukrainische Volksrepublik*, 34ff.

66 On Kholm, see Klaus Kindler, *Die Cholmer Frage 1905–1918* (Frankfurt am Main, 1990), 281–350.

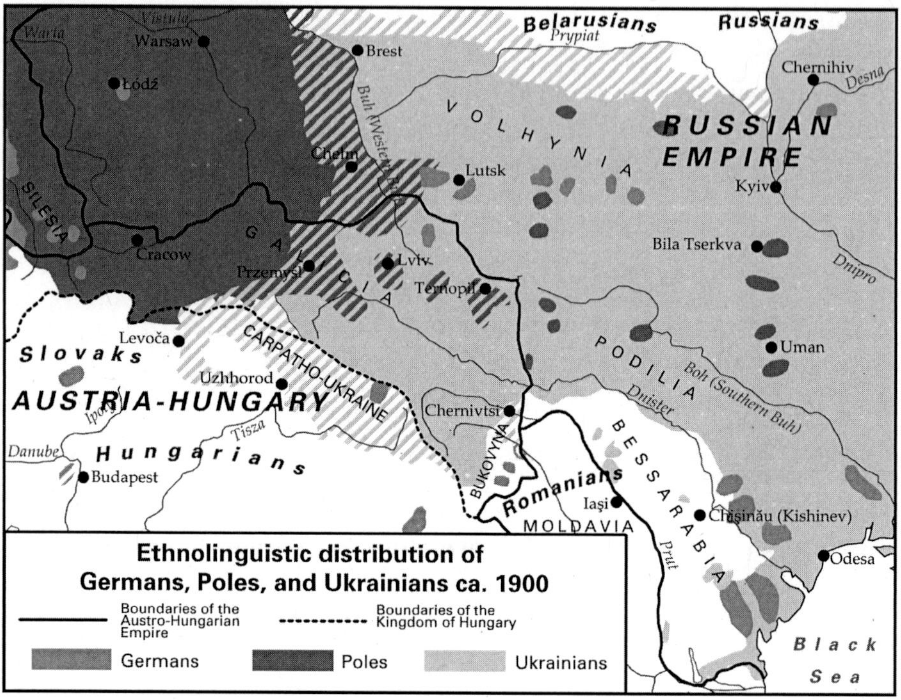

Map 2: Ethnolinguistic distribution of Germans, Poles, and Ukrainians ca. 1900 (Magocsi, *Historical Atlas of East Central Europe*, 99)

Kholm region should be separated from the Kingdom of Poland and, together with Austrian Volhynia, under the leadership of officers and officials of Ukrainian nationality...should be organized as a military governorate." In addition, Levytsky believed that "the only solution... would be to organize the Ukrainian regions of the Monarchy, in particular the onetime old Ukrainian Lodomerian-Galician Principality (Kholm, Volhynia, and present-day Eastern Galicia east of the San), incorporating the Ukrainian parts of Bukovyna, as a united crownland with a national parliament and a Ukrainian administration and to set up this crownland in such a way...that this Ukrainian province of Austria would be completely comparable to Russian Ukraine."[67] The steps toward independence taken by their fellow nationals in Russian-ruled Ukraine increased the self-confidence and status of the Austro-Hungarian Ukrainians. This was not the last proposal for a Ukrainian crownland as a solution to the national conflict between Poles and Ukrainians in Galicia.

67 ÖStA, HHStA, MdÄ, PA 1, Liasse Krieg 58, Ukraine, Kt. 1042, Fol. 572–74, Pro memoria der Ukrainischen Parlamentarischen Vertretung, August 1917.

The Central Powers and Ukraine in Brest-Litovsk

In sum, neither the Germans nor the Austro-Hungarians had a clear policy on Ukraine before 1917. The German Empire officially had no interest in the country. Nothing illustrates this more clearly than the demands of General Erich Ludendorff before the peace negotiations in Brest-Litovsk. On 16 December 1917 this prominent and certainly most powerful supporter of annexations in the whole German discussion of war aims[68] gave Major General Max Hoffmann the guidelines for negotiations with Bolshevik Russia. Among other things, Ludendorff demanded: German annexation of Lithuania and Courland, Polish independence, and respect for the right of national self-determination. Russia should therefore get out of Finland, Livonia, Estonia, Romanian territories, Eastern Galicia, and Armenia.[69] Still, Ludendorff made no mention whatever of Ukraine.[70] It was only the foreign minister, Richard von Kühlmann, who put Ukraine on the agenda before the departure for Brest-Litovsk, but he wanted to consult with the Russian Bolsheviks before recognizing the political independence of Ukraine.[71]

It was only in the course of negotiations between the Central Powers and Bolshevik Russia that Germany's Ukrainian policy began to take on concrete form but, even then, remained essentially part of its policy toward Russia.[72] It was not an independent goal, but more a means of pressure. On 24 December the Ukrainian Central Rada issued a general appeal for defensive measures, referring to its declaration of independence of 17 November 1917. The Central Powers recognized the opportunity, with the help of Ukraine, to exert diplomatic pressure on Russia.

On 16 December the first delegates from the Ukrainian Rada arrived in Brest-Litovsk. The German emissaries wanted to recognize the new state as soon as possible. They pointed out that this would

---

68 See Michael Epkenhans, "Die Politik der militärischen Führung 1918," in *Kriegsende 1918. Ereignis, Wirkung, Nachwirkung,* ed. Jörg Duppler and Gerhard P. Gross (Munich, 1999), 217–33. On the eastern policy of the navy, see the relevant sections of Gerhard P. Gross, *Die Seekriegführung der kaiserlichen Marine im Jahre 1918* (Frankfurt am Main, 1989).

69 Fischer, *Griff nach der Weltmacht*, 421.

70 Imperial Chancellor Georg von Hertling declared to the Reichstag on 29 November 1917 that the German Empire wished to respect the right of self-determination of the population of Poland, Lithuania, and Courland. Hertling did not mention Ukraine. See Baumgart, *Deutsche Ostpolitik 1918*, 15.

71 Fischer, *Griff nach der Weltmacht*, 423.

72 On the peace negotiations, see Borowsky, *Deutsche Ukrainepolitik*, 49–63; Fischer, *Griff nach der Weltmacht*, 415–48; Baumgart, *Deutsche Ostpolitik*, 13–28.

mean a "definite weakening" of the Bolsheviks and could only be in the interests of the Central Powers.[73] On 3 January the German emperor gave the order: "In the meantime, negotiate with the Ukrainians and, if possible, form an alliance with them."[74] He later repeated his demand to pay "special attention" to these negotiations. Ludendorff also thought that a separate peace with the Ukrainians would be "desirable," and Paul von Hindenburg, the chief of the German general staff, believed that with "the creation of a Ukrainian state...the Polish threat to Germany could be moderated."[75] German heavy industry had already shown an interest in Ukraine's reserves of manganese and iron and had sent memoranda on this subject to the government.

The first conversations between the Rada representatives and the Central Powers took place between 1 and 5 January and, on 6 January, the negotiations began. But these did not run as had been hoped. The main problem concerned the Kholm region, a bone of contention between Ukraine and Austria-Hungary: the latter feared negative repercussions on its own Polish population. The negotiations with the Bolsheviks also stalled very quickly. The cause here was, on the one hand, the excessive demands of the Germans with regard to annexations in the Baltic countries and in Poland that Hindenburg, expressing his "intense concern for the fatherland,"[76] regarded as minimal. On the other hand, the Bolsheviks failed to comprehend the limits of their ability to maneuver, given their hopeless military situation, and made completely unrealistic demands, such as the renunciation of annexations or compensation.[77] Similarly, the multinational Habsburg Monarchy could never have accepted the Bolshevik demand for referenda to allow national self-determination.

On 13 January the Ukrainians put forward their demands. They wanted the Kholm region as well as other territory south of Białystok and a referendum in Eastern Galicia. On the following day, the whole

73 ÖStA, HHStA, MdÄ, PA 1, Liasse Krieg 70, Kt. 1056, Mappe "Krieg 70/6 Friedensvertrag mit der Ukraine Dez 17–Mai 18," Fol. 72ff., Telegramm von Merey, 16.12.1917.

74 Quoted in Golczewski, *Deutsche und Ukrainer*, 186.

75 BA–MA, PH 1/55, Brief Kaiser Wilhelm an Lyncker v. 7.1.1918; BA–MA, PH 1/55, Brief Ludendorffs an den Reichskanzler v. 27.12.1917; BA–MA, PH 1/55, Brief Hindenburgs an Kaiser Wilhelm II v. 7.1.1918.

76 BA–MA, PH 1/55, Brief Hindenburgs an den Reichskanzler v. 3.12.1917.

77 On 26 December 1917 Hindenburg wrote to the imperial chancellor, Hertling: "I must express my serious concern that, without any limitation, we have renounced acquisition by force and war reparations.... One has the impression that, in these negotiations, it is not we but the Russians who are making demands." See BA–MA, PH 1/55, Brief Hindenburgs an den Reichskanzler v. 26.12.1917.

basis of the negotiations changed: hunger strikes broke out in Wiener Neustadt and soon spread to the whole of the Austrian part of the empire. Austria-Hungary desperately needed grain, and it was the Ukrainians who could provide it. Ukrainian dealers were aware of their advantage and could drive up the price of grain.[78] This issue hung over further negotiations in Brest. On 17 January the Austrian foreign minister, Count Ottokar von Czernin, announced in a telegram to Vienna that agreement had been reached with the Ukrainians. He expressed his annoyance that officials had allowed "public" reporting of the hunger strikes that had broken out in Cisleithania: "When I am stabbed in the back, as Austrian officials have now done by not suppressing these revolutionary appeals from the workers' newspapers, then everything is in vain.... Now that this appeal is known here and in Russia, there is no prospect of an agreement with Petersburg, and probably not with Kyiv either."[79] In the following days, negotiations took place mainly between the Austro-Hungarians and the Ukrainians about the exact amounts of provisions, but the Ukrainians could not and did not wish to guarantee either precise tonnage or delivery times. Czernin knew that he could only justify concessions to the Ukrainians on the question of a Ukrainian crownland within the Habsburg monarchy and Kholm. But he needed a generous delivery of provisions from the Ukrainians to restore stability in Austria-Hungary.

A few days later, Czernin traveled to Vienna to take part in a meeting of the Privy Council on 22 January. There he summarized the state of the negotiations and presented for discussion the Ukrainian demands with regard to the Kholm region and the creation of a Ukrainian crownland in Eastern Galicia and Bukovyna.[80] He also requested permission to sign a separate peace agreement with the Bolsheviks in case of the failure of their negotiations with the Germans concerning Livonia and Courland. There followed a lively discussion about the creation of a Ukrainian crownland. The participants were unanimous that such a policy would require them at least to rethink the Austro-Polish solution if not to drop it entirely. Emperor Karl intervened in the discussion only at the end and offered his own summary. He allowed Czernin to sign a separate peace with the Russian Bolsheviks,

---

78 Golczewski, *Deutsche und Ukrainer*, 187ff.

79 ÖStA, HHStA, MdÄ, PA 1, Nachlass Czernin, Kt. 1092a, Fol. 159, Telegramm von Czernin an Flotow, 17.1.1918.

80 Bihl, "Einige Aspekte," 542ff. According to Golczewski (*Deutsche und Ukrainer*, 189–91), the Ukrainian delegation had not, up to that point, officially asked for a crownland; it was Zalizniak who arrived in Brest-Litovsk on 25 January and brought the crownland into the discussion between the Ukrainian and Austro-Hungarian delegations.

to enter into negotiations with the Ukrainians about a partition of Galicia,[81] and, "as regrettable as it may be, to postpone the Austro-Polish solution for now and, in its place, consider an annexation of Romania to the Monarchy."[82] As unrealistic as this may seem, it is still remarkable that the emperor allowed Czernin to negotiate over Eastern Galicia and the creation of a Ukrainian crownland.

Before returning to Brest-Litovsk, the Austro-Hungarian and German leaders met in Berlin on 5 February to discuss future strategy in the negotiations. They agreed that Ukraine should be used to put pressure on the Bolsheviks and, if the negotiations were to break down, to offer military and political support to the young state. For in the meantime, on 25 January (backdated to 22 January), the Rada in Kyiv had issued its Fourth Universal proclaiming Ukraine an independent state.[83] The Germans had strongly impressed on the Ukrainians that, for tactical reasons, they should take this step, in accordance with international law, so that they could sign an internationally valid peace treaty.[84] As early as 1 February 1918 the Central Powers recognized Ukraine as an "independent, free, and sovereign state."[85] Events, however, came thick and fast in the second week of February. With the declaration of independence, Rada Ukraine found itself at war with the Ukrainian and Russian Bolsheviks. On 8 February, after day-long battles, the Bolsheviks drove the Rada out of Kyiv.[86] The Rada desperately needed help, even though the question of territories and grain remained to be clarified with the Central Powers.

Against this background, the negotiations between the Ukrainians and the Central Powers in Brest-Litovsk entered their decisive phase in the early days of February. Agreement was reached on just about all essential points.[87] On 7 and 8 February, the protocols were signed

---

81 As he had already done in the spring of 1917, Karl surrendered Galicia to a foreign power, not to the Germans this time but to the Ukrainians: Gaul, "The Austro-Hungarian Empire and its Political Allies," 208; Rauchensteiner, *Der Tod des Doppeladlers*, 520.

82 ÖStA, HHStA, MdÄ, PA 1, Nachlass Czernin, Kt. 1092a, Fol. 163–75, Kronrats-Protokoll, 22.1.1918.

83 For a contemporary translation, see ÖStA, KA, FA, AOK, OpAbt, Kt. 469, Nr. 1481, Berichte über die politische Lage in der Ukraine Mitte April, 15.4.1918.

84 Golczewski, *Deutsche und Ukrainer*, 189.

85 As the Austro-Hungarian legation in Bern informed the Swiss president on 11.2.1918: BA Bern, EPD, E 2001 B, 1000/1502, 13, B.15.11.2.

86 It is strange that this key event is either mentioned only in passing or completely ignored by Fischer and Borowsky.

87 ÖStA, KA, FA, AOK, OpAbt, Kt. 465, Nr. 940, Telegram von Csicserics an AOK, 2.2.1918; ÖStA, KA, FA, AOK, OpAbt, Kt. 465, Nr. 949, Notizen zur Hauptkommission in Brest-Litowsk von Csicserics, 2.2.1918.

regarding the Ukrainian crownland and the delivery of one million tons of grain. The protocol signed on 8 February stipulated that the government of Cisleithania would establish the Ukrainian crownland by the summer (20 July) at the latest.[88] Austria-Hungary was not able to resolve the question of grain deliveries in a satisfactory manner. The Ukrainians had agreed, in a separate protocol, to deliver one million tons, but the formulation alone suggests how vague this agreement was: "Concerning the amount of grain that the Ukrainian People's Republic will deliver, we believe we can state that this amount is available; collection and transport, however, will depend on whether the grain producers receive an equivalent amount of goods that we need and whether the four allied powers participate in the transport and in the improvement of transport organization." The Austro-Hungarian diplomats added a handwritten remark that the ratification of the peace treaty by the Imperial Council would depend on the delivery of one million tons of grain.[89]

With both these protocols accepted, the peace treaty could now be signed on the night of 8–9 February.[90] Czernin telegraphed immediately to Vienna: "Peace with Ukraine has just been signed at two o'clock at night. I ask Your Majesty to allow all bells to be rung in Vienna as thanks to the Almighty for this first peace."[91] A few hours later, he sent a telegram admitting the price for this agreement: the transfer of the Kholm region.[92] When news of the treaty broke, there was a storm of protest in Poland and Galicia. Flags of the German Empire and the Habsburg Monarchy were publicly burned, as well as portraits of both emperors. Soldiers of the Polish Legion and Polish administrative officials left their posts in outrage, and the Polish Regency Council objected with a letter to the Austro-Hungarian emperor.[93] Numerous protest letters were sent to the ministry in Vienna from local assemblies in the Austro-Hungarian occupation

---

88 *Ereignisse in der Ukraine 1914–1922. Deren Bedeutung und historische Hintergründe*, ed. Theophil Hornykiewicz, vol. 2 (Philadelphia, 1967), 209–11.

89 ÖStA, HHStA, MdÄ, PA 1, Kt. 523, Liasse XLVII, Krieg 1914–1918, Mappe 12g.

90 Wolfdieter Bihl, *Österreich-Ungarn und die Friedensschlüsse von Brest-Litowsk* (Graz, 1970), 97–100; Rauchensteiner, *Der Tod des Doppeladlers*, 537–39.

91 ÖStA, HHStA, MdÄ, PA 1, Liasse Krieg 70, Kt. 1056, Mappe: "Krieg 70/6 Friedensvertrag mit der Ukraine Dez 17–Mai 18," 120.

92 ÖStA, HHStA, MdÄ, PA 1, Liasse Krieg 70, Kt. 1056, Mappe: "Krieg 70/6 Friedensvertrag mit der Ukraine Dez 17–Mai 18," 72ff., 116ff., 121. For contents, see Borowsky, *Deutsche Ukrainepolitik*, 60.

93 The letter is in the archive of a member of the emperor's court staff, August Demblin: ÖStA, HHStA, MdÄ, PA 1, Nachlass Demblin, Kt. 1092a, Karl an Czernin, 10.2.1918.

zone in Poland and in Galicia.[94]

The policy of the Central Powers toward Poland in previous years had had little success. On 5 November 1916, in the so-called Two Emperors' Manifesto, the emperors of Germany and Austria-Hungary had promised an independent Polish kingdom at the end of the war. But very little had been done since then with regard to concrete steps toward the establishment of a Polish state. In 1917 the German Empire and the Austro-Hungarian Empire had flirted with the idea of Romania rather than Poland as a zone of influence. This had been welcomed in Warsaw and Lublin, but now the Central Powers were "giving away" ancient Polish territory—a loss of trust that could never be repaired. Poland now turned to the Entente. After all, President Woodrow Wilson, in his Fourteen Points, had called for an independent Poland. Although the Austro-Polish solution revived briefly after Istvan Burián took over the Foreign Ministry in April 1918, for many Poles, after Brest-Litovsk, this was just an empty phrase.[95] The most contentious part of the Brest-Litovsk treaty, the Crownland Protocol, was still a secret.

Finally, there was agreement in the treaty about withdrawal from occupied territories, an exchange of prisoners of war, renunciation of war reparations, and the establishment of diplomatic and economic relations. The peace treaty did not offer any military assistance from the Central Powers for the extremely hard-pressed Rada, although some thought had already been given to this.[96]

The peace treaty of Brest-Litovsk between the Central Powers and Ukraine, signed on 9 February 1918, was the first peace treaty of the First World War. In assessing this, one thing should be emphasized: in order to arrive at this treaty, both Ukraine and Austria-Hungary had to make concessions. The Ukrainians had to reduce their ambitions with regard to Eastern Galicia and be satisfied with a vague commitment to establish a crownland in the future. On the other side, Czernin knew that giving the Kholm region to Ukraine would be an affront to Poland and would be "a serious blow to the Austro-Polish solution."[97] The treaty as a whole, because of the vague compromises

---

94 ÖStA, HHStA, MdÄ, PA 1, Liasse "Krieg 56/32b, Aufregung wegen Abtretung Cholms in Galizien, Februar-April 1918" and "Aufregung wegen Abtretung Cholms an die Ukraine (im Friedensvertrag vom 9 Februar 18), Febr–Mai 1918."

95 Gaul, "The Austro-Hungarian Empire and its Political Allies," 205–9; Rauchensteiner, *Der Tod des Doppeladlers*, 520ff.

96 Golczewski, *Deutsche und Ukrainer*, 192. See the text of the treaty in ÖStA, KA, FA, AOK, OpAbt, Kt. 466, Nr. 1035, Friedensvertrag von Brest-Litowsk vom 9 Februar 1918, 21.2.1918.

97 As Czernin had already warned at the meeting of the Privy Council on 22 January: ÖStA, HHStA, MdÄ, PA 1, Nachlass Czernin, Kt. 1092a, Fol. 163–75, Kronrats-Protokoll, 22.1.1918.

reached under time pressure, would create serious difficulties in the long run. Changes with regard to Kholm, dealt with below, would not pacify the Poles, since the loss of what they regarded as ancient Polish territory was unacceptable. For the non-Polish representatives in the Dual Monarchy, the treaty was a blessing. Letters of congratulations arrived at the Foreign Ministry by the dozen. The mayor of Vienna, Richard Weiskirchner, spoke of the "Bread Peace" (*Brotfrieden*), for now the hungry population would have its needs met.[98]

The Reichstag in Berlin, especially the Social Democrats and the Center Party, welcomed the treaty as a very positive step, as did the press generally, since it recognized the right of national self-determination. Industry welcomed the promise of a new market and trading partner. Some media indicated difficulties in obtaining provisions and problems that would arise from the solution of the Kholm question. There were fears that even higher prices would have to be paid for provisions, and the news that the Rada had been driven out of Kyiv promised nothing good. The only party to reject the treaty totally was the USPD (*Unabhängige Sozialdemokratische Partei Deutschlands,* Independent Social Democratic Party). In line with the Bolshevik argument, it rejected the legitimacy of the signatures to the treaty and voted against ratification.[99] Bulgaria and the Ottoman Empire ratified the treaty quickly, as it really did not affect their own state interests. On the contrary, they hoped for rapid economic cooperation. The Ukrainian Central Rada accepted the treaty on 17 March, after the Germans had taken Kyiv.

But Austria-Hungary remained a problem. In the weeks following, Vienna began to move away from ratifying the treaty. First, there were the irreconcilable differences between the Polish and Ukrainian representatives in the Imperial Council concerning the Kholm region. Were Austria-Hungary to ratify the treaty, it would have to leave the region and hand it over to a commission. The Foreign Ministry was anxious about having to implement the crownland protocol, which could lead to a civil war in the northeast of the Dual Monarchy. Second, the ministry also did not want to ratify the treaty before the million tons of grain had been delivered from Ukraine. Until the summer of 1918, the Germans and the provisional Ukrainian representatives in

---

98 ÖStA, HHStA, MdÄ, PA 1, Liasse Krieg 70, Kt. 1056, Mappe: "Krieg 70/6 Friedensvertrag mit der Ukraine," Fol. 214–79, Glückwünsche und Danksagungen anlässlich des am 9.2.1918 erfolgten Friedensschlusses mit der Ukraine.

99 Golczewski, *Deutsche und Ukrainer*, 240–44.

Vienna[100] attempted to persuade the Austro-Hungarian government to change its mind, but without success. As late as 9 October 1918, Burián telegraphed Warsaw that Vienna had finally decided, "in view of the change in the general situation...to put off the ratification of the Brest treaty." The Polish and Ukrainian governments would settle the borders of the Kholm region in bilateral negotiations, and only then would Vienna ratify the treaty.[101]

For the Entente, Brest-Litovsk was a Rubicon that the Germans had crossed. Diplomatic recognition and the separate peace treaty with "Ukraine," which they regarded as a German construct, was to them an annexation of part of united Russia. The true face of German militarism had finally shown itself. The Brest treaty with the Bolsheviks that followed on 3 March was, for the Entente, the final revelation of Germany's annexationist aims in Eastern Europe. The broad support of the German *Reichstag* for both treaties confirmed that it was not just a military clique that had kidnapped the German population. The democratic part of the German Empire also shared this idea. President Wilson of the United States was disappointed, sent more troops to Europe, and set his sights on total victory over the German Empire—with this Germany, compromise was clearly impossible.

Policies of the Central Powers during the Occupation of Ukraine

Whereas the Central Powers were willing to move some way to meet Ukrainian demands, they were completely unwilling to offer any compromises to the Bolsheviks. Their representatives left Brest-Litovsk on 10 February, and Trotsky declared the situation to be one of "neither war nor peace." The Central Powers saw this as a welcome opportunity to blame the Bolsheviks for the breakdown in negotiations. Two days later, the Central Powers and the Rada met in Brody to discuss the issue of military intervention. The Ukrainian negotiators explained that the problems in their country could only be resolved with the assistance of foreign troops. They emphasized that

100 *Pavlo Skoropads'kyj. Erinnerungen 1917 bis 1918,* ed. Günter Rosenfeld (Stuttgart, 1999), 299ff.

101 ÖStA, HHStA, MdÄ, PA 1, Liasse Krieg 70, Kt. 1056, Mappe: "Krieg 70/6 Friedensvertrag mit der Ukraine," Fol. 349, Telegramm von Forgach an Ministerium des Äußern, 25.5.1918; ibid., Mappe: "Krieg 70/6 Friedensvertrag mit der Ukraine Dez 17–Mai 18," Fol. 146, Czernin an Hohenlohe und Storck, 18.2.1918; ibid., Mappe: "Krieg 70/6 Verhandlungen über die Revision und Ratifikation des mit der Ukraine geschlossenen Brester Vertrages, Juni–Oktober 1918," Fol. 360, Diplomatische Mission der UVR in Wien an Ministerium des Äußern, 15.6.1918; ibid., Fol. 373, Larisch an Ministerium des Äußern, 20.6.1918; ibid., Fol. 561ff., Forgach an Ministerium des Äußern, 5.8.1918; ibid., Fol. 701ff., Burián an Ugron, 9.10.1918; ibid., Fol. 701ff., Burián an Ugron, 6.10.1918.

there should be no Slavic troops, only German and Hungarian.[102] The Ukrainian foreign minister, Mykola Liubynsky, and Major General Max Hoffmann met at Brest-Litovsk and worked jointly on a Ukrainian appeal.[103] The Rada's appeal for assistance arrived in the capitals of the Central Powers on 16 February. At the same time, the Supreme Commander of all German Forces in the East (*Ober Ost*) declared that the Brest-Litovsk ceasefire would end at noon on 18 February.[104] In Berlin, active preparations were made for a broad thrust from the Baltic to the Black Sea.

While there was agreement in Berlin on the way forward, in Vienna there were still differences. Czernin telegraphed the Austro-Hungarian ambassador in Berlin and the German AOK[105] that he considered assistance for the Rada expedient, but, because of Polish protests, he wanted to negotiate with the Rada about a change with regard to the Kholm region. He asked his German allies to postpone their military operation. Unlike Czernin, however, the military had its doubts. On 17 February the Austro-Hungarian chief of the general staff, Arthur Arz von Straußenburg, telegraphed Hindenburg that he did not think an intervention in Ukraine would be expedient; politically, the Rada lacked support, and "events in Ukraine would have to burn themselves out"; militarily, there was a lack of adequate supply routes and, at this time of year, large-scale military operations would not be possible.[106] He thought that an operation against Russia would make more sense. In the next few days, however, Arz was persuaded to take part in the operation in Ukraine.

The decisive individual was Emperor Karl, who was at first strictly opposed to any Austro-Hungarian participation. After all, he had just begun a peace initiative with the Entente. Occupation of foreign territory would run wholly counter to his wish for peace. The units of the 12th Cavalry Schützen Division, which were ready to march on 17 February, were ordered back to barracks the next day.[107] On 19 February the Austro-Hungarian prime minister, Ernst Seidler von Feuchtenegg,

102 ÖStA, HHStA, MdÄ, PA 1, Liasse Krieg 3f/Russland 1918, Kt. 836, Mappe: "Krieg 2 Russland k," Arz an Ministerium des Äußern, 16.2.1918.

103 Golczewski, *Deutsche und Ukrainer*, 193.

104 ÖStA, KA, FA, AOK, OpAbt, Kt. 466, Nr. 1043, Heeresbefehl des Obost, 16.2.1918.

105 ÖStA, KA, FA, AOK, OpAbt, Kt. 466, Nr. 1040, Arz an Hindenburg, 17.2.1918.

106 ÖStA, HHStA, MdÄ, PA 1, Liasse Krieg 3f/Russland 1918, Kt. 836, Mappe: "Krieg 2 Russland k," Arz an Hindenburg, 17.2.1918; ÖStA, KA, FA, AOK, OpAbt, Kt. 466, Nr. 1040, Arz an Hindenburg, 17.2.1918.

107 ÖStA, KA, FA, AOK, OpAbt, Kt. 466, Nr. 1055, Teilnahme k.u.k. Truppen an den Operationen gegen Ukraine, 19.2.1918.

made a speech in the Imperial Council that had the approval of the emperor and the foreign minister. He gave assurances that Austria-Hungary would not participate in any military advance into Eastern Europe. To put pressure on the Ukrainians, however, he suggested the possibility of abandoning the peace treaty if the promised food supplies were not delivered.[108] Arz was extremely irritated, as he had been convinced by Czernin in the previous days that imperial troops should participate in the advance.[109] Czernin, however, stuck to his guns. On 18 February he reached an agreement with the Rada that the Crownland Protocol should be given to the German Foreign Office for safekeeping[110] and that the borders in the Kholm region would be established by both Poles and Ukrainians.[111] Until the very end of the war, the Central Powers delayed any final solution of the border question in the Kholm region.[112]

But the emperor also stuck to his position: no Austro-Hungarian troops were to join the German intervention. The Austro-Hungarian ambassador in Berlin, Gottfried zu Hohenlohe-Schillingfürst, telegraphed desperately a number of times to Vienna that Austria-Hungary should join the Germans with a symbolic contingent of troops to avoid the threat of loss of prestige and lessen the chance of any cancellation of the grain deliveries from Ukraine. Behind the back of the emperor, Czernin attempted to work out some way to join the Germans. He told his diplomats in Brest-Litovsk to persuade the Ukrainians to issue an appeal for help to Austria-Hungary.[113] The Ukrainian delegates did indeed repeat their appeal on 27 February.[114] The emperor then bowed to the pressure but attempted to save face.[115] The press was to emphasize that the political situation had

108 "Reichsrat. Abgeordnetenhaus," in *Christlich-Soziale Arbeiter-Zeitung*, no. 8, 23 February 1918; 60th sitting of session XXII on 19 February 1918, in *Stenographische Protokolle. Abgeordnetenhaus. Sitzungsprotokolle*, 3161–3167, http://alex.onb.ac.at/, accessed 19 October 2010, 11:02.

109 ÖStA, KA, FA, AOK, OpAbt, Kt. 466, Nr. 1082, Parlamentsrede Dr. von Seidlers am 19.2.1918, 23.2.1918.

110 In the summer, the protocol was burned in the courtyard of the Foreign Office.

111 ÖStA, KA, FA, AOK, OpAbt, Kt. 466, Nr. 1035, Friedensvertrag von Brest-Litovsk vom 9.2.1918, 21 Februar; ibid., Nr. 1044, Telegramm zwischen Arz und Czernin, 16–17.2.1918; ibid., Kt. 467, Nr. 1147, Csicserics an AOK, 4.3.1918.

112 ÖStA, KA, FA, AOK, OpAbt, Kt. 468, Nr. 1419, Räumung des Cholmer Gebiets, 13.4.1918.

113 ÖStA, KA, FA, AOK, OpAbt, Kt. 466, Nr. 1094, Hughes-Gespräche zwischen Glaise und Gayer, 26.2.1918.

114 ÖStA, KA, FA, AOK, OpAbt, Kt. 467, Nr. 1102, Depeche von Csicserics aus Brest-Litovsk, 27.2.1918.

115 Arz informed Czernin that on 25 February he had given Emperor Karl "only very superficial

fundamentally changed in recent days as a result of the many appeals from Ukraine for assistance, the German advance, and insecure transport of grain resulting from chaotic conditions in the country. Therefore an occupation "of a peaceful character" had become necessary.[116] The loss of image caused by the Dual Monarchy's hesitation, however, could no longer be undone.[117]

For the Central Powers, their entry into Ukraine in those February days seemed to offer a window of opportunity to give Bolshevik Russia, already militarily weakened, the final political knockout. Rather appropriately, the action was given the code name "Punch" (*Faustschlag*). On 18 February German troops made a rapid advance eastward on a broad front: the whole Baltic region, Belarus, and Ukraine came under German control. The Bolsheviks had to make a humble return to Brest-Litovsk. But they were not there to negotiate, only to add their signature. On 3 March the Central Powers signed the peace treaty with Russia. Seen in this light, the occupation of Ukraine represented an immediate tangible success. But this view of the situation was short-sighted because none of the long-term problems in the East had been resolved. Quite the contrary. Whereas in the past the Central Powers had taken advantage of internal Russian tensions and exploited them for their own ends, now they were directly involved.[118] They were now the protectors and custodians of a chaotic state. This was recognized correctly by the supreme commander of German forces in the East at the time, Field Marshal General Prince Leopold of Bavaria: "Actually, the situation on the Eastern Front has become more complex; now we really cannot distinguish friend from foe."[119] Leopold had been unsympathetic to this deep thrust into Ukraine, as he feared a fragmentation of German forces.[120] But the *Ober Ost* lacked

---

information about the military operations" to secure the rail line to Odesa "in order not to be held back again": ÖStA, HHStA, MdÄ, PA 1, Liasse Krieg 3f/Russland 1918, Kt. 836, Mappe: "Krieg 2 Russland k," Czernin an Demblin, 25.2.1918.

116 ÖStA, KA, FA, AOK, OpAbt, Kt. 467, Nr. 1121, Telegramm von Beyer an Weisner, 27.2.1918.

117 ÖStA, HHStA, MdÄ, PA 1, Liasse Krieg 3f/Russland 1918, Kt. 836, Mappe: "Krieg 2 Russland k," Hohenlohe an Ministerium des Äußern, 7.3.1918.

118 The then leader of rail transport in Kyiv, Stefan von Velsen, made this very apt assessment after the war: "We were the unwise neighbors when, in the spring of 1918, we decided to intervene in the internal strife of the Russian peoples and believed that, in so doing, we would establish useful political and economic relations with the great Slavic nations." Stephan von Velsen, "Ukraine. Die Ukrainer und wir. Ein Rückblick auf die deutsche Okkupation," *Preußische Jahrbücher*, no. 176 (1919): 266.

119 BayHSta, BayHA, Geh, StA, Nachlass Leopold von Bayern, Bd. 239, 1, Tagebucheintrag v. 23.1.1918.

120 Ibid., Tagebucheintrag v. 26.2, 7.3.1918.

both the power and the personality to enforce his ideas. Ludendorff in particular brushed these considerations aside, even though he himself had not originally intended any permanent presence in Ukraine.[121] The Supreme Army Command was unable to offer a clear strategy with regard to relations between the German Empire and Ukraine.

In 1918, Germany's eastern policy faced a fundamental dilemma with two opposing options: support for the Bolsheviks in Moscow or restoration of the old Russian regime. Should Germany proceed with the first option and maintain Brest-Litovsk and the "pact with the devil" in Moscow, as a way of accelerating the internal weakening and collapse of Russia? In the short term this was certainly an attractive solution, as it secured German influence in Ukraine for a certain time. But over the long term this option had its dangers, since it threatened to spread Bolshevik ideas into Central Europe. Or should Germany choose the second option and give its support to the representatives of restoration, the Whites? This would have been an ideologically more natural position for Imperial Germany, but it would have meant immediate Russian demands for the restoration of the Russian Empire. This would have its effect on Ukraine and the other occupied territories in the East. And one could not overlook the fact that most Germans, including the highest strata in the military, had shed no tears for the overthrown tsarist empire. After all, tsarist Russia had been a constant security risk in the East and was seen as the warmonger in 1914.

To this general dilemma of German eastern policy was now added a particular dilemma in its Ukrainian policy. Was it worth all the effort and resources to create an independent state from all this chaos, or should Germany rule the territory directly, using the Ukrainian government merely as a puppet? There were different opinions on this among both the politicians and the military. There was most support for a viable Ukrainian state in the Foreign Office and the Ministry of the Economy. The representative of this view in Kyiv, Privy Councillor Otto Wiedfeldt, saw the indirect rule in the British Empire as an inspiration and hoped to be able to apply that model in Ukraine.[122] Among the military there was also support for an independent Ukraine, though not for indirect rule. The most prominent advocate of this position was undoubtedly General Field Marshal Hermann von Eichhorn,

121 See TNA, GFM 6/35, Telegramm von Regierungsrat Schwarzkopf an Unterstaatssekretär Radowitz v. 6.3.1918.

122 Cf. BArch, R 3101/1168, Brief von Geheimrat Wiedfeldt an den Staatssekretär des Reichswirtschaftsamts v. 7.5.1918.

who, from 2 April, was supreme commander of German forces in Ukraine. Eichhorn warned against any support for tsarist forces and called instead for the creation of an independent state in Ukraine. This would also create a counterweight to Russia and Poland. With chaos reigning in Russia, success in stabilizing Ukraine would give this new state an even stronger appeal.[123] Richard von Kühlmann's successor as state secretary in the Foreign Office, Paul von Hintze, wanted to "Ukrainize" Russia from Kyiv.[124] Hintze had taken this idea from the emperor. For Wilhelm, Kyiv "should become the Russian force for order in the rebirth of Russia," but, unlike Eichhorn, he saw a future reunification of Ukraine with Russia as inevitable.[125] The Ukrainian state, in this way of looking at things, was just a historical interlude.

There was certainly a lot of optimism and wishful thinking in Eichhorn's idea. His more modest and realistic chief of staff, Wilhelm Groener, had a rather different view of the situation: "If the foundations of a healthy state are a capable army and good finances, then the Ukrainian state has no foundations at present."[126] Ludendorff agreed: "A viable independent Ukrainian state will never come into being. The national conception of Ukraine stands and falls with the presence of our troops."[127] Ludendorff and Groener would be proved right, for at no time were the Rada government or the Hetmanate that followed it viable; they survived by the grace of Germany and Austria-Hungary. For Groener, the Ukrainian government was merely a "cloak," nothing more. He was annoyed with the "fiction of an independent state" and the "intricate maneuvering" (*Eiertanz*) around the Rada.[128] The only solution, in this view, was to use the political and economic power of the German Empire. Eichhorn endorsed this view, although he wanted to support a stable

---

123 Cf. TNA, GFM 6/52, Notizzettel Eichhorns zu "Russland und Ukraine," 17.6.1918.

124 Cf. Johannes Hürter, ed., *Paul von Hintze. Marineoffizier, Diplomat, Staatssekretär. Dokumente einer Karriere zwischen Militär und Politik, 1903–1918* (Munich, 1998), 480. Telegram from Hintze to Ludendorff, 9.8.1918. Also the general thoughts of *Ober Ost*: "The events in Russia are without parallel. It is to be hoped that, in the not too distant future, we shall manage to restore stable relations to some extent." See BayHStA, BayHA, Geh, StA, Nachlass Leopold von Bayern, Bd. 27, Brief des Kronprinzen Rupprecht an Prinz Leopold, 16.5.1918.

125 See TNA, GFM 6/52, Protokoll über die Besprechung der schwebenden politischen Fragen unter Vorsitz seiner Majestät zwischen den Vertretern der Reichsregierung und der Obersten Heeresleitung, Zu AS 3086, 9.7.1918.

126 BA-MA, N 46/172, Heeresgruppe Eichhorn Kr, Zusammenfassender Bericht über die wirtschaftliche und politische Lage in der Ukraine, Nr. 190 geh., 18.5.1918.

127 GFM 6/52, Protokoll über die Besprechung der schwebenden politischen Fragen unter Vorsitz seiner Majestät zwischen den Vertretern der Reichsregierung und der Obersten Heeresleitung, Zu AS 3086, 9.7.1918.

128 Baumgart, *Deutsche Ostpolitik*, 124ff.

independent state. German policy would then have to be "supported unreservedly by military power...regardless of how this might affect our relations with Austria-Hungary or whether we would incur the hatred of the Great Russian-oriented section of the population."[129] Thus, for Eichhorn and the other military leaders, direct rule over the Ukrainians was the only feasible way. More subtle forms of rule were alien to them. One should not forget, however, that within the military there were also divergent opinions about the goal of Germany's eastern policy. Prince Leopold and especially Groener repeatedly criticized the escalating and overly ambitious plans of Ludendorff.[130]

On the Austro-Hungarian side, opinions on Ukrainian policy were also sharply divided. The first military men to arrive in Ukraine warned that the Rada was powerless outside Kyiv. It was only when the grain did not arrive quickly enough and in the agreed amounts that Czernin wanted to rethink Ukrainian policy.[131] For the troops in Ukraine, the situation became increasingly contradictory. They were there to secure and transport the grain. But the 2nd Army considered that "sooner or later, it will have to be a military occupation with all that this implies." The troops were required to behave in a manner appropriate to the fact that they were not on enemy territory. It was completely clear to the AOK that, with such a small number of troops, an occupation was not possible. The head of the quartermaster division of High Command argued "that it is more in our interest today to support and maintain the present government, in spite of its mistakes and its meager executive power, than to remove it by force and create a chaotic, anarchic situation in Ukraine."[132] As a consequence, Vienna rejected any discussion concerning the responsibilities of the troops or a date for their withdrawal.[133]

---

129 BArch, R 3101/1314, Bericht des Feldmarschalls Eichhorn über die politische und wirtschaftliche Lage in der Ukraine, 4.6.1918. For similar statements by Groener, see Baumgart, *Deutsche Ostpolitik*, 135.

130 Winfried Baumgart, ed., *Von Brest-Litovsk zur deutschen Novemberrevolution. Aus den Tagebüchern, Briefen und Aufzeichnungen von Alfons Paquet, Wilhelm Groener und Albert Hopman, März bis November 1918* (Göttingen, 1971), 443, 445, 449. Leopold also criticized the Supreme Army Command (OHL) for its lack of goals and its "adventurist attitudes that border on megalomania." See BayHStA, BayHA, Geh. StA, Nachlass Leopold von Bayern, Bd. 239.1, Tagebucheintrag v. 8.5.1918. As a qualification, however, one must add that Leopold later revised his journal. There is a similar critical remark about the OHL in the entry for 18.8.1918. This is absent, however, from the original journal.

131 ÖStA, KA, FA, AOK, OpAbt, Kt. 468, Nr. 1329/1, Verhältnisse in Odesa, 29.3.1918.

132 ÖStA, HHStA, MdÄ, PA X, Russland Liasse XI d 1, Kt. 152, Fol. 238ff., Zur Situation in der Ukraine, 11.4.1918.

133 Ibid., Kt. 153, Mappe: "Geplante Militärkonvention der Mittelmächte mit der Ukraine März und

The status of the Crimea became a particularly difficult issue between the occupying powers and the Ukrainian government. Since the peninsula in the Black Sea was part of the German zone, the Ukrainian leadership came increasingly to the view that Ukraine should lay claim to it. There were fears that Germany wanted long-term control of the strategic Crimea. The authorized representative of the Austro-Hungarian AOK to the Ukrainian government, Major Fleischmann, intervened to emphasize that the Crimea was essential to a prosperous Ukraine. Austria-Hungary wanted a strong Ukraine and therefore supported a Ukrainian claim to the peninsula. With this trick, he hoped "that from now on more mature elements, less influenced by the Germans, as well as the military leaders, would gradually get a chance to have their say and create a more favorable environment for Austria."[134] At the same time, the Rada increased its activities to support its claims to the Crimea.[135] Once Hetman Pavlo Skoropadsky came to power, the government would become more active on this question in the late summer.[136] But with the withdrawal of the Central Powers and the loss of the protecting power, the government's priorities shifted to the struggle against the Bolsheviks.

When Burián replaced Czernin at the Foreign Ministry on 14 April, there was initially no obvious change in Vienna's Ukrainian policy. But dissatisfaction with the Rada did not abate. On 23 April there was a meeting between the chief of staff of the Army Group Eichhorn-Kiew, General Groener; the Austro-Hungarian high representative in Kyiv, Ambassador János Forgách; and the authorized representative of AOK to the Ukrainian Rada, Major Fleischmann. The participants agreed that "cooperation with the current Ukrainian government, acting as it does, is not possible." In the absence of an alternative, however, they should stick with it for now but make it "dependent" on the Central Powers. At this point there was no suggestion of a change of government.[137] But Groener acted on his own, without informing his

---

April 1918."

134 ÖStA, KA, FA, AOK, OpAbt, Kt. 468, Nr. 1364, Chiffrentelegramm von Fleischmann an AOK, 2.4.1918.

135 At the end of April a Ukrainian otaman (Cossack commander) was chosen for the defense of the Crimea. He was to raise the Ukrainian flag on ships, fortifications and other buildings, which the defenders of an independent Crimea interpreted as an attack on their sovereign rights. See ÖStA, KA, FA, AOK, OpAbt, Kt. 468, Nr. 1438, Ukraine-Ansprüche, 15.4.1918.

136 ÖStA, KA, FA, AOK, OpAbt, Kt. 470, Nr. 1550, Schreiben der Muselmanischen Gesellschafts-Organisation zur Befreiung der Krim, 25.4.1918. Further on the question of the Crimea, cf. *Pavlo Skoropads'kyj*, 264, 293ff., 312; Baumgart, *Deutsche Ostpolitik*, 151–55.

137 ÖStA, KA, FA, AOK, OpAbt, Kt. 469, Nr. 1517, Vorgänge im Kiew, 29.4.1918.

allies. The very next day, he spoke with Skoropadsky, who had already been in contact with the German occupiers for some time. Groener made a number of demands to which Skoropadsky basically agreed,[138] paving the way for a change of government a few days later.[139]

Even after the overthrow of the Rada, neither the Austro-Hungarian Foreign Ministry nor the AOK saw Ukraine officially as an occupied country.[140] However, relations between Austria-Hungary and the Ukrainian state leadership did not improve. On the contrary, Skoropadsky was highly distrustful of the diplomats of the Habsburg Monarchy, whom he saw as intriguing and interested mainly in the Galician Ukrainians. He also regarded the Austro-Hungarian military as "brutal and corrupt."[141] In mid-May the head of the Austro-Hungarian military, Arz, warned the foreign minister, Burián, against a new change of government, as this would further delay the grain deliveries and, in addition, there were insufficient resources to install a military administration.[142] The main concern was still the delivery of large quantities of grain. Burián praised Eichhorn's "energetic action" in overthrowing the Rada. He hoped that this would break the resistance of some ministers to grain export and finally improve the delivery.[143] But Vienna remained reticent in relation to the Hetman government. The Foreign Ministry's representative in Kyiv was to "enter into de facto relations...with the government but not recognize it officially."[144] Throughout 1918 Austria-Hungary did not take up

138 ÖStA, KA, FA, AOK, OpAbt, Kt. 469, Nr. 1529, Vorgänge im Kiew III, 2.5.1918. For Skoropadsky's account, which emphasizes some points but significantly changes others, see *Pavlo Skoropads'kyj*, ed. Rosenfeld, 160–62. A major problem with this publication is that the differences between various versions are not adequately dealt with and are seldom pointed out. Passages that offer an assessment of personalities or situations going beyond description should be treated with great caution and attention to sources.

139 On the change of government, see chapters 2a and 3b in the present volume. In his recollections of the event, Skoropadsky emphasizes his own independent role in the change of government. That may have been so from his viewpoint, but the success of the coup depended entirely on German support: *Pavlo Skoropads'kyj*, 152–72, 217. Note in particular the statement that, according to Skoropadsky, Groener repeatedly made about the installation of the Hetmanate: "We do not intervene in your affairs."

140 ÖStA, KA, FA, AOK, OpAbt, Kt. 475, Nr. 1906, Darstellung der materiellen Lage der Armee im Felde, 18.8.1918.

141 *Pavlo Skoropads'kyj*, 191, 210, 235ff., 269–72.

142 ÖStA, KA, FA, AOK, OpAbt, Kt. 470, Nr. 1572, Lage in der Ukraine, Okkupationsfrage, 19.5.1918.

143 ÖStA, HHStA, MdÄ, PA X, Russland Liasse XI d 1, Kt. 152, Fol. 336f., Vorgänge in der Ukraine, 21.5.1918; ÖStA, KA, FA, AOK, OpAbt, Kt. 469, Nr. 1530, Telegramm des AOK an Burián, 1.5.1918.

144 ÖStA, KA, FA, AOK, OpAbt, Kt. 470, Nr. 1548, Vertrag mit Skoropads'kyj, 5 Mai.

official diplomatic relations or open an embassy.[145] But it maintained a diplomatic representation, led by Ambassador Baron János Forgách of Ghymes and Gács.[146] The Foreign Ministry also sent Heinrich Zitovsky of Szemeszova and Szohorad[147] as its representative to the army command in Odesa. He was to strengthen the political component of the sometimes arbitrary Austro-Hungarian military in Ukraine.[148]

It was not until June that Austria-Hungary's diplomats recognized the advantages of having the Hetman in power: "In the present situation, the Central Powers are able to enforce their will almost as if it were an occupation, with the advantage that the orders come from an indigenous government, the executive of which is dependent on our support and forced to align itself with us completely."[149] A direct military occupation would have provoked major resistance from the Ukrainian population, but Skoropadsky's Ukrainization measures seemed to have a pacifying effect. Shortly after the change of government, Burián had given up all hope with regard to any improvement in the grain deliveries. He believed that the delivery of one million tons of grain was no longer possible and considered the Brest-Litovsk treaty null and void. His central policy now became one of making a concession to the Poles, hoping thereby to keep them on the side of the Central Powers.[150]

But the commander of Austria-Hungary's Eastern Army (*Ostarmee*) saw things differently. At the beginning of June, Alfred Krauss warned against Germany's pursuit of colonial and long-term economic goals

---

145 ÖStA, HHStA, MdÄ, PA X, Russland Liasse XI d 1, Kt. 153, Mappe: "Ukrainische Vertreter im Auslande (für Wien: Yakovlev & Lipinsky)," Fol. 1–55, Sammelakt zu ukrainischen Vertretern in Österreich-Ungarn.

146 Forgách was born on 24 October 1870 and, from the 1890s, had been ambassador in St. Petersburg, Sofia, Belgrade, Rome, Brazil, and Saxony. From August 1914 his title was Ambassador Extraordinary and Plenipotentiary: Erwin Matsch, *Der Auswärtige Dienst von Österreich(-Ungarn) 1720–1920* (Vienna, Cologne, and Graz, 1986), 96, 136. Until May, Forgách had been responsible for economic matters alongside Walter Ritter Princig von Herwalt, who in turn was followed by Prince Emil zu Fürstenberg. Fürstenberg took over the leadership of the representation in Kyiv in the autumn. (The latter is not to be confused with Prince Karl Emil zu Fürstenberg, born 16 February 1867, who was ambassador to Spain between 1911 and 1918): Matsch, *Der Auswärtige Dienst*, 112, 136, 154.

147 Representatives of the Orient and Overseas Society of the Imperial Austrian Trade Museum in Vienna: *Hof-und Staats-Handbuch der österreichisch-ungarischen Monarchie für das Jahr 1918*, vol. 44 (Vienna, 1918), 388.

148 ÖStA, KA, FA, AOK, Ukraine Akten, Kt. 2.618, Nr. 4597, Verzeichnis des öster-ung. und deutschen Behörden und Funktionäre in Kiew, 7.8.1918.

149 Underlined in the original, probably by one of the staff of AOK: ÖStA, KA, FA, AOK, OpAbt, Kt. 472, Nr. 1710, Forgách an Burián, 28.6.1918.

150 ÖStA, HHStA, MdÄ, PA X, Russland Liasse XI d 1, Kt. 152, Burián an Hohenlohe, 29.5.1918.

in Ukraine and in the Crimea and concurrently insisted on clarity about the economic and political goals of Austria-Hungary in Eastern Europe, which could be achieved "with them [the Germans], using all diplomatic and military means." Colonel Kreneis, chief of the Ukrainian section of the quartermaster division of AOK, proposed three options for binding Ukraine to the Central Powers, with a stronger role for the Habsburg Monarchy: first, the creation of a monarchy, allied with Austria-Hungary and Germany, under a Habsburg or a German prince; second, "maintenance of the fiction of a Ukrainian state" that would in fact be militarily and economically "completely in the hands" of the Central Powers; third, annexation by the Monarchy of the Austro-Hungarian "area of operations as far as the Dnipro" and the creation of a "Kingdom of Odesa under a Habsburg prince that would be joined with Eastern Galicia."[151] The AOK saw a strong Russia as a long-term threat to the Habsburg Monarchy. Ukraine, supported by Austria-Hungary, would be an ideal tool to weaken Russia, although this would carry the risk of strengthening an irredentist Ukrainian movement.[152] Although these options may appear utopian today, they gave expression to the colonialist approach, the excessive overestimation of one's own position, and the wishful thinking of many military decision-makers.

But the chief of AOK did not want to tie himself down to any of these plans and asked the Foreign Ministry to state its position. In early June the ministry ordered an occupation regime more strongly linked with its German ally and acting, in general, with greater force. Thus economic life was to be restored more quickly and improvements made to the delivery of provisions. Clearly, the Foreign Ministry wanted to be the key player in Ukraine once again and to get the military under its control.[153] But it was not until 10 July that Burián established clear goals. They should seek a loyal agreement with the Germans and have an open discussion of any differences. In the short term, the goal was to secure the delivery of provisions and raw materials. Ukrainian national and separatist tendencies were to be encouraged as a means of strengthening the state in relation to Great Russia. The "thin elitist layer" was to be empowered to "lead an orderly state." In the long run,

151 Perhaps the AOK favored the last option; it was commented with "yes."

152 ÖStA, KA, FA, AOK, OpAbt, Kt. 471, Nr. 1684, Ukraine-Bericht, 6.6.1918.

153 ÖStA, HHStA, MdÄ, PA X, Russland Liasse XI d 1, Kt. 152, Fol. 781f., Repressivmaßnahmen gegen die Unruhen auf dem Lande in der Ukraine und Proteste dagegen, 12.6.1918; ibid., Fol. 857–59, Burián an Forgách und Larisch, 3.7.1918; ÖStA, KA, FA, AOK, OpAbt, Kt. 472, Nr. 1729, Ziele der Monarchie in der Ukraine, 6.7.1918; ibid., Nr. 1733, Ostarmee an AOK, 12.7.1918.

it was important to secure the greatest possible amount of economic influence.[154] The military leadership was dissatisfied with this vague response from the Foreign Ministry, especially with the absence of any strategy for achieving these goals.[155]

The activities of Archduke Wilhelm were extremely embarrassing to Austro-Hungarian diplomacy. The son of Archduke Karl Stephen,[156] who played an important role with regard to the Austro-Polish solution, wanted to establish a Habsburg monarchy in Ukraine with the help of the Ukrainian Legion.[157] This led to powerful protests in both Berlin and Kyiv.[158] It was only following interventions from just about every relevant level of the German Empire, including the emperor himself, and from the Austro-Hungarian Foreign Ministry as well, that Emperor Karl, in a "most high letter," "requested" that Archduke Wilhelm take no further action against Skoropadsky. A Habsburg archduke for Ukraine would have damaged relations with the German Empire.[159] But it required another series of protests before Archduke Wilhelm and the Ukrainian Legion left Ukraine at the beginning of October 1918.[160]

---

154 ÖStA, HHStA, MdÄ, PA X, Russland Liasse XI d 1, Kt. 153, ohne Nr., Telegramm von Burián an Arz, 10.7.1918; ÖStA, KA, FA, AOK, OpAbt, Kt. 474, Nr. 1862, Politische Ziele in der Ukraine, 18.8.1918.

155 ÖStA, HHStA, MdÄ, PA X, Russland Liasse XI d 1, Kt. 153, Fol. 419–29, Politische Ziele in der Ukraine, 18.9.1918; ÖStA, KA, FA, AOK, OpAbt, Kt. 474, Nr. 1862, Politische Ziele in der Ukraine, 18.8.1918; ibid., Nr. 1863, Klärung von Fragen in der Ukraine, 26.9.1918; ibid., Nr. 1864, Spanocchi an AOK, 27.9.1918.

156 The Habsburg Archduke Karl Stephen of Austria was suggested by the Germans in 1916 as regent for Poland, but Kaiser Franz Joseph himself wanted to be the Polish king. This idea was taken up again under Karl, but Karl, too, entertained hopes for the Polish crown: Gaul, "The Austro-Hungarian Empire and Its Political Allies," 203–22; Timothy Snyder, *Der König von Ukraine. Die geheimen Leben des Wilhelm von Habsburg* (Vienna, 2009), 77–81.

157 See Vasyl Rasevych, "Ein habsburgischer König für die Ukraine? Wilhelm von Habsburg und Kaiser Karl I," in *Karl I. (IV.)*, ed. Gottsmann, 223–30; Snyder, *The Red Prince*, 77–120. See also ÖStA, KA, FA, AOK, OpAbt, Kt. 470, Nr. 1595, 2, Armeekommando an AOK, 8.5.1918; ibid., Kt. 472, Nr. 1709, Vertrauliche Nachrichten aus der Ukraine, 25.5.1918; ibid., Nr. 1712, Aktenkonvolut zu den Verhältnissen in der Ukraine, 29.5–30.6.1918; ibid., Nr. 1728, Ostarmee an AOK, 30.6.1918.

158 *Pavlo Skoropads'kyj*, 235ff., 269ff.

159 ÖStA, HHStA, MdÄ, PA I, Liasse XLVII, Krieg 1914–1918, Kt. 523, Konvolut 12d, Beziehungen Erzherzog Wilhelm zu ukrainischen Nobilitäten, Mai 1918. Interventions by the Ukrainian government may also have played a role when members of the Ukrainian Legion tended toward revolutionary propaganda and warned the people in advance of weapons searches. See ÖStA, HHStA, MdÄ, PA X, Russland Liasse XI d 1, Kt. 153, Mappe: "Unsere Truppen in der Ukraine, März–Nov 1918," Zitkovsky an Ministerium des Äußern, 13.7.1918.

160 ÖStA, HHStA, MdÄ, PA X, Russland Liasse XI d 7–12, Kt. 154, Mappe: "Russland XI d/8 Tätigkeit Erzherzog Wilhelms in der Ukraine und seine Abberufung, Juni–Okt 1918"; ÖStA, KA, FA, AOK, OpAbt, Kt. 472, Nr. 1728, Ostarmee an AOK, 30.6.1918.

Although the unrest in Ukraine declined in the course of the summer of 1918,[161] the military situation on the Western Front deteriorated at the same time. Following the British tank breakthrough at Amiens on 8 August 1918 ("Black Day of the German Army"), Arz painted a somber picture of Ukraine in a consultation with Hindenburg and Ludendorff in Spa on 14 August: Austria-Hungary would no longer have any military interest in Ukraine if its economic exploitation did not bring adequate returns. The maintenance of security was taking up too many forces that were desperately needed elsewhere. The defense of the Don region was doubtful and economically of little value.[162]

From 4 to 15 September, on his own initiative, Skoropadsky traveled around Germany with his whole entourage. An official state visit to the German emperor, as well as talks with top-level military and economic personnel, were meant to raise his status both at home and in Germany. Although talks were held at the highest level, nothing substantial was achieved. Skoropadsky was committed to deeper relations, in return for which he was promised help in building an army and support in the removal of Archduke Wilhelm from Ukraine. With regard to Ukrainian-Polish relations (Kholm), the Germans attempted to commit Skoropadsky to moderation in order not to drive Poland further into the arms of the Entente. The visit had high symbolic value and demonstrated the German Empire's interest in an independent Ukraine and its desire for the long-term stability of the Hetman regime that it had created. For the opponents of an independent Ukraine, however, this was grist to their mill, as it demonstrated the dependence of Ukraine, especially the Hetman, on Berlin.[163]

It was only toward the end of the occupation that both the Germans and the Austro-Hungarians started to rethink their Ukraine policy. At the beginning of October Arz, Austria-Hungary's chief of AOK, saw the breakup of Russia as one of the most important goals, in order that "no new enemy arise, either militarily or economically." In his view, the peace treaty with the Bolsheviks at Brest-Litovsk had been militarily necessary to gain respite on the Eastern Front.[164] In view of the threat of defeat in the West, and with its own occupation troops in

161 See chapter 3a in the present volume.

162 ÖStA, KA, FA, AOK, OpAbt, Kt. 473, Nr. 1848, Besprechung in Spa, 14.8.1918.

163 Golczewski, *Deutsche und Ukrainer*, 328–30. The Hetman himself, in retrospect, assessed this journey rather modestly and with nuances, perhaps with too much of a critical distance: *Pavlo Skoropads'kyj*, 305–14.

164 ÖStA, KA, FA, AOK, Ukraine Akten, Kt. 2626, Nr. 3658, Klärung der Fragen in der Ukraine, 4.10.1918.

short supply, the German OHL fundamentally changed its Ukrainian policy. The maintenance of Ukraine was "militarily necessary," but the occupation should be "Ukrainized." The "internal state structure" should be built up in accordance with the "needs and wishes" of the Hetman government.[165] There should also be "fundamental democratic reforms."[166] At the end of October, the OHL contacted the Foreign Ministry once again concerning the future of an independent and friendly Ukraine. It stressed in particular the importance of international recognition and even suggested membership in Wilson's League of Nations.[167] Ukraine should be supported "as long as possible, so that this friendly nation is never again abandoned to anarchy."[168] As early as the beginning of October, Groener and Ludendorff had considered a partial withdrawal from Ukraine. With the remaining troops, they hoped to maintain order and eventually to halt or even drive back the Entente troops landing in southern Ukraine.

The recall of the German ambassador in Kyiv, Philipp Alfons Mumm vom Schwarzenstein, and especially Groener's recall at the beginning of October were, however, the first indications of a German withdrawal. Skoropadsky then asked the new chargé d'affaires of the Austro-Hungarian representatives in Ukraine, Prince Emil Egon Fürstenberg, whether the troops of the Central Powers would remain in Ukraine after the cessation of hostilities.[169] In the truce of Compiègne, small contingents of German troops were told to stay in Ukraine. But for Austria-Hungary, this was no longer possible. At the end of October, the Habsburg Monarchy and its army disintegrated into total chaos.

Conclusion

Was the occupation of Ukraine in 1918 a step toward a German "reach for world power" (Fritz Fischer)? In some of the documents of

---

165 Cf. TNA, GFM 6/99, Telegramm Nr. 2464, Der K. Staatssekretär Hintze an AA, 16.10.1918.

166 Ibid., Kaiserlich Deutsche Gesandtschaft Ir Nr. 8947, An den Reichskanzler Prinz Max von Baden, 31.10.1918.

167 See TNA, GFM, 6/99, Telegramm Nr. 2170 K. Gesandte an AA, 27.10.1918. It is unclear who made this amazing suggestion. Maybe Groener provided the impulse. On the previous day he had removed Ludendorff as First Quartermaster.

168 Reichsarchiv, ed., *Der Weltkrieg, 1914–1918. Die Kriegsführung im Sommer und Herbst 1918. Die Ereignisse ausserhalb der Westfront bis November 1918*, vol. 13 (Berlin, 1942), 390.

169 ÖStA, HHStA, MdÄ, PA X, Russland Liasse XI d 1, Kt. 153, Nr. 1088, Fürstenberg an Ministerium des Äußern, 10.10.1918.

important decision-makers, one does indeed find such thoughts,[170] and Ludendorff's policy does appear *ex post* to fulfill the demands of the Pan-German League. His comprehensive annexation plans in the East as well as the founding of vassal states such as Ukraine could hardly be surpassed in their excessiveness. But this policy can also be interpreted differently. The *Generalquartiermeister* was well known to be an efficient and competent military leader but, at the same time, an unbelievable dilettante in matters of strategy. "We'll simply bash in a hole. The rest will take care of itself. That's what we did in Russia," is what he is known to have said about the goal of the German offensive on the Western Front in the spring of 1918. This was Ludendorff's catastrophic understanding of strategy: tactics determine strategy, which is known today as the tacticization of strategy.[171]

Ludendorff's words about the Western Front aptly describe his Ukrainian policy: the Germans simply marched into the country, and the rest would somehow take care of itself. The power vacuum in Eastern Europe was simply too tempting for the OHL (as it was for other German elites). They could achieve quick and simple military victories there, occupy large areas without major resistance, and exploit them for the German Empire. In addition, they could exert long-term pressure on the Bolsheviks in Moscow. A political plan for occupied Ukraine was a minor matter, but this policy overextended German power.[172] It was a constant of 1918 that rapid tactical victories took precedence over long-term strategic planning. This led to the "unusual aimlessness and inconsistency"[173] of the Central Powers' Ukrainian policy.

It was also a German pecularity that the military, more than the government, determined the fundamentals of eastern policy. The territory of *Ober Ost* was officially under military administration[174] and, even in formally independent Ukraine, it was the military and not the politicians that took the lead. The OHL gave general guidelines

170 Cf. TNA, GFM 6/52, Notizzettel Eichhorns zu "Russland und Ukraine," 17.6.1918.

171 Herwig is quite right to point out that Ludendorff never rose above the intellectual level of a regimental commander. See Herwig, *The First World War*, 420.

172 We cannot go into any more detail here about Ludendorff's plans to support the Don Cossacks or his Caucasus adventure in the summer and autumn of 1918. See Baumgart, *Deutsche Ostpolitik*, 139–46 and 174–207. At many points, Baumgart revises Fischer's claims about policy in the Caucasus. Cf. Fischer, *Griff nach der Weltmacht*, 486–95.

173 Baumgart, *Deutsche Ostpolitik*, 25ff. Fischer, in *Griff nach der Weltmacht*, 441–44, and Borowsky, in *Deutsche Ukrainepolitik* generally, stress that both the military and the imperial government pursued the same aims. They differed only about the way to achieve these.

174 Liulevicius, *War Land on the Eastern Front*.

but left the concrete execution of policy on the ground to Army Group Eichhorn-Kiew. It was this group that also frequently formulated long-term political and economic goals. Groener expressed it quite bluntly: "We do what we think is good and necessary and ask no further what Berlin Wilhelmstrasse and Erzberger and his comrades would have to say about it."[175] Nevertheless, it was precisely because of the boastful Groener that the military frequently sought a compromise with the political representatives of their own German government in Kyiv and with the Hetman government. In general, it is a bit of an exaggeration to speak of a "military dictatorship" in Ukraine.[176] The German economy certainly had its own interest in Ukraine, but the representatives of the Ministry of the Economy were very weak advocates.

Austria-Hungary's Ukrainian policy was similarly inadequate. It was characterized by a pronounced cacophony and an absence of clearly defined goals. The AOK and the commanders of the *Ostarmee* wanted to establish their own Ukrainian policy but, at the same time, the Foreign Ministry wanted to hold the reins firmly in its own hands. At the conclusion of military operations in March–April 1918, when a concrete Ukrainian policy should have been developed, Czernin was busy with Romania and later with the Sixtus affair. The two self-confident commanders in Ukraine, Eduard von Böhm-Ermolli and later Alfred Krauss, stepped into this vacuum and attempted to act as independently as possible. This changed very little under Czernin's successor, Burián. He attempted to reactivate the Austro-Polish solution and was reluctant to formulate medium- or long-term goals in Ukraine, as that would have run counter to his amicable relations with Poland. For Burián, the key was the largest and fastest possible delivery of provisions. This was the task of the German and Austro-Hungarian troops, and everything else was subordinated to it. Even at the end of the occupation, Austria-Hungary was unclear about the long-term existence of a sovereign Ukrainian state. Reunification with a united Russia liberated from the Bolsheviks was a possibility. Admittedly, this united Russia was not supposed to become too strong.

175 Quoted in Baumgart, *Deutsche Ostpolitik*, 124. The Wilhelmstrasse in Berlin is the location of the Foreign Office.

176 This is the explicit view of Grelka, *Die ukrainische Nationalbewegung*, 115ff. This view is shared by Golczewski, *Deutsche und Ukrainer*, 194.

2a. Ukraine between Revolution, Independence, and Foreign Dominance

Georgiy Kasianov

In terminological discussions among Ukrainian historians since the end of the 1980s, the academic community has agreed that the concept of the "Ukrainian Revolution" comprises all events on Ukrainian territory between 1917 and 1920. Although the issue is not settled for good, the debate is now essentially about the precise time frame. Some experts suggest that this time frame should be extended to 1921 or 1922 to include the insurgent movement of 1921 and the peasant uprisings in Soviet Ukraine in 1922. Others consider the revolution to have finally ended with the loss of Eastern Galicia to Poland in 1923.[1] One should also mention the approach that sees the Ukrainian Revolution as lasting from 1914 to 1921. This would include the period of the First World War as the time in which the Ukrainian national movement mobilized and would take in the movement outside the Russian-ruled part of Ukraine. In the present article, we hold to the view that sees the Ukrainian Revolution as lasting from March 1917 (the creation of the Central Rada) to 21 November 1920, when Ukrainian troops engaged in the Soviet-Polish war retreated to Galicia.

In this period there were half a dozen state or quasi-state bodies[2] that succeeded one another, existed side by side, and were proclaimed or dissolved. These included the Ukrainian People's Republic, first as part of Russia and then independent (7 November 1917 to 28 April 1918); the Ukrainian State (29 April to 15 November 1918); the Western Ukrainian People's Republic (18 October 1918 to 21 January 1919); the Ukrainian People's Republic (26 December 1918 to 21 January 1919 and 16 July 1919 to 20 November 1920); the Ukrainian Soviet Republic (12 December 1917 to July 1918) and the Ukrainian Soviet Socialist Republic

---

1 Originally, this term signified the events associated with the Ukrainian struggle for independence and national statehood. In the 1990s the concept of the "Liberation Struggle" (*Vyzvol'ni zmahannia*), adopted from the historiography of the emigration/diaspora, was also frequently used. Some historians use the phrase "Ukrainian National-Democratic Revolution." Some Russian historians are critical of the term "Ukrainian Revolution," seeing the events on Ukrainian territory, even if characterized by specific national features, as part of the Russian Revolution and Civil War.

2 D. Ianevs'kyi, *Politychni systemy Ukraïny 1917–1920 rokiv: sproby tvorennia i prychyny porazky* (Kyiv, 2003), 428–30.

(6 January 1919 to December 1919 and February to May 1920). We could also include in this list a number of local bodies, for example, the Soviet Republic of Donetsk and Kryvyi Rih, which was formally part of the Russian Socialist Soviet Republic (27 December 1917 to 19 March 1918); the Soviet Republic of Odesa (3 January to 13 March 1918); the Socialist Soviet Republic of Tavria (19 March to 30 April 1918), and the Galician Socialist Soviet Republic (15 July to 21 September 1920). Ukrainian territory was occupied by German, Austro-Hungarian, Romanian, Polish, French, and Russian troops and was a theater of war between the White and Red armies. There were also large insurgent peasant armies (Nestor Makhno, Nykyfor Hryhoriiv, Zeleny [Danylo Terpylo], Yevhen Anhel), as well as hundreds and thousands of smaller units of partisans, deserters, or plain bandits.

From the Fall of Tsarist Russia to the Hetmanate (February 1917 to April 1918)

In the events of the Ukrainian Revolution between February 1917 and April 1918, there are a number of different strands of action: the fall of the autocracy and the establishment of the Provisional Government's rule on Ukrainian territory; the consolidation of the Ukrainian national movement as a political force and its evolution from a demand for political autonomy to a program for Ukrainian political sovereignty (independence); the political conflicts within the Ukrainian movement and its conflicts with other political forces, especially the Provisional Government and the Bolsheviks; the revolution of October 1917 in St. Petersburg and the subsequent political and military confrontation between the Central Rada and the Bolsheviks; the development of the peasant movement and the spontaneous "black repartition";[3] the attempts to create a state (the Ukrainian People's Republic); the peace of Brest-Litovsk and the occupation of Ukraine by German and Austro-Hungarian troops; the overthrow of the Central Rada and the establishment of the Hetmanate in April 1918.

In March 1917, almost immediately after the fall of the tsarist autocracy, parties that had long been forbidden resumed their activity, among them Ukrainian parties. The number of parties in Ukraine at this time is usually given as more than twenty, but this number includes the Russian as well as the newly formed or readmitted Ukrainian parties and other national parties (Jewish, Polish, etc.).[4]

---

3 The spontaneous redistribution of land and the expropriation of property by the peasants.

4 Olena Liubovets', "Ideino-politychni protsesy v ukraïns'kykh partiiakh u konteksti al'ternatyv revoliutsiinoï doby (1917–1920 rr.)" (Ph.D. diss., Kyiv, 2006).

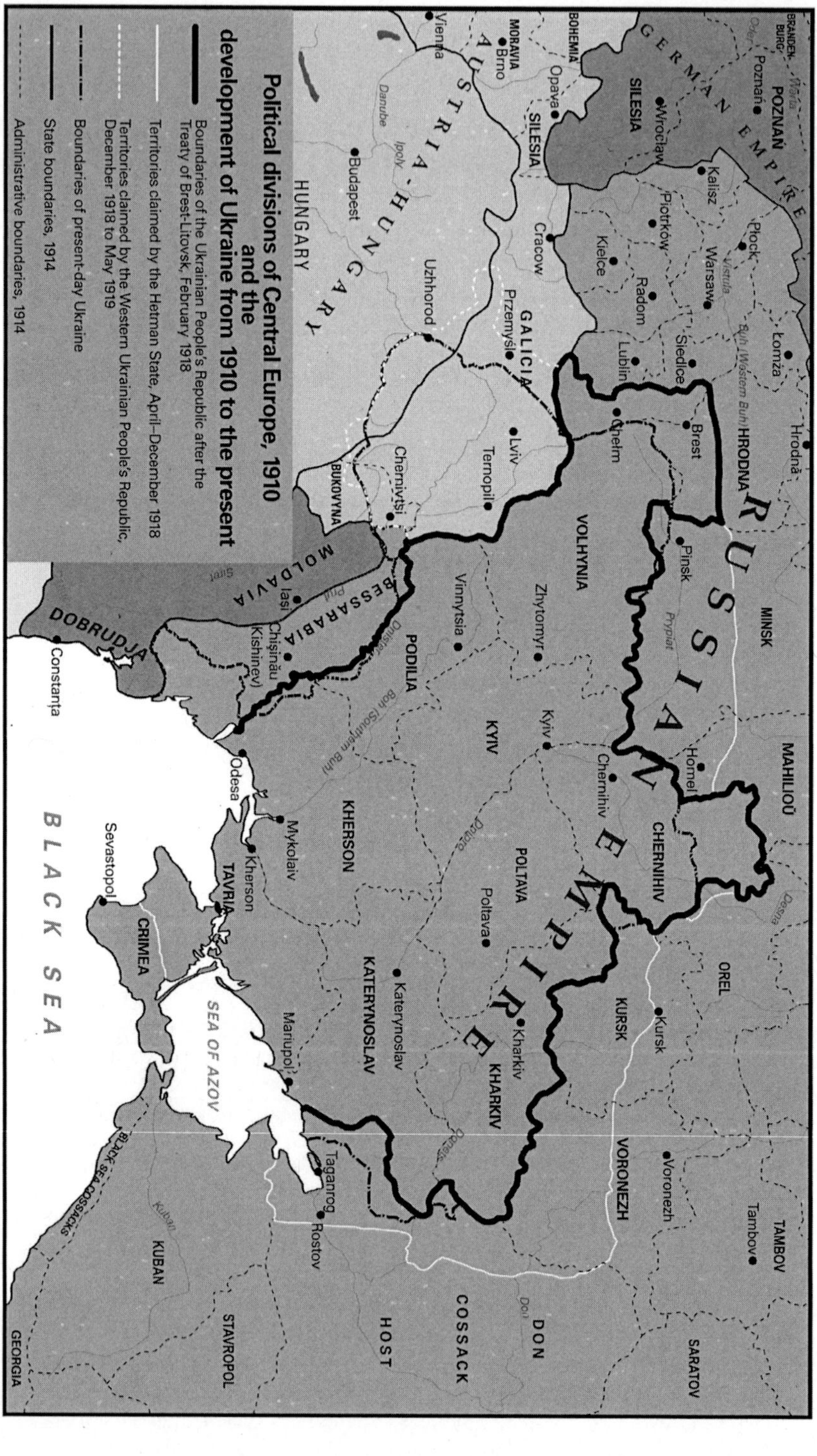

Map 3: Political borders of Ukraine, 1918 (Magocsi, *Historical Atlas of East Central Europe*, 138)

Ukrainian historians have traditionally argued that, from the beginning, there were two competing currents in the Ukrainian national movement in 1917, autonomists and supporters of an immediate declaration of independence. The most recent documents, however, offer no evidence for this standpoint. In its first public declaration of 8 March 1917, the Society of Ukrainian Progressives (TUP)[5] spoke of the implementation of Ukrainian national cultural rights through the principle of autonomy. On 25–27 March 1917, at the founding congress of the Union of Ukrainian Autonomists and Federalists, formed on the basis of the TUP, the slogan produced was "autonomy of Ukraine,"[6] by which they understood political or national and territorial autonomy. This was also the position of the Ukrainian People's Socialist Party, the Ukrainian Party of Labor, the Ukrainian Social Democratic Party, and the party with the largest membership, the Ukrainian Party of Socialist Revolutionaries.[7] The autonomy solution was also supported initially, perhaps for tactical reasons, by the Ukrainian parties and associations that stood for the idea of independence, the Ukrainian People's Party and the Union for Ukrainian Statehood.[8] Immediately after the fall of the autocracy, therefore, in spite of numerous differences of opinion, there was at least a declared unity on the question of strategy, namely the achievement of national territorial autonomy within a federal democratic Russia. This relatively moderate position was supported not only by the parties but also by a variety of other organizations and movements, such as teachers' organizations, soldiers' and peasants' congresses, cooperatives, and Ukrainian military formations.[9]

At the same time, practically all the national Ukrainian parties and organizations declared their support for the Provisional Government. In spite of this, the Provisional Government did not welcome and indeed resisted the rapid and initially successful organizational and institutional development of the Ukrainian movement, especially its demand for autonomy. Between the spring and autumn of 1917, the

---

5 *Nova Rada*, 25 March 1917.

6 Ibid., 2 March 1917.

7 O. M. Liubovets', "Problema ukraïns'koï derzhavnosti v prohramakh i diial'nosti ukraïns'kykh politychnykh partii (berezen'-lystopad 1917)," *Ukraïns'kyi istorychnyi zhurnal,* 2003, no. 4: 22–25.

8 V. F. Verstiuk, "Ukraïns'kyi natsional'no-vyzvol'nyi rukh (berezen'-lystopad 1917)," *Ukraïns'kyi istorychnyi zhurnal,* 2003, no. 3: 65–67.

9 The First Ukrainian Military Congress (5–8 May 1917), the All-Ukrainian Peasant Congress (28 May–2 June 1917), and the Congress of Free Cossacks (16–20 October 1917) were among those that supported Ukrainian autonomy within a democratic Russia.

struggle between the Central Rada and the Provisional Government over the division of powers and responsibilities was a constant feature of politics in Ukraine.

The Ukrainian Central Rada was established in Kyiv at the beginning of March 1917.[10] It was originally an attempt to create an all-Ukrainian political coordinating body under the leadership of the TUP but, under pressure from the Ukrainian Social Democrats, the "older" representatives of the Ukrainian movement had to recognize the equal rights of the other Ukrainian organizations. The conflict between the older political generation, represented by the TUP, and the younger generation, represented especially by the Social Democrats, was clear from the very founding of the Central Rada. The older generation attempted to restrict the Rada to the traditional functions of a national cultural movement, while the younger generation demanded, first of all, that more attention be paid to social and economic issues and, secondly, that the Rada have a stronger representation of non-Ukrainian organizations. In the first official announcement of the formation of the Central Rada and its leading bodies, it was said to have representatives of student, educational, scientific, and cooperative organizations, as well as the army and the Social Democrats.[11] Its tactical and ideologically conditioned desire to have the widest possible representation resulted in the number of delegates expanding initially from 15 to 118 (April 1917), and then to 798 (August 1917). At its height, the Rada had 822 delegates, according to participants (Dmytro Doroshenko and Pavlo Khrystiuk). This rapid growth was the result of the collective entrance of whole organizations into the Rada, for instance, workers', soldiers', and peasants' councils. There were delegates from the National Congress (elected at the beginning of April 1917), representatives of the above-mentioned councils (the most numerous), members of Ukrainian military committees, representatives of gubernia, district, and city organizations, Russian and national parties,[12] as well as

---

10 There is no agreement among historians or direct participants about the exact date of this event. The following dates are proposed: 3 March (a meeting of Ukrainian public figures at which the words "Central Rada" were first used), 4 March (a meeting of leaders of the TUP and the Ukrainian Social Democrats at which it was decided to establish a body to coordinate and direct the work of Ukrainian organizations), 7 March (election of leading bodies; this date was first celebrated in 1918 as the founding date of the Central Rada), 9 March (the first minutes of a session of the Central Rada). See V. Verstiuk, "Ukraïns'ka Tsentral'na Rada. Period stanovlennia," *Ukraïns'kyi istorychnyi zhurnal,* 2007, no. 2: 33–34; Ianevs'kyi, *Politychni systemy Ukraïny 1917–1920*, 67–71.

11 *Ukraïns'ka Tsentral'na Rada. Dokumenty i materialy u dvokh tomakh*, vol. 1 (Kyiv, 1996), 44–45.

12 According to estimates by historians, there were altogether nineteen parties represented in the Rada.

from organizations of ethnic minorities, professional, economic, and educational organizations.[13] The Little Rada, a kind of executive committee, was established to manage the day-to-day affairs of the Central Rada. At the end of March 1917 the Central Rada called for an All-Ukrainian National Congress, which met in Kyiv from 6 to 8 April. More than a thousand delegates from a great variety of Ukrainian organizations attended.

It was the general opinion of contemporaries and later historians that this was the first and most impressive demonstration of the unity and influence of the Ukrainian movement. As things turned out, it was also the last. The congress unanimously accepted the slogan of Ukrainian national territorial autonomy within a "federal and democratic Russian republic." There were similar national congresses throughout April at the gubernia level, as well as peasant congresses in the gubernias and districts, and the topic everywhere was national territorial autonomy. All this strengthened the arguments of the Central Rada in its discussions with the Provisional Government about the redistribution of power.

The Provisional Government reacted negatively to the relatively cautious demands for national territorial autonomy[14] from the Ukrainian delegation when it arrived in St. Petersburg on 15 May 1917. At this time the minister of war in the Provisional Government, Aleksandr Kerensky, was in Kyiv. He met with the leaders of the Central Rada, discussed their demands, and requested that they "wait a little." On 1 June the Provisional Government rejected the Central Rada's demands for a nationally autonomous Ukrainian administration, claiming that, as a provisional government, it did not have the authority to make such a decision before the convocation of an all-Russian constituent assembly; moreover, the Central Rada was not a legitimate representative of the whole Ukrainian people. In the course of the negotiations, the Provisional Government expressed its concern that the territorial borders of the proposed autonomy were unclear, and this could create an extremely delicate situation.

The reaction of the Ukrainian Central Rada was predictable. At the beginning of June 1917 the All-Ukrainian Peasant Congress, led by the Socialist Revolutionaries, supported the demands of the Central Rada

---

13 *Ukraïns'ka Tsentral'na Rada,* 1: 233–41.

14 Initially, the issues were the creation of the post of Commissar for Ukrainian Affairs in the Provisional Government and the post of Government Commissar for Ukraine in Kyiv, elected by the Central Rada, limited financial autonomy, and public recognition of Ukraine's right to autonomy.

and instructed the All-Ukrainian Council of Peasant Deputies, present in full strength in the Central Rada, to draft a statute of autonomy for Ukraine.[15] On 10 June 1917, at the second All-Ukrainian Military Congress, which had been prohibited by Kerensky, the Central Rada issued its Universal (proclamation) to the Ukrainian people, declaring that "from this day forth we shall build our own life" and calling on all Ukrainian organizations and local government bodies to establish "the closest organizational ties with the Central Rada." It called on them to raise, on 1 July, a special tax "for our native cause" and to pay this tax to the treasury of the Central Rada.[16] The Universal was unanimously supported by the Ukrainians but rejected by all the all-Russian parties and movements in Ukraine except the Bolsheviks, who became a kind of ally in this conflict with the Provisional Government.

On 15 June the Central Rada established an executive body, the General Secretariat. This was de facto a proto-government with responsibilities for land, finance, food supplies, the peasantry, relations among nationalities, and the maintenance of public order. The majority of the Secretariat was made up of Ukrainian Social Democrats. Its leader was Volodymyr Vynnychenko. The other Social Democrats were Borys Martos, Symon Petliura, Valentyn Sadovsky, and Ivan Steshenko. The Ukrainian Socialist Revolutionaries were represented by Pavlo Khrystiuk and the Socialist Federalists by Serhii Yefremov. There were also two non-party socialists, Mykola Stasiuk and Khrystofor Baranovsky.

The next two weeks were taken up with informal negotiations between St. Petersburg and Kyiv aimed at clarifying the positions of both sides. The contacts in Kyiv, members of the Constitutional Democrats and Mensheviks, argued that more attention should be paid to the demands of the Ukrainians.[17] The Provisional Government itself, mired in a permanent political crisis, did not have the leverage to control the situation in Ukraine.

On 27 June the General Secretariat issued a declaration summarizing in broad terms, not very clearly for the most part, what it saw as its principal tasks and the main focus of its activity: reorganization of local authorities and administration (its nebulous

---

15 *Ukraïns'kyi natsional'no-vyzvol'nyi rukh. Berezen'-lystopad 1917 r. Dokumenty i materialy* (Kyiv, 2003), 347. The peasant enthusiasm for autonomy was easily explained: this was seen as the quickest way to resolve the land question.

16 *Ukraïns'ka Tsentral'na Rada,* 1: 105.

17 O. B. Kudlai, "Perehovory Tsentral'noï Rady i predstavnykiv Tymchasovoho uriadu. 28–30 chervnia 1917 r.," *Ukraïns'kyi istorychnyi zhurnal*, 1999, no. 6: 46–47.

sentences could be interpreted to mean that they were to be subordinate to the Central Rada); Ukrainization of the educational system, the army, and financial organizations; preparation of a land law; normalization of the situation in the villages, and so on. On 29 June 1917 there was a meeting between a delegation of the Provisional Government (Irakli Tsereteli, Mykhailo Tereshchenko, Nikolai Nekrasov, Aleksandr Kerensky) and the Committee and General Secretariat of the Central Rada. The Ukrainians demanded that the Provisional Government recognize the Central Rada as the supreme power in the region, that it accept a document regulating the autonomy of Ukraine until such time as it could be regulated by a constituent assembly, and that it prepare a document containing the principles of land reform. The Russian delegation demanded that the Central Rada accept representatives of non-Ukrainian nationalities and insisted that the General Secretariat required the approval of the ministerial cabinet of the Provisional Government.

The results of the negotiations were made public in the Second Universal of the Central Rada on 3 July 1917. This included the promise that it would accept "representatives of the revolutionary organizations of the other peoples who live in Ukraine," prepare legislation for Ukraine's autonomous structure to be submitted for confirmation to the Constituent Assembly, and support the Provisional Government in the Ukrainization of the army (formation of separate units composed exclusively of Ukrainians).[18] One month later, on 4 August 1917, there came the "Provisional Instructions of the Provisional Government to the General Secretariat," in which the General Secretariat, appointed by the Provisional Government on the basis of recommendations from the Central Rada, was designated the supreme organ of the Provisional Government in Ukraine. According to this document, the authority of the General Secretariat extended to the gubernias of Kyiv, Volhynia, Poltava, Chernihiv, and Podilia, encompassing internal affairs, finance, agriculture, education, trade and industry, labor law, and nationalities.[19] It was only from this point that the General Secretariat really began its activity.

---

18 The publication of the Universal coincided with the events of 3 and 4 July in St. Petersburg, where there was mass unrest and military encounters between government troops and revolutionary soldiers and sailors.

19 *Konstytutsiini akty Ukraïny, 1917–1920. Nevidomi konstytutsiï Ukraïny* (Kyiv, 1992). The document is also available in English in *The Russian Provisional Government, 1917: Documents*, ed. Robert Paul Browder and Alexander Kerensky, vol. 1 (Stanford, 1961), 396.

Negotiations, appeals, conflicts over the division of responsibilities between St. Petersburg and Kyiv, plans and declarations about the organization of administration—all these had increasingly symbolic and little practical significance. In both St. Petersburg and Kyiv, the powers of the central organs became increasingly volatile. Between the spring and autumn of 1917 there was a constant fragmentation of power, both horizontally across the territory and vertically among the different political forces. From the center, the Provisional Government attempted to establish a vertical order appropriate to the administrative territorial structure of the empire (gubernia and district commissars as executive authorities, with zemstvos and city dumas as organs of local self-administration). The Central Rada, on the other hand, with its executive and provisional organs (General Secretariat, Committee for the Defense of the Revolution), was also very quickly attempting to establish its own division of powers within the framework of national autonomy. The workers' councils (soon followed by soldiers' and peasants' councils) were a third actor. And, finally, there were the factory committees in the enterprises and the garrisons and logistic units, whose role in the summer of 1917 was becoming increasingly volatile, given the growing revolutionary mood and the disintegration of the army.[20]

The horizontal fragmentation of power was expressed by the fact that orders from the central authorities were ignored, sabotaged, or even disobeyed and by the increasing de facto independence of local authorities. In the case of cities, this might be the city duma, the district commissar, or the local soviet; in the countryside, it might be the village assembly or the leaders of the local self-defense units.

By the autumn of 1917, the already difficult social and economic situation had deteriorated sharply. The weakness of the bodies responsible for law and order, the expropriation propaganda of the left-wing parties, especially the Bolsheviks and Socialist Revolutionaries, the weakness of the central government, the constant decline in living standards (rising prices, lack of basic food and industrial commodities, speculation), the disintegration of the army—all these factors were leading to chaos. There was an increase in criminality in the cities, especially in the district centers and larger market towns. Shops and houses were plundered, wine cellars and factories were laid waste,

---

20 The advance of the Russian army on the southwestern front collapsed completely because of the disintegration of the advancing units between 16 and 20 June 1917. Soldiers discussed their orders and refused to carry them out. Whole lower-level detachments left the front line.

and various forms of street crime were a daily occurrence. Not just criminal elements but increasingly soldiers and "ordinary citizens" were engaging in robbery and theft.[21]

The relatively peaceful summer of 1917 in the countryside was followed in the autumn by a flare-up of peasant expropriations. A growing sense of impunity, of "everything-is-permitted," was increased by Socialist Revolutionary agitation for the redistribution of land. A contemporary observer recalls the ferment among the peasants caused by demobilized soldiers, deserters, and amnestied criminals: "They poisoned the village," wrote Volodymyr Leontovych, "with their rage, their disrespect, yes even their hatred of law, morality, and justice, their hatred of everything that could restrict or rein them in. They incited the peasants to arbitrariness, destruction, and murder."[22] Another contemporary and chronicler of the events of 1917–20, Dmytro Doroshenko, writes that by the end of the summer of 1917, "all appeals from the center to maintain peace and order and to await the decisions of the constituent assembly had lost all force. There were disturbances everywhere: theft of cattle and property from the estate owners, unauthorized expropriation of land, chopping down trees, arson, and the plundering of distilleries."[23] According to official data, there were as many as 525 such incidents perpetrated by dissatisfied peasants in the Ukrainian gubernias between July and the first half of October 1917.[24]

Between August and October 1917, there was an evident radicalization of the Ukrainian movement. The Social Democratic and Socialist Revolutionary congresses, the meeting of the All-Ukrainian Soviet of Peasant Deputies, and the congress of the "enslaved nations of Russia," which took place in September and October, all demanded an extension of the powers of the Central Rada and the General Secretariat (both politically and territorially) up to the creation of an autonomous republic. At the initiative of the Ukrainian Socialist Revolutionaries, the Third All-Ukrainian Military Congress passed a resolution on 20 October 1917 on the independent creation of a

---

21 V. Boiko, T. Demchenko, and O. Onyshchenko, *1917 rik na Chernihivshchyni* (Chernihiv, 2003), 44–50.

22 National Archives of the Czech Republic, F. Ukrainian Museum. Kart. 57, inv. c. 784 (Leontovych V.) "Spohady i vrazhennia z chasiv ahrarnoï reform," typescript 5.

23 D. Doroshenko, *Istoriia Ukraïny 1917–1923 rr. Doba Tsentral'noï Rady*, vol. 1 (Uzhhorod, 1932; repr. New York, 1954), 75.

24 V. Verstiuk, *Selians'ka problema v politytsi ukraïns'kykh politychnykh syl ta uriadiv 1917–1920 rr. Istoriia ukraïns'koho selianstva*, vol. 1 (Kyiv, 2006), 535.

"Ukrainian democratic republic." On 25 October the Bolsheviks seized power in St. Petersburg. The Provisional Government fell. Relations with the central authorities changed radically. The Provisional Government was replaced by a power that saw extreme forms of demagogy and the use of force as the solution to political and social problems. On the nationality issue, the Bolsheviks supported the principle of self-determination for tactical reasons but, in the concrete instance of Ukraine, this was subordinate to "class" and to "revolutionary necessity."

Subsequent to the events in St. Petersburg, the Ukrainian Bolsheviks attempted to repeat the 25 October scenario in Kyiv. The uprising led to armed clashes with troops of the Kyiv military district. The Central Rada later resumed power peacefully. It did not approve of the coup in St. Petersburg but did nothing to support the Provisional Government. The Bolsheviks, who had left the Central Rada immediately after the coup, initially took a loyal attitude to the developments.

On 1 and 3 November 1917 the Ukrainian Central Rada declared that it was taking all military installations in Ukraine under its control except the detachments at the front.[25] Posts were created in the General Secretariat for ministers of military affairs (Petliura), food, justice, post and telegraph, and transport. The Central Rada also declared the extension of its rule to the gubernias of Kherson, Kharkiv, Katerynoslav, and Tavria (not including the Crimea).

The Third Universal was proclaimed on 7 November. This Universal declared the founding of the Ukrainian People's Republic (UNR) while remaining in federation with the Russian Republic. It proclaimed that all power in Ukraine (the nine gubernias) now rested with the Central Rada and the General Secretariat. The Universal also announced the abolition of estates and other forms of land "not worked directly by the proprietors," which would now become the "property of the toiling people" without compensation. Until such time as the constituent assembly met, the administration of all matters pertaining to land would be in the hands of the General Secretariat and the land committees.[26] It proclaimed the eight-hour day, the abolition of the death penalty, freedom of the press, religion, and association, and the

25 The entire staff of the Kyiv military district left the city on 31 October at the time of the truce negotiations between the Central Rada, the various parties, and the workers' and soldiers' councils.

26 In the Ukrainian gubernias there were 9 gubernia, 94 regional, and 1,528 district land committees that had been created by the Provisional Government.

inviolability of person and domicile. It also proclaimed the principle of national-personal autonomy for non-Ukrainian national minorities living in Ukraine and demanded immediate peace negotiations.[27]

When the Central Rada and the General Secretariat published their principles and slogans, they obviously did so with the intention of continuing to act within a legal framework. All local organs that had previously functioned under the Provisional Government would continue to operate until the constituent assembly, to be elected on 27 December 1917 and convoked on 9 January 1918, had made its decisions. According to decisions and orders of the Central Rada and the General Secretariat, decisions of the Provisional Government would remain in force on the territory of the Ukrainian People's Republic, except where they had already been overruled by the Ukrainian authorities. Instructions were given to local authorities prohibiting unauthorized appropriation of land or property and deforestation. Attempts were made (unsuccessfully) to reunite the southwestern and Romanian front into one Ukrainian front. At the level of intentions, resolutions, and declarations, everything was directed toward the maintenance of law and order and a certain status quo until the convocation of the constitutional assembly.

In most cases, these intentions, resolutions, and declarations had little effect. The Ukrainian authorities had practically no real leverage to make them a reality. There was a colossal shortage of human resources, and the Ukrainian movement itself was not united in its intentions or actions. The social base of the movement was small and unreliable. At the time of the Third Universal, the leaders of the Central Rada and the General Secretariat had the support of the Ukrainian intelligentsia[28] (the social base of the new rule), the politicized elements of the Ukrainian peasantry, the Ukrainized troops, and representatives of the Ukrainian zemstvos and the Ukrainian cooperative movement. The overwhelming majority of the Russian intelligentsia, the urban middle

27 *Ukraïns'ka Tsentral'na Rada*, 1: 399–401.

28 In the census of 1897, under the heading "nature of activity," the possible answers were: social and public service, private legal practice, teaching and educational activity, science, literature and art, and therapeutic and medical activity. The total number of Ukrainians engaged in these activities was 27,900, two-thirds of whom lived in rural areas. Figures from *Pervaia vseobshchaia perepis' naseleniia Rossiiskoi imperii 1897 g.*, in 89 volumes (St. Petersburg, 1887–1905), vol. 8: 172ff., 176, 180ff., 184; vol. 13: 152ff., 156, 158ff., 162; vol. 16: 178ff., 182; vol. 18: 212–14, 216, 218, 220, 222; vol. 32: 178–83, 185; vol. 33: 192, 194, 196, 198, 200, 202; vol. 47: 200–2, 204; vol. 48: 208, 211, 214, 216, 218; vol. 51: 198–200, 204–7, 210. The criterion for nationality was language. A Ukrainian was anyone who selected "Little Russian" as his mother tongue. Among the working population, 90 percent of the Ukrainians were peasants.

stratum, the industrial workers, representatives of urban government, officials, and the officer corps all opposed the Ukrainian movement or were neutral at best.

The potentially strongest support for the Ukrainian Revolution, the peasantry, rapidly lost all interest in politics with the advent of the "black repartition."[29] The prospect of a redistribution or appropriation of land that entailed no sanctions and was not controlled by anyone was far more attractive than waiting for the solution to the land question promised by the Central Rada. In any case, the relevant sections of the Third Universal could be interpreted as a call for a "black repartition," and there were many who saw it that way.

In such a situation, the villages sank very quickly into anarchy. The "organization of national life," previously seen as the pathway to "owning our land," lost all relevance. District commissars reported in November that "there is no longer any authority in the village." According to these reports, "the government attempted to implement the Central Rada's Universal, but local people just plundered and did not recognize the authority of the Central Rada," and "everyone just does as he wishes."[30]

In November and early December 1917 the General Secretariat, now the government of the Ukrainian People's Republic, established the Ukrainian Central Bank, recognized the Council of People's Commissars that had been created in St. Petersburg on 27 October 1917 as a regional government, and established the General Court. Initial talks were begun with Germany about a truce. At the same time, attempts were made to reach an understanding with the Entente. All this was happening against the background of drastically worsening relations with Bolshevik organizations in Ukraine and with the Bolshevik government in St. Petersburg. On 17 November 1917, in telephone negotiations between Mykola Porsh and Joseph Stalin, a member of the Council of People's Commissars, it became clear that the government in St. Petersburg recognized only the Ukrainian Congress of Workers', Peasants', and Soldiers' Deputies as the supreme power in Ukraine. Some workers' and soldiers' councils in Ukraine, influenced by the Bolsheviks, had already passed resolutions in support of this idea in November.

---

29 This land decree was issued on 26 October 1917 at the Second All-Russian Congress of Soviets at the initiative of the Bolsheviks, who had made use of the Socialist Revolutionary slogan of "socialization of the land."

30 V. V. Sokal's'kyi, *Guberns'ki selians'ki z'ïzdy iak skladovi ukraïns'koï revoliutsiï 1917–1921 rr.* (Kyiv, 2009), 107.

Elections to the All-Russian Constituent Assembly took place at the end of November 1917. The results alarmed the Bolsheviks. They received only 10 percent of the popular vote in Ukraine, while the Ukrainian parties received 77 percent. They were also worried by resolutions passed by councils in the larger cities of Ukraine (Kyiv, Kharkiv, Odesa, Poltava, Katerynoslav), which, while supporting the Council of People's Commissars in St. Petersburg, also recognized the Ukrainian Central Rada as the authority in Ukraine.[31] The Ukrainian Bolsheviks pursued their traditional methods. While they took part in relatively legitimate forms of political struggle, such as preparing the All-Ukrainian Congress of Soviets, they also made preparations for an armed coup and carried out intensive agitation against the Central Rada. In mid-November the Kyiv Revolutionary Committee, led by the Bolsheviks, declared the Central Rada to be counterrevolutionary and began preparations for an armed uprising.

For the Central Rada and the General Secretariat, the moment had now come in which the use of military force was necessary. The leaders of the Ukrainian Revolution, however, were not prepared for this development. Practically all the fighting units that could have been deployed to protect the Ukrainian People's Republic were either independent of the Ukrainian leaders or had actually been trained in opposition to their principles and ideals. The representatives of the Ukrainian Social Democrats and Socialist Revolutionaries, who dominated in the Central Rada, were opposed to the formation of a regular national army. In a time of war, they were satisfied with the Ukrainization of units in the Russian army.

Ukrainian units had already begun to emerge spontaneously in the army in March 1917. Ukrainian conscript clubs were formed. *Vicha*[32] were convened at which demands were made for the formation of Ukrainian units. Although in April 1917 the Central Rada supported an initiative of Ukrainian recruits to form a volunteer regiment named after Bohdan Khmelnytsky, the Rada played no role in its organization (the regiment had 3,500 soldiers and was sent to the front in July 1917). At the first All-Ukrainian Military Congress, in May 1917, a Ukrainian General Military Committee was formed under the leadership of Petliura. This committee was subordinate to the Central Rada and was in charge of the organization of Ukrainian

---

31 O. Boiko, "Politychne protystoiannia Ukraïns'koï Tsentral'noï Rady i bil'shovykiv (zhovten'–hruden' 1917)," *Ukraïns'kyi istorychnyi zhurnal*, 2003, no. 4: 18.

32 *Viche* (Ukr., pl. *vicha*; Russ. *veche*) was the name for a traditional old Slavic democratic "assembly" and was revived by contemporaries.

units in the army. In reality, the Ukrainization of troop units depended on individual commanders. The First Ukrainian Corps (about sixty thousand soldiers and officers)[33] was formed on the southwestern front in the summer of 1917 under the command of Pavlo Skoropadsky. This fact is often given as an example of the successful Ukrainization of the army. Vynnychenko gave an account of the general situation: "The military units themselves began to reform. Regiments arose under the leadership of various hetmans and other Ukrainian individuals: the Sahaidachny Regiment, the Gonta Regiment, the Doroshenko Regiment, and so on. Once those regiments came into existence on their own initiative and had been officially recognized, they considered themselves somewhat independent, not subject to the general order. They only wanted to be part of the Ukrainian Corps at the front. But the famous 'three corps' did not really exist. The Russian command was frightened into giving approval for their formation but had no intention of doing anything about it. So these regiments could not be sent anywhere. This created confusion and chaos in troop movements and groupings. The commanders were angry and blamed the General Committee for disorganizing the army and interfering in its affairs. The regiments and soldiers were angry and accused the General Committee of inaction and inability to carry out its tasks. The General Committee was also angry and made superhuman efforts to put an end to the confusion."[34]

The truly scandalous and tragic fate of the Hetman Pavlo Polubotok Regiment was indicative of relations between the Central Rada and the General Secretariat on the question of military organization. The leaders of the Central Rada not only distanced themselves from this initiative but thwarted it.[35] The Free Cossacks,[36] with a strength

33 This is the number usually quoted, but other sources suggest that the number was no more than 25,000 to 30,000. See I. Ie. Petrenko, "Diial'nist' P. Skoropads'koho shchodo ukraïnizatsiï chastyn rosiis'koï armiï u 1917 r.," in *Problemy istoriï Ukraïny XIX – poch. XX st.*, vyp. XV.SC (Kyiv, 2008), 136.

34 V. Vynnychenko, *Vidrodzhennia natsiï*, 3 vols. (Kyiv and Vienna, 1920), 1: 197ff.

35 The regiment was formed in May 1917 at the initiative of recruits from the village of Hrushky near Kyiv. Many writers have pointed out that the Ukrainization of regiments and stationing them in Kyiv to protect the Central Rada only served eventually to prevent their movement to the front. Between 5 and 7 July, the soldiers (about five thousand men), reduced to despair by the shortage of food and lack of support from the Central Rada, stormed Kyiv, appropriated weapons, blockaded a number of establishments (bank, telegraph office), and occupied the headquarters of the militia and the arsenal. The disturbance was brought to an end through the mediation of the Central Rada, but the Rada refused official recognition to the regiment. See V. F. Soldatenko, *Vynnychenko i Petliura. Politychni portrety revoliutsiinoï doby* (Kyiv, 2007), 128–46.

36 The Free Cossacks began to organize themselves in March 1917 from local self-defense units for the maintenance of public order.

estimated to have been around sixty thousand men, was another armed force formed on an initiative from below but was ignored by the Central Rada and the General Secretariat alike. The statute of the Free Cossacks was not confirmed until November 1917, but even afterwards its sections were basically civilian organizations without any real status. It was not until January 1918, when armed conflict with the Bolsheviks had already broken out, that small units of Free Cossacks were formed in Kyiv. They then took part in the conflict, but without any noteworthy success. The creation of battle-ready Ukrainian units took place literally *en passant*, always lagging behind events. At the initiative of Petliura and the commander of the Kyiv military district, Viktor Pavlenko, two Serdiuk (Cossack) divisions were started in November that then defeated an attempted Bolshevik uprising in Kyiv on 30 November 1917.

As the winter of 1917–18 began and the Ukrainian People's Republic feared for its existence, it lacked a serious military force. Its overall strength was a little over 25,000 bayonets, 1,680 swords, and 44 guns, around 16,000 of which were concentrated in Kyiv and the surrounding area.[37] These would need to be strengthened by the Ukrainized units on the southwestern and Romanian fronts (at least 50,000 soldiers).[38] However, when fighting began between the troops of the Petrograd Council of People's Commissars, the Ukrainian Bolsheviks, and the military units of the Central Rada, these units existed only on paper.

On 3 December the All-Ukrainian Congress of Soviets opened in Kyiv. The Ukrainian Bolsheviks were in a minority (they represented 86 of the 300 soviets). On 4 December the Petrograd Council of People's Commissars sent a manifesto to Kyiv signed by Lenin and Trotsky. This was the "Manifesto to the Ukrainian People with an Ultimatum to the Ukrainian Rada." In this document, which recognized the right of the Ukrainian People's Republic to independence, there was a protest against the actions of the Central Rada, which was allegedly trying to disorganize the common front (this refers to the movement of Ukrainian units on the northern and northwestern front to the Ukrainian front, formed from the merging of the southwestern and Romanian fronts in November 1917). The manifesto demanded that the disarming of Soviet troops and Red Guards in Ukraine cease, that

---

37 Ia. Tynchenko, *Persha ukraïns'ko-bil'shovyts'ka viina (hruden' 1917–berezen' 1918)* (Kyiv and Lviv, 1996), 40–41. The data concerning strength and location of troops are given in tables.

38 Ibid., 66.

transit be refused to military units heading for the Don and the Kuban to join Aleksei Kaledin (who was fighting against the Council of People's Commissars), and that armed units of the Council of People's Commissars be allowed free passage to the front to fight Kaledin. In case the Ukrainian People's Republic did not give a satisfactory reply within forty-eight hours, the Council of People's Commissars "would deem the Rada to be in a state of open war with Soviet power in Russia and Ukraine."

The majority of delegates rejected the ultimatum. The Bolshevik delegates,[39] having assessed the situation, moved to Kharkiv, which was already in the hands of Bolshevik forces.[40] In Kharkiv, they met with the delegates of the Third Congress of Soviets from the Donbas and Kryvyi Rih, which declared itself the All-Ukrainian Congress of Soviets. The congress elected a Central Executive Committee which, in turn, formed a government, the People's Secretariat, under the leadership of Evgeniia Bosh. The Ukrainian Soviet Republic was proclaimed. There were now two governments in Ukraine that would soon enter into armed conflict with each other. On 17 December 1917 the Executive Committee in Kharkiv proclaimed the Ukrainian Central Rada a "counterrevolutionary force" and declared war against it.[41]

At the end of 1917, the general situation in Ukraine was as follows. The administrative organs of the Provisional Government (gubernia and district commissars) were still formally in charge in the towns, gubernias, and districts, as were the city dumas. The Central Rada and the General Secretariat were formally the government in Kyiv and in the nine Ukrainian gubernias. These were in confrontation with the Central Executive Committee and the People's Secretariat in Kharkiv. Bolshevik Revolutionary Committees were also active in the big cities. This list would be incomplete without the land committees, the zemstvos, and the local workers', soldiers', and peasants' councils,

---

39 This move by the Council of People's Commissars in St. Petersburg came as a surprise to the Ukrainian Bolsheviks. According to one contemporary observer, "the Central Committee of the party had not forewarned the Ukrainian organizations and had not attempted to discuss the advisability of such a major step. The ultimatum, right at the beginning of the All-Ukrainian Soviet Congress, put the Ukrainian Bolsheviks in an extremely difficult position because there was an explosion of chauvinism at this congress that bound all nationally inclined elements even more strongly to the Rada." See S. K. Shreiber, "K protokolam pervogo vseukrainskogo soveshchaniia bol'shevikov," *Letopis' revoliutsii*, 1926, no. 5: 61.

40 Kharkiv was taken by units from the Siversk region.

41 Military operations took place mainly in the cities of Kharkiv, Katerynoslav, and Kyiv. The Soviet government in Kharkiv at this time had neither military forces of its own nor any real lever of power. It was basically an appendage of the Bolshevik military forces.

which were controlled in some cases by the Bolsheviks, in other cases by the Socialist Revolutionaries, Mensheviks, Ukrainian Social Democrats, and Ukrainian Socialist Revolutionaries. Finally, there were the command headquarters at the front and the administrative bodies in the rear. The country teemed with armed men over whom there was little or no control. In the towns, there were the army garrisons and army units with their command headquarters (at this time the army was rapidly disintegrating), Red Guard units, armed formations of Russian Bolsheviks, the armed forces of the Ukrainian People's Republic, officers in training in military training centers and schools, and Red Cossacks. In the countryside there were the self-defense units, the Free Cossacks, groups of army deserters, and criminal elements.

It was against this background of chaos that armed conflict broke out between the Ukrainian People's Republic and the Bolsheviks. In December 1917 the Bolsheviks had established control over Kharkiv and then captured Poltava, Chernihiv, and Katerynoslav. The General Secretariat was active in reorganizing the military forces of the Ukrainian People's Republic and, at the same time, commenced negotiations with representatives of the Central Powers in Brest-Litovsk.[42]

To forestall a Bolshevik uprising in Kyiv, on the night of 17–18 January 1918[43] military units of the Central Rada took control of thirty sites in the city from which an uprising could be launched or that could be attacked (factories, workshops, the administration of the southwestern railway). On the day before, the Revolutionary Committee in Kyiv had called for an uprising against the Central Rada. In this dramatic situation, on the night of 24–25 January, as an armed uprising hung in the air in Kyiv and the troops of the Ukrainian Soviet government (whose strongest units had come from Soviet Russia) were successfully advancing against Kyiv from the east, the Ukrainian Central Rada proclaimed its Fourth (and last) Universal.

The Universal declared the Ukrainian People's Republic to be "independent, subject to no one, a free sovereign state of the

---

42 These negotiations, which had begun in early December, were initially private. The delegation of the Central Powers regarded the Council of People's Commissars in St. Petersburg, which was now trying to arrange a separate peace, as the only representative of political power. Following the publication on 11 December 1917 of the General Secretariat's note to all warring and neutral states, the delegation began official negotiations with the representatives of the Ukrainian People's Republic on 22 December.

43 Here and in the remainder of the text, dates are given according to the new Gregorian calendar.

Ukrainian people." The Council of People's Ministers (the former General Secretariat) was given the task of making peace with the Central Powers. Once peace had been achieved, the army would be dissolved and replaced by a "people's militia." All the democratic rights proclaimed in the previous Universal were confirmed, as was the law passed the day before on national-personal autonomy. Elections to regional and district councils and city dumas were set for the time when the demobilized soldiers would return from the front. The previous decision to transfer land to the "toiling people" without compensation was also confirmed. A state monopoly of land was introduced, as was control of the banks "by the state and the people." The Universal called for a struggle against the Bolsheviks.[44] This Universal, which most scholars regard as a final declaration of independence, was the result of tense discussions between the two leading parties in the Rada, the Social Democrats and Socialist Revolutionaries, and between these and the non-Ukrainian parties (the Russian Mensheviks and Socialist Revolutionaries and the Bund were against declaring independence). What is clear is that the leaders of the major Ukrainian parties saw this action as something forced on them, since they continued to speak of a federation of "democratic nations." This declaration of independence was, on the one hand, a response to Bolshevik aggression and, on the other hand, an important step in the context of the negotiations at Brest-Litovsk.

The Bolshevik-led uprising in Kyiv began on 29 January 1918. At the same time, Bolshevik forces advanced on Kyiv from Poltava and Chernihiv.[45] The strongest forces of the Central Rada were concentrated in Kyiv to suppress the uprising, which is why the Bolsheviks were able to advance on Kyiv without too much difficulty. (Recent estimates suggest that the ratio of forces between the Bolsheviks and the Central Rada was seven to one;[46] other sources suggest three to one.) On 5 February 1918, the commander of the military forces under

---

44 Doroshenko, *Istoriia Ukraïny 1917–23 rr.*, 1: 264–68.

45 Battles were fought mainly over control of railway junctions and towns capable of offering supplies to the warring sides. Control was often achieved without the use of force, as when units formally under the control of the Rada declared themselves "neutral" or went over to the Bolsheviks. There were also instances of conflict not with the troops of the Ukrainian People's Republic but with troops in transit to the Don or Kuban or with garrison units that would not allow transit to "foreigners." It should also be remembered that in Ukraine, when Bolshevik troops approached a town, events tended to follow a standard schema in which there would be an outbreak of workers' uprisings and strikes led by local revolutionary committees assisted by Red Guards.

46 V. Holubko, *Armiia Ukraïns'koï Narodnoï Respubliky* (Lviv, 1997), 168.

the People's Secretariat of the Ukrainian Soviet Socialist Republic gave the order to storm Kyiv, where the uprising was still in progress. On 8 February Soviet forces occupied the city, and the Central Rada abandoned it. It might be thought ironic that during those same days, with cannons thundering all around, the Central Rada was discussing the draft law on workers' control of enterprises and the eight-hour day.[47] The city was subjected to the most brutal terror. The Bolshevik commander, Mikhail Muraviev, ordered that officers, haidamakas, monarchists, and "all enemies of the revolution" be killed in the streets. These "enemies" also included residents who spoke Ukrainian and individuals with a cultivated appearance.[48] On 12 February the Ukrainian Soviet government moved from Kharkiv to Kyiv, where it remained until 28 February. It then fled before the advancing German army toward Poltava, Katerynoslav, Taganrog and beyond.

In the situation at the time, it was only assistance from the Central Powers that could have rescued the Central Rada and its government. On the night of 8–9 February, a peace treaty was signed between the Ukrainian People's Republic and the Central Powers. On 18 February, after a formal request for military assistance from the UNR, German troops began to advance into Ukrainian territory. They were followed ten days later by Austro-Hungarian units. On 8 May 1918 German troops occupied Rostov on the Don, having crossed the Ukrainian border and driven the Bolsheviks from Ukrainian territory. Earlier, on 28 March 1918, an agreement was signed on establishing the "zones of influence" of the "occupying powers."[49] All this was portrayed as military assistance for an ally. In the initial period the occupying troops were forbidden to take military action against the local population in the event of "unfriendly actions" (which rarely occurred then). They would have to seek redress from the UNR authorities.[50]

---

47 *Ukraïna. Khronika XX stolittia. Rik 1918* (Kyiv, 2005), 64.

48 Volodymyr Zatonsky, a member of both the Ukrainian and the Russian Soviet governments, reported in his memoirs that he was almost shot by a patrol. An official Ukrainian identity paper made him suspect, but he was saved by a document signed by Lenin showing him to be a member of the Council of People's Commissars. See V. P. Zatons'kyi, "Iz spohadiv pro ukraïns'ku revoliutsiiu," *Litopys revoliutsiï*, 1929, nos. 5–6: 116–17. The total number of victims was about three thousand.

49 See chapters 3a and 3b in the present volume.

50 Peter Lieb, "Pryborkannia povstans'koho rukhu — stratehichna dylema. Nimets'ka okupatsiia Ukraïny 1918 roku," in *Okupatsiia Ukraïny 1918 roku. Istorychnyi kontekst – stan doslidzhennia – ekonomichni ta sotsial'ni naslidky*, ed. Wolfram Dornik and Stefan Karner (Chernivtsi, 2009), 110–40; Wolfram Dornik, "Okupatsiia Ukraïny avstro-uhors'kymy viis'kamy u 1918 rotsi," ibid., 141–83. For more detail, see chapter 3b in the present volume.

When the Central Rada and the UNR Council of People's Ministers returned to Kyiv on 5 March, they found themselves in an extremely difficult situation. The whole vertical power structure had to be reestablished. At the same time, however, they had to pay attention to the obligations to their new allies (especially the deliveries of food), which in turn required an effective power structure. But this power structure was lacking. The Central Rada passed laws, made regulations, and took decisions in many areas, from the organization of the army to the introduction of Ukrainian as the official language of the state, from the minting of money to the creation of national holidays (for instance, 9 March, the birthday of Taras Shevchenko), from the establishment of a state sugar monopoly to the founding of a Ukrainian national university. At the beginning of March 1918, the national currency (the hryvnia), the state coat of arms (the trident of Volodymyr the Great), and the citizenship law of the Ukrainian People's Republic were introduced. The main problem was that most of these decisions were never actually implemented, whether because of the lack of an effective administrative apparatus, the continued failure of the government to implement them owing to personnel changes caused by differences of opinion among the various parties, or because of an elementary lack of organizational ability and political will on the part of the state's leaders. One need only realize that the Council of People's Ministers spent the whole month of March on its own reorganization. According to a communication from the German Foreign Office, "It is completely out of the question that the Rada, with its own officials, could manage to carry out the delivery and transport of food, since it has no regular and functioning organization. And that cannot be changed quickly, for the Rada lacks both money and an effective executive apparatus (army, gendarmerie, courts, police)."[51]

The Central Rada and the Council of People's Ministers held only nominal power, maintained by the bayonets of the German and Austro-Hungarian armies.[52] In the towns and at railway junctions, order was maintained by garrisons of the "allies." There was practically no control over the villages, where anarchy ruled. The peasantry recognized no power, while spontaneous land redistribution and plundering of estates continued as before. This was often accompanied by conflicts

---

51 Doroshenko, *Istoriia Ukraïny 1917–1923 rr.*, 2: 11.

52 The attitude of the "allies" is expressed very clearly in the words of General Hoffmann: "I am interested in Ukraine only until the next harvest. I do not care what happens after that." See "Bericht des Leiters der operativen Abteilung der deutschen Ostfront über die Lage in der Ukraine im März 1918," *Archiv der Russischen Revolution*, vol. 1 (Berlin, 1922), 288n.

among the peasants themselves, and there were open battles between individual villages. As the journalist Colin Ross reported to German headquarters on the Eastern Front, "There is no central power in the state capable of occupying an area of reasonable size. The whole country is divided into individual areas that sometimes do not extend beyond the borders of a district, a town, or even a village. In these areas, power is in the hands of political parties, individual political adventurers, robbers, and dictators. One finds villages surrounded by trenches, in conflict with each other over estate land. Some areas are ruled over by otamans who enforce their rule with the help of stewards and mercenaries. They have machine guns, artillery, and tanks, just as the population itself has acquired a host of weapons."[53]

In April, the commanders of the German and Austro-Hungarian military forces themselves began to "maintain order," especially in the villages. On 6 April the commander of German troops in Ukraine, Field Marshal Hermann von Eichhorn, issued his cultivation order at the start of the spring sowing.[54] The Central Rada overruled his order and issued one of its own, thereby entering into open conflict with its allies. By this time, the latter were searching intensively for an alternative to the Rada. Its dissolution was made easier by the fact that it had no noticeable influence on the situation in the country, as well as by the presence of an active opposition in the form of large and middle landowners, from estate owners to wealthier peasants. They were the principal victims of the "black repartition," which they attributed equally to Bolshevik demagogy, spontaneous land division, and the laws passed by the Central Rada that had the effect of practically legalizing it. A number of congresses and assemblies of representative organizations and political parties of the large and middle landowners stated openly, in March and April 1918, that a change of power was necessary and that the German and Austro-Hungarian military should be asked for help "in restoring order." Similar attitudes prevailed in an influential part of the Ukrainian movement that stood in sometimes hidden and sometimes open opposition to the leaders of the Central Rada and the government controlled by the Socialist Revolutionaries and Social Democrats. In early April 1918 Yevhen Chykalenko, a leading representative of the Ukrainian movement, made a note about conversations in this milieu: "Everyone is waiting for the Germans to take everything into their own hands and appoint ministers, as our

53 Ibid., 288.

54 Two weeks later, the German command installed military courts for civilians.

own people will not manage to establish order and bring peace to our young state."[55]

A large part of the Russian-speaking urban population, as well as the overwhelming majority of the urban bourgeoisie and petty bourgeoisie, were passive allies of the opposition. By April 1918 the Central Rada had no serious social base. The Ukrainian peasants, having themselves divided up the land, had "forgotten" about national self-determination, while the intelligentsia was too weak. Nor did the Rada have an adequate battle-ready army (the consequence of ideological experiments) or external allies. Under such circumstances, a change of regime was a mere "technicality."

The initiative was taken by the German military commander in Ukraine and the German ambassador in Kyiv, Philipp Alfons Mumm von Schwarzenstein. In mid-April contact was established with Pavlo Skoropadsky, founder of the Ukrainian People's Hromada (Community), the core of which consisted of ex-military and personally loyal officers. The informal negotiations resulted in the assumption of certain formal obligations. Skoropadsky was confronted with concrete demands whose implementation would guarantee him the "friendly neutrality" of the German military leaders.[56] The same demands were presented to the Council of People's Ministers of the Ukrainian People's Republic, where they were certain to be rejected.

The circumstances of the overthrow are generally known. On 23–24 April, a meeting took place between the military commanders of the occupation and the ambassadors of Germany and Austria-Hungary. The decision was taken at this meeting for a change of regime in Ukraine (at the same time, negotiations were being held and documents signed for an "economic agreement" with the government of the Ukrainian People's Republic).[57] On 26–27 April, German units in Kyiv disarmed the units of the First Ukrainian Division (the so-called *Syn'ozhupannyky*) and the Ukrainian artillery regiments. On 28 April a German military group entered the chamber of the Pedagogical Museum, where the Little Rada was meeting, broke up the meeting, and arrested some of those present (the pretext for this was the kidnapping of the banker Adam Dobry). On 29 April there took place what turned out to be the final session of the Ukrainian Central Rada (Little Rada), at which the constitution of the Ukrainian

---

55 Ievhen Chykalenko, *Shchodennyk, 1918–1919*, vol. 2 (Kyiv, 2004), 9.

56 Doroshenko, *Istoriia Ukraïny*, 2: 31–32.

57 See the detailed discussion in chapter 3b of the present volume.

People's Republic was approved (titled "Statute Concerning the State Structure, Rights and Freedoms of the Ukrainian People's Republic"). The Congress of the All-Ukrainian Union of Landowners, called by the Ukrainian Democratic Agrarian Party, met on the same day in the Kyiv circus. This congress not only announced the overthrow of the Central Rada and of the government of the Ukrainian People's Republic but also proclaimed a new ruler, Hetman Skoropadsky. In a parallel move, forces of the Ukrainian People's Hromada took all the essential junctions and centers in Kyiv under their control, while the Germans maintained their "neutrality." The overthrow took place with little bloodshed. Three Ukrainian Sich Riflemen who were guarding the Pedagogical Museum lost their lives when the building was stormed.

The Hetman's first act as legislator, his "Manifesto to the Whole Ukrainian People," announced the formation of the Ukrainian State, annulled all the laws and decrees of the Central Rada and the Provisional Government, dissolved the land committees, and restored private ownership of land.[58] The Ukrainian People's Republic and the Ukrainian Central Rada de facto ceased to exist.

Skoropadsky's Ukrainian State

The regime that came to power following the coup of 29 April 1918 differed little from its predecessor from the point of view of legitimacy and representativeness. It was supported by the large landowners, prosperous peasants, industrialists, and the financial bourgeoisie. The parties and organizations that supported Skoropadsky included the very small Ukrainian Democratic Agrarian Party, the Union of Landowners (a grouping of large landowners), and the Union of Industry, Commerce, Finance, and Agriculture (Protofis), a conglomerate of branch organizations from trade, industry, and finance. Finally, there was the Constitutional Democratic Party, which formed the government for just about the whole period of Skoropadsky's rule.

In conditions of revolution, civil war, general anarchy, and economic collapse, the political strength and capacity of these social strata, parties, and organizations to influence events were very limited. The only real force that could be relied on to maintain law and order were the German and Austro-Hungarian troops. But their actual task in the country was a very narrow one—that of maintaining

---

58 *Konstytutsiini akty Ukraïny, 1917–1920*, 82.

the structures necessary for the "exchange of goods" between Ukraine and the Central Powers. The ranks of Skoropadsky's allies and supporters were also disunited when it came to his policies. The Democratic Agrarian Party soon went into opposition over his choice of Russian-speaking officials from the tsarist period to fill the posts in the bureaucracy, army, and police. Influential members of the Union of Landowners disagreed with Skoropadsky's plans for land reform, the basic idea of which was to create a broad stratum of small and medium landowners. Representatives of the Union who were members of the Committee on the Land Question, which was meant to prepare the reform, blocked the committee's work and delayed the implementation of the reform. Similarly, representatives of the Protofis forced the Hetman to take extremely unpopular measures against the workers (abolition of the eight-hour day, repression of trade unions) and hindered, where possible, the Ukrainization of the state. The same could be said of the representatives of the dominant Constitutional Democrats in Skoropadsky's government who, in their majority, were opposed to an independent Ukrainian state from the outset.

In present-day studies, one finds quite different assessments of the political nature of Skoropadsky's state. Some claim that "the Hetmanate of 1918 was an authoritarian bureaucratic regime in which the head of state had almost dictatorial powers. It lacked a representative body, had no separation of executive and legislative functions in government, and clearly restricted basic democratic freedoms. It had a small social base, and the exercise of government had a very makeshift character."[59] Others describe the Hetmanate as a "military-bureaucratic dictatorship."[60] The Hetmanate is also often described in the traditional manner as a "puppet regime."[61] It is a commonplace of apologetic historical writing that Skoropadsky restored the state-building tradition of the Cossacks. In any case, no one questions the small social base of the state or its critical dependence on an external force.

It should not be overlooked that for all its attributes of dictatorial power (the Hetman personally appointed and dismissed the

59 R. Pyrih, "Derzhavna sluzhba Het'manatu Pavla Skoropads'koho (kviten'–hruden' 1918)," *Ukraïna XX stolittia: kul'tura, ideolohiia, polityka* (Kyiv), no. 15 (2009): 67.

60 Ia. Pelens'kyi, "Peredmova. Spohady het'mana Pavla Skoropads'koho (kinets' 1917–hruden' 1918)," in *Pavlo Skoropads'kyi. Spohady. Kinets' 1917–hruden' 1918* (Kyiv, 1995), 23.

61 V. Soldatenko, *Ukraïna v revoliutsiinu dobu. Istorychni ese-khroniky. Rik 1918*, vol. 2 (Kyiv, 2009), 201. This work can be found on the home page of the Ukrainian Institute of National Remembrance: http://www.memory.gov.ua/.

government, was commander in chief, and exercised the functions of the highest court), this regime was politically very weak. Although censorship and various prohibitions and restrictions on the freedom of speech and assembly were imposed in the first few days, political forces and individuals continued to act legally or semi-legally in the Ukrainian state, often opposing the Hetman, holding congresses, and publishing newspapers prohibited by the government. It was typical of this period that in May 1918 the opposition parties organized their congresses in the environs of Kyiv "in the underground" after they had been banned in the city or even broken up by force. This was a symbolic demonstration of the limits of the ruler's influence.

The brief imprisonment of some representatives of the Ukrainian People's Republic was the sharpest form of repression of the political opposition.[62] Vynnychenko's imprisonment, on 10 July 1918, was typical. He was arrested under suspicion of having organized an uprising. His imprisonment lasted less than twenty-four hours and ended with the Hetman personally apologizing to the "injured party" through his chief of staff.[63] This also indicates the difference between the Hetman and the German commanders, who were demanding that Vynnychenko be handed over to them. The arrest of Petliura, the head of the All-Ukrainian Union of Zemstvos, in July 1918 is another example, except this time it was the Germans who were demanding proper treatment of the arrested person because the German command was then trying to create a broader base for the political spectrum represented in the Hetman government. Skoropadsky was also inclined toward cooperation with the Ukrainian socialists.

The best-known instance of "severe" repression against representatives of the Ukrainian People's Republic is that of the trial of members of the Central Rada by a military court. Vsevolod Holubovych, Oleksandr Zhukovsky, and four government officials were arrested in connection with the kidnapping of the banker Dobry. All the accused received short prison sentences. What is

---

62 In close proximity to the Hetman there were people (such as Dmytro Doroshenko) who were in constant contact with the leaders of the Ukrainian opposition parties. Skoropadsky himself was not inclined to use radical measures against representatives of the Ukrainian movement. It is worth mentioning that Symon Petliura was released on 12 November 1918 on personal instructions from the Hetman, whereupon he immediately joined the organizers of the uprising against the Hetman in Bila Tserkva (Skoropadsky, *Spohady*, 376n).

63 V. Vynnychenko, *Shchodennyk, 1911–20,* vol. 1 (Edmonton and New York, 1980), 289–96.

also remarkable is that preparations by the Ukrainian parties for an uprising against the Hetman were made in an almost legal manner through cultural and educational organizations.

The weakness of Skoropadsky's government was particularly evident in its attempts to "maintain order" in the villages. The armed units of the Hetmanate (the Hetman Guards) were unable to gain control because the situation in the villages had been radicalized by the government's attempts at normalization. They were unable to achieve their goal without the assistance of the occupation troops. The efforts of the occupying troops and the Hetman's security forces to restore order also demonstrated a lack of understanding of local conditions. They underestimated the ability of the villages to organize themselves and offer military resistance, notwithstanding all the available information about massive arsenals of weaponry that existed after the collapse of the front and about the fighting ability of soldiers just recently returned from the war. The punitive expeditions and executions carried out by those in power just poured more oil on the flames and provoked the peasants into actions that in many cases grew into organized uprisings.

The first encounters with the occupying troops took place at the beginning of March in Podilia in the Austro-Hungarian zone. The conflict here was provoked by Polish volunteer formations whose members were often owners of businesses and estates that had been plundered. Revenge was frequently a motive in such conflicts and often led to extreme cruelty.[64] Peasant uprisings began in mid-May 1918. Sometimes they were provoked by attempts to confiscate weapons owned by the peasants, sometimes by the requisitioning of grain, and sometimes by attempts on the part of landowners to reclaim expropriated land. News that the Hetman intended to implement a land reform, in which the peasants would have to pay compensation for the land they had acquired, was a cause of unrest, as were the instructions on the distribution of the harvest issued in late May and early June 1918.[65] Unrest was further increased by measures to confiscate harvests, collect compensation, and reclaim the property

---

64 P. Zakharchenko, *Selians'ka viina v Ukraïni: rik 1918* (Kyiv, 1997), 49.

65 The "Law on Rights to the Harvest of 1918 on the Territory of the Ukrainian State" of 27 May required that one-third of the harvest (or a corresponding compensation) from land sown without authorization would have to be given to the owner of the land. On 14 June it was declared that the sugar-beet harvest on fields sown without authorization belonged to the owners of the factories.

of the returning landowners, as well as by attempts to use force to compel the peasants to harvest grain.[66]

The actions of the peasantry varied in scale. There were local rebellions that involved armed attacks and murders (sometimes of whole families) of landowners who had returned to their estates. Prosperous peasants were also sometimes the object of such attacks. There were also organized actions that sometimes extended over whole districts. One such uprising was that organized by the Ukrainian Socialist Revolutionaries in the districts of Tarashcha and Zvenyhorod, in the Kyiv gubernia, between May and August 1918, in which, according to various sources, between twenty and forty thousand people were involved. The uprising was suppressed only with the help of the German military.

By the end of July, the uprisings had spread to the gubernias of Kyiv, Chernihiv, Katerynoslav, and Poltava. According to the estimates of Field Marshal Eichhorn, 10 to 12 percent of the peasants had taken part in "agrarian unrest," in other words, 2.5 million people.[67] According to calculations of the modern historian Viktor Savchenko, in the period up to the autumn of 1918 the occupying troops in Ukraine lost 22,000 officers and men, the forces of the Hetman more than 30,000. The number of insurgents between May and September 1918 is estimated to have been around 80,000.[68] With the assistance of the occupying troops, the situation in the villages was stabilized by the autumn of 1918.

During this period, government institutions took reasonable steps to resolve the agrarian problem in a civilized manner. In June 1918 the government passed a law permitting the state land bank to purchase land for the purpose of selling it to the peasants (the maximum area of each land parcel purchased was limited to 27 hectares) and allowing the private sale of land without limitation. But the estate owners were in no hurry to sell their "surplus" parcels of land, while the peasants, like the land bank that was meant to provide the loans for

66 The "liquidation commissions" established by the government attempted without much success to manage locally the return of property to the owners and reach some amicable settlement regarding compensation. The peasants were unwilling to return what had been taken, and the landowners made unrealistic demands. The situation was made worse by the government's instruction of 4 July 1918, according to which it was the landowners themselves who would determine the value of losses. A number of measures were taken in July and August to force the peasants to bring in the harvest (which was very good), whereby the sanctions for sabotage included fines, imprisonment, and forced labor.

67 Soldatenko, *Ukraïna v revoliutsiinu dobu*, 2: 317. Archival source: TsDAVO, f. 2311, op. 1, spr. 120, 143.

68 V. A. Savchenko, *Pavlo Skoropads'kyi – ostannii het'man Ukraïny* (Kharkiv, 2009), 223–24. These data require scrutiny.

this purchase, lacked the necessary funds. So the Hetman's intention to create a broad social stratum of small agricultural enterprises as the social foundation of the state came to nothing. It was also a project that everyone opposed: the peasants who had appropriated land without payment; the large landowners, who wanted to maintain their monopoly; the left-wing Ukrainian parties, which favored the socialization of land; and the occupying troops, which wanted the kind of large-scale economy that would guarantee them the deliveries of grain they required. So the Hetman's plans, not infrequently sabotaged in small ways by the governing institutions themselves, remained hanging in the air, with the result that the Hetman had to do without the broad social support he had hoped for. Even as a project, it took a long time for the agrarian reform to get off the ground. It was only at the end of October that documents became available with concrete instructions about the implementation of the reform.

In the meantime, the situation in the towns was becoming critical. Speculation flourished in both food and industrial commodities, and food deliveries sometimes were not carried out. The Hetman's policies toward labor (the removal of restrictions on working hours, the expansion of the rights of employers, the restriction of trade-union activities) led to a growing number of strikes, in which the Bolsheviks and Socialist Revolutionaries played an active role. Here as well, the Ukrainian State was not master of the situation, and the occupying troops had to intervene. The most telling example was the railworkers' strike of July 1918.[69] The strike ended only when the German and Austro-Hungarian troops took control of a number of railway junctions and carried out reprisals[70] against the organizers and participants in the strike.[71] But it should be noted that in this case as well the Hetman government looked for a civilized solution to the problem. A number of the strikers' economic demands were met (payment of wages and provision of food).

In spite of all these problems that resulted from the consequences of war and revolution, with their destruction and disorganization of social life, Skoropadsky's Ukrainian State was an area of relative peace and order, especially when compared with Bolshevik Russia, where a

---

69 According to the (exaggerated) numbers in the Bolshevik press, more than two hundred thousand workers were involved in the strike.

70 The term "reprisal" included arrest, detention, and expulsion. Extreme forms of violence, such as regularly existed in Soviet Russia or in areas involved in civil war, happened very seldom.

71 See the detailed discussion in chapters 3a and 3c in the present volume.

bitter civil war was raging. The period from May to September 1918 was a period in which, to some extent, systematic and thoughtful efforts were made to create the structures and infrastructure of Ukrainian statehood. It was a very impressive period when seen against the background of the chaotic experiments and organizational incompetence of the Central Rada.

The first months of Skoropadsky's rule saw the creation of a central state administration, a government (Council of Ministers), and a centralized system of justice (courts, Senate). Under the Hetman, a more or less stable network of financial institutions was reestablished, and the work of local organs of self-administration was resumed (gubernia and district starostas). Where problems had arisen with organs of local self-administration (city dumas, zemstvos),[72] they had been resolved by the autumn of 1918. Skoropadsky established an organization with police powers to maintain public order, the Hetman Guard. He took concrete steps to establish an army, one of his major achievements. He persuaded the Central Powers to give him what remained of the Black Sea fleet. Preparations for the organization of a future army were begun in May and June 1918. A general staff was created and a system of service grades and ranks established, as was the army structure. A law was passed on general conscription, and the leading personnel of the army were named. Most of Skoropadsky's army (eight army corps, four cavalry divisions) was of course made up of these military leaders. Training and demonstration units were also established in the autumn (once again made up mostly of leading personnel). By November 1918 the armed forces of the Ukrainian State included the cadre units already mentioned, a Zaporozhian Division (Kharkiv gubernia), the Zaporozhian and Black Sea Cossacks (*Zaporoz'kyi kozats'kyi kish, Chornomors'kyi kozats'kyi kish)* stationed in Koziatyn and Berdychiv, the Serdiuk Division in Kyiv, the Sich Riflemen (Bila Tserkva), and the hundreds of the Guard. In October, a beginning was made to create a special volunteer corps consisting of officers from the tsarist army.[73] The total strength of the army and other armed formations in the Ukrainian State was sixty-five thousand.[74]

---

72 In a whole series of cases, gubernia starostas, whose powers were similar to those of prerevolutionary governors, simply dissolved local organs of self-administration that they considered an annoyance, which led to strenuous protests and central government intervention.

73 This special corps was to maintain order in the border regions.

74 A. O. Buravchenkov, "Zbroini syly Ukraïns'koï Derzhavy 1918 r.," in *Entsyklopediia istoriï Ukraïny*, vol. 3 (Kyiv, 2005), 311. See also the detailed discussion in chapter 3b in the present volume.

Ukrainization had a special place in Skoropadsky's domestic policies. A network of Ukrainian primary schools was initiated in May and June 1918. The Hetman began a systematic process of Ukrainizing the state apparatus, the army, and the universities, although this caused some conflicts. Skoropadsky was the founder of the Ukrainian Academy of Sciences. His attempt to create a state apparatus represented the only systematic effort to do so during the whole course of the Ukrainian Revolution. In these attempts, he relied on the support of the occupying troops (an essential factor of political stability) and on a relatively small stratum of large landowners, as well as members of the old bureaucracy and officialdom. One could say that Skoropadsky was successful in creating a state infrastructure, but his system-building plans were clearly in contradiction with reality and met with resistance, both open (from the workers and peasants) and covert (from his "allies" in the country).

The situation of the Hetman and of the state he had created became less and less secure as the influence of the occupying troops waned. The German and Austro-Hungarian defeats on the Western Front and in the Balkans in the second half of 1918, as well as the partial withdrawal of troops from Ukraine, reduced their physical support for the regime. The Hetman became more active in probing the possibility of an alliance with the Whites, not least because of pressure from the Russians in his entourage. Whether because of the weakness of Skoropadsky's regime or as a result of its being not harsh enough, a well-organized opposition covering a broad political spectrum had emerged by November 1918. A circular of 31 October from the Ministry of the Interior listed the clandestine and illegally active organizations that were hostile to the state and had to be combated. It included the Russian Communist Party (Bolshevik), the Communist Party (Bolshevik) of Ukraine, anarchist parties and circles, the left-wing Ukrainian Socialist Revolutionaries, and the right-wing Russian Socialist Revolutionaries.[75] It is remarkable that in their agitation against the government in Ukraine[76] all the organizations listed, to the extent that they did not seek open conflict, met with no special problems. It suffices to note that local revolutionary committees carried out quite successful agitation against the government in the spring and autumn of 1918. The Bolsheviks in the neutral zone were practically unhindered as they prepared partisan groups for

75 *Ukraïna. Khronika XX stolittia. Rik 1918* (Kyiv, 2005), 349–50.

76 The leading bodies of the Ukrainian Bolsheviks were outside the country.

an uprising against the Hetman. The left-wing Ukrainian parties likewise had no special problems in their oppositional activity, which went as far as participating in the organization of peasant uprisings and strikes. The Ukrainian National Union was formed in August 1918, a coalition of left-wing Ukrainian parties and the social and professional organizations that they controlled.

There were other opposition forces not mentioned in the ministry's circular. These included the All-Ukrainian Peasant Union, influenced by the Ukrainian Socialist Revolutionaries; the All-Ukrainian Union of Zemstvos, led by the Ukrainian Social Democrat Symon Petliura; and organizations such as the Kyiv National Center, which brought together Russian nationalists and monarchists dissatisfied with the Hetman's Ukrainization efforts. As already mentioned, the Hetman's allies completely rejected Ukrainian statehood. The Constitutional Democrats, who were dominant in the government, accepted the need for a Ukrainian state only as a transition to the restoration of Russian unity. The big bourgeoisie and the industrialists saw the Ukrainian state merely as a tactical ruse. The "restoration and reunification of the fatherland" was a major theme in the speeches of delegates to the last congress of Protofis at the end of October 1918.[77] On 17 October 1918 a declaration of nine members of the Council of Ministers spoke of the necessity of establishing a federation with a non-Bolshevik Russia.

At the same time, the declarations and actions of the Ukrainian National Union became increasingly radical. They demanded the neutralization of "anti-Ukrainian elements" in the government and the promotion of patriotic forces. Its leaders (Vynnychenko and Mykyta Shapoval) negotiated with Skoropadsky on the formation of a coalition government and the calling of a national congress (planned for 17 November), while simultaneously planning an uprising against him. At the beginning of November they secured the support of the commanders of the Sich Riflemen, the Black Sea Cossacks, and the Zaporozhian Division,[78] all of which were units of the Ukrainian State army. The military aspects of the plan were prepared by Yevhen Konovalets and Andrii Melnyk, commanders of the Sich Riflemen. Skoropadsky had been informed of the preparations for an uprising but undertook no serious countermeasures. What is more, on 9 November 1918 he secured the release of Petliura, Porsh, and Yurii Kapkan from

---

77 Pavlo Khrystiuk, *Zamitky i materiialy do istoriï ukraïns'koï revoliutsiï 1917–1920 rr.*, vol. 3 (New York, 1969), 115–16.

78 Mykyta Shapoval, *Velyka revoliutsiia i ukraïns'ka vyzvol'na prohrama* (Prague, 1928), 120–21.

prison, individuals who would certainly join the uprising. On the night of 13–14 November there was an illegal meeting, in the building of the Ministry of Transport, of representatives of the Ukrainian Party of Socialist Revolutionaries, the Ukrainian Social Democratic Labor Party, the Ukrainian Socialist Federalist Party, the Ukrainian Party of Socialist Independentists, and representatives of the army (Sich Riflemen). The decision was made to mount an uprising against the Hetman. A Directory[79] under the leadership of Vynnychenko was elected at the same meeting.

The international situation prompted the search for strong new allies. The Bolshevik government was preparing a military intervention.[80] The capitulation of Turkey and Bulgaria in October had accelerated the military as well as the political collapse of Austria-Hungary and the German Empire. The withdrawal of their troops had begun at the end of October and continued until the beginning of 1919. The Whites on the eastern border of Ukraine were becoming increasingly stronger, and secret negotiations were being carried out with some of their representatives. Skoropadsky was looking for a compromise or a temporary resolution of the conflicting pressures from the Ukrainian movement and from those who supported the restoration of a "united and indivisible Russia." Having lost his main supporters, Austria-Hungary and Germany, he needed to turn to another external power that could deal with the elemental violence of the peasant war. The Entente states were then negotiating over future zones of influence, and "southern Russia," in other words, the territory of the Ukrainian State, was being mentioned.

On 14 November 1918 the Hetman signed an "edict" that has been described in later literature as "federalist,"[81] in which he declared that "Ukraine must take the lead in the establishment of an all-Russian federation, the final goal of which will be the restoration of Great Russia." The edict was a signal to the Entente and to the anti-Bolshevik forces allied with the Entente, as well as to the Hetman's own allies

---

79 The intention was to elect the Directory for the period of the uprising, after which power would pass to a representative body. In addition to Vynnychenko, the Directory included Petliura, Andrii Makarenko, Fedir Shvets, and Opanas Andriievsky.

80 A fact worth mentioning here is that, during the preparations for the uprising, Vynnychenko met secretly with representatives of the Council of People's Commissars, Khristian Rakovsky and Dmytro Manuilsky, who promised him the "neutrality" of the communist underground, demanding in return the legalization of the Communist Party (Bolshevik) of Ukraine in the future Ukrainian state.

81 P. Hai-Nyzhnyk, *Finansova polityka uriadu Ukraïns'koï Derzhavy Het'mana Pavla Skoropads'koho (29 kvitnia–14 hrudnia 1918 r.)* (Kyiv, 2004), 346.

in Ukraine who wanted Ukraine to be reunified with Russia. It was published on 15 November. The uprising, led by the Directory, began on the same day. Troops that had gone over to the Directory advanced on Kyiv from Bila Tserkva, Berdychiv, and Kharkiv. As they approached Kyiv, they were joined by increasing numbers of insurgent peasants. The Ukrainian National Union occupied government offices, driving out representatives of the Hetman administration. The counteroffensive of troops loyal to the Hetman had little effect. In some cases (the Serdiuk Division), they joined the uprising. On 19 November the troops of the Directory and the insurgent groups were outside Kyiv but decided not to storm it because the German command had abandoned its neutrality and placed its units at the entrances to the city. This move was forced on them, as an entrance of insurgents into the city would have hindered the withdrawal of German troops. In addition, the Entente had demanded that the German command allow no insurgents to enter Kyiv because, at this time, they were negotiating with Skoropadsky. The army of the Directory withdrew to Vinnytsia and Fastiv.

The Hetman declared a general mobilization, but it was only the large number of tsarist officers in Kyiv that responded. The Directory countered on 27 November by declaring its own general mobilization. Petliura, in charge of the Directory's troops, issued an order in which he promised an extra parcel of land to those peasants who joined the Directory's troops "on time."[82] By the end of November, the Directory's troops and the insurgents had taken control of most of the district centers of Left- and Right-Bank Ukraine. In the first half of December they captured Odesa and Mykolaiv, only to give them up under pressure from the Entente, which had a large military presence there.

On 14 December the troops of the Directory took Kyiv, having broken the resistance of a small number of officer groups. The Hetman's military formations in the city went over to the insurgents. On the same day, Skoropadsky published his instrument of abdication and, some days later, left the city and the country in a German sealed train. The Directory entered the city in triumph on 19 December 1918.

The Directory and the "Second" Ukrainian People's Republic

On 26 December 1918, the Declaration of the Directory of the Ukrainian People's Republic was published. This document proclaimed the rule of the workers and peasants in Ukraine. The Directory abolished all

82 The mass of recruits increased its numerical strength while decreasing its fighting capacity.

the laws of the Hetmanate and reintroduced the eight-hour day and the right to strike. The land of the "small and laboring peasantry" was declared to be their inalienable property. The remaining land would be given to peasants who had little or no land "to be worked," first of all to those who had taken part in the uprising. The "overall administration" of all land was in the hands of the Directory and would be carried out by the National Land Administration. This decision applied not only to estates but also to lands owned by monasteries, the church, and the state. The definitive decision on the exercise of power would be taken by a Labor Congress. The "exploiting classes" would lose their right to participate in government institutions (the expropriation of their property was not mentioned in the declaration).

On the same day, the Directory named the government of the Ukrainian People's Republic, the Council of People's Ministers, under the leadership of the Social Democrat Volodymyr Chekhivsky. The government would consist of representatives of the Ukrainian Social Democratic Labor Party, the Ukrainian Socialist Revolutionaries, the Socialist Independentists, and the Ukrainian Socialist Federalists.[83] A representative of the Poalei Zion Party also joined the government as minister for Jewish affairs. There were no representatives of Russian or Polish parties. As events would later show, this government was really more of a technical body of the Directory, with the latter making all important decisions itself. The task of the government was to implement those decisions. But this turned out to be highly problematic. From the very first days of the second Ukrainian People's Republic, the country experienced a kind of *déjà-vu*: extreme weakness of the central authority, disorganization and anarchy in the provinces, political and personal intrigue and conflict at the top, organizational inability of the leaders, and local power structures that were either lacking or weak. All this was painfully reminiscent of the experience of the Central Rada and General Secretariat. Added to this was a whole series of difficult internal and external circumstances.

The support of the masses during the month of the uprising against the Hetman disappeared as soon as the Directory entered Kyiv. The soldiers in the Directory's army, estimated to have been between 150,000 and 250,000 men, returned to the villages to take part in the distribution of land. By January 1919, the army had only around 50,000

83 Between the summer and winter of 1918, left-wing factions split from the two main parties in Ukraine, the Social Democrats and Socialist Revolutionaries. These left-wing factions supported Bolshevik ideology and fought against the Directory.

men.[84] In reality, it was the units established under the Hetman that formed the core of the army of the Ukrainian People's Republic. The army established following Petliura's mobilization of 27 November 1918, after the fall of the Hetman, when masses of volunteers joined, required significant organizational effort for which resources were not available. Among the population, especially among the peasantry, there were very few who wanted to be "mobilized."

On 8 January 1918, the Directory passed a law that would give recruits an extra five dessiatines (one dessiatine = 2.7 acres) of land and a loan for the purchase of equipment. But this measure made little difference, as the peasants had already appropriated both in the course of the "black repartition." The size of the army was increased at the last minute, when fighting was already under way. Recruits were generally regarded as unreliable, and desertion was a mass phenomenon. In contemporary memoirs, one finds examples of recruits who disappeared the day after receiving their uniform and weapon. The fighting ability of the reliable units was decreased by this mobilization. For example, a unit of Sich Riflemen that had begun the uprising against Skoropadsky, most of whose senior and junior officers came from Galicia, was expanded during the uprising to a division and later to a corps. According to one observer, "Nobody asked—and, under the circumstances, this was not possible anyway—who was joining the ranks of the Riflemen, who this or that volunteer was: the most important thing was to reach full strength; the main thing was a first, a second, a third company.[85] It is no wonder that many unreliable elements joined the corps, of little military value and even less moral worth." The same observer writes that in the corps, following the capture of Kyiv, there were ten to fifteen desertions daily.[86]

Building the army was also hindered by the already mentioned disputes among the leading politicians of the Ukrainian People's Republic.[87] Leading individuals in the parties represented in the Directory and in the government competed for influence over the

84 Zh. V. Mina, "Zbroini syly Dyrektoriï na pochatku ïï isnuvannia (lystopad 1918–traven' 1919 r.)," *Visnyk Natsional'noho Universytetu "L'vivs'ka politekhnika" "Derzhava ta armiia"* (Lviv), no. 408 (2000): 49–54.

85 A Cossack expression for a military unit having the strength of a battalion.

86 Antin Krezub (Osyp Dumin), "Hrupa polkovnyka Rogul's'koho," *Kalendar "Chervonoï kalyny"* (1929), 57–58. Quoted from the National Archives of the Czech Republic, f. Ukrainian Museum, Kt. 44, inv. c. 710/5, 452–53.

87 These differences of opinion did not pertain only to the organization of the army. The left-wing factions of the Social Democrats and Socialist Revolutionaries did not want to fight against the Bolsheviks and eventually went over to their side.

military, each one championing his own ideas about state-building. The sharpest conflict was the one between the two most influential members of the Directory, Petliura and Vynnychenko, over the organization of the army.[88] In the selection of leading personnel, the differences were often not about professional suitability, experience, or competence but about ethnic origin and commitment to "the Ukrainian cause." Moreover, in order to secure influence over and gain real support from the military, these various leaders of the Directory sought to ingratiate themselves with the otamans. Petliura, for instance, regularly gave large sums of money to individual otamans for "the organization of the army."[89]

During the period of Skoropadsky's rule, the leadership had been expanded and a general staff had been created. In the assessment of specialists, this leadership personnel of fifteen thousand men was adequate, with a competently organized mobilization, to establish an operational army. The left-wing leadership of the Directory, however, had no trust in those officers who had served under the *ancien régime*. This created confusion and disorganization in the building of the army, angered the officers, and had a negative effect on the fighting morale of the army's leading personnel. The career soldiers were also unhappy with the way in which the army was increased by incorporating whole groups of insurgents.

This form of mobilization, incorporating already existing insurgent units commanded by otamans into the army, was forced on the UNR by the circumstances of war, which made normal mobilization very difficult. The active army that was created was therefore made up not just of regular soldiers trained according to military rules but also of insurgents whose leaders, although they formally recognized the authority of the Directory and its military commanders and acted in their name, actually brought in armed detachments that were under no one's control, used partisan methods of warfare, and were not suited for regular military engagements. Such units operated under the official aegis of the Directory. Units under Otaman Zeleny (Danylo Terpylo) were active in the Kyiv gubernia, those under Yevhen Anhel in the Chernihiv gubernia, those under Yukhym Bozhko in the Kherson and Mykolaiv gubernias, and units under Matvii Hryhoriiv in part of the Katerynoslav gubernia. Dozens of smaller insurgent groups had become part of the UNR army. According to contemporary estimates,

88 Soldatenko, *Vynnychenko i Petliura*.

89 Vynnychenko, *Vidrodzhennia natsiï*, 3: 351.

the total strength of these insurgent units and "armies" in mid-1919 was between 15,000 and 200,000.[90]

Hundreds of these insurgent units and peasant "armies" had leaders whose political orientation was unclear and changed according to the situation and the leaders' interests. Some of the insurgents were influenced by the Social Democrats and Socialist Revolutionaries, and many supported the Bolsheviks or went over to their troops as they approached. One of the largest insurgent armies, that of the anarchist Nestor Makhno, controlled a large part of the Katerynoslav gubernia and was fundamentally opposed to rule of any kind (although it used Bolshevik slogans and allied itself with them for certain periods). The leaders of the smaller units were mainly interested in the defense of their own villages or local areas under their control. Otamans in the provinces sometimes proclaimed their own republics[91] or declared their personal rule over a certain territory. There were about 120 different "peasant republics" during the Ukrainian Revolution.[92] These otamans frequently fought not only against the Directory, the Bolsheviks, the Whites, and the intervening foreign troops, but also against one another. The leadership of the Directory was unable to deal with this elemental form of violence. Having to fight a war on many fronts, it failed not only to establish a stable leadership over the insurgents but also to maintain stable lines of communication and information.

The otamans were autonomous to such an extent that at critical moments they changed sides. At the height of the struggle against the Bolsheviks in January 1919, Otaman Zeleny left his position outside Kyiv and withdrew with his units to the forest. The gap that this created in the front made it significantly easier for the Bolsheviks to take the city. In the battle against the Bolsheviks at Bila Tserkva in June of that year, it was only after a gala dinner in his honor and the promise of a share in the war booty that Zeleny agreed to join the UNR army and work with Yurii Tiutiunnyk. After the successful defense of Bila Tserkva against the Bolsheviks in August 1919, Zeleny and his "army" again left the Directory.

---

90 P. Hai-Nyzhnyk, "Otamanshchyna v period Dyrektoriï UNR: sotsial'na baza, rol' i mistse v natsional'no-vyzvol'nii borot'bi," *Literatura ta kul'tura Polissia*, no. 58: *Problemy filolohiï, istoriï ta kul'tury XX stolittia u suchasnykh doslidzhenniakh* (Nizhyn: Vyd-vo NDPU im. M. Hoholia, 2010), 105–14.

91 The best-known of these, the Kholodnyi Yar Republic in the Cherkasy gubernia, existed (with interruptions) until the autumn of 1921.

92 V. Savchenko, *Atamany kazach'ego voiska* (Moscow, 2006), 14.

At the beginning of February 1919 Hryhoriiv, who had fought on the side of the Directory, went over to the Bolsheviks. The occasion for this was a secret agreement between the Directory and the Entente (French commanders) to withdraw Directory troops behind the Tiraspol–Voznesensk–Kherson line. First of all, Hryhoriiv, against Petliura's orders, fought the Entente troops that had begun to occupy the area. Then, on 2 February, he joined the Bolsheviks.[93] In the midst of fighting the Bolsheviks, in August 1919, Otaman Bozhko also refused to obey orders from supreme command. He commanded the Second Division of the UNR, made up of insurgents who had chosen their own commander.

These examples give some idea of the extent of the chaos that existed in the army of the Ukrainian People's Republic as a consequence of "otamanship" and the narrow scope that the leaders of the UNR had in their direction of the war. Added to this was the situation within the leadership, which did not exactly promote efficiency. Following the successful overthrow of the Hetman, there was acute political and personal competition among the leaders, which had to do not only with ideological differences but also with personal ambition.

Attempts to move forward with the creation of state structures remained fragmentary and unsystematic, proceeding against the background of a war on many fronts, anarchy, peasant warfare, and economic disorganization. The Labor Congress, called by the Directory to resolve issues of state power, failed to do so because of differences of opinion among the delegates and disputes within the Directory itself, where the alternatives of soviets or dictatorship were debated endlessly. At the final session of the congress, total power was given to the Directory until the next congress. This, alongside the Act of Union with the Western Ukrainian People's Republic on 22 January 1918, was the most important decision of the congress and the most significant for the state-building of the second Ukrainian People's Republic.[94] Events at the front made it impossible to create functioning institutions, rebuild the economy, or resolve social problems. The Directory, which had come to power thanks to the uprisings of the peasant masses, very quickly lost the support of this largest sector

---

93 Both representatives of the Volunteer Army and Makhno's people attempted to win Hryhoriiv to their side. See A. A. Lysenko, "Viis'kova ta politychna diial'nist' otamana N. Ia. Hryhor'ieva (Servetnyka) u 1918–1919 rr.," *Ukraïns'kyi istorychnyi zhurnal*, 2009, no. 6: 63–80.

94 Other efforts at state-building included the revocation of the decisions of the Hetmanate and the replacement of its institutions by "new" ones, the State Senate by the Supreme Court and the State Guard by the People's Militia.

of society because it had nothing to offer them. The peasants had already divided up the land. The land law of 8 January 1918, which allowed fifteen dessiatines of land to "working" peasant households and five dessiatines to the poorest peasants, did not arouse any great enthusiasm among the peasantry.[95]

The law had practically no influence in the towns. Among the politically active population, the workers supported the Bolsheviks, while the Russian-speaking bourgeoisie, officials, and the petty bourgeoisie supported the Whites. The Directory's inability to keep its own people under control also made it unpopular. Although the Directory had restored civil liberties, commanders of regular troop units and insurgent detachments acted according to their own discretion. For instance, the commander of the Sich Riflemen, Yevhen Konovalets, prohibited the activities of a number of trade-union organizations in Kyiv on 22 December 1918, justifying this by the need to fight the Bolsheviks. Otaman Petro Bolbochan, commander of the Directory's troops in Left-Bank Ukraine, closed down a workers' congress in Kharkiv (controlled by the Mensheviks) and a peasant congress in Poltava. This led to arrests and public executions, which understandably undermined support for the Directory, as it was identified with this assault in public opinion and in oppositional propaganda. Most of the urban population was mainly interested in survival and would accept any government that could ensure stability.

The attack by Bolshevik troops[96] against Left-Bank Ukraine and the Donbas began from the area around Kursk toward the end of December 1918. A response to the four notes sent by the Directory to the Russian government arrived on 6 January. The Russian government rejected the "unjustified assumption" of the Directory that Russian troops were responsible for the fighting and maintained, as it had done in 1918, that it was a conflict between the Directory and the Provisional Workers' and Peasants' Government of Ukraine, established by the Bolsheviks in November 1918. The Directory declared war on Soviet Russia on 16 January 1919, when Bolshevik troops had already pushed deep into Ukrainian territory and captured Kharkiv and Chernihiv. To the very end, Vynnychenko had hoped for an agreement with the Bolsheviks and had even offered the Moscow government various forms of treaty and proposed a united effort against the Whites and

95 *Ukraïna. Khronika XX stolittia, Rik 1919* (Kyiv, 2005), 12.

96 These were units of the All-Ukrainian Military Revolutionary Central Committee in Kursk, as well as units of the Red Army in "neutral guise," both from Russia.

the Entente. However, the military (Petliura, Bolbochan) put pressure on Vynnychenko. One of their arguments was that a declaration of war against Soviet Russia would increase the chances of support from the Entente. On the same day the Directory, the Ukrainian parties, and the Peasant Union had a meeting with the UNR military command to discuss the question of power. Some of those present (the military) argued for a military dictatorship, others for a "dictatorship of the working peasantry." The demand was also raised to establish a Soviet republic. In the end, they decided to leave things as they were.[97]

In the southern gubernias, the few operational army units of the UNR[98] withdrew to the southwestern gubernias after some brief successes in January in Katerynoslav, Kherson, and Mykolaiv. The insurgent units either declared themselves neutral or went over to the Bolsheviks and fought against the Directory. The south of the country sank into total chaos. Simultaneously active in this region were the troops of the Directory, volunteer officer units, Bolshevik units, military revolutionary committees, large insurgent groups (Makhno, Hryhoriiv), as well as dozens and hundreds of small groupings of peasants, bands of deserters, self-defense units created by German settlers, Entente troops, and the remaining German and Austro-Hungarian garrisons that were waiting to be evacuated.

The situation was similar in Left-Bank Ukraine and parts of the Right Bank that were controlled by the Directory. The great mass of the population, the peasantry, were waiting for the Bolsheviks because they expected to benefit from their definitive resolution of the land question. A communication from the information bureau of the UNR army in February stated: "It is the opinion among the peasantry that they will be given the land in the winter, but in the summer it will be the *pany*[99] who control the land.... The people want the Bolsheviks to come as soon as possible because they will crush the *pany* and give their possessions to the people."[100]

In the towns and around the major railway junctions, the scenario of 1918 was repeated. As Bolshevik troops approached, the local revolutionary committees established by the Ukrainian Bolsheviks

97 V. F. Soldatenko, *Ukraïna v revoliutsiinu dobu. Istorychni ese-khroniky. Rik 1919*, vol. 3 (Kyiv, 2010), 43.

98 According to the estimates of the UNR's minister of military affairs, General Oleksandr Hrekov, the UNR's total troop strength was around twenty-one thousand men. See Vynnychenko, *Vidrodzhennia natsiï*, 3: 244ff.

99 *Pan* is a Ukrainian term for "landowner."

100 Soldatenko, *Ukraïna v revoliutsiinu dobu*, 3: 76.

would start an uprising. Southern Ukraine and the Crimea became a theater of war between the Bolsheviks, the Whites, and the troops of the Entente.

At the beginning of February 1919, the Directory[101] and the government were forced to move to Vinnytsia, then on 6 March to Proskuriv, and on 18 March to Kamianets-Podilskyi. In April and May, the greater part of the Directory was in Rivne, with some in Stanyslaviv. The government was scattered between Stanyslaviv, Rivne, and Odesa. Negotiations with the French occupying troops had been taking place in Odesa since January.[102] Although the Directory restructured the government a number of times, and the government made laws and regulations, its rule was often restricted to its location at the time. Authority at the front, in the best of cases, was in the hands of the army command (Petliura and the general staff); at worst, it was in the hands of the otamans. In the towns and villages formally under the control of the Directory, power was effectively exercised either by the military stationed there or by no one.

In March 1919, the Directory lost its last hope of international support. Under pressure from Hryhoriiv's troops, who were fighting on the side of the Bolsheviks, the Entente troops and the volunteer officer units left Kherson and Mykolaiv and, in April, left Odesa. The UNR's few forces in the south were forced to withdraw to the Romanian border. The situation was brought to a head by the action of Otaman Omelian Volokh, who, on 21 March, formed a "military revolutionary committee" and began separate negotiations with the Bolsheviks. The latter knew how to take advantage of the situation and defeated the disorganized Ukrainian troops under Volokh's command. Under pressure from the Bolsheviks (eight thousand men), the Zaporozhian Corps, which was loyal to the Ukrainian People's Republic, withdrew to Romanian territory, where they were interned. At the same time, the Directory's troops began an offensive from Volhynia that reached the outskirts of Kyiv but then lacked the forces to continue.

In April and May 1919, the leaders of the Directory managed to reorganize their remaining troops and expand their numbers

101 On 9 February, under pressure from the French, who were negotiating with the UNR, Vynnychenko resigned from the Directory. Petliura, who was also persona non grata for the Entente, remained in the Directory but resigned from his party.

102 The French were making impossible demands that would effectively have abolished Ukrainian sovereignty: control of the UNR army, railway junctions, and finances. Ukraine would be recognized at an international peace conference, after which it would become a French protectorate.

by mobilization. At this time, the Directory's rule extended over a narrow stretch of land in Podilia and Volhynia, along a line from Lutsk through Sarny and Rivne to Kremianets. Bolshevik advances separated the Directory's three military groups. There were disputes among members of the Directory and, on 29 April, there was an attempted uprising behind the lines when Otaman Volodymyr Oskilko, dissatisfied with being dropped as leader of the forces in Volhynia, made an unsuccessful attempt to overthrow Petliura. It was at this time that the disintegration of the state apparatus reached its lowest point: corruption, abuse of office, and embezzlement of public funds had become part of daily life.

On 1 May Petliura ordered the evacuation of the army from Volhynia to Galicia. On 5 May the Directory and the UNR government occupied some railway cars at the Radyvyliv border station. On 18 May they rode to Zolochiv in their railway cars, and on 25 May to Ternopil. Their rule now extended over a few kilometers of railway track and the town of Brody. The situation was a catastrophe. On 25 May, having taken Rivne, the Bolsheviks declared the liquidation of the "Petliura front." They could not decide whether to continue their advance into Galicia, as it was formally part of another state. The Poles were advancing from the west against the troops of the Western Ukrainian People's Republic, which, since 22 January, had formally been part of the UNR army. Trains with troops, munitions, officials of the UNR and their families had now gathered on a narrow strip of land along the railway line. In this hopeless situation, a decision was made to gather the remaining troops of the UNR and, according to a plan of Tiutiunnyk's, to advance toward Proskuriv. Thus began the summer offensive of the UNR army. In the truest sense of the word, it had nothing to lose. In mid-July 1919, after difficult battles with varying degrees of success, they were caught in a vise on a small strip of land between Kamianets-Podilskyi and the Zbruch and Dnister Rivers. The situation was saved by the Ukrainian Galician Army of the Western Ukrainian People's Republic, which crossed the Zbruch and attacked the Bolsheviks.[103]

On 1 August Petliura issued his Kyiv Directive, and a month later, on 30 August, troops of the Ukrainian People's Republic entered Kyiv. This success was due to the fact that the Bolsheviks had to fight on three fronts: against the UNR, against the White army advancing from the south and east, and against uprisings in the rear that were

103 As usual, the battles were fought over control of the railway junctions.

the result of their "war communism" and requisitioning of grain. At practically the same time, units of the White army from the east entered Kyiv, and the UNR army again withdrew. The attitude of the White leaders to the UNR and to the "Ukrainian question" was uncompromising. They refused to recognize the right of the Ukrainians to an independent state. On 17 September, in a message on behalf of the UNR to the "people of united (*soborna*) Ukraine," Petliura announced his government's program: independence for the Ukrainian People's Republic, recognition of the peasants' right to land without compensation, introduction of the eight-hour day, and direct elections to the Great State Council (parliament).[104] On 24 September the UNR declared war against Denikin. The People's Revolutionary Army of Makhno, the anarchist peasant leader, allied itself with the army of the UNR.

The war against the Whites in Left-Bank Ukraine went on, with varying degrees of success, until October 1919. It was temporarily quiet on the Ukrainian-Bolshevik front and, in September, there were even negotiations with Trotsky over a common military front against the Whites. In the meantime, the policies of the Whites in Ukraine,[105] especially their plan to hand the land back to the estate owners, had led to mass resistance. In the southern gubernias, Makhno's army disrupted the Whites' areas of retreat, while insurgents in Left-Bank Ukraine did the same, with the support of the Bolsheviks and the left-wing faction of the Ukrainian Socialist Revolutionaries (the Borotbists). Nonetheless, by the end of October 1919 the situation on the front against the Whites was critical. The most competent military unit, the Ukrainian Galician Army, had lost members to a typhus epidemic. On 6 November 1919 a truce was signed between the Whites and the Galician Army.

To make matters worse, differences of opinion with the leadership of the Western Ukrainian People's Republic, which was formally the western region of the Ukrainian People's Republic, gave rise to military as well as political friction and disorganization. There were disagreements in particular with Yevhen Petrushevych and with the UNR over the lack of clarity with regard to its attitude to Poland. At that time, Kost Levytsky was in Warsaw, where he was holding negotiations with Poland on behalf of the UNR. There was a

---

104 Oleksandr Dotsenko, *Litopys Ukraïns'koï revoliutsiï. Materiialy i dokumenty do istoriï Ukraïns'koï revoliutsiï, 1917–1923*, vol. 2, bk. 4 (Lviv, 1923), 243–45.

105 For a detailed discussion, see chapter 1a in the present volume.

meeting of the State Council in Kamianets-Podilskyi on 25 October, with representatives of the UNR government, the Western Ukrainian People's Republic, as well as the Ukrainian and Jewish political parties, but it made no decisions. In November, fighting flared up again with the Bolsheviks, who were successfully advancing against the Whites. The army of the UNR was no longer capable of carrying on a serious war on three fronts—against the Bolsheviks attacking from the north, against the Whites from the south and east, and against the Poles advancing from the west. On 14 November two members of the Directory, Andrii Makarenko and Fedir Shvets, went on an "official journey" to the peace conference in Paris. On 16 November the UNR government withdrew from Kamianets-Podilskyi, which was in the process of being occupied by the Poles. It moved first to Proskuriv, then to Starokostiantyniv, and was finally "stranded" in Chortoryia. Symon Petliura was now effectively the sole ruler of the Ukrainian People's Republic, which then had something more than ten thousand exhausted soldiers. The UNR army found itself in a "triangle of death" in Chortoryia, surrounded by Denikin's troops, who were retreating from the Bolsheviks, the Red Army, and the Poles.

On 28–29 November, there were meetings in Lviv between representatives of the Directory and the government at which it was agreed to submit to the demands of the Poles (the UNR-Polish border to be established along the Zbruch, i.e., loss of the western region) in return for military assistance. On 2 December, the military command and the leaders of the Directory decided to shift to partisan warfare behind the lines of the Bolsheviks and Denikin's army.[106] On 5 December, following a decision by the UNR government, Petliura left for Warsaw (although Isaak Mazepa, the head of the government, later wrote that no one knew the purpose of Petliura's journey). At this time, both the Directory and the government of the UNR had in fact collapsed. Things had gone so far that after an unsuccessful attempt to overthrow Petliura, a group of otamans of the UNR army (Omelian Volokh, Yukhym Bozhko, and Oleksandr Danchenko) took the government coffers that had been stored at some railway station and divided the money among themselves[107] (one of the conspirators, Bozhko, lost his life under dubious circumstances). Part of the UNR army crossed into Poland and was interned there. Another part (about ten thousand men), led by the new commander in chief, Mykhailo

---

106 Dotsenko, *Litopys Ukraïns'koï revoliutsiï*, 46.

107 I. Mazepa, *Ukraïna v ohni i buri revoliutsiï* (Kyiv, 2003), 324–25.

Omelianovych-Pavlenko, managed to carry on a five-month "winter campaign" behind the Bolshevik lines that has been described among apologetic historians as a "successful attempt to preserve the army."

On 25 December 1919 the Socialist Revolutionaries in Khmilnyk, in the Podilia gubernia, established a "Council of the Republic" that, in their view, was to take over from the Directory. On the following day, a party conference of Socialist Revolutionaries, Social Democrats, and Galicians decided to convene a "pre-parliament" that would dismiss the Directory. These events took place in an area controlled by the army as it advanced in its "winter campaign" along a line from Vinnytsia to Uman. These plans to reorganize the government of the UNR were given a boost at the beginning of 1920 as negotiations were under way with Poland. In February, the UNR government under Mazepa returned to Kamianets-Podilskyi. It was there that the essential decisions were made concerning the pre-parliament (the People's Council of State) and the sharing of power between the government and the Directory (decisions that remained on paper).

On 22 April 1920, a treaty was signed in Warsaw between the Ukrainian People's Republic and Poland in which the UNR relinquished its claim to the Western Region of the UNR. Two days later a joint offensive of the UNR army, formed anew on Polish territory, and the Polish army was undertaken against Bolshevik-occupied Ukraine. Kyiv was captured on 6 May. This final phase of the existence of the Ukrainian People's Republic (May to November 1920) was characterized by an intensive effort to rebuild the state and by the usual "organizational chaos" resulting from the critical shortage of professional experts and the inability of politicians to agree. But the obvious instability on the military front against the Red Army made any kind of stable policy impossible. The successful Soviet counteroffensive began in June. Before the final onslaught, the UNR government retreated along the familiar route to Zhmerynka, then to Proskuriv, and finally to Kamianets-Podilskyi. In mid-July 1920 the UNR army and government crossed the Zbruch to Polish territory. Bolshevik troops advanced as far as Warsaw, where they suffered defeat in August. By the end of September, a kind of border had begun to exist between the UNR and Soviet Ukraine along the line from Korosten through Zhytomyr to Berdychiv. On 18 October, a truce was signed between Poland and the Russian Soviet Federative Socialist Republic (RSFSR), as a result of which the UNR army lost its Polish ally. The balance of forces was too unequal. The UNR government withdrew for the last time to Kamianets-Podilskyi, but on 16 November it was forced to flee to Tarnów. Toward the end of the year, the last fighting troops of the UNR followed it across the Polish border. On 21 May 1921, a peace treaty was signed in Riga between Poland and the RSFSR that buried any last hopes of support for the Ukrainian People's Republic.

The Bolsheviks and Soviet Power in Ukraine

Like all the other regimes that succeeded one another in Ukraine between 1917 and 1920, the Soviets never controlled the whole of Ukrainian territory (the nine gubernias) before the end of 1920. Their efforts to build state structures, like those of all the others, were affected by extreme circumstances: large-scale political and military conflicts with "external forces" (foreign intervention troops, White Guards, Ukrainian parties and state structures) and "internal" enemies, i.e., dissidents of every kind.[108] The most important slogan with regard to building the new state was "All power to the soviets," which initially referred to the soviets (councils) of workers' deputies, later to the soviets of workers' and soldiers' deputies, and eventually included the peasant soviets. The main actors in establishing such a soviet system in Ukraine were to be the Ukrainian and all-Russian left-wing parties, although, during the civil war, other more mobile forms of the organization of power also played a role, such as revolutionary or military revolutionary committees.

As was the case with all other regimes at the time of the Ukrainian Revolution, the social base of Soviet power was very small, essentially the industrial proletariat in eastern Ukraine and a section of the poorest peasantry, some of whom had sunk to the level of lumpenproletariat. The zealously nurtured social demagogy and the programmatic calls for expropriation made allies of a large section of the landless peasantry, depending on the situation. In Bolshevik theory, property-owing peasants were regarded as part of the petty-bourgeois class.

On 18 April 1918 the Central Executive Committee of Ukrainian Soviets, having fled from the occupying armies to Taganrog, created (practically as a substitute for itself) the "All-Ukrainian Bureau to Lead the Insurgent Struggle against the German Occupiers." This included Ukrainian Bolsheviks, Russian left-wing Socialist Revolutionaries, and a Ukrainian Social Democrat. At a meeting of representatives of Bolshevik organizations of Ukraine, which were still illegal, it was decided to establish a Communist Party (Bolshevik) of Ukraine or

108 See chapter 4b in the present volume.

CP(B)U.[109] It was a very small party, with just 4,364 members in early June 1918.

On 4 May 1918, the supreme commander of the armed forces of the Ukrainian Soviet Socialist Republic,[110] Volodymyr Antonov-Ovsiienko, informed the Council of People's Commissars in a memorandum that the units assigned to him had ceased all activity. They were to be disarmed on the territory of the RSFSR.[111] The All-Ukrainian Bureau then began to redeploy some of these "disarmed troops" in the neutral zone that separated the Ukrainian State from the RSFSR. By the autumn of 1918, it had put together two divisions with a total of six thousand men.

The First Party Congress of the CP(B)U, meeting in Moscow at the beginning of July 1918, decided that the main task of the All-Ukrainian Bureau, now renamed the All-Ukrainian Central Military Revolutionary Committee, was to prepare an uprising against Hetman Skoropadsky and the occupying troops. On 28 November this body ceased to exist. Some of its members joined the Provisional Workers' and Peasants' Government of Ukraine,[112] formed in Kursk under the leadership of Georgii Piatakov. This government issued a manifesto on 29 November 1918 in which it proclaimed the overthrow of the Hetman and called for a struggle against the Directory. Military operations against the Directory now began, involving the two above-mentioned insurgent divisions and units of the Red Army, with a deployment of 22,000 soldiers.[113]

On 4 January 1919, following a decision of the Military Revolutionary Committee of the RSFSR, a Ukrainian front was created. By 6 February, its troops had taken the Donbas and the whole of Left-Bank Ukraine, including Kyiv. With the assistance of Makhno's Revolutionary People's Army and Hryhoriiv's units, "Soviet power"[114]

---

109 This was to be a Ukrainian Bolshevik party, although a number of representatives, led by Emmanuil Kviring, were demanding a regional section of the All-Russian Communist Party (Bolshevik).

110 The Ukrainian Soviet Socialist Republic proclaimed in Kharkiv in December 1917 is meant here.

111 *Grazhdanskaia voina na Ukraine 1918–1920 gg.*, vol. 1, bk. 1 (Kyiv, 1967), 134.

112 It is noteworthy that the decision to form the government was made by five people: TsDAVO, f. 2, op. 1, spr. 14, 1ff. Real power was in the hands of the Military Revolutionary Committee of the Kursk Direction, which was set up on instructions from Moscow and whose members were Antonov-Ovsiienko, Stalin, and Zatonsky.

113 *Ukraïna: politychna istoriia XX – pochatok XXI stolittia* (Kyiv, 2007), 409.

114 This term is a euphemism. Real power in the cities was exercised by the military revolutionary committees, which were dominated by members of the CP(B)U and, in the countryside, by the committees of poor peasants. One should not forget the Extraordinary All-Ukrainian

was established in most of the southern gubernias of Ukraine (the troops of the Entente had hastily withdrawn from Odesa, Kherson, Mykolaiv, and the Crimea). On 6 January 1919, the Provisional Workers' and Peasants' Government in Kharkiv proclaimed the establishment of the Ukrainian Soviet Socialist Republic. The new state was formally legitimized by the Third All-Ukrainian Congress of Soviets at the beginning of March.

The establishment of the "second Soviet power" in Ukraine met certain strategic needs. First of all, the large war effort and the maintenance of the army depended on the industrial resources of the Donbas and on the grain and food resources of the Dnipro region. Second, Ukraine was a staging area for the offensive against Europe where, the Bolshevik leaders believed, the world revolution would take place. Bolshevik policy in Ukraine pursued both these goals and demanded a rapid mobilization of resources. Under wartime conditions, this required extraordinary measures whose radical nature was only deepened by the Bolsheviks' ideological postulates—the "dictatorship of the proletariat," the abolition of private property, and the end of money-commodity relations.

Where the Bolsheviks were in control in Ukraine, they applied the same methods as in the RSFSR: requisitioning of grain and food directly from the peasants by means of armed "food detachments," a centralized system for the distribution of food and industrial commodities with the use of ration cards, prohibition of private commerce, and the establishment of agricultural communes and state farms (*sovkhozy*) to replace the estates and large private agriculture.

In January 1919, the government of Soviet Ukraine began to nationalize large industry, mining, and sugar factories and introduced a state monopoly on grain and food. In February 1919, the Central Committee of the Russian Communist Party passed a resolution on forced deliveries of food in Ukraine. The plan was to requisition 139 million poods of grain (1 pood = 16.38 kg), practically half the entire supply. In April 1919, there was a decree on the forced delivery of "surplus grain" from 1918. Special detachments were posted at railway and marine stations to prevent the transport of flour, grain, sugar, oil, and other types of food. Food detachments made up of armed communist workers raided villages.

Commission, formed on 3 December 1918 as a regional branch of the Extraordinary All-Russian Commission to Combat Counterrevolution, Speculation, and Sabotage (VChK or Cheka). It organized class terror, and its power was unrestricted.

The reaction was predictable: there were widespread uprisings in the villages. According to official statistics, there were 93 actions by the peasants against the Bolsheviks in April 1919; by July of the same year, the number had increased to 207. In Left-Bank Ukraine alone, there were 57 insurgent groups numbering altogether 22,000 men.[115] The leaders of the large peasant insurgent armies that had been allied with the Bolsheviks shortly before—Hryhoriiv, Otaman Zeleny, and even Makhno—now turned their arms against the Bolsheviks. At this time, Bolshevik power in the areas they controlled existed only in the towns (mainly gubernia and district centers). The countryside was dominated by anti-Bolshevik uprisings. To fight this "Ukrainian *jacquerie*," the Bolsheviks had to create a so-called "internal front" in April 1919 that mobilized 21,000 fighters, artillery, cavalry, and even an inland fleet.[116]

The disintegration of the armies of the Ukrainian front reached a critical point in May and June. Upon hearing reports of the excesses of the food detachments and the Special Commission (Cheka), soldiers and lower-ranking officers refused to carry out orders, convened assemblies, discharged their superiors, or deserted. Not infrequently, a unit sent to suppress a peasant rebellion actually joined it. The uprisings behind the lines and the unrest at the front helped the Whites win. At the end of June, the Bolsheviks, under pressure from Denikin's troops, withdrew from Kharkiv and Katerynoslav, and the Whites took over all of Left-Bank Ukraine. In June 1919, in view of the economic and military situation, the state administrative bodies of Soviet Ukraine and the RSFSR were consolidated. At the end of August, the government of Soviet Ukraine fled from Kyiv. The government established by the Whites, from the viewpoint of the mass of the population, especially the peasantry, was no less foreign than that of the Bolsheviks. Denikin's restorationist policy,[117] his complete ignorance of the real situation in the villages, and his Great Russian chauvinism led to mass spontaneous as well as organized actions by the peasantry behind the lines of Denikin's army by the autumn of that year. The activity of Makhno's army, with a force that varied between 50,000 and 100,000 men, soon became the main problem for the Whites.

115 O. V. Mykhailiuk, *Selianstvo Ukraïny v pershi desiatylittia XX st.: sotsiokul'turni protsesy* (Dnipropetrovsk, 2007), 333–34.

116 *Ukraïna: politychna istoriia XX – pochatok XXI stolittia* (Kyiv, 2007), 412.

117 For more details on Denikin's policies, see chapter 1a in this volume.

On 10 July 1919 the Central Committee of the CP(B)U, under the leadership of Stanislav Kosior, established the "Bureau behind the Lines," whose task was to organize underground activity and uprisings in the rear of Denikin's army and coordinate the activities of the 108 CP(B)U committees working in the underground.[118] In October 1919, the bureau began to establish revolutionary committees that were to organize local uprisings and diversions. In Moscow, in December 1919, the Ukrainian government created an extraordinary administrative organ in Ukraine, the All-Ukrainian Revolutionary Committee, under the leadership of Hryhorii Petrovsky. In the meantime, the situation at the front had changed radically. A mobilization of resources that had been accompanied by the most brutal terror and a reorganization of the army had made it possible for the Bolsheviks to mount a successful counterattack. In the course of December 1919 they took the Donbas and, on 16 December, the Red Army entered Kyiv. Following the wishes of the Central Committee of the Russian Communist Party, they chose "proletarian" Kharkiv as the capital city, which was also the location of the All-Ukrainian Revolutionary Committee. At the end of December 1919, the White armies were concentrated in the Crimea. By the end of January 1920, most of the Ukrainian gubernias were under Bolshevik rule.

In January 1920 the All-Ukrainian Revolutionary Committee, according to previous agreements concerning the military and political union of both republics, decided that all decrees and orders issued by the Council of People's Commissars of the RSFSR were also valid on Ukrainian territory. The armed forces of both countries were finally merged under Moscow's control. In mid-February 1920, the All-Ukrainian Central Executive Committee decided to end the activity of the All-Ukrainian Revolutionary Committee and reinstate the Council of People's Commissars of the Ukrainian SSR. In March and April there were elections to the village and county soviets. Based on the results of those elections, the congresses of soviets at the district and gubernia levels were elected. When the competing left-wing parties (Mensheviks, Ukrainian Socialist Revolutionaries) had been suppressed, the CP(B)U managed to obtain a decisive majority in the executive committees of the soviets at all levels, from 70 percent at district level to 85 percent at the level of the gubernias. Communist Party policies were implemented in the villages mainly

118 A. V. Lykholat, *Rozhrom natsionalistychnoï kontrrevoliutsiï na Ukraïni (1917–1933)* (Kyiv, 1955), 404.

by the Committees of Poor Peasants (*komnezamy*), which had begun to be formed in March 1920. By November 1920 there were about ten thousand of these committees, which actively supported the communists in their requisitioning of food.

It seemed at first that the "third Soviet power" had learned the lessons of the recent past. In a resolution of the Central Committee of the Russian Communist Party "On Soviet Power in Ukraine" that was personally prepared by Lenin himself, the errors made with regard to the nationality question, land, and food would not be repeated. The resolution recognized the independence of Ukraine and contained a clause on the need for free development of Ukrainian culture (language, education) in order, as the resolution said, "to be able to explain, in a comradely manner, the common interests of the working people of Ukraine and Russia." With regard to land, the plan was for the complete elimination of estates. The policy on food suggested that "surplus grain" would be appropriated mainly from the kulaks.

Representatives of Ukrainian left-wing parties would be allowed to share power. In December 1919, an agreement on collaboration was reached between the CP(B)U and the Ukrainian Communist Party (the left wing of the Ukrainian Socialist Revolutionaries, the *Borot'bisty*). One of the Borotbists, Hryhorii Hrynko, became a member of the All-Ukrainian Revolutionary Committee, and representatives of his and other left-wing parties were accepted as members of local revolutionary committees.[119]

On 5 February 1920, the All-Ukrainian Revolutionary Committee confirmed the land law, which dealt with the distribution of land and imposed limits on the size of land parcels that could be made available to state farms. The establishment of agricultural communes would be voluntary. All the land that had previously belonged to estate owners, the state, the tsar's family, or the monasteries was declared to be the "property of the working people" (the confiscation of estate land continued to the end of 1920). Further events demonstrated, however, that these intentions were no more than declarations. Soviet power found itself in the midst of a real and anticipated war, and its actions corresponded to the laws of war and to the Bolsheviks' ideological principles, which formally aspired to a dictatorship of the proletariat

---

119 A. Voinovych, "Uchast' livykh politychnykh partii v diial'nosti mistsevykh orhaniv vlady na Pivdni Ukraïny v 1920 r.," *Problemy istoriï Ukraïny: fakty, sudzhennia, poshuky* (Kyiv), no. 14 (2005): 60–61.

but, in practice, strove to maintain a one-party dictatorship of professional revolutionaries.

The Bolsheviks themselves considered the situation to be just a "peaceful breather." Petr Wrangel still controlled the Crimea (a problem that was not resolved until the end of 1920) and, between April and November 1920, the country was at war with Poland. In the countryside, the peasant war that the Bolsheviks had ignited continued to rage. Forced deliveries of food continued in spite of the directive on surplus grain and led to large-scale requisitioning of grain supplies. The size of the surplus, according to the Ukrainian government, was estimated to be 160 million poods, less than what had been demanded by the previous Soviet rulers, but the harvest in the autumn of 1919 was only 25 percent of what it had been the previous year.[120] The attempt to obtain grain at "fixed prices" was unsuccessful, first because the peasants had no confidence in the currency (there were ten different types of currency at that time, from the tsarist to that of the Provisional Government to that of the Ukrainian People's Republic) and, second, because the term "fixed prices" meant that the grain would be acquired gratis, since the government was not in a position to offer even the most elementary industrial goods in exchange.

The end result was that Ukrainian grain was, to a large extent, once again "pumped out" (the Bolshevik expression) by force. The food detachments began their work again and succeeded in "pumping out" 70 million poods (4.3 million tons) of grain, a result that was achieved by means of massive force and repression against the unwilling peasants. In the spring and summer, food policy in the countryside took on an explicit class character. Those who resisted the delivery of grain were declared to be kulaks (this category included all the well-off peasants, and often middle peasants as well). In the autumn of 1920, the "campaign for bread" and the "campaign against the kulaks" were one and the same in official rhetoric.

In addition to the food detachments, Red Army units were deployed in the confiscation of grain "surpluses" and agricultural products.[121] We can get some idea of the scale of the forces engaged from the fact that the staffs of the special food committees in the gubernias,

120 I. Khmel', *Agrarnye preobrazovaniia na Ukraine (1917–1920 gg.)* (Kyiv, 1990), 105–12.

121 The forced deliveries also involved fodder, cattle, hay and straw. The activists of the local committees of poor peasants were allowed to take clothing, personal objects, and even meals as payment.

regions, and districts comprised about sixty thousand people. In the autumn of 1920, the army became involved in food collection.[122] The best-known (and most extreme) example of this was the Red Cavalry of Semen Budenny, which was involved in forced deliveries in the Poltava gubernia in the late summer of 1920.

The result was a new outbreak of civil war. Once again the peasants reached for their weapons. The struggle against the insurgents was made difficult by the particular partisan tactics that the peasants had mastered during the years of the civil war after 1917. As a rule, there was just a small stable core (the otaman and his staff) around whom, depending on the situation, dozens or hundreds of peasants came together and constituted the mass of fighters. They attacked the activists and representatives of Soviet power, food detachments, or army units, mainly by night. By day, these insurgents became ordinary peasants. These groups generally avoided open conflict with the Red Army units deployed against them.[123]

By the autumn of 1920, the Bolsheviks had again lost control over large parts of rural Ukraine. Outside the towns, it was hundreds of small peasant detachments that set the tone. They melted away as the regular army approached, only to reappear when it left. In late 1920 and early 1921, according to official statistics, there were as many as one hundred thousand men in the larger insurgent units in Ukraine.[124] By the late spring of 1920, Nestor Makhno's army had been organized again and advanced during the summer far into Left-Bank Ukraine, which was then behind the lines of the southwestern front in the war against Poland. All military efforts to localize, encircle, or destroy Makhno's army in 1920 failed.[125]

The response of Soviet power was total terror. In April 1920, kidnapping and family liability were introduced in the villages.

---

122 In the early autumn of 1920, there were 482,000 men in the army on the territory of Soviet Ukraine.

123 Descriptions of this kind are to be found mostly in the apologetic literature. See, for instance, V. Ia. Revehuk, *U borot'bi za voliu Ukraïny (Vyzvol'ni zmahannia na Poltavshchyni 1920–1925)* (Poltava, 2000).

124 O. I. Hanzha, *Opir selian stanovlenniu totalitarnoho rezhymu v USRR* (Kyiv, 1996), 5ff.

125 In October 1920, a military and political agreement was signed with Makhno according to which the rear of the Red Army, now advancing toward the Crimea, would be kept free, and Makhno's army would join in the fighting against the Whites. In return, Makhno's supporters and the anarchists who had not fought against Soviet power would be granted an amnesty and a guarantee of security. The treaty was violated as early as November of the same year, but the attempt to destroy Makhno's army was unsuccessful. It was not until the autumn of 1921 that Soviet forces managed to drive the remnants of Makhno's army as far as the Romanian border, which they finally crossed on 28 August.

Following the capture of the Crimea, the end of the Polish-Soviet war, and the final defeat of the UNR army, Soviet power had massive resources available to defeat the peasants, but neither military operations nor punitive expeditions achieved the desired effect. On the contrary, peasant uprisings spread even farther, to the gubernias of Tambov and Voronezh, to western Siberia and the Volga region. By the spring of 1921, Soviet power had put an end to the uprisings in Ukraine, but there was no guarantee that they would not break out again at the first relaxation of military pressure.

In the meantime, the situation had become critical in the towns, traditionally considered the strongholds of the "dictatorship of the proletariat." The policy of "war communism" reached its high point in 1920. The complete nationalization of all strategically important branches, even the militarization of coal and iron production, the introduction of universal compulsory labor, the rejection of money-commodity relations,[126] the abolition of private property, and the extremely centralized direction of industry all led to economic collapse. The Soviets attempted to overcome the crisis by force: the creation of a "labor army," persecution (imprisonment in camps) of "labor deserters," and brutal repression of speculators and anyone described as such. By the spring of 1921, production in the metal industry was 5 percent of its prewar level, coal production was 22 percent, and the sugar factories produced 4 million tons of sugar, down from 85 million tons before the war.

Economic decline undermined the position of the sector of the population declared by the Bolsheviks to be the social base of the regime, the industrial working class. The daily bread ration available with the ration card fell to 100 grams daily in the industrial centers. The market, which continued to exist in spite of all efforts to wipe it out, went over to bartering. The most sought-after "currencies" were salt, matches, sugar, flour, and fuel. The shortage economy and widespread hunger forced many workers to rescue themselves by leaving the city and returning to the land or engaging in some kind of small enterprise not approved by the state.

By the spring of 1921, Soviet power in Ukraine (as in the RSFSR generally) had reached an extremely dangerous point. The economic collapse threatened to become a political one. In view of this

126 Along with other measures, such as the centralized distribution of food and industrial commodities by means of ration cards, payment for the use of public transport, post, telegraph, and communal services was also abolished.

situation, the Bolsheviks, on Lenin's initiative, were prepared to make concessions. The Tenth Party Conference of the Russian Communist Party introduced the New Economic Policy. Forced deliveries were replaced by a food tax, and the peasants were now able to sell their remaining grain on the market. Nonstrategic branches were denationalized, and private enterprise was permitted, as was private capital and free trade. These and other measures eased the social situation and made possible the political consolidation of the Bolshevik regime. This, however, meant the end of the Ukrainian Revolution.[127]

127 On the integration of Ukraine into the USSR, see chapter 4b in the present volume.

2b. The Western Ukrainian People's Republic of 1918–1919

Vasyl Rasevych

When the Western Ukrainian People's Republic was proclaimed, on 1 November 1918, on the Ukrainian ethnic territory of the former Austria-Hungary, this did not happen spontaneously or by chance. The creation of the new republic was simply the high point in the development of the Ukrainian national movement in the Habsburg lands. The establishment of a Ukrainian state came as a shock, however, to the Polish elite of Galicia, which had never paid serious attention to the "Ukrainian question." The newly created state, with its capital in Lviv (Lemberg), where the politically active Ukrainians were in a minority in relation to the Poles, was threatened from the outset by the outbreak of a bloody Polish-Ukrainian conflict that could soon put an end to its existence. The republic lasted only a little more than eight months, but it was the first major step of the Ukrainian movement in its struggle for independent statehood.

The Ukrainian National Movement within the Habsburg Monarchy

The Ukrainian political movement was in some ways less developed than other national movements in Austria-Hungary. It began only very gradually to address the masses, and the political leadership limited its demands to a partition of Galicia according to ethnic criteria and the unification of Eastern Galicia and Northern Bukovyna to form a separate Ukrainian province within the Habsburg Monarchy. In view of its internal weakness, the Ukrainian movement in Austria-Hungary saw it as one of its priorities to mobilize external support. As a way of dealing with difficulties in relations with Poland, the movement had long oriented itself on the central government in Vienna, and its leadership was traditionally loyal to the Habsburgs.

With the advent of the First World War, the political demands of the Galician Ukrainians became more radical, but this did not affect their program. Before the war, the leadership of the Ukrainian movement had been in the hands of the Ukrainian National Democratic Party (UNDP), distinguished by the fact that its leading bodies consisted mainly of jurists and lawyers. They had grown up in the Austrian legal system, and nothing was further from their minds, even theoretically, than a violent seizure of power, even one that might be formally legitimate. In their ambitions for a state of their own, the Galician political leaders, such as Kost Levytsky, Yevhen Olesnytsky, Yevhen Petrushevych, and even Lonhyn Tsehelsky, remained strictly within the Habsburg paradigm. From being an arbiter in the Polish-Ukrainian conflict, the Austro-Hungarian Monarchy would become the source of legitimacy for the new Ukrainian state that was to be created.

Until the outbreak of the First World War, there had been no essential changes in the programs of the most important Ukrainian parties in Galicia and Bukovyna as regards their national and political ideal. The program of the *Narodovtsi* (1899) stated: "It is our wish, in an Austrian state that is respected internationally and strengthened by the harmony and satisfaction of all its peoples, to achieve for the Ruthenian people, on the basis of a constitution and by legal means, a political status that is its due among the peoples of this state."[1] This postulate remained later in the program of the UNDP, which described its national political ideal more precisely: "We, the Galician Ruthenians, part of the Ukrainian-Ruthenian nation that once possessed independent statehood, after which it fought for centuries for its right to political sovereignty, which has never relinquished the rights of an independent nation and does not relinquish them now, declare it to be the final goal of all our strivings to continue working until the whole Ukrainian-Ruthenian people has achieved cultural, economic, and political independence and, in time, is united in a single national organism, in which the whole people can make use of its cultural, economic, and political rights for the general good. In our striving for this goal, and in recognition of our affiliation to the Austrian state, we are working to ensure that the territory occupied by Ruthenians in the Austrian state becomes a province in its own right, with the most far-reaching autonomy in legislation and administration."[2] Until October 1918, the maximal demand of the Ukrainians was for a federalist transformation of the Monarchy and the creation of an autonomous Ukrainian province. As far as the Ukrainian population of Transleithania was concerned, what the Galician Ukrainians wanted, considering that national life there was only in its initial stages, was to establish "close mutual relations" in

---

1 TsDIA Lviv, f. 146, op. 7, spr. 4529, 12, Narodna prohrama. Nakladom Tovarystva "Narodna Rada," pid zariadom K. Bednars'koho (Tekst prohramy narodovtsiv, pryiniatoi zboramy muzhiv doviria politychnoho tovarystva "Narodna Rada" u L'vovi 25 bereznia 1892 roku).

2 Ibid., 9.

order "to create a national movement similar to that which already exists in Galicia and Bukovyna."[3] On the nationality question, neither the program of the Ruthenian-Ukrainian Radical Party nor that of the Ukrainian Social Democratic Party was particularly radical. What distinguished them from the National Democratic Party were their more progressive social and economic demands and their theoretical plans for agriculture.

On the eve of the war, the leading Ukrainian parties in Galicia and Bukovyna began gradually to move away from their principle of loyalty to the Habsburg Empire, even though this was not reflected in official documents. The discussions over strategy and tactics for building the Ukrainian political movement led to the formation of two competing groups. The dividing line was not between the parties. The polarization grew out of mutual accusations that loyalty to the Austro-Hungarian government was given priority over the concerns of the oppositional Ukrainians. That there was no strategic difference between the aims of both groups is demonstrated by the fact that the "unofficial group," that is, the opposition, did not create its own structures. Within the then leading political force, the UNDP, the oppositional members did not come together as a group either.

At the head of the official group, which was completely loyal to the Austro-Hungarian government and state, were well-known political figures such as Mykola Vasylko from Bukovyna and Kost Levytsky, the leader of the Galicians. With his aristocratic origins and his study at the Theresian Academy in Vienna, Vasylko was able to establish good contacts with the government and with financial circles in the empire. His political credo rested on two pillars: he stood for a strong Austro-Hungarian state and was unable to imagine life outside the Habsburg Empire.[4] In a letter to Wilhelm von Habsburg he defined his political orientation, calling himself a "truly faithful Austrian patriot of the Habsburg dynasty."[5] His unchallenged leadership in the political movement in Bukovyna and his successes in Viennese governing circles even allowed him to control Galician Ukrainian politics for a time. He worked in tandem with Levytsky, both pursuing an ultra-loyal political course.

A group of Galician politicians came together to oppose this orientation. Led by Yevhen Petrushevych, this group included Yevhen

3 "Nova partiia, ieï prohrama i orhanizatsiia," *Buduchnist'*, 15 December 1899.

4 Stepan Baran, "Mykola Vasyl'ko (Nekroloh)," *Dilo*, 8 August 1924: 1–4.

5 TsDIA Lviv, f. 309, op. 2, spr. 109, Lyst M. Vasyl'ka do Vil'hel'ma Habsburga vid 24 kvitnia 1917.

Levytsky, Lonhyn Tsehelsky, Volodymyr Bachynsky, and others. The core of the group was made up of representatives in the Cisleithanian Imperial Council (*Reichsrat*), with the base consisting of the oppositional forces among the Ukrainian Parliamentary Representation (UPR) in Vienna. Having removed the Bukovynian representatives from the UPR, they now had a majority there. The General Ukrainian Council (*Zahal'na Ukraïns'ka Rada*, ZUR) and the People's Committee (*Narodnyi Komitet*), the leading organ of the Ukrainian National Democratic Party, remained in the hands of Kost Levytsky's supporters. As conflict developed between these two currents, the opponents of the loyalist course not only did not produce new slogans but also did not question the methods of political struggle. They shared the idea of autonomy and regarded petitioning as their principal political activity.

The first hard blow to the pro-Austrian loyalist position was the Two Emperors' Manifesto of Kaiser Franz Joseph I and Kaiser Wilhelm II in November 1916. It announced the intention of Austria-Hungary and Germany to establish a Polish kingdom in the foreseeable future on territory wrested from Russia. The Polish factor was much more important to the Habsburg Empire than the young and confused Ukrainian movement. The Habsburgs depended on Polish support. Vienna did not intend incorporating Galicia into the Kingdom of Poland, but regional autonomy would be further extended.[6] Among the Ukrainian population of the empire, the manifesto provoked a storm of outrage that continued even after the death of the emperor. The Ukrainians of Galicia protested, and the new emperor, Karl I, promised to take account of Ukrainian demands, but only after the war. Ukrainian political circles in Galicia considered the very fact that such a manifesto could appear to be a declaration of bankruptcy for the loyalist policies of the group around Levytsky and Vasylko.

The politicians who had opposed this course forced the previous leadership to resign, and Vasylko was also forced to resign as vice president of the General Ukrainian Council, thereby losing the right to speak in the name of the whole Ukrainian movement in Austria-Hungary. This shift in the balance of forces had a negative effect on Ukrainian politics generally. Shortly before the publication of the manifesto, Vasylko had attempted to establish contact with influential government circles in Germany. He was able to have a number of talks with the German side that gave him clearly to understand that their

6 Tadeusz Dąbkowski, *Ukraiński ruch narodowy w Galicji Wschodniej, 1912–1923* (Warsaw, 1985), 80.

position on the future of Galicia and the whole of Ukraine differed on a number of points from that of their Austro-Hungarian allies. In a letter of 25 November 1916, Vasylko summarized the German position on the Ukrainian question as follows: "Of course, all measures here are dictated first and foremost by German interests. On the other hand, it is a fact that the Germans are absolutely clear that our interests are also exceptionally important and decisive for them. In this respect, they really want to support us and offer serious assistance. There is therefore no basis for the exaggerated pessimism that is widespread among uninformed circles with regard to Germany, just as there was also no basis for the previous exaggerated hopes."[7] Even Vasylko's main opponents, the group around Petrushevych, had to admit that after his departure from the Ukrainian stage Germany's interest in the "Ukrainian card" began to wane.[8] Having lost any influence over Galician politics, Vasylko concentrated on leading the Ukrainian clubs of Bukovyna, where he pursued his previous line. The split in the Ukrainian movement between the Galician and Bukovynian politicians certainly did not contribute to a positive image abroad, especially in the central government in Vienna.

When parliament resumed in 1917, the demands from representatives of the various national groups concerning national autonomy had become much more radical. The Ukrainian Parliamentary Representation declared that the continuing subordination of the Ukrainians to the Poles, in a single province, was nothing but disregard for national rights and for the principle of national self-determination. Under the leadership of Yevhen Petrushevych, the UPR categorically rejected any form of community of Ukrainians and Poles in one and the same province.[9] The partition of Galicia was now a minimal demand. Vienna answered with delaying tactics.

An analysis of all the documents and the press (including the oppositional ones) leads one to the conviction that in 1918 the Austro-Hungarian Ukrainians saw themselves pressured by circumstances into choosing between an all-embracing Ukraine and loyalty to the empire. Most were inclined to support autonomy within a reformed Habsburg Monarchy. There were many reasons for this. When the war began, the Ukrainians had decided unequivocally to fight on the

7 TsDIA Lviv, f. 746, op. 1, spr. 6, 5.

8 Ievhen Levyts'kyi, *Lysty z Nimechchyny* (Vienna, 1916), 13.

9 P. Mahochi, *Istoriia Ukraïny* (Kyiv, 2007), 439.

side of the Central Powers.[10] This had to do with the weakness of the Ukrainian movement and with the fact that Russia was part of the Entente. The Austro-Hungarian orientation was the firm foundation of the policy of the Ukrainian parties. In the preface to his book *Zoloti vorota*,[11] in which he assessed Ukrainian politics at the time, Vasyl Kuchabsky explained its source: "In view of the weakness of the Ukrainian people, the afflictions imposed by the occupying states, Austria and Russia, were absolutely unwelcome, but they were the least unwelcome. One of the essential tasks of Ukrainian policy, then, was to convince these powers that the increasing national consciousness and culture of the Ukrainian people would not lead to a derogation of its loyalty. The tactic of loyalism, on which, in Ukraine's national interest, no shadow should fall, became an axiom of Ukrainian political thought."[12]

This policy of loyalty to Austria-Hungary on the part of the Ukrainians within the empire did not prevent them, however, from forging radical plans for territory wrested from the Russian Empire. At the start of the First World War, a political organization of Ukrainians from Russia was formed in Lviv, the Union for the Liberation of Ukraine (*Soiuz vyzvolennia Ukraïny*, SVU). The SVU was a nonparty organization that represented the political interests of Ukrainians under Russian rule. Its political plans were linked to a defeat of Russia in the war and the overthrow of tsarism so that, "out of its ruins," a "free and independent Ukraine" could emerge.[13] The SVU received considerable financial support from the Austro-Hungarian government on condition that it be used solely for propaganda in the Russian Empire.[14] Galician politicians were deeply involved in this, and there is no doubt that some SVU material was distributed in Bukovyna and Galicia. With the formation of the SVU, a "legal" basis existed for the development of a concrete program for a future independent Ukrainian state. The Galicians eagerly began developing concrete plans for Ukrainian territory in Russia.[15] Kost Levytsky continued to

10 Mykhailo Lozyns'kyi, *Halychyna v rr. 1918–1920* (Vienna, 1922; repr. New York, 1970), 11.

11 Ukrainian for "golden gate."

12 Vasyl' Kuchabs'kyi, *Zoloti vorota. Istoriia Sichovykh Stril'tsiv 1917–1919* (Lviv, 1937), 6.

13 I. Pater, *Soiuz vyzvolennia Ukraïny: problemy derzhavnosti i sobornosti* (Lviv, 2000), 74; *Nasha platforma* (Vienna), no. 1, 5 October 1914: 2.

14 For more detail, see chapter 1b in the present volume.

15 Wassyl Rassewytsch (Vasyl' Rasevych), "Außenpolitische Orientierungen österreichischer Ukrainer (1912–1918)," in *Confraternitas. Ukraïna: kul'turna spadshchyna, natsional'na svidomist', derzhavnist'*, vol. 15 (Lviv, 2006–7), 623–36.

insist throughout 1917 that the main task of the Ukrainian political movement was "the liberation of Ukrainian territory from foreign rule and the creation of state constitutional organs of self-determination for the Ukrainian people."[16] The implementation of this demand was, for him, unequivocally bound up with Austria-Hungary. It was his view that this initiative would allow the Galician Ukrainians to maintain "clear and unambiguous" relations with Austria.[17] This was also the position of the oppositional Ukrainian Parliamentary Representation, which adopted the following resolution in February 1917: "The Ukrainians wish for nothing other than a close affiliation with Austria; not one, however, that is dependent on other constitutionally equal factors, but one that affiliates us directly with the Empire."[18]

Possible unification in an all-embracing Ukraine was mentioned only when the task was to wrest political concessions from the government in office, such as the founding of a Ukrainian university or the partition of Galicia. This tactic was explained by Levytsky in 1919. In 1918 the Ukrainian National Democrats had formulated very clear demands on the central government in Vienna: "either the Ukrainian territory within the Austrian Monarchy obtains the independent constitutional order under Austria that is its due, with an end to Polish sovereignty, or, regardless of how much Austria might not want this or be able to accomplish it, our road will lead not to Warsaw but to Kyiv, to unite us with the Ukrainian state whose independence has been proclaimed by the Central Rada in Kyiv."[19]

Cautious Preparations for Autonomous Statehood in 1918

The radicalization of other national movements in the Austro-Hungarian Monarchy in 1918 prompted the Ukrainians to make preparations for a possible collapse of the empire. From September–October, Ukrainian politicians began to play a double game in that they worked out the modalities for a federalist transformation of the empire while, at the same time, preparing the foundations for an independent state. Lonhyn Tsehelsky, a deputy in the Cisleithanian Imperial Council and one of the best-known representatives of the opposition, described this period in his memoirs: "We were outwardly

---

16 Kost' Levyts'kyi, "S'ohochasnyi stan ukraïns'koï spravy. 1917 rik," *Dilo*, 6 January 1917: 1.

17 Ibid.

18 "Rishennia parliamentarnoï komisiï UPR," *Ukraïns'ke slovo*, 20 January 1917: 1.

19 Kost' Levyts'kyi, "Natsiolnal'no-demokratychne storonnytstvo v 1918 r.," *Republyka*, 1 April 1919: 1ff.

loyal to Austria but were preparing its overthrow. If Austria managed to survive, we would be part of its federal structure. In the event of its disintegration, we were determined and prepared to proclaim our own independent state and, should the occasion arise, to unite with greater Ukraine."[20]

Hopes for possible reform of the Austro-Hungarian Monarchy were strengthened, to some extent, by the events connected with the Brest-Litovsk peace treaty, for it was here that the Central Powers not only recognized the existence of a sovereign Ukrainian People's Republic (UNR) in Kyiv but also, in a secret appendix to the treaty, guaranteed the establishment of Ukrainian national political autonomy within the Habsburg Monarchy (the Crownland Protocol). There had also been agreement on a border favorable to the Ukrainians in the Kholm region. On this occasion, the People's Committee of the UNDP met in extraordinary session. The resolution passed by the People's Committee greeted the recognition of the fact that the Ukrainian state existed and proclaimed that "the whole Ukrainian people of Galicia will exercise its right to statehood within the borders of the Habsburg Monarchy."[21] At an extraordinary session of the People's Committee on 18 February 1918, it was resolved that in all the districts of Galicia a festival would be held on 3 March under the slogan, "Long live Ukrainian statehood in the Habsburg Monarchy."

The Polish population of Eastern Galicia responded to the Brest-Litovsk treaty, especially to the losses in the Kholm region, with strikes and protests aimed at preventing Austria-Hungary from implementing these undertakings. And although the Ukrainian parties succeeded in mobilizing a mass movement such as had never been seen before in support of the undertakings given in Brest-Litovsk, the Austro-Hungarian government never risked implementing the secret Crownland Protocol.[22]

Another blow to the positions of the committed Austro-Hungarian autonomists was the coup in Kyiv. German troops supported Hetman Skoropadsky's seizure of power and recognized his Ukrainian State. This severely restricted the Austro-Hungarian Ukrainians' freedom of action, as threats to unite with Kyiv in a single Ukrainian state were no longer effective. Kost Levytsky considered three ways out

---

20 Lonhyn Tsehel's'kyi, *Vid lehend do pravdy. Spomyny pro podiï v Ukraïni zv'iazani z Pershym Lystopadom 1918 r.* (New York and Philadelphia, 1960), 33.

21 "Z Narodnoho Komitetu," *Ukraïns'ke slovo,* 15 February 1918: 1.

22 *Ukraïns'ke slovo*, 20 February 1918: 1.

of this situation: "First, an understanding with the Hetman, since he nourishes good intentions with regard to an independent Ukrainian state; second, an alliance with Ukrainian parties to fight the Hetman for the democratization of the Ukrainian State; or, third, support for the Austro-German movement in Ukraine."[23]

A resolution was passed at a meeting of the People's Committee on 11 May 1918 that clearly condemned Germany's "brutal interference" in the internal affairs of Ukraine.[24] The UNDP also recognized the right of the political organization that had created the Ukrainian People's Republic, the Central Rada, to continue to exercise state power. The committee also declared that "the Central Powers, which demand that the UNR adhere to the Brest-Litovsk treaty and its additional provisions, are also themselves legally and morally obliged to fulfill those undertakings into which they entered with the UNR and with the whole Ukrainian people in the Brest-Litovsk treaty and its additional provisions, whether publicly or confidentially." This meant that the Central Powers should hand over Kholm and Pidliashia (present-day Podlachia) to the UNR. The strong condemnation of Germany for its brutal interference in Ukraine's internal affairs did not cause the Galicians to change their position with regard to the Austrian government. They wanted it "to partition Galicia, in keeping with its commitments, and to establish a separate state organism in Eastern Galicia and Bukovyna within the framework of Austria."[25]

In the summer of 1918 Yevhen Petrushevych, head of the Ukrainian Parliamentary Representation in the Austrian paliament, said that "the star of the Habsburg dynasty still shines bright and clear in our firmament."[26] By the autumn of 1918, however, there were few politicians who did not see that what was coming was a victory of the Entente and the inevitable collapse of Austria-Hungary. From this time on, secret groupings emerged throughout the empire that worked on different models for the future restructuring of the state. With the announcement of President Woodrow Wilson's "fourteen points," at the latest, the principle of self-determination of nations had become a fundamental postulate of international politics. Wilson's

---

23 Levyts'kyi, "Natsional'no-demokratychne storonnytstvo v 1918 r.," 1ff.

24 "Narodnyi Komitet pro derzhavnyi perevorot u Kyïvi i parliamentarnu krizu v Avstriï," *Dilo*, 14 May 1918: 1–4.

25 Ibid.

26 O. Karpenko, "Lystopadova 1918 r. Natsional'no-demokratychna revoliutsiia na zakhidnoukraïns'kykh zemliakh," *Ukraïns'kyi istorychnyi zhurnal*, 1993, no. 1: 18.

program promised independence for Poland. For the peoples of Austria-Hungary, he promised "the freest opportunity for autonomous development." The Ukrainians took this declaration very seriously. It prompted the Galicians to pursue their struggle for independence even more vigorously.[27] Educated in the spirit of Austro-Hungarian constitutionalism, they continued to rely on international resolutions and "thereby underestimated the potential of their own people."[28]

The Ukrainian politicians of Galicia found it very difficult to depart from their basic principle of the unconditional legitimacy of power, which is why, even as they developed their own plans, they always did so with reference to Austria. Even when Emperor Karl rejected the Ukrainian demand for the partition of Galicia, and it became clear that Ukrainian autonomy was not to be part of the planned transformation of the Monarchy, the Galician Ukrainians still hoped for a legislated solution. It was for this reason that they did not proclaim the unity of all Ukrainian territories in Austria-Hungary until after Karl's manifesto of 16 October 1918 announcing the transformation of Austria into a federal state.[29] But even then, the group around Kost Levytsky did not go beyond demanding agrarian reform, which they saw as an extremely radical step, equivalent to an attack on Austro-Hungarian power: "At that time (autumn 1918), it was clear to us that the collapse had to come. It was suggested in the People's Committee that our response to this should be a demand for agrarian reform, since our program called for land, especially the large estates, to become the property of the people, without compensation, and for this land to be distributed to the peasants with little or no land."[30] The fact that the Ukrainians made this demand at a time when the other peoples of the empire, no longer satisfied with federalism, were declaring their own independent states, demonstrates their "backwardness" and their late entry into this process. What is more, the Ukrainian political leaders tried for a long time to ignore the fact that the Entente had given up any plans for a separate peace with Austria-Hungary, which meant, in practice, that the disintegration of the empire into nation-states was inevitable. It was not until the autumn of 1918 that the leadership of

27 Matvii Stakhiv, *Zakhidna Ukraïna. Narys istoriï derzhavnoho budivnytstva ta zbroinoï i dyplomatychnoï oborony v 1918–1923*, vol. 3 (Scranton, 1960), 102.

28 Valerii Soldatenko, *Ukraïna v revoliutsiinu dobu. Istorychni ese-khroniky. Rik 1918*, vol. 2 (Kyiv, 2009), 313.

29 Vasyl Kuchabsky, *Western Ukraine in Conflict with Poland and Bolshevism, 1918–1923* (Edmonton and Toronto, 2009), 24.

30 Levyts'kyi, "Natsional'no-demokratychne storonnytstvo v 1918 r.," 1–2.

the People's Committee adopted a new slogan and began to prepare for the collapse. Stepan Baran later recalled this historic decision: "There was only one thing left for us to do: to make ourselves ready, at the last minute, to ensure that the Ukrainian lands in Austria-Hungary did not come under a foreign yoke. Therefore, when I returned from the country at the beginning of September, at the first session of the People's Committee on 7 September 1918, which had been put off until then by the leaders of political life in our region, as secretary of the committee I took a decisive step by pointing out the need for our forces to prepare for the moment of Austria-Hungary's collapse and, when necessary, to establish our own state organism."[31] At this highly conspiratorial session, it was decided to establish a coordinating body to prepare for the collapse of the empire. Two commissions of the People's Committee were created: "An organizational commission to instruct the organs with a view to taking over administration in Eastern Galicia and a military commission to prepare the armed forces to carry out a coup."[32]

The members of the organizational commission were Volodymyr Okhrymovych, Vasyl Paneiko, and Stepan Baran. Since its activity was "strictly conspiratorial,"[33] the committee left no documents behind. The decisions of the People's Committee were only reported verbally. Levytsky was the liaison to the Ukrainian Parliamentary Representation, and his task was to inform the UPR about the decisions of the People's Committee. Some members of the UPR had their own plans for the overthrow of the empire. This alternative group was led by Yosyf Folys, Ivan Kyveliuk, and Lonhyn Tsehelsky. Originally they had tended to support the idea of a "transformation of Austria-Hungary on a federal basis,"[34] and their ultimate aim was to persuade the Austro-Hungarian emperor "to carry out a coup from above, in other words, to dissolve or suspend parliament and introduce a new constitution by imperial edict that would create autonomous regional national states united in a federal state, with a federal parliament responsible for foreign and military affairs."[35] To realize this plan, Folys and Tsehelsky made contact with representatives of the Slovenian, Croatian, and Czech national movements. At a joint meeting in the

31 Stepan Baran, "Do istoriï povstannia ZUNR," *Dilo*, 6 January 1923: 1ff.

32 Levyts'kyi, "Natsional'no-demokratychne storonnytstvo v 1918 r.," 1–2.

33 Baran, "Do istoriï povstannia ZUNR," 1–2.

34 Tsehel's'kyi, *Vid lehend do pravdy*, 25.

35 Ibid.

autumn of 1918, they decided to propose to Emperor Karl "that, before the coup, military commanders and units in the national capitals be replaced by those that would be subordinate to the national constituent assemblies and would prevent any unrest directed against the coup."[36] Galician politicians and religious dignitaries, among them Yuliian Romanchuk, Yevhen Levytsky, Volodymyr Bachynsky, Yevhen Petrushevych, Tyt Voinarovsky, Stepan Smal-Stotsky, Sydir Holubovych, Ivan Kyveliuk, Oleksander Stefanovych, Andrei Sheptytsky, Vasyl Paneiko, Volodymyr Okhrymovych, and Teodosii Lezhohubsky, were informed of these intentions.[37]

The Cossack officer Petro Bubela, assisted by two other officers, Volodymyr Ohonovsky and Dmytro Paliiv, was chosen to make the necessary preparations and carry out agitation among Ukrainians in the Austro-Hungarian army.[38] Tsehelsky wrote in his memoirs: "The coup had already been decided secretly by the leaders of the Ukrainian National Council in August 1918 as it became clear that Austria could not escape catastrophe. The organizer of the coup was to be a liutenant in the Austrian army, Petro Bubela, a determined, quiet, even-tempered, and discreet man." The plan was thwarted to some extent by the sudden death of Folys. Nonetheless, the "trio for carrying out the military coup" performed its main task in that it not only designed the scenario for the transfer of power but also identified the pro-Ukrainian forces inside the imperial army and consolidated them in a system of secret organizations. The trio was led politically by a commission established by the Ukrainian National Council and consisting of Kyveliuk, Tsehelsky, and Paneiko.[39] According to Tsehelsky, this commission, which was also secret, was already in a position on 25 October 1918 "to inform the delegates of the Ukrainian National Council in Lviv and the delegates in Vienna generally about preparations for the coup on the territory between the Zbruch and the San."[40]

But the implementation of the UNDP People's Committee's plan was an entirely different matter. According to Stepan Baran, the People's Committee had set up its own commission to carry out the coup, and it actually made preparations. Baran wrote in 1923 that it was his initiative to establish the military committee: "Knowing that

36 Ibid.

37 Ibid., 26.

38 Ibid., 17.

39 Ibid., 35.

40 Ibid., 36.

a military organization would be necessary in order to perform our task, we decided at the second meeting to seek out reliable people among the Ukrainian officers in Lviv and set up our own military committee with the task of carrying out the military organization. I turned to Cossack officers known to me, Liubomyr Ohonovsky, Vasyl Baranyk, and Ivan Vatran. We enlarged the commission by bringing in Dr. Stepan Tomashivsky, Dr. Mykhailo Lozynsky, and Omelian Saievych."[41] The officers called upon to join the commission were in agreement with the creation of their own Ukrainian military committee. There is reason to believe that this committee played a decisive role in the events of 1 November 1918. Its membership and essential tasks were later confirmed by one of the participants in those events. Vasyl Paneiko wrote that, having returned from Switzerland, he was active in the organization of a secret committee that included Okhrymovych, Stepan Rudnytsky, Mykhailo Lozynsky, Stepan Tomashivsky, and Osyp Nazaruk.[42] The meetings of the committee, which was in touch with the military committee, were held in the museum of the Shevchenko Scientific Society.[43]

On behalf of the committee, Vasyl Paneiko traveled to Bukovyna to make contact with the Ukrainian Legion in order to expedite its move to Lviv and choose the commander of the uprising. He was uncertain about the extent to which the commander of the Legion, Archduke Wilhelm von Habsburg, was committed to the Ukrainian cause and, with the help of Ostap Lutsky, selected Dmytro Vitovsky for that role.[44] In the end, however, he was not happy with this choice, and so, in the military committee, he insisted on naming another organizer for the uprising. He was allowed to travel to Kyiv "in order for the Hetman to select a commander."[45] The Galician politicians had thought of Oleksandr Udovychenko, but the Hetman did not agree.

Stepan Baran invited the Ukrainian otamans Teodor Rozhankovsky and Nykyfor Hirniak to Lviv for consultations. It was then decided that the Ukrainian Legion should organize the military coup. Representatives of the Legion reached agreement on their plans with the military committee and began to prepare the uprising.[46] Knowing that the other Ukrainian parties did not have such a dense

41 Baran, "Do istoriï povstannia ZUNR," 1–2.

42 Vasyl' Paneiko, "Pered Pershym Lystopada," *Dilo*, 1 November 1928: 1.

43 "Viis'kovyi komitet," *Dilo*, 1 November 1928: 2.

44 Paneiko, "Pered Pershym Lystopada," 1.

45 Ibid.

46 Baran, "Do istoriï povstannia ZUNR."

network in the regions, Baran decided to consolidate forces for the preparation of the uprising that was to take place on 1 November and invited the best-known politicians from the districts, regardless of party affiliation, to a meeting. His main demand to the political activists was that they establish district committees to assume the functions of state administration at the given time.[47]

It was decided that the general political direction of the state-building process should be entrusted to an assembly designated as the "Ukrainian National Council."[48] This decision was taken on 10 October 1918 at a session of the UPR at which Petrushevych, Romanchuk, Metropolitan Andrei Sheptytsky, and other prominent Ukrainian representatives were present. Yevhen Levytsky was given the task of producing the statute for the Ukrainian National Council, and Bachynsky was made responsible for the convocation of the constituent assembly.[49]

On 18 and 19 October 1918, an assembly was held in Lviv with public officials and representatives of the various political parties. Those attending included the Ukrainian representatives in the Vienna parliament and in the Galician Diet, along with representatives of the Greek Catholic Church. On the basis of Emperor Karl's manifesto, the assembly declared itself to be the Ukrainian National Council with parliamentary authority. At the head of the Council was a representative to the Vienna parliament, Yevhen Petrushevych. In accordance with the principle of national self-determination, the Council proclaimed the formation of a Ukrainian state on Ukrainian ethnic territories in Austria-Hungary. Although not all the territories claimed were represented at the assembly, the National Council declared that the new state included not only Eastern Galicia and Northern Bukovyna but also Transcarpathia (which had no representatives at the assembly).[50] The relation of the newly proclaimed state to Austria-Hungary remained undefined. That would depend on the decisions taken by the Entente with regard to the future of the Monarchy.[51] In the event that the Entente decided to dissolve the Monarchy, the Ukrainian National Council reserved for itself the right to form a

---

47 Ibid.

48 Lozyns'kyi, *Halychyna,* 27.

49 Baran, "Do istoriï povstannia ZUNR."

50 Kost' Levyts'kyi, *Istoriia politychnoï dumky halyts'kykh ukraïntsiv. Na pidstavi spomyniv i dokumentiv* (Lviv, 1926), 106.

51 O. Krasivs'kyi, *Halychyna u pershii chverti XX st.: Problema ukraïns'ko-pol's'kykh stosunkiv* (Lviv, 2000), 107.

union of Ukrainian territories in Austria-Hungary with Ukrainian territory previously part of the Russian Empire.

The resolutions announced by Petrushevych to the assembly of 19 October 1918 did not satisfy the representatives of the Ukrainian Social Democratic Party. Some of the Radicals and National Democrats were also opposed. The problem was the absence of any clause providing for the unification of Ukrainian territory in Austria-Hungary with the Ukrainian State.[52] On the following day, Petrushevych headed a delegation to Vienna for further negotiations with the Austro-Hungarian emperor. Some of the participants in the Lviv assembly hoped for the proclamation of an independent Ukrainian state and demanded a complete break with Vienna. The political leaders of the Ukrainian movement in the Habsburg Monarchy based their position on the claim that their forces were too weak to be able to declare the unity of all territories in an all-embracing Ukraine. The Ukrainians in Cisleithania were not such a significant revolutionary force that they could separate their territory from Austria-Hungary, confront Poland's ambitions for power in the region, and implement a unification with the Ukrainian People's Republic, which had existed since the beginning of 1918.

But it was not just the relative weakness of the Ukrainian movement in Austria-Hungary that led to this moderate decision. When they thought about an all-inclusive Ukraine, the Austrian Ukrainians knew they could not count on political agreement with the Ukrainian State of Hetman Skoropadsky. There had been poor relations right from the start between the Ukrainian State and Austro-Hungarian politicians. The Hetman was mistrustful of Germany's Austro-Hungarian ally. The plans of the Galician politicians and the Habsburg Monarchy regarding the future of the Ukrainian political order worried him. He championed a plan for a "Greater Ukraine" that would include not only all ethnic Ukrainian territories but also the Crimea and the Kuban. The Austro-Hungarians favored a "Little Russian" solution, with Eastern Galicia and Northern Bukovyna remaining outside, or a unification of all Ukrainian territory with the Habsburg Crown. Skoropadsky was especially disturbed by the "Greek Catholic" plan for the postwar period. According to that plan, the Habsburg Archduke Wilhelm, whose Ukrainian name was Vasyl Vyshyvany, would mount the Ukrainian throne and unite all Ukrainian territory in a personal union with the Habsburg Crown. Galician Ukrainian

---

52 Lozyns'kyi, *Halychyna*, 31.

support for that plan was the cause of the intra-Ukrainian conflict. But what most divided the Ukrainians on both sides of the border were their conceptions of Ukrainian statehood, the nation, and the Greek Catholic Church.[53]

The activities of Archduke Wilhelm not only provoked Hetman Skoropadsky's resistance but also created confusion in the plans of the Galician politicians. Not all of them shared the idea of a monarchist future under the house of Habsburg. Most of them did not know what the archduke's plans were. Unlike the majority of the Galician Ukrainian politicians, however, Wilhelm had had a good deal of personal experience of the Hetman. In a letter of 18 October 1918 to Metropolitan Sheptytsky, he warned against a union of Galicia and Bukovyna with the Ukrainian State.[54] In this letter he described Skoropadsky as a "colossus with feet of clay" that could come crashing down at any moment and bury with it any hope of Ukrainian independence. In his view, the optimal form of statehood would be national autonomy within the borders of the Habsburg state. In the same letter, he expressed his agreement with the strategy and plans of the group around Kost Levytsky.

That Ukrainian politicians, as late as October 1918, did not want a complete break with Austria-Hungary is demonstrated by the fact that, at the session of the Ukrainian National Council on 19 October that decided on the composition of delegations, the Council chose not only a Galician delegation under Kost Levytsky and a Bukovynian delegation under Omelian Popovych but also an executive delegation in Vienna.[55] The National Council found it extremely difficult to make a complete break with Vienna. Its presidium continued to negotiate with the Austro-Hungarian government as if it were not aware of the catastrophic situation in Vienna. On 23 October, when the Ukrainian delegation informed the Austrian prime minister, Max Hussarek von Heinlein, about the decision of the Ukrainian National Council in Lviv, they assured him that the new state would maintain close links with the empire. They wanted the prime minister to appoint Levytsky governor of Galicia so that he could introduce reforms that

---

53 Ia. Pelens'kyi, "Peredmova: Spohady Het'mana Pavla Skoropads'koho (kinets' 1917–hruden' 1918)," in Pavlo Skoropads'kyi, *Spohady (kinets' 1917–hruden' 1918)* (Kyiv and Philadelphia, 1995), 21.

54 TsDIA Lviv, f. 358, op. 3, spr. 166, 36–40.

55 Lozyns'kyi, *Halychyna*, 31.

would give the Ukrainians predominance over the Poles.[56] What is also remarkable is the fact that, not just in October but even after the proclamation of the Western Ukrainian People's Republic, a significant number of Ukrainian politicians remained in Vienna, even the president of Western Ukraine, Yevhen Petrushevych.

The Race against the Poles

The Ukrainians were forced to act quickly by news of the planned arrival of the Polish Liquidation Commission, formed in Cracow on 28 October 1918, which was to take over power in the region. Lviv was to come under Polish rule on 2–3 November. The decisive action of the Poles made it necessary for the Ukrainians to be more determined.[57] The Lviv delegation began concrete preparations on 25 October. Under the leadership of Roman Perfetsky, an organizational bureau was created that issued instructions at district and local levels for the establishment of Ukrainian rule. On 31 October, the People's Committee of the UNDP entrusted all preparations to the delegation of the Ukrainian National Council in Lviv.[58]

Polish preparations for the proclamation of an independent state, unlike those of the Ukrainians, were more systematic and better organized. No one had any doubts as far as a future renewal of Poland was concerned. As early as 15 September 1917, the Regency Council of the Kingdom of Poland was established, with the agreement of Germany and Austria-Hungary. This was the first and most important step toward the creation of a Polish state administration for all Polish territories. On 7 October 1918 the Regency Council proclaimed the independence of Poland and, on the next day, took over command of troops from the occupying Central Powers. As the supreme organ of the Polish state, the Regency Council declared that it was necessary to establish both economic and political independence, guaranteed by international treaty, as well as territorial integrity.[59] The goal of Poland's political leadership was the unification of all of Poland's "historical" territory, and it regarded the problem of Galicia as an "internal Polish affair." This made the outbreak of Polish-Ukrainian conflict practically unavoidable.[60]

---

56 Krasivs'kyi, *Halychyna u pershii chverti XX st.*, 108.

57 Mahochi, *Istoriia Ukraïny*, 439.

58 Levyts'kyi, "Natsional'no-demokratychne storonnytstvo v 1918 r."

59 Soldatenko, *Ukraïna v revoliutsiinu dobu*, 314.

60 Lozyns'kyi, *Halychyna*, 36–37.

In all their preparations for the founding of new states, both Poland and Ukraine continued to look to Vienna, still the capital of the empire. The Liquidation Commission under Wincenty Witos, established in Cracow on 28 October, proclaimed the takeover of power in all of Galicia and informed the Austrian prime minister, Heinrich Lammasch, and the Galician governor, Karl von Huyn. The Poles, considering the transfer of power from the Austrian governor to the Polish side legitimate and justified, planned a journey of their representatives to Lviv, where this act was to take place. The Ukrainian National Council also proclaimed its authority over the territory. Neither the Poles nor the Ukrainians paid any attention to what the other side was doing, but both wanted a legitimate transfer of power from the Galician governor. The Ukrainian delegation in Vienna had apparently succeeded in getting recognition from the Austrian Council of Ministers of the right of the Ukrainians to their own state, but that decision never reached Lviv. Therefore the Galician governor, von Huyn, did not have the formal authority to relinquish power and transfer it to the Ukrainians. In response to the demands of the Ukrainian delegation, he declared on 31 October that he would not transfer power to either the Ukrainians or the Poles, since the problem would have to be resolved by a peace conference.[61] But there is no agreement about this fact. Some politicians declared that Prime Minister Lammasch, in response to the demands of the Vienna delegation of the Ukrainian National Council, had instructed the Galician governor to hand over power to the Ukrainian representatives, but that the telegram with this instruction had been intercepted by the Poles in Cracow.[62]

During the night of 31 October/1 November the Ukrainian military command, led by an officer of the Ukrainian Legion, Dmytro Vitovsky, carried out the uprising, seized power in the Galician capital, and later took administrative control of more than fifty districts. In its appeal to the "Ukrainian people," the Ukrainian National Council announced the establishment of a Ukrainian state: "The Ukrainian state and its supreme organ, the Ukrainian National Council, were established according to your will on 19 October in the Ukrainian lands of the former Austro-Hungarian Monarchy. The Ukrainian National Council has this day taken power in the capital, Lviv, and on the whole territory of the Ukrainian state."[63]

---

61 Levyts'kyi, *Istoriia politychnoï dumky halyts'kykh ukraïntsiv*, 131.

62 Mykhailo Demkovych-Dobrians'kyi, *Ukraïns'ko-pol's'ki stosunky u XIX storichchi* (Munich, 1969), 16.

63 Lozyns'kyi, *Halychyna*, 42ff., 58.

Western Ukraine's Struggle for Survival

The Ukrainian National Council announced that until political power was properly reorganized, the local Ukrainian district and village organizations would continue to carry out their usual functions. All soldiers of Ukrainian nationality were mobilized to defend the young state. A special summons was issued to Ukrainian soldiers in the Austro-Hungarian army outside Galicia. They were to return as rapidly as possible to their new state and serve in its defense. Until a new Ukrainian army was created, the maintenance of public order and defense would be carried out by so-called military units, which would include members of the general public capable of bearing arms.

Everyone living on its territory, regardless of nationality or religion, would be a citizen of the new Ukrainian state. National minorities (Poles, Jews, Germans) were guaranteed equal rights and would elect their own representatives to the Ukrainian National Council. All former laws would remain in force on the territory of the Ukrainian state except those that contradicted the principles of the new state. Once the new state structure had been consolidated, a constitutional assembly would be elected on the basis of direct and universal franchise. Jurists would be charged with getting to work immediately on drafting a constitution.

The seizure of power in Lviv was peaceful, and the leadership of the National Council rejected the suggestion that three hundred leading representatives of the Polish population should be arrested as security in case of Polish resistance. The new Ukrainian government did not want to provoke any violence on the part of the Poles. Nevertheless, on 1 November, the Poles began to mobilize their forces for battle against the Ukrainians. In Lviv, a Polish National Committee was established under the leadership of Tadeusz Cieński. The military leader of Polish forces was Czesław Mączyński.[64] The battle began for the key parts of the city.[65] Unfortunately for the Ukrainians, the Ukrainian Legion did not arrive on time from Chernivtsi. The Legion was supposed to defend the city while the rest of the Ukrainian military forces were being organized. The fact that the Legion did not arrive until three days later had a negative effect on the defensive capacity of the Ukrainian forces. The first military units that fought against the Poles and later joined the Legion were the basis on which the Ukrainian Galician Army would be built, the army of Western Ukraine.

---

64 Mieczysław Wrzosek, *Wojny o granice Polski Odrodzonej 1918–1921* (Warsaw, 1992), 168.

65 Mykola Lytvyn and Kim Naumenko, *Istoriia ZUNR* (Lviv, 1995), 47.

The fighting between the Poles and Ukrainians in Lviv lasted from the very first day on which the Western Ukrainian state was proclaimed until 21 November. The leadership of the new state was then forced to leave the city along with its troops. In this short time, however, the Ukrainians managed to establish the most important state agencies. On 9 November 1918 the National Council established its provisional executive organ, the State Secretariat of the Western Ukrainian People's Republic, which then functioned as government from 13 November.[66] On the same day, the constitutional foundation of the new state was established, the "Provisional Basic Law on the Sovereign Independence of the Ukrainian Lands of the Former Austro-Hungarian Monarchy," and the official name of the new state was the Western Ukrainian People's Republic (*Zakhidnoukraïns'ka Narodna Respublika*, ZUNR). In a very short time, the ZUNR had been able to develop the essential juridical foundation to regulate the most important areas of public life: organization of the military, the provisional organization of legal jurisdiction, official language, the educational system, citizenship, and land reform. An analysis of the documents shows that the basic principles underlying ZUNR law were democratic and, to some extent, liberal. The state that claimed, even if only declaratively, 70,000 square kilometers and 6 million people did not intend to become monoethnic.[67] The ZUNR guaranteed its national minorities freedom of development and proportional representation in the supreme legislative body, even if, in practice, the national minorities refused to send representatives to the Ukrainian National Council and it remained in reality an exclusively Ukrainian body.[68]

On 25 October 1918, simultaneously with the events in Galicia, the Ukrainian Regional Committee of Bukovyna was established in Chernivtsi under the leadership of Omelian Popovych as the Bukovynian central administration. The committee lacked both a widespread network in the province and support in the city. Two days later, Romanian representatives in the Vienna parliament established the Romanian National Council, which began immediately to secure its power in Bukovyna. On 3 November, the Ukrainians held a mass

66 Mykola Chubatyi, *Derzhavnyi lad na Zakhidnii oblasti Ukraïns'koï Narodnoï Respubliky* (Lviv, 1921), 16–17.

67 V. S. Kul'chyts'kyi, M. I. Nastiuk, and B. I. Tyshchyk, *Istoriia derzhavy i prava Ukraïny* (Lviv, 1996), 177.

68 Pavlo Hai-Nyzhnyk, *UNR ta ZUNR: stanovlennia orhaniv vlady i natsional'ne derzhavotvorennia (1917–1920)* (Kyiv, 2010), 212.

assembly in Chernivtsi that declared Bukovyna part of a united Ukrainian state. Popovych became president of the province. In view of the internal weakness of the Ukrainian movement in Bukovyna, and based on its experience with Austria-Hungary's constitutional management of inter-ethnic problems in the Habsburg Monarchy, the Ukrainian Regional Committee began negotiations with moderate Romanian representatives. They were able to reach agreement with only one of the Romanians, Aurel Onciul, who had limited influence on the situation. On 6 November, the provincial administration of Bukovyna handed power to Popovych and Onciul, who proceeded to act on behalf of both the Ukrainian and Romanian national organizations. These institutions would govern the respective parts of the province in which their ethnic group was in the majority. The Romanian National Council, however, led by Jancu Flondor, had no intention of sharing power with the Ukrainians. The council's leaders immediately asked Romania to send troops.[69] The Romanian army did not hesitate and, on 11 November, occupied the whole of Bukovyna, including Chernivtsi. Although Bukovyna was only nominally part of the Western Ukrainian People's Republic, it was military intervention from outside that brought down its legitimate government.[70]

There were no representatives of Transcarpathia at the meeting of the Ukrainian National Council on 19 October. The separatist process began here much later than in Galicia and Bukovyna, and under very different circumstances. The new Hungarian Republic under Mihály Károlyi laid claim to all territories that had been under the jurisdiction of the Hungarian Kingdom.[71] Among the Transcarpathian regions, the most strongly pro-Ukrainian were Máramarossziget (present-day Sighetu Marmației) and the area around the city of Huszt (present-day Khust). However, the fact remains that, apart from a brief presence of Ukrainian troops, Transcarpathia was never under ZUNR control.

The State Secretariat and the National Council left Lviv on 21 November and moved to Ternopil. The loss of the capital had a negative effect on the fighting morale of the Ukrainian Galician Army. When the Poles finally captured Lviv, they not only closed Ukrainian institutions and carried out searches and arrests but also instigated a bloody pogrom against the Jewish population of the city.

---

69 Mahochi, *Istoriia Ukraïny*, 444.

70 I. Piddubnyi, "Politychne zhyttia Bukovyny 1918–1940 rr.," in *Bukovyna 1918–1940 rr.: zovnishni vplyvy na vnutrishnii rozvytok* (Chernivtsi, 2005), 58.

71 Mahochi, *Istoriia Ukraïny*, 445.

It has been argued that this pogrom was an act of revenge for Jewish neutrality toward the Ukrainian state, but in reality it was a typical bloody anti-Semitic action that involved robbery, murder, and rape. It is estimated that 78 people were killed and 453 wounded in this pogrom. Altogether 13,375 people had their belongings plundered or lost their homes.[72] Ukrainians, too, were not spared by the new authorities. Those regarded as the greatest security risks were sent to an internment camp in Dąbie, while the rest, including priests, were imprisoned in Lviv.

The Ukrainian government remained in Ternopil until 2 January 1919, when it moved to Stanyslaviv (present-day Ivano-Frankivsk). A meeting of the Ukrainian National Council was held here on 3 January and declared its intention to unite with the Ukrainian People's Republic "in an undivided sovereign republic."[73] The act of union, which took place on 22 January 1919 in St. Sophia Square in Kyiv, was purely symbolic. Following the union with the UNR, the official name of the ZUNR was Western Province of the Ukrainian People's Republic. The two governing bodies, however, continued to operate separately. In spite of the union and the military assistance and food supplies that the Galicians obtained from the UNR, the leadership in the Western Province continued to follow its own line in both domestic policy and international relations.

The war between Western Ukraine and Poland continued with mixed results.[74] On two occasions, the Ukrainians almost reached Lviv but never succeeded in capturing it. Attempts on the part of the Entente to mediate failed a number of times. Symon Petliura, the head of the Directory in Kyiv, visited Western Ukraine once but was really on the side of the Entente. He tried to get the Western Ukrainians to compromise, hoping that they would then be able to redirect their army from fighting the Poles to fighting the Bolsheviks. For the Galician Ukrainians, however, the Poles were the main enemy. They could not let the Poles take their territory, to say nothing of making an agreement that would amount to a capitulation.[75] All attempts by the Entente to end the Polish-Ukrainian conflict would have been at

72 M. Lytvyn, "Stolytsia ZUNR," in *Istoriia L'vova. U tr'okh tomakh*, vol. 3 (Lviv, 2007), 25; Christoph Mick, "Ethnische Gewalt und Pogrome in Lemberg 1914 und 1941," *Osteuropa* 53, no. 12 (December 2003): 1810–30.

73 Lytvyn and Naumenko, *Istoriia ZUNR*, 126.

74 For a detailed account, see chapter 4f in the present volume.

75 Stakhiv, *Zakhidna Ukraïna*, 48ff.

the expense of the Western Ukrainian People's Republic, which is why they all failed. The final warning to the Western Ukrainians was the threat from the mission led by Joseph Berthélemy on 28 February 1919 that if the ZUNR rejected the Entente's conditions, it would face the army of General Józef Haller, a Polish army created in France. It was well armed and would pose a serious threat to the weakened Ukrainian Galician army. Under cover of the fight against the Bolsheviks, it was moved to Eastern Europe to fight the ZUNR.

By June 1919, after exhausting battles, the Petrushevych government controlled only a tiny amount of territory, consisting of parts of the Borshchiv, Husiatyn, Chortkiv, and Horodenka districts. On 9 June, faced with the threat of defeat, Petrushevych abolished the office of president and the State Secretariat and proclaimed himself dictator. The government and the State Secretariat were replaced by the plenipotentiaries of the Dictator and the Military Chancellery. He removed the military command, which led to some short-term successes. On 25 June, however, Poland received official permission from Paris to extend its military operations over the whole territory as far as the Zbruch, which amounted to approval from the Entente for the occupation of Galicia.[76] Approval for the deployment of the Haller army on the Galician front came at the same time. Polish troops reached the Zbruch on 17 June and forced the Western Ukrainian government out of Galicia.

The brevity of the existence of the Western Ukrainian People's Republic had to do with a number of factors. Among the internal factors were the asymmetrical structure of Ukrainian society (the complete absence of a nobility and a stratum of major industrialists), the lack of competent officials (a small number of Ukrainians in the Austrian civil service), the shortage of experienced military commanders, and weak support for the Ukrainian demand for independence among the urban population. There was no Ukrainian majority in almost all the larger and smaller towns in Galicia; furthermore, neither their economic nor social status enabled them to have significant influence on the socioeconomic and political conditions in the towns. Among the external factors were the international community's lack of familiarity with the Ukrainian question and the unfavorable international circumstances.

---

76 "Sprawy polskie na konferencji pokojowej w Paryżu w 1919 r." Dokumenty i materiały, vol. 2 (Warsaw, 1967), 353.

3a. Military Operations

Peter Lieb and Wolfram Dornik

The Invasion of Ukraine by the Central Powers, February to May 1918

"It is the strangest war that I have ever experienced—it is being carried out almost exclusively on the railway and with railway carriages. They put a handful of infantrymen with machine guns and a cannon on the track and head off for the next station, which they capture, then arrest the Bolsheviks, bring in more troops by rail, and then set off again. But this has, in any case, the attraction of novelty."[1] That is how the chief of staff of *Ober Ost*, Major General Max Hoffmann, described the advance of German troops at the beginning of Operation *Faustschlag* (Punch), the occupation of parts of the Baltic states, Belarus, and Ukraine.

The original deployment of forces for Operation *Faustschlag* was very small. Army Group Linsingen was set to invade Ukraine with six weak divisions[2] and one cavalry brigade.[3] Their destination, according to the orders of their commander in chief, was Kyiv. The Germans initially advanced only along the railway lines and reached the Ukrainian capital very quickly because most of the Ukrainian railway personnel supported the German (and, later, Austro-Hungarian) troops. On 2 March the 45th Landwehr Division entered the suburbs of Kyiv. On the following day, the whole city was liberated from Bolshevik rule. This did not mean, however, the complete overthrow of Bolshevik power, since they still controlled the east of the country. The key question for the German military leadership was how to organize this further eastward advance. A proper plan of operations

---

1 *Die Aufzeichnungen des Generalmajors Max Hoffmann*, ed. Karl Friedrich Nowak, vol. 1 (Berlin, 1929), Eintrag v. 22.2.1918.

2 ÖStA, KA, FA, AOK, OpAbt, Kt. 466, Nr. 1090, Militärischer Stimmungsbericht über die Lage im Osten, 26.2.1918.

3 These were the 91st, 215th, and 224th Infantry Divisions, the 7th und 45th Landwehr Divisions, as well as the 2nd Cavalry Division, joined later by the 4th Bavarian Cavalry Brigade. See Reichsarchiv, ed., *Der Weltkrieg, 1914–1918. Die Kriegführung im Sommer und Herbst 1918. Die Ereignisse außerhalb der Westfront bis November 1918*, vol. 13 (Berlin, 1942), 376. For a general account of the military operations in Ukraine, see ibid., 376–99. On the problems of official historical writing between the wars, see Markus Pöhlmann, *Kriegsgeschichte und Geschichtspolitik. Der Erste Weltkrieg. Die amtliche deutsche Militärgeschichtsschreibung, 1914–1956* (Paderborn, 2002).

simply did not exist.[4] Kyiv was taken, but then the Germans found it necessary to advance on "the Bolshevik center, the city of Kharkiv."[5] Then, in April, they moved into the Donets Basin toward Rostov on the Don.[6] Moreover, in order to gain complete control of the east-west railway line in Ukraine, they had to take the railway junction at Homel, which was on Russian territory. All these ad hoc military decisions demonstrate the previous lack of interest in this country. Throughout the campaign, the Germans had to improvise in order to make up for inadequate military preparations. At the beginning of March, the troops were increased to nine divisions, later to twelve, organized in three army corps: *Korps Gronau* (later renamed the XXXXI Reserve Corps) in the north covered the border with Soviet Russia; Groener's I Army Corps in the center was to advance on Poltava and Kharkiv; in the south, *Korps Knoerzer* was to advance in the direction of the Sea of Azov and later into the Donets Basin.[7] The Germans wanted in particular to gain control of the fertile agricultural land in the Crimea, while providing the new Ukrainian state with a solid economic foundation by taking the coal reserves of the Donets Basin. In the far south, from 6 March, the 52nd Corps advanced from Romania toward the Black Sea ports with two infantry divisions, the Bavarian Cavalry Division, and the Austro-Hungarian 145th Infantry Brigade, which all came from the 9th Army (Army Group Mackensen).[8]

Austria-Hungary had taken part in the operation only after 28 February in order to prevent its German allies from getting all the rich booty. This decision, however, was a difficult one. Emperor Karl had resisted being part of this operation, which was at first solely German. But the Ukrainians kept up the pressure. On 25 February, two emissaries came to Eduard von Böhm-Ermolli, the commander

---

4 *Von Brest-Litovsk zur deutschen Novemberrevolution. Aus den Tagebüchern, Briefen und Aufzeichnungen von Alfons Paquet, Wilhelm Groener und Albert Hopman. März bis November 1918*, ed. Winfried Baumgart (Göttingen, 1971), 288. Letter from Groener to his wife, 9 March 1918: "The measures taken by Obost and Linsingen for the Ukrainian operation are not impressive; they were taken on the spur of the moment and given little thought."

5 HStA Stuttgart, M 46/21, Korps Knoerzer, Abt. Ia, Nr. 1707, Die Operationen des Korps Knoerzer nach Einnahme von Kiew bis zur Einnahme von Rostow, 29.5.1918.

6 BA-MA, N 46/171, Heeresgruppe Eichhorn, Abt. Ia, Nr. 14902 op an Ob.Ost, 9.4.1918.

7 Reichsarchiv, ed., *Der Weltkrieg, 1914–1918*, 378, 384.

8 These were the 217th Infantry Division and the 11th Landwehr Division. The 212th Infantry Division came later. See Österreichisches Bundesministerium für Landesverteidigung – Kriegsarchiv, ed., *Österreich-Ungarns letzter Krieg 1914–1918*, vol. 7, *Das Kriegsjahr 1918* (Vienna, 1938), Supplement VII, 5, Map "Vormarsch der k.u.k. 2. Armee bis Odessa 28. Februar bis Mitte März 1918."

of the 2nd Army.[9] "In the name of the whole Ukrainian people" and "on their own authority, in the absence of any link with the Central Rada," they asked for Austro-Hungarian assistance in the struggle against the Bolsheviks. On the previous day, the troops selected for the advance had already been given their orders.[10] Böhm-Ermolli gave the instructions: "The troops advancing into Ukraine should be reminded once again that our intervention is to offer peaceful support for the new and as yet unconsolidated state and should under no circumstances lead to hostilities. Special measures will be necessary to protect supplies in the rear of the troops and for the proper evaluation of the country's resources. Waste nothing!"[11]

Like the Germans, the Austro-Hungarian troops advanced along the railway lines from the borders of Galicia and Bukovyna into Podilia.[12] Their first task was to secure the railway line to Odesa in order to guarantee supplies and the export of provisions. Only when they had reached Odesa did the Austro-Hungarians begin to expand their operations and advance further eastward. But already in these first operations there were constant disputes and conflicts between the Germans and the Austro-Hungarians over their respective zones and plans of operation and sharing of railway capacity. Unlike in Italy or in the campaigns against Serbia in 1915 or against Romania in 1916, in the Ukrainian operation the Central Powers were unable to agree on a joint command, even though Emperor Wilhelm of Germany had sought agreement on this a number of times with the Austro-Hungarian emperor. Of course, a German was supposed to be in overall command. But the Austrians, as was often the case, had a strong aversion to the typical representatives of the Prussian military. They were annoyed at "the dictatorial tone of General [Erich] Ludendorff" and rejected "the unlikeable [Alexander von] Linsingen." Their suggestion that Böhm-Ermolli should take command with a German chief of staff[13] would have inversely reflected the actual relation of forces between them. The Germans, of course, refused to accept this.[14]

---

9 They were Dr. Stepura, commissar for the Podilia gubernia, and Major Mykolaiv, staff officer for the commander in chief of the southwestern front: ÖStA, KA, FA, AOK, OpAbt, Kt. 466, Nr. 1095, Telegramm des 2. Armeekommandos an AOK und Obost, 26.2.1918.

10 ÖStA, KA, AdT, Kt. 754, FJB 13, 6. Tagebuch des Feldjägerbataillon Nr. 13, Einträge vom 26. und 27.2.1918.

11 ÖStA, KA, FA, AOK, OpAbt, Kt. 467, Nr. 1110, Hindenburg an Arz via Cramon, 26.2.1918.

12 See the uncritical account of Austro-Hungarian military operations in Ukraine: *Österreich-Ungarns letzter Krieg*, 103–50, 406–16, 798–800.

13 TNA, GFM 6/36, Telegramm Nr. 24, von Mumm an AA, 18.3.1918.

14 For more detail, see chapter 3b in the present volume.

The growing rivalry between the two allies over political influence and honor on the battlefield had been there from the start of the war and was now set to continue in Ukraine.[15] Tension between these allied powers was not new,[16] but it reached a new intensity in the spring of 1918.[17] This was the case not only in the course of the military operations but also later, during the whole period of occupation. Wilhelm Groener observed in the German army a "powerful hatred" of the Austrians, and he himself hoped that "the Italians would mount a strong attack" in order to put a brake on the demands from Vienna.[18]

This competitive approach was manifest in the "absurd race"[19] to see who would reach a railway station or town first.[20] As a result, at Slobidka in Podilia, the German Ehrenstein Battalion fell into a trap and suffered great losses.[21] Something similar happened during the capture of Odesa. In this case, it was not just military prestige that was at stake but also economic interests. Both attempted to be the first to gain control of the remaining ships in the harbor and the military supplies stored in the city.[22] However, in spite of these rivalries and mutual dislike, military comradeship functioned more or less at the regional level, as, for instance, in southern Ukraine, with the 52nd Corps under General Robert Kosch.

From mid-March the advance of the Central Powers slowed, especially in the cities along the Black Sea coast and in the eastern

15 The complaints about military recognition continued after the war. See Alfred von Dragoni, "Die Kämpfe um Nikolajew und Cherson im Frühjahr 1918," *Österreichische Wehrzeitung*, no. 18 (1928): 2ff.

16 Holger H. Herwig, *The First World War: Germany and Austria-Hungary, 1914–1918* (London and New York, 1997).

17 Oleh S. Fedyshyn, *Germany's Drive to the East and the Ukrainian Revolution, 1917–1918* (New Brunswick, N.J., 1971), 255.

18 *Von Brest-Litovsk zur deutschen Novemberrevolution*, "Brief an seine Frau v. 9.3.1918," 288. Hoffmann had similar thoughts. See *Die Aufzeichnungen des Generalmajors Max Hoffmann*, vol. 1, Eintrag v. 14.3.1918.

19 *Von Brest-Litovsk zur deutschen Novemberrevolution*, Eintrag v. 7.3.1918, 280.

20 ÖStA, KA, FA, AOK, OpAbt, Kt. 467, Nr. 1153, Hetzjagd Žmerinka–Odessa, 4.3.1918; ÖStA, KA, FA, AOK, OpAbt, Kt. 467, Nr. 1162, Regelung der Verhältnisse in der Ukraina, 5.3.1918; ÖStA, KA, FA, AOK, OpAbt, Kt. 467, Nr. 1164, Arz an Hindenburg, 5.3.1918; ÖStA, KA, FA, AOK, OpAbt, Kt. 467, Nr. 1176, Telegrammsammlung, 6.3.1918; ÖStA, KA, FA, AOK, OpAbt, Kt. 467, Nr. 1177, Ludendorff an Arz, 6.3.1918; ÖStA, KA, AdT, UR 13, Kt. 801, III. Tagebuch, Eintrag v. 25.3.1918.

21 ÖStA, KA, FA, AOK, OpAbt, Kt. 467, Nr. 1211, Vorfälle bei Žmerinka und Slobidka, 20.3.1918. See *Österreich-Ungarns letzter Krieg*, 124. German and Austro-Hungarian losses at Slobidka were three hundred, including seven officers. See *Von Brest-Litovsk zur deutschen Novemberrevolution*, 280.

22 ÖStA, KA, FA, AOK, OpAbt, Kt. 467, Nr. 1273, Vorgänge bei Odessa, 20.3.1918.

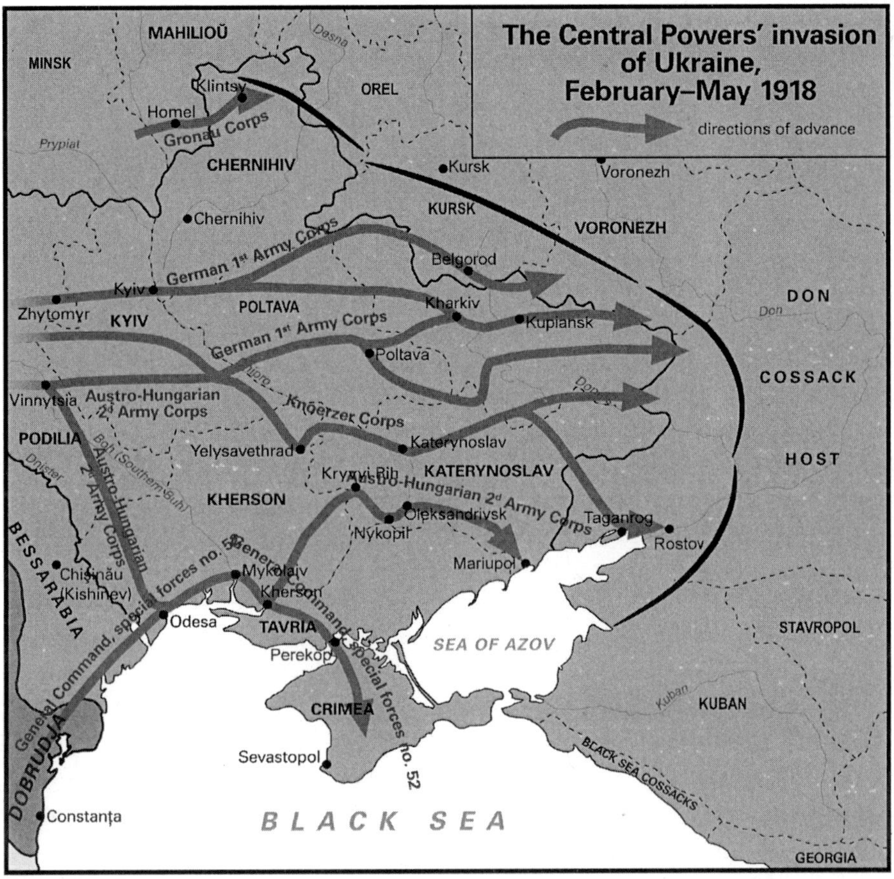

Map 4: The Central Powers' invasion of Ukraine, February to May 1918 (ÖStA, KA, AOK, OpAbt, Kt. 469, No. 1492; ibid., Kt. 308, Fol. 271; Österreichisches Bundesministerium für Landesverteidigung – Kriegsarchiv, ed., *Österreich-Ungarns letzter Krieg 1914–1918*, vol. 7, supplement 6; Reichsarchiv, ed., *Der Weltkrieg, 1914–1918*, vol. 13, 376–86)

industrial region of Ukraine.[23] The retreating Bolsheviks blew up bridges and railway lines. Heavy losses were sustained in battles for important railway junctions and towns.[24] The advancing troops had to go forward on foot in some places. In some regions there were even major setbacks. In Mykolaiv, for instance, a few days after the German and Austro-Hungarian troops had captured the city, an uprising

23 See the assessment made by the command of the Austro-Hungarian XII Corps in the second half of March: ÖStA, KA, FA, NFA, HHK AK/KorpsKdo, 12. Korps, Kt. 1661, ohne Nr., Beurteilung der Lage durch das XII. Korpskommando, 31.3.1918.

24 See the report of the command of the Austro-Hungarian XII Corps to the 2nd Army: ÖStA, KA, FA, NFA, HHK AK/AGKdo, 2. Armee, OpAK, Kt. 308, 1918 Situations- und Tagesmeldungen, Op. Nr. 3454/8, 2. Armeekommando an QuAbt des 2. Armeekommandos, 18.4.1918.

began that lasted from 22 to 25 March: the staff of 52nd Corps briefly found themselves in the midst of a full-fledged battle.[25] Kherson had to be evacuated on 20 March because of an uprising that began on the day after the city was occupied, and it was not retaken until 5 April. There were also heavy battles in Kharkiv at the beginning of April and in Rostov in early May.[26]

Naval forces were also employed. On 12 April Austria-Hungary's Danube Flotilla arrived in Odesa and was able to support the advancing troops with minor actions at sea and on rivers. German submarines were also in use to capture departing cargo ships or warships of the old tsarist navy that had been taken over by the Bolsheviks.[27] Bulgarian and Turkish ships joined the action later.

But in spite of these reinforcements, the obvious shortage of troops was increasingly having its effect as the armies advanced. In mid-March, Ludendorff needed more troops for the large German spring offensive in the West, but *Ober Ost* successfully insisted that at the moment no troops could be withdrawn. In fact, in order to secure the harvest, the 1st Cavalry Division and the 92nd Infantry Division had to be sent to Ukraine. The advance continued eastward, but every kilometer of land gained also meant a further stretching of the supply routes, and consequently even more troops were then needed to secure the railway lines.[28]

With the capture of Rostov on the Don on 8 May 1918, the campaign in Ukraine finally ended. On 28 May Kaiser Wilhelm issued a decree that there should be no further military operations beyond the already captured territory in order not to endanger the peace with Russia.[29] In spite of this, however, skirmishes on the border with Bolshevik Russia continued until the autumn of 1918. In mid-June the Bolsheviks even attempted a large amphibious landing at Taganrog, to which we shall return below.

---

25 Letters from Kosch to his wife: BA-MA, N 754/10.

26 In Kharkiv, the Germans lost sixty, including three officers and thirty-nine wounded, among them two officers. Seven soldiers were missing. In Rostov, *Korps Knoerzer* lost twenty-one soldiers, with fifty-four wounded. See BA-MA, N 46/171, Heeresgruppe Eichhorn-Kiew, Lage am 10.4.1918 morgens; BA-MA, N 46/171, Heeresgruppe Eichhorn-Kiew, Lage am 13.5.1918. In its situation report, the Supreme Command of the Austro-Hungarian forces emphasized the increasing intensity of the battles: ÖStA, KA, FA, AOK, OpAbt, Kt. 469, Nr. 1492, Über die Lage XII., 23.3.–25.4.1918.

27 ÖStA, AVA, Nachlässe, Nachlass: Böhm-Ermolli, B 1466, Mikrofilm B 1466, Eintrag v. 12.4.1918.

28 Reichsarchiv, ed., *Der Weltkrieg, 1914–1918*, 378.

29 Ibid., 338.

Although this "railway campaign"[30] in Ukraine impressed contemporaries and excited the military "railway experts" in particular,[31] this novel experience received very little attention or examination in the interwar period.[32] The conditions of the "railway campaign" were too unique, and a repetition of that constellation in the future seemed too improbable for the military to believe that they could draw general lessons from it. Nevertheless, there were certain principles evident in the operations in Ukraine that resembled the overwhelming military successes of the German *Wehrmacht* more than twenty years later in their *Blitzkrieg* campaigns against Poland, France, and other countries.[33]

The Central Powers did not operate on a broad front, as so often happened in this war, but aimed at winning key points.[34] *Korps Knoerzer,* which acted as a spearhead in the first weeks, summarized this principle succinctly: "In view of the strength of our troops, it was not possible to occupy the whole of Ukraine. What was needed, therefore, was to capture the provincial capitals and the main commercial centers quickly."[35] But, as was the case in the lightning campaign against the Soviet Union in the summer of 1941, such tactics had the long-term disadvantage that the hinterland could be controlled only superficially with a small number of troops and, beyond the main transport routes, hostile partisan groups were able to form.[36]

In order to achieve a successful advance away from the railway lines, the German troops in Ukraine in 1918 created "flying columns"

---

30 See *Österreich-Ungarns letzter Krieg*, 7: 121.

31 Wilhelm Groener, *Der Weltkrieg und seine Probleme. Rückschau und Ausblick* (Berlin, 1920); Stefan von Velsen, "Deutsche Generalstabsoffiziere im 1. Weltkrieg 1914–1918. Erinnerungen," *Die Welt als Geschichte,* no. 16 (1956): 250–93.

32 Shortly after the war ended, Groener wrote: "The advance along the railway in Ukraine in 1918 was particularly exciting. The diversity brought great joy to leaders and troops and showed how control of the railway lines makes it possible to control a large country." See Groener, *Der Weltkrieg und seine Probleme*, 74. On the development of German policy in the interwar period, see Matthias Strohn, *The German Army and the Defence of the Reich: Military Doctrine and the Conduct of the Defensive Battle, 1918–1939* (Cambridge, 2010).

33 See the discussion of this comparison in the chapter "Looking Ahead" in the present volume.

34 The storm troops on the Western Front operated according to this principle, although only tactically. See Bruce Gudmundson, *Stormtrooper Tactics: Innovation in the German Army, 1914–1918* (Westport and London, 1989); Ralf Raths, *Vom Massensturm zur Stoßtrupptaktik. Die deutsche Landkriegstaktik im Spiegel von Dienstvorschriften und Publizistik 1906–1918* (Freiburg, 2009).

35 HStA Stuttgart, M 46/16, Korps Knoerzer, Abt. Ia, Nr. 214, An Generalkommando I. A.K., 6.3.1918.

36 On 22 March Groener wrote urgently to Ludendorff: "We desperately need more troops for these vast spaces, otherwise our authority will go down the drain." See *Von Brest-Litovsk zur deutschen Novemberrevolution*, 317.

equipped with armored vehicles, infantry, and artillery, in other words, ad hoc groups that anticipated the "battle groups" of the Second World War. But these "flying columns" were an exception, used only when working railway lines were not available.[37] The most important means of transport in the First World War, especially in Ukraine, was indeed the railway, closely followed by the horse. In Operation *Faustschlag* the Germans achieved rates of advance that no other army in both world wars was able to repeat and that are difficult to match even today. The US Army, in its "lightning campaign" during Operation Iraqi Freedom in 2003, took twenty days (21 March to 9 April), with the most modern technology, to advance the 550 km from the Kuwait-Iraq border to Baghdad and finally take the city. The Germans in 1918, by comparison, needed only fourteen days (18 February to 3 March) to cover the same distance between Kovel and Kyiv and take control of that city. The remaining advance, over the 900 km to Rostov, engaging in battles along the way, took only another two months.

The speed of the advance had much to do with the fact that officers on the spot were able to react quickly and flexibly to any particular situation, without contacting their superiors. After three years of static trench warfare with murderous artillery fire in the West (and, to a certain degree, also in the East), this mentality was astonishing. At first Linsingen wanted to advance only as far as Kaunas (Kovno), but the continued advance to Kyiv was a result of "pressure from the troops to keep moving forward.... To be surprised by both friend and foe was a pleasure,"[38] as Groener smugly remarked.

The rapid advance of the Central Powers created confusion and amazement among the enemy, as well as among the Ukrainian population. The liaison officer attached to the Foreign Office reported from Ukraine that everywhere there was an "almost fairy-tale dread" of the "approach of the *Germanski*. The maintenance of this moral prestige appears to be the basis for further successes."[39] What was the significance of this "fairy-tale dread"? Did it indicate respect for

---

37 For instance, in the advance of 52nd Corps toward Odesa. See Kosch's letters to his wife: BA-MA, N 754/10.

38 *Von Brest-Litovsk zur deutschen Novemberrevolution*, Eintrag v. 8.3.1918, 285.

39 BArch, R 3101/1314, Bericht über Eindrücke in der Ukraine von Oblt.d.Res. Colin Ross, Verbindungsoffizier der militärischen Stelle des Auswärtigen Amtes. Although Ross only held the rank of first lieutenant, his report aroused great interest at the top levels of the empire. Copies of his report were remarked on favorably by the Foreign Office, the Ministry of the Economy, and the OHL. General Hoffmann also approved of the report. See the correspondence in TNA, GFM 6/35.

the military achievements of the Germans or fear of their use of terror against the enemy and the civilian population?

This is a controversial point in the historical evaluation of the *Blitzkrieg* in Ukraine in 1918. Was the "measured terrorization" of the civilian population and of the enemy an integral element of a German plan to spread chaos among their opponents?[40] With regard to Ukraine, the picture is highly ambivalent. First of all, one should not lose sight of the overall context. In the early spring of 1918, conditions in Ukraine were extremely chaotic and unclear. The authority of the Rada was not properly recognized anywhere. On the Black Sea coast, for instance, "every town wanted to be independent."[41] There were, in addition, ethnic tensions between Ukrainians, Russians, Tatars, German settlers, Cossacks, Poles, and Jews. Countless criminal bands, paramilitary groups, remnants of the tsarist army, fighting groups such as the anarchist Makhno movement, as well as the Polish and Czechoslovak Legions were hanging around in the towns or looking for hideouts in the country away from the railway lines. Disbanded soldiers and officers of the old tsarist army wanted to find their way home or stayed where they were and sought to keep their heads above water by taking on small jobs. Most of them were still armed and joined one of the fighting groups, mainly the Bolsheviks. An order of the German 2nd Cavalry Division showed very clearly the difficulties that the troops were facing: "Conditions in the new area of operations are difficult in that the local rural population, not having enough clothes, often wear Russian military uniforms, and the external appearance of the Rada troops is no different from that of the Bolshevik groups. It would be practical to recruit German-speaking Ukrainians as interpreters. We should not, without any more ado, shoot at every person wearing a Russian uniform but should first try to ascertain whether the person concerned has hostile intentions."[42] It was therefore difficult to get a clear view of the situation, and very hard or impossible for the soldiers of the Central Powers to distinguish between friend and foe.

---

40 On the Polish campaign, see Jochen Böhler, *Auftakt zum Vernichtungskrieg. Die Wehrmacht in Polen 1939* (Frankfurt am Main, 2006); Alexander B. Rossino, *Hitler Strikes Poland: Blitzkrieg, Ideology and Atrocity* (Lawrence, Kans., 2003).

41 BA-MA, N 754/10, Brief Koschs an seine Frau, 21.3.1918.

42 BayHStA-KA, 5, Chev. Regt., Bd. 1, 2. Kavalleriedivision, Abt. Ia, Allgemeine Anordnungen, 17.2.1918. Even in September 1918, masses of unemployed disbanded Russian soldiers living in the towns wore full or partial uniforms. See BayHStA-KA, Kav.Div., Bd. 21, Bezirk Wolhynien West. Bay.Kav.Division, Abt. Ia, Nr. 3276 W, Stimmung im Lande, 19.9.1918.

However, the political direction for the German soldiers had been made very clear. Both before and shortly after the invasion, they were strongly reminded of their task: "We are in a friendly country. The government and the population are ready to make available to us everything we need to carry out our task, but they expect of us that we behave according to the appropriate rules, whatever the requirement. This is the only way to maintain the trust of the population or to win it where it does not yet exist."[43] The commander of the 91st Infantry Division, Lieutenant General Hermann Clausius, ordered leaflets to be distributed to the population informing them that the Germans were in their country as friends.[44]Requisitioning of food should therefore be absolutely avoided.

In fact, many Ukrainians, including Jews,[45] welcomed the German troops as liberators from Bolshevism. This was particularly apparent in towns that had been occupied by the Bolsheviks for some time, such as Feodosiia or Rostov.[46] But the Germans also frequently encountered "very unfriendly" sentiments from the local population in response to their invasion.[47] The orders to the troops then changed: the population was not to be trusted.

---

43 BayHStA-KA, 15. Res.Inf.Brig., Bd. 7, Generalkommando I. A.K., Abt. Ib, Nr. 4122, 16.3.1918. See BayHStA-KA, 15. Res.Inf.Brig., Bd. 7, Korps Knoerzer, Abt. Ib, Nr. 528, 24.3.1918. Besondere Anordnungen (Zusammenfassung der bisher erlassenen wichtigsten Bestimmungen). This contains the statement: "We find ourselves in a friendly country. Our behavior toward Ukrainian officials and the population must reflect this." See also BayHStA-KA, Kav.Div., Bd. 18, Generalkommando 52, Nr. 4412, Besondere Anordnungen, 19.3.1918. These orders relate back to a central order of the Linsingen Army Group: HStA Stuttgart, M 46/15, Fernspruch Heeresgruppe Linsingen, Abt. Ia, Nr. 13204, 16.2.1918. By way of explaining the German intervention, *Ober Ost* commanded that "the sins of the Bolshevik Government should be made clear once again to the Russians." See BayHStA-KA, 15. Res.Inf.Brig., Bd. 7, Verst. 93. Res.Inf. Brigade, Abt. Ia, Nr. 2296, ObOst drahtet, 17.2.1918.

44 HStA Stuttgart, M 46/21. 91, Infanteriedivision, Abt. Ia, Nr. 605/18, Bericht über die Ereignisse vom Verlassen der Stochodstellung an bis zur Einnahme von Kiew, 16.3.1918.

45 HStA Stuttgart, M 46/21. 91, Infanteriedivision, Abt. Ia, M 46/16. 91, Infanteriedivision, Abt. Ia, Nr. 513/18, Funkspruch an Korps Knoerzer, 9.3.1918. However, this positive attitude of the 91st Infantry Division did not seem to be shared by *Korps Knoerzer,* which added a handwritten question mark on the margin.

46 BayHStA-KA, Kav.Div., Bd. 18, Kaiserl. Deutsches Gouvernement Sewastopol, Abt. Ia, Nr. 120, Bericht über die Tätigkeit der B.K.D. von Bierislawa bis zur Besetzung von Feodossija, 13.5.1918; HStA Stuttgart, M 413/1214, III./württem. Landwehr Feld-Artillerieregiment, 1. KTB, Eintrag v. 8.5.1918; HStA Stuttgart, M 46/21, Korps Knoerzer, Abt. Ia, Nr. 1707, Die Operationen des Korps Knoerzer nach Einnahme von Kiew bis zur Einnahme von Rostow, 29.5.1918. See Max Fritsche, *Das königlich sächsische Landwehr Infanterieregiment Nr. 106* (Dresden, 1925), 163; Oberst Fromm, *Das Württembergische Landwehr Infanterieregiment Nr. 126 im Weltkrieg 1914–1918* (Stuttgart, 1921), 55, 65.

47 TNA, GFM 6/35, Telegramm des K. Legationsrats an AA, 9.3.1918.

As was demonstrated by the many counter-orders, there were many excesses and instances of indiscipline on the part of the German troops. The XXII Reserve Corps warned, for instance, that "the establishment of orderly conditions" also depended on "how our troops observe the existing regulations and laws."[48] In retrospect, a representative of the German Ministry of the Economy stated: "It cannot be denied that our military and civilian authorities in this wild country, with its insecure conditions, did not always behave completely legally and considerately, especially in the early period."[49] Not least because of this, the mood in the country threatened to turn against the Central Powers. But there was certainly no conscious or planned terrorization of the population during the invasion in the spring of 1918. Even though the extent of the excesses is still unknown, they did not reflect the general policy of the Central Powers.

The Radicalization of the Struggle against the Bolsheviks

But with the actions of the Bolsheviks, the military opponent that most frequently brought weapons and propaganda to bear against the Central Powers, the situation was quite different. They sometimes fled at the approach of enemy troops but frequently engaged in delaying actions. They had some support in the countryside but more in the towns.[50] Often they fought without uniforms and, in many cases, killed soldiers of the Central Powers whom they took prisoner.[51] In most cases, the German and Austro-Hungarian troops recognized the Bolsheviks only when they had opened fire. The latter did not respect the Hague Conventions of 1899 and 1907, according to which they were to make themselves known as combatants. Kosch summarized this kind of warfare with the following words: "A very difficult war against the inhabitants of a country is always bad because it is unpredictable and prey to a thousand accidents."[52]

---

48 BayHStA-KA, Kav.Div., Bd. 20, Bezirk Wolhynien, Generalkommando XXII. R.K., Abt. Ia, Nr. 222 op, 29.3.1918.

49 BArch, R 3101/1168, Reichswirtschaftsstelle bei der Deutschen Ukrainedelegation an den Staatssekretär des Reichswirtschaftsamts, 17.8.1918.

50 ÖStA, KA, FA, AOK, Evidenzbüro 1918, Nachrichtenabteilung, Kt. 3669, NA Nr. 11222, Die militärische Lage Großrusslands im März und April 1918.

51 Cf. HStA Stuttgart, M 46/16, Morgenmeldung Korps Knoerzer, Abt. Ia, 5.3.1918; Fromm, *Das Württembergische Landwehr Infanterieregiment Nr. 126*, 80. There were, however, cases where the Bolsheviks treated their prisoners well. See BA-MA, N 754/10, Brief Koschs an seine Frau vom 25.3.1918.

52 BA-MA, N 754/10, Brief Koschs an seine Frau v. 26.3.1918.

At the beginning of the campaign, explicit orders were given to the German troops that the Bolsheviks should be taken prisoner, whether armed or not.[53] This is also suggested by general orders to erect prisoner-of-war camps, as well as by reports about Bolshevik prisoners.[54] There is a lack of clarity, however, in German orders issued at the end of March: "Organized Bolsheviks and the Czech divisions are our enemies and are to be treated according to the laws of war." In other words, they were to be shot. But the following sentence is perplexing: "Officers, military officials, and staff of the Entente are likewise to be regarded as enemies."[55] It is, however, unthinkable that Entente officers were shot in the East without more ado, as this would have led to a massive wave of international protest.[56] In sum, this order was not unambiguous, but there are clear indications that in late March and early April most Bolshevik prisoners were shot immediately.[57] A postwar German regimental history claimed that Bolsheviks who resisted were shot, while the remainder were handed

---

53 BayHStA-KA, Landsturm Regt 1, Bd. 4, Armee Abt. Gronau, Abt. Ia, Nr. 09570 geheim, Verhalten dem Feinde gegenüber beim Vorgehen aus unseren Linien, 17.2.1918.

54 Cf. HStA Stuttgart, M 46/16, HGr Linsingen, Abt Ic, Nr. 17960 geh, Besondere Anordnungen für die Unternehmung des Korps Knoerzer, 16.2.1918; HStA Stuttgart, M 46/16, Korps Knoerzer, Abt. Ia, Fernspruch an 92. I.D., 28.2.1918; HStA Stuttgart, M 46/21, 91. Inf.-Division, Abt. Ia, Nr. 605/18, Bericht über die Ereignisse vom Verlassen der Stochodstellung an bis zur Einnahme von Kiew, 16.3.1918; BayHStA-KA, 15. Res.Inf.Brig., Bd. 1, 15. Bayerische Reserve-Infanteriebrigade, KTB, Eintrag v. 19.2.1918; BayHStA-KA, 5. Chevauleger Regiment, Bd. 4, 2. Kavalleriedivision, Abt. Ia, Nr. 476/18, 23.2.1918; BayHStA-KA, 5. Chevauleger Regiment, Bd. 4, 2. Kavalleriedivision, Abt. Ia, Nr. 476/18, Divisionsbefehl für den 24.2.1918; Ludwig Freiherr von Gebsattel, *Das K.B. 1. Ulanen-Regiment "Kaiser Wilhelm II. König von Preußen." Nach Kriegsakten, Kriegstagebüchern und Mitteilungen ehemaliger Angehöriger des Regiments* (Augsburg, 1924), Eintrag v. 22.2.1918, 201.

55 Cf. BayHStA-KA, 15. Res.Inf.Brig., Bd. 7, Korps Knoerzer, Abt. Ib, Nr. 528, Besondere Anordnungen (Zusammenfassung der bisher erlassenen wichtigsten Bestimmungen), 24.3.1918. Cf. also: BayHStA-KA, 5. Chevauleger Regiment, Bd. 4, 2. Kavalleriedivision, Abt. Ia, Nr. 656/18, 23.3.1918. This states that "When Czechs are taken prisoner, and when procedures are undertaken in keeping with the laws of war, brief reports are to be made to the leader of the escort battalion containing statements made by participants in the battle and any written materials found in the possession of the Czechs."

56 In March 1918 there were French, British, Belgian, and Serbian officers in Kyiv whom the Ukrainian government expelled by 19 March under German pressure. Cf. TNA, GFM 6/36, Telegramm von Mumm an AA v. 16.3.1918.

57 Cf. BA-MA, N 46/171, Heeresgruppe Eichhorn-Kiew, Lage am 6.4.1918 morgens. In the battle for Katerynoslav, *Korps Knoerzer* counted five hundred enemy dead, with their own losses at seven dead and fourteen wounded. Cf. HStA Stuttgart, M 46/21.215, Infanteriedivision, Abt. Ia, Nr. 6111/18 op, 24.5.1918; HStA Stuttgart, M 62/2, KTB der 52. k.w. Landwehr Infanteriebrigade, Eintrag v. 30.4.1918.

over to the Ukrainian government.[58] Obviously, the orders left individual German units a certain scope for interpretation.

The state of command for the Austro-Hungarian troops was similar. In the early months, there were no clear orders on how to treat the Bolsheviks. It was not until 9 May, when the advance had ended, that a corresponding order was sent to the 59th Infantry Division: "No matter how difficult the battles in this country may seem, the Bolsheviks, who are not recognized by us in international law—whether we confront them as individuals, in groups, or in larger formations—and who, since they are acting against the laws of the Ukrainian People's Republic, have no right to be treated according to international law, are to be regarded as irregulars and not as regular troops. Similarly, any attack on our troops by such unauthorized persons is a serious crime that, according to the principles of self-defense in war, can only be atoned by immediate death."[59] In the following months, orders and reports from the command of the Austro-Hungarian 2nd Army (*Ostarmee*) to the divisions always portray the Bolsheviks as troublemakers among the population and prisoners of war. They should therefore be treated with "special severity." But what this meant was not specified unambiguously.[60] Not surprisingly, the shooting of individual Bolsheviks or whole groups was a daily occurrence throughout the occupation.[61]

The radicalization of the fighting against Bolshevik units can be demonstrated by two instances in which German troops massacred large numbers of Bolsheviks: the massacre at Perekop in the Crimea in April and the mass killing at Taganrog in June 1918. Both events are very well documented and allow certain conclusions to be drawn.

---

58 Fromm, *Das Württembergische Landwehr Infanterieregiment Nr. 126*, 65. The regimental history of the 106th Landwehr Infantry Regiment says that the Bolsheviks, "according to orders, were to be treated as irregulars." Cf. Fritsche, *Das königlich sächsische Landwehr Infanterieregiment Nr. 106*, 151.

59 ÖStA, KA, AdT, FAR 59, Kt. 832, Abfertigung Nr. 57, 9. Mai 1918. First quoted in Wolfram Dornik, "Die Besatzung der Ukraine durch österreichisch-ungarische Truppen 1918," in *Die Besatzung der Ukraine 1918. Historischer Kontext – Forschungsstand – wirtschaftliche und soziale Folgen,* ed. Wolfram Dornik and Stefan Karner (Graz, 2008), 168.

60 ÖStA, KA, AdT, FABrig 59, Kt. 4131, Nr. 307, Verhalten der Zivilbevölkerung gegenüber, 20.8.1918.

61 At the level of troops in the field, see the examples of the 13th Military Police Battalion and the 3rd Uhlan Regiment: ÖStA, KA, AdT, FJBat 13, Kt. 754, 6. Tagebuch des Feldjägerbataillons Nr. 13; ÖStA, KA, AdT, FJBat 13, Kt. 754, 7. Tagebuch des Feldjägerbataillons Nr. 13; ÖStA, KA, AdT, UR 3, Kt. 800, Lagebücher, Einträge vom 25., 26.6.1918, 2., 17., 24., 27.7.1918, 5., 6.10.1918. See also the situation reports and daily reports to the 2nd Army: ÖStA, KA, FA, NFA, HHK AK/AGKdo, 2. Armee, OpAK, Kt. 308, 1918 Situations- und Tagesmeldungen.

In the fighting at Perekop between 17 and 19 April 1918, the Germans made a breakthrough to the Crimea. According to German reports, about two thousand Bolsheviks were defending the isthmus. The 217th Infantry Division should have led the attack[62] but was unable to arrive in time in sufficient numbers. The commander of the Bavarian Cavalry Division, Major General Moritz Freiherr von Egloffstein, requested that 52nd Corps allow his division to begin the attack immediately. Permission was granted and, in a single day, the Bavarian Cavalry, with the 9th Jäger Battalion and the 29th Bavarian Jäger Regiment, broke through the Bolshevik defense lines. Then a wild pursuit of the fleeing Bolsheviks ensued; no prisoners were taken. The commander of the 1st Bavarian Cavalry Brigade, Colonel Joseph von Tannstein, commented: "This had the effect of spreading great fear among the enemy (especially after the battle at Perekop). All the local population said so." Since Tannstein's brigade was outnumbered in battle, this psychological shock element had a very welcome effect, according to this Bavarian cavalry officer: "Bolsheviks who have been beaten do not offer any more resistance."[63] Kosch praised the Bavarian Cavalry Division for its "ruthless courage in the attack against the barbarous and treacherous enemy," which was a "model for all future undertakings."[64]

In these battles in the Crimea, why did the Bavarian Cavalry not take any prisoners? The issue cannot be resolved simply by the questionable and brutal utilitarian considerations quoted above, since the division, in the previous war years on the Eastern Front, had been quite concerned to deal correctly with prisoners of war.[65] It was rather

---

62 Cf. BayHStA-KA, Kav.Div., Bd. 18, Generalkommando (z.b.V.) Nr. 52, Chef/Ia, Nr. 4863, 14.4.1918.

63 BayHStA-KA, Kav.Div., Bd. 19, 1. bayer. Kavallerie Brigade. Kommandeur. Erfahrungen aus den Operationen und Kämpfen gegen die Bolschewisten in Taurien und in der Krim in der Zeit v. 16.4.–2.5.1918, 20.5.1918. The division's report admitted that no prisoners had been taken. Cf. BayHStA-KA, Kav.Div., Bd. 18, Kaiserl. Deutsches Gouvernement Sewastopol, Abt. Ia, Nr. 120, Bericht über die Tätigkeit der B.K.D. von Bierislawa bis zur Besetzung von Feodossija, 13.5.1918. See also Kosch's letter of 21.4.1918 to his wife: BA-MA, N 754/10: "Well, the defeat at Perekop, where the Bavarians wiped out just about everyone, will hopefully instill some salutary fear in them [the Bolsheviks]."

64 Cf. BayHStA-KA, Kav.Div., Bd. 18, Generalkommando (z.b.V.) Nr. 52, Abt. Ia, Nr. 4920, Korpsbefehl, 19.4.1918.

65 Cf. BayHStA-KA, Kav.Div., Bd. 28, Bayerische Kavalleriedivision, Abt. Ib, Nr. 2428, Divisionsbefehl, 18.1.1917. Cf. the general order of the War -Ministry, in BayHStA-KA, Kriegsministerium, Nr. 546/15 g.U.3. geheim, Betrifft: Misshandlung von russischen Gefangenen, 29.7.1915. This says: "It must be emphasized explicitly that it does not correspond to German interests to handle the Russians badly. Among the majority of Russian soldiers, there was no previous hatred of the Germans. It would be impolitic to provoke such sentiment by bad treatment. On the contrary, every effort must be made, while maintaining order and discipline, to treat them in a manner that is just and humane."

a mixture of different factors that led to this radicalization. From mid-March, the troops of the Central Powers had witnessed Bolshevik atrocities against the Ukrainian population.[66] The victims were mainly nobles and officers. For instance, hundreds if not thousands of officers were executed in Kyiv.[67] In his personal diary, the commander in chief of the Austro-Hungarian 2nd Army, Böhm-Ermolli, wrote about "bestial horrors carried out by the Bolsheviks, but also by the peasantry." Thirty-two "Russian" officers, members of a Ukrainian unit, were "found killed, stripped, and mutilated" by the peasants.[68] It is seldom possible to verify today exactly what happened and the number of victims, but there is no doubt that massacres became daily occurrences quite early on in the Russian Civil War. Widespread reporting of such horrors must have poisoned the mood and radicalized the attitude of the troops. Since the officer corps not only of the Bavarian Cavalry Division but also of most of the Austro-Hungarian military came almost exclusively from the nobility, these reports would not have had a moderating effect on their behavior. Added to this was the fact that, in southern Ukraine, the Bavarian Cavalry would frequently have encountered German settlers. There were no linguistic barriers to communication here, and a sense of ethnic community would have bound them together. These German settlers would have had very little good to say about the Bolsheviks. Since they were the wealthiest group among the peasantry, they had been subject to Bolshevik plundering and destruction. Many of them had been abducted. Before and after 1917, they were regarded by the population, and later by the Bolsheviks, as allies of the enemy.[69]

---

66 Army Group Eichhorn-Kiew did not issue an order to make a collection of these atrocities until July 1918: BayHStA-KA, Kav.Div., Bd. 22, Nachrichtenoffizier der OHL beim Generalkommando XXII, Res.-Korps, Nr. 1076, An alle Nachrichtenoffiziere der Divisionen und Etappenkommandanturen, 24.7.1918.

67 Different numbers are to be found in the literature and in sources. The number 900, which appears in the history of the 133rd Landwehr Infantry Regiment, seems to be the most credible, as this regiment was the first to enter the capital. Cf. Max Romstedt, *Das Kgl. Sächs. Landwehr Infanterieregiment Nr. 133* (Dresden, 1924), 108. The number 3,000 is mentioned two years after the event in a report by a Swiss citizen to the Swiss foreign ministry: BAR Bern, E 2300, 1000/716, 282, Bericht des Schweizers Carl Heinrich Würgler "Die Bolschewistische Diktatur" an das Eidgenössische Politische Departement, Abteilung für Auswärtiges, 12.7.1920, 13ff. See also the report of the American consul, Summer: NARA, US Department of State, relating to internal Affairs in Russia and Soviet Union 1910–1929, War Series 6, RG 59, Russia, IV Reports from Consul General Moscow on Conditions in Russia, Cable message from American Consul at Moscow via Vladivostok, No. 222, 1.3.1918. The historian Mark von Hagen writes of more than 2,500 victims in his *War in a European Borderland: Occupations and Occupation Plans in Galicia and Ukraine, 1914–1918* (Seattle and London, 2007), 87.

68 ÖStA, AVA, Nachlässe, Nachlass: Böhm-Ermolli, B 1466, Mikrofilm B 1466, Eintrag v. 19.3.1918.

69 Cf. BA-MA, N 754/10, Briefe Koschs an seine Frau vom 21.3., 29.3. und 31.3.1918; Fromm, *Das*

The German troops, including the Bavarian Cavalry Division, had been deployed to southern Ukraine from Romania with an order from the 9th Army that did not encourage moderation: "All troops being sent into Ukraine are to be instructed about the conditions there, which are reminiscent of the invasion of Belgium in the summer of 1914. They are also to be instructed about the nature of irregular warfare, with special attention to fighting in built-up areas.... Weapons are to be used ruthlessly against an armed enemy. Insurgencies are to be nipped in the bud before they can grow.... A friendly reception and peaceful behavior of the population by light of day should not lead to carelessness."[70] But the first reports from the Bavarian Cavalry Division did not have anything negative to say about the country.

In the second half of March, however, this changed in Mykolaiv. The events there were an almost traumatic experience. This southern Ukrainian industrial city was regarded as a Bolshevik stronghold and was home to many unemployed and armed workers. Once the Central Powers had occupied Mykolaiv on 17 March, the German and Austro-Hungarian troops continued their rapid advance eastward in the direction of Kherson without waiting for reinforcements. On 23 March, after a funeral of comrades who had been killed by troops of the Central Powers, the Bolsheviks staged a demonstration that led to an uprising in the city. This quickly became a mass uprising that created extreme difficulties for the German troops and staff of the 52nd Corps. After some tense hours, German and Austro-Hungarian reinforcements were able to restore order. But their intervention had led to fierce street battles with the use of artillery. "Behind the lines of the troops, everyone was disarmed." Anyone found afterwards in possession of a weapon was killed on the spot or, during a new search of the city some days later, was shot following a summary court martial.[71] German troops did not even hesitate to break their promise of an amnesty for Bolsheviks who surrendered.[72]

Württembergische Landwehr Infanterieregiment Nr. 126, passim.

70 BayHStA-KA, 2. S.R.R., Bd. 7, AOK 9, Abt. Ia, Nr. 6654 op, Armeebefehl betreffend Verhalten der Truppen in der Ukraine, 26.3.1918. On the troops sent into Kyiv, cf. BayHStA-KA, 5. Chev. Regt., Bd. 1, 2. Kavalleriedivision, Abt. Ia, Allgemeine Anordnungen, 17.2.1918: "It is likely that the Bolsheviks will carry on a kind of Francs-tireurs war."

71 Cf. BA-MA, N 754/10, Briefe Koschs an seine Frau vom 24.3. und 31.3.1918. See also the drastic order of the 217th Infantry Division in BayHStA-KA, 29. InfRegt, Bd. 2, 29. bay.Inf.Regt. (Jäg. Regt.), Auszug aus Divisionsbefehl (217. ID) v. 23.3.18, Abt. Ia, Nr. 47, 26.3.1918.

72 Cf. BayHStA-KA, 29. InfRegt, Bd. 2, Bayer. Res. Jäger Batl. 1; *Auszug aus dem Kriegstagebuch mit Gefechtsbericht. Das K.B. Reserve Jägerbataillon Nr. 1,* ed. Hans Muggenthaler et al. (Munich, 1935), 363–68.

For the Central Powers, the uprising in Mykolaiv clearly demonstrated their vulnerability, given their small number of troops in this large country permeated in parts by hostile units. This incident also exposed the problem of advancing rapidly without having secured the territory in the rear. The experience of the battle in Mykolaiv and the conclusions drawn from it would now become a yardstick for future actions. The command of the Austro-Hungarian Army Group Command Kherson (*k.u.k. Armeegruppenkommando Cherson*) and the German 52nd Corps circulated a short and succinct report.[73] The attitude of the officers and units deployed in Mykolaiv had now clearly become more radical. Army Group Command Kherson indicated that "right from the start, one has to proceed with the greatest ruthlessness against the rabble."[74] The Germans adopted a similar tone. According to Kosch, "the Russian bows only to brute force, to which he is accustomed from his former government. This worked here [in Mykolaiv], and it will also work in Kherson, which was fortunately taken after heavy fighting. There is no place for weakness here."[75] The Bavarian Cavalry Division also drew its conclusions: "The experiences in Mykolaiv have demonstrated that the only thing that works against the population is to be ruthlessly strict. Every man we meet with a weapon in his hand has to be shot immediately. Arrests, followed by a court-martial, are only seen as weakness." But the division also cautioned that "of course, the use of force" was permissible "only to maintain order,"[76] and "the strictness that is required against the population" had to be "accompanied by irreproachable and disciplined behavior on the part of the troops."[77] Nevertheless, these orders did not as yet mean that the whole population was to be seen as an enemy. Even in Perekop, the

73 ÖStA, KA, FA, NFA, HHK AK/AGKdo, 2. Armee, OpAK, Kt. 308, Nr. 234, Erfahrung aus den Straßenkämpfen in Nikolajew, 25.3.1918; BayHStA-KA, Kav.Div., Bd. 18, Generalkommando z.b.V. Nr. 52, Abt. Ia, Nr. 4608, Erfahrungen bei den Straßenkämpfen in Nikolajew, 3.4.1918. Since the German report is abridged and was published later, it may be assumed that the original report was written by the Austro-Hungarians.

74 ÖStA, KA, FA, NFA, HHK AK/AGKdo, 2. Armee, OpAK, Kt. 308, Nr. 234, Erfahrung aus den Straßenkämpfen in Nikolajew, 25.3.1918.

75 BA-MA, N 754/10, Brief Koschs an seine Frau vom 5.4.1918. See also the letter from Kosch to his wife on 2.4.1918: "Calm has gradually been restored here; the bloody lesson and the many death sentences passed later seem to have borne fruit. The Russian needs a firm hand, and then he complies."

76 BayHStA-KA, Kav.Div., Bd. 18, Bay.Kav.Div., Abt. Ia, Nr. 943, Divisionsbefehl, 4.4.1918.

77 BayHStA-KA, Kav.Div., Bd. 18, Bay.Kav.Div., Abt. Ia, Nr. 966, 6.4.1918. See also: BayHStA-KA, 1. Kav.Brig., Bd. 7, 217. Infanteriedivision, Abt. Ia, Nr. 47 op, Divisionsbefehl, 25.3.1918.

Bavarian Cavalry did not bother *unarmed* Bolshevik party members.[78] But with regard to *armed* Bolsheviks, the orders were now clear.

Before the battle at Perekop, there was one other concrete reason why the Bavarian Cavalry took no prisoners: the Bolsheviks had shot prisoners from the 2nd Bavarian Heavy Cavalry Regiment.[79] In the battle itself, the division suffered severe losses. There were 220 dead and wounded, almost all of them shot with handguns, indicating that these battles were fought in close combat.[80] Shortly after the battle, the Bavarian Cavalry Division sharpened its tone against the enemy in an order of 29 April 1918: "Let us go forward now until we have finally eliminated these hateful bandits, whom we must recognize not as soldiers but as robbers and murderers."[81]

Yet the 52nd Corps could also find practical and flexible solutions to the issue of armed captured Bolsheviks, as was demonstrated in the capture of Sevastopol. While the Bavarian Cavalry Division, after its breakthrough at Perekop, moved toward the Kerch peninsula and captured Feodosiia, Kosch sent the 217th Infantry Division and 15th Landwehr Division to Sevastopol, where the fleeing Bolsheviks had gathered and had the Russian Black Sea Fleet under their control.

78 BayHStA-KA, Kav.Div., Bd. 19, 1. Bayer. Kavalleriebrigade, Kommandeur. Erfahrungen aus den Operationen und Kämpfen gegen die Bolschewisten in Taurien und in der Krim in der Zeit vom 16.4.–2.5.1918, 20.5.1918. This report says: "A report that a place was a strong nest of Bolsheviks led to an unnecessary splintering of forces, as the population seeking help understood the Bolsheviks to be everyone who agreed with their basic principles (distribution of land, etc.). The place in question was then generally found to be peaceful.... In all places, only those Bolsheviks were sought who had previously been seen with weapons [underlined in the original] and, in such cases, they were immediately sentenced to death."

79 See Eugen Frauenholz, *Das K.B. 2. Kürassier- und Schweres Reiterregiment* (Munich, 1921), 293: "While on patrol, First Lieutenant Baron von Gohre, Private Riepl, and Cavalryman Johann Huber were taken prisoner by the Bolsheviks. Some days later, according to local residents, and based on the autopsy, it was established that the prisoners had been taken to Bolshevik headquarters and, since all three refused to reveal the strength of our forces, they were, contrary to international law, made to stand against the wall and shot. An enemy like this could no longer be treated as an honest adversary. Once these facts were known, our regiment took no more prisoners." This account, given after the war, is confirmed by BA-MA, N 754/10, Brief Koschs an seine Frau v. 19.4.1918; BayHStA-KA, 29. InfRegt, Bd. 3, 29. Bayerisches Jägerregiment, Nachrichtensammlung v. 18.4.1918.

80 BayHStA-KA, Kav.Div., Bd. 19, 1. Bayer. Kavallerie Brigade. Kommandeur, Erfahrungen aus den Operationen und Kämpfen gegen die Bolschewisten in Taurien und in der Krim in der Zeit vom 16.4.–2.5.1918, 20.5.1918. The 29th Bavarian Jäger Regiment also suffered major losses, with 29 dead and 151 wounded. Cf. BayHStA-KA, 29. InfRegt, Bd. 3. 29, Bayerisches Jägerregiment, KTB, Eintrag v. 19.4.1918.

81 Cf. BayHStA-KA, 29. InfReg, Bd. 3. BayKavDiv. Divisions-Tagesbefehl, 20.4.1918. The brutalization of the Bavarian cavalrymen is also confirmed by statements from their own side, for instance, in the history of the 126th Landwehr Regiment: Fromm, *Das Württembergische Landwehr Infanterieregiment Nr. 126*, 79.

Kosch feared renewed street fighting, as had happened in Mykolaiv. His situation was not a simple one, particularly as a Ukrainian brigade was based in the Crimea and wanted to assert the authority of the Rada.

Before the feared storming of Sevastopol, Kosch received three delegations from the city. While he immediately rebuffed the representatives of the Rada, he promised the mayor that peace and order would be established if the citizens did not take up arms against the Germans. It was, however, only with the representatives of the workers' soviet that Kosch engaged in a proper negotiation. He promised that he would not intervene in their organization if they reined in the workers. The Bolsheviks were guaranteed their lives if they handed over the fortress peacefully. The coup took place and, on 30 April, Sevastopol came under German control practically without a fight. Kosch thought it would be "quite impossible to have all 5–8,000 Bolsheviks shot."[82]

His colleague Colonel Arthur Bopp, on the other hand, as commander of the 52nd Württemberg Landwehr Brigade, showed no scruples only a few weeks later about shooting thousands of captured Bolsheviks at Taganrog. This was by far the greatest German mass crime during the whole period of occupation.[83] After the initial campaign had been completed, there were still conflicts, especially on the eastern border of Ukraine. On 11 June the Bolsheviks carried out a major coup. In an amphibious operation, eight thousand men landed on a peninsula between Taganrog and the Miius Firth[84] in order to attack the German troops in the vicinity of Rostov. *Korps Knoerzer* briefly considered withdrawing from the city but then decided against it on account of "the lack of initiative constantly shown by these opponents, their poor discipline and lack of leaders." Instead, Knoerzer sent the 52nd Württemberg Landwehr Brigade and the 7th Bavarian Cavalry Brigade against the enemy.[85]

---

82 BA-MA, N 754/10, Brief Koschs an seine Frau v. 30.4.1918.

83 In the works written about the period of occupation in Ukraine, the battle at Taganrog merits a footnote at most. For the only detailed analysis, see Reinhard Nachtigal, "Krasnyj Desant: Das Gefecht an der Mius-Bucht. Ein unbeachtetes Kapitel der deutschen Besetzung Südrusslands 1918," *Jahrbücher für Geschichte Osteuropas*, no. 53 (2005): 221–46.

84 The Miius Firth is actually the wide estuary of the river as it flows into the Black Sea. The battles at Taganrog are often referred to as the Battle on the Miius Firth.

85 HStA Stuttgart, M 46/20, 7. Landwehrdivision Stab, Gefecht am Mius-See 9.6.–13.6.1918, Abschriften.

Colonel Bopp was given the task of leading the attack. He divided the units under his command into three groups[86] and, after two days, drove his opponents back to the sea. Only between one and two thousand Bolsheviks could be rescued by the landing craft. The Germans took no prisoners during the battle from among the "Bolsheviks who were defending themselves desperately"[87] and, after the battle, Bopp issued a written order to shoot all prisoners. Only ten were kept for interrogation and later executed. On 14 June, the day after the battle, the battlefield was searched once again for scattered Bolsheviks, and they covered the many bodies because "with the high temperatures...the numerous bodies of dead men and animals lying around were creating intolerable and unhealthy conditions."[88] The war journal of the Württemberg Landwehr Brigade speaks of 6,000 enemy dead against 39 of their own troops, with 169 wounded and two missing.[89] Army Group Eichhorn-Kiew published the outcome of the battle and hoped that this would give a "severe fright" to the Bolsheviks with regard to any future undertakings. The German delegation in Kyiv also considered the shootings justified but feared that publication in Germany or in neutral countries would "create a bad impression...because it could be concluded from this that we are conducting this war in a brutal manner."[90]

If this mass execution of Bolsheviks was already a horrible war crime, there is still some question as to whether there was also another one: among these shot, were there women and children from surrounding villages? As the German delegation in Ukraine

86 Taking part were one cavalry regiment, six and one-half infantry battalions, and three and one-half artillery groups. Cf. HStA Stuttgart, M 62/2, KTB der 52. k.w. Landwehr Infanteriebrigade, Eintrag v. 12.6.1918. Nachtigal estimates the number of German soldiers to have been 3,000 but, with this military structure, there may have been as many as 4,000. See Nachtigal, "Krasnyj Desant," 234.

87 HStA Stuttgart, M 62/2, KTB der 52. k.w. Landwehr Infanteriebrigade, Eintrag v. 13.6.1918.

88 HStA Stuttgart, M 413/1214, KTB der III./württem. L.F.A.R. 1, Eintrag v. 14.6.1918.

89 HStA Stuttgart, M 62/2, KTB der 52. k.w. Landwehr Infanteriebrigade, Eintrag v. 13.6.1918. The Austro-Hungarian general staff officer assigned to the commander of Army Group Eichhorn-Kiew, Waldbott, reported to AOK on 15.6.1918: "The destruction of the 10,000 Bolsheviks who landed at Taganrog (5,000 killed, 5,000 driven into the sea, 10 taken prisoner) was announced immediately in Kyiv by means of wall posters." Cf. ÖStA, KA, FA, AOK, OpAbt, Kt. 472, Nr. 1707, Bericht über die Aufbringung der Lebensmittel durch den k.u.k. bevollmächtigten Generalstabsoffizier beim Oberkmdo der HG Eichhorn-Kiew, 15.6.1918.

90 TNA, GFM 6/52, Deutsche Ukraine Delegation, An Reichskanzler Hertling, Kiew, 16.6.1918. The press release said: "Those remaining on land were killed, only 10 men surrendered." Cf. BA-MA, N 46/171, Neueste Kriegs-Nachrichten. Presse-Abteilung–Heeresgruppe Eichhorn, Kiew, 15.6.1918.

feared, letters appeared in the German press from German soldiers who had taken part in the battle containing "similar descriptions" of mass executions of "civilians, among them women and children."[91] The incident was even going to be debated in the Reichstag,[92] which is why Army Group Eichhorn-Kiew demanded an explanation from *Korps Knoerzer.* The commanding general of the corps, Karl Albrecht von Knoerzer, replied an hour later by telephone that this involved "civilian bandits without uniform or other identification, among them some women and adolescents."[93] In spite of receiving other war documents from *Korps Knoerzer, Ober Ost* was not satisfied with this answer. Accordingly, on 11 August, Colonel Bopp had to give a personal and detailed response to the accusations.[94] Bopp indicated the previous atrocities committed by the Bolsheviks against German soldiers[95] as well as against the civilian population, such as the murder of the former tsarist general Pavel von Rennenkampf. Moreover, the Bolsheviks were not wearing uniforms, were "nothing but murderers," and "had pretended to be harmless villagers so that they could shoot at our people again." Bopp frankly admitted the shooting of prisoners early in the morning of 14 June, among whom were a few armed women.[96] But the colonel vigorously rejected the accusation that women and children from the civilian population had been killed. In addition, he emphasized that the shooting was broadly supported by the Ukrainian population.[97]

A detailed study of the numerous after-action reports from various German units deployed at Taganrog give us a comparatively clear picture of what happened. The order to shoot prisoners is

---

91 HStA Stuttgart, M 46/20, Heeresgruppe Eichhorn, Abt. Ia, Nr. 2604/18, Fernspruch v. 12.7.1918. The location of these letters is unknown.

92 Friedrich Ebert may have raised this. See Nachtigal, "Krasnyj Desant," 237

93 HStA Stuttgart, M 46/20, Korps Knoerzer, Abt. Ia, Nr. 2779, Fernspruch Nr. 359 aus dem Felde, 12.7.1918.

94 HStA Stuttgart, M 46/20, Korps Knoerzer, Abt. Ia, Nr. 2779, Bericht über das Gefecht bei Taganrog im Besonderen und über die nach dem Gefecht erfolgte Erschießung der gefangenen Bolschewiki, 11.8.1918.

95 According to a report by the 4th Bavarian Chevauleger Regiment, the Bolsheviks were taking no German prisoners at the start of the battle. Cf. BayHStA-KA, 4. Chevauleger Regiment, Bd. 1, Meldung Chev. 4. an 7. Brigade, vom 12.6.1918, 3.30 Uhr Nachm.

96 Other sources support the claim that there were women in the ranks of the Bolsheviks. See Fromm, *Das Württembergische Landwehr Infanterieregiment Nr. 126*, 92ff.

97 Lieutenant General von Arnim, leading the corps in Knoerzer's absence, confirmed what Bopp had said and, in an additional written statement, confirmed the correctness of his decision. See HStA Stuttgart, M 46/20, Korps Knoerzer, Abt. Ia, Nr. 3487, Erschießung gefangener Bolschewisten, 13.8.1918.

explicitly confirmed,[98] and an instruction regarding the digging of mass graves can also be found in the documents.[99] But there is no mention of a mass execution of civilians.[100] It is possible that this was not written down in official war journals or after-action reports, but there would have been some mention of the participation of local residents in the battle. But there is no such mention. It appears that the Bolsheviks forced the local population to carry out some logistical tasks,[101] but the civilians clearly did not take part in the battle and do not appear to have assisted the landed Bolsheviks in any other way.[102] There are two possible reasons why civilians still might have been killed. During the battle, there was some bitter close combat in the villages and on the farms where the Bolsheviks, according to German reports, "hid in mounds of straw, behind houses, hedges, etc....to fire on our companies, and some defended themselves to the last."[103] Civilians might have become victims in this way. On 14 June there was another order to "ruthlessly" cleanse and disarm the local towns and villages.[104] Here as well, it cannot be ruled out that local residents were executed. But in general there is no sound evidence for a mass killing of civilians at Taganrog. To claim, on the basis of such

---

98 HStA Stuttgart, KTB des Stabes Korps Knoerzer vom 16.2.–3.10.1918, Eintrag v. 14.6.1918; HStA Stuttgart, M 411/394, III./Landwehr Infanterieregiment 121, KTB, Eintrag v. 14.6.1918. Das KTB der 52. The Württemberg Landwehr Infantry Brigade was silent about the execution.

99 BayHStA-KA, 5. Chevauleger Regiment, Bd. 4, Kommando Bezirk Taganrog, Artillerie Kommandeur 149, Nr. 356, Bezirks-Befehl v. 19.6.1918, Abschrift Korps Knoerzer IVb/Ib/2086, 17.6.1918.

100 In an East German publication dealing with crimes committed by the Germans in Ukraine in 1918, based on limited sources, the execution of prisoners is mentioned, but not the execution of civilians. When the order to shoot had been made known there was, according to one veteran, "no limit to our outrage. Some others of our comrades were indifferent. It was war." Some other units described his battalion as a "murder battalion." See Albert Norden, *Zwischen Berlin und Moskau. Zur Geschichte deutsch-sowjetischer Beziehungen* ([East] Berlin, 1954), 117.

101 Cf. HStA Stuttgart, M 411/395, III./L.I.R. 121, Bericht über die Gefechte bei Federowka am 12.6 und bei Cristoforow am 13.6.1918, 22.6.1918.

102 A communist account of 1965 claimed that five hundred local residents had joined the landing force. Cf. Nachtigal, "Krasnyj Desant," 236, n. 61. However, this data should be regarded with caution, since Soviet historians wanted to portray partisan warfare in the First and Second World Wars as a people's war. The reality was different. Nachtigal also describes the quoted account as "semiofficial."

103 See BayHStA-KA, 5. Chevauleger Regiment, Bd. 1, Gruppe Nord (Stab 5. Bayr. Chevaulegers-Regiment), Gefechtsbericht über die Gefechte nordw. u. westl. Taganrog vom 10.–14.6.1918, 17.6.1918. Cf. also HStA Stuttgart, M 411/395, III./L.I.R. 121, Bericht über die Gefechte an der Miusbucht, 24.7.1918.

104 BayHStA-KA, 4. Chevauleger Regiment, Bd. 11, 7. Bayr. Kav.Brig, Brigadebefehl v. 14.6.1918; HStA Stuttgart, M 62/2, 52. Württembergische Landwehr Infanteriebrigade, KTB, entry of 14.6.1918.

examples, that the local population was an *integral part* or an *object of war* for the Germans is highly questionable,[105] quite apart from the fact that, with regard to numbers, the incidents at Taganrog were an absolute exception during the German occupation of Ukraine in 1918. Before the start of the invasion, the order of *Korps Knoerzer* stated: "Treat the local population well. They have already suffered enough at the hands of the Bolsheviks, those murderers and thieves."[106] In the weeks that followed, the local population certainly became more mistrustful of the Germans, but the soldiers did attempt, at Taganrog as well, to distinguish between the Bolsheviks and the uninvolved local population.[107]

Still, there is no doubt that this incident, as well as the previous battles in the Crimea, demonstrated a radicalization of the German troops in their campaign against the Bolsheviks. Prisoners were no longer taken, even if they numbered in the thousands. And no one appeared to be bothered by this any longer.[108] For Bopp, the incident had no career consequences. He kept his command and was even promoted to major general in November 1918. Knoerzer, however, maintained after the war that it was because of the Taganrog incident that he did not receive a decoration for the war in the East.[109] The incident may also have played a role in his demotion in rank: on 2 October the corps named after him was disbanded, and he became commander of his old 7th Landwehr Division.

Finally, it is interesting to note the argument of Bopp's direct superior, Lieutenant General von Arnim.[110] In his justification of this mass execution, he wrote: "For the reasons given, I consider the shooting of the prisoners to be not only humane and completely legal but also militarily necessary and correct."[111] This argumentation

---

105 As claimed by Michael Geyer, "War and Terror: Some Timely Observations on the German Way of Waging War," in *War and Terror in Historical and Contemporary Perspective*, ed. Michael Geyer (Chicago, 2003), 47–69, http://www.aicgs.org/documents/warandterror.pdf, accessed 13 June 2010.

106 HStA Stuttgart, M 46/15, 7. Landwehrdivision, Befehl v. 16.2.1918.

107 Nachtigal, "Krasnyj Desant," also starts from the assumption that there was no mass execution of civilians.

108 It seems fairly clear from the morning report of Army Group Eichhorn-Kiew for 15 June 1918 that no prisoners were taken. The incident, then, was no secret to the staff of the Army Group. See BA-MA, N 46/171, Heeresgruppe Eichhorn, Lage am 15.6.1918 morgens.

109 Cf. HStA Stuttgart, M 660/131, Die Befreiung der Ukraine vom Bolschewismus durch das Korps Knoerzer 1918, written in 1925.

110 Knoerzer was on leave at this time.

111 HStA Stuttgart, M 46/20, Korps Knoerzer, Abt. Ia, Nr. 3487, Erschießung gefangener

reminds us of the Second World War: with the firm conviction that they were acting out of the necessities of war, combined with the belief that they had right on their side, it seemed to the German military that they could use any means to assert their claim.

Uprisings during the Period of Occupation

Although incidents on this scale did not occur again during the period of occupation, the occupying troops often had to deal with uprisings. These disturbances had a number of causes. The country's social problems remained unresolved and were exacerbated by rising prices, unpaid wages, and the continuing lack of urgently needed land reform. Ethnic and religious conflicts were also a constant source of trouble. The occupiers believed that Entente agents were at work. Among the rural population, many saw the troops of the Central Powers as supporters and defenders of the widely unpopular Rada, and later especially of the Hetmanate.[112] Military requisitioning or enforced purchases also did little to calm the situation. Disturbances were also facilitated by the small numbers of troops. In August, for instance, the number of German troops in Chernihiv was "so small that they were by and large powerless to confront this ferment."[113]

The German Zone of Occupation

Since the Central Powers entered Ukraine not as enemy territory but as supporters of a friendly power, they were legally bound to hand over criminals to the Ukrainian courts. But this was not, of course, how the army saw it; moreover, the Ukrainian justice system was extremely rudimentary.[114] As early as March 1918, some German units sought to circumvent this regulation and ordered that anyone attacking the occupation forces should be brought before a German military court.[115] This order, however, had to be withdrawn shortly

---

Bolschewisten, 13.8.1918. On returning from leave, Knoerzer felt it necessary to write again directly to Groener. He had "never given the order to execute the prisoners" but regarded it as legally "defensible": HStA Stuttgart, M 46/20, Brief Knoerzers an Groener v. 9.9.1918.

112 Von Hagen, *War in a European Borderland*, 96–98.

113 BayHStA-KA, Etappenkommandantur 54, Bd. 22, Etappenbezirk Czernigow, Abt. Ia, Nr. 1049/18, Monatsbericht v. 22.7.–21.8.1918, 21.8.1918.

114 When prisoners were handed over to the Ukrainian authorities, it seems that they were immediately shot without any lengthy process. Cf. Fromm, *Das Württembergische Landwehr Infanterieregiment Nr. 126*, 61.

115 HStA Stuttgart, M 46/16, Korps Knoerzer, Abt. Ib, Nr. 528, Besondere Anordnungen (Zusammenfassung der bisher erlassenen wichtigsten Bestimmungen), 24.3.1918.

afterwards.[116] Other units used a similar artifice and ordered that, in accordance with art. 18 of the imperial decree of 28 December 1899, armed Bolsheviks "should be treated according to military procedure [*Kriegsbrauch*]," in other words, they should be shot. Only in cases of doubt should a witness be required.[117] The imperial decree of 1899, however, only applied to occupied enemy territory; consequently, the court of the Bavarian Cavalry Division described this new regulation as "not unobjectionable."[118] In any case, the Germans had thereby bypassed the Ukrainian justice system and questioned Ukrainian state sovereignty or, rather, circumvented it.

Army Group Eichhorn-Kiew gradually moved away from the legal regulations regarding operations in friendly territory: if Ukrainian authorities failed to proceed against agitators, "the German General Command should act on its own discretion." German commanders were "fully responsible on their own" for the disarming of localities if the Ukrainian authorities "cannot or will not carry out...their duty."[119] The great break came on 25 April, when the Army Group ordered the use of military courts in case of attacks on German or other allied troops in the city of Kyiv.[120] Two days later the order was extended to the whole German zone in Ukraine and in the Crimea.[121]

This extension of the authority of military courts was one of the issues that led to conflict with the Rada. Under German pressure, and before Skoropadsky's takeover of power, the Rada confirmed

116 BayHStA-KA, 15. Res.Inf.Brig., Bd. 30, Generalkommando I. A.K. Abt III, Nr. 4387/243, 19.3.1918 mit dem Zusatz des Korps Knoerzer v. 26.3.1918.

117 BayHStA-KA, 2. S.R.R., Bd. 6, 2. Schweres Reiterregiment, Regimentsbefehl v. 7.4.1918. This order came from the Bavarian Cavalry Division on 5 April 1918.

118 BayHStA-KA, Kav.Div., Bd. 51, Bayerische Kavalleriedivision, Gericht der Division. Kriegstagebuch, Eintrag 1.–30.4.1918. The division commander therefore refused confirmation of two death sentences and asked the 52nd Corps to clarify. The Supreme Command of the 9th Army declared the judgement unlawful. For the wider German discussion concerning the legal status and sentencing of irregular troops, see Andreas Toppe, *Militär und Kriegsvölkerrecht. Rechtsnorm, Fachdiskurs und Kriegspraxis in Deutschland 1899–1940* (Munich, 2008).

119 BayHStA-KA, 15. Res.Inf.Brig., Bd. 30, Heeresgruppe Eichhorn, Abt. G., Nr. 13, 10.4.1918. Cf. also BayHStA-KA, Kav.Div., Bd. 21, Bezirk Wolhynien. Generalkommando XXII. R.K., Abt. Ia, Nr. 578 op. geh., Befehl der Heeresgruppe Eichhorn, 14.4.1918.

120 HStA Stuttgart, M 46/5e, Korps Knoerzer, Abt. Ic, Nr. 1121, Heeresgruppe Eichhorn drahtet am 25.4.1918, 29.4.1918. Printed in *Die Deutsche Okkupation der Ukraine. Geheimdokumenten* (Strasbourg, 1937), 59.

121 BayHStA-KA, 1. Kav.Brig., Bd. 12, Heeresgruppe Eichhorn, Nr. 377/18, 5.5.1918. Using the reference number for this order, one finds in another document that it was already given on 27 April 1918. Cf. BayHStA-KA, Kav.Div., Bd. 22, Bezirk Wolhynien, Generalkommando XXII. R.K., Abt. Ia, Nr. 1103 op., 4.5.1918.

the authority of military courts.[122] As before, this order did not apply to all instances where public security was threatened. In the case of offenses by Ukrainians committed against Ukrainian authorities, the offenders had to be handed over to a Ukrainian court. This regulation did not please some hardliners, such as the commander of the Bavarian Cavalry Division, who feared that it could be "interpreted as a weakness."[123] Moreover, some German commanders believed that because of this new regulation they no longer needed to rely on cooperation with the Ukrainian authorities.[124]

But Army Group Eichhorn-Kiew very quickly countered this trend, since cooperation with the local Ukrainian authorities was a cornerstone of what was perhaps the only successful chapter in the German period of occupation—combating partisan groups and pacifying the country. The initial conditions here were extremely unfavorable, as the demobilized Russian soldiers returned from the front with their weapons. Social and political tensions exacerbated the situation. The systematic disarmament of the villages was therefore "the only way to pacify the country,"[125] and this was the central task of the Central Powers' troops during the months of occupation.[126] Shortly after the Hetman came to power, there were two joint instructions from the Army Group and the Ukrainian government concerning the billeting of troops in public and private quarters and cooperation "with the Ukrainian authorities in maintaining peace, order, and security."[127]

An order from Army Group Eichhorn-Kiew on 23 May 1918 undermined this policy. The Army Group demanded "the sharpest measures against rebellious elements" and recourse to "the practices of warfare" in dealing with resistance. It recognized, at the same time, that only a minority of peasants, about 10 or 12 percent, were

---

122 Cf. BayHStA-KA, 1. Kav.Brig., Bd. 12, Heeresgruppe Eichhorn, Nr. 377/18, 5.5.1918.

123 BayHStA-KA, Kav.Div., Bd. 21, Bezirk Wolhynien West. Bay.Kav.Division, Abt. Ia, Nr. 2349 W, Innere Lage im Bezirk Wolhynien West, 18.8.1918.

124 BayHStA-KA, Kav.Div., Bd. 22, Bezirk Wolhynien, Generalkommando XXII. R.K., Abt. Ia, Nr. 1103 op., 4.5.1918. An addendum from the General Command states that "According to this order, the participation of Ukrainian authorities in disarmament is no longer necessary."

125 HStA Stuttgart, M 46/16, Heeresgruppe Eichhorn, Abt. Ia, Nr. 3086/18, 26.7.1918.

126 As an example of the concrete disarmament process carried out by Austro-Hungarian troops, see the daily entries, especially from May to July: ÖStA, KA, AdT, FJBat 13, Kt. 754, 6. Tagebuch des Feldjägerbataillons Nr. 13; ÖStA, KA, AdT, UR 3, Kt. 800, Lagebuch I.

127 The written instructions reached the Austro-Hungarian AOK through Waldbott, the Austro-Hungarian liaison officer to Army Group Eichhorn-Kiew: ÖStA, KA, FA, AOK, OpAbt, Kt. 472, Nr. 1712, Aktenkonvolut zu den Verhältnissen in der Ukraine v. 29.5.–30.6.1918.

terrorizing "the whole country." "Foolhardy measures such as mistreatment and the burning of houses" only damaged "Germany's reputation."[128] Whatever the ambivalence of this order, it was a clear rejection of indiscriminate terror methods. From mid-May, Eichhorn could no longer assume that more troops would be sent to the East, so he had to rely increasingly, *nolens volens*, on assistance from the native population in pacifying the country.[129]

But these measures had no rapid effect, as it appeared in some regions that the Germans had lost control to the rebels. In June 1918 there were large uprisings,[130] particularly in the area of Smila, Zvenyhorodka, and Uman (Cherkasy oblast). At the end of June, the Austro-Hungarian liaison officer to Army Group Eichhorn-Kiew, Captain Klemens Waldbott, reported that the German troops "had proceeded vigorously and forcefully against the revolutionary peasants," although, in the previous months, they had been critical of the brutal behavior of the Austro-Hungarian troops: "Today they resort to drastic measures, perhaps a little late."[131] On 27 June, Mumm had delivered a handwritten note from the Kaiser to the Hetman in which he was called upon to "Ukrainize the Kyiv government" in order to pacify the country.[132]

The suppression of these uprisings in the vicinity of Zvenyhorodka deserves closer analysis in order to better understand the evolution of the German approach. The XXVII Reserve Corps was responsible for security in the town as well as in the areas affected by the uprisings. Its commander, General Bernhard von Watzdorf, had arrived in Ukraine at the beginning of April, that is, before the outbreak of the rebellion. In spite of the generally chaotic conditions, he was "determined," as he wrote in his journal, "to establish order here and to create trust in us among the population."[133] In an order issued a few days later,

---

128 BayHStA-KA, Kav.Div., Bd. 21. Heeresgruppe Eichhorn, Abt. Ia, Nr. 1094/18, 23.5.1918. On the burning of villages, see Fritsche, *Das königlich sächsische Landwehr Infanterieregiment Nr. 106*, 181.

129 BayHStA-KA, Kav.Div., Bd. 22, Heeresgruppe Eichhorn, Abt. Ia, Nr. 1093/18, 23.5.1918.

130 ÖStA, KA, FA, NFA, HHK AK/AGKdo, 2. Armee, OpAK, Kt. 308, 1918 Situations- und Tagesmeldungen, Nr. 4185/1, Morgenmeldung vom 10.5.1918.

131 ÖStA, KA, FA, AOK, OpAbt, Kt. 472, Nr. 1712, Aktenkonvolut zu den Verhältnissen in der Ukraine, 29.5.–30.6.1918.

132 ÖStA, KA, FA, AOK, OpAbt, Kt. 472, Nr. 1712, Aktenkonvolut zu den Verhältnissen in der Ukraine, 29.5.–30.6.1918. According to rumors that Waldbott relayed in his report, Eichhorn and Groener had threatened to leave Kyiv and had threatened Mumm with decommissioning. This claim has not been able to be verified with reference to German or Ukrainian documents.

133 BA-MA, N 776/45, Tagebuch Generalleutnant v. Watzdorf, Eintrag v. 7.4.1918.

he stressed the need for explicit cooperation with the Ukrainian authorities in all administrative questions and in the disarmament of the villages. Mistakes would thereby be avoided. Although Watzdorf admitted that executing administrative tasks "contradicts our soldierly feelings," the German officer and soldier should set an "example" to "win the trust of the whole nation."[134] This Saxon general thus showed himself to be an extremely level-headed and moderate officer. In the following months, with the 15th Bavarian Reserve Infantry Brigade subordinated to him, he managed to pacify this turbulent region with a comparatively modern approach to combating insurgency.

The Bavarian Reserve Infantry Brigade had to begin its mission under difficult circumstances. True, at first the Bolsheviks seldom attacked German soldiers, but they plundered and murdered the Ukrainian population in the brigade's area of deployment. Initially the brigade was unable to deploy enough troops to put an end to the disturbances. At the end of March, a battalion of the 126th Landwehr Infantry Regiment was unable, on its own, to disarm the city of Yelysavethrad (present-day Kirovohrad). The situation escalated. In the opinion of the brigade commander, Major General Franz Samhaber, the villages could not be disarmed effectively without the "sharpest measures," i.e., the death penalty.[135] In mid-April, to ensure the surrender of weapons, units of the brigade began taking hostages in some villages, even though these hostages were not shot. But this measure brought only modest success, as, according to the brigade, the peasants seldom gave up their weapons.[136] The weapons recovered demonstrated the existence of an enormous threat: 2 cannon, 39 machine guns, 10,119 rifles, and 494 pistols were surrendered in May alone.[137] On 20 May, an aroused group of peasants in the village of Okhrimove threatened a detachment of the 11th Landwehr Cavalry Schützen Regiment and killed a German soldier. The brigade requested permission from the XXVII Reserve Corps to burn the village, since it was impossible to

134 BayHStA-KA, Etappenkommandantur 54, Bd. 22, Militärbezirk Kiew, XXVII. Res.Korps, Abt. Ia, Nr. 1100, 13.4.1918.

135 BayHStA-KA, 15. Res.Inf.Brig., Bd. 7, Bayr. 15. Res.Inf.Brigade, Nr. 1489, An den Militärbezirk Kiew. XXVII, Res.Korps, Bericht über die Ereignisse vom 8., 9., 10., 11.4.1918.

136 BayHStA-KA, 15. Res.Inf.Brig., Bd. 7, K.bayr. 15. Res.Inf.Brigade, Nr. 2602, Brigadebefehl, 23.5.1918.

137 BayHStA-KA, 15. Res.Inf.Brig., Bd. 7, K.bayr. 15. Res.Inf.Brigade, Nr. 2374, Entwaffnungen. Nachweisung der abgenommenen Waffen vom 1.–15.5.1918, 17.5.1918; BayHStA-KA, 15. Res.Inf.Brig., Bd. 7, K.bayr. 15. Res.Inf.Brigade, Nr. 2907, Entwaffnungen. Nachweisung der abgenommenen Waffen vom 16.–31.5.1918, 2.6.1918.

investigate who was guilty.[138] The corps rejected this. Even earlier, at the end of April, Watzdorf had prohibited "the burning of houses and villages" and had explicitly ordered the protection of the innocent, namely women and children.[139]

It was shortly afterward that the above-mentioned uprising took place in the area of Smila, Zvenyhorodka, and Uman, which was in the brigade's area of responsibility. It was to become the largest uprising during the period of occupation. Beginning on 5 June, incited and led by the Bolsheviks and onetime Rada supporters, poor peasants and decommissioned soldiers in a wide area south of Kyiv rebelled against the Hetman government and the German troops.[140] The rebels took the entire German Gotha Landsturm Battalion and a squadron of the 4th Hussar Regiment prisoner. At first, these prisoners were generally well treated. The "murder of German soldiers" happened "in only a few cases."[141] Influenced by these events, Army Group Eichhorn-Kiew issued a strict order. The uprising was to be suppressed using "the harshest measures." This meant that all participants in the uprising and all those engaged in acts of sabotage were "to be judged in accordance with the customs of warfare and shot." German officers were to make use of "all measures" to combat "the blind confidence that resides in the character of our men." The XXVII Reserve Corps, extremely moderate until then, added to this command: "in the villages concerned, ruthless examples are to be set."[142] The corps now approved even the burning of houses or whole villages, although only in "individual cases, when the villages are particularly rebellious" and "the male population has left."[143]

Shortly afterward, however, the XXVII Reserve Corps qualified these instructions. The burning of villages was again prohibited because this created "homeless elements" that would be "new replacements" for

---

138 BayHStA-KA, 15. Res.Inf.Brig., Bd. 1, 15. Bayerische Reserve Infanteriebrigade, KTB, Eintrag v. 20.5.1918.

139 BayHStA-KA, 15. Res.Inf.Brig., Bd. 7, Militärbezirk Kiew. XXVII, Res.Korps, Abt. Ia, Nr. 1370, 28.4.1918. Similar requests were made by the XXII. Reserve Corps: BayHStA-KA, Kav.Div., Bd. 21, Bezirk Wolhynien. Generalkommando XXII. R.K, Abt. Ia, Nr. 578 op.geh., 14.4.1918.

140 A daily report from Army Group Eichhorn-Kiew speaks of at least 5,000 insurgents: BA-MA, N 46/171, Heeresgruppe Eichhorn, Lage am 10.6.1918 morgens.

141 BayHStA-KA, 15. Res.Inf.Brig., Bd. 7, K.Bayr. 15. Res.Inf.Brigade, Nr. 9417 Adj., Gekürzte Truppenberichte über die Unruhen in und bei Zvenyhorodka, 18.6.1918; BayHStA-KA, 15. Res. Inf.Brig., Bd. 7, Militärbezirk Kiew. XXVII. R.K., Abt. Ia, Nr. 2300, Korpsbefehl, 13.6.1918.

142 BayHStA-KA, 15. Res.Inf.Brig., Bd. 7, Heeresgruppe Eichhorn, Abt. Ia, Nr. 1595/18, Brieftelegramm an das Generalkommando XXVII, Res.Korps, 9.6.1918.

143 BayHStA-KA, 15. Res.Inf.Brig., Bd. 7, K.Bayr. 15. Res.Inf.Brig., Nr. 3298, 13.6.1918.

the bands. The burning of individual houses and farms was, "for this reason, to be restricted to the most urgent exceptional cases."[144] The counterproductive effects of these indiscriminate measures had been recognized very quickly. The 15th Bavarian Reserve Infantry Brigade also prohibited firing on villages as a way of forcing them to give up weapons.[145] At the same time, it prohibited the taking of hostages, since this way of exerting pressure on villages to disarm had proved ineffective. In future, rebellious communities would have to give up money, cattle, or grain.[146] This, in 1918, was what was generally understood in Ukraine to be "the harshest measures."[147] It should be recalled that orders in Ukraine in 1918 to set "ruthless examples" did not mean wiping out entire villages, civilians included, as happened in the Second World War.

There are also no indications of massacres in the documents relating to the suppression of revolt in Zvenyhorodka. The orders in existence left very little room for arbitrary action. The 15th Bavarian Reserve Infantry Brigade had already issued an order that, in the case of large operations, a legal councillor (*Kriegsgerichtsrat*) was to accompany the troops. This allowed judgments to be enforced immediately, and it also meant that the troops were acting within a legal framework. It was emphasized that there should be clear evidence in cases brought before a military court.[148] Finally, "a German court" could "condemn no one...whose guilt had not been proven to the court."[149] Before the outbreak of the unrest, the brigade commander, Samhaber, had impressed on his troops that "our appearance must be resolute and calm."[150] "Harshness" was to be

---

144 BayHStA-KA, 15. Res.Inf.Brig., Bd. 7, Militärbezirk Kiew, XXVII. Res.Korps, Abt. Ia, Nr. 2793, Bestrafung und Entwaffnung von Ortschaften, 18.7.1918.

145 BayHStA-KA, 15. Res.Inf.Brig., Bd. 7, K.bayr. 15. Res.Inf.Brigade, Nr. 3365, Adj. Brigadebefehl v. 15.6.1918.

146 BayHStA-KA, 15. Res.Inf.Brig., Bd. 7, K.bayr. 15. Res.Inf.Brigade, Nr. 3239, Adj. Brigadebefehl v. 12.6.1918.

147 BayHStA-KA, 15. Res.Inf.Brig., Bd. 7, Militärbezirk Kiew. XXVII, Res.Korps, Abt. Ia, Nr. 1755, Zusätze des Generalkommandos v. 19.5.1918. This says, among other things: "When penal measures are being applied, all villages nearby should be involved and, through the imposition of contributions in kind, should be forced to give up the guilty parties."

148 BayHStA-KA, 15. Res.Inf.Brig., Bd. 7, K.bayr. 15. Res.Inf.Brigade, Nr. 4460, Merkblatt für Unterweisung von Führern und Mannschaften für ihr Verhalten im besetzten Gebiet und bei Unternehmungen, 15.7.1918.

149 BayHStA-KA, 15. Res.Inf.Brig., Bd. 7, Bez.Komdtr. Smiela, Merkblatt, 10.6.1918; BayHStA-KA, 15. 4. Kav.Brig., Bd. 4, Gruppe Tannstein. Nr. 3020/I, Gerichtliches Verfahren gegen Landeseinwohner, 11.9.1918.

150 BayHStA-KA, 15. Res.Inf.Brig., Bd. 7, K.Bayr. 15. Res.Inf.Brigade, Nr. 2602, Brigadebefehl, 23.5.1918.

avoided in future so that "the well-disposed part of the population does not have to suffer for the actions of evil-minded minorities." "Friendly inhabitants" should "be well treated and protected in every respect."[151] Collective liability of the civilian population for the actions of individuals was thereby rejected.[152]

A widespread railway strike in late July/early August as well as further disturbances in the Chernihiv region in August 1918 certainly showed that Ukraine had not been completely pacified. But these uprisings in the summer of 1918 remained "local."[153] By August, the 15th Bavarian Reserve Infantry Brigade managed to suppress the last flickers of the June uprisings and pacify the area constructively, although initially this peace was very fragile. The brigade was able to restore peace and order by means of a "systematically constructed network of agents," close cooperation[154] with Ukrainian officials, and local auxiliaries. A program for deserters who had participated in uprisings began to bear fruit. A longer deployment of individual units in particular locations proved particularly effective because they could then win the trust of the local population. Also, cooperation with the Ukrainian administration could be improved through personal contact.[155] In fact, troops in transit or troops brought in for a short period to deal with uprisings were much more often to be blamed for attacks on the local population than units that were stationed locally.[156]

There were, however, also voices demanding harsher action. These came from the cavalry, in other words, precisely from those units that were frequently called in to act as "fire engines" and quickly put down local uprisings. During the uprisings south of Kyiv, the 4th Bavarian Cavalry Brigade requested its superior, the 93rd Infantry Division, to allow the destruction of whole villages, even though their superiors had long ago adopted a moderate approach. "Only immediate punishment

---

151 BayHStA-KA, 15. Res.Inf.Brig., Bd. 7, K.Bayr. 15. Res.Inf.Brigade Nr. 4460, Merkblatt für Unterweisung von Führern und Mannschaften für ihr Verhalten im besetzten Gebiet und bei Unternehmungen, 15.7.1918.

152 See the explicit instruction of the XXVII Reserve Corps: BayHStA-KA, 15. Res.Inf.Brig., Bd. 30, Militärbezirk Kiew, XXVII. Res.Korps, Abt. Ib, Nr. 12406, Zwangsauflagen, 7.7.1918.

153 BayHStA-KA, Kav.Div., Bd. 20, Nachrichtenoffizier der OHL, Heeresgruppe Eichhorn, Zentral-Abt., Tgb. Nr. 703, Innere Lage, 28.6.1918.

154 Skoropadsky later claimed that the initiative for cooperation came from him: *Pavlo Skoropads'kyj. Erinnerungen 1917 bis 1918,* ed. Günter Rosenfeld (Stuttgart, 1999), 280ff.

155 BayHStA-KA, 15. Res.Inf.Brig., Bd. 7, K.Bayr.15. Res.Inf.Brigade, Nr. 7701/Adj., Monatsbericht über die allgemeine Lage, 22.9.1918.

156 BayHStA-KA, 15. Res.Inf.Brig., Bd. 30, Militärbezirk Kiew, XXVII. Res.Korps, Abt. Ia, Nr. 3919, 13.9.1918.

will create a deterring example so that other villages do not dare to join the insurrection, and the conditions that enable the bands to exist will be removed." According to the 4th Bavarian Cavalry Brigade, little would be achieved by taking provisions from these villages.[157] Unfortunately, the response of the Infantry Division to this request has not been preserved, but it seems that the request was not granted.[158]

The Austro-Hungarian Zone of Occupation

There was a similar evolution in the strategy for combating insurgency in the area controlled by Austro-Hungarian troops. At first, insurgents or those found sabotaging provisions, crops, or infrastructure were "immediately killed," but this changed as the months passed.[159] At the beginning of June, the Austro-Hungarian Army High Command (AOK) recommended fines for killed and wounded soldiers (40,000 and 10,000 rubles respectively) instead of the burning of villages. This would be a "more practical" approach, as this money would make it possible to finance new purchases.[160] Until then, it had been common practice to burn houses or whole villages as a way of forcing the inhabitants to hand over provisions or weapons.[161] In spite of this, in June, troops were still being instructed to adopt a ruthless approach to restoring order, especially in the search for weapons.[162]

On 1 June, at the request of Germany's ally, martial law was declared in the Katerynoslav and Kherson gubernias. Following criticism from the Foreign Ministry and AOK about a too lax approach, Krauss felt under pressure to act. In his report to AOK at the beginning of July, he summarized a number of stricter measures being used to combat unrest. In agreement with the Ukrainian government, the use of military courts was to be extended to cases of activities "aimed directly

---

157 BayHStA-KA, 4. Kav.Brig., Bd. 4, Bayer. 4. Kav.Brig., Nr. 1648/I, An 93. Infanteriedivision, Tätigkeit der verst. 4. Bay. Kav.Brig. v. 26.6.–30.6.18, 30.6.1918.

158 The brigade commander, von Poschinger, was appointed shortly afterwards to take command of 93rd Infantry Division. In a divisional order issued just fourteen days later, Poschinger made it clear that contributions, rather than the burning of houses or localities, were to be the method of punishment. Cf. BayHStA-KA, 2. S.R.R., Bd. 7, 93. Infanteriedivision, Abt. Ia, Nr. 595 op, Divisionsbefehl, 15.7.1918.

159 ÖStA, KA, AdT, 145. IBrig, Kt. 1378, F. 68, Nr. 979, Expositur des 2. Armeekommandos (QAbt) an k.u.k. Stationskommando Sinielnikowo, 18.5.1918. This was announced in both Russian and Ukrainian: ÖStA, KA, AdT, 145. IBrig, Kt. 1378, F. 69.

160 ÖStA, KA, FA, AOK, OpAbt, Kt. 471, Nr. 1681, Überfälle an Soldaten, 6.6.1918.

161 ÖStA, KA, AdT, FJB 13, Kt. 754, 6. Tagebuch des Feldjägerbataillons Nr. 13, Einträge v. 11.5.1918, 20.–31.5.1918.

162 ÖStA, KA, AdT, UR 3, Kt. 800, Lagebuch I, Eintrag v. 5.6.1918.

or indirectly against our interests" and "agitation and incitement against the Ukrainian government." Acts of sabotage against railways, harvest, and property would be more severely punished (by "heavier fines," among other things), and the disarmament of the population would be continued vigorously. "Sailors of the Black Sea Fleet known to be particularly dangerous" would be arrested and assigned to worker formations. Since citizens of the Entente states were also suspected of sabotage and incitement, they would be placed under control, and the Italian and French consuls would be expelled from Odesa. "Politically unreliable elements would soon be interned."[163]

As in the German zone, there were three phases in the counterinsurgency measures in the Austro-Hungarian zone of occupation. These were in May and June, when the insurgency was at its height; in July and August, when the situation was relatively calm; and in September and October, when the resistance had almost completely faded away, although it flared up again briefly at the end of the occupation.

According to a report from AOK's chief of staff, the resistance movement had grown after the formation of the Hetman government, and the prestige of the Central Powers had suffered thereby.[164] As a reaction to this, an extensive disarmament was begun on 7 May in which the units involved proceeded quite rigorously. Böhm-Ermolli allowed only German settlers and former Russian and Romanian officers to carry weapons.[165] These disarmament actions seem to have led to an embarrassing number of Austro-Hungarian losses, which

---

163 ÖStA, KA, FA, AOK, OpAbt, Kt. 472, Nr. 1706, Repressivmaßnahmen gegen die Unruhen auf dem Land in der Ukraine und Proteste dagegen, 12.6.1918; ÖStA, KA, FA, AOK, Ukraine Akten, Kt. 2.615, Nr. 3070, Bericht des k.k. Eisenbahnministeriums an Ukraine-Abteilung, 10.7.1918. Although not as explicit as Forgách, a report from Waldbott, on 15 June, emphasized the uncertainty of the situation and implied repeatedly that a more vigorous approach was necessary: ÖStA, KA, FA, AOK, OpAbt, Kt. 472, Nr. 1707, Bericht über die Aufbringung der Lebensmittel durch den k.u.k. bevollmächtigten Generalstabsoffizier beim Oberkmdo der HG Eichhorn-Kiew, 15.6.1918. On the Austro-Hungarian system of military courts, see Hans Hautmann, "Fragen des Strafvollzuges in der Endphase des Habsburgerreiches (1872–1918)," in *Justiz und Geschichte. Symposionsbeiträge 1976–1993,* ed. Erika Weinzierl et al., vol. 1 (Vienna, 1995), 664–84; Mathias Preuschl, "Österreichische Militärstrafgerichtsbarkeit 1914 bis 1918. Rechtliche Grundlagen und Judikatur" (Ph.D. diss., Vienna, 1999).

164 ÖStA, KA, FA, AOK, Ukraine Akten, Kt. 2.626, Mappe "Ukraine. Geheimakten," Nr. 77, Lage in der Ukraine, 7.8.1918; ÖStA, KA, AdT, 145. IBrig, Kt. 1378, Nr. 823, Verbreitung von Proklamationen, 12.5.1918.

165 ÖStA, KA, AdT, 145. IBrig, Kt. 1378, F. 69, ohne Nr., Befehl Böhm-Ermollis, 7.5.1918; ÖStA, KA, AdT, 145. IBrig, Kt. 1379, Nr. 922, Vollständige Entwaffnung der Ukraine, 7.5.1918.

the XII Corps attributed to too much "blind confidence."[166] Again at the beginning of May, the command urgently instructed its troops: "Anyone bearing a weapon who commits an offense against our troops is to be killed immediately on the spot." Austro-Hungarian prisoners of war guilty of a punishable offense (especially agitation against the Monarchy, the Imperial Army, or the Central Powers) were to be arrested immediately and handed over to the nearest military court. All Russians, Ukrainians, and "other foreigners" found "inciting or agitating against our military" were to be arrested and handed over to the Army Command in the city of Katerynoslav, where they would be remanded to a Ukrainian military court.[167] Ukrainians whose offenses against the Austro-Hungarian military were not of a military nature were generally handed over to a Ukrainian court.[168] At the end of May, Ambassador Forgách praised the success that had been achieved by "these vigorous and harsh measures" and recommended that this approach be continued in spite of Ukrainian protests.[169]

One of the most serious incidents in the Austro-Hungarian zone occurred on 18 May 1918. Fourteen kilometers north of Yampil in Podilia, a food transport with an eighteen-man escort was captured by armed peasants. Two battalions of the XXV Corps were sent on a punitive expedition and were attacked from the village. The Austro-Hungarian units returned fire and burned the village to ashes. "About 100 peasants were killed and 9 executed. Among our own men, 1 dead, 3 wounded, 1 missing." At the same time, farther north, three hundred "mounted peasants/free Cossacks" attacked Austro-Hungarian troops. Following unsuccessful negotiations, the attack on Pysarivka was extended. The peasants surrendered the next day, and eighteen field guns with munitions as well as a large cache of weapons were seized. A similar incident occurred on 16 June in the vicinity of Kanizh, where

166 ÖStA, KA, AdT, FABrig 59, Kt. 4131, Nr. 276, Bemerkungen aufgrund letzter Inspizierung, 17.6.1918; ÖStA, KA, AdT, FABrig 59, Kt. 4131, Nr. 307, Verhalten der Zivilbevölkerung gegenüber, 20.8.1918.

167 This order was issued again at the end of May and included additional instructions concerning the type of custody. It was emphasized that this order should be strictly enforced: ÖStA, KA, AdT, FABrig 59, Kt. 4131, Nr. 197, Abänderung der Bestimmungen bzgl. Behandlung, 26. Mai; ÖStA, KA, AdT, 145. IBrig, Kt. 1378, F. 68, Nr. 471, Definition des Kriegsnotwehrrechtes, 25. April.

168 ÖStA, KA, AdT, UR 3, Kt. 800, Lagebücher, Einträge vom 6., 14., 16.6.1918, 12., 19., 29.7.1918, 16.9.1918.

169 ÖStA, HHStA, MdÄ, PA X, Kt. 152, Russland: Liasse XI d, Brief von Forgách an Burian vom 31.5.1918.

62 insurgents were executed.[170] In the area where the XII Corps was stationed, there were also frequent serious incidents. According to a succinct evening report of 22 June to the *Ostarmee*, "On an expedition in the area of Myloradivka and Huliaipole...47 Bolshevik murderers were killed; on a patrol along the west bank of the Dnipro south of Katerynoslav, 37 robbers were executed. Seized weapons were given to German colonists. Order restored." The report does not give any reason for this rigorous approach.[171]

Since these many attacks caused great disquiet among the Ukrainian population, at the end of June the XII Corps issued a directive concerning behavior toward civilians during disarmament operations. Care should be taken when making an arrest, and enquiries should be made concerning the information and sources on the basis of which the arrest was made. Attacks on arrestees would not be tolerated, and those arrested should be handed over immediately to a military court. Following a successful disarmament, weapons and firearms passes should be given to "trustworthy people," and a start should be made to setting up a village militia. Nevertheless, "People bearing weapons who commit offenses against Austro-Hungarian military personnel are of course to be killed immediately, i.e., at the place where the offense was committed."[172]

Perhaps as a result of this more cooperative approach, there was a decline in the numbers killed in July and August. According to the daily reports of the various sections of the *Ostarmee*, in May and June alone more than five hundred individuals were "executed," shot, or "lost their lives" in flight during these "punitive expeditions," "patrols," and "weapons searches." In the following months until October—double the amount of time—only 380 deaths were reported. Most of these, described as "Bolsheviks," were individuals or units made up of workers, Red Guards, insurgent peasants or, in some cases, Cossacks

170 ÖStA, KA, FA, NFA, HHK AK/AGKdo, 2. Armee, OpAK, Kt. 308, 1918 Situations- und Tagesmeldungen, Nr. 4493/8, Abendmeldung v. 20.5.1918; ÖStA, KA, FA, NFA, HHK AK/AGKdo, 2. Armee, OpAK, Kt. 308, 1918 Situations- und Tagesmeldungen, Nr. 4525/8, Abendmeldung v. 21.5.1918; ÖStA, KA, FA, NFA, HHK AK/AGKdo, 2. Armee, OpAK, Kt. 308, 1918 Situations- und Tagesmeldungen, Nr. 5772/8, Abendmeldung vom 18.6.1918; ÖStA, KA, AdT, 145. IBrig, Kt. 1378, Nr. 1093, Verlautbarung von Vorfällen gegen die k.u.k. Truppen, 21.5.1918. For more detail, see chapter 3d in the present volume.

171 Underlining in original: ÖStA, KA, FA, NFA, HHK AK/AGKdo, 2. Armee, OpAK, Kt. 308, 1918 Situations- und Tagesmeldungen, Nr. 5901/8, Abendmeldung v. 22.6.1918.

172 ÖStA, KA, AdT, FABrig 59, Kt. 4131, Nr. 307, Verhalten der Zivilbevölkerung gegenüber, 20.8.1918.

fighting the Central Powers.[173] In July and August, reports continued concerning the formation of bands and local insurrections.[174] There were fewer shootings and "executions." Instead, the imposition of fines was stepped up. In addition, positive behavior toward the population could lead to a commendation from Division Command.[175]

Nevertheless, bloody incidents continued in the summer. On 16 July the XII Corps reported 48 persons killed during patrols over a number of days. The reason given was that "there is evidence that they had taken part in the earlier murder of hussars at Volodymyrivka or were robbers."[176] There was another more significant incident when a planned attack by 600–800 Bolsheviks on Austro-Hungarian troops in Mariupol was betrayed. In spite of this, on the night of 23–24 July they managed for a time to occupy the field hospital and steal provisions as well as money. In the street fighting that then occurred, there were dead and wounded on both sides. Most of the rebels fled to the harbor, where they were surrounded and, "in the hunt that followed, numerous Bolsh[eviks] were killed." A number of Bolsheviks attempted to flee in a sailing ship but were prevented by artillery and planes. They then withdrew to the railway station, where they were bombarded with artillery. Although they scattered throughout the town and in the surrounding villages, some were captured and "court-martialed." On 25 July the situation was calm again, and the Austro-Hungarian troops began the search for weapons so as to prevent new uprisings.[177] It is not clear from the documents how many Bolsheviks were killed but, in view of the large numbers involved in the attack, it was probably several hundred.

---

173 See the daily reports to the Command of the *Ostarmee*/2nd Army: ÖStA, KA, FA, NFA, HHK AK/AGKdo, 2. Armee, OpAK, Kt. 308, 1918 Situations- und Tagesmeldungen. See also the note in Dornik, "Die Besatzung der Ukraine 1918 durch österreichisch-ungarische Truppen," 166, n. 84.

174 ÖStA, HHStA, MdÄ, PA X, Kt. 153, Russland Liasse XId/1 Fortsetzung bis Schluss, Juni–November 1918, Nr. 13.290, Telegramm von Zitkovsky an das Ministerium des Äußern, 18.8.1918; ÖStA, HHStA, MdÄ, PA X, Kt. 153, Russland Liasse XId/1 Fortsetzung bis Schluss, Juni–November 1918, Nr. 9004, Ordre de bataille der Ostarmee, 20.8.1918.

175 ÖStA, KA, AdT, FABrig 59, Kt. 4131, Nr. 307, Verhalten der Zivilbevölkerung gegenüber, 20.8.1918.

176 ÖStA, KA, FA, NFA, HHK AK/AGKdo, 2. Armee, OpAK, Kt. 308, 1918 Situations- und Tagesmeldungen, Nr. 6834/8, Abendmeldung v. 16.7.1918.

177 ÖStA, KA, FA, NFA, HHK AK/AGKdo, 2. Armee, OpAK, Kt. 308, 1918 Situations- und Tagesmeldungen Nr. 7142/8, Abendmeldung v. 24.7.1918; ÖStA, KA, FA, NFA, HHK AK/AGKdo, 2. Armee, OpAK, Kt. 308, 1918 Situations- und Tagesmeldungen, Nr. 7176/8, Auszug aus der Abendmeldung vom 25.7.1918; ÖStA, KA, FA, NFA, HHK AK/AGKdo, 2. Armee, OpAK, Kt. 308, 1918 Situations- und Tagesmeldungen, Nr. 7217/8, Abendmeldung vom 26.7.1918.

Although a bit later than the Germans, from the summer of 1918 the Austro-Hungarians began to cooperate more closely with the Ukrainian administration. On 10 July the commander of the 59th Infantry Division announced to his troops that, in future, "in cases of unrest, uprisings, arrests, and other similar official actions," they were to cooperate with the Ukrainian militia. With the approval of higher-level command, Austro-Hungarian troops were to offer military support to the Ukrainian militia. The Austro-Hungarians would decide how the action was to be carried out, but the relevant Ukrainian official was responsible for the action.[178] Nevertheless, this did not prevent the continued use of collective punitive violence in the following months. For instance, on 26 August the XXV Corps reported that bands in its area had been suppressed during previous days. The bands had been dispersed, weapons searches carried out and, with the help of informers, a number of band members had been arrested. "Twenty-nine members of bands were immediately shot. A number of houses belonging to residents who joined bands were destroyed."[179]

Even when the situation had become calmer,[180] the Austro-Hungarian commanders of the occupation troops did not have complete confidence in this calmness in August and September. The troops were constantly warned of imminent unrest, strikes, and uprisings. This was because appeals to the peasants to rebel cropped up again and again.[181] It was believed that Moscow was pulling the strings here,[182] but there were no major uprisings, although some incidents occurred in September and October. Suspects were generally handed over to the Ukrainian authorities, who then undertook investigations into minor acts of sabotage.[183] In the final days of

---

178 ÖStA, KA, AdT, FABrig 59, Kt. 4131, Nr. 317, Militärische Mitwirkung bei Aktionen der ukrainischen Miliz, 10.7.1918.

179 ÖStA, KA, FA, NFA, HHK AK/AGKdo, 2. Armee, OpAK, Kt. 308, 1918 Situations- und Tagesmeldungen, Nr. 8441/8, Abendmeldung v. 26.8.1918.

180 According to the Austro-Hungarian liaison officer at the German-Austro-Hungarian Economic Headquarters, this was generally apparent from the end of July: ÖStA, KA, AOK, Qu. Abt., Ukraine-Bestand, Kt. 2.617, Nr. 4204, Tätigkeitsbericht der deutsch-österreichisch-ungarischen Wirtschaftsabteilung, 29.7.1918; ÖStA, KA, AOK, Qu. Abt., Ukraine-Bestand, Kt. 2.621, Nr. 6218, Bericht der wirtschaftlichen Aufklärungszentrale beim AK Ost, 7.9.1918; ÖStA, KA, AOK, Qu. Abt., Ukraine-Bestand, Kt. 2.621, Nr. 6300, 19. Wochenbericht, 18.–24.8.1918.

181 ÖStA, KA, FA, AOK, Ukraine Akten, Kt. 2.621, Nr. 6072, Übersetzung eines Aufrufes des Allukrainischen Zentral-Kriegs-Revolutions-Komitees, 26.8.1918.

182 ÖStA, KA, FA, AOK, Ukraine Akten, Kt. 2.626, Mappe "Ukraine.Geheimakten," Nr. 77, Lage in der Ukraine, 7.8.1918; ÖStA, KA, FA, AOK, Ukraine Akten, Kt. 2.626, Mappe "Ukraine. Geheimakten," Nr. 140, Bericht über Bolschewiki in der Ukraine, 27.9.1918.

183 ÖStA, KA, FA, NFA, HHK AK/AGKdo, 2. Armee, OpAK, Kt. 308, 1918 Situations- und

October, the occupying troops again grew increasingly nervous. On 24 October the commander in Odesa, Eduard von Böltz, issued a warning to the troops that disturbances were to be feared the next day (the anniversary of the October Revolution).[184] On the previous day there had been a dramatic incident with numerous killings. On 23 October, units of the 15th Infantry Division and the 59th Search Party Detachment (*Streifdetachement*) began action against a band in which 39 Bolsheviks were shot and a similar number of local residents were stabbed to death. A village was reduced to ashes by artillery fire.[185]

The tactical withdrawal of Russian and Ukrainian Bolsheviks as well as the anti-Hetman movement between August and October also contributed to calming the situation. The Bolsheviks in particular had to rethink their strategy, especially after the failure of the uprisings against Skoropadsky and of the strike in late July and early August. The tough approach of the occupying troops suppressed local uprisings in June and July, and the widespread railway strike had no major effect, as the occupying troops continued to be able to use the railway. The Russian Bolsheviks were facing collapse in the spring and summer of 1918. The Czechoslovak Legion controlled nearly the whole of the Trans-Siberian Railway, while the Whites had had some successes and were receiving support from the Entente. To make matters worse, the Red Army was only in the process of being formed and had suffered heavy losses in the previous months. Lenin now had to concentrate all his forces on maintaining power and winning back or securing the core area of Russia.[186] In a report of 10 October, Klemens Waldbott surmised that "The Bolsheviks are lying in wait for the withdrawal of our troops and are not mistaken in believing that they can then take power in Ukraine." It was Waldbott's opinion that if the Central Powers wanted to prevent the Bolsheviks from coming to power,

---

Tagesmeldungen, Nr. 9711/8, Abendmeldung vom 5.10.1918; ÖStA, KA, FA, NFA, HHK AK/AGKdo, 2. Armee, OpAK, Kt. 308, 1918 Situations- und Tagesmeldungen, Nr. 9745/8, Abendmeldung vom 6.10.1918; ÖStA, KA, FA, NFA, HHK AK/AGKdo, 2. Armee, OpAK, Kt. 308, 1918 Situations- und Tagesmeldungen, Nr. 9938/8, Tagesmeldung vom 11.10.1918.

184 ÖStA, KA, FA, NFA, HHK AK/AGKdo, 2. Armee, QuAbt, Kt. 697, Nr. 7003, Kundmachung, 24.10.1918.

185 ÖStA, KA, FA, NFA, HHK AK/AGKdo, 2. Armee, OpAK, Kt. 308, 1918 Situations- und Tagesmeldungen, ohne Nr., Telegramm des 4. Generalkommandos, 23.10.1918.

186 Orlando Figes, *A People's Tragedy: Russian Revolution 1891–1924* (London, 1996), 589–649; Peter Gosztony, *Die Rote Armee. Geschichte und Aufbau der sowjetischen Streitkräfte seit 1917* (Vienna, Munich, Zurich, and New York, 1980); Verena Moritz, "'Ein Missverständnis, das sich in Kürze aufklären wird.' Der Zwischenfall von Tscheljabinsk und der Bürgerkrieg in Russland," in Verena Moritz and Hannes Leidinger, *Die Nacht des Kirpitschnikow. Eine andere Geschichte des Ersten Weltkriegs* (Vienna, 2006), 171–205. See also chapters 1a, 1b, 2a, and 4b in the present volume.

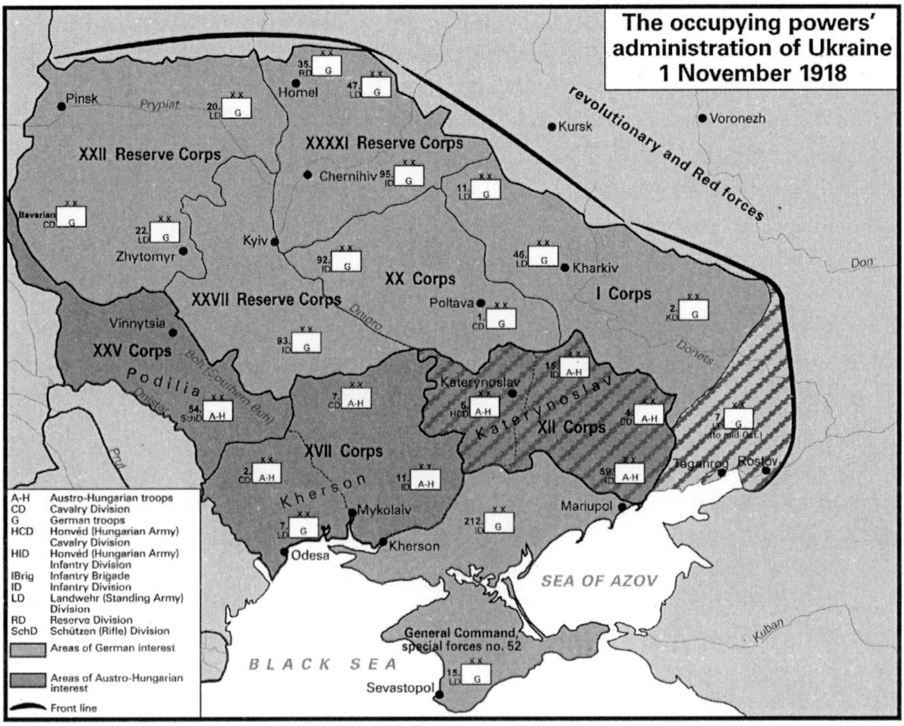

Map 5: The occupying powers' administration of Ukraine, 1 November 1918 (Österreichisches Bundesministerium für Landesverteidigung – Kriegsarchiv, ed., *Österreich-Ungarns letzter Krieg 1914-1918*, vol. 7, supplement 27/2)

then they would have to continue the occupation and, in the event of withdrawal, get a start on "the rapid creation of a Ukrainian national army."[187] This then happened, but much too late for the Ukrainian army to take over the security of the country.

The Withdrawal of Troops from Ukraine, October–December 1918

On 14 October, at Austro-Hungarian Army High Command, a general conference of the chiefs of general staff of all armies took place. They discussed initial preparations for a withdrawal of the armies from the occupied territories "to the peripheral regions of Austria-Hungary." It was agreed that the first priority was the maintenance of law and order and support for the regions concerned on their own territory.[188] Preparations for withdrawal were begun at all levels in the last days

187 ÖStA, KA, FA, AOK, OpAbt, Kt. 474, Nr. 1866, Beurteilung der politischen Lage in der Ukraine, 11.10.1918.

188 ÖStA, KA, FA, AOK, OpAbt, Kt. 476, Nr. 1985, Maßnahmen bei Räumung der besetzten Gebiete, 16.10.1918; ÖStA, KA, FA, NFA, HHK AK/AGKdo, 2. Armee, OpAK, Kt. 309, 1918 Befehle und Verlautbarungen, Allgemeine Verlautbarungen des Kommandos der Ostarmee, 30.10.1918.

of October. It was particularly important that the railway lines and coastal areas of the *Ostarmee* be secured as long as possible.[189]

There were still ten Austro-Hungarian divisions in Ukraine in September, and these were reduced to six by early October. When the Bulgarian front collapsed at the end of September, the emperor ordered Krauss to withdraw his last troops from Ukraine as rapidly as possible and send them to the Balkans. Bulgaria had agreed to a truce and made a peace offer to the Entente on 26 September. The Balkan front thereby collapsed, and the southeastern flank of the Monarchy was directly threatened. At the end of September, the 15th, 30th, and 59th Infantry Divisions as well as the 4th Cavalry Division were moved by ship and rail from Ukraine to the Balkans. This was followed by the return of the Hungarian units, which had started to mutiny at the end of October.[190]

On 25 October, the Hetman asked Major General Lelio von Spannocchi to ensure that Austro-Hungarian troops would remain in Ukraine. At the same time, the Ukrainian foreign ministry asked the United States and other Entente states to allow troops of the Central Powers to stay in Ukraine, since they would "provide the greatest service in fighting all-destroying Bolshevism."[191]

Requests from village elders to the XII Corps at the end of October show that this fear was not unfounded. They requested that not all troops should leave, since insurgents were taking over more and more areas; the environs of Oleksandrivsk (present-day Zaporizhia) and Mariupol were already being terrorized by about five hundred insurgents. The local Austro-Hungarian commanders hesitated to move against them without orders from above, and the

189 ÖStA, KA, AdT, UR 3, Kt. 800, Nr. 167, 21. IBrigKmdo an GrpKdo Nowo-Ukrainka, 30.10.1918; ÖStA, AVA, Nachlässe, Nachlass: Spannocchi, B 760, Fas. 3. Because of the increasing separation of army units, comprehensive measures had already begun in early September to secure the railway lines. The head of railway administration within AOK envisaged an "extensive and thorough destruction of rail lines" during the withdrawal that would "completely paralyze railway transport for a long time." Whether this was done during the withdrawal, and how thoroughly, is not clear from the Austrian documents: ÖStA, KA, NFA, Korpskommanden, 12. Korps, Kt. 1662, ohne Nr., Vorbereitende Maßnahmen auf ukrainischen Bahnen, 1.9.1918. Troops were withdrawn from the Katerynoslav gubernia at the beginning of October. From mid-October these measures were strengthened: ÖStA, KA, FA, NFA, HHK AK/KorpsKdo, 12. Korps, Kt. 1661, Nr. 2599, Sammelakt "Fangstoß"; ÖStA, KA, FA, NFA, HHK AK/KorpsKdo, 12. Korps, Kt. 1661, Nr. 2716, Sammelakt zur Räumung und Zerstörung der Bahnanlagen 8–28.10.1918.

190 ÖStA, AVA, Nachlässe, Nachlass: Krauß, B 60, Fas. 14c, Schreiben von General Alfred Krauß an das Österreichische Kriegsarchiv, 15.4.1932.

191 ÖStA, AVA, Nachlässe, Nachlass: Spannocchi, B 760, Fas. 3, Nr. 1803/9, Spannocchi an AK Ost, ohne Datum.

Ukrainian troops there were too weak to fight against the bands. The corps was unwilling and unable to offer protection and attempted instead to assist Ukrainian military units in arming the population for self-defense.[192]

On 30 October, two days after the Austrian emperor had sought peace and a truce with Italy, the staff of the *Ostarmee* withdrew to Vinnytsia; the security of the city was taken over by the XVII Corps. Krauss later claimed that the withdrawal was justified because, following the removal of the mutinous Hungarian troops, there were not enough troops to secure Odesa (there was fear of a Bolshevik uprising), and he wanted to save the city from an expected attack by the British fleet on the Black Sea.[193] Chaos reigned everywhere. The troops of the *Ostarmee,* with mostly Hungarian and Galician and some South Slav units, were already attempting on their own initiative to get back to their home countries. Since early September, these had been moving inexorably toward independence. Even with his manifesto of 16 October proposing federalization, the emperor was no longer able to halt this development.[194] Ten days later, Karl officially dissolved the alliance with the German Empire.

On 29 October, the Hungarian government ordered its troops to lay down their arms immediately. The soldiers refused to acknowledge the orders of their mostly German- or Hungarian-speaking officers, with whom they ceased to feel a bond. These officers represented the old rulers and no longer had the authority of their new nation-states. Some regiments, such as the 97th Infantry Regiment, sent their German officers home, declared themselves "subject to the Entente," and attempted to reach Belgrade through Romania. In the meantime, parts of the Habsburg Monarchy had become involved in disputes about claims to particular regions, which were also hindering the return transport of troops.

On 4 November the *Ostarmee* made a desperate appeal for an orderly withdrawal. The soldiers were warned that there was a great distance and an unfriendly population between them and their homeland. There was even reference to the withdrawal of Napoleon's

---

192 ÖStA, KA, FA, NFA, HHK AK/KorpsKdo, 12. Korps, Kt. 1662, Nr. 2870/2869, Sammelakt zu Bandaufständen, 26.10.1918.

193 ÖStA, AVA, Nachlässe, Nachlass: Krauß, B 60, Fas. 14c, Schreiben von General Alfred Krauß an das Österreichische Kriegsarchiv, 15.4.1932.

194 For greater detail, see Feliks J. Bister, *"Majestät, es ist zu spät..."Anton Korošec und die slovenische Politik im Wiener Reichsrat bis 1918* (Vienna, Cologne, and Weimar, 1995).

troops in 1812, which had famously ended in catastrophe, as a way of encouraging the troops to stay together and have patience. Lack of discipline and "Bolshevik ideas" were to be "dealt with ruthlessly" by commanders. Krauss ordered: "I appeal finally to everyone to be mindful of their duties to their homeland, to the widows and orphans of their comrades who have died a hero's death on the field of honor. They call on you to make every effort, after a happy return home, to join in the work for the reconstruction and renewal of your fatherland for the good of all."[195]

The fate of the military governor of Odesa, Lieutenant Field Marshal Eduard vonBöltz, can be seen as a symbol of the dramatic and chaotic situation. Having handed over command of the Odesa region to the infantry general Ludwig von Fabini, he committed suicide in Odesa on 9 November.[196] One can only speculate about the reasons for his death, as he did not leave a letter. It remained unclear for weeks what had become of Böltz, and the exact details of the event are still unknown.

In the meantime, communication was interrupted for days between Krauss and Army High Command. Krauss and his staff had no information about the situation at home and were dependent on rumors. On 5 November, a telegram arrived from Army High Command stating that the *Ostarmee* had to stay in Vinnytsia. With his personnel, who were pushing to return home, Krauss decided to move to Rivne, where he was imprisoned for weeks and humiliated by a soldiers' council. It was not until 30 November that they received permission from the Western Ukrainian (Polish) authorities to leave Rivne and return to Vienna through Czechoslovakia. Divested of all their possessions, they arrived in Vienna on 1 December. Only part of the operation's funds was able to be rescued.[197]

Acting individually, the commanders of the various sections of troops sought desperately to maintain order and coordinate the

---

195 ÖStA, KA, AdT, UR 3, Kt. 800, Nr. 1463, Armeebefehl, 4.11.1918. First quoted in: Dornik, "Die Besatzung der Ukraine 1918 durch österreichisch-ungarische Truppen, " 176ff.

196 ÖStA, AVA, Nachlässe, Nachlass: Spannocchi, B 760, Fas. 10, Hughesgespräch zwischen Spannocchi, Kreneis und Belitska, 10.11.1918. Krauss was accused of responsibility for Böltz's suicide, against which he defended himself vigorously. For his own account on the suicide, see ÖStA, AVA, Nachlässe, Nachlass: Krauß, B 60, Fas. 14c, Schreiben von General Alfred Krauß an das Österreichische Kriegsarchiv, 15.4.1932.

197 ÖStA, AVA, Nachlässe, Nachlass: Krauß, B 60, Fas. 14c, Schreiben von General Alfred Krauß an das Österreichische Kriegsarchiv, 15.4.1932.

withdrawal.[198] On 9 November, the corps were made independent and had to find their own way back individually to their garrisons. The return was a test of patience, and most units did not arrive until December. Eastern Galicia had already declared its independence as the Western Ukrainian People's Republic[199] and blocked the railway lines to foreign troops. It was only after lengthy negotiations that the *Ostarmee* was able to reach agreement on the transit of troops with the Ukrainian authorities in Lviv on 20 November and with the Polish authorities in Warsaw on 24 November. Organizational problems exacerbated the difficulty: the change from Russian to Central European gauge, lack of coal, as well as lack of locomotives and rolling stock. The troops were constantly exposed to pillaging by the local population and often had to wait for days at stations before continuing their journey.[200] Of the previous Austro-Hungarian contingent, only Spannocchi, with a small staff, remained in Ukraine. His task was to organize the repatriation of the remaining troops from Ukraine and of the prisoners of war who were now streaming back from civil war-torn Russia. He also had to recover army property or sell it where possible. Spannocchi did not reach Vienna until January 1919.[201]

The situation for German troops in Ukraine was somewhat different. Although the front in Belgium and France was close to collapse, there was still a wish, even in October 1918, to hold on to territory in the East. On 16 October, that is, before Ludendorff's dismissal, Supreme Army Command (OHL) saw "the retention of Ukraine, under present circumstances, as a necessity of war."[202] With their own forces, they thought it possible to deal with a withdrawal of Austro-Hungarian troops east of the Dnipro. But if they were to withdraw across the Buh, Army Group Kiew would not be able to fill

198 ÖStA, KA, AdT, UR 3, Kt. 800, Nr. 1107, Regimentsabfertigung vom 9. November. For the 155th Hungarian Infantry Division, see KA Budapest, F. II.220, Kt. 1, Magyar királyi 155. honvéd gyaloghadosztály. I am grateful to Éva Kosa and Nicole-Melanie Goll for their research in the Hungarian archives and for bringing this document to my attention.

199 For more detail, see chapter 2b in the present volume.

200 ÖStA, KA, FA, NFA, HHK AK/AGKdo, 2. Armee, OpAK, Kt. 308, 1918 Situations- und Tagesmeldungen, Die Ereignisse bei der Ostarmee und beim 4. General-Kommando in der Zeit von Ende Oktober 1918–Jänner 1919.

201 *Österreich-Ungarns letzter Krieg,* 7: 798–800; ÖStA, KA, NFA, 2. Armee, Op. AK, Kt. 308, 1918 Situations- und Tagesmeldungen, Die Ereignisse bei der Ostarmee und beim 4. General-Kommando in der Zeit von Ende Oktober 1918–Jänner 1919. See also Spannocchi's report and the accompanying documents concerning the operations of the *Ostarmee* in November and December 1918: ÖStA, KA, FA, NFA, HHK AK/AGKdo, 2. Armee, QuAbt, Kt. 723.

202 TNA, GFM 6/99, Telegramm Nr. 2464, Der K. Staatssekretär Hintze an AA, 16.10.1918.

the vacuum.[203] As Groener informed Waldbott on 23 October, the Army Group thought it could prevent a possible landing of Entente troops in Ukraine by force of arms. German troops in the Crimea and Tavria had been given the appropriate orders.[204] Shortly afterwards, Groener replaced Ludendorff as first general quartermaster in OHL. The recall of the most capable senior German military leader from Ukraine was not a good sign for any further presence of German troops in the country.

The truce of Compiègne on 11 November fundamentally changed the situation, even though the German Empire had committed itself to leaving German troops in the East until the arrival of Entente troops in order to stop a westward Bolshevik advance. The situation was not a simple one. With the revolution in Germany, soldiers' councils had also been established among the occupation troops in Ukraine.[205] The already ramshackle discipline threatened to disintegrate entirely. Everyone wanted to go home. Some units, though unauthorized to do so, left their posts and abandoned important stretches of railway.[206] The Ukrainian population became increasingly hostile to the occupation troops. The country was in turmoil, and a civil war developed between the troops of the Hetman, the Directory, the Makhno movement, and the Bolsheviks. The remaining troops of the Central Powers found themselves between the various fronts. The partial withdrawal of German troops began on 16 November and was seriously threatened. Organizing the withdrawal presented the military authorities with a central question: should they undertake a long but secure march on foot or use the railway, which was more rapid but significantly riskier, as it exposed them to attack? The great distance and the age structure of most of the regiments led them to choose the second option, which turned out to be the right one.[207]

---

203 See TNA, GFM 6/99, Telegramm Nr. 2154 K. Geschäftsträger an AA, 25.10.1918.

204 ÖStA, AVA, Nachlässe, Nachlass: Spannocchi, B 760, Fas. 3, Nr. 4099, Groener an Waldbott, 23.10.1918.

205 The official regimental history of the 2nd Bavarian Heavy Cavalry Regiment claims that soldiers' councils had been rejected in the regiment and that the soldiers trusted only their officers. If this claim is correct, it sheds interesting light on the self-image of this cavalry regiment. See Frauenholz, *Das K.B. 2. Kürassier- und Schweres Reiterregiment*, 306.

206 BA-MA, PH 6-I/89, XX. Armeekorps. Generalkommando, Abt. Ia, Nr. 3287, 29.12.1918, Ia Mitteilung Nr. XXII.

207 Cf. Velsen, "Deutsche Generalstabsoffiziere im 1. Weltkrieg 1914–1918," 291; ÖStA, KA, NFA, 2. Armee, Op. AK, Kt. 308, 1918 Situations- und Tagesmeldungen, Die Ereignisse bei der Ostarmee und beim 4. General-Kommando in der Zeit von Ende Oktober 1918–Jänner 1919.

German troops were to withdraw from Ukraine in six phases, first from the Crimea and then gradually from east to west.[208] The troops retreated from their outlying garrisons and concentrated themselves along the railway lines in order to secure them. Against all expectations, there was good cooperation between the soldiers' councils and the officers.[209] Both explicitly pointed out the danger of being caught between the fronts in the civil war. The German troops were ordered to remain strictly neutral in the internal battles for control of Ukraine. Only in case of attack on their own troops were they authorized to defend themselves. In Kyiv, the Germans more or less maintained peace and order for a while.[210] On 13 December Army Group Eichhorn-Kiew and the Soldiers' Council signed an agreement with the Directory to hand over the city peacefully and mount a joint struggle against the Bolsheviks.[211] The evacuation of the German troops thus proceeded more or less satisfactorily in spite of quite a few attacks by Bolsheviks and some by Directory troops. On 18 January, Army Group Kiew left the Ukrainian capital, and the last German soldiers came home in mid-February 1919 to a country shaken by revolution.

Conclusion

Communist accounts of Ukraine in 1918 have always attempted to create the image of a growing people's war against which the Germans were powerless.[212] The reality at the time was completely different. By the end of August 1918, the Germans had by and large succeeded in pacifying their zone of occupation. At the beginning of October 1918, Groener wrote home to his wife: "It is so peaceful and quiet in Ukraine

---

208 BArch, R 3101/1180, Oberbefehlshaber Ost, Abt. Ic, Nr. 11826/18, 12.11.1918.

209 See, for example, the joint appeal in: BA-MA, PH 5-I/7, Heeresgruppe Kiew, Abt. Ia, Nr. 7476/18, 18.11.1918; BA-MA, PH 5-I/5, Beschlüsse des Großen Soldatenrats der Heeresgruppe Kiew v. 27.11.1918. See also the warning of Army Group Eichhorn-Kiew to its officers concerning cooperation in BayHStA-KA, 15. Res.Inf.Brig., Bd. 30, Heeresgruppe Kiew, Abt. Ia, Nr. 7448/18, 16.11.1918.

210 See the appeal in BA-MA, PH 5-I/5, An die Einwohner von Kiew. It is interesting that the text was in German and Russian but not in Ukrainian.

211 BayHStA-KA, 15. Res.Inf.Brig., Bd. 30, Heeresgruppe Kiew, Abt. Ia, Nr. 8346/18, 13.12.1918. Near Bilhorod, for instance, German troops killed fleeing Bolsheviks and even received a gift of money "from the grateful population." See BayHStA-KA, Kav.Div., Bd. 20, Gen.Kdo. XXII. R.K., Abt. Ia, Nr. 5245 op, 2.12.1918; BayHStA-KA, Kav.Div., Bd. 20, Bezirk Wolhynien West, Bay.Kav.Div, Abt. Ia, Nr. 5179 W, Tagesbefehl v. 2.12.1918.

212 See *Die Deutsche Okkupation der Ukraine. Geheimdokumenten,* 14; also, for a general account, Joachim Petzold et al., *Deutschland im Ersten Weltkrieg*, vol. 3, *November 1917 bis November 1918* (Berlin, 1969).

at the moment that life would be quite pleasant were it not for the shadows cast by the uncertainties from the other theaters of war and from Berlin."[213] The generals in command of the various German army corps[214] in Ukraine had a similar view of the situation. At a meeting in October, they agreed that the domestic situation in Ukraine was developing favorably and was likely to improve even further.[215] With security established, the conditions required for successful state-building were in place. The Germans also benefited from the fact that the Ukrainian Bolsheviks had held back in the summer.

But the Germans were unable to win the sympathy of the Ukrainian population. As in every uprising, the government and the occupiers were judged by the modest reality, while the rebels, that is, the supporters of the Rada or the Bolsheviks, as well as the other groups fighting the Central Powers or the Hetmanate in either an organized or a sporadic manner, were able to influence the population with promises and propaganda.[216] The peace was an unstable one, as shown by the murder of Field Marshal Eichhorn on 30 July 1918 by a Socialist Revolutionary. The country was unable to overcome its internal divisions and, following the withdrawal of the Central Powers, degenerated into a brutal and bloody civil war.

Winfried Baumgart's assessment was correct: "On the whole, the eight months of the Hetman government were a period of relatively stable peace and order that, one must emphasize, was ensured by the bayonets of the allied troops."[217] If there is a positive aspect to the German and Austro-Hungarian occupation of Ukraine, it was precisely this partial establishment of internal security and a functioning administration in the unstable country. The passage of months was also a learning process for the occupying troops. It is certainly the case that, in suppressing uprisings, they sometimes had recourse to drastic deterrents, but in their subsequent efforts at pacification they very quickly abandoned these terror methods. The core elements of

---

213 *Von Brest-Litovsk zur deutschen Novemberrevolution*, 442.

214 It is unclear from this document whether the reference is to the chiefs of staff, as the term used is "Korpschefs." Militarily, the chief of staff takes the place of the general in the latter's absence.

215 BayHStA-KA, Etappenkommandantur 54, Bd. 22, 18. Kavalleriebrigade. I, Nr. 70 per.geheim, 28.10.1918.

216 See the recognition of this in BayHStA-KA, Etappenbezirk Czernikow, Abt. Ia, Nr. 1049/18, Monatsbericht v. 22.7.–21.8.1918, 21.8.1918.

217 *Von Brest-Litovsk zur deutschen Novemberrevolution*, 33. Subtelny also makes a positive assessment of this period as a "relatively calm hiatus imposed by the German occupation." Orest Subtelny, *Ukraine: A History* (Toronto, Buffalo, and London, 1994), 355–57.

this latter approach were: building up systematically an intelligence network that gave early warning of new unrest; the creation of local self-defense units and a militia, although the latter was more often brutal than efficient;[218] a flexible approach to insurgents at a tactical level designed to catch them off guard; and, finally, close cooperation with Ukrainian officials by making use of lists of names, interpreters, people familiar with a locality, and the like in order to avoid errors. Reports indicate that this cooperation worked well in most cases in the German zone of occupation, but not in the Austro-Hungarian zone. The civilian population was to be protected, and violent measures were to be avoided. In the search for the genuinely guilty, greater emphasis was placed on the military courts. In extreme cases, at the beginning of the occupation, the sinister phrase "punitive expedition" could mean reducing a whole village to ashes, but not the shooting of innocent people. The most common measure was the imposition of contributions. But the occupiers continued to be ruthless against the insurgents themselves. In case of an uprising, they were to be shot immediately or later court-martialed.[219] When it came to daily contacts of the occupying soldiers in the villages, it was difficult to distinguish between insurgents and civilians, but they generally attempted to make this distinction.

218 BayHStA-KA, Kav.Div., Bd. 21, Bezirk Wolhynien West, Bay.Kav.Division, Abt. Ia, Nr. 3276 W.8., Stimmung im Lande, 19.9.1918. The 15th Bavarian Reserve Infantry Brigade made a more positive assessment of the militia: BayHStA-KA, 15.Res.Inf.Brig., Bd.7, K.Bayr.15.Res.Inf. Brigade, Nr. 7701/Adj., Monatsbericht über die allgemeine Lage v. 22.9.1918.

219 For the central orders of Army Group Eichhorn-Kiew on combating insurgency, see BayHStA-KA, Kav.Div., Bd. 22, Heeresgruppe Eichhorn, Abt. Ia, Nr. 1093/18, 23.5.1918; BayHStA-KA, Kav.Div., Bd. 21, Bezirk Wolhynien (Generalkommando XXII. Res.-Korps), Abt. Ib/III, Nr. 680, 4.7.1918; BayHStA-KA, Kav.Div., Bd. 20, Heeresgruppe Eichhorn-Kiew, Abt. Ic, Nr. 22803, Anweisung v. 29.5.1918; BayHStA-KA, Kav.Div., Bd. 20, Heeresgruppe Eichhorn-Kiew, Abt. Ia, Nr. 2825/18, 18.7.1918; BayHStA-KA, 1. Kav.Brig., Bd. 13, Heeresgruppe Kiew, Abt. Ia/III, Nr. 4864/16, 7.9.1918; BayHStA-KA, 15. Res.Inf.Brig., Bd. 30, Heeresgruppe Eichhorn-Kiew, Abt. Ia, Nr. 1781/18, Brieftelegramm an XXVII. Res.Korps, 17.6.1918; BayHStA-KA, 15. Res.Inf. Brig., Bd. 30, Heeresgruppe Eichhorn-Kiew, Abt. Ia, Nr. 2636/18, 13.7.1918. HStA Stuttgart, M 46/16, Heeresgruppe Eichhorn, Abt. Ia, Nr. 3086/18, 26.7.1918.

3b. The Administration of the Occupation

Wolfram Dornik and Peter Lieb

Negotiations between the German Empire and Austria-Hungary over the Zones of Occupation

Ever since the Brusilov catastrophe in the summer of 1916, Austria-Hungary had been under almost complete German control in its military, foreign, and economic policy and, to some extent, in its domestic and administrative policy as well. These control measures were implemented through the Hindenburg Front and the Combined War Leadership. The military and political leadership in Vienna therefore attempted, at every opportunity, to demonstrate its independence of Berlin. This was also the case in its Ukrainian policy. Thus the tensions that emerged in these negotiations were not just a result of personal vanity. Austria-Hungary feared, rather, that at the end of the war it would find itself still under the "German wheel." From the very beginning, the negotiations between Germany and Austria-Hungary over a possible combined command of the troops in Ukraine proved extremely difficult. Since the beginning of the Austro-Hungarian advance on 28 February, there had been disputes over the allocation of zones of operation, that is, future areas of interest, in Ukraine. Paul Hindenburg and Erich Ludendorff on the one side and Ottokar von Czernin and Arthur Arz von Straussenburg on the other jealously sought to maintain control of areas each had already captured.[1] Arz complained bitterly to Hindenburg on 3 March: "I would like to ask Your Excellency to look at the map of Russia and see what a small territory is being claimed by Austria-Hungary and what Germany has already occupied and what would thereby fall to it as an

1 ÖStA, KA, FA, AOK, OpAbt, Kt. 467, Nr. 1126/1, Abgrenzung des österreichisch-ungarischen und deutschen Operationsgebietes in der Ukraine, 2. März; ÖStA, KA, FA, AOK, OpAbt, Kt. 467, Nr. 1138, Ludendorff an Arz und seine Antwort, 2. März; ÖStA, KA, FA, AOK, OpAbt, Kt. 467, Nr. 1146, Bahn Zmerinka-Odessa, 4. März; ÖStA, KA, FA, AOK, OpAbt, Kt. 467, 1160, Arz an Hindenburg und Antwort, 5. März; ÖStA, KA, FA, AOK, OpAbt, Kt. 467, 1162, Regelung der Verhältnisse in der Ukraina, 5. März; ÖStA, KA, FA, AOK, OpAbt, Kt. 467, 1164, Arz an Hindenburg und Antworten, 5. März.

area of interest."[2] In the following days they were only able to agree on a provisional division of operational zones during the advance.[3]

Nevertheless, negotiations over possible combined command and over zones of occupation continued. On 14 March the commander in chief, Arz, rejected the German proposal that the troops in Ukraine be led by the German Army Group Linsingen. There were concerns about placing the commander of Austria-Hungary's 2nd Army, Baron Eduard Böhm-Ermolli, under Linsingen's command. Emperor Karl rejected a joint command, "supposedly out of annoyance at the dictatorial tone of General Ludendorff and because of dislike for [Alexander von] Linsingen, who was intended as commander of combined forces and whom the Austrians regarded unsympathetically." Arz proposed that either both zones of operation be placed under the command of Böhm-Ermolli or that they be administered separately.[4] For Wilhelm Groener, the first was unthinkable; as for the second, he had some formal concerns but no material ones.[5]

Austria-Hungary's stubborn attitude provoked a stormy reaction in Germany's Supreme Army Command (OHL). In the early hours of 15 March, Hindenburg sent a note to Arz in which he threatened to station a number of German troops in Odesa to equal the number of Austro-Hungarian troops already there. The city would then have to be divided. In addition, he demanded that German troops in Kherson, east of the Boh (Southern Bug), be placed under German command and that there be a combined administration of the Zhmerynka–Odesa railway line.[6] Austria-Hungary's Army High Command (AOK) chose not to reply to this note because Emperor Karl now intervened in the debate: a combined command here was simply not desirable and did not come under the provisions concerning combined command as agreed in September 1916.[7] In their respective areas, "each party...in agreement with the Ukrainian government, should be in unrestricted control."

2 ÖStA, KA, FA, AOK, OpAbt, Kt. 467, Nr. 1138, Ludendorff an Arz und seine Antwort, 2. März.

3 ÖStA, KA, FA, AOK, OpAbt, Kt. 467, Nr. 1171, Ukraina, März; ÖStA, KA, FA, AOK, OpAbt, Kt. 467, Nr. 1174, Ukraina-Regelung, 6. März; ÖStA, KA, FA, AOK, OpAbt, Kt. 467, Nr. 1176, Telegrammsammlung bzgl. Befehlsverhältnisse, 6. März; ÖStA, KA, FA, AOK, OpAbt, Kt. 467, Nr. 1177, Ludendorff an Arz, 6. März; ÖStA, KA, FA, AOK, OpAbt, Kt. 467, Nr. 1183, Weisung für die Ukraine-Kommission, 10. März.

4 ÖStA, KA, FA, AOK, OpAbt, Kt. 467, Nr. 1214, Leitung der Operation, 14. März.

5 Cf. TNA, GFM 6/36, Nr. 24, Telegramm von Mumm an AA, 18.3.1918.

6 ÖStA, KA, FA, AOK, OpAbt, Kt. 467, Nr. 1224, Hindenburg an Arz, 15. März.

7 See Holger H. Herwig, *The First World War: Germany and Austria-Hungary, 1914–1918* (London and New York, 1997), 212–22.

The emperor, however, attached great importance to maintaining the February agreements regulating the sharing of provisions from the East.[8] Karl wished to show independence and hoped that this independent approach would assure the quickest possible delivery of food from Ukraine to relieve the famine in Cisleithania. Groener had already frequently insisted at General Headquarters that joint command was absolutely necessary for the reputation of the allied troops and for dealings with the Rada. Wilhelm, the German emperor, had asked Karl on a number of occasions to see reason and give way. A few hours later, Wilhelm reacted to the definitive decision of the Habsburgs with just a few words expressing his "great regret." He could "not suppress the fear" that thereby the procurement of provisions for "our peoples" and "the internal situation in Ukraine, which is friendly to us, will now become even more difficult."[9] On 20 March, therefore, the Austro-Hungarian 2nd Army, advancing into Ukraine, was removed from the command of *Ober Ost* (command of all German forces in the East) and again placed directly under Austria-Hungary's AOK.[10] The troops in the Linsingen area, the 4th Army, as well as the 3rd and 7th Armies, stationed in Romania, remained under the command of *Ober Ost*.

It took days before an agreement could be reached on spheres of influence. Both army leaderships obstructed each other with demands concerning jointly administered port cities and railway lines or threatened that sections of their own troops would not be placed under allied command. There was also mutual suspicion about hidden agendas behind these demands. On the one hand, as early as mid-March, the Austro-Hungarian emissaries suspected that the German troops were aiming to take over the government in Kyiv and, for that reason, did not want any Austro-Hungarian troops there. On the other hand, the general staff officer in *Ober Ost*, Major Brinckmann, reported to OHL that he was convinced "that Austria-Hungary is pursuing extensive political goals in southern Ukraine. While it is our wish that Ukraine soon become a viable state, and we therefore promote the creation of a sovereign government and an army, Austria-Hungary seems to have no interest in this." The Austro-Hungarians,

---

8 ÖStA, KA, FA, AOK, OpAbt, Kt. 467, Nr. 1220/1, Vereinbarungen wegen der Ukraine, 15. März.

9 ÖStA, KA, FA, AOK, OpAbt, Kt. 467, Nr. 1282, Schriftverkehr zwischen Wilhelm, Karl und Arz, 16.–19. März.

10 ÖStA, KA, FA, NFA, HHK AK/AGKdo, 2. Armee, OpAK, Kt. 309, 1918 Befehle und Verlautbarungen, Armeekommandobefehl Nr. 41 vom 31. März; ÖStA, KA, FA, NFA, HHK AK/AGKdo, 2. Armee, OpAK, Kt. 309, Armeekommandobefehl Nr. 8 vom 20. März; ÖStA, KA, FA, NFA, HHK AK/AGKdo, 2. Armee, OpAK, Kt. 309, Armeekommandobefehl Nr. 9 vom 21. März.

it was thought, wanted to establish themselves permanently, both politically and economically, in Odesa.[11]

It was not until 28 March that "a military agreement between both army commands with respect to Ukraine" could be signed. According to this agreement, Austria-Hungary would get the southwestern part of Volhynia as well as the Podilia, Kherson, and Katerynoslav gubernias.[12] Germany got all the other gubernias, including the Crimea. Military operations already begun in Katerynoslav would be completed under German command; those already begun in Tavria (part of the present-day Kherson and Zaporizhia oblasts) and the Crimea would be completed under Austro-Hungarian command. Mykolaiv, Mariupol, and Rostov would be occupied jointly, but Mykolaiv and Rostov would be under German command, Mariupol under Austro-Hungarian command. Taganrog and Novorossiisk would be administered by the Germans. The German head of railways in Kyiv, with an Austro-Hungarian deputy, would be in charge of railways and canals and rivers. The precise regulations would be left to them. The coal and iron area in Katerynoslav would be administered and exploited on a one-to-one basis. Other raw materials would be shared according to the articles of the Berlin agreement of February 1918.[13] Kyiv would have an Austro-Hungarian garrison with at most two battalions without higher-level command officials. This reduced Austro-Hungarian influence in the capital to a minimum. Austro-Hungarian facilities for the repatriation of prisoners of war situated in the German zone would be placed under the respective German command of that area. Officers and other organs "coordinating economic relations...under the terms of the Berlin Economic Agreement" should "not be hindered by either side." "Only Austro-Hungarian troops of German nationality" were to be used in settlements of German colonists. Since this was not possible, German troops would have to be stationed in those areas.[14] The communications link in Odesa would be administered by a parity commission.[15]

The Austro-Hungarians were not entirely satisfied with the result of the negotiations. The commander of the 145th Infantry Brigade, Major

---

11 TNA, GFM 6/36, Nr. 599, Telegramm des Leg.Sekr. v. Lersner an AA, 20.3.1918.

12 The eastern part of the Katerynoslav gubernia would be assigned as hinterland to the German I Army Corps and the *Korps Knoerzer*: ÖStA, KA, FA, AOK, OpAbt, Kt. 470, Nr. 1585, Überlassung von Teilen des G. Jekaterinoslaw an Deutsche, 14.5.1918.

13 For more details on economic arrangements, see chapter 3c in the present volume.

14 ÖStA, KA, AdT, FJBat 13, Kt. 754, 6. Tagebuch des Feldjägerbataillons Nr. 13, Eintrag v. 5. Mai.

15 ÖStA, KA, FA, AOK, OpAbt, Kt. 468, Nr. 1326, Übereinkommen über Ukraine.

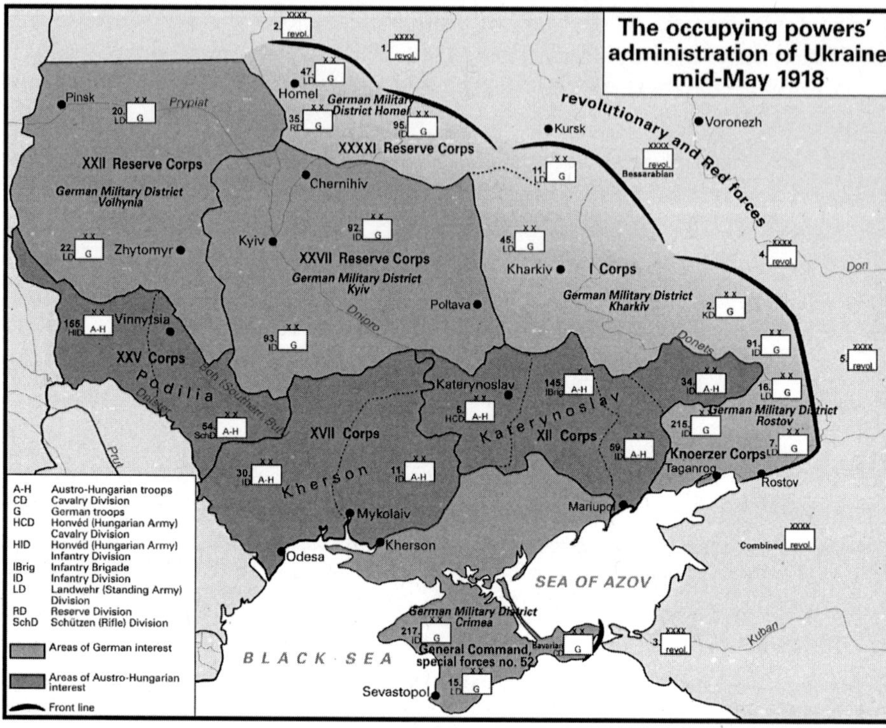

Map 6: The administration of the occupation in Ukraine, mid-May 1918. (ÖStA, KA, NFA, 2. Armee, Op. AK, Kt. 308, Fol. 275)

General Oskar von Hranilovic-Czvetassin, agreeing with Czernin, stated that a combined command would be useful only for the duration of military operations. But in the case of a lasting occupation of those areas, once peace had been established, this was to be avoided, since it would not serve long-term economic interests.[16] In addition, Austria-Hungary hoped that the approach in Ukraine would establish a model for Romania. Because of the smooth transition from military operations to the subsequent occupation, the Germans had been in overall command in Romania since the summer of 1916. This subordination, in the longer term, was to change as a result of the peace then being negotiated with Romania. It was thought that this demonstrative independence in Ukraine would give Austria-Hungary a better position in future peace negotiations, as well as in the secret talks undertaken with the Entente. Of course, those talks failed in the end.

16 ÖStA, KA, FA, AOK, OpAbt, Kt. 467, Nr. 1226, Telegrammsammlung, 15.–16.3.1918.

The Administration of the German Zone of Occupation

Although the military operations to occupy Ukraine had not yet been completed, on 16 March Army Group Linsingen announced guidelines for the German troops in Ukraine. In consultation with Ukrainian and civilian German departments, there were three tasks to be accomplished: the pacification of the country, the promotion of trade, and the stimulation of the agricultural economy.[17] All three turned out to be more difficult than previously thought, mainly because there were never enough troops available.

The top military command in Ukraine was initially Army Group Linsingen. Its commander in chief, General Alexander von Linsingen, was generally considered to be a difficult person, and the judgments made about him confirm this. Groener called him "an old boot" (*olle Knackstiefel*), Max Hoffmann doubted his military abilities, and the Austrians and Hungarians completely refused, as we have seen above, to place themselves under his command.[18] On 25 March 1918 Linsingen was replaced by Field Marshal General Hermann von Eichhorn and Army Group Eichhorn-Kiew (later officially renamed Army Group Eichhorn).[19] The new commander in chief was described as "a general who was full of character, highly educated, and possessed of inner nobility"[20] but, given his age of seventy, he was thought to be "quite old and no longer as capable."[21] As chief of staff he was therefore assigned the experienced, diplomatically educated, and organizationally brilliant Lieutenant General Wilhelm Groener.[22]

---

17 Cf. BayHStA-KA, Kav.Div., Bd. 22, Heeresgruppe Linsingen, Abt. Ic, Nr. 19061, Abschrift, 21.3.1918.

18 Cf. *Von Brest-Litovsk zur deutschen Novemberrevolution. Aus den Tagebüchern, Briefen und Aufzeichnungen von Alfons Paquet, Wilhelm Groener und Albert Hopman. März bis November 1918*, ed. Winfried Baumgart (Göttingen, 1971), Eintrag vom 9.3.1918, 288; ibid., Brief Groeners an seine Frau vom 15.4.1918, 344; *Die Aufzeichnungen des Generalmajors Max Hoffmann*, ed. Karl Friedrich Nowak, vol. 1 (Berlin, 1929), Eintrag vom 29.3.1918; TNA, GFM 6/36, Nr. 24, Telegramm von Mumm an AA, 18.3.1918.

19 In the interests of clarity, the name "Eichhorn-Kiew" will be used for this army group with reference to the period from April to August.

20 Stefan von Velsen, "Deutsche Generalstabsoffiziere im 1. Weltkrieg 1914–1918. Erinnerungen," *Die Welt als Geschichte*, no. 16 (1956): 286.

21 *Von Brest-Litovsk zur deutschen Novemberrevolution*, Brief Groeners an seine Frau vom 29.3.1918, 332.

22 As successor to Ludendorff in OHL, Groener was later to play an important role through his part in the "Ebert-Groener pact." Also later, as defense minister in the late phase of the Weimar Republic, he figured prominently in German domestic politics with his banning of the SA. Cf. Gerhard W. Rakenius, *Wilhelm Groener als Erster Generalquartiermeister. Die Politik der Obersten Heeresleitung 1918* (Boppard am Rhein, 1977); Johannes Hürter, *Wilhelm Groener.*

Although Groener had criticized Ludendorff more than once, he was regarded as a protégé of OHL. While *Ober Ost* was in fact the direct superior of the army group, Groener frequently communicated directly with Berlin, and *Ober Ost* largely gave the general a free hand in Ukraine. The supreme commander of *Ober Ost*, Field Marshal General Prince Leopold of Bavaria, described Army Group Eichhorn-Kiew as "absolutely the most important command post on my eastern front,"[23] but he actually visited the Ukrainian capital only once, and that at the beginning of November 1918. Following the murder of Eichhorn by a Ukrainian Socialist Revolutionary at the end of July,[24] General Günther Graf von Kirchbach took command; the Army Group was now renamed Army Group Kiew. Sixty-eight years old at the time, Kirchbach was also considered "too old and without the necessary abilities for this difficult post"[25] and therefore did not concern himself "too much with political and military questions."[26] There is no doubt that the real "ruler" in Ukraine during all these months of occupation was Groener.

In May 1918, once the military operations to occupy the country had come to an end, Army Group Eichhorn-Kiew assigned to each of the six corps subordinate to it a Ukrainian gubernia as its military district.[27] The troops of occupation consisted of a number of second- and third-class formations, that is, mostly Landwehr divisions or infantry divisions that had only been raised late in the war. There were also some dozens of territorial (*Landsturm*) battalions. The average age of the occupying soldiers was quite high. A good example is the 387th Landwehr Infantry Regiment, part of the 11th Landwehr Division. Practically wiped out at Cambrai in 1917, the regiment was reassembled in the East. All soldiers between the ages of twenty and thirty-five were then moved to the West, and their places were taken by soldiers from

---

Reichswehrminister am Ende der Weimarer Republik (1928–1932) (Munich, 1993). See also his memoirs: Wilhelm Groener, *Lebenserinnerungen. Jugend, Generalstab, Weltkrieg* (Osnabrück, 1972).

23 BayHStA-Geheimes Hausarchiv, Nachlass Leopold von Bayern 239 I, Eintrag v. 31.7.1918.

24 See also Skoropadsky's account of this: *Pavlo Skoropads'kyj. Erinnerungen 1917 bis 1918*, ed. Günter Rosenfeld (Stuttgart, 1999), 274ff.

25 Velsen, "Deutsche Generalstabsoffiziere im 1. Weltkrieg 1914–1918," 289.

26 *Von Brest-Litovsk zur deutschen Novemberrevolution*, Brief Groeners an seine Frau vom 13.8.1918, 420.

27 I. Army Corps: Kharkiv; XXII Reserve Corps: Volhynia; XXVII Reserve Corps: Kyiv; XXXXI Reserve Corps: Homel; 52nd Corps: Crimea; Corps Knoerzer: Rostov. When *Korps Knoerzer* was disbanded, the XX Army Corps came to Ukraine for the final weeks of the occupation. It took the district around Poltava. There were no *Armeeoberkommandos* in Ukraine in 1918.

various territorial units. So the average age of the regiment was thirty-eight, and a fifth of the men were already over forty. Since the regiment in Ukraine was used to reinforce positions on the Soviet Russian border and to assist in the harvest, adequate training was impossible.[28] In some units, discipline and morale were not very high. Some of the junior officers and older soldiers seemed to show little enthusiasm for the service.[29] From the early autumn of 1918, there were some serious cases of insubordination.[30] In addition to the German troops, there were also a number of more exotic units, such as the Muslim Battalion, which, from May until its dissolution in October 1918, served in the district of the XXII Reserve Corps in Volhynia.[31] This battalion was put together in Germany from among Muslims who had been Russian prisoners of war and was meant to be a friendly gesture toward the Ottoman ally. The Ottoman Empire was concerned about the protection of Muslim Tatars in the Crimea and had been thinking of sending a large Turkish contingent to the region.[32]

There were also German elite units in the Crimea, or at least units that considered themselves as such. They included the cavalry, with its "old German horse-riding spirit."[33] In the industrialized trench warfare of the Western Front, the cavalry very soon had no place and, even in the East, it never managed to regain its previous dominance on the field of battle. In the spring of 1918, therefore, the German army disbanded the majority of its cavalry divisions or reconstituted them as dismounted cavalry rifle divisions.[34] The 1st and 2nd Cavalry Divisions

---

28 BayHStA-KA, 1. Kav.Brig., Bd. 11, Generalkommando I. A.K., Abt. Ia, Nr. 1887 op., v. 6.11.1918.

29 See the urgent order of the commanding general of the XXVII Reserve Corps, Lieutenant General Gustav Bernhard von Watzdorf, in BayHStA-KA, 15. Res.Inf.Brig., Bd. 30, Militärbezirk Kiew. XXVII. R.K., Abt. Ia, Nr. 17800, v. 31.8.1918. See also BayHStA-KA, Etappenkommandantur 54, Bd. 22, 18. Kavalleriebrigade, Abt. I, Nr. 70 per.geheim, v. 28.10.1918.

30 BayHStA-KA, Kav.Div., Bd. 51, Bayerische Kavalleriedivision, Gericht der Division, KTB, Eintrag v. 1.–30.9.1918. There is a description of an incident that occurred during a transport of parts of the 1st Bavarian Landsturm Regiment to the West. The soldiers refused to obey orders and demanded leave from the front. Four men were sentenced to death by a military court. The division commander of the Bavarian Cavalry Division confirmed only two of the sentences. King Ludwig III of Bavaria eventually pardoned the men.

31 BayHStA-KA, Kav.Div., Bd. 20, Bezirk Wolhynien West. Bay.Kav.Div, Abt. Ia, Nr. 4631 w., v. 25.10.1918. Betr.: Auflösung des muselman. Batls. One of the reasons given for the dissolution of the Muslim Battalion was the poor pay its soldiers received for their service in Ukraine. This resulted in around 350 soldiers deserting the battalion.

32 ÖStA, KA, FA, AOK, OpAbt, Kt. 469, Nr.1481, Berichte über die politische Lage in der Ukraine Mitte April, 15.4.1918.

33 BayHStA-KA, Kav.Div., Bd. 18, Bay.Kav.Div, Abt. Ia, Nr. 1125, v. 1.7.1918. The quotation is from General Kosch on the occasion of the Bavarian Cavalry Division leaving his district.

34 The 5th, 8th, and 9th Cavalry Divisions were dissolved. The 6th and 7th Cavalry Divisions as well as the Guard Cavalry Division were reestablished as Cavalry Rifle Divisions. The staff of 3rd Cavalry Division became the staff of 65th Corps. The 4th Cavalry Division had already been stood down.

and the Bavarian Cavalry Division were the only remaining mounted cavalry divisions. These three divisions were sent to Ukraine in 1918 along with a number of independent regiments. Some venerable regiments, rich in tradition, with such resonant names as the Prussian Garde du Corps Regiment or the Bavarian 4th Chevauleger Regiment "König," were to fight the last skirmish of their regimental history here against insurgent Bolsheviks and peasants. Mounted squadrons of regimental cavalry were deployed throughout the country as police troops and "tactical firefighters," so the dying cavalry had one last brief historical renaissance in Ukraine in 1918.

The military administrative posts throughout the country were the Etappe Commands (*Etappenkommandanturen*). The Germans installed the first of these etappe commands in eastern Ukraine at the beginning of March. There were 45 of them by mid-June and almost 90 by the end of the occupation.[35] They were under the command of older or reactivated reserve or Landwehr officers, mostly having the rank of captain, major, or lieutenant colonel. They had a small staff of officers, mostly just one adjutant with the rank of lieutenant, and a military court advocate. The shortage of officers in the fourth year of war forced them "temporarily" to do without interpreters, medical officers, and officers for raw materials and trade.[36] The etappe commands were supposed to support Army Group Eichhorn-Kiew by dealing with the economy, trade, and deliveries of grain. They also dealt with the recruitment of Ukrainians for volunteer labor in Germany.[37] The occupation troops, by contrast, were responsible for the protection of railway lines, the maintenance of internal security, and the disarmament of the villages.[38]

---

35 Cf. HStA Stuttgart, M 46/16, Heeresgruppe Kiew, Abt. Ic, Nr. 26546 v. 16.8.1918, Die mit K.M. 3851.5.18 A.M. v. 15.6.1918 genehmigten Etappen-Kdten; BA-MA, PH 5-I/3, Heeresgruppe Kiew, Abt. Ib, Nr. 7110/18 v. 1.11.1918.

36 HStA Stuttgart, M 46/16, Heeresgruppe Kiew, Abt. Ic, Nr. 26546 v. 16.8.1918, Die mit K.M. 3851.5.18 A.M. v. 15.6.1918 genehmigten Etappen-Kdten.

37 See BayHStA-KA, 15.Res.Inf.Brig., Bd. 30, Heeresgruppe Eichhorn-Kiew, Abt. Ic, Nr. 22586, Anwerbung landwirtschaftlicher Arbeiter-Familien für Deutschland, 28.5.1918. According to this source, at the end of May there were five recruitment offices in Ukraine, with five more planned. A shortage of officials meant that no further offices were established. There are many documents confirming the existence of such recruitment offices in the Austro-Hungarian zone (model contracts, advertising placards, provisions regarding unemployment, etc.): ÖStA, KA, FA, AOK, Ukraine Akten, Kt. 2.613, Nr. 1816, Anwerbung landwirtschaftlicher Arbeiterfamilien für Deutschland. To date, no concrete indications of the numbers of workers involved have been found either in the German or in the Austro-Hungarian documents.

38 BayHStA-KA, 15. Res.Inf.Brig., Bd. 7, K.bayr. 15. Res.Inf.Brigade, Nr. 1752, An das K.bayr. Kriegsministerium, 23.4.1918.

The relations of command and responsibility between the occupation troops and the etappe commands, in case of disturbances, were unclear. It was not until September that Army Group Kiew drew up comprehensive instructions, but these do not appear ever to have been published. So every corps managed things differently. The XXVII Reserve Corps, for instance, left it to its 92nd Infantry Division and 15th Bavarian Reserve Infantry Brigade to decide how to handle their command relations with the etappe commands.[39] In the case of the XXII Reserve Corps, on the other hand, the etappe command was given "a certain administrative power over the troops"; it was "tactically...responsible for peace, security, and order in its district."[40] This regulation, however, met with widespread rejection on the part of the troops for the simple reason that the troop leaders were generally of higher rank.[41] Moreover, the troop leaders had much more experience of combat than the older and mostly reactivated etappe commanders. This regulation was rescinded in November.[42]

It is difficult to estimate the total number of German occupation troops in Ukraine in 1918. In the middle of 1918 there were 20 divisions,[43] shrinking to 16 by November.[44] It is problematic to take these divisions as the only basis for reckoning numbers, since a number of independent brigade staffs, such as that of the 15th Bavarian Reserve Infantry Brigade, de facto fulfilled the function of a divisional staff.[45] Added to these were a number of reserve battalions. The

39 BayHStA-KA, Etappenkommandantur 54, Bd. 22, Militärbezirk Kiew. XXVII. R.K, Abt. Ia, Nr. 1100, Richtlinien v. 13.4.1918. The 15th Bavarian Reserve Infantry Brigade placed itself under the *Etappenkommandanturen*. See also BayHStA-KA, 15. Mkr 1824, K.Bayr.15. Res.Inf.Brigade Nr. 7347/Adj, An das Kgl. Bayr. Kriegsministerium, 16.9.1918.

40 BayHStA-KA, Kav.Div., Bd. 18, Bezirk Wolhynien West. Bay.Kav.Div., Abt. Ia, Nr. 2889 W., Etappenkommandanturen, 6.9.1918.

41 BayHStA-KA, Kav.Div., Bd. 20, Bay.Kav.Div., Abt. Ia, Nr. 4898 W, An das Generalkommando XXII. Res.Korps, 8.11.1918.

42 BayHStA-KA, Kav.Div., Bd. 20, Bay.Kav.Div., Abt. Ia, Nr. 4987 W, Regelung des dienstl. Verhältnisses zwischen Et.K'drn. u. Truppenführern, 18.11.1918.

43 BA-MA, N 46/171, Truppen der Heeresgruppe, außer Etappe (o.D.). The fifteen divisions mentioned here were soon joined by the 1st Cavalry Division, as well as four divisions of the 52nd Corps in the Crimea.

44 BA-MA, PH 5-I/3, Heeresgruppe Kiew, Abt. Ib, Nr. 7110/18 v. 1.11.18. The 7th Württemberg Landwehr Division, not shown on this map, was in Odesa at the time, waiting there (in vain) for transport to another theater of war. See Reichsarchiv, ed., *Der Weltkrieg, 1914–1918. Die Kriegführung im Sommer und Herbst 1918. Die Ereignisse außerhalb der Westfront bis November 1918*, vol. 13 (Berlin, 1942), 397ff.

45 In September, this brigade commanded two infantry regiments, an infantry battalion, five cavalry regiments (including brigade staff), an artillery regiment, and a small number of engineer and intelligence troops. See BayHStA-KA, MKr 1824, K.Bayr. 15. Res.Inf.Brigade, Nr. 7347/Adj, Bericht zu K.M.E. v. 20.8.1917, 16.9.1918.

number of etappe troops and supply troops was insignificant. The number of German occupation troops in Ukraine in the summer of 1918 was therefore probably around 250,000,[46] shrinking by the end of the occupation to around 200,000.[47] The number repeated in the literature of 500,000 troops in Ukraine is clearly too high.[48] In the entire East occupied by German troops at the time of the collapse in November 1918, from the Baltic Sea to the Black Sea, the number of German troops was probably not more than 300,000.[49] The "occupation density" of German soldiers in this very large country was therefore very low, as is clear from the example of the Bavarian Cavalry Division. With ten battalions under it, around 8,000 men, it had to secure 35,000 sq. km.[50] This would be equivalent to the current size of North Rhine Westphalia or Styria and Lower Austria taken together.[51]

Alongside the military hierarchy, and parallel to it, there was the civilian representation of the German Empire in the form of the German delegation to Ukraine in Kyiv, headed by the ambassador, Baron Philipp Alfons Mumm von Schwarzenstein. In spite of his title, Mumm did not administer an embassy but a "diplomatic representation." Consulates with both a consular and an economic mission were also opened in Katerynoslav, Odesa, Kharkiv, and Mykolaiv.[52] Since Ukraine was

46 See BA-MA, N 46/171, Truppeneinteilung 13.6.1918. To this must be added about twenty thousand men of the *Etappeninspektion Bug*. On the basis for reckoning the strength of individual battalions, see Hermann Cron, *Imperial German Army 1914–18: Organisation, Structure, Orders of Battle* (Solihull, 2001) (Original German title: *Geschichte des Deutschen Heeres im Weltkrieg 1914–18*, Berlin, 1937). Individual units in Ukraine appear to have reached their target strength. See BayHStA-KA, 5. Chevauleger Regiment, Bd. 1, 5. Chevauleger Regiment, KTB, Eintrag v. 1.6.1918; BayHStA-KA, 5. Landsturmregiment 1, Bd. 4, Bayerisches Landsturmregiment 1. Anlagen zum KTB, 1.7.1918.

47 BA-MA, PH 5-I/3, Heeresgruppe Kiew, Abt. Ib, Nr. 7110/18, 1.11.1918.

48 See Peter Borowsky, "Germany's Ukrainian Policy during World War I and the Revolution 1918–19," in *German-Ukrainian Relations in Historical Perspective,* ed. Hans-Joachim Torke and John-Paul Himka (Edmonton and Toronto, 1994), 86.

49 See BA-MA, RH 61/2315, Verteilung der deutschen und k.u.k. Divisionen am 26.10.1918. According to this, AOK 8 had four divisions and AOK 10 had three. Three further divisions were in the process of being transported to the Western Front. There were about thirteen thousand German soldiers in the Caucasus. See BA-MA, RH 61/2315, Übersicht über die deutschen Truppen im Kaukasus.

50 BayHStA-KA, Kav.Div., Bd. 18, Bezirk Wolhynien West, Bay.Kav.Div, Abt. Ia, Nr. 2198 W, 13.8.1918. Bericht über die Lage im Bezirk Wolhynien West.

51 This was relatively better than in the case of the Second World War. For the example of the 707th Infantry Division in Belarus in 1941, see Peter Lieb, "Täter aus Überzeugung? Oberst Carl von Andrian und die Judenmorde der 707. Infanteriedivision 1941/42," *Vierteljahreshefte für Zeitgeschichte*, no. 50 (2002): 545.

52 Frank Golczewski, *Deutsche und Ukrainer 1914–1939* (Paderborn, 2010), 245.

officially a friendly country and therefore did not come under German or Austro-Hungarian administration, it was the Foreign Office in Berlin that was theoretically responsible for Ukrainian policy. But the reality was different, as it was the military that determined strategy. However, because of the good personal relations between Groener and Mumm, the two men were often able to find compromises on particular issues, bridging the faulty parallel hierarchies of civil and military representatives. But there was no unity of command among the German occupation apparatus.

Since the Central Powers were officially in the country as a protection force, they frequently had to show restraint, at least superficially. Many German officers thought that this had an unsatisfactory effect on their daily work. As much as Groener and other military leaders might have been annoyed at this privately, they still ordered their subordinate officers to exercise restraint in expressing opinions on Germany's Ukrainian policy. They could be "politically engaged only insofar" as necessary "to encourage the inhabitants of this country to do what is reasonable and useful."[53]

Eichhorn, Groener and their entourage in Kyiv got along quite well, privately and personally, with their Ukrainian counterparts, even with representatives of the Rada. Yet, at the same time, Groener castigated the Rada as a "government club"[54] and as a "conventicle of immature students and other youthful visionaries and bad elements."[55] In mid-April he decided that cooperation with the Rada was no longer possible. That Groener was involved in the overthrow of the Rada on 29 April is no longer open to doubt.[56] Not for nothing, a few days previously, had the Army Group issued its "guidelines for behavior in case of a change of government." This would come into force with the cue "change."[57] General Gustav Bernhard von Watzdorf, commander of the XXVII Reserve Corps, which was stationed in Kyiv, wrote in his personal diary on 28 April about the planned arrest of some Ukrainian government members the next

---

53 BayHStA-KA, Etappenkommandantur 54, Bd. 22, Heeresgruppe Eichhorn, N.O., Nr. 692, 27.6.1918.

54 BA-MA, N 46/172, Brief Groeners an Ludendorff v. 23.3.1918.

55 *Von Brest-Litovsk zur deutschen Novemberrevolution*, 348.

56 For an opposing view, see ibid., 357, n. 365.

57 BayHStA-KA, 15. Res.Inf.Brig., Bd. 7, Heeresgruppe Eichhorn-Kiew, Abt. Ia, Nr. 254/18 [o.D., allerdings kurz vor 24.4.1918], Richtlinien für Verhalten der Truppen im Falle Regierungswechsel. According to an appendix added by the XXVII Reserve Corps, only officers could give this command. No junior officers or troops could be used even for writing services. See also HStA Stuttgart, M 46/5e, Korps Knoerzer, Abt. Ic, Nr. 1121, Heeresgruppe Eichhorn drahtet, 29.4.1918.

day. On 29 April he noted: "Troops are on heightened alert. Everything is being prepared for the overthrow of the government."[58]

Two previous orders issued by Eichhorn had sharply crystallized as points of conflict between the Germans and the Rada. One was the cultivation order, which required the immediate tillage of fields and the reversal of the land expropriations that had taken place after the revolution. The other was the command concerning the jurisdiction of German military courts in Ukraine, which aroused powerful opposition in the Rada. After its session on 28 April, the Rada sent a telegraphic protest to Berlin and issued a public decree declaring that the cultivation order was not valid. It also demanded the immediate recall of Field Marshal Eichhorn. This was an open provocation of the German occupying power and provided it with the opportunity to move against the Rada. The ministers for war, foreign affairs, and agriculture as well as a number of other important persons were arrested, and the Rada session was dispersed. On the next day the German ambassador, Mumm, apologized to Vsevolod Holubovych for the "unintended dispersal of the Rada." At the same time, Pavlo Skoropadsky, with some of his confidants, had prepared a congress of peasants and estate owners who would proclaim him Hetman.[59] The Rada reacted to this putsch by bringing Socialist Federalists and other independent parties into the government, forming a new State Council and adopting a more moderate constitution, but it was too late. On the afternoon of the same day, supporters of Skoropadsky began to occupy major posts according to a previously agreed plan. On the night of 29 April there were exchanges of fire between troops loyal to the Rada and supporters of Skoropadsky.[60] On the same night, with only a few units, Skoropadsky was able to gain control of the internal affairs and war ministries and the state bank. He now had the power centers in his hands.[61]

---

58 BA-MA, N 776/45, Tagebuch Generalleutnant v. Watzdorf, Einträge vom 28. und 29.4.1918.

59 See the report of the signals intelligence service concerning the inauguration of Skoropadsky: ÖStA, KA, FA, AOK, Evidenzbüro 1918, Nachrichtenabteilung, Kt. 3670, Nr. 14.321, Bericht über die ukrainischen Verhältnisse, 10.6.1918.

60 ÖStA, KA, FA, AOK, OpAbt, Kt. 469, Nr. 1498/3, Lage in der Ukraine, 28.4.1918; ÖStA, KA, FA, AOK, OpAbt, Kt. 469, Nr. 1517, Vorgänge in Kiew, 29.4.1918; ÖStA, KA, FA, AOK, OpAbt, Kt. 469, Nr. 1525, Nachrichten aus der Ukraine, 30.4.1918; ÖStA, KA, FA, AOK, OpAbt, Kt. 469, Nr. 1526, Nachrichten aus Kiew, 30.4.1918; ÖStA, KA, FA, AOK, OpAbt, Kt. 469, Nr. 1527, Burian an Trauttmansdorff, 30.4.1918; ÖStA, KA, FA, AOK, OpAbt, Kt. 469, Nr. 1528, Burian an Trauttmansdorff, 30.4.1918; ÖStA, KA, FA, NFA, HHK AK/AGKdo, 2. Armee, OpAK, Kt. 308, 1918 Situations- und Tagesmeldungen, Chronologische Zusammenstellung der Kiewer Vorgänge.

61 *Pavlo Skoropads'kyj*, 152–72. These memoirs are based on different versions of notes compiled by Skoropadsky after the war. There are difficulties in assessing the value of this source, as there is no indication of the variations between the different versions and very few references to the fact that there are variations.

Even before being proclaimed in that position, the Hetman had secured the support of the Germans, who had been in contact with him since mid-April. Shortly before the overthrow of the Rada, he made far-reaching concessions to Groener. These included the recognition of the Brest-Litovsk peace treaty, the dissolution of the Rada, an agreement not to establish a Ukrainian army, recognition of the jurisdiction of German military courts, the dismissal of "all undesirable persons" from "state administration," the cancellation of all regulations limiting trade with the Central Powers, the resolution of "the agrarian question by restoring all property rights" (that is, extensive reversal of the expropriations and compensation for nationalized or distributed land), the recognition of finance and currency arrangements in accordance with already established agreements, and compensation for the military assistance being provided to Ukraine. Skoropadsky agreed, with very few reservations, to these German demands.[62] On 30 April, influenced by the Central Powers, especially by Groener and Fleischmann, Skoropadsky attempted to form a new government. The occupying powers pressured him to bring left-wing ministers into the government in order to make it more widely acceptable to the population.[63] That same day he issued a declaration announcing his takeover of the government and the dissolution of the Rada. The remaining supporters of the Rada were arrested, and the building was occupied by Skoropadsky's guards.[64] However, his method of seizing power and his conservative anti-revolutionary policies would create permanent enemies among the majority of Rada supporters, and this, in the end, would lead to his own overthrow half a year later.[65]

Although the Germans had now achieved their political goals, namely the removal of the Rada and the creation of a reliable point of contact, they were not entirely satisfied with the way in which this had been done. The city commandant in Kyiv, General Gaspard von

62 In mid-May the *Ostarmee* expressed concerns to the AOK and to the Austro-Hungarian Foreign Ministry about the agreement between Groener and Skoropadsky. The Foreign Ministry, however, regarded these agreements not as a state treaty but as "informal agreements" in which the representatives of the Austro-Hungarian Foreign Ministry had also been involved. They were therefore not "bound" by these agreements, which did not mean that individual points would be revised: ÖStA, KA, FA, AOK, OpAbt, Kt. 470, Nr. 1548, Vertrag mit Skoropadsky, 5.5.1918.

63 See details in chapter 2a of the present volume.

64 ÖStA, KA, FA, AOK, OpAbt, Kt. 469, Nr. 1529, Die Vorgänge in Kiew III, 2.5.1918. For the list of ministers and Fleischmann's assessment, see ÖStA, KA, FA, AOK, OpAbt, Kt. 470, Nr. 1547, Vorgänge in Kiew IV, 3. Mai; ÖStA, KA, FA, AOK, OpAbt, Kt. 470, 1564, Vorgänge in Kiew VI, 8.5.1918.

65 See chapters 2a and 2b in the present volume.

Eberhardt, had made the arrests during a session of the Rada. Two days later, Eberhardt had to exchange his post with the commander of the 33rd Landwehr Brigade in Poltava, Major General von Dittfurth.[66] The Germans appeared not to be bothered, however, by the internal political implications of the overthrow of the Rada, according to the assessment of Army Group Eichhorn-Kiew: "One should not exaggerate the extent to which our intervention has made us disliked. The Russian [*sic*] has great respect for firm action. On the other hand, this experience has demonstrated that our patience with the Rada has not won us the love of the Social Revolutionaries."[67]

With the Hetman, the German military had a negotiating partner whom they respected socially and personally, if for no other reason than that he had once been a Russian general. A product of tsarist Russia and "a passionate soldier," Skoropadsky had been "a supporter of the war party" and had fought against the Germans "with enthusiasm."[68] But his past did not bother the German military at all. They harbored no feelings of revenge or other emotions against the Hetman—an unmistakable sign of the last remnants of "cabinet warfare" in the midst of total war. This respect was based on reciprocity.[69] The Hetman also did not fail to respect the diplomats of the Foreign Ministry. This contrasted quite strongly with his reaction to some representatives of the German economy and to the Austrians and Hungarians. He accused the latter of corruption and deceit[70] and, according to German documents, showed contempt for their limited military abilities.[71]

---

66 BA-MA, N 776/45, Tagebuch Generalleutnant v. Watzdorf, Eintrag v. 1.5.1918. According to *Von Brest-Litovsk zur deutschen Novemberrevolution*, 359, n. 375, Eberhardt was given command of an infantry brigade in the West.

67 BayHStA-KA, 15.Res.Inf.Brig., Bd. 7, N.O. der OHL, Heeresgruppe Eichhorn, Zentral-Abt., Tgb. Nr. 390, Innere Lage, 17.5.1918.

68 Cf. BayHStA-KA, Kav.Div., Bd. 21, N.O.d.O.H.L. Heeresgruppe Eichhorn, Zentral-Abt., Tgb. Nr. 503, Innere Lage unter besonderer Berücksichtigung des Hetmantums, 30.5.1918.

69 Jaroslaw Pelenski, "Hetman Pavlo Skoropadsky and Germany (1917–18) as Reflected in his Memoirs," in *German-Ukrainian Relations in Historical Perspective*, 73; *Pavlo Skoropads'kyj*, 276–79.

70 Pelenski, "Hetman Pavlo Skoropadsky and Germany," 75.

71 BayHStA-KA, Kav.Div., Bd. 21, N.O.d.O.H.L. Heeresgruppe Eichhorn, Zentral-Abt, Tgb. Nr. 503, Innere Lage unter besonderer Berücksichtigung des Hetmantums, 30.5.1918. In this document, it is said of the Hetman that "His dislike of the militarily and politically incompetent Poles is just as well founded and credible."

The Administration of the Austro-Hungarian Zone of Occupation

On 27 March, the day before signing the agreement on the administration of the occupation, the chief of the operations section of the general staff, Major General Alfred Freiherr von Waldstätten, presented a report on Ukraine. He drew a somber picture of a chaotic state led by the "old" and "powerless" Rada president, Mykhailo Hrushevsky, who was being exploited by all sides. Neither the Rada, the government, nor the idea of Ukrainian national identity were accepted by most of the population. Kyiv in particular was a dangerous place in which there were thousands of tsarist officers who had fled from the Bolsheviks and were engaged in political intrigue. Entente officers were also turning public opinion against the Central Powers. In addition, revolutionary and counterrevolutionary activists were adding to the chaos. Waldstätten was also critical of the influence of the German allies and demanded that money be set aside for propaganda activity in Ukraine to counter German activities aimed at controlling the Rada.[72]

Austro-Hungarian generals also reported chaotic conditions in provincial cities such as Odesa, which was taken by German and Austro-Hungarian troops on 12 March after some heavy fighting.[73] In a report from the 30th Infantry Division on 18 March, the situation was described as still extremely chaotic and difficult. The Central Rada had practically no support, as Ukrainian speakers were only a minority there. The jerry-built structures of the Central Rada had less popular support than the better organized City Duma, whose goal was to make Odesa a free city. A well-disciplined Polish Legion, which saw itself as the protector of the Poles in Odesa, did not support the Rada. There were also tens of thousands of soldiers from the dissolved Russian army in the city who belonged to various national committees and pursued their own interests. There was a catastrophic shortage of food, coal, oil, and ore, which, it was feared, would soon lead to riots.[74]

It soon became clear that the Austro-Hungarians lacked experts with a knowledge of the recently occupied country. At the beginning of April, they began efforts "to resume trade with Ukraine...to attract all those Austro-Hungarian subjects who had had relations with the country before the war and knew conditions there." In the following

72 ÖStA, KA, FA, AOK, OpAbt, Kt. 468, Nr. 1328, Waldstätten an AOK, 29.3.1918.

73 For the specifics on the revolutionary year 1917 in Odesa, see Tanja Penter, *Odessa 1917. Revolution an der Peripherie* (Cologne, Weimar, and Vienna, 2000).

74 ÖStA, AVA, Nachlässe, Nachlass: Spannocchi, B 760, Fas. 9.

months, lists arrived from all parts of the army with names of Gagists[75] and troop members who, in some cases, had had long experience of the country and knew its language.[76] But because of the limited personnel resources throughout the army, very few people with knowledge of the country were deployed in Ukraine.

The 2nd Army and parts of the 4th and 7th Armies took part in the invasion of Ukraine. The advance was linked to the dismantling of the Eastern Front, which was now to be organized by the General Commands (*Generalkommando*). The Commands of the 2nd and 4th Armies (the latter was dissolved and its units integrated into the 2nd Army) departing for Ukraine were replaced by the 4th General Command. The Command of the 7th Army was replaced by the 7th General Command.[77] The 4th General Command, made up of the quartermaster sections of the 2nd and 4th Army, was stationed in Lviv; attached to it were the 2nd and 25th Infantry Divisions, the 45th Schützen Division, the 12th Cavalry Schützen Division, and the 4th Cavalry Division.[78] The commandant of this General Command was the infantry general Viktor von Webenau. Its sector of deployment was the area of Volhynia occupied by Austro-Hungarian troops, parts of the military district of Lublin, and the northern part of Bessarabia, as well as Galicia and Bukovyna. Divided into etappe commands (*Etappenkommandos*) and manned with weak *Landsturm* units, the General Command managed a variety of tasks. These included administration of the return home of prisoners of war, the rebuilding of destroyed infrastructure,[79] the dismantling of military installations erected during the war, the preparation of harvest detachments, the reception and further transmission of looted property, the purchase of goods in Ukraine for the military administration, transport

75 *Gagist* was a term used in the Austro-Hungarian military to refer to long-serving officers and noncommissioned officers. See *Die Habsburgermonarchie 1848–1918. Die Bewaffnete Macht*, ed. Adam Wandruszka and Peter Urbanitsch, vol. 5 (Vienna, 1987), 552, 593–98, 743.

76 ÖStA, KA, FA, NFA, HHK AK/AGKdo, 2. Armee, OpAK, Kt. 309, 1918 Befehle und Verlautbarungen, Allgemeine Verlautbarungen des 2. Armeekommandos am 8.4.1918.

77 The Austro-Hungarian General Commands during the First World War should not be confused with the German units of the same name at that time and, later, in the Second World War. A General Command in the Austro-Hungarian army was equivalent to a corps in the German army: ÖStA, KA, FA, NFA, HHK AK/AGKdo, 4. Armee, Kt. 484, Beilagen zum Tagebuch des Generalkommandos 4 v. 8.4.–30.10.1918, Beilage 1.

78 ÖStA, KA, FA, NFA, HHK AK/AGKdo, 4. Armee, Kt. 484, Beilagen zum Tagebuch des Generalkommandos 4 vom 8.4.–30.10.1918, Beilage 6.

79 Formally the task of repairing infrastructure fell to the military command in Lviv (formerly in Ostrava in Moravia), but this was placed under the General Command.

management and supervision, border security, the construction of facilities in the rail transit stations (making use of prisoner-of-war companies), support for the post in Lviv, the maintenance of peace and order, reinforcing troop numbers from among those returning home, and recruitment among the local population for *Landsturm* units.[80] In the course of late summer, all General Command areas in the northeast of the Monarchy were placed under the authority of the Military Centers in the Rear (*Militärische Zentralstellen im Hinterland*). Galicia, for instance, was subordinated to the military command in Lviv.[81] The remaining troops were placed under the *Ostarmee* or moved to other sections of the front.[82]

The troops advancing into Ukraine had to deal not only with their own military duties but also with managing the thousands of returning Austro-Hungarian prisoners of war. Negotiations between Bolshevik Russia, Germany, and Austria-Hungary on the question of prisoners had begun on 31 December 1917 in St. Petersburg. Although the talks dealt with what was only a limited problem, they dragged on. An agreement was finally signed at the beginning of February but was rendered ineffective by the breakdown of negotiations at Brest-Litovsk on 10 February 1918 and the end of the truce. In spite of this, thousands of former prisoners had been making their own way home since December. In a Russia stricken by revolutionary chaos, this was no simple journey. Austria-Hungary was particularly troubled by this because it feared that the returning prisoners would carry the "virus of revolution" into the already poisonous mood behind the lines and radicalize the situation in the army. AOK was pushing for a legal resolution of the prisoner-of-war issue and relied on the Red Cross.[83]

---

80 For the variety of activities of 4th General Command, see ÖStA, KA, FA, NFA, HHK AK/AGKdo, 4. Armee, Kt. 484, Beilagen zum Tagebuch des Generalkommandos 4 vom 8.4.–30.10.1918.

81 The 7th General Command was dissolved on 15 June, and its responsibilities in the Austro-Hungarian area were given to the 4th General Command. Its troops were used to form the XI Corps, which was subordinated to the *Ostarmee*. On the dissolution of the 7th General Command, see ÖStA, KA, FA, NFA, HHK AK/AGKdo, 7. Armee, Kt. 289, Separat-Reservat-Generalkommandobefehl Nr. 2 v. 14.6.1918.

82 The much reduced 4th General Command remained responsible for the administration of Bessarabia (until it was taken over by Romanian authorities) and Volhynia, as well as for the administration of march formations and the security of the border with Romania: ÖStA, KA, FA, NFA, HHK AK/AGKdo, 4. Armee, Kt. 484, Beilagen zum Tagebuch des Generalkommandos 4 vom 8.4.–30.10.1918, Übergabe des 4. GenKmdos an MilKmdo Lemberg, 18.8.1918. For a general account, see ÖStA, KA, FA, NFA, HHK AK/AGKdo, 4. Armee, Kt. 485, Nr. 45.587, Ausscheiden der innerhalb der Monarchie gelegenen Gebietsteile des 1. und 4. Genkmdos aus dem Bereich der A.i.F., 14.8.1918.

83 Verena Moritz and Hannes Leidinger, *Zwischen Nutzen und Bedrohung. Die russischen*

During the advance into Ukraine, thousands of their own onetime soldiers volunteered, and others were picked up in the villages and towns. In his diary, Böhm-Ermolli wrote of 66,273 prisoners of war[84] who "arrived" in March at the advancing 2nd Army.[85] At the end of April, corps commands were given guidelines for the treatment of returning prisoners of war. Collection points were to be established in Ukraine from which the returning soldiers could be taken back to Austria-Hungary in the area of the 4th General Command.[86] Those being repatriated were to be set up with adequate funds for the return journey in order to avoid dissatisfaction on their part. To attract greater numbers of these ex-prisoners, posters were put up and information points established at the returnee mission in Kyiv and at collection points in Kharkiv.[87] But these measures may not have achieved the desired success since, as late as September, the military reconnaissance (*Nachrichtenstelle*) in Volodymyr-Volynskyi reported that, in Kyiv, "there are many of our prisoners of war who do not want to leave the good work that they have found there."[88]

Two weeks after the Hetman came to power, the Austro-Hungarian troops in Ukraine were also restructured. Field Marshal Eduard von Böhm-Ermolli was replaced on 16 May by General Alfred Krauss. Krauss was assisted by the chief of general staff, Major General Alexander Belitska. The 2nd Army was renamed the *Ostarmee,* with its headquarters in Odesa.[89] The Austro-Hungarian *Ostarmee* consisted of the XII Corps in the Katerynoslav gubernia (the 15th, 34th, and 59th Infantry Divisions, the 5th Honved Cavalry Division,

Kriegsgefangenen in Österreich (1914–1921) (Bonn, 2005), 210–29; ÖStA, KA, FA, AOK, OpAbt, Kt. 466, Nr. 1018, Csicerics an AOK, 11.2.1918; ÖStA, KA, FA, NFA, HHK AK/AGKdo, 2. Armee, QuAbt, Kt. 696, Nr. 4017, Disziplinäre Verhältnisse beim ErsBaon SchR 31, 8.7.1918.

84 These numbers may be realistic, since the 2nd Army, on 9 March, reported 3,000–5,000 returning daily: ÖStA, KA, FA, NFA, HHK AK/AGKdo, 2. Armee, QuAbt, Kt. 694, Nr. 1334, Heimkehrerzahlen, 9.3.1918.

85 ÖStA, AVA, Nachlässe, Nachlass: Böhm-Ermolli, B 1466, Mikrofilm B 1466, Eintrag v. 28.–31.3.1918.

86 Existing buildings and housing complexes served as collection points, since the shortage of materials meant that new sites could not be constructed: ÖStA, KA, FA, NFA, HHK AK/KorpsKdo, 12. Korps, Kt. 1663, Nr. 8069, Regelung des Heimkehrerwesens in der Ukraine durch das 2. Armee-Kommando, 28.4.1918.

87 ÖStA, KA, FA, NFA, HHK AK/AGKdo, 2. Armee, QuAbt, Kt. 693, Nr. 2923, Regelung des Heimkehrerwesens in der Ukraina, 13.6.1918.

88 ÖStA, KA, FA, AOK, Evidenzbüro 1918, Nachrichtenabteilung, Kt. 3674, Nr. 24.107, Verhältnisse in der Ukraine, 16.9.1918.

89 ÖStA, KA, FA, NFA, HHK AK/AGKdo, 2. Armee, QuAbt, Kt. 695, Nr. 1872, Kommandoverhältnisse, 29.3.1918.

and the 145th Infantry Brigade), the XXV Corps in Podilia (the 155th Honved Infantry Division and the 54th Schützen Division), and the XVII Corps in Kherson (2nd and 7th Cavalry Divisions, as well as the 11th and 30th Infantry Divisions).[90] The units were made up mainly of soldiers from the South Slav (Slovenian, Croatian) regions of the Habsburg Monarchy and from the northwestern and southeastern regions of Hungary, Bohemia, Moravia, Galicia, and Bukovyna.[91] The 36th Infantry Division, the 21st Schützen Division,[92] and the 4th Cavalry Division also took part in the invasion.[93] By early October, the troops had shrunk to just six divisions. All three corps had only two divisions each.[94] In addition, the 2nd Cavalry Division (with only the 3rd Cavalry Brigade) and the 145th Infantry Brigade were placed under the command of the *Ostarmee*.[95] As in the case of the German troops, the numerical data for the Austro-Hungarian troops in Ukraine need to revised downward. The *Ostarmee* itself assumed a maximum of 240,000 troops in Ukraine at the end of August,[96] and by the beginning of October it may have been less than half that.[97]

By the summer, an entire network of Austro-Hungarian military and civilian officials had been established in Ukraine.[98] The general in charge in Kyiv was Major General Lelio von Spannocchi, assisted by

---

90 ÖStA, KA, FA, NFA, HHK AK/AGKdo, 2. Armee, OpAK, Kt. 309, 1918 Befehle und Verlautbarungen, Allgemeine Verlautbarungen des Kommandos der Ostarmee am 20. Mai 1918.

91 Allthough it has to be admitted that the national/ethnic structure of the military units became more and more mixed throughout the war: Rudolf Hecht, *Heeresergänzung – Österreich-Ungarn im 1. Weltkrieg* (Vienna, 2010), 449–57.

92 ÖStA, KA, FA, NFA, HHK AK/AGKdo, 2. Armee, QuAbt, Kt. 693, Nr. 853, Sammelakt zur militärischen Teilnahme an der wirtschaftlichen Ausnutzung der Ukraine, Februar/März 1918.

93 See *Österreich-Ungarns letzter Krieg, Das Kriegsjahr 1918*, no. VII, supplements 6 und 27.

94 XII Corps: 5th Honved Cavalry Division and 15th Infantry Division; the 59th Infantry and 4th Cavalry Division were already departing; XVII Corps: 11th Infantry and 7th Cavalry Division; XXV Corps: 155th Honved Infantry and 54th Schützen Division.

95 ÖStA, KA, FA, AOK, Ukraine Akten, Kt. 2626, Nr. 8399, Kriegsgliederung der k.u.k. Ostarmee, 1.10.1918.

96 Their monthly maintenance cost was around 97.4 million crowns: ÖStA, KA, FA, NFA, HHK AK/AGKdo, 2. Armee, QuAbt, Kt. 710, Nr. 43.295, Stellungnahme zur beabsichtigten Aufbringung des Heeresbedarfes in der Ukraina, 26.9.1918.

97 ÖStA, KA, FA, AOK, Ukraine Akten, Kt. 2626, Nr. 8399, Kriegsgliederung der k.u.k. Ostarmee, 1.10.1918; *Österreich-Ungarns letzter Krieg, Das Kriegsjahr 1918*, no. VII, supplement 32, "Letzte Kriegsgliederung der öst.-ung. und der dem k.u.k. AOK unterstellten deutschen Streitkräfte am 15. Oktober 1918"; Alfred Krauss and Franz Klingenbrunner, *Die Besetzung der Ukraine 1918* (Vienna, 1928), 389. See also John Ellis and Michael Cox, *The World War I Databook: The Essential Facts and Figures for All the Combatants* (London, 2001), 247.

98 For individual persons and positions in Kyiv on 8 August, see ÖStA, KA, FA, AOK, Ukraine Akten, Kt. 2618, Nr. 4597, Verzeichnis der öster.-ung. und deutschen Behörden und Funktionäre in Kiew, 7.8.1918.

Major Moritz Fleischmann von Theissruck (he was also the "authorized representative of Austro-Hungarian High Command to the Ukrainian Rada"). Spannocchi took his orders directly from Austria-Hungary's AOK, and all Austro-Hungarian military personnel stationed in Kyiv and in the German zone of influence were formally under his command. The Austro-Hungarian general staff officers of the Army Group Eichhorn-Kiew, the Austro-Hungarian representatives at the German-Austro-Hungarian Economic Center, and the prisoner-of-war missions were subject to his instructions in military and economic matters. Spannocchi was to cooperate with the ambassador, Forgách, as much as possible and, in political matters, it was Forgách who was the leader.[99] Lieutenant Field Marshal Georg Alexich in Kyiv was responsible for the repatriation of prisoners of war. The representative of the War Ministry in Kyiv was Gustav Riemer (replacing the Military Commission of Colonel Milan Lennoch).[100] The liaison officer to Army Group Eichhorn-Kiew was Cavalry Captain Klemens Waldbott zu Bassenheim-Bornheim. The military representatives, also with economic responsibilities, were Captain Josef Daróczy, general staff officer at the German-Austro-Hungarian Economic Center, and Major Franz Buchar, general staff officer to the director of the railways and chief of Austro-Hungarian staff at the Railway Center in Kyiv. The governor of Odesa[101] was Lieutenant Field Marshal Eduard Edler von Böltz.[102]

In general, Krauss attempted to establish Odesa as an economic and political counterweight to Kyiv and make use of existing separatist tendencies. In an agreement signed between the Ukrainian government and the Austro-Hungarian military, there was a promise of an authorized representative of the Ukrainian government at the headquarters of the *Ostarmee* in Odesa and a certain amount of consultation in matters that would affect the occupying troops. The Germany army in Ukraine was indignant about the agreement, suspecting that Austria-Hungary was attempting to establish its own Ukrainian state in southern Ukraine, with Odesa as its capital. And this suspicion was not altogether unfounded. Krauss had repeatedly

99 ÖStA, KA, FA, AOK, Ukraine Akten, Kt. 2626, Mappe "Ukraine. Geheimakten," Nr. 20, Befehlsverhältnisse in der Ukraine, 20.6.1918.

100 ÖStA, KA, FA, NFA, HHK AK/AGKdo, 2. Armee, OpAK, Kt. 309, 1918 Befehle und Verlautbarungen, Allgemeine Verlautbarungen des Kommandos der Ostarmee am 20.7.1918.

101 Previously group commandant, later also military governor of Odesa.

102 For the military organization of the Austro-Hungarian *Ostarmee* after 1 October 1918, see ÖStA, KA, FA, AOK, Ukraine Akten, Kt. 2626, Nr. 8399, Kriegsgliederung der k.u.k. Ostarmee, 1.10.1918.

brought this idea forward, particularly when it came to thinking about an official military occupation of the country.[103] When this agreement was signed, Eichhorn protested both to Skoropadsky and to the command of the *Ostarmee*. He saw it as a violation of the Brest-Litovsk treaty and feared a partition of Ukraine.[104] However, Krauss continued to insist that a representative of the Ukrainian government be sent to Odesa.[105] The Hetman, too, was not enthusiastic about the actions of the Austro-Hungarians in southern Ukraine and remained mistrustful of the Austrians and Hungarians.[106]

Krauss's intention with these actions was to get around not only the German troops, with their monopoly of power in Kyiv, but also the Austro-Hungarian Foreign Ministry, whose representatives in Kyiv were becoming increasingly powerful. Since taking over the post in mid-April, the foreign minister, Burián, had been attempting to get control of the political agenda in Ukraine and repeatedly reminded the military representatives of their proper place. Between February and April, Czernin had been losing control of affairs in Ukraine as a result of the tough peace negotiations with Romania, the completion of the Treaty of Brest-Litovsk with Bolshevik Russia, the Polish question, and the Sixtus affair.

In spite of this dense network of newly created Austro-Hungarian institutions in Ukraine, the separation of responsibilities remained problematic. Time and energy were repeatedly being lost as a result of tensions between military and political authorities. One particular area of dispute concerned control of the migration of Ukrainians to Austria-Hungary. There was a fear that the Ukrainians in Galicia and Bukovyna could join with those of the old Russian Empire and become an uncontrollable centrifugal political force. Basically, it

---

103 Krauss had suggested, at the time, a division of Ukraine into two general governorates and had proposed a detailed administrative plan for the "Southern Ukrainian general governorate"; ÖStA, KA, FA, AOK, OpAbt, Kt. 472, Nr. 1729, Ziele der Monarchie in der Ukraine, 6.7.1918.

104 Both Germans and Ukrainians protested against the influence on Ukrainian internal affairs in Odesa. It was only after some maneuvering by Krauss himself, as well as by Waldbott and Ambassador Forgách, that the situation calmed down. See ÖStA, KA, FA, AOK, OpAbt, Kt. 470, Nr. 1614, Komorny-Absetzung, 20.5.1918; ÖStA, KA, FA, AOK, OpAbt, Kt. 470, Nr. 1629, Ostarmee an AOK, 22.5.1918; ÖStA, KA, FA, AOK, OpAbt, Kt. 470, Nr. 1644, Beratungen mit Staatssekretär Kistiakowski, 23.5.1918; ÖStA, KA, FA, AOK, OpAbt, Kt. 472, Nr. 1707, Aktenkonvolut zur Situation in der Ukraine, 13.–25.6.1918.

105 ÖStA, KA, FA, AOK, OpAbt, Kt. 471, Nr. 1679, Fragen der Ostarmee, 5.6.1918.

106 ÖStA, KA, FA, AOK, OpAbt, Kt. 472, Nr. 1712, Aktenkonvolut zu den Verhältnissen in der Ukraine, 29.5.–30.6.1918; *Pavlo Skoropads'kyj*, 269–73.

was the Austro-Hungarian military commission in Kyiv that was responsible for issuing permits for Ukrainians wishing to travel to Austria-Hungary; it was also responsible for the military intelligence service of the 2nd Army. It was only in very urgent cases that the representative of the Foreign Ministry, Forgách, could issue such a travel permit.[107] Not until the beginning of August were they able to agree on a new regulation according to which the passport authorities of the Foreign Ministry in Kyiv and Odesa had the authority to accredit passports for the whole of Ukraine. However, the passport authority of the AOK would also have to issue a permit. Guidelines were also approved concerning local border traffic. It was hoped that this would improve trade between Ukraine, Galicia, and Bukovyna and thus also increase the amount of provisions for Austria-Hungary.[108] Local border trade, however, led to very active smuggling not only of goods but undoubtedly also of propaganda.

On 1 June, after long deliberation and following the example of the Germans, the jurisdiction of military courts was introduced into the Austro-Hungarian zone in Ukraine. The increase in the numbers of military police helped in the suppression of uprisings,[109] although their numbers, around 4,000 men (1,500 in Odesa alone), were quite small for such a large area of occupation.[110] Generally, after June 1918, a bit later than the Germans, the Foreign Ministry in Vienna and the command of the *Ostarmee* were insisting more strongly on cooperation between the troops and Ukrainian officials,[111] from prohibiting direct

---

107 ÖStA, KA, FA, NFA, HHK AK/AGKdo, 2. Armee, OpAK, Kt. 309, 1918 Befehle und Verlautbarungen, Allgemeine Verlautbarungen des 2. Armeekommandos am 10.5.1918. On Zitkovsky (born 2.10.1883), see *Jahrbuch des k.u.k. Auswärtigen Dienstes 1916*, 26. May 1916, vol. 20 (Vienna, 1916), 460.

108 ÖStA, KA, FA, NFA, HHK AK/AGKdo, 2. Armee, OpAK, Kt. 309, 1918 Befehle und Verlautbarungen, Allgemeine Verlautbarungen des Kommandos der Ostarmee am 13.8.1918.

109 ÖStA, KA, FA, AOK, OpAbt, Kt. 472, Nr. 1707, Aktenkonvolut zur Situation in der Ukraine, 13–25.6.1918.

110 After Serbia and the Lublin area, which were much smaller, this was the area with the third largest number of military police: ÖStA, KA, FA, AOK, OpAbt, Kt. 475, Nr. 1906, Darstellung der materiellen Lage der Armee im Felde, 18.8.1918, Beilage 12.

111 ÖStA, KA, FA, AOK, OpAbt, Kt. 470, Op. Geh. Nr. 1560, Gerichte, Kriegsleistungsgesetz Ukraine, 6.5.1918; ÖStA, KA, FA, AOK, OpAbt, Kt. 470, Op. Geh. Nr. 1568, Kriegsleistungsgesetz in der Ukraine, 9.5.1918; ÖStA, KA, FA, AOK, OpAbt, Kt. 470, Op. Geh. Nr. 1581, Regelung der Verhältnisse in der Ukraine, 12.5.1918; ÖStA, KA, FA, AOK, OpAbt, Kt. 470, Op. Geh. Nr. 1583, Gerichtsbarkeit, Kriegsleistungsgesetz in der Ukraine, 13.5.1918; ÖStA, KA, FA, AOK, OpAbt, Kt. 470, Op. Geh. Nr. 1586, Anordnungen der Deutschen in der Ukraine, 14.5.1918; ÖStA, KA, FA, AOK, OpAbt, Kt. 470, Op. Geh. Nr. 1612, Gerichtsbarkeit und Kriegsleistungsgesetz in der Ukraine, 19.5.1918.

intervention in rail transport (this intervention was now to take place only through official channels) to promoting cooperation with their corresponding military and civilian officials.[112]

In spite of all these efforts, the Austro-Hungarian authorities never came close to having as much influence in Ukraine as their German allies. This was made particularly clear at the time of Skoropadsky's coup, engineered by Groener, in which Fleischmann and Forgách were mere onlookers. They had got wind of events, but all they could do was discreetly sound out the persons involved to get better information.[113] Fleischmann in particular attempted, through a network of "Austrophile" "loyal" individuals, to improve his access to information, but ultimately he had only limited success.

Combined Executive Bodies of Administration

Although the Austro-Hungarians and Germans were unable to agree on a combined military structure in Ukraine, they were nonetheless forced to cooperate in organizing the economic administration in order to better exploit the occupied territory. The organizational agreement of 28 March had contained the first economic arrangements, including the organization of the railways and shipyards as well as agreements that regulated shipping on the rivers and on the Black Sea. A Combined Railway Center (*Gemeinsame Eisenbahnzentralstelle*) was established in Kyiv to organize the railways and a similar River Transport Center to oversee shipping (which, given Austria-Hungary's dominance in shipping on the Danube, was to be led by one of its officers).[114] In about two dozen treaties, agreements, and protocols signed between April and September, the Central Powers agreed among themselves and/or with the Ukrainian government on the regulation of economic matters. These included the creation of institutions to improve the exploitation of resources, regulation of food prices, contribution quotas, and formulas for the allocation of war materials and procured goods. There were just two agreements that did not focus mainly

112 ÖStA, KA, FA, NFA, HHK AK/AGKdo, 2. Armee, OpAK, Kt. 309, 1918 Befehle und Verlautbarungen, Allgemeine Verlautbarungen des Kommandos der Ostarmee am 20.5.1918; ÖStA, KA, FA, NFA, HHK AK/AGKdo, 2. Armee, OpAK, Kt. 309, 1918, Beilage zu Allgemeinen Verlautbarungen Nr. 152; ÖStA, KA, FA, NFA, HHK AK/AGKdo, 2. Armee, QuAbt, Kt. 693, Nr. 2856, Organisation der ukrainischen Militär- und Zivilbehörden, 23.6.1918; ÖStA, KA, FA, NFA, HHK AK/AGKdo, 2. Armee, QuAbt, Kt. 696, Nr. 4111, Verkehr mit ukrainischen Behörden, 16.7.1918.

113 For what Skoropadsky had to say about Fleischmann, see *Pavlo Skoropads'kyj*, 155.

114 ÖStA, KA, FA, AOK, OpAbt, Kt. 468, Nr. 1430, Regelung von einigen Fragen in der Ukraine, April 1918.

on economic matters—the already mentioned agreement on the administration of the occupation and the agreement with Ukraine concerning the handover of the 1st Cavalry Schützen (Cossack) Division, which will be discussed below. The central institutions for the administration of the economy were the Ukrainian Food Council, the German-Austro-Hungarian Economic Center, and the Ukrainian State Grain Bureau.[115]

But in spite of these extensive regulations, there was constant friction in the day-to-day work of the allied troops. According to a report submitted to AOK at the end of May by the Austro-Hungarian liaison officer to Army Group Eichhorn-Kiew, Captain Waldbott, the main reason for this may have been the personal dislike between Groener and Krauss. Krauss jealously guarded Austria-Hungary's independent interests in Ukraine, while Groener, with great self-confidence, was intent on exploiting Ukraine in an amicable arrangement with the new government he had himself created. Groener frequently told Waldbott that he was dissatisfied with the Brest-Litovsk treaty, the Berlin agreement of February, and the Kyiv treaty signed in May because they were all based on the "illusion" of an independent Ukrainian state. They had "built on this false foundation. In fact, Ukraine is a country without borders, without a language, and without a government." Waldbott, however, tried to soothe relations between Army Group Eichhorn-Kiew and the *Ostarmee* and, in some cases, managed to accomplish this.[116]

It was only in the maritime area that military relations among the Central Powers were relatively free of friction. The Wulff section of the Austro-Hungarian Danube flotilla was in the ports of Odesa and Kherson; German U-boats as well as Bulgarian and Turkish warships were in the port of Odesa; Turkish naval forces were at Sevastopol.[117] They were to ensure control of the Black Sea and the navigable rivers of Ukraine in order to accelerate the export of procured goods. At first they also intervened in the battles for the military conquest of Ukraine. The Turkish presence was to support that country's (unsuccessful) claims with regard to the Crimea.

115 For more detail, see chapter 3c in the present volume.

116 ÖStA, KA, FA, AOK, OpAbt, Kt. 470, Nr. 1649, Waldbott an AOK, 28.5.1918.

117 *Österreich-Ungarns letzter Krieg. Das Kriegsjahr 1918*, supplements VII/6, Map, "Kräftegruppierung im Südosten nach Besetzung der Ukraine am 1. Juni 1918."

The Hesitant "Ukrainization": Ukrainian Military Formations during the Occupation by the Central Powers

Although the Germans wanted Ukrainian cooperation in combating insurgency, they were also very skeptical about building an Ukrainian army. Shortly after its return to power in Kyiv, the Rada began to create at least provisional militias and volunteer formations (red and black Haidamakas, a Zaporozhian Corps, and Sich Riflemen) that were to serve as the military arm of the government until the creation of an organized army. The old army[118] had been largely dissolved in April 1918 because of its unreliability. German military leaders such as Groener and the Austro-Hungarian High Command saw a new army as an unpredictable factor.[119] However, the Rada attempted, in contact with the Central Powers, to build a stand-alone Ukrainian army. Officers, non-commissioned officers, and soldiers were to be given their ranks from the time before the "Bolshevik upheavals."[120] The men to be enlisted in this army were eighteen- and nineteen-year-old youths, as they would have been less affected by the "corrosive influence of the soldiers' councils and Bolshevik theories." Recruitment was to have begun in June 1918, but the date continued to be postponed. It was still unclear at that point to what extent the militias and volunteer formations, as well as the Ukrainian Cossack Schützen Division created by the Central Powers, would be integrated into the new army.[121]

The few Ukrainian formations created by Germany and Austria-Hungary from among Ukrainians who had been Russian prisoners of war were extremely controversial within the Central Powers. There were fears in Vienna and Berlin that these units would one day turn against their own troops. Shortly after the signing of the Brest-Litovsk treaty with Ukraine, a "division" was being put together in Cisleithania, and preparations were being made for its transfer to the Rada.[122] In the spring of 1918, however, the German Empire dissolved its division, described as "bluecoats" (*Blauröcke, syn'ozhupannyky*) because of the

118 "Old army" means the remnants of the army from the period of the Provisional Government, which in turn had been based on the tsarist army.

119 Cf. BA-MA, N 46/172, Niederschrift über die Besprechung, An ObOst v. 23.4.1918.; ÖStA, KA, FA, AOK, Ukraine Akten, Kt. 2614, Nr. 2387, Ukrainasitzung, 28.6.1918.

120 ÖStA, KA, FA, NFA, HHK AK/AGKdo, 2. Armee, OpAK, Kt. 309, 1918 Befehle und Verlautbarungen, Allgemeine Verlautbarungen des Kommandos der Ostarmee am 14.7.1918.

121 ÖStA, KA, FA, AOK, OpAbt, Kt. 468, Nr. 1407, Lage in der Ukraina Ende März 1918, 16.4.1918.

122 ÖStA, KA, FA, NFA, HHK AK/AGKdo, 2. Armee, QuAbt, Kt. 692, Nr. 702, Ukrainische Kriegsgefangene – Formierung zu Abteilungen, 19.2.1918.

color of their uniform, but Austria-Hungary continued with this project, although there was still some skepticism about it.[123] Ukrainians from among the prisoners of war, often described as "graycoats" (*Grauröcke, sirozhupannyky*), were gathered together from the areas of the 2nd and 4th Armies[124] and from the upper Austrian prisoner-of-war camps in Kleinmünchen and Freistadt. Those Russian prisoners of war accommodated at the Eastern Front were collected in Volodymyr-Volynskyi. Selected officers were trained in upper Austria, and they would "form the basis of a disciplined, soldierly feeling, combat-ready army that was well disposed to the Monarchy."[125] They would later be sent to Volhynia. The signals service of AOK and some of their own "propaganda organs" from the ranks of the Union for the Liberation of Ukraine were responsible for training the officers.[126] These troops were to be a future basis for the internal security of Ukraine. This military formation was also a sign to the Ukrainians within the Austro-Hungarian Monarchy that it took the Ukrainian movement seriously and supported it, even though it saw the movement as something mostly outside the Monarchy itself.[127] In the political education of the officers, the focus would be the friendly relationship between the two countries and the mutual advantages of cooperation between Austria-Hungary and Ukraine. On social questions, "Bolshevik ideas" were to be combated and shown to be absurd. A Ukrainian newspaper, *Vidrodzhenie* (Rebirth), was provided for this purpose, as well as other newspapers and pamphlets.[128] Although the Ukrainian formation was described as a "division," it consisted of only 7,227 Ukrainians deployed in infantry companies, a divisional cavalry and artillery, a technical company and a telephone company, a medical unit, and a divisional train. For purposes of training, a further 220 Austro-Hungarian officers and soldiers were attached to the division.[129]

---

123 ÖStA, KA, FA, AOK, Ukraine Akten, Kt. 2614, Nr. 2387, Ukrainasitzung, 28.6.1918.

124 ÖStA, KA, FA, NFA, Sonstiges, Ukrainische Formationen, Kt. 1952, Nr. 1, Anweisung zur Formierung ukrainischer Baone des k.u.k. 4. Armeekommandos, 18.2.1918.

125 ÖStA, KA, FA, AOK, Evidenzbüro 1918, Nachrichtenabteilung, Kt. 3669, Nr. 7370, Formierung der ukrainischen Armee, 3.4.1918.

126 ÖStA, KA, FA, AOK, Evidenzbüro 1918, Nachrichtenabteilung, Kt. 3669, Nr. 6815, Propaganda bei ukrainischen Truppen, 22.3.1918.

127 ÖStA, KA, FA, AOK, OpAbt, Kt. 470, Nr. 1632, Ukrainische Division, 29.5.1918.

128 ÖStA, KA, FA, AOK, Evidenzbüro 1918, Nachrichtenabteilung, Kt. 3669, Nr. 7370, Formierung der ukrainischen Armee, 3.4.1918.

129 The structure of the division was extremely unusual and did not correspond to the standard strength: ÖStA, KA, NFA, Sonstiges, Ukrainische Formationen, Kt. 1952, Nr. 28, Organisation der 1. Ukrainischen Schützen-Kosakendivision.

After months of intervention and pressure from the Hetman,[130] the 1st Ukrainian Schützen Division[131] was handed over to the Ukrainian government.[132] There was no further recruitment of Ukrainians from Russian prisoners of war.[133]

In addition to this military formation, which was created under Austro-Hungarian control, the Rada established a number of units of Sich Riflemen (*Sichovi Stril'tsi*). One of them raised the delicate question of a battalion made up of Austro-Hungarian prisoners of war on Ukrainian territory in 1917–18 (*Halyts'ko-Bukovyns'kyi Kurin' Sichovykh Stril'tsiv*).[134] The Austro-Hungarian High Command raised serious concerns about this shortly after the occupation because these soldiers were Austro-Hungarian citizens fighting for a foreign country, which constituted "high treason." On 27 April, the day before the Hetman came to power, Fleischmann recommended that no action be taken with regard to the Sich Riflemen for the moment. On 6 May, AOK's legal consultant called for the immediate withdrawal of Austro-Hungarian citizens from the Sich Riflemen and their repatriation. Because of their breach of "sworn duty and loyalty," which was a punishable offense, they had to be dealt with by legal means.[135] During the Skoropadsky putsch, the *Stril'tsi*, not least because of their anticipated repatriation to the Habsburg Monarchy, were the last troops to remain loyal to the Rada and refused to recognize the Hetman in the months that followed. In mid-May some hundreds of them joined the (Oleksandr) Natiiv Brigade in Oleksandrivsk (present-day Zaporizhia), which was also hostile to the Hetman.[136]

The Sich Riflemen mentioned here are not to be confused with the Ukrainian Sich Riflemen (*Ukraïns'ki Sichovi Stril'tsi*). They were a Galician volunteer organization created at the beginning of the war

130 ÖStA, KA, NFA, Sonstiges, Ukrainische Formationen, Kt. 1952, Nr. 724, Telegramm des AOK-Verbindungsoffiziers bei den ukrainischen Truppen an die Operative Abteilung des AOK v. 11.7.1918; *Pavlo Skoropads'kyj*, 216.

131 The division was frequently referred to as the "1st Ukrainian Schützen Cossack Division," but the term "Cossack" was removed from official references in the summer.

132 ÖStA, HHStA, MdÄ, PA X, Russland Liasse XI d/9, Plan der Aufstellung einer ukrainischen Armee, Juli–Oktober 1918. For further detail, see chapter 2a in the present volume.

133 ÖStA, KA, FA, AOK, Evidenzbüro 1918, Nachrichtenabteilung, Kt. 3673, Nr. 23.750, Ronge an Kriegsministerium/Abt. 10, Oktober 1918; ÖStA, HHStA, MdÄ, PA I, Kt. 1041, Liasse Krieg, 58 Ukraine, Fol. 228–233, AOK an Ministerium des Äußern, 24.8.1918.

134 On the different military units of the Rada, see Peter Abbott and Eugene Pinak, *Ukrainian Armies 1914–55* (Oxford and New York, 2004), 9–13.

135 ÖStA, KA, FA, AOK, OpAbt, Kt. 469, Nr.1513, Stellungnahme des Justizreferenten des AOK, 6.5.1918.

136 ÖStA, KA, FA, AOK, OpAbt, Kt. 472, Nr. 1709, Vertrauliche Nachrichten aus der Ukraina, 25.5.1918.

to take part in the campaign against Russia. Their demands were too extreme for the Austro-Hungarian authorities. They wanted better arms, training, and treatment and, on top of that, the establishment of a Ukrainian state.[137] As Austria-Hungary feared offending Poland by creating a strong Ukrainian Legion, it did not want to offer too much support to the Ukrainian movement in Galicia. Consequently these demands were not met as the initiators would have wanted. Instead, only a small number of the Ukrainian Sich Riflemen were taken into the k.k. Ukrainian Legion. The Legion was poorly armed and, with 2,500 men, was very small but all the more motivated.[138]

By June 1918 the Hetman had created his own State Guard, made up mostly of onetime tsarist officers and consisting of five infantry companies and one cavalry company.[139] At the beginning of July, Groener had ordered that no obstacles be raised against the recruitment of onetime Russian officers to the Ukrainian army.[140] By that time, there existed two pioneer battalions, a technical regiment, the 1st Kyiv Infantry Division, the 121st, 122nd, and 123rd Regiments, an artillery brigade, and four guard cavalry regiments. The Free Cossacks, however, who were meant to be a "special army" in the struggle against the Bolsheviks, were disarmed by German troops.[141] The recruitment of the army proceeded at a very slow pace during the summer. According to reports from the Austro-Hungarian signals intelligence service in Ukraine in September and October, the organization was extremely uneven, discipline and training poor, and recruitment slow, but provisions and armaments relatively good. In spite of these efforts, the army had only 85,000 men as of 25 October, according to the Ukrainian minister of war,[142] totally inadequate to bring stability to the state.

---

137 StA, HHStA, MdÄ, PA I, Kt. 902, Liasse Krieg 8b, Ukraine 1914 VIII–1915 VII, Fol. 461–465, Forderungen der Sitschower-Schützen, August 1914.

138 See chapter 1b in the present volume.

139 See Abbott and Pinak, *Ukrainian Armies 1914–55*, 13–16.

140 ÖStA, KA, FA, AOK, Ukraine Akten, Kt. 2615, Nr. 2788, Groener an AOK, 3.7.1918.

141 ÖStA, KA, FA, AOK, Evidenzbüro 1918, Nachrichtenabteilung, Kt. 3670, Nr. 13.754, Militärische Daten über ukrainische Armee, 12.6.1918; ÖStA, KA, FA, AOK, Evidenzbüro 1918, Nachrichtenabteilung, Kt. 3671, Nr. 15.956, Ostarmee an AOK, 24.6.1918.

142 ÖStA, KA, FA, AOK, Evidenzbüro 1918, Nachrichtenabteilung, Kt. 3674, Nr. 24.107, Verhältnisse in der Ukraine, 16.9.1918; ÖStA, KA, FA, AOK, Evidenzbüro 1918, Nachrichtenabteilung, Kt. 3674, Nr. 26.131, Militärpassstelle Kiew an AOK, 2.10.1918; ÖStA, KA, FA, AOK, Evidenzbüro 1918, Nachrichtenabteilung, Kt. 3674, Nr. 26.587, Ostarmee an AOK, 12.10.1918; ÖStA, KA, FA, AOK, Evidenzbüro 1918, Nachrichtenabteilung, Kt. 3674, Nr. 26.588, Aktenkonvolut zur ukrainischen Armee, 12.7.–5.10.1918; ÖStA, KA, FA, AOK, Evidenzbüro 1918, Nachrichtenabteilung, Kt. 3675, Nr. 28.065, ukrainische Armee, 25.10.1918.

The Ukrainian Border Guard was also a cause of concern for the Central Powers. It was made up of 28 brigades (about 120,000 men) and was directly subordinate to the War Ministry. But this formation was also disunited, chaotic, and poorly armed. Its personnel were recruited from ex-Russian soldiers of all ranks. They had not been paid any wages until June, so there were high levels of corruption and desertion.[143] In spite of all this, the Border Guard, in cooperation with the German troops, was supposed to secure the border with Bolshevik Russia, thousands of miles long and still contested in many areas.

But the Central Powers were not alone responsible for the sluggish pace in establishing the Ukrainian army or for the desolate state of the paramilitary formations. The Hetman himself was also part of the problem, as he believed that the Central Powers would not withdraw before the spring of 1919 and saw no urgency in the creation of his own armed forces.[144] It was only when the Central Powers began their preparations for withdrawal that they wanted to "use all means" to drive forward the establishment of the Ukrainian army, "even at the cost of the mobility of our own troops."[145] This army was to be a counterweight to the Entente and the Bolsheviks. The plans were very ambitious. The army was to consist of sixteen infantry divisions, four cavalry divisions, an independent cavalry brigade, and some smaller already existing units. Its military equipment was to come from captured Russian matériel.[146] Assistance in building the Ukrainian army was embedded in the larger policy of "Ukrainizing" the occupation.[147] The impetus for this new policy, however, came from outside. The imminent defeat in the West made it extremely unlikelythat the Central Powers would stay in Ukraine.

143 ÖStA, KA, FA, AOK, Evidenzbüro 1918, Nachrichtenabteilung, Kt. 3670, Nr. 14.707, Ukrainische Grenzwache, 14.6.1918; ÖStA, KA, FA, AOK, Evidenzbüro 1918, Nachrichtenabteilung, Kt. 3671, Nr. 15.701, Militärpassstelle an AOK, 23.7.1918.

144 Cf. Pelenski, "Hetman Pavlo Skoropadsky and Germany," 77; *Pavlo Skoropads'kyj*, 203.

145 BayHStA-KA, Etappenkommandantur 54, Bd. 22, 18. Kavalleriebrigade, Abt. I, Nr. 70 per. geheim v. 28.10.1918; ÖStA, KA, FA, AOK, Evidenzbüro 1918, Nachrichtenabteilung, Kt. 3674, Nr. 27.007, Karte über Grenzeinteilung der ukrainischen Korpsbezirke 12.10.1918; ÖStA, KA, FA, AOK, Evidenzbüro 1918, Nachrichtenabteilung, Kt. 3674, Nr. 27.683, Militärpassstelle an AOK, 12.10.1918; ÖStA, KA, FA, AOK, Evidenzbüro 1918, Nachrichtenabteilung, Kt. 3674, Nr. 27.684, Militärpassstelle an AOK, 15.10.1918.

146 Cf. BayHStA-KA, Etappenkommandantur 54, Bd. 22, Chef des Generalstabes des Feldheeres, Abteilung Fremde Heere, Nr. 19210, Die Ukrainische Wehrmacht Ende Oktober 1918, 1.11.1918.

147 Groener wrote on 20 October that the new government was to be more "Ukrainized" and more to the left. See *Von Brest-Litovsk zur deutschen Novemberrevolution*, 446ff.

The Cultural and Propaganda Activities of the Central Powers

Propaganda, as an aspect of policy with regard to the press, culture, and information, was soon a central area of activity for the occupation administration. German efforts in this respect are difficult to assess because of the shortage of documentation, even though one finds repeated demands for targeted propaganda activity in the military documents and in spite of the fact that Groener arranged for journalists from the empire to attend a major press conference in Kyiv in August.[148] We know from Ukrainian sources that German troops in Kyiv engaged in a certain amount of censorship and, in the early phase of the occupation, repeatedly closed down newspapers at short notice on account of critical press reports.[149]

The documentation for the Austro-Hungarian side is significantly better. Just a few days after the start of the eastward advance, the signals service of the XII Corps issued guidelines stating that care should be taken to prevent the infiltration of propaganda material through the thinly occupied front and via returning prisoners of war. Bolshevik attempts to foment revolution were seen as a special danger. This development was to be countered by means of espionage networks, civilian agents,[150] and propaganda among the Russian soldiers as well as the civilian population in order to "bring about the final overthrow of the Bolsheviks." The chaos in Russia, as well as Trotsky's antidemocratic measures and contradictory statements, were to be presented as evidence.[151] There is a certain irony in the fact that the Monarchy should be pointing to antidemocratic measures in Russia when it had itself suspended parliament until spring 1917, used weapons against its own citizens who staged hunger strikes, and executed or interned in 1914, without any evidence, thousands of citizens whom it described as "Russophiles."

At the end of March, Austria-Hungary's AOK set up the newspaper *Nedelia* (The Week) as a way of better implementing its policy. Its task was to combat Bolshevik ideas, strengthen future relations between the Habsburg Monarchy and Ukraine, and emphasize the good treatment of Ukrainian prisoners of war in Austro-Hungarian custody (especially

148 Ibid., 425–37.

149 Mark von Hagen, *War in a European Borderland: Occupations and Occupation Plans in Galicia and Ukraine, 1914–1918* (Seattle and London, 2007), 90ff.

150 ÖStA, KA, FA, NFA, Kmdo. Odessa (Gouv.), Kt. 3870, Nr. 1013/1039, Bericht der NA-Stelle des Gruppenkommandos Odessa, 31.5.1918.

151 ÖStA, KA, AdT, Kt. 4131, FABrig 59, Nr. 208, Richtlinien für die Fortsetzung der Propagandatätigkeit, 5.3.1918.

the cultural education of prisoners in the Freistadt camp). It would also provide a "favorable interpretation" of the Brest-Litovsk peace treaty with Ukraine, underlining especially the economic and political advantages as well as the amicable solution of the Kholm question. In addition to the newspaper, pamphlets were to be "distributed as widely as possible in the country."[152] With regard to the domestic Ukrainian press, there was also an urgent need for action, as demonstrated by the example of Odesa. Except for one Russian newspaper, *Odesskii listok* (Odesa Leaflet), and one German, *Odessaer Rundschau* (Odesa Review), the rest of the press was "absolutely hostile, spreading reports about defeat at Mykolaiv and exploiting every incident in the city to our disadvantage." There had also been a widespread rumor that the Central Powers would restore tsarist rule.[153] The basic principles of press policy in Ukraine were laid down on 15 April and, the very next day, a journalist from the War Press Bureau (*Kriegspressequartier*), Josef Hermann, was dispatched to Ukraine.[154] Hermann was directly subordinate to Fleischmann, and his task was to make sure that the press bulletins from the army commands in Kyiv, Odesa, and other cities were distributed as widely as possible: "The guiding idea must be that skillful journalistic and commercial propaganda will open up stores of provisions for us in Ukraine." They had to pull out all the stops: Sunday supplements, provision of filtered information to journalists, photos, films, radio programs, publication of articles, even operas, concerts, and variety shows were being considered.[155]

The Austro-Hungarian communications sections were to praise the friendship between Austria-Hungary and Ukraine and the advantages of cooperation to both states. They were also to emphasize that Austro-Hungarian troops would not change domestic Ukrainian conditions in any way and would take nothing from "the peasantry." Because of the multi-ethnic composition of the Ukrainian population, officers were instructed that, in those areas "where there are no or very few Ukrainians," of course "they should emphasize not so much

---

152 ÖStA, KA, AdT, Kt. 1378, IBrig 145, F. 68, Nr. 354, Ukrainische Propaganda.

153 ÖStA, AVA, Nachlässe, Nachlass: Spannocchi, B 760, Fas. 9, Politischer Bericht Nr. 2 des Kommandanten der k.u.k. Besatzungstruppen in Odessa v. 26.3.1918.

154 ÖStA, KA, FA, AOK, OpAbt, Kt. 468, Op. Geh. Nr. 1440, Journalisten nach Kiew senden, 16.4.1918; ÖStA, KA, FA, AOK, Ukraine Akten, Kt. 2.611, Nr. 1150, Ukraine-Tätigkeit des KPQu, 6.6.1918.

155 ÖStA, KA, FA, NFA, AOK, KPQ, Kommandobefehle, Kt. 22, Sonder-Kommandobefehl Nr. 5, 18.4.1918.

their friendship with Ukraine as with the inhabitants in general."[156] At the end of June, the communications sections were entrusted with the task of providing the newspapers with "brief notices" about combating insurgencies and disarmament activities so that the latter would not rely on their own "false" investigations.[157]

However, coverage of Ukraine never got into full swing either in Ukraine or on the home front. Many reports in the home press failed to correspond to the conceptions of the military leadership.[158] The *Kriegspressequartier* issued an order on 1 September that, in the home press, there should be one reporter on Ukraine assigned to "take an interest and make sure that inaccurate articles in certain leading papers be immediately refuted." Abroad as well, especially in Russia and Germany, the coverage of Ukraine and of the Austro-Hungarian troops was to be directed and intensified in a similar manner.[159]

In spite of all these measures and efforts, coverage of Ukraine on the home front and influence on the Ukrainian press in the occupied areas never had the success hoped for. This may have been due to the shortage of time or the inadequate resources. But a much more important reason was that the "home front" had to deal with the fact that no food or far too little food was coming from Ukraine. And in Ukraine itself, it was no longer possible to combat the negative sentiment that had become widespread among the population during the first half of the occupation period as a result of the military attacks during the invasion, the counterinsurgency campaign, the procurement of food supplies, and the occupation forces' support for the unloved Skoropadsky regime.

---

156 ÖStA, KA, AdT, Kt. 1379, IBrig 145, Nr. 466, NA und AW-Dienst-Leitlinien, 16.4.1918.

157 ÖStA, KA, AdT, Kt. 4131, FABrig 59, Nr. 307, Verhalten der Zivilbevölkerung gegenüber, 20.8.1918.

158 ÖStA, KA, FA, NFA, AOK, KPQ, Kommandobefehle, Kt. 22, Reservatbefehl Nr. 64, 1.9.1918; ÖStA, KA, FA, NFA, AOK, KPQ, Reservatbefehl Nr. 66, 7.9.1918; ÖStA, KA, FA, NFA, AOK, KPQ, Sonderkommandobefehl Nr. 22, 29.9.1918.

159 ÖStA, KA, FA, NFA, AOK, KPQ, Reservatbefehl Nr. 64, 1.9.1918.

3c. Economic Utilization

Wolfram Dornik and Peter Lieb[1]

The Economic Interests of the Central Powers in Ukraine

From the beginning of 1918, a central aspect of Austria-Hungary's Ukrainian policy was the acquisition of food from "Russia's granary." Myths circulated about the mass of grain and raw materials stored in Ukraine. These desires were also aroused by Ukrainian politicians who attempted, with promises of grain deliveries, to draw the attention of the Entente and the Central Powers as well as neutral states to their own political goals, such as diplomatic recognition, support in the struggle against the Bolsheviks, and trade agreements.[2] But it was clear, even in Ukraine itself, that such claims were illusory.[3]

The food situation in the Habsburg Monarchy at the beginning of 1918 was dire. As early as the autumn of 1914, large parts of the agriculturally important northeast of the empire had been occupied by Russia. At the same time, there were none of the traditional deliveries of grain or raw materials from such sources as Russia, Romania, or South America, which were now hostile or neutral. Since the beginning of the war, Hungary had also closed its borders within the Dual Monarchy to the export of food, although it did contribute to provisions for the army. At the same time, the tight transport situation, the lack of manure, and military conscription had all reduced productive capacity and the distribution of food. The Austrian part of the empire was now dependent on itself, on the assistance of its German ally, and on the utilization of the occupied territories.

The first shortages in Austria-Hungary's war economy appeared in the winter of 1914–15, and the situation deteriorated from one year to the next, especially in the cities. The high costs of the war drove up prices, but wages did not keep pace. It was only after long negotiations that Hungary was persuaded to offer more than its share of provisions for the imperial army from 1916, but these deliveries continued to be disputed. In the autumn of 1916, following the Russian successes

1 We would like to thank Vasyl Rasevych for valuable information on Ukrainian documents and literature for this chapter.

2 Switzerland, for instance. See details in chapter 4g of the German edition of the present volume.

3 V. Soldatenko, *Ukraïna v revoliutsiinu dobu. Istorychni ese-khroniky*, vol. 2, *Rik 1918* (Kyiv, 2009), 69.

in the Brusilov offensive, the economy of the Danube Monarchy became completely dependent on Germany, but that did not relieve the catastrophic food situation. Goods from the occupied territories in Poland, Serbia, Montenegro, and Italy did not fundamentally improve the situation.[4] The Austro-Hungarian economic structure was simply too weak and had suffered for decades from fundamental problems that had never been overcome. The food crisis reached its peak in the "January strikes" between 3 and 25 January 1918, involving three-quarters of a million workers. Starting in the big cities and industrial regions, it had spread throughout the country. Even earlier, there had been hunger riots in smaller towns that had been put down with military force. In the early months of 1918, it had become clear to everyone that the limits of endurance had been reached and, as the emperor stated in a handwritten note to Eduard von Böhm-Ermolli at the end of March, the continuation of the war itself was in question.[5] In the meantime, Hungary was unable to deliver the provisions demanded, and by spring it was on the verge of its own food crisis.[6]

On the German side, the invasion of Ukraine served a political purpose—the weakening of Soviet Russia. But even the Germans regarded a plentiful delivery of provisions as a welcome by-product that could improve their own tight food situation. The "turnip winter" of 1916–17 had been a catastrophe. Average consumption per day had been only 1,200 calories.[7] During the First World War, there was a horrendous number of deaths from malnutrition in the German Empire. According to the Imperial Health Ministry in December 1918, the figure had reached almost 763,000 for the whole period of the war.[8] The food supply improved in the winter of 1917–18 because of better government management of nutrition, tighter regulation of

4 Maureen Healy, *Vienna and the Fall of the Habsburg Empire: Total War and Everyday Life in World War I* (Cambridge, 2004), 31–86; Herbert Matis, *Leitlinien der* österreichischen *Wirtschaftspolitik 1848–1918* (Vienna, 1973), 29–67; Manfried Rauchensteiner, *Der Tod des Doppeladlers. Österreich-Ungarn und der Erste Weltkrieg* (Graz, Vienna, and Cologne, 1994), 144–46, 262–67; Roman Sandgruber, *Ökonomie und Politik. Österreichische Wirtschaftsgeschichte vom Mittelalter bis zur Gegenwart* (Vienna, 1995), 322ff.; Max-Stephan Schulze, "Austria-Hungary's Economy in World War I," in *The Economics of World War I*, ed. Stephen Broadberry and Mark Harrison (Cambridge, 2005), 95–97; Robert J. Wegs, *Die österreichische Kriegswirtschaft 1914–1918* (Vienna, 1979), 29ff

5 Rauchensteiner, *Der Tod des Doppeladlers*, 409–12, 533–37.

6 ÖStA, KA, FA, AOK, OpAbt, Kt. 470, Nr. 1612, Aktenkonvolut zu Gerichtsbarkeit und Kriegsleistungsgesetz in der Ukraine, 18–20.5.1918.

7 Anver Offner, *The First World War: An Agrarian Interpretation* (Oxford, 1989), 45–53.

8 See "Aus einer Denkschrift des Reichsgesundheitsamtes," 16.12.1918, in *Ursachen und Folgen. Vom deutschen Zusammenbruch 1918 und 1945 bis zur staatlichen Neuordnung Deutschlands in der Gegenwart*, ed. Herbert Michaelis and Ernst Schraepler, vol. 1 (Berlin, 1958), 283–88.

rations, and a satisfactory potato harvest, but it still remained tight. The daily bread ration in the empire was just 250 grams, and 600–700 grams at the front. From the beginning of 1918, there was no more pork for the urban population.[9] This did not help ease the social and political difficulties in the country, as demonstrated by the January strikes of 1918.

The Central Powers were concerned not just about providing food for the population but also about fodder for the horses. The 1917 grain harvest was very poor and was more or less a failure east of the Elbe. At the beginning of 1918, the War Ministry believed that, with stocks at home and supplies from Romania, they would make it through only to May. The ministry estimated that, until the new harvest in the autumn of 1918, there would be a shortage of 500,000 tons of fodder. Grain and fodder from Ukraine seemed the only solution.[10] In return, chemicals, medicines, textiles, and agricultural machinery would be delivered to Ukraine.[11]

Substantial German and Austro-Hungarian interest in Ukrainian resources was already clear in the Berlin Agreement signed on 5 February 1918, five days before the signing of the Brest-Litovsk treaty with Ukraine. This agreement regulated the delivery of "grain, grain products, and fodder" from Ukraine over land or water. Until 31 August, these would essentially be shared one-to-one. A temporary modification of the allocation formula allowed Austria-Hungary to exceed its share of deliveries until 31 May, for which Germany would be compensated in the period from June to August. On 21 February, the agreement was extended to the "other areas of Russia" and to other product groups (pulses, oil seeds, oil and fat, meat, cattle, eggs, and other food products), the latter being shared six-to-four in favor of Germany.[12]

The high level of expectations from Ukraine is clear in the reports from German representatives in Ukraine even many weeks after the

---

9 BA-MA, RH 61/810, Manuskript "Die deutsche Ernährungslage im Frühjahr 1918," von Dr. Mehrens, Februar 1942.

10 BArch, R 3101/1190, Kriegsministerium, Nr. 1369.18.B2, Berlin, 15.2.1918. The ministry estimated that the army would need 130,000 tons of fodder per month. But in the case of major battles, experience showed that much more would be needed.

11 See ibid., Antwort zu Abschrift II Fr 89, Wirtschaftliche Fragen der zweiten Verhandlungszeit, Bericht Nr. 2 v. 13.1.1918.

12 ÖStA, KA, FA, AOK, Ukraine Akten, Kt. 2.609, Nr. 61, Teilungsschlüssel für Nahrungsmittel zwischen Österreich-Ungarn und Deutschland, 23.3.1918; ÖStA, KA, FA, AOK, Ukraine Akten, Kt. 2.634, Vereinbarungen über ein gemeinschaftliches Vorgehen Deutschlands und Österreich-Ungarns bei der Wiederanknüpfung von Handelsbeziehungen mit den einzelnen Teilen des ehemaligen russischen Reiches, 21.2.1918.

invasion, for instance, that from the leader of the German Economic Office in Kyiv, Privy Councillor Otto Wiedfeldt, who described the situation there in the brightest of colors: as a "raw materials country," Ukraine was "an excellent extension to our agriculturally intensive and industrially highly developed economy." Wiedfeldt's report to the state secretary in the Ministry of the Economy culminated in this assessment: "Ukraine offers us such favorable future economic possibilities as may never appear again."[13] In light of such descriptions, it is no wonder that, as early as mid-March, Groener complained that "people in Berlin see Ukraine as a pot of fat that you can just dip your finger into and lick. And they believe I'm the magician who can make grain and pork out of nothing, or at least put them on a train bound for home."[14]

The Austro-Hungarian War Ministry was somewhat more modest. In mid-April, it accused the various departments dealing with the export of food of being in the dark "as regards supplies of Ukrainian grain and other foodstuffs and raw materials.... The most contradictory reports are being circulated." Liaison officers or other officials were therefore to be sent to every divisional command in order to draw up accounts of supplies, production possibilities, prices, and other economic developments.[15] But reports to general staff during the whole period of occupation remained unsatisfactory.[16]

The Economic Situation in Ukraine in 1918

Ukraine had been the "granary" of the tsarist empire before and during the war and had produced the greater part of its grain exports. According to German figures, a "cautious estimate" would indicate that Ukraine's average annual production of surplus grain between 1909 and 1913 was 5.5 million tons (340 million poods),[17] of which almost 80 percent was exported to other parts of the empire or abroad. Some economists went so far as to describe Ukraine "quite rightly as an exceptional country"

13 BArch, R 3101/1168, Brief von Geheimrat Wiedfeldt an den Staatssekretär des Reichswirtschaftsamts vom 7.5.1918.

14 *Von Brest-Litovsk zur deutschen Novemberrevolution. Aus den Tagebüchern, Briefen und Aufzeichnungen von Alfons Paquet, Wilhelm Groener und Albert Hopman. März bis November 1918*, ed. Winfried Baumgart (Göttingen, 1971), "Tagebuch Groener, Eintrag v. 10.3.1918," 291.

15 ÖStA, KA, FA, AOK, Ukraine Akten, Kt. 2.609, Nr. 157, Vereinbarungen über Getreidelieferungen aus der Ukraine, 20.4.1918.

16 ÖStA, KA, FA, AOK, Ukraine Akten, Kt. 2.619, Nr. 5230, Oberquartiermeisterei der Ostarmee an die Ukraine-Abteilung des AOK, 22.8.1918.

17 1 pood = 16.38 kilograms.

with "the most promising future" ahead.[18] Ukrainian emigrants and Galician Ukrainians also promoted this view.[19]

The reality at the turn of the year 1917–18, however, looked completely different and, indeed, very grim. The commencement of regular trade and the fulfillment of contractual agreements proved extremely difficult for a number of reasons. Economic life in Ukraine had almost come to a halt following three and a half years of war, revolution, and civil war. Occupation by the Central Powers could initially do little to change that. The Rada government had neither a functioning administration nor a system for the collection of taxes or other income. Its financial foundation consisted of the printing of bank notes, which drove up inflation. The *karbovanets'* was introduced in April, but trust in this new currency remained low, and people resorted to the ruble or the currency of the Central Powers.[20] The Central Powers themselves flooded the country with their own currencies through their purchases. Austria-Hungary made 180,000 crowns available to the troops for the purchase of food and other goods but without any agreement about price limits, which caused prices to rocket.[21] From the very beginning, then, the Central Powers were confronted with the problem that they lacked the necessary means to buy goods in Ukraine. Rampant inflation meant that the peasants had plenty of money but lacked confidence in the various currencies, as they were unable to buy anything with them. In any case, they were able to make more money by using the grain to distill spirits rather than selling it directly.[22]

Whereas the Austrians and Hungarians requisitioned grain by force and did not even inform their German allies about the quantities

18 BArch, R 3101/1137; *Handelsstatistische Blätter*, ed. S. Zuckermann, 1918, no. 4.

19 See, e.g., Michael Hruschewskyj, *Die ukrainische Frage in historischer Entwicklung* (Vienna, 1915); Eugen Lewicky, *Die Ukraine, der Lebensnerv Rußlands* (Stuttgart and Berlin, 1915).

20 ÖStA, KA, FA, AOK, OpAbt, Kt. 468, Nr. 1407, Lage in der Ukraina Ende März 1918, 16.4.1918; ÖStA, KA, FA, AOK, OpAbt, Kt. 475, Nr. 1906, Darstellung der materiellen Lage der Armee im Felde, 18.8.1918. The *karbovanets'* as the sole means of payment for purchases by the Austro-Hungarian troops was not introduced until the end of September: ÖStA, KA, FA, NFA, HHK AK/AGKdo, 2. Armee, OpAK, Kt. 309, Allgemeine Verlautbarungen des Kommandos der Ostarmee v. 27.9.1918.

21 ÖStA, KA, FA, AOK, Ukraine Akten, Kt. 2.619, Nr. 4962, Bericht Zitkovskys an das Ministerium des Äußern, August 1918.

22 See BArch, R 3101/1314, Bericht über die Eindrücke in der Ukraine von Oblt d.R. Colin Ross, Verbindungsoffizier der militärischen Stelle des Auswärtigen Amts, verfasst Mitte März 1918. See also BArch, R 3101/1314, Stand der Dinge am 31.3.1918. Bericht von Herrn Geheimrat Wiedfeldt. It says, in this report: "Catching colds and freezing here, we ourselves are a test of how it is absolutely impossible, in this climate, to get by without the use of alcohol."

exported,[23] the Germans were undecided as to whether they should follow this bad example or attempt some method for the exchange of goods.[24] Yet even among civilian officials in the Habsburg Monarchy there was dissatisfaction with the ruthless methods of the military. At the end of May, the leader of the Austro-Hungarian delegation to the Economic Center, Court Councillor Emil Heindl, proposed a system of coupons "whereby the Ukrainian who delivers grain receives a coupon for the purchase of certain goods." These goods were to be imported from both Germany and Austria-Hungary; however, the Ukrainian administration opposed this.[25] One of the liaison officers from the German Foreign Office made a somewhat unusual proposal: by "introducing a new vice such as opium smoking," the peasants could easily be persuaded to exchange their grain for the drug.[26]

The most important and protracted stumbling block for the export of grain from Ukraine was the land question. But this "most burning problem"[27] was not resolved right up to the time of withdrawal of the Central Powers, neither by the Rada nor later by the Hetman government. In 1916, altogether 30 percent of agricultural land (not including forests) was in the hands of the large estate owners. The proportion varied greatly from region to region. Whereas large estate owners had only 9.5 percent of the land in the Chernihiv gubernia and 18.7 percent in the Kharkiv gubernia, they held 45.2 percent in the southern Ukrainian gubernia of Tavria and 43.5 percent in the Kherson gubernia.[28] The farmland not in the possession of the large estates belonged, as rustic land,[29] to the peasantry. The average independent Ukrainian peasant owned 7.4 hectares, but he would have required between eight and eleven hectares to earn his own

23 See BA-MA, RM 41/62, Der Staatssekretär des Reichs-Marine-Amts, Nr. A. VI.S. 7605, 29.4.1918.

24 Except for Groener, the military wanted forced requisitioning. See BArch, R 3101/1314, Bericht von Herrn Geheimrat Wiedfeldt, 31.3.1918.

25 ÖStA, KA, FA, AOK, Ukraine Akten, Kt. 2.611, Nr. 1189, Situationsbericht von Heindl an die Kriegs-Getreide-Verkehrsanstalt, 1.6.1918. His proposal was also attacked by his German colleagues. See BArch, R 3101/1137, Der Unterstaatsekretär in der Reichskanzlei, 4.7.1918.

26 BArch, R 3101/1314, Bericht über die Eindrücke in der Ukraine von Oblt d.R. Colin Ross, Verbindungsoffizier der militärischen Stelle des Auswärtigen Amts, Mitte März 1918. This was not, after all, a new means of economic policy, as the British had used similar methods in the mid-nineteenth century to force the Chinese to open their markets, leading to the opium wars.

27 BA-MA, N 46/172, Heeresgruppe Eichhorn, Kr Nr. 190 geheim, Zusammenfassender Bericht über die wirtschaftliche und politische Lage in der Ukraine, 18.5.1918.

28 BArch, R 3101/1316, Heeresgruppe Kiew, Wirtschaftsnachrichten Nr. 2, Kiew, 15.10.1918. The statistics are based on tsarist figures. In the richly forested gubernia of Volhynia, estate owners had 48.2 percent of the land and forest, but that figure fell to 27.4 percent for agricultural land.

29 Rustic land belonged to the peasantry by law (especially since the abolition of serfdom in 1861).

living.[30] There were great regional differences here as well. The smallest average farm sizes were in the gubernias of Podilia (4.2 hectares) and Poltava (5.4 hectares). The largest were in the gubernias of Katerynoslav (10.2 hectares) and Tavria (16.2 hectares). These larger sizes were partly the result of the above-average size of farms in the possession of German colonists.[31] In sum, the great mass of peasants and peasant smallholders were not able to live independently from their agricultural production. Only about 15 percent of the peasantry had more than eleven hectares, the amount necessary to secure an independent existence.[32] A powerful socially explosive situation had therefore developed on the land, and it exploded in the February Revolution of 1917. The resolution of the land question was also a key element in the widespread revolutionary thinking and action in the collapsing Russian Empire. The demand for a just distribution of land headed the list of demands in Ukraine in the revolutionary year of 1917 and in the first legislative measures taken by the Central Rada.[33] In the Rada's Fourth Universal, the land was de facto nationalized.[34] But the Rada was also divided about the way forward, as there was massive resistance to the socialization of land planned for April: it was seen as absolutely essential to preserve smallholdings.[35] The peasants did not want to till their fields in the spring of 1918 because of the lack of clarity about the future. They frequently hid their grain supplies from the occupying troops or even deliberately destroyed the sown fields.[36] Even though there was a Ukrainian decree that every peasant had to till his land, it remained unclear whether the harvest would be his. In addition, the Rada lacked the administrative apparatus that could have overseen the implementation of its laws and decrees.

The Central Powers were also not united on how to resolve the problem. At the end of March, the Austro-Hungarian Finance Ministry proposed a comprehensive distribution of land by means of cooperation between the independent peasantry, the Ukrainian

---

30 See BArch, R 3101/1316, Heeresgruppe Kiew, Wirtschaftsnachrichten Nr. 3, Kiew, 1.11.1918. The figures are based on surveys made in 1905.

31 In the Katerynoslav gubernia in 1905, the average size of a German farm was 30.3 hectares; in Tavria, 40 hectares.

32 BArch, R 3101/1316, Heeresgruppe Kiew, Wirtschaftsnachrichten Nr. 3, Kiew, 1.11.1918.

33 ÖStA, KA, FA, AOK, OpAbt, Kt. 469, Nr. 1481, Fleischmann an das AOK, 15.4.1918.

34 *Ukraïns'ka Tsentral'na Rada. Dokumenty i materialy u dvokh tomakh*, vol. 2 (Kyiv, 1997), 22ff. For a contemporary German translation, see ÖStA, KA, FA, AOK, OpAbt, Kt. 469, Nr.1481, Berichte über die politische Lage in der Ukraine Mitte April, 15.4.1918, Beilage 3.

35 ÖStA, KA, FA, AOK, OpAbt, Kt. 469, Nr. 1481, Fleischmann an das AOK, 15.4.1918.

36 BA-MA, N 46/172, Heeresgruppe Eichhorn-Kiew, Abt. Ic, Nr. 19961, 8.4.1918.

state organs, and the occupying powers. The new land distribution was to legalize the existing pattern of ownership while compensating the estate owners for lost land.[37] But the Austro-Hungarian Foreign Ministry, out of concern for Polish estate owners, adopted no part of this plan except the basic principle that there should be no expropriation without compensation. The German Foreign Office, at least officially, attempted not to intervene in this internal Ukrainian affair.[38] But that was not the case with the German military. In March, Groener complained that the Ukrainian prime minister, Vsevolod Holubovych, was "making problematic attempts to create a socialist state instead of taking care of what is most urgent, ensuring that the spring sowing is carried out."[39] Words were followed by deeds. On 6 April 1918, Field Marshal Eichhorn issued his so-called "cultivation order". Whoever sowed the field would reap the harvest. As these regulations contradicted certain elements of the Fourth and Fifth Universals, they provoked a great deal of unrest in Ukraine.[40] From a German point of view, however, this made for clarity about the harvest, and the German army corps were soon reporting on the good effect of the cultivation order, since the estate owners and peasants with larger holdings were now beginning to till the soil.[41] Nevertheless, the cultivation order was disputed even on the German side,[42] as it had three serious consequences. First, it was an intervention in Ukrainian internal affairs, thus undermining the sovereignty of the Rada government. The order was consequently a prelude to the overthrow of the Rada only a few weeks later. Second, the order did not resolve the land question; it remained only a provisional resolution. And third, it created a great deal of unrest among the smallholders, who

---

37 ÖStA, KA, FA, AOK, QuAbt, Ukraine Akten, Kt.: 2.627, Nr. 216, Bericht von Dr. Schwarzwald v. 29.3.1918.

38 BArch, R 3101/1166, Telegramm des K. Botschafter z.D. an Auswärtiges Amt v. 9.4.1918.

39 *Von Brest-Litovsk zur deutschen Novemberrevolution*, 302.

40 Włodzimierz Mędrzecki, *Niemiecka interwencja militarna na Ukrainie w 1918 roku* (Warsaw, 2000), 141.

41 BA-MA, N 46/172, Heeresgruppe Eichhorn, Oberkommando G. Nr. 158, Auszug aus den Berichten der Generalkommandos über die Wirkung des Befehles des Generalfeldmarschalls, betr. Landbestellung, 6.4.1918.

42 The plans of Army Group Eichhorn-Kiew began to emerge as early as the beginning of April. The German delegation to Ukraine telegraphed about this to the German Ministry of the Economy: "The military, who appear to want to establish a military dictatorship over the whole country, seem to want to issue a very firm regulation. But that will make no difference, since they lack the means to carry it out." See BArch, R 3101/1096, Deutsche Ukrainedelegation an Reichswirtschaftsamt, 8.4.1918; BA-MA, N 46/172, Heeresgruppe Eichhorn-Kiew. Abschrift eines Fernspruches v. 7.5.1918.

had hoped for a distribution of land and now feared a return to the pre-revolutionary situation. When the Rada attempted to give voice to this unrest about the order and to resist it, it was overthrown.

The cultivation order did little to change the economic situation in Ukraine for the time being. Hardly any grain was procured by the Central Powers. They themselves were partly to blame for this. During the invasion, their own troops had taken over the railway network.[43] Similarly, the German Reichsbank had not yet made funds available to begin the purchase of Ukrainian grain.[44] Austria-Hungary's military requisitioning had also aroused mistrust and unrest among the peasants. Any delivery of grain in the quantities hoped for at Brest-Litovsk was now out of the question. However, the Central Powers still pushed for an agreement with Ukraine. For not only in Austria-Hungary but now also in the German Empire, there was a threat that bread rations would have to be reduced.[45]

Exports from Ukraine to the Central Powers

First Phase: Chaos

From the very beginning, German officials doubted whether the Rada government would be able to deliver the amounts agreed upon at Brest-Litovsk. In addition, "the whole procurement activity" had to be "extensively supported by military measures."[46] Parts of the country were still not pacified and would remain so until the summer of 1918, which meant that the most important transport routes had to be kept under military supervision. The inability of the Rada to deliver the grain initially promised at Brest-Litovsk and later contractually agreed upon very soon became a burden on relations between Ukraine and the Central Powers. This non-delivery was also the main reason for the overthrow of the Rada at the end of April.

Certainly at the beginning of the occupation, the greater part of the German and Austro-Hungarian military were interested in taking short-term advantage of Ukraine.[47] The complex situation in Ukraine

---

43 See *Von Brest-Litovsk zur deutschen Novemberrevolution*, "Tagebuch Groener, Eintrag v. 8.3.1918," 284.

44 BA-MA, N 46/172, Generalleutnant Groener an Obost, Zusammenfassender Bericht der Heeresgruppe über die derzeitige Lage in der Ukraine v. 18.4.1918; BArch, R 3101/1096, Telegramm des Kaiserlichen Botschafters an Auswärtiges Amt, Kiew, 29.3.1918.

45 See BArch, R 3101/1220, Telegramm Nr. 245, von Mumm an AA v. 9.4.1918.

46 BArch, R 3101/1136, Deutsche Ukrainedelegation. Der Vorsitzende der Gesamt-Kommission, J. Nr. 74, 13.4.1918.

47 See *Karl Freiherr von Bothmer. Moskauer Tagebuch 1918*, ed. Gernot Böhme (Paderborn, 2010), "Eintrag vom 28.7.1918," 100. Bothmer was a representative of Supreme Command at the embassy in Moscow.

meant that their focus was mostly a purely military one. Ludendorff had advised quite early on that, to procure the grain and raw materials, they would have to "use such measures as are unbefitting the dignity of the highest representatives of the German Empire."[48] The representative of German Supreme Army Command (OHL) in Kyiv, Colonel von Stolzenberg, expressed this most clearly: "Bread and fodder are essentials of life for us. In the West, we are facing the most difficult final battle. Diplomatic and long-term considerations cannot be decisive when we have to take by force what is essential to our life and struggle and when nothing else is possible. Whether it is with this government, which cannot last, or with another is a matter of indifference. Commissions, at this time, have no place here, only military orders."[49]

The Foreign Office and especially the Ministry of the Economy had a completely different view of the situation. They had the best intentions of helping Ukraine develop a functioning state system by advising on all economic, sociopolitical, financial, and administrative matters.[50] It was here that Germany policy differed fundamentally from that of Austria-Hungary.

Orders to the Austro-Hungarian troops corresponded more to Stolzenberg's approach. Even during the invasion and in the early phase of the occupation, the most important goal was "to acquire food supplies." Requisitions were part of the daily routine of troops stationed in the countryside.[51] At the end of March Emperor Karl himself, in a handwritten memo to Böhm-Ermolli, ordered that "requisitions have to be carried out ruthlessly, even by force."[52] According to the emperor, if deliveries of food from Ukraine did not arrive quickly, the continuation of the war was in question. In

---

48 TNA, GFM 6/35, Telegramm Nr. 466 von Ludendorff über AA an Reichskanzler, 6.3.1918.

49 TNA, GFM 6/35, Telegramm des K. Legationssekretärs Bülow an AA v. 10.3.1918. Oberst Stoltzenberg telegrafiert am 9. d. M. aus Kiew an ObOst. Colonel Stolzenberg sent this telegram just two days after the arrival of the Rada in Kyiv. See Winfried Baumgart, *Deutsche Ostpolitik 1918. Von Brest-Litowsk bis zum Ende des Ersten Weltkrieges* (Vienna and Munich, 1966), 125, n. 39.

50 Cf. BArch, R 3101/1170, Der Staatssekretär des Reichswirtschaftsamts, IDR 1870. V. Anlage, 11.6.1918; BArch, R 3101/1164, Zentral-Einkaufsgesellschaft m.b.H. Vorstand, Nr. 3105, Berlin, 17.7.1918.

51 Examples can be seen in the following troop journals: ÖStA, KA, AdT, Kt. 754, FJB 13, 6. Tagebuch des Feldjägerbataillon Nr. 13, 85–111; ÖStA, KA, AdT, Kt. 754, UR 13, Tagebuch vom Dezember 1917–20. November 1918, Eintrag v. 23.3.1918.

52 ÖStA, KA, FA, AOK, OpAbt, Kt. 468, Nr. 1372, Handschreiben Kaiser Karls an Böhm-Ermolli v. 31.3.1918.

Böhm-Ermolli's procurement order, issued following this memo, he explained what was meant by requisitioning: "Basically, one buys and then pays in cash. But if there is no agreement between buyer and seller, then there has to be an enforced purchase, taking into account the target prices that have been ordered." If there was not enough money available,[53] then a certificate would be issued that could be cashed at the nearest military cash point. It was clear, however, that force was to be used where necessary: "If we do not properly make use of Ukraine, something to which it has agreed in the peace treaty, then the whole operation in Ukraine is worthless."[54]

Just a few weeks after the capture of the city, Austria-Hungary's supreme political representative in Kyiv, Ambassador Forgách, was also keen to give his own troops clear instructions about their dealings with Ukrainian officials in economic matters. There were constant problems with border officials who did not want to grant export licences. On 26 March, the Foreign Ministry informed civilian and military officials dealing with Ukraine in Vienna, Budapest, Kyiv, and Odesa that there should be no delay in negotiations with the Rada concerning the procurement and export of food. The ministry insisted, however, that this procurement should "not be carried out by means of requisitioning but by means of cash payments" or exchange for other products. Collection and purchase for the territory behind the lines were to be carried out by commissioners and buyers from cartels but under military supervision.[55]

To acquire the rubles necessary for purchasing, a financial agreement had been entered into as early as 21 February for the establishment of a German-Austro-Hungarian bank syndicate. This was to be organized by a joint Central Bureau for Russian Currency located in Berlin.[56] But the early results were unsatisfactory, so in late April the Austro-Hungarians began purchasing rubles in Lublin and established currency exchange offices for Austro-Hungarian prisoners of war returning from Russia.[57] In addition to the financial agreement,

53 The 13th Ulanen Regiment, for instance, did not carry out a procurement that had been ordered because of a lack of funds: ÖStA, KA, AdT, UR 13, Tagebuch vom Dezember 1917–20. November 1918, Eintrag v. 25.3.1918.

54 ÖStA, KA, FA, NFA, HHK AK/AGKdo, 2. Armee, OpAK, Kt. 308, Abschrift des AOK-Befehls mit Qu. Nr. 121.055, 9.4.1918.

55 ÖStA, KA, FA, AOK, Ukraine Akten, Kt. 2.609, Nr. 74, Sammelakt zur Aufbringung in der Ukraine, 19.–26.3.1918.

56 ÖStA, KA, FA, AOK, Ukraine Akten, Kt. 2.611, Nr. 1255, Vereinbarung mit den Türken und Bulgaren, 10.6.1918; ÖStA, KA, FA, AOK, Ukraine Akten, OpApt, Kt. 467, Nr. 1210, Zusatzvertrag zum Friedensvertrag mit Rußland, Anlage 11a, 7.3.1918.

57 ÖStA, KA, FA, AOK, Ukraine Akten, Kt. 2.609, Nr. 199, Ministerium des Äußern an AOK, 28.4.1918.

the Central Powers signed an agreement on transport. According to it, the Black Sea and the Danube would be open to naval transport, and a Black Sea Bureau[58] would be established with a mixed staff. For the management of goods coming across "dry borders," that is, by rail, canals, and rivers (except the Danube), two "land offices" were established. Each was subordinate to its respective military leadership. The land office in Brest-Litovsk[59] was under Army Group Eichhorn-Kiew, while that in Lviv[60] was under the 2nd Army/*Ostarmee*.[61] Assisted by border posts, the land offices were to supervise the transport of goods in Ukraine, gather economic information, guide the activities of the cartel organizations, and handle the accounts for the goods purchased.[62]

The central economic institution on the Austro-Hungarian side was the Department for Trade with Ukraine, established in the Foreign Office in March. In June it was merged with the Ukrainian section of the Quartermaster Staff within Army High Command (AOK) to become the Ukrainian Department of AOK.[63] Led by Colonel Emil Kreneis, it was involved in all organizational matters at the interface of politics,

58 On the organization of Austro-Hungarian naval transport, see ÖStA, KA, FA, AOK, Ukraine Akten, Kt. 2.611, Nr. 1340, Organisation der Marine-Behörden am Schwarzen Meer, 7.6.1918.

59 Until 15 May it had been the land station in Biała (Biała Podlaska).

60 ÖStA, KA, FA, AOK, Ukraine Akten, Kt. 2.612, Nr. 1735, k.u.k. Kriegsministerium an das AOK, 17.6.1918; ÖStA, KA, FA, NFA, HHK AK/AGKdo, 2. Armee, QuAbt, Kt. 695, Nr. 2162, Bestimmungen für die Rohstoffstellen für die bei dem russischen Handel tätigen Offizieren der Kriegs-Rohstoff-Abteilung, 30.3.1918.

61 ÖStA, KA, FA, AOK, Ukraine Akten, Kt. 2.611, Nr. 1255, Vereinbarung mit den Türken und Bulgaren, 10.6.1918; ÖStA, KA, FA, AOK, OpAbt, Kt. 466, Nr. 1096, Vereinbarung zur Regelung der Transportfragen im Verkehr über das Schwarze Meer und die Donau sowie über die trockene Grenze des ehemaligen Russland, 27.2.1918.

62 ÖStA, KA, FA, AOK, Ukraine Akten, Kt. 2.609, Nr. 92, Bezahlung der in der Ukraine für die KGV und die OeZEG eingekauften Waren, 3.4.1918.

63 ÖStA, KA, FA, AOK, Ukraine Akten, Kt. 2.633, Nr. 122.442, Errichtung der Ukrainischen Abteilung beim AOK, 24.5.1918; ÖStA, KA, FA, NFA, HHK AK/AGKdo, 2. Armee, QuAbt, Kt. 693, Nr. 2839, Errichtung der Ukrainischen Abteilung beim AOK, 2.6.1918. The Ukrainian Department of AOK was later placed under the command of the quartermaster section of the *Ostarmee*. It was led by Lieutenant Colonel Richard Skubec. He was also the leader of War Group R, responsible for Ukraine, Volhynia, Galicia, Bukovyna, Transylvania, and Romania and, following the formation of the Ukrainian Department, deputy head of the department. The management of raw materials, to the extent that this affected military administration, was moved on 1 October to the War Ministry. The previous head of the Ukrainian Department, Colonel Kreneis, was made quartermaster general of the *Ostarmee*. Some of the personnel of the Ukrainian Department moved to the quartermaster staff of AOK, others to the War Ministry: ÖStA, KA, FA, AOK, Ukraine Akten, Kt. 2.616, Nr. 3401, Ukraineangelegenheiten – Kompetenz-Festsetzung, 17.8.1918; ÖStA, KA, FA, AOK, Ukraine Akten, Kt. 2.616, Nr. 3402, Personal der Ukraineabteilung, 22.7.1918; ÖStA, KA, FA, AOK, Ukraine Akten, Kt. 2.623, Nr. 7024, Unterstellung der Ukraine-Abteilung unter den Chef der Quartier-Abteilung des AOK, 24.9.1918.

economics, and the military. But there were no substantive initiatives from there regarding Ukrainian policy. Arz, Krauss, and Spannocchi on the military side, and Burián and Forgách on the political side were the key figures, and it was they who also directed economic policy. In Ukraine itself, it was Major General Karl von Sendler, quartermaster general of the 2nd Army/*Ostarmee*, who was responsible for economic acquisitions for the troops. He was directly subordinate to Krauss and led both the technical-industrial group in the quartermaster staff and the Austro-Hungarian shipping section.[64] The problems of this dual structure were already apparent in April. First, the civil and military authorities operated in the same territories in a way that was mutually obstructive. Second, the military authorities offered much higher prices than their civilian counterparts. Third, this dual structure gave the Ukrainians an excuse for not fulfilling their own obligations. The Germans were also unhappy with this situation.[65]

In spite of or precisely because of these multilateral attempts to make use of Ukraine, very few goods were being exported to the homelands. Numerous railway carriages were waiting at the border because they had not been released by the Ukrainian authorities.[66] There was also a shortage of rolling stock, locomotives, and fuel. In addition, the capacity of the railways to carry goods to the border was very limited.[67] In order to preserve at least the appearance of a "bread peace" with Ukraine, AOK ordered twenty carriages each to be sent to Vienna, Prague, and Budapest.[68]

In addition to food supplies, war material found in the country played an important role. Materials captured from the Red Guards during the invasion were put to use immediately. But stored equipment previously belonging to the tsarist army, the troops of the Russian Provisional Government, the Ukrainian Rada, or Romania was considered to be "war material" whose status needed clarification.[69]

64 ÖStA, KA, FA, AOK, Ukraine Akten, Kt. 2.612, Nr. 1446, Geschäftseinteilung des AK-Ost, 14.6.1918.

65 ÖStA, KA, FA, AOK, Ukraine Akten, Kt. 2.609, Nr. 90, Militärische Aufbringungsorganisation in der Ukraine, 5.4.1918.

66 ÖStA, KA, FA, AOK, Ukraine Akten, Kt. 2.633, Nr. 121.211, Ausfuhrschwierigkeiten in der Ukraine, 10.4.1918; ÖStA, KA, FA, AOK, Ukraine Akten, Op. Geh. Akten, Kt. 467, Nr. 1218, Meldung des 2. Armeekommandos an AOK, 17.3.1918.

67 ÖStA, KA, FA, AOK, OpAbt, Kt. 468, Nr. 1397, Telegramm des 2. Armeekommandos an AOK, 7.4.1918.

68 ÖStA, KA, FA, AOK, Ukraine Akten, Kt. 2.628, Nr. 120.805, Befehl des AOK, März 1918.

69 ÖStA, KA, FA, AOK, OpAbt, Kt. 468, Nr. 1426, Einschreiten des ukrainischen Kriegsministers, 13.4.1918.

On 8 March, however, the 2nd Army ordered that stored equipment was also "to be confiscated by our own troops and used where necessary...in that regard, any validly asserted claims of ownership by the Ukrainian government would have to be recognized."[70] War materials definitely considered Ukrainian were to be left to the Ukrainian government. This requirement remained in place during the summer.[71]

Food procurement in Bessarabia was a special case, since northern Bessarabia was not part of Ukrainian territory and had been occupied by Austro-Hungarian troops in March. Initially a provisional arrangement was made whereby the advancing 7th Army did the requisitioning. Lack of adequate infrastructure meant that no military administration would be established.[72] The export of provisions for Bukovyna had to be canceled at the beginning of June because of shortages in Bessarabia itself.[73] In mid-July the 4th General Command took over military administration.[74]

Second Phase: Creating a Procurement System

After the first few weeks, the Central Powers sought to bring order out of the chaos of their previous economic policy and began to construct a regular procurement system for the agricultural products they wanted. But this turned out to be a difficult task, since it remained unclear just how much food and fodder the Central Powers could expect. Representatives of the Rada gave detailed estimates at the beginning of April. After a number of deductions—among them 2.6 million tons (160 million poods) exported, 328,000 tons (20 million poods) requisitioned for the troops of the Central Powers, 164,000 tons (10 million poods) for the brewing of alcohol, 328,000 tons (20 million poods) stolen by the Bolsheviks—only 442,000 tons (27 million poods) remained for export to the Central Powers. With existing stores, that

70 ÖStA, KA, FA, NFA, HHK AK/AGKdo, 2. Armee, QuAbt, Kt. 694, Nr. 1251, Zweck der Expedition in der Ukraina, 8.3.1918.

71 ÖStA, KA, FA, AOK, Ukraine Akten, Kt. 2.611, Nr. 1110, Russische Munitionsdepots in Woloczyska, 8.6.1918.

72 ÖStA, KA, FA, AOK, Ukraine Akten, Kt. 2.633, Nr. 122.446, Militärverwaltung in Nordbessarabien, 28.5.1918.

73 ÖStA, KA, FA, AOK, Ukraine Akten, Kt. 2.613, Nr. 1788, Schreiben der bukowinischen k.k. Landesregierung an den Präsidenten des Volksernährungsamtes v. 10.6.1918.

74 ÖStA, KA, FA, AOK, Ukraine Akten, Kt. 2.614, Nr. 2281, Verwaltung von Bessarabien, 16. Juli. Documents from 4th General Command in ÖStA, KA, FA, NFA, HHK AK/AGKdo, 4. Armee, Kt. 485, Nr. 42.304, Sammelakt zur Verwaltung Bessarabiens. See also chapter 3b in the present volume.

left a maximum of 655,220 tons (40 million poods) and represented only about two-thirds of the amount agreed at Brest-Litovsk. This was clearly less than the Central Powers had hoped for. The Ukrainian representatives in Brest-Litovsk, after all, had boasted of potential exports of 3.3 million tons (200 million poods). The Germans consoled themselves with the thought that these statistics were "incorrect" and that a more efficient organization of procurement by the Central Powers would increase this amount.[75]

On 9 April, in a new agreement,[76] the Rada committed itself, for the period until 31 July 1918, to deliver 60 million poods,[77] just under one million tons, of grain and grain products, fodder, pulses, seeds, and oil seeds to the German Empire and Austria-Hungary. Prices would be established for each product that could be changed only by mutual agreement,[78] although Groener described the prices as "outrageously high."[79] In this agreement, just as in the Berlin agreement of February, Austria-Hungary was to receive more in April and May because of its severe food crisis. In the days following, the agreement was extended to include delivery of 50,000 tons of sugar, 200,000 cattle, and 400–500 million eggs.[80]

In order to put life into this agreement, the three parties established a German-Austro-Hungarian-Ukrainian Economic Center with branches in the provinces.[81] The Economic Center would take over from the Ukrainian Food Ministry, deal with settling accounts, arrange and supervise transport, eliminate misunderstandings, receive statistical

---

75 BArch, R 3101/1314, Sitzung vom 1. April 1918 betr. Getreide u. Futtermittel, Vorsitz Gawriloff, Berichterstatter Goldstein.

76 On 23 April this new agreement was incorporated into the general economic agreement.

77 This amount had been unanimously agreed some days previously by the Rada government, although there had been some concerns about it. See the minutes of the session of the UNR Council of Ministers of 3 April 1918 in *Ukraïns'ka Tsentral'na Rada*, 244ff.

78 BArch, R 3101/1220, Telegramm der Handelskommission an AA v. 9.4.1918, Vereinbarungen über Getreidelieferungen aus der Ukraine. Six million poods were to be delivered by the end of April, another 15 million by the end of May, 20 million again by the end of June, and another 19 million by the end of July. The German delegation was pleased with the outcome of the negotiations but believed that they could have got more if the Austro-Hungarians had not repeatedly indicated the precarious food situation at home. See BArch R 3101/1136, Deutsche Ukraine Delegation, An den Herrn Staatsekretär des Reichswirtschaftsamts, Freiherrn von Stein, Kiew, 10.4.1918.

79 *Von Brest-Litovsk zur deutschen Novemberrevolution*, "Tagebucheintrag v. 9.4.1918," 340.

80 BArch, R 3101/1136, Deutsche Ukraine Delegation. Der Vorsitzende der Gesamt-Kommission, J.Nr. 74, 13.4.1918; TsDAVO Ukraïny, fond 1118, op. 1, spr. 37, 14. See *Ursachen und Folgen*, 188; ÖStA, KA, FA, AOK, OpAbt, Kt. 469, Nr. 1477, Zusatzverträge zu den Friedensverträgen mit Rußland und der ukrainischen Volksrepublik, 17.6.1918.

81 On the territorial distribution of these economic centers, see ÖStA, KA, FA, AOK, Ukraine-Akten, Kt. 2.613, Nr. 2030, Organisation der Getreide-Ausfuhr aus der Ukraine.

information, and exercise control over the organs subordinate to it. Goods would be received at rail, river, sea, and border stations. The Economic Center would also have the authority, in procurement areas with inadequate infrastructure, to install commissioners from the local population.[82] The most important task of the Economic Center, however, was to allocate the procured goods to the land offices and the Black Sea Bureau according to a complex allocation formula.[83] The Austro-Hungarian delegation was made up of Court Councillor Emil Heindl[84] and Mr. Lorant,[85] as well as other representatives from the Austrian Central Purchasing Syndicate (ÖZEG), the Austrian and Hungarian Finance Ministry, and the Austro-Hungarian Bank. AOK's general staff officer at the Economic Center was Captain von Daróczy.[86] The German delegate to the Economic Center was a certain Mr. Meyer, head of the Central Purchasing Syndicate in Berlin.[87]

Although the new agreement definitely prohibited military procurement except for the purpose of meeting the needs of the troops themselves,[88] Austria-Hungary was very slow to implement this.[89] Its Ukrainian Department ordered that military procurement was to be maintained but emphasized that this "applied to purchase and not requisitioning." The reason for this was the critical food situation in Austria and the still unresolved issue of whether Kyiv was at all "in a position to begin immediately with the delivery of the food that we so urgently need." But the goods procured heretofore and in the future should conform to the accepted amounts and prices. Military requisitioning should cease when the civilian authorities, with the

82 ÖStA, KA, FA, AOK, Ukraine-Akten, Kt. 2.609, Nr. 157, Vereinbarungen über Getreidelieferungen aus der Ukraine, 20.4.1918.

83 ÖStA, KA, FA, AOK, Ukraine-Akten, Kt. 2.626, Nr. 8400, Richtlinien für die militärische Mithilfe bei der wirtschaftlichen Ausnützung der Ukraine.

84 He was a representative of the Orient and Overseas Company and of the Austrian Trade Museum in Vienna. See *Hof- und Staats-Handbuch der österreichisch-ungarischen Monarchie für das Jahr 1918*, vol. 44 (Vienna, 1918), 507.

85 In the *Staatshandbuch* for 1918 there is just one Ernst Lorant, secretary of the Hungarian *Allgemeine Creditanstalt* in Budapest (ibid., 1324).

86 ÖStA, KA, FA, AOK, Ukraine Akten, Kt. 2.618, Nr. 4597, Verzeichnis der öster.-ung. und deutschen Behörden und Funktionäre in Kiew, 7.8.1918.

87 ÖStA, KA, FA, AOK, Ukraine-Akten, Kt. 2.610, Nr. 365, Organisation der Aufbringung in der Ukraine, 15.5.1918.

88 See Groener's instructions to Army Group Eichhorn-Kiew: ÖStA, KA, FA, AOK, Ukraine-Akten, Kt. 2.618, Nr. 4597, Verzeichnis der öster.-ung. und deutschen Behörden und Funktionäre in Kiew, 7.8.1918.

89 ÖStA, KA, FA, AOK, Ukraine-Akten, Kt. 2.610, Nr. 365, Organisation der Aufbringung in der Ukraine, 15.5.1918.

assistance of the Ukrainian government, had delivered the agreed amounts in the different procurement areas.[90] It was only following strong protests from the Germans and the Ukrainians that this practice ceased in May.[91] But instances of this continued to occur in the Austro-Hungarian zone throughout the occupation.[92] Many troops employed it as a disciplinary measure. Sometimes individual soldiers did it to improve their own food situation.[93]

It was the Berlin agreements of 18 May that almost completely deprived Austria-Hungary of its power in the matter of procurement.[94] Two days before, Krauss had replaced Böhm-Ermolli, who had been considered responsible for the failures up to then. Shortly before the agreements were signed, Krauss had protested strongly against the new regulations.[95] Krauss was considered to be a forceful man, and the emperor had sent him to Ukraine as a "dictator"[96] in order to improve procurement at least in southern Ukraine. But his scope for action disappeared with the Berlin agreements. These agreements complemented the February agreement and gave Germany, until 15 August, "according to the agreed allocation...the right to all cereals, those in Ukraine, in the other parts of the former Russian Empire, in

90 ÖStA, KA, FA, AOK, Ukraine-Akten, Kt. 2.609, Nr. 121, Beibehalten der militärischen Aufbringungsaktion, 12.4.1918; ÖStA, KA, FA, AOK, Ukraine-Akten, Kt. 2.609, Nr. 138, Militärische Aufbringungsaktion, 16.4.1918; ÖStA, KA, FA, AOK, Ukraine-Akten, Kt. 2.609, Nr. 157, Vereinbarungen über Getreidelieferungen aus der Ukraine, 20.4.1918.

91 ÖStA, KA, FA, AOK, OpAbt, Kt. 470, Nr. 1565, Streitigkeiten in der Ukraine wegen Aufbringung, 9.5.1918; ÖStA, KA, FA, AOK, OpAbt, Kt. 470, Nr. 1580, Telegramm-Sammlung zur militärischen Aufbringung, 12.–14.5.1918.

92 ÖStA, KA, FA, AOK, Ukraine Akten, Kt. 2.617, Nr. 4204, Tätigkeitsbericht der Deutsch-österreichisch-ungarischen Wirtschaftsabteilung, 29.7.1918; ÖStA, KA, FA, AOK, Ukraine Akten, Kt. 2.619, Nr. 5249, Schreiben der Kriegsgetreideverkehrsanstalt an das AOK, 21.8.1918.

93 ÖStA, KA, FA, AOK, Ukraine Akten, Kt. 2.609, Nr. 211, Störung der ukrainischen Aufbringungsaktion durch militärische Käufe, 1. Mai; ÖStA, KA, FA, AOK, Ukraine Akten, Kt. 2.610, Nr. 325, Situationsbericht Nr. 10, 5.5.1918; ÖStA, KA, FA, AOK, Ukraine Akten, Kt. 2.624, Nr. 7410, Bericht des Obersten Kreneis über die Bereisung der Ukraine, 7.10.1918. See also ÖStA, KA, AdT, FAR 59, Kt. 832, Abfertigung Nr. 95 vom 20.7.1918; ÖStA, KA, AdT, FAR 59, Kt. 832, Abfertigung Nr. 118, 19.8.1918; ÖStA, KA, AdT, FAR 59, Kt. 832, UR 3, Lagebuch v. 17.10.1918, Eintragungen vom 14., 21., 24., 29.7.1918; ÖStA, KA, AdT, FAR 59, Kt. 832, UR 13, Tagebuch vom Dezember 1917–20. November 1918, Einträge vom 16.3.1918, 3.6.1918.

94 On the background to this agreement, see *Theodor Ritter von Zeynek. Ein Offizier im Generalstabskorps erinnert sich,* ed. Peter Broucek (Vienna, Cologne, and Weimar, 2009), 294ff.

95 ÖStA, KA, FA, AOK, OpAbt, Kt. 470, Nr. 1633, Verwendung k.u.k. Truppen in Ukraine, 25.5.1918. He confirmed this in an account of the situation in Ukraine written in 1932: ÖStA, AVA, Nachlässe, B 60 Krauß, 14c, Schreiben von General Alfred Krauß an das Österreichische Kriegsarchiv, 15.4.1932.

96 It is not completely clear whether Karl himself had used this term, but Krauss referred to it twice in his memoirs and expressed his unhappiness with this description, which, he wrote, had an "unpleasant sound" and "was not necessary": Alfred Krauß, *Die Ursachen unserer Niederlage. Erinnerungen und Urteile aus dem Weltkrieg* (Vienna, 1923), 253ff.

Romania, and in the Bessarabian territories occupied by Romania until the new harvest."[97] Until 15 July, 150,000 tons of grain would be delivered from the German Empire to Austria-Hungary.[98] Austro-Hungarian influence in the common institutions in Ukraine shrank considerably in the following months. Austria-Hungary withdrew increasingly to its own zone of occupation. Criticism from Berlin or Kyiv about its behavior was met with either demonstrative protest or formal concessions that were hardly ever adhered to. But, in the meantime, even AOK had recognized that procurement could only be influenced by the civilian authorities,[99] and important military figures, such as the governor of Odesa, Eduard von Böltz, questioned the existing approach: "Even the forced requisitions with military support yielded very few results: around 22,000 poods[100] of grain in two and a half months from the 30th Infantry Division! In my view, one should at least attempt to leave the grain to free purchase. The stores of grain that are certainly hidden in the country and have not been discovered will suddenly appear...."[101] The extensive military procurement ceased, and cooperation with the Ukrainians improved dramatically.[102]

The food obtained by the new procurement organizations established between April and June was to go mainly over land to the German Empire via the stations at Holoby and at Baranowicze in Poland. Since most of the deliveries were going to western Germany and to the places where they were needed on the Western Front, the "wet route" by way of the Danube was not suitable, as it would take too long. It would take eight weeks on the river but only two weeks by rail. Only a small amount was sent by ship to the Black Sea port of Brăila in

97 ÖStA, KA, FA, AOK, OpAbt, Kt. 470, Nr. 1634, Neuer Berliner Vertrag, 25.5.1918.

98 ÖStA, KA, FA, AOK, Ukraine Akten, Kt. 2.612, Nr. 1465, Wirtschaftliche Ausnutzung der Ukraine, 23.6.1918; ÖStA, KA, FA, AOK, Ukraine Akten, Kt. 2.612, Nr. 1577, Kriegsgetreideverkehrsanstalt an Ukraine-Abteilung, 17.6.1918; ÖStA, KA, FA, NFA, HHK AK/AGKdo, 2. Armee, QuAbt, Kt. 693, Nr. 2972, Ernteaufbringung in den okkupierten Gebieten, 31.5.1918. According to a report from the Austro-Hungarian High Command on 18 August, Germany was unable to deliver all the grain that had been agreed: ÖStA, KA, FA, AOK, OpAbt, Kt. 475, Nr. 1906, Darstellung der materiellen Lage der Armee im Felde, 18.8.1918.

99 ÖStA, KA, FA, AOK, OpAbt, Kt. 470, Nr. 1634, Neuer Berliner Vertrag, 25.5.1918; ÖStA, KA, FA, AOK, OpAbt, Kt. 474, Nr. 1863, Klärung von Fragen in der Ukraine, 26.9.1918.

100 360.36 tons.

101 ÖStA, AVA, Nachlässe, B 760 Böltz, Fol. 9. This is an undated report on his experiences as city commandant and governor of Odesa. Since he speaks of the five months "since we arrived," this report must have been written in August.

102 ÖStA, KA, FA, AOK, Ukraine Akten, Kt. 2.610, Nr. 432, Bericht Nr. 13, 17.5.1918.

Romania, from where it was transported by rail to Germany.[103] Austria-Hungary was more open to using the Black Sea and the Danube but also used its rail lines through Bukovyna and Galicia.

In this second phase of economic policy, the Central Powers were able to implement their preferred trade policies. This involved a comprehensive reorganization of their economic centers in Ukraine. On the German side, it was the Foreign Office that was mainly responsible for trade policy, but the Ministry of the Economy attempted to exercise some influence "in order to develop the economic forces of Ukraine" and "guide this development."[104] The Imperial Ministry of the Economy (*Reichswirtschaftsamt*) was first established only in October 1917 as the central economic authority of the German Empire.[105] It was therefore responsible for the procurement of goods in Ukraine. The War Food Office (*Kriegsernährungsamt*) then took over responsibility for its distribution at home. The Imperial Economic Office of the German Ukraine Delegation functioned as an extended arm of the Ministry of the Economy. It was subordinate to the German Ukraine Delegation of the Foreign Office in Kyiv and provided it with expert advice.[106] The head of this Economic Office in Kyiv was Privy Councillor Otto Wiedfeldt, who had exercised some influence on the organization of the German war economy through his previous positions in the Ministry of Internal Affairs and in the Ministry of the Economy.[107] Of course, power rivalries were unavoidable throughout these months. The Foreign Office kept close watch and was successful in preventing any independent organizations from emerging in the Economic Office in Kyiv.[108] On the other hand, both the Foreign Office and the Ministry of the Economy joined forces in competing with "the military authorities" in Kyiv, "who were so excessively equipped with means and personnel."[109] In general, however, there was "harmonious

103 BA-MA, RH 61/847, Ergebnis der Besprechung am 30.4.1918 in Berlin über die in der Heimat zu treffenden Beförderungsmaßnahmen für die aus der Ukraine zu erwartenden Lebensmittel.

104 BArch, R 3101/1170, Der Staatssekretär des Reichswirtschaftsamts, IDR 1870. V, 11.6.1918.

105 See Hans Gotthard Ehlert, *Die wirtschaftliche Zentralbehörde des Deutschen Reiches 1914 bis 1919. Das Problem der "Gemeinwirtschaft" in Krieg und Frieden* (Wiesbaden, 1982).

106 See BArch, R 3101/1170, Telegramm Ludendorffs an Reichskanzler v. 21.6.1918.

107 On Wiedfeldt, see Peter Borowsky, *Deutsche Ukrainepolitik 1918 unter besonderer Berücksichtigung der Wirtschaftsfragen* (Lübeck and Hamburg, 1970), 81ff.; Ernst Schröder, *Otto Wiedfeldt. Eine Biographie* (Neustadt and Aisch, 1981).

108 See BArch, R 3101/1170, Auswärtiges Amt, Nr. Ap 1554. 107085, An den Staatssekretär des Reichswirtschaftsamts, Berlin, 26.7.1918.

109 BArch, R 3101/1170, Auswärtiges Amt, Nr. Ap 1554. 107085, Telegramm des Botschafters Mumm an Auswärtiges Amt v. 15.6.1918.

cooperation" at a personal level in day-to-day work.[110]

The Ukrainian State Grain Bureau had been established before Skoropadsky came to power. It had sole authority, assisted by trade networks in Ukraine, to purchase Ukrainian agricultural products. It was the executive agent of the food ministry in which wholesalers, mill owners, and agricultural associations were represented. The State Grain Bureau assumed responsibility for cooperation with the Economic Center. But it was only after the Hetman had taken power that the newly created institutions began to function.[111] Following protests from the Central Powers about the inadequate performance and escalating corruption in the State Grain Bureau,[112] the Ukrainian Food Council was established on 24 May.[113] The Food Council was a kind of coordinating body to which the State Grain Bureau and the German-Austro-Hungarian-Ukrainian Economic Center were subordinate. It was here that meetings were held and agreements reached between representatives of the occupation troops, the German government, the Ukrainian Food Ministry, the various centers of the Central Powers (among them the Central Purchasing Syndicate Berlin, the Austro-Hungarian Central Purchasing Syndicate, and the War Grain Transport Office). These agreements dealt with the procurement of food and fodder for the armies in Ukraine, the transport of food and provisions for cities and industrial areas, and exports to the Central Powers. The Food Council met regularly, and all the difficulties that arose between the various parties were discussed here. Although many of its sessions were quite stormy, it was a well-functioning institution in which decisions could be made on short notice.[114] The Food Council intervened repeatedly in the summer to protect Kyiv or Odesa from shortages or from famine.[115]

---

110 Stefan von Velsen, "Deutsche Generalstabsoffiziere im 1. Weltkrieg 1914–1918. Erinnerungen," *Die Welt als Geschichte*, no. 16 (1956): 286.

111 ÖStA, KA, FA, AOK, Ukraine Akten, Kt. 2.610, Nr. 325, Situationsbericht Nr. 10, 5.5.1918; ÖStA, KA, FA, AOK, Ukraine Akten, Kt. 2.610, Nr. 365, Organisation der Aufbringung in der Ukraine, 15.5.1918.

112 This was confirmed by Skoropadsky in his memoirs: *Pavlo Skoropads'kyj: Erinnerungen 1917 bis 1918,* ed. Günter Rosenfeld (Stuttgart, 1999), 250.

113 ÖStA, KA, FA, AOK, Ukraine Akten, Kt. 2.633, Nr. 122.595, Schreiben der Militärkommission Kiew an AOK, 25.5.1918.

114 ÖStA, KA, FA, AOK, Ukraine Akten, Kt. 2.611, Nr. 1221, 6. Wochenbericht der Eisenbahnzentralstelle Kiew, 30.5.1918; ÖStA, KA, FA, AOK, Ukraine Akten, Kt. 2.612, Nr. 1752, Deutsch-österreichisch-ungarische Wirtschaftszentrale an AOK, 16.6.1918; ÖStA, KA, FA, AOK, Ukraine Akten, Kt. 2.617, Nr. 3779, Organisation der Kartelle, 19.7.1918.

115 ÖStA, KA, FA, AOK, Ukraine Akten, Kt. 2.617, Nr.3688, Bericht Nr. 14, 17.7.1918.

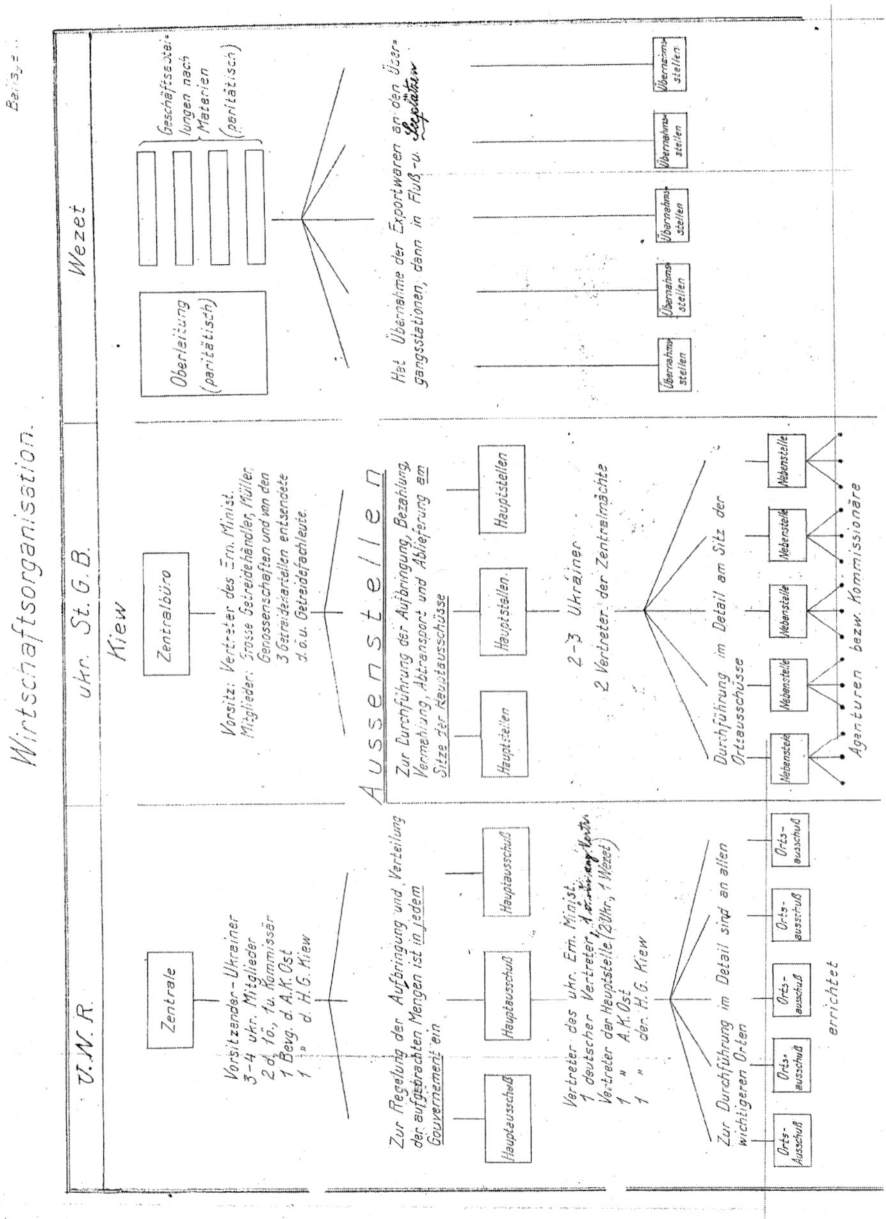

Facsimile 1: Economic organization (ÖStA, KA, AOK, Ukraine Akten, Kt. 2622, Nr. 6906).

Beginning in May, a dense network of purchasers from the cartels and centers was established in the German zone of occupation in Ukraine. They operated locally in the gubernias, which in turn had been divided into purchasing areas, and they bought the goods that had been allocated to their cartels and centers.[116] A common Raw Materials Center was established in Kyiv to coordinate the purchases supplied until mid-July by all the German and Austro-Hungarian centers.[117] Exports from Ukraine to the Central Powers were handled by export syndicates. For Austria-Hungary, these included the Trade Association East from Vienna, the Import and Export Trading Syndicate (MERX), the International Import and Export Syndicate (INTAK), the Northern Bohemian Import and Export Syndicate, and the Hungarian-Ukrainian Export Syndicate (EXUKRAN). The goods were then transported further by rail or ship to the land offices, for which the Black Sea Bureau or the Central Staff for Railways (*Eisenbahnzentralstelle*) in Kyiv were responsible. The land offices then sent these products on to the centers and cartels in the homeland that were responsible for their distribution. In Austria-Hungary the goods were received by the Imperial Food Office (*k.k. Amt für Volksernährung*), which sent them on to the Austrian Central Purchasing Syndicate (ÖZEG).[118] Most of the products were distributed in Austria (Cisleithania), especially in the cities. Only a small proportion of the products were sent to Hungary.[119]

116 See the agreements for the Metal Centers, the Egg-Importing Company, and the Leather Centers: ÖStA, KA, FA, AOK, Ukraine Akten, Kt. 2.614, Nr. 2396, Vertrag zwischen den Metallzentralen Deutschlands und Österreich-Ungarns über die Aufbringung in der Ukraine; ibid., Nr. 2458, Vertrag zwischen OeZEG und Eier-Import-Gesellschaft über Aufbringung in der Ukraine; ibid., Nr. 2462, Abkommen zwischen der deutschen und österreichisch-ungarischen Lederzentrale über Aufbringung in der Ukraine.

117 The Austro-Hungarian cartels and centers complained of a shortage of staff that put them at an unfair disadvantage vis-à-vis their German counterparts: ÖStA, KA, FA, AOK, Ukraine Akten, Kt. 2.617, Nr. 3681, Bericht des Verbindungsoffiziers bei der Rohstoffabteilung, 17.7.1918.

118 ÖStA, KA, FA, AOK, Ukraine Akten, Kt. 2.611, Nr. 1321, Bericht des Österreichischen Warenverkehrsbüros an die Ukraine-Abteilung, 9.6.1918; ÖStA, KA, FA, AOK, Ukraine Akten, Kt. 2.612, Nr. 1735, Zusammenwirken der deutschen zivilen und militärischen Stellen bei Wiederaufnahme des Handelsverkehrs mit Russland, 17.6.1918; ÖStA, KA, FA, AOK, Ukraine Akten, Kt. 2.617, Nr. 3779, Organisation der Kartelle, 19.7.1918.

119 ÖStA, KA, FA, AOK, Ukraine Akten, Kt. 2.611, Nr. 1300, Ukrainische Importe – Teilung zwischen Österreich und Ungarn, 11.6.1918; ÖStA, KA, FA, AOK, Ukraine Akten, Kt. 2.614, Nr. 2253, Niederschrift über die Verteilung der ukrainischen Einfuhren an Zucker zwischen Ungarn und Österreich.

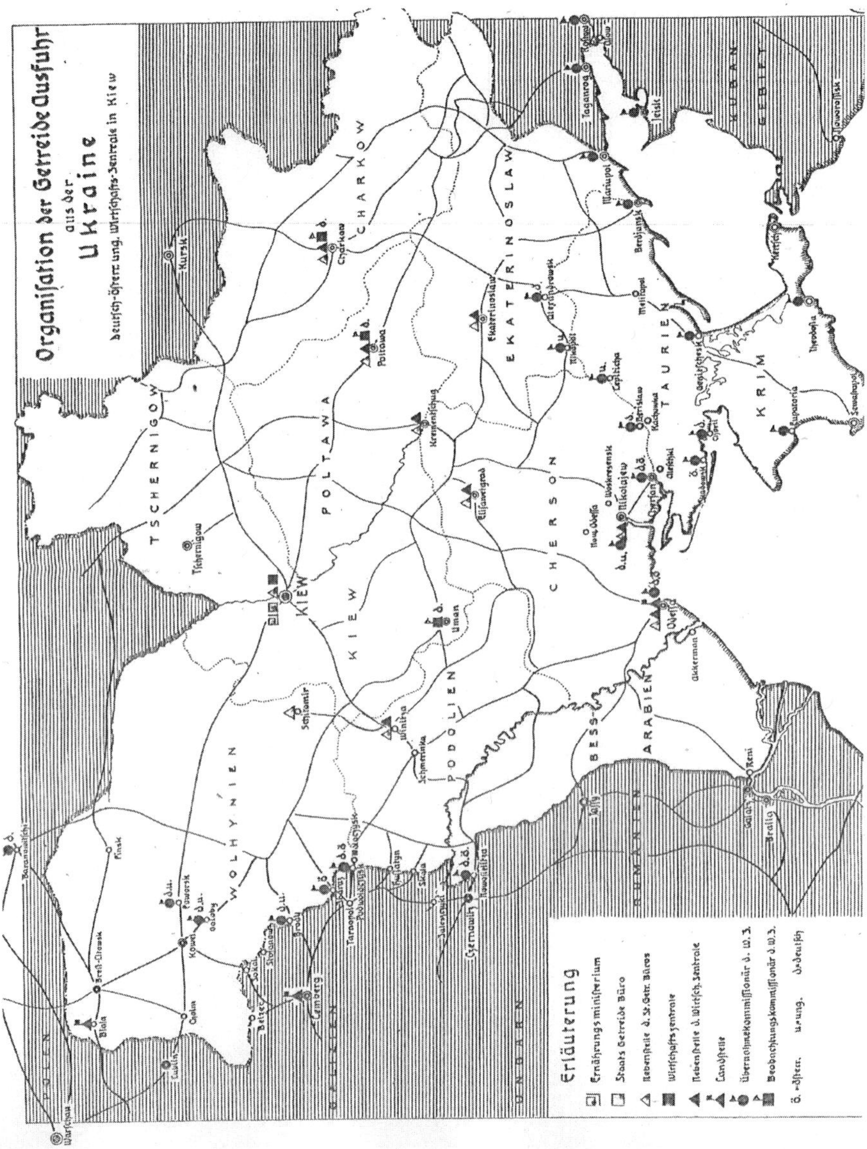

Facsimile 2: Organization of grain export from Ukraine, German-Austro-Hungarian-Ukrainian Economic Center, Kyiv (ÖStA, KA, AOK, Ukraine Akten, Kt. 2613, Nr. 2030).

Once purchases by the troops had ceased,[120] apart from provisions for the troops themselves, the Austro-Hungarian units were called on by Ukrainian organizations or private individuals to undertake measures for supervision or security.[121] At the beginning of July, they were moved into economically important areas to help with the harvest. The areas settled by German colonists played an important role because the Central Powers expected higher crop yields there, and a greater willingness to cooperate. Austro-Hungarian troops were also required to replace the German troops still stationed in the Austro-Hungarian zone. The goal of the action was, by means of this support, to gain control of the harvest and receive a share in return for the labor.[122] As before, the troops may have been negligent in implementing the new guidelines that prohibited military requisitioning. At the beginning of October, the command of the *Ostarmee* reissued its "guidelines for military assistance in the economic utilization of Ukraine," which stressed once more that "members of the army, except in case of dire necessity, are not to act as buyers." These guidelines also contained concrete instructions for participation of the troops in procurement. In the case of "normal procurement," they were to provide only "beneficial influence, support, and supervision." In the case of "procurement under military pressure," they were to "provide military assistance or carry out military requisitioning." But military requisitioning was defined as an "extreme means of coercion" that had to be requested by the Ukrainian Food Council and carried out in the presence of Kyiv officials. Use of weapons by military commanders was prohibited. Goods required by the military were to be handled by civilian organizations, paid for, and loaded in the usual way. Only if supplies were hidden should there be "confiscation without compensation."[123] There were similar orders on the German side. Purchasing was to be undertaken only to cover current needs and was to involve Ukrainian officials so as

---

120 ÖStA, KA, FA, AOK, Ukraine Akten, Kt. 2.612, Nr. 1465, Wirtschaftliche Ausnutzung der Ukraine, 23.6.1918.

121 ÖStA, KA, AdT, UR 3, Kt. 800, Lagebuch vom 17. Oktober 1918, Eintragungen v. 26.7.1918.

122 ÖStA, KA, FA, AOK, Ukraine Akten, Kt. 2.614, Nr. 2455, AK Ostarmee an AOK, 4.7.1918; ÖStA, KA, FA, AOK, Ukraine Akten, Kt. 2.622, Nr. 6906, Bericht der Ostarmee über Aufbringung und Einfuhr, 25.9.1918.

123 ÖStA, KA, FA, AOK, Ukraine Akten, Kt. 2.626, Nr. 8400, Richtlinien für die militärische Mithilfe bei der wirtschaftlichen Ausnützung der Ukraine.

not to impair procurement by shared institutions and not to incur the hostility of the local population.[124]

An integral part of every agreement was the maximum price for particular products, but this was always exceeded in practice.[125] The reason for this was that traders as well as peasants held back grain in the hope of getting much better prices on the black market. The Austro-Hungarian troops, however, offered prices above the maximum. In exceptional cases, such as supply shortages, Ukrainian officials were also able to pay more than the maximum price. Captain Daróczy, the Austro-Hungarian general staff officer at the Economic Center in Kyiv,[126] stated rather laconically in a report on 29 July: "It is a fact that, as soon as permission is given to exceed maximum prices, stores from the old harvest can be brought out very quickly."[127]

The system thus established was a mixed government-military-private system in which, under the circumstances, the Ukrainian, German, and Austro-Hungarian institutions cooperated relatively well. Mistrust, mutual accusations, and irritation still arose among the various parties, but most of the organizational problems that actually arose were generally able to be discussed and resolved in the Ukrainian Food Council. But the old rifts still existed between the allies and their Ukrainian counterparts. According to a report by the director of the Austrian Central Purchasing Syndicate, Lukacs, the Austrians and Hungarians felt themselves circumvented by their German colleagues on many issues.[128] Vienna was also dissatisfied with the Ukrainians: "Experience has shown that the Ukrainian organizations are completely incapable of fulfilling the tasks assigned to them; hence their own civilian organizations are essentially hindered in their activity." A report from AOK on 20 June stated that the

---

124 See BayHStA-KA, Kav.Div., Bd. 19, Bezirk Wolhynien West, Bay.Kav.Division, Abt. Ia, Nr. 2769 W, Beitreibungen zur Deckung des laufenden Truppenbedarfs, 1.9.1918.

125 For example, the maximum prices for September: ÖStA, KA, FA, NFA, HHK AK/AGKdo, 2. Armee, OpAK, Kt. 309, Allgemeine Verlautbarungen des Kommandos der Ostarmee v. 3.10.1918, Nr. 226. According to a report of the Bavarian Cavalry Division, the maximum prices were sometimes exceeded by a factor of four to six. The division was then in a dilemma. The Ukrainian government could not provide for the troops, nor was the division itself able to buy food, since purchases above the maximum price were forbidden by command of Army Group Eichhorn-Kiew. See BayHStA-KA, MKr 1824, Bay.Kav.Div, Abt. Ia, Nr. 1131, Verwendung der B.K.D, 4.6.1918.

126 He was also a representative in the Ukrainian Food Council.

127 ÖStA, KA, FA, AOK, Ukraine Akten, Kt. 2.617, Nr. 4204, Tätigkeitsbericht der Deutsch-österreichisch-ungarischen Wirtschaftsabteilung, 29.7.1918.

128 ÖStA, KA, FA, AOK, Ukraine Akten, Kt. 2.612, Nr. 1400, Wahrnehmungen des Vertreters der österreichischen Zentraleinkaufs-Gesellschaft bei der Wirtschaftszentrale in Kiew, 8.6.1918.

daily number of railway carriages leaving for the Habsburg Monarchy had decreased from 190 at the end of April to fewer than 60 at the end of May. For Austria-Hungary, this meant that the briefly improved situation was again becoming acute owing to reduced deliveries and their own as yet unreaped harvest.[129]

The overall result of the deliveries in the first months of occupation was worse than poor. Up to 31 July, 43,158 tons of food and other goods passed through the land station in Lviv, 11,000 tons of which were sent to Vienna. The food delivered to the capital city (fat and bacon, animals for slaughter, eggs, and sugar) provided some short-term relief. Altogether, the deliveries to the Central Powers that passed through the stations in Lviv, Brest-Litovsk, and the Black Sea and that crossed Austria-Hungary's eastern border by 31 July amounted to roughly 152,229 tons. Even if ore, sulphur, rubber, rags, skins, rope, and other products were to be included, the total would not amount to the one million tons promised at Brest-Litovsk.[130]

It was becoming increasingly clear to the occupying powers that the state institutions of Ukraine had too little support in the gubernias, right down to the individual villages, and that state directives could only be implemented by force or by the use of coercive measures, such as withholding salt provisions in retaliation for uncooperative behavior. Numerous solutions were discussed, including the introduction of a free market. But it was the view of the Austro-Hungarian army that a purely commercial organization could not function because of poor security, the mistrust of the rural population, and the inadequate infrastructure.[131]

When the Berlin agreements of February ran out in the summer, the new agreements of 27 July prohibited the troops from contracting deliveries of monopolized goods. Purchase of provisions for the troops required the agreement of local Food Office officials, and requisitioning was allowed only in extreme cases. Monopolized goods needed by the troops could only be purchased by Ukrainian government officials. Non-monopoly goods were available for free

129 ÖStA, KA, FA, AOK, Ukraine Akten, Kt. 2.612, Nr. 1465, Wirtschaftliche Ausnutzung der Ukraine, 23.6.1918; ibid., Nr. 1598, Hughes-Gespräch zwischen Kiew und Ukraine-Abteilung, 17.6.1918.

130 ÖStA, KA, FA, AOK, Ukraine Akten, Kt. 2.636, Aufstellungen über die Lebensmitteleinkäufe, 21.3.–31.7.1918.

131 ÖStA, KA, FA, AOK, Ukraine Akten, Kt. 2.615, Nr. 2752, Gesichtspunkte zur Frage der Lebensmittelaufbringung, 10.7.1918.

purchase. A monthly sum of 97.4 million crowns[132] was made available to the quartermaster section of the *Ostarmee* for such purchases for its 240,000 men.[133]

Although the procurement and purchasing system between the Central Powers and Ukraine had been put on a new footing, the main problem—the land question—remained unresolved. The expropriation of large estates remained the same great bone of contention under the Hetman as it had been under the Rada.[134] On 23 May 1918, Skoropadsky issued a law regulating the cultivation of fields that accorded with Eichhorn's decree: whoever sowed the fields in the autumn of 1917 had the right to harvest them, and whoever sowed in the spring of 1918 had the right to the summer harvest.[135] The socialization of the land was thereby put to rest. There was a significant restriction, however, on the ownership of large amounts of land: no one could acquire more than 27.5 hectares (25 dessiatines).[136] Wiedfeldt was satisfied with this law, since he saw it as strengthening the wealthier peasants, "the pioneers of agrarian culture."[137] The German military was to support this and, "hand in hand with the Ukrainian government, restore peace, order, and security to the country so that farming, industry, and trade may bloom again."[138] The most urgent task for the troops was to support the export of grain. But all this was still a long way from resolving the land question.

A new law came into force on 15 July that nationalized the greater part of yields. The producers could retail a portion to meet their own needs and to feed the animals. Anyone who resisted this

---

132 For details of the account, see ÖStA, KA, FA, NFA, HHK AK/AGKdo, 2. Armee, QuAbt, Kt. 710, Nr. 37.024, Stellungnahme zur beabsichtigten Aufbringung des Heeresbedarfes in der Ukraine, 26.9.1918.

133 ÖStA, KA, FA, AOK, Ukraine Akten, Kt. 2.626, Nr. 8400, Richtlinien für die militärische Mithilfe bei der wirtschaftlichen Ausnützung der Ukraine; ÖStA, KA, FA, NFA, HHK AK/AGKdo, 2. Armee, QuAbt, Kt. 710, Nr. 43.295, Stellungnahme zur beabsichtigten Aufbringung des Heeresbedarfes in der Ukraina, 26.8.1918; ibid., Kt. 717, Nr. 2661, AOK an Expositur der Ostarmee, Jekaterinoslaw, 9.8.1918; ibid., Nr. 2694, Einlieferungen der St.G.B., 9.9.1918.

134 For Skoropadsky's view on the land question, see *Pavlo Skoropads'kyj*, 195–201, 228–30, 314–19.

135 See ÖStA, KA, FA, AOK, Ukraine Akten, Kt. 2.611, Nr. 1312, Bericht des Warenverkehrsbüros, 6.6.1918; Soldatenko, *Ukraïna v revoliutsiinu dobu*, 233.

136 1 dessiatine=1.1 hectare.

137 BArch, R 3101/1166, Geheimrat Wiedfeldt an Staatssekretär des Reichswirtschaftsamts v. 29.5.1918.

138 BayHStA-KA, 15. Res.Inf.Brig., Bd. 7, Militärbezirk Kiew. XXVII. Res.Korps, Abt. Ia, Nr. 2000, 30.5.1918; ibid., Richtlinien im Anschluss an G.K.O, Abt. Ia, Nr. 1756, 19.5.1918.

could lose his property and agricultural stock.[139] Three months later came Skoropadsky's next thunderbolt in the agrarian question. Under pressure from the large landowners, he issued a new law in mid-August according to which tenants had to hand over their surpluses to the estate owners. Wiedfeldt quite rightly criticized this law, as it removed any incentives for the tenants to produce more. And it was precisely the tenants who had shown themselves to be most productive. Wiedfeldt also feared the political repercussions of this law, which was a slap in the face to the tenants, who had been hoping to acquire more land or revenue from their harvest.[140] So the land question remained a stumbling block, a bone of contention, and a source of conflict. It was also one of the main reasons why the deliveries fell far short of what had been agreed.

In spite of the failure to resolve the land question, some calm was restored in the internal political situation[141] during the summer, but Ukraine remained economically, socially, and politically unstable. This was demonstrated by the railway strike, which lasted from 15 July until the first week of August. The main issue in the strike was the fact that wages were not being paid and, in any case, were failing to keep up with rapidly increasing prices. Trade union recognition was also an issue.[142] The Central Powers suspected that the Entente was behind the strike. The intelligence section of the *Ostarmee* interpreted the event as a protest against both the occupying powers and the unpopular Ukrainian government over the export of Ukrainian grain. The strikers knew that a transport blockade would hit the Central Powers hardest.[143] German authorities, however, regarded the strike as a purely internal Ukrainian affair.[144] The occupying military took

139 Soldatenko, *Ukraïna v revoliutsiinu dobu*, 237.

140 See BArch, R 3101/1166, Reichswirtschaftsstelle bei der Deutschen Ukrainedelegation, Kiew, 29.8.1918.

141 ÖStA, KA, FA, AOK, Ukraine Akten, Kt. 2.617, Nr. 4204, Tätigkeitsbericht der Deutsch-österreichisch-ungarischen Wirtschaftsabteilung, 29.7.1918.

142 See also *Pavlo Skoropads'kyj*, 250–53.

143 BayHStA-KA, Kav.Div., Bd. 18, Fernspruch der Heeresgruppe Eichhorn, Abt. Ia, Nr. 2928/18, o.D.; ibid., XXII. R.K., Abt. Ia, Nr. 2716, 18.7.1918. ÖStA, KA, FA, AOK, Evidenzbüro 1918, Nachrichtenabteilung, Kt. 3672, Nr. 18.568, Eisenbahnstreik und Vorgänge in der Ukraine, August 1918. The Bavarian Cavalry Division repeated its most radical order, in which it stated: "Anyone who offers the least resistance is to be shot on the spot." See BayHStA-KA, Kav.Div., Bd. 18, Bezirk Wolhynien West. Bay.Kav.Division, Abt. Ia, Nr. 2009 W., 6.8.1918.

144 See BayHSt-KA, MKr 1779, Chef des Generalstabes des Feldheeres, Abteilung Fremde Heere, Nr. 15100 geh., 15.8.1918. Die militär-politische Lage im Osten; BArch, R 3101/1194, Eisenbahnzentralstelle Kiew, Besprechung v. 2.8.1918. The Bavarian Cavalry Division, on the other hand, saw hostility to the Germans as one of the motives behind the strike. See BayHStA-

charge of the railways on the important stretches and proceeded "vigorously" against the strikers, imprisoning the "ringleaders" and sending them behind the lines to Brest. Army Group Eichhorn-Kiew also ordered that those willing to work should be given better protection and provisions.[145] In general, the Central Powers were able to cushion the effects of the strike on transport capacity. Nonetheless, in the final weeks of July only 33 carriages a day were moving in Ukraine. From the second week of July to the beginning of August, the number of daily carriages carrying food sank rapidly[146] but, because there had been a high level of transport in early July, it was still a successful month for the export of food.[147] At the beginning of August, when the troops had almost completely restored rail transport, the strike came to an end.[148] From the second half of August and into October, the situation was very calm, a fact confirmed by the secretariat of the Economic Center in its weekly report in the second half of September: "There is no news of serious strike agitation on the railways or in workers' circles, and reports agree that German and Austro-Hungarian troops are increasingly winning the trust of the population. One of our representatives has written: 'They do not love us, but there would be lamentations if we were to withdraw.'"[149]

Furthermore, Turkey and Bulgaria also tried to gain some economic influence in Ukraine. Between February and May 1918, Germany and Austria-Hungary signed trade deals with these two countries. Both agreed initially not to purchase or export goods independently from Ukraine. On 19 April, during negotiations in Berlin concerning a common approach on the part of Germany, Austria-Hungary, and Bulgaria to the resumption of economic relations with the various territories of the former Russian Empire, a secret agreement was signed. According to this agreement, Bulgaria was to receive between

---

KA, Kav.Div., Bd. 51, B.K.D. Gericht, KTB, Eintrag 1.–31.8.1918.

145 ÖStA, KA, FA, NFA, HHK AK/AGKdo, 2. Armee, QuAbt, Kt. 696, Nr. 4152, Eisenbahnstreik – Anordnungen, 17.7.1918.

146 See the facsimile below. See also ÖStA, KA, FA, AOK, Ukraine Akten, Kt. 2.625, Nr. 8193, 24. Wochenbericht der Eisenbahnzentralstelle Kiew, Oktober 1918.

147 See BArch, R 3101/1303, Eisenbahnzentralstelle Kiew, 21. Wochenbericht, 1.–7.9.1918; ibid., Bildliche Darstellung der monatl. Ausfuhr aus der Ukraine.

148 ÖStA, KA, FA, AOK, Ukraine Akten, Kt. 2.617, Nr. 4096, Wirtschaftliche Nachrichten aus Kiew, 12.8.1918; ibid., Nr. 4204, Tätigkeitsbericht der Deutsch-österreichisch-ungarischen Wirtschaftsabteilung, 29.7.1918; ibid., Kt. 2.618, Nr. 4418, Bericht von Waldstätten an Ukraine-Abteilung, 8.8.1918; ibid., Kt. 2.619, Nr. 5425, Regelung der Lohnverhältnisse bei den ukrainischen Eisenbahnen, 27.8.1918.

149 ÖStA, KA, FA, AOK, Ukraine Akten, Kt. 2.625, Nr. 8123, Wochenbericht der Deutsch-österreichisch-ungarischen Wirtschaftszentrale Nr. 11 und 12, 16.–30.9.1918.

2 and 5 percent of procured food and fodder, depending on the product. Separate allocations were established for raw materials and other products. There was a similar agreement with Turkey a week later in which Turkey agreed not to procure goods in any part of the former Russian Empire but retained the right to send its agents as observers to the various organizations. A complicated allocation formula was established, according to which Turkey was to receive between 3 and 12.5 percent of the food and fodder imported by the Central Powers. Separate allocation formulas were worked out for certain raw materials and goods.[150] In spite of this, however, there were repeated incidents where the two allies exported goods from Ukraine without any consultation.[151] At the end of September, Austria-Hungary's High Command ordered the *Ostarmee* to make it "difficult from now on for Bulgaria to export from Ukraine, but without attracting attention."[152] A month later, the Austro-Hungarians ceased all deliveries to Bulgaria and Turkey.[153] But over all these months the proportion of goods exported by Bulgaria and Turkey was very small. Altogether, only 130 carriages from Ukraine went to Bulgaria, 271 to Turkey.[154]

Third Phase: Attempts to Establish Free Trade

At the end of July, when the spring agreement between Ukraine and the Central Powers had run out and had been only provisionally extended,[155] intensive efforts were made to establish new regulations.[156] These led, on 10 September, to a new agreement for the

150 ÖStA, KA, FA, AOK, Ukraine Akten, Kt. 2.611, Nr. 1064, Türkischer und Bulgarischer Einkauf in der Ukraina, 6.6.1918; ibid., Nr. 1255, Vereinbarung mit den Türken und Bulgaren, 10.6.1918.

151 ÖStA, KA, FA, AOK, Ukraine Akten, Kt. 2.611, Nr. 1252, Ausfuhr von Waren aus der Ukraine durch Bulgaren ohne schlüsselmäßige Teilung, 13.6.1918. In early June, for instance, the captain of a Bulgarian steamer, Boris, attempted to export various goods without the permission of the Austro-Hungarian command in Odesa: ÖStA, KA, FA, AOK, Ukraine Akten, Kt. 2.611, Nr. 1207, Vertragswidriger Abtransport von Waren durch Bulgaren aus Odessa, 9.6.1918.

152 ÖStA, KA, FA, AOK, Ukraine Akten, Kt. 2.626, Mappe "Ukraine. Geheimakten," Nr. 124, Bulgarische Ausfuhr, 28.9.1918.

153 ÖStA, KA, FA, AOK, Ukraine Akten, Kt. 2.624, Nr. 7718, Freier Handel in der Ukraine, 12.10.1918; ibid., Kt. 2.625, Nr. 8221, Einstellung der Lieferung an Bulgarien und Türkei, 21.10.1918.

154 BArch, R 3101/1303, Ukraine-Ausfuhr nach den Zentralmächten bis zum 30.9.1918; ibid., Ukraine-Ausfuhr nach den Zentralmächten im Oktober 1918.

155 ÖStA, KA, FA, AOK, Ukraine Akten, Kt. 2.617, Nr. 4096, Wirtschaftliche Nachrichten aus Kiew, 12.8.1918.

156 See also the agreement on the German and Austro-Hungarian approach that served as a basis for the negotiations: ÖStA, KA, FA, AOK, Ukraine Akten, Kt. 2.617, Nr. 3934, Berliner Vereinbarungen v. 27.7.1918, 2.8.1918.

year 1918–19.[157] Part of this was an agreement on grain that contained a detailed plan for the procurement, delivery, and allocation of grain until August 1919. The procurement organization was also improved. The Ukrainian Food Council was required to open offices of the State Grain Bureau in all important locations.[158] During this period, the State Grain Office would procure 5.1 million tons (313 million poods) of grain, of which 1.6 million tons (about 100 million poods) would be for export.[159] In a separate financial agreement, Berlin specified the printing of bank notes that the Central Powers would use to pay for these exports. In addition, Ukraine was granted preferential credits from German banks to the amount of 1 billion Reichsmarks.[160]

There had been previous attempts to replace the existing state monopoly with free trade, and in mid-July a Ukrainian law took the first step in this direction. From then on, only a certain number of goods would remain state monopoly: rye, wheat, millet, buckwheat, lentils, beans, peas, maize, barley, oats, all sorts of flour, bran, groats, by-products from the processing of grains, sugar, spirits, oilseeds, and all sorts of oilcakes.[161] But it was only in the autumn that there was any fundamental change in this third and final phase of economic policy, when free trade replaced the state monopoly for most of these key products. The German military had previously opposed free purchase because they feared that they would then become dependent on Ukrainian officials in providing for the occupation troops.[162] In the early autumn, however, the representatives of the German economy prevailed. They hoped that this would revitalize the Ukrainian economy and create opportunities for procurement for their own

---

157 ÖStA, KA, FA, AOK, OpAbt, Kt. 474, Nr. 1865, Wirtschaftsabkommen mit der Ukraine, 25.9.1918. See also ÖStA, KA, FA, AOK, Ukraine Akten, Kt.: 2.626, Nr. 8400, Richtlinien für die militärische Mithilfe bei der wirtschaftlichen Ausnützung der Ukraine.

158 Text in BArch, R 3101/1169, Niederschrift über ein Wirtschaftsabkommen zwischen dem Ukrainischen Staate einerseits sowie Deutschland und Österreich-Ungarn andererseits für das Wirtschaftsjahr 1918/19, Berlin 1918; see also ÖStA, KA, FA, AOK, Ukraine Akten, Kt. 2.622, Nr. 6474, Wirtschaftsabkommen zwischen der Ukraine sowie Deutschland und Österreich-Ungarn für das Wirtschaftsjahr 1918/19, 10.9.1918.

159 According to this agreement, the peasants would provide for themselves, while the State Grain Bureau would take charge of provisions for the rest of the population, for the troops, and for export.

160 P. Hai-Nyzhnyk, *Finansova polityka uriadu Ukraïns'koï Derzhavy Het'mana Pavla Skoropads'koho (29 kvitnia – 14 hrudnia 1918 r.)* (Kyiv, 2004), 78ff.

161 ÖStA, KA, FA, AOK, Ukraine Akten, Kt. 2.626, Nr. 8400, Richtlinien für die militärische Mithilfe bei der wirtschaftlichen Ausnützung der Ukraine.

162 See BArch, R 3101/1097, Heeresgruppe Eichhorn. Chef des Generalstabes, Abt. Ic, Nr. 20265, 17.4.1918.

industry.[163] On the Austro-Hungarian side, it was the governor of Odesa, Böltz, who strongly supported free purchase and an end to military requisitioning.[164]

The Ukrainian government was now also sympathetic to free purchase and, in August and September, the Ukrainian Food Ministry raised the maximum price for bacon, vegetables, butter, milk products, potatoes, and fish. Ukrainian sellers and German buyers could now have direct contact with one another. The export organizations in this area were now superfluous.[165] The Ukrainian state continued to hold a monopoly in grain but, from September 1918, was also playing with the idea of free trade here as well.[166] The trade minister, Sergei Gerbel, stated this publicly. This arrangement was also good for the large landowners: once they handed over a certain percentage of their grain, it would leave them free to dispose of the rest.[167] But the imminent withdrawal of the Central Powers meant that the tender plant of free trade would have no impact.

At the beginning of October, Hindenburg asked the Foreign Office and the Ministry of the Economy for their assessment of the consequences of a withdrawal from Ukraine. While the Foreign Office feared "serious difficulties" with the supply of provisions to Germany, the Ministry of the Economy took a more sober view of the situation. Of course, a withdrawal from the country would "have an adverse effect on the food situation and on the economy." However, "if we were to take a close look at current imports," then the loss "would not be of such great importance that we would have to maintain the occupation under all circumstances." From the viewpoint of future economic relations, however, a withdrawal from Ukraine would have negative effects.[168] At the same time, the Reich Treasury (*Reichschatzamt*) indicated the general failure of economic policy in Ukraine. German

163 See BArch, R 3101/1169, Telegramm Auswärtiges Amt an Diplomatische Vertretung Kiew v. 30.10.1918.

164 ÖStA, KA, FA, AOK, Ukraine Akten, Kt. 2.621, Nr. 6304, Zustände in der Ukraine, 15.9.1918.

165 Cf. BArch, R 3101/1169, Reichswirtschaftsstelle bei der deutschen Ukraine-Delegation. Tgb Nr. 1672. Kiew, 6.11.1918; ÖStA, KA, FA, AOK, Ukraine Akten, Kt. 2.624, Nr. 7718, Freier Handel in der Ukraine, 12.10.1918.

166 Cf. BArch, R 3101/1169, Reichswirtschaftsstelle bei der Ukrainedelegation, Tgb Nr. 1997/I, 6.12.1918.

167 Cf. BArch, R 3101/1341, Handelsvereinigung für Getreide, Futtermittel u. Saaten GmbH, Berichte, Verlademeldungen der Deutsch-österreichisch-ungarischen Wirtschaftszentrale Kiew, Berlin, 11.10.1918.

168 BArch, R 3101/1180, Der Staatssekretär des Reichswirtschaftsamts I D R 8547, An den Herrn Staatssekretär des Auswärtigen Amts, Berlin, 17.10.1918.

economic and financial expenditure bore no relationship to output. Advances paid to Ukraine would never flow back to the Reich. The treasury saw only one solution: "In this situation, from the viewpoint of the Reich's financial administration, it is absolutely necessary to begin a gradual withdrawal from Ukraine immediately, with a short time frame for the liquidation of the undertaking."[169]

Austria-Hungary was initially more optimistic. During the withdrawal from the Katerynoslav gubernia, its economic officials were ordered to stay at their posts and continue trading.[170] But when the headquarters of the *Ostarmee* withdrew, it seems that the civilian officials left Ukraine as well. There is no evidence of the "lamentations" over the withdrawal of Austro-Hungarian troops foretold by the economic centers. Once those troops withdrew, the Germans considered themselves no longer bound by their agreements with their erstwhile ally. They did hope, however, that they would be able to take over their treaty rights from the treaties that Austria-Hungary had signed with Ukraine.[171]

Even in the autumn of 1918, after the truce of 11 November, when the export of grain and food from Ukraine was no longer practically possible owing to the shortages in that country, Germany still wanted to "maintain...a certain control over the procurement and distribution of Ukrainian grain."[172] In the new political situation, however, it soon became clear that this was completely illusory. From the late autumn of 1918, as a consequence of the civil war, Germany's economic relations with Ukraine ceased altogether.

The Results of Ukrainian Exports

It was already clear in the summer that, despite all efforts, exports from Ukraine to the Central Powers were very modest. Not a single product was delivered in the quantity agreed in the treaty. Of the 50,000 tons of sugar agreed to be delivered to the Central Powers by 31 July, 37,750 tons (about 75 percent) were delivered by the end of August; of the 200,000 cattle, 91,000 (45 percent) were delivered, and

169 TNA, GFM 6/99, Der Staatssekretär des Reichsschatzamts (Graf Roedern) IV.A.6347, An den Herrn Chef des Generalstab des Feldheeres, 22.10.1918.

170 ÖStA, KA, FA, AOK, Ukraine Akten, Kt. 2.625, Nr. 8121, Räumung der Ukraine, 19.10.1918.

171 BArch, R 3101/1304 [Reichswirtschaftsamt] IDR 9518, Niederschrift über die Sitzung des Ständigen Russischen Ausschusses am Freitag, 8.11.1918 um 9:30.

172 BArch, R 3101/1304, Reichswirtschaftsstelle bei der Deutschen Gesandtschaft, Tgb.Nr. 1777, An den Herrn Staatssekretär des Reichswirtschaftsministeriums, 15.11.1918.

of the 400–500 million eggs, only 60 million (12–15 percent).[173] But the most glaring shortfall was in grain, the very item for which the Central Powers had invaded Ukraine in the first place. By 31 August, exactly 102,000 tons (about 10 percent) of grain, pulses, fodder, and seeds had been exported to the Central Powers.[174] According to the Ukrainian Food Ministry, of the 8,260 wagons of food that were sent by rail to the Central Powers by 16 August, 2,324 (28.14 percent) went to Germany and 4,326 (52.37 percent) to Austria. Another 1,610 (19.49 percent) went by sea.[175]

Figure 1: Agreed deliveries and actual deliveries (BArch, R 3101/1341. Handelsvereinigung für Getreide, Futtermittel und Saaten. Ukraine-Bericht Nr. 98 für den 31. August)

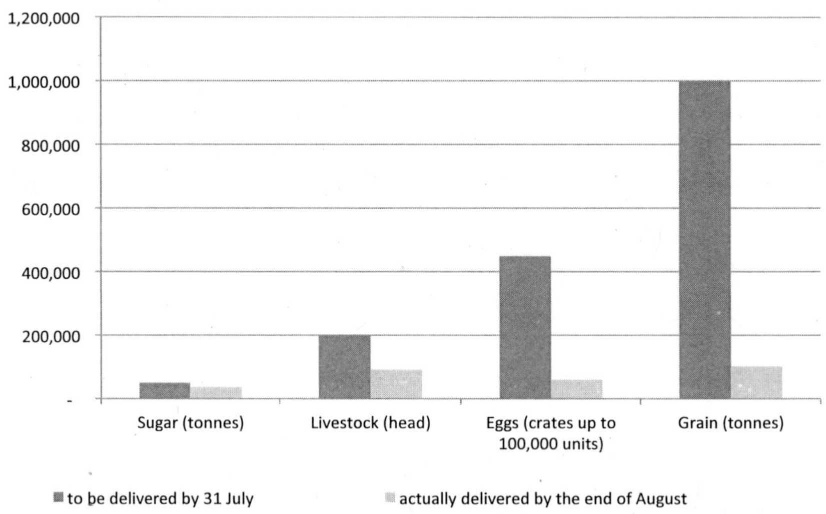

173 BArch, R 3101/1316, Heeresgruppe Kiew, Wirtschaftsnachrichten Nr. 1, Kiew, 20.9.1918.

174 At the end of July, the announced figure of 110,000 was higher than had actually been exported. The cause of this discrepancy—perhaps a computational error—is not clear. But the fact remains that the quantities exported from Ukraine were far below the levels agreed. See BArch, R 3101/1341, Handelsvereinigung für Getreide, Futtermittel und Saaten, Ukraine-Bericht Nr. 73 für den 30.7.1918. The figures from the Quartermaster General of the Austro-Hungarian *Ostarmee* are even smaller and suggest that by 31 July only 7 percent of agreed grain had been delivered, and 18 percent of cattle: ÖStA, KA, FA, AOK, Ukraine Akten, Kt. 2.622, Nr. 6906, Bericht der Ostarmee über Aufbringung und Einfuhr, 25.9.1918.

175 ÖStA, KA, AOK, Qu. Abt., Ukraine Akten, Kt. 2.620, Nr. 5574, Bericht des Bevollmächtigten Generalstabsoffiziers bei der Deutsch-österreichisch-ungarischen Wirtschaftszentrale, 25.8.1918.

Figure 2: Deliveries to the Central Powers until 16 August 1918 (ÖStA, KA, AOK, Qu. Abt., Ukraine-Bestand, Karton 2.620, Nr. 5574)

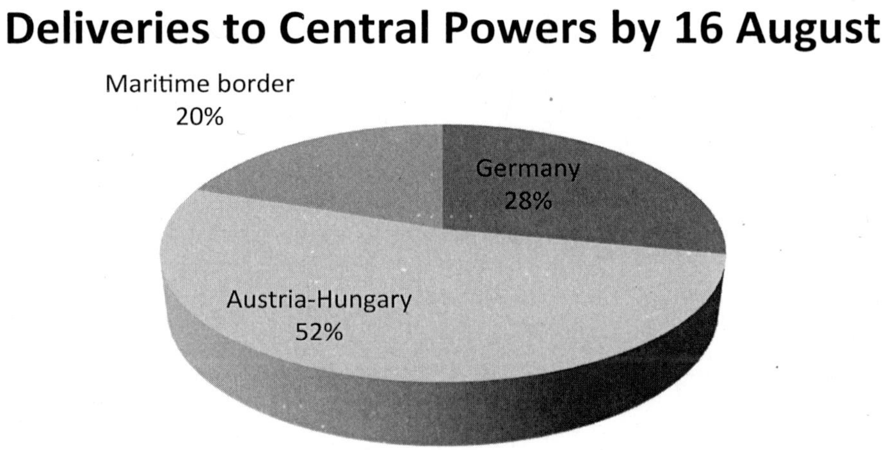

Although Ukraine was unable by far to carry out its contractual obligations in the period up to the summer, it continued to give optimistic forecasts for the future throughout the period of occupation.[176] The Central Powers also seemed to live in a dream world and did not want to see the country's limited economic capacity.[177] Only a few of those involved saw the situation differently.[178] An

176 See BArch, R 3101/1316, Heeresgruppe Kiew. Wirtschaftsnachrichten Nr. 2, Kiew, 15.10.1918.

177 ÖStA, KA, FA, AOK, Ukraine Akten, Kt. 2.615, Nr. 2896, Die Ukraine. Auszug aus dem Vortrag von Major Konrad John, 13.7.1918; BArch, R 3101/1304, Kt. 2.617, Nr. 4167, Waldbott an Ukraine-Abteilung, 30.7.1918.

178 BArch, R 3101/1304, Kt. 2.617, Nr. 4204, Tätigkeitsbericht der Deutsch-österreichisch-ungarischen Wirtschaftsabteilung, 29.7.1918; ibid., Kt. 2.619, Nr. 4937, Bericht des Schweizer Geschäftsmannes Edgar Brun, 10.8.1918; ibid., Kt. 2.622, Nr. 6906, Bericht der Ostarmee über

external observer, the American general consul in Moscow, DeWitt U. Poole, made a more realistic assessment in April of the amount of grain available for export. Although his sources suggested that eight million tons of grain could be gained from the harvest of 1917, the Central Powers were only able to procure half a million tons by the time of the 1918 harvest.[179]

In the final phase as well, the Ukrainian state was unable to deliver the amounts contracted in the September agreement. From the time of the agreement until the end of October 1918, the last date of regular deliveries, the amount of grain that should have been made available for export according to the agreement was 460,000 tons (27.3 million poods). But only 30,000 tons were loaded during this period, less than one-tenth of the agreed amount,[180] although the autumn harvest, with 15.3 million tons, was relatively good.[181]

Although grain, fodder, and pulses were at the top of Germany's list of priorities,[182] and although the Austro-Hungarian ambassador in Berlin also emphasized that food and fodder had "priority over all other exports from Ukraine,"[183] this grain policy was a disaster by the end of the occupation. The million tons promised at Brest-Litovsk never came close to being achieved. By 23 December 1918, 137,854 tons of grain and fodder had been loaded, 129,310 tons had crossed the border, and 48,575 tons had eventually arrived in the German Empire.[184] Since these statistics from the Trade Syndicate for Grain, Fodder, and Seeds agree almost exactly with the figures from the *Eisenbahnzentralstelle* in Kyiv, the figure of roughly 130,000

Aufbringung und Einfuhr, 25.9.1918.

179 NARA, US Department of State, relating to internal Affairs to Russia and Soviet Union 1910–1929, War Series 6, RG 59, Russia, Department of State Periodical Report of Matters relating to Russia (681.00/1161), Present Food Resources of the Ukraine. Paraphrase of Telegram from DeWitt U. Poole, American Consul General at Moscow, Nr. 331, 10.4.1918.

180 See BArch, R 3101/1341, Handelsvereinigung für Getreide, Futtermittel und Saaten, Ukraine-Bericht Nr. 98 für den 31.8.1918; ibid., Ukraine-Bericht, Nr. 139 für den 31.10.1918.

181 Mędrzecki, *Niemiecka interwencja militarna na Ukrainie w 1918 roku*, 249.

182 See BArch, R 3101/1304, Geheimrat Wiedfeldt an Herrn Staatssekretär des Reichswirtschaftsamts. 25.5.1918. The list of priorities was: 1) grain, including flour, 2) fodder, 3) pulses, 4) eggs, 5) fat, including bacon and oil, 6) meat, 7) sugar, 8) raw materials and tobacco. The most important raw materials for export were: 1) rubber, tires, old rubber, 2) hemp, 3) Japanese camphor. See also BArch, R 3101/1304, Kriegsministerium, Kriegsamt, Z Ia 232/5.18 KRA. Dringlichkeitsliste für die Zufuhr von Rohstoffen aus der Ukraine v. 1.6.1918.

183 BArch, R 3101/1304 K.u.k Österreichisch-Ungarische Botschaft. Kommerzdirektion, Nr. K 14901/Res, 7.5.1918.

184 BArch, R 3101/1341, Handelsvereinigung für Getreide, Futtermittel und Saaten, Ukraine-Bericht, Nr. 149 für den 23.12.1918.

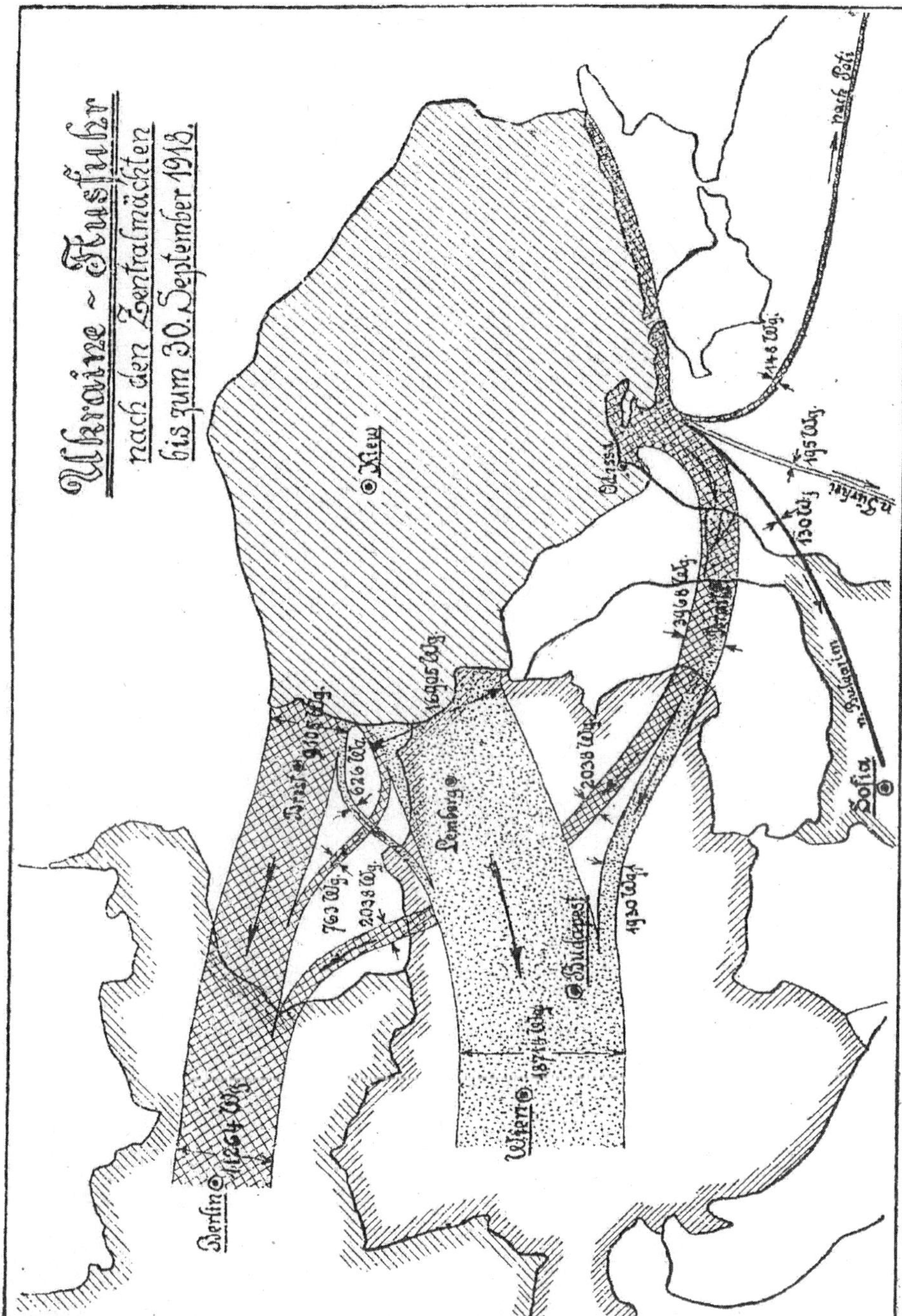

Facsimile 3: Ukrainian exports until 30 September and in October 1918 (BArch, R 3101/1303f.).

tons is the definitive one for total exports of grain from Ukraine to the Central Powers.[185]

There was obviously an extensive black market on the border to Soviet Russia and to Austria-Hungary.[186] It was probably larger on the Austro-Hungarian border and was noticed by officials of the Habsburg Monarchy. In the guise of "small border trade," this smuggling at least helped improve provisions in the border areas. Following strong protests about "colossal smuggling" at the Lviv land office,[187] AOK issued "stricter instructions" in order to reduce it "to an acceptable minimum."[188] Soldiers were encouraged to purchase food packets privately and send them to their families. Their allowances were even increased for that purpose,[189] and offices were established from which they could send the food packets.[190] But no valid figures are available for smuggling[191] or for private food packets.

The Central Powers had to get by as best they could with these faltering deliveries of grain and fodder. The Vienna mayor at the

---

185 According to the Trade Syndicate, 105,530 tons had crossed the border by the end of September. The Railway Center's figure for grain exports in this period was 7,770 wagons. If we assume 13.5 to 14 tons per wagon, then the figures agree. See BArch, R 3101/1341, Handelsvereinigung für Getreide, Futtermittel und Saaten, Ukraine-Bericht Nr. 120 für den 30.9.1918; BArch, R 3101/1303, Bildliche Darstellung der monatl. Ausfuhr aus der Ukraine. Using figures from Czernin, Fedyshyn claims that altogether 1.5 million tons of grain and food reached the Central Powers from Ukraine by legal and illegal routes: Oleh S. Fedyshyn, *Germany's Drive to the East and the Ukrainian Revolution, 1917–1918* (New Brunswick, N.J., 1971), 259. This figure is clearly too high.

186 See the reports on petroleum smuggling in Brody: ÖStA, KA, FA, AOK, Ukraine Akten, Kt. 2.611, Nr. 1029, Schmuggel mit Mineralölprodukten in Brody, 8.6.1918.

187 ÖStA, KA, FA, AOK, Ukraine Akten, Kt. 2.617, Nr. 4112, Bericht der Landstelle Lemberg über Schmuggelwesen, 31.7.1918; ÖStA, KA, FA, AOK, Ukraine Akten, Kt. 2.626, Nr. 8400, Richtlinien für die militärische Mithilfe bei der wirtschaftlichen Ausnützung der Ukraine; ÖStA, KA, FA, AOK, Ukraine Akten, Kt. 2.617, Nr. 4292, Schmuggel zwischen Ukraine und Österreich, 2.8.1918.

188 ÖStA, KA, FA, NFA, HHK AK/AGKdo, 2. Armee, OpAK, Kt. 309, Allgemeine Verlautbarungen des Kommandos der Ostarmee vom 14.9.1918, Nr. 207. The following document suggests that there may have been a "loss" of products during transport, since goods were pilfered from trains on the way to the border: ÖStA, KA, FA, AOK, Ukraine Akten, Kt. 2.616, Nr. 3335, Schmuggel an der Grenze, Eindämmung, 22.7.1918.

189 ÖStA, KA, FA, NFA, HHK AK/AGKdo, 2. Armee, OpAK, Kt. 309, Allgemeine Verlautbarungen des Kommandos der Ostarmee vom 15.10.1918.

190 ÖStA, KA, FA, NFA, HHK AK/AGKdo, 2. Armee, OpAK, Kt. 309, O.Q. Nr. 3000, Errichtung von Heimatpaket-Abschubstellen im Bereiche der Ostarmee.

191 According to official Austro-Hungarian estimates, these "unofficial Ukrainian exports" were twice the size of official exports: ÖStA, KA, FA, AOK, Ukraine Akten, Kt. 2.612, Nr. 1711, Protokoll des Russischen Ausschusses des AOK, 13.6.1918; Ottokar Czernin, *Im Weltkriege* (Berlin and Vienna, 1919), 346. The Hungarian government was annoyed by the smuggling, since it felt robbed of the quantities it had been promised: ÖStA, KA, FA, AOK, Ukraine Akten, Kt. 2.612, Nr. 1658, Einfuhr aus der Ukraina nach Österreich im Schmuggelwege, 1.7.1918.

time, Richard Weiskirchner, coined the term "bread peace," which is still sometimes used today, but the biggest export from Ukraine to the Central Powers was not grain but other foodstuffs and cattle. In particular, the Austro-Hungarian Monarchy improved its stock of horses with the much better horses from Ukraine.[192] By the end of July, altogether 90,000 horses had been procured, one-third for the army in the field, two-thirds for civilian use.[193] In addition to grain, oilseeds, and fodder, the most important exports from Ukraine were eggs, bacon, lamb, fowl, canned goods, cattle, butter, and cheese. Added to these were raw materials and booty. The export of these goods required almost three times more railway capacity than the export of grain. Between April and September, these goods were carried by 23,000 wagons to the German Empire, Austria-Hungary and, to a lesser extent, to Turkey and Bulgaria.[194] The number of wagons carrying grain was 7,800.[195] Even including these, the total amount of goods delivered to the Central Powers was less than half the value of the grain and grain products that were promised at Brest-Litovsk to be delivered by the end of June.[196]

What were the reasons for these very low export figures? First of all, the occupying troops required a certain amount of food for their own use. This, however, was a relatively small proportion overall and accounted for only around 10 percent of the deliveries of the State Grain Bureau. This is a smaller amount than expected because the number of occupying troops was far smaller than has been assumed in studies up to now.[197]

German officials listed a number of other reasons. The poor harvest, the shortage of money for purchases, and the failures of the State Grain Bureau were all blamed. According to its "admittedly not impeccable figures," only 1.3 million tons (80 million poods) of the promised 3 million tons (181 million poods) from the new harvest were purchased

192 ÖStA, KA, FA, NFA, HHK AK/AGKdo, 2. Armee, QuAbt, Kt. 693, Nr. 853, Sammelakt zur militärischen Teilnahme an der wirtschaftlichen Ausnutzung der Ukraine, Februar/März 1918.

193 ÖStA, KA, FA, AOK, OpAbt, Kt. 475, Nr. 1906, Darstellung der materiellen Lage der Armee im Felde, 18.8.1918.

194 See, for example, the permit to export 300 poods of tin and four tons of castor oil and glycerine for the Ottoman navy: ÖStA, KA, FA, AOK, Ukraine Akten, Kt. 2.611, Nr. 1263, Schlüsselmäßige Anrechnung Türkischer Importe aus Ukraine, 13.6.1918.

195 BArch, R 3101/1303, Bildliche Darstellung der monatl. Ausfuhr aus der Ukraine.

196 Ukrainian sources speak of about 20 percent of the agreed amounts for July and August: I. Dats'kiv, "Ekonomichni aspekty Brests'koho dohovoru 1918 roku," *Istoriia Ukraïny* (Kyiv, 2008), 46.

197 See chapter 3b in the present volume.

from September to November. Also, according to German statements, the "encroachments by the withdrawing Austro-Hungarian troops" had a negative influence on procurement. Similarly, they were unable to stop the booming black market on the borders with Russia and Austria-Hungary. Other factors were the "transport difficulties" after October caused by the withdrawal of Austro-Hungarian troops and the civil war that flared up at the beginning of November.[198]

Exports from the Central Powers to Ukraine

Trouble-free use of the railways was an essential precondition for getting the Ukrainian economy moving. In the spring of 1918, the Germans had continued their advance in order to take advantage of the coal reserves in the Donets Basin, but hopes that the Ukrainian state would be able to provide itself with coal were not fulfilled.[199] Much less would Ukraine be able to export coal—indeed, the German Empire soon found it necessary to export coal to Ukraine.[200] Throughout the occupation, coal was the most important export from the German Empire. At first it was estimated that 105,000 tons per month would be needed to secure grain transport on the railways.[201] In April 1918, the German Empire contracted to deliver 315,000 tons of coal to Ukraine until 31 July and then an additional 144,000 tons until 31

---

198 BArch, R 3101/1318, Wirtschaftsnachrichten der Heeresgruppe Kiew, Nr. 1 v. 20.9.1918; BArch, R 3101/1341, Handelsvereinigung für Getreide, Futtermittel und Saaten GmbH, Berlin, Berichte (bis 2. Okt.18). Verlademeldungen (bis 10. Okt. 1918) der Deutsch-österreichisch-ungarischen Wirtschaftszentrale Kiew, 11.10.1918; BArch, R 3101/1169, Reichswirtschaftsstelle bei der Ukraine Delegation, Tgb Nr. 1997/I, 6.12.1918.

199 On 16 June, the Austro-Hungarian captain and engineer Gutmann, having traveled through the district, wrote a report on the coal mines in the Donets Basin. He was very optimistic about the capacities and technical equipment of the mines. But his report dealt mostly with the poor administration of the mines and the transport system, the wage-price spiral, the lack of food, the poor training of the workers and officials, and their political unreliability: ÖStA, KA, FA, NFA, HHK AK/KorpsKdo, 12. Korps, Kt. 1663, Nr. 10.686, Bericht über die Kohlenwerke im Steinkohlegebiet des Donezbeckens in der Ukraine von Hauptmann Ing. Gutmann, 16.6.1918.

200 Studies have often claimed that the Germans wanted to exploit the coal reserves for their own use. Cf. Peter Borowsky, "Germany's Ukrainian Policy during World War I and the Revolution of 1918–19," in *German-Ukrainian Relations in Historical Perspective,* ed. Hans-Joachim Torke and John-Paul Himka (Edmonton and Toronto, 1994), 89; Caroline Milow, *Die ukrainische Frage 1917–1923 im Spannungsfeld der europäischen Diplomatie* (Wiesbaden, 2002), 160, although, on the following pages, German exports of coal are described in detail. In view of the massive coal reserves in the Ruhr, the Saarland, and Silesia, this argument is not convincing.

201 BArch, R 3101/1136, Deutsche Ukrainedelegation, Der Vorsitzende der Gesamt-Kommission, J.Nr. 74, 13.4.1918. Ludendorff had originally insisted that "coal deliveries to Ukraine" would only come into question "as occasional assistance." See TNA, GFM 6/36, Telegramm Nr. 576 des K. Legationssekretärs Lersner an AA, 18.3.1918.

October 1918.[202] Ukraine wanted 8,175 tons of naphtha petroleum, but the Central Powers agreed to only 750 tons of oil products: gasoline, benzol mixture, kerosene, paraffin candles, grease, and machine oil. All other products requested by Ukraine, such as agricultural machinery, manufactured goods, paper and parchment, chemical/pharmaceutical goods, and textile machinery, would be delivered according to surplus capacity.[203]

The Germans wanted to use coal initially as "one of the most important means of leverage"[204] with regard to grain deliveries, but this very soon proved illusory. The volume of coal exports to Ukraine very quickly exceeded the amount of goods that Ukraine was able to deliver to the Central Powers. By the end of May, Germany had delivered 5,300 wagons of coal (and other goods) to Ukraine. During the same period, only 1,800 wagons of grain, food, and raw materials were delivered to Germany.[205] This relationship did not improve much by the end of September, the last date for valid data. From April to September, Germany delivered 23,500 wagons of coal (plus a small proportion of agricultural machinery and oil products) to Ukraine. During the same period, only about 10,700 wagons arrived in Germany.[206] Although the amount of coal exported did not reach the level agreed, what Germany had to export was more than just "some of its own coal."[207]

Until June 1918, in spite of these coal exports, there was no central German organization that dealt with the export of German goods to Ukraine. Until then, German goods were frequently purchased by Austro-Hungarian traders and exported to Ukraine. At the beginning of June, the Federation of German Wholesalers and the War Committee of German Industry established the Export Syndicate, which was given the sole right to export to Ukraine by the Ministry

---

202 Milow, *Die ukrainische Frage 1917–1923 im Spannungsfeld der europäischen Diplomatie*, 161.

203 ÖStA, KA, FA, AOK, Ukraine Akten, Kt. 2.610, Nr. 365, Organisation der Aufbringung in der Ukraine, 15.5.1918.

204 BArch, R 3101/1096, Deutsche Ukrainedelegation an Reichswirtschaftsamt v. 8.4.1918.

205 BArch, R 3101/1303, Bildliche Darstellung der monatlichen Ausfuhr aus der Ukraine; BArch, R 3101/1303, Eisenbahnzentralstelle Kiew. 27. Wochenbericht 13.–19.10.1918. See also an article by the onetime head of the Railway Center, Stefan von Velsen, "Ukraine. Die Ukraine und Wir. Ein Rückblick auf die deutsche Okkupation," *Preußische Jahrbücher*, no. 176 (1919): 261. Velsen's figure of 6,000 wagons of coal by the end of May is too high. He gives the number of wagons leaving Ukraine as 2,000.

206 BArch, R 3101/1303, Eisenbahnzentralstelle Kiew, 27. Wochenbericht vom 13.–19.10.1918; ibid., Bildliche Darstellung der monatlichen Ausfuhr aus der Ukraine.

207 Borowsky, "Germany's Ukrainian Policy during World War I and the Revolution of 1918–19," 89.

of the Economy.[208] The syndicate was thus responsible for the export of German industrial products. It purchased or ordered goods in Germany and exported them to Ukraine. The situation of German exports to Ukraine improved after that. Within one month of the founding of the Export Syndicate, products to the value of 100 million marks were exported or being prepared for export to Ukraine.[209]

Compared with German exports, those of Austria-Hungary were quite modest. Its main exports to the end of September were mineral oil products from Galicia (707 wagons) and 648 wagons with enamelware, agricultural machinery, scythes and other industrial products. With a few other smaller product groups, the total amount was 1,937 wagons.[210] The creation of an organization to deal with exports to Ukraine was also very slow here, even though officials dealing with purchasing were pressing hard for goods to be sent to Ukraine as quickly as possible as a way of improving procurement. All exports to Ukraine were processed by the Austrian and Hungarian Goods Transport Bureau (*Waren-Verkehrs-Büro*), which received goods from the export organizations. The bureau sent the goods to the land office in Lviv or the Black Sea office at Brăila, which in turn passed them on to the branches of the transport bureau in Ukraine or to the command of the *Ostarmee*. Their route (*Instradierung*)[211] then took them by rail or ship along the field transport system of the Austro-Hungarians or that of the Railway Center in Kyiv.[212] There was very active smuggling that affected imports to Ukraine across the border from Bukovyna and Galicia, just as there was in the case of Ukrainian exports. The German Empire protested repeatedly about this.[213]

However, as the quartermaster general of the *Ostarmee* bitterly complained at the beginning of September, these exports to Ukraine

208 ÖStA, KA, FA, AOK, Ukraine Akten, Kt. 2.614, Nr. 2555, Gesellschaftsvertrag der Ausfuhrgesellschaft, 2.7.1918.

209 BArch, R 3101/1137, Der Unterstaatsekretär in der Reichskanzlei, 4.7.1918.

210 ÖStA, KA, FA, AOK, Ukraine Akten, Kt. 2.613, Nr. 1862, Telegramme betreffend die Bereitstellung von Mineralölprodukten für die Ukraine vom 23.–25.6.1918; ÖStA, KA, FA, AOK, Ukraine Akten, Kt. 2.624, Nr. 7718, Freier Handel in der Ukraine, 12.10.1918.

211 *Instradiere* is a military term, especially in Austria, meaning to begin a march along a marching route or by rail; in the postal service, it indicated the determination of a route for postal transmission.

212 ÖStA, KA, FA, AOK, Ukraine Akten, Kt. 2.612, Nr. 1655, Schematische Darstellung der Durchführung des Exportes nach der Ukraine, 19.6.1918; ÖStA, KA, FA, AOK, Ukraine Akten, Kt. 2.618, Nr. 4842, Schematische Darstellung des Exports in die Ukraine, 20.8.1918.

213 ÖStA, KA, FA, AOK, Ukraine Akten, Kt. 2.614, Nr. 2557, Protokoll über die in der Zentral-Einkaufsgesellschaft in Wien abgehaltene Besprechung, 7.7.1918.

did not have the positive effects that had been hoped for. There had been hopes for a reduction of inflation, an improvement in public attitudes to the Austro-Hungarian occupying power, and a corresponding long-term improvement in its economic positioning after the war. In early October, Arz stated that the strategy was to direct Austro-Hungarian exports toward the Dual Monarchy's own zone of occupation "in order to gain a foothold in the economy there for the transition period and for the period of peace that would follow."[214]

Exploitation or Utilization?

In spite of the coal exports and the various efforts to establish economic structures, the economic motor of Ukraine never started up. To the Ukrainian population, the occupation by the Central Powers and their support for the Hetman and his counterrevolutionary measures regarding the land question were the root of all their problems. The initially optimistic Wiedfeldt expressed it clearly in August: "All economic misfortunes are more or less blamed on us. If we intervene, those disadvantaged by our intervention denounce us, whether it be large landowners, entrepreneurs, or workers. If we keep our distance, it is even worse, as the accusation is then made that the Germans are intentionally letting things go to ruin."[215]

How should we assess the economic policy of the Central Powers in Ukraine? First of all, there was no single economic policy. While short-term utilization was at the forefront for the Austro-Hungarian and German military, foreign-policy and economic officials in Vienna and Berlin had long-term plans to stabilize Ukraine economically and, in the medium term, to tie it in to their own economies. For them, it was more than just a question of grain and food imports from an occupied country. It was not for nothing that the German Ministry of the Economy complained in October 1918 that, while the withdrawal from Ukraine would create no short-term problems concerning provisions for the homeland, it would be "a great loss" for potential future economic relations.[216] Wiedfeldt always had in mind "the great English model in the English colonies": "There, everything proceeds

214 ÖStA, KA, FA, AOK, Ukraine Akten, Kt. 2.622, Nr. 6681, Bericht der Quartiermeister-Abteilung der k.u.k. Ostarmee, 4.9.1918; ibid., Kt. 2.626, Nr. 3658, Klärung der Fragen in der Ukraina, 4.10.1918.

215 BArch, R 3101/1168, Reichswirtschaftsstelle bei der deutschen Ukrainedelegation an den Staatssekretär des Reichswirtschaftsamts v. 17.8.1918.

216 BArch, R 3101/1180, Der Staatssekretär des Reichswirtschaftsamts I D R 8547. An den Herrn Staatssekretär des Auswärtigen Amts, Berlin, 17.10.1918.

along civilian lines, hardly apparent on the outside, while the military is the power in the background."[217] Using the rhetoric of debates of the 1960s, Peter Borowsky describes the long-term economic policy of the Foreign Office and the Ministry of the Economy as "more imperialist" than that of the OHL.[218] From today's perspective, however, one cannot get away from the fact that this policy was more purposeful and progressive than any economic policy aimed at short-term advantage. Present-day state-building is essentially no different.

Shortly before the end of the occupation, the German Economic Office in Kyiv affirmed that Austria-Hungary had pursued a much more vigorous economic policy than Germany, but this report also added: "One cannot claim, however, in the meantime, that Austro-Hungarian exports surpassed those of Germany or that Austria-Hungary was more commercially successful in Ukraine."[219] From today's perspective, there is nothing to add to this summary.

When one of the architects of this alliance with Ukraine, Czernin, attempted in retrospect to pass a more differentiated judgment, he nevertheless had to admit "that the hopes generally raised by the conclusion of the Brest-Litovsk peace treaty were far from fulfilled."[220] From today's perspective, there is only one judgment that can be rendered about the results of the Central Powers' economic policy: it was a grandiose failure.[221] The amount of grain expected to reach Austria-Hungary and Germany was not achieved even to a small extent. Instead, the German Reich had to export large amounts of coal to Ukraine and, in addition, had to pay 110 million marks monthly in occupation costs.[222] Economically, the Ukrainian undertaking ended up costing money, and the invested money was lost when the civil war broke out. The Paris peace settlements created a final barrier to Germany's wishes in Eastern Europe and in the Caucasus. Thus the economic policy of the Central Powers in Ukraine cannot be

---

217 BArch, R 3101/1168, Brief von Geheimrat Wiedfeldt an den Staatssekretär des Reichswirtschaftsamts v. 7.5.1918.

218 Borowsky, *Deutsche Ukrainepolitik*, 298.

219 BArch, R 3101/1169, Reichswirtschaftsstelle bei der deutschen Ukraine-Delegation, Tgb Nr. 1672, Kiew, 6.11.1918.

220 Czernin, *Im Weltkriege*, 344. He hoped that the thousands of wagons that came from Ukraine had saved "millions" of lives (ibid., 347).

221 As Colonel Kreneis had already claimed in a comprehensive report to AOK at the end of September: ÖStA, KA, AOK, OpAbt, Kt. 476, Nr. 1987, Kreneis an AOK, 28.9.1918.

222 BArch, R 3101/1168, An die Regierung des ukrainischen Staates, Entwurf eines Militär- und Wirtschaftsabkommens, Juni 1918.

described as "exploitation," although such plans did exist, above all on the Austro-Hungarian side, at the start of the occupation. In sum, the term "utilization" would be more appropriate here or, more exactly, "failed utilization."

3d. The View from Within: Everyday Life during the Occupation

Vasyl Rasevych

When German and Austro-Hungarian troops marched into Ukraine, they were confronted with a catastrophic situation. The Central Rada had effectively lost control over the territory. The greatest insecurity factor was the complete demoralization of the old Russian army and the large number of deserters. Most of them were armed and, as they attempted to make their own individual way home, they took by force whatever they needed from the civilian population. Large areas were afflicted by bands of plundering marauders. The Bolsheviks were also terrorizing their opponents and inciting the population to plunder the large estate holders.[223] When the Bolsheviks withdrew, they left small groups behind in the occupied territory. Strengthened by the local proletariat, these soon formed mobile bands that went on to terrorize and rob the civilian population. Bolshevik agitators were active everywhere, telling the people that the occupying troops intended to take away their democratic freedoms and return the land to the estate owners. Under such circumstances, it was only small circles among the more educated population who appreciated the reasons for the invasion by the troops of the Central Powers and hoped that they would restore order.[224]

The Germans' first impression of Ukraine was a positive one, since they did not encounter any particular hostility and even noticed that people were relieved that they had arrived. They hoped that the people would be so exhausted by the rule of the Bolsheviks and their plundering and anarchic conditions that it would be relatively easy for them to build up the administration of the occupation. At first the German troops were impressed by the large amounts of food they

223 ÖStA, HHStA, PA I, Kt. 500, Liasse XLVII/2 b 20, Über die Lage 26. Jänner bis 24. Februar 1918. Östlicher Kriegsschauplatz; Dmytro Doroshenko, *Moï spomyny pro nedavnie-mynule* (Lviv, 1923), 57ff.; Pavlo Skoropads'kyi, *Spohady. Kinets' 1917–hruden' 1918* (Kyiv and Philadelphia, 1995), 110–16, 172ff.; Volodymyr Vynnychenko, *Vidrodzhennia natsiï (Istoriia ukraïns'koï revoliutsiï)*, vol. 2 (Vienna, 1920), 216–60.

224 ÖStA, HHStA, PA I, Kt. 500, Liasse XLVII/2 b 20, Über die Lage XI. 24.2 bis 22/III. 1918; Valerii Soldatenko, *Ukraïna v revoliutsiinu dobu. Istorychni ese-khroniky. Rik 1918*, vol. 2 (Kyiv, 2009), 112ff.; Skoropads'kyi, *Spohady*, 209.

found, especially meat, since they had had so little along the whole invasion route. There also appeared to be plenty of grain that the peasants had no motivation to sell. What kind of money would they get for it anyway?[225]

The very different goals pursued by the left-wing Rada and the command of the German and Austro-Hungarian troops would eventually have to give rise to conflict between these two actors in Ukrainian politics. It was the intention of the Rada, which had returned from Zhytomyr to Kyiv with the German troops, to continue its previous agrarian policies. The goal of the German and Austro-Hungarian troops, however, was to procure food in Ukraine as quickly as possible and transport it back to the homelands. It soon became very clear to the new military powers that the Rada lacked the capacity to carry out the undertakings it had made in the Brest-Litovsk peace treaty. In addition, the left-wing parties in the Rada were now engaging in confrontation with the German command over the latter's intervention in Ukraine's internal affairs. When the German commander, Field Marshal Hermann von Eichhorn, issued his "cultivation order" and introduced military courts[226] in Ukraine, some members of the Rada threatened to abrogate the Brest-Litovsk treaty. They began to see the policies of the Central Powers as those of an occupying power. The Ukrainian government, under Vsevolod Holubovych, did not dare to oppose Eichhorn, but the Rada continued to protest and called on the peasants to resist the orders of the occupying power. Ukrainian politicians also completely rejected the way in which the German and Austro-Hungarian troops were procuring food. They attempted to prohibit unauthorized requisitioning by the occupying power or to allow it only under supervision by Ukrainian officials.[227]

The Occupying Powers between the Fronts in the Struggle over Land

The invasion of Austro-Hungarian and German troops in Ukraine was a signal for the estate owners, who had had their lands expropriated, and for other entrepreneurs that there was at last going to be a change of government and that they could count on the return of their

225 Włodzimierz Mędrzecki, *Niemiecka interwencja militarna na Ukrainie w 1918 roku* (Warsaw, 2000), 137.

226 *Grazhdanskaia voina na Ukraine 1918–1920. Sbornik dokumentov i materialov v trekh tomakh, chetyrekh knigakh*, vol. 1, bk. 1 (Kyiv, 1967), 131.

227 Pavlo Khrystiuk, *Zamitky i materiialy do istoriï ukraïns'koï revoliutsiï 1917–1920 rr.*, vol. 2 (Vienna, 1921), 164.

illegally expropriated property. The estate owners and the average well-off peasants saw the troops as their "natural allies," for whom the inviolability of private property was an absolute principle.[228] Practically from the very first day of the occupation, the estate owners began to reclaim their lost property. Theirs was their initiative behind the formation of the "punitive units" that would force the peasants to return what they had stolen. The situation in the villages was thus more than tense.

The Ukrainian foreign minister, Dmytro Doroshenko, wrote that in the villages in 1917–18 a number of antagonisms had come to a head, especially between the social classes: "It was not just hostility between the peasants and the estate owners, incited by a variety of agitators from the spring of 1917; it was generally a struggle between the better off and the poorest. In the autumn, under the Central Rada, everything centered on the property of the large estate owners, which was burned, plundered, and destroyed. With the arrival of the Bolsheviks, this class hostility took the form of an equally drastic and destructive conflict between the various hostile categories of the peasant and Cossack masses."[229] Taking advantage of the temporary power vacuum in February–March 1918, according to Doroshenko, "the estate owners and the well-off peasants themselves began to reclaim their stolen property and, for this purpose, formed so-called punitive units that attracted the worst social scum, which used the most hideous methods of violence in their activity. The Polish landowners in Podilia and Volhynia set the example. They simply asked Austria-Hungary to occupy Right-Bank Ukraine, restore order, and force the peasants to compensate for the damage they had caused by either money or labor."[230]

The return of land to estate owners and the obligation forced on the peasantry to restore stolen property to its owners began under the Rada, at the same time as the requisitioning by Austro-Hungarian and German troops and the attacks of the "punitive expeditions." The new Hetman regime was supposed to limit this, if not stop it altogether, and bring it into some legal framework. The proclamation of Skoropadsky as hetman, however, was seen as an additional signal to the estate owners to activate their punitive units and have them act in even

---

228 Ibid., 156.

229 Doroshenko, *Moï spomyny pro nedavnie-mynule*, 51.

230 Ibid., 58.

more brutal fashion.[231] The estate owners, bypassing officials of the Hetmanate, often turned directly to the Austro-Hungarian or German units for assistance, which very soon not only created a negative image of the occupiers but also led to the view that the Ukrainian state was not really so independent. When the new Ukrainian regime attempted to bring an end to the anarchy and achieve a return to legality, it met with resistance not just from the rural proletariat, which did not want to lose what it had gained in the revolution, but also from the well-off peasants, who did not want to part with their harvested produce and food for a scant return in cash. The peasants raised their concerns, especially about the introduction of forced labor on the fields of the estate owners.

Following the coup of 29 April, Skoropadsky began an approach that differed fundamentally from what had gone before. He relied on previous tsarist officials and did not pay even formal attention to the national element in the state. Even more, he was a supporter of the "greater Ukrainian" concept of the Ukrainian nation, in which ethnicity played no role. He completely rejected Ukrainian national political ideas, which, in his view, were a "Galician" creation. He regarded the previous policies of Symon Petliura and Volodymyr Vynnychenko as "pro-Galician," in other words, as extreme socialism in danger of tipping over into Bolshevism.[232]

Skoropadsky held the view that the restoration of strong rule was necessary to fight chaos and anarchy, at least as strong as the Russian imperial power before the revolution. Consequently, the restoration of the inalienability of private property became a cornerstone of the new Hetmanate. He said, in his Manifesto to the Whole Ukrainian People: "The right to private property, as the foundation of culture and civilization, will be completely restored; all the laws of the previous Ukrainian government and the Russian Provisional Government are null and void.... In the area of finance and economy, completely free trade is restored, and greater scope will be given to enterprise and individual initiative...."[233] In the thinking of the Ukrainians, especially the peasantry, the arrival of the occupying troops and the Hetman's restrictive policies were inextricably linked together. The fact that previous representatives of the Central Rada were now

231 Ibid.

232 Skoropads'kyi, *Spohady*, 183.

233 *Derzhavnyi Vistnyk,* 16.5.1918, no. 1; *Konstytutsiini akty Ukraïny, 1917–1920. Nevidomi konstytutsiï Ukraïny* (Kyiv, 1992).

dispersed throughout the country and were agitating against the new state leadership contributed to the negative image of this policy. They proclaimed that the German occupation was the product of a "union of large estate owners" who "had elected the Hetman and called in the Germans to take the land away from the peasantry."[234] The Bolsheviks also contributed to the demoralization.

Having experienced the plundering of estates during the Bolshevik advance, as well as life under the Provisional Government and the Central Rada, the people returned gradually and not very willingly to peaceful conditions in which the law should now rule. The return, with help from the occupying troops, of orderly conditions and the restoration of property to the estate owners that now took place under the newly constructed administrative apparatus led to the Hetmanate being seen as a foreign power. Good and even friendly relations now existed between the Hetman and the German representatives in Kyiv. These people generally belonged to the same social class. The Germans were impressed by the Hetman's way of restoring order. The Austro-Hungarians, on the other hand, were not only far away, stationed in Odesa, but were regarded by the Hetman through a disagreeable Galician prism. He not only mistrusted the Galician Ukrainians but also had reservations about the presence of Austro-Hungarian troops in Ukraine. He perceived here the hidden danger of a "Uniate" expansion, as well as plans to bring all Ukrainian lands into a personal union with the Habsburg throne.[235] Skoropadsky was particularly annoyed by the activities of Archduke Wilhelm and his Ukrainian Legion.[236]

For Skoropadsky, the Galician and Russian Ukrainians were two different peoples from two different countries: "The whole culture, religion, and outlook of the inhabitants are completely different. The Galicians would like to convey to the Entente the image of an allegedly united Ukraine that is totally hostile to Russia and in which it is the Galicians themselves who play the major role. Our people will never agree to this. It is logical that the Galicians behave in this manner; they can only gain from it. That our socialist parties joined in this is also understandable. Neither I nor the government want this extreme socialism, certainly not our 'abysmal' Russian variety, which

234 Skoropads'kyi, *Spohady*, 209.

235 Ibid., 239.

236 See chapter 3b in the present volume.

very soon degenerates into raging Bolshevism."[237] He transferred his rejection of the Galician model of Ukrainianism almost automatically to the policy of the Austro-Hungarian occupiers. He thought that conditions were much better in the German occupation zone than in the Austro-Hungarian, where, in his view, plundering was almost legal and corruption widespread.[238]

The rigorous policies of the armies of the Central Powers as well as the Hetman's policy of restoring the land to the estate owners created opposition to the occupying powers among the Ukrainian peasantry.[239] The lack of understanding for the situation in the countryside and the misguided direction of agrarian policy alienated the peasantry from the idea of a Ukrainian national state and made the populist promises of the Bolsheviks even more attractive. Their promise to distribute the land of the large estates was far more attractive than the policy of expropriation. The Hetman's government refused to recognize that the land had now been handed over to the peasants who had little or no land, even though this had been done in a revolutionary, chaotic, and illegal manner. The only way out of this situation would have been an attempt to reach a compromise between the peasants and the large landowners, but such a compromise could not be achieved.[240]

Combating Insurrection in Early Summer after the Fall of the Central Rada

The peasants began to see the Hetman and the occupying power as the enemy, and war began in earnest. There were some uprisings, but the struggle frequently took the form of a "guerilla war." This partisan tactic emerged spontaneously and was partly successful. The peasants armed themselves, attacked Austro-Hungarian or German units or estates, then returned to their homes and hid their weapons until the next action. Meanwhile, local unrest reached such dimensions that one can describe it as a real uprising. The Ukrainian politician Serhii Shemet wrote to Skoropadsky on 17 May 1918: "The party has received information from southern areas of the Poltava gubernia that in many villages, members of peasant organizations who returned to their villages after the peasant congress in Kyiv was banned have decided to kill everyone who traveled to Kyiv to elect the Hetman. The uprising

---

237 Skoropads'kyi, *Spohady*, 184ff.

238 Ibid., 184.

239 Petro Zakharchenko, *Selians'ka viina v Ukraïni: rik 1918* (Kyiv, 1997), 68.

240 Soldatenko, *Ukraïna v revoliutsiinu dobu*, 237.

against the Hetman has already begun. They have begun to kill the landowners as well as their wives and children, burn their houses, and steal their grain. Around the villages of Buromka, Denysivka, and Khrestyteleve, in the districts of Lubny and Zolotonosha, conflict has been raging for four days between the insurgents and the *Haidamaky*. The insurgents are forcibly recruiting farmers. The agitation against the Hetman was a great success."[241]

Almost the entire top political leadership of the Ukrainian state spoke of the coarseness of German and Austro-Hungarian policy in Ukraine. Not only did they make no effort to win the people's sympathy, but they did everything to turn the people against them. Germany's top military and diplomatic personnel frequently remarked that the Ukrainians had little say, as it was the Germans who "had rescued them and now protect them."[242] The brutal behaviour of the occupation troops, the propaganda of the left-wing parties and the Bolsheviks, as well as the wrath of the punitive expeditions triggered a series of uprisings. Peasant attacks on units of the Central Powers led to greater repression, which in turn infuriated the peasantry even more. As Doroshenko describes it, it was a vicious circle: "Insurgent peasants attacked the Germans, the Germans retaliated, whereupon the peasants formed bands to avenge themselves, and so it went throughout the summer."[243] It was not only the Austro-Hungarian and German troops that began to feel the negative attitude of the Ukrainian peasantry that summer: "the Hetman regime began to sense the danger" as well.[244]

From mid-May, the wave of uprisings spread to Podilia. The first uprisings had already been provoked in March, when Polish landowners, with the help of Austro-Hungarian troops, began to reclaim their land and stolen property. The first mass explosion occurred on 8 March in the Yampil area, when a volunteer unit came to the village of Ihnativka to oversee the restoration of property to the previous owners. Before peace could be restored in the village, four people were killed. One officer was killed in a shootout during a village assembly. The remaining soldiers were disarmed by the peasants. The leader of the unit had his right hand cut off before being torn apart by

241 Quoted ibid., 240; *Dokumenty o razgrome germanskikh okkupantov na Ukraine v 1918 godu* (Moscow, 1942), 142ff.

242 Doroshenko, *Moï spomyny pro nedavnie-mynule*, 7.

243 Ibid., 59.

244 Mykhailo Omelianovych-Pavlenko, *Spomyny* (Lviv, 1930), 47.

the crowd, which then killed the rest of the attackers. This incident led the peasants to organize their own self-defense. The insurgents then occupied a large part of the area to control entry to their villages and attack neighboring estates and even smaller towns. In mid-May the Austro-Hungarian troops moved in and put down the uprising.[245]

The occupying troops frequently used artillery against insurgent peasants, thus destroying whole localities. Once the insurgency had ended, the activists would be arrested, and significant amounts of money then had to be paid. These uprisings took place in the Poltava, Kyiv, Kharkiv, Volhynia, and Podilia gubernias. The peasant uprising that took place in Kanizh and its surrounding area in May 1918 is particularly well known. It involved more than 700 insurgents and lasted for some time. When the insurgency was finally suppressed by Austro-Hungarian troops, 117 people were either shot or hanged.[246]

Ukrainian village heads in the various districts of the Podilia gubernia repeatedly informed their superiors of encounters between armed peasants and Austro-Hungarian units. The head of the militia in the district of Kremianets, Voloshyn, reported on peasant resistance in the villages of Tsvyklivtsi, Ruda, and Havrylivtsi to Habsburg troops who wanted to arrest the members of the local land committees. After these had got away in time, the Austro-Hungarian troops took four hostages.[247] This practice of hostage taking was widely used by the Habsburg army as a means of putting pressure on the local population.

The commanders of the occupying troops understood very well that the only way to resolve the insurgency problem was to disarm the peasants. Most conflicts broke out in the villages when an army unit attempted to do this. This kind of conflict arose in almost every district. On 18 May 1918 the interior minister, Fedir Lyzohub, declared that everything movable that had been stolen from the estate owners had to be returned. This was to apply not only to what the peasants themselves had expropriated but also to everything that

245 Zakharchenko, *Selians'ka viina v Ukraïni*, 49.

246 Vladyslav Verstiuk, Olena Dziuba, and Volodymyr Repryntsev, *Ukraïna vid naidavnishykh chasiv do s'ohodennia. Khronolohichnyi dovidnyk* (Kyiv, 1995), 273; *Ukraïns'ka RSR v period hromadians'koï viiny. 1917–1920 rr.*, vol. 1 (Kyiv, 1967), 413–14. Austrian sources speak of 62 insurgents killed: ÖStA, KA, FA, NFA, HHK AK/AGKdo, 2. Armee, OpAK, Kt. 308, 1918 Situations- und Tagesmeldungen, Nr. 4493/8, Abendmeldung v. 20.5.1918; ibid., Nr. 4525/8, Abendmeldung v. 21.5.1918; ibid., Nr. 5772/8, Abendmeldung v. 18.6.1918; ÖStA, KA, AdT, 145. IBrig, Kt. 1378, Nr. 1093, Verlautbarung von Vorfällen gegen die k.u.k. Truppen, 21. Mai. See also chapter 3a in the present volume.

247 "Telehrama nachal'nyka militsiï Kremenets'koho povitu Voloshyna vid 10.5.1918" in *Grazhdanskaia voina na Ukraine 1918–1920*, 140.

had been handed over to the peasants for temporary use according to decisions of the land committees. This order further stated that, if these enforced restitutions were not carried out, the police or, in extreme cases, the military would intervene, and those guilty would be punished according to law. All previous activities of these land committees would be examined, and the results would be handed over to officers of the law. Destruction of seed or woodlands would be severely punished.[248]

As a rule, attempts by the occupying troops to disarm the peasants in this or that village met with determined resistance. The response of the peasants to demands to hand over their weapons voluntarily was to fire those weapons. In May 1918, the typical outcome in all such instances was suppression of the resistance by means of artillery, the burning of houses, or the taking of hostages. The peasants, nonetheless, did not hand over their weapons, which meant that the hostages were brought before military courts.[249]

Austro-Hungarian and German soldiers frequently requisitioned food and cattle without paying for them or offered fixed prices that had been arranged with the Ukrainian authorities but offered little value to the peasants because of inflation. The district and village heads reported such instances, emphasizing that the troops had been adequately provided with food and fodder.[250] Such robbery and the burning of houses that accompanied it were frequently justified by the claim that the peasant family had refused to say where all the family members or their remaining supplies were.[251] Although this was not always possible in wartime conditions, it was seen as disloyalty. Hostility to the Austrians was aroused especially by the methods used to pacify the villages: use of the rod, threats, arrests, and forced requisitioning of grain, cattle, and horses.

As time passed, the nature of the armed conflicts between the peasants and the military changed. The peasants no longer just resisted attempts to take their property or weapons: they formed armed groups and carried out attacks on German and Austro-Hungarian units. The

---

248 "Rozporiadzhennia ministra vnutrishnikh sprav pro povernennia pomishchykam ïkh vlasnosti vid 18.5.1918," ibid., 154.

249 "Postanova Lubens'koho povitovoho starosty pro peredachu voienno-pol'ovomu sudu uchasnykiv protynimets'koho povstannia v selakh Denysivka i Zolotukha vid 18.5.1918," ibid., 154–55.

250 "Informatsiia holovy Bilhorods'koï hromads'koï upravy Iakovenka kyïvs'komu povitovomu komisaru pro hrabezhi z boku nimets'kykh soldat vid 18.5.1918," ibid., 156.

251 "Protokol nachal'nyka militsiï 6-ho viddilu Odes'koho povitu pro spalennia avstriis'kymy soldatamy khaty selianyna Kravchuka s. Avdotivka Kovalevs'koï volosti vid 16.5.1918," ibid., 149.

initiative to form such groups came mostly from demobilized soldiers of the old tsarist army or from Bolshevik agitators. In May 1918, in the village of Kachkivka in the Yampil district of the Podilia gubernia, the onetime commander of the Winter Palace in Petrograd, Mykola Kryvoruchko, gathered together three hundred peasants, armed them, and set off. The insurgents even had sixteen cannons in their arsenal. Led by Kryvoruchko and convinced that they would pick up at least another forty thousand peasants on the way, they advanced on the town of Yampil. Capturing the town, they added 26 machine guns to their armory.[252] When attacked by Austro-Hungarian troops, they withdrew to the surrounding forest and regrouped. This cat-and-mouse game lasted into the summer.[253]

The most common forms of protest were refusal to hand over weapons or pay taxes, illegal deforestation, and the sowing of grain in fields where sugar beet was to be grown. They also resisted Bolshevik agitation.[254] Faced with the danger that a village might be destroyed, the peasants could turn against the insurgent activists. On 18 May 1918, in the district of Yampil, some peasants under the leadership of Kryvoruchko captured Austrian carts with bread but, on the very next day, Austro-Hungarian troops took the village of Kachkivka. One Austro-Hungarian soldier and thirty-five peasants were killed. The troops also burned about two hundred homes. Some of the insurgents managed to capture an Austro-Hungarian cannon and opened fire on the village. The frightened peasants of Pysarivka, fearing that their village would also be burned, captured the insurgents and handed them over to the Austrians and Hungarians.[255]

At the end of May, there was an increase in the incidence of sabotage in the villages. The command of the *Ostarmee* set out a detailed set of measures to combat this. According to order no. 4344 of 14 May 1918, cattle put to pasture in grain fields were to become the property of the Austro-Hungarian army. If those guilty of sabotage could not be investigated and shot on the spot, then suspects were to

252 "Materialy administratyvnoho viddilu viis'kovoho ministerstva za 21 travnia pro povstannia selian v Podil's'kii huberniï," ibid., 158.

253 According to Soviet sources, troops of the Hetman and the Central Powers burned the villages but, in the months that followed, did not dare to leave the main roads, which was why the battles lasted so long. See "Donesennia vchytelia Smilians'koï himnaziï het'mans'komu Ministerstvu vnutrishnikh sprav pro povstans'kyi rukh v Zvenyhorods'komu poviti Kyïvs'koï huberniï vid 20.6.1918," ibid., 190ff.

254 Ibid.

255 "Informatsiia Iampil's'koho povitovoho starosty Han'ka pro povstannia v poviti," ibid., 157.

be arrested and held until they could be tried by a military court. If, in cases of poisoning or the destruction of sowings, no suspects could be identified, the peasants would be fined 36.6 kg of grain per hectare of arable fields damaged. The carts in which the requisitioned grain was delivered would also be confiscated.[256] Anyone who destroyed sowings could be executed on the spot or sentenced to ten years' imprisonment and a fine of 10,000 rubles. If no guilty individuals could be found, the whole district would be fined.[257]

In June 1918, peasant resistance began to take on the form of full-scale uprisings. Peasants in the districts of Zvenyhorodka and Tarashcha rebelled not just against the occupying troops but also against the Hetman regime. By 10 June there were uprisings in fourteen villages in the Tarashcha district alone. There were nearly four thousand insurgents, all of whom were armed, and they even had machine guns.[258] Insurgent peasants from the village of Stryzhavka took four junior officers from Captain Ivzhenko's unit and shot them. On 9 June Burkov's punitive unit, with thirty Germans, entered Stryzhavka. The insurgents were dispersed by artillery. But on 10 June the crowd disarmed and arrested the heads of militia in Piatyhory and Zhashkiv, Voitsekhovsky and Pozharnytsky. A German unit supported by Ivzhenko's men captured the insurgents near the village of Stavyshcha. After the battle, the village of Yanyshivka was burned. On 12 June, the Germans and the Hetman's units had to withdraw from Tarashcha and retreat toward Bila Tserkva. Not only the representatives of the Hetmanate but also most of their intelligence agents withdrew with the Germans. The insurgents then dealt with twenty-seven officers in a number of villages and plundered the sugar factory in Luka.[259]

June was one of the "hottest" months in Ukraine. Uprisings and attacks on occupying troops spread in the areas around Kyiv, Chernihiv, Kherson, and in the Donbas. In many regions, these formations had a large number of fighters, sometimes led by career officers, at other times, as in the case of Nestor Makhno, under the black flag of anarchism. In the Zvenyhorodka region, "Free Cossacks"

256 "Nakaz 12-ro avstro-uhors'koho korpusu pro pokarannia za otruiennia abo pidpaly posiviv na pomishchyts'kykh zemliakh," ibid., 159.

257 "Informatsiia pro pokarannia za znyshchennia vrozhaia u Smilians'komu poviti Kyïvs'koï huberniï," ibid., 174.

258 "Povidomlennia het'mans'koho henshtabu pro povstannia v Tarashchans'komu poviti vid 11.6.1918," ibid., 175.

259 "Donesennia Tarashchans'koho povitovoho starosty Dubinenka vid 14.6.1918," ibid., 178.

arose under the command of Yurii Tiutiunnyk. An uprising led by Levko Shevchenko was ruthlessly suppressed. In August 1918, Matvii Hryhoriiv formed a group of insurgents in the village of Verbliudka in the Kherson gubernia. It had 175 peasants armed with Austro-Hungarian guns, hay forks, and axes. They began with attacks on the Hetman's guards, on Austro-Hungarian troops, and frequently also on estate owners. The Hetman sent a unit of 350 men armed with a number of machine guns to fight the partisans. But Hryhoriiv's men defeated the Hetman's unit in spite of being outnumbered. Later, in October 1918, they captured an Austro-Hungarian military train. Eventually, Otaman Hryhoriiv's partisan army numbered about six thousand armed insurgents.[260]

In almost all instances, the cause of insurgency was the same: accompanied by German or Austro-Hungarian troops, a landowner would appear in the village to reclaim his property. As a rule, these actions, in which goods taken from the landowner were restored to him by force, were very brutal. The suspects included not only the peasants on whose property the stolen goods were found but also the activists of the local self-government. The soldiers were not satisfied just to burn the houses of those suspected of criminal activity; they usually executed them.[261] The landowners "offended" by the previous socialist regime wanted to reclaim their lost property, but also to take revenge on their "offenders" and teach them a lesson.[262] The Hetman himself stated in his memoirs that there were by no means few instances in which landowners reclaimed more than they had lost as a way of improving their material situation.[263] The participation of units of occupying troops in these punitive actions, especially when there were executions of local people, created an extremely negative image of the occupying powers. Misunderstandings were added to this, as none of the German troops spoke Ukrainian. Without knowing the language, it was difficult for the German officers to get an accurate picture of the situation, with the result that they almost always sided with the landowners.

To fight the insurgents more effectively, the occupying army declared martial law, forbidding assemblies, demonstrations, and

---

260 V. Horak, "Makhno, Hryhor'iev, Tiutiunnyk. Dolia tr'okh otamaniv," *Voienna istoriia*, 2006, nos. 4-6, http://www.warhistory-ukrlife.ru/4_6_06_3.htm, 21.3.2011.

261 Mędrzecki, *Niemiecka interwencja militarna na Ukrainie w 1918 roku*, 221.

262 Soldatenko, *Ukraïna v revoliutsiinu dobu*, 239.

263 Skoropads'kyi, *Spohady*, 184.

even meetings in private dwellings. In some districts, the soldiers of the Central Powers, supported by the Hetman's forces, succeeded in driving out the rebels. But the latter only withdrew to the forests, from where they were able to attack neighboring locations. The insurgents killed not only numerous landowners but also official representatives of the Hetman regime and intelligence agents.[264] In order to frighten the local inhabitants and prevent them from joining the insurgency, the military executed by hanging, frequently in the village center. The gallows, with bodies hanging from them, remained standing for days.[265]

Not every Austro-Hungarian soldier shared the same attitude to these punitive operations. Quite a few village heads from the Katerynoslav gubernia requested that ethnic German and Hungarian units not take part in these actions. Units made up of Austrian Galicians were more passive, out of solidarity with the local population. Hungarian units, on the other hand, which carried out actions in the district of Verkhniodniprovsk, acted with extraordinary brutality. In the village of Volodymyrivka, on 17 June 1918, 16 persons suspected of subversive activity on behalf of the Bolsheviks were handed over to a Hungarian unit. The military court sentenced all of them to execution and burned their homes. On 19 June, this unit shot fourteen people in Huliaipole. Other forms of punishment were frequently used to punish lack of loyalty to the Hetman. Lesser offences were punished with public whipping or caning.[266]

Winning Hearts and Minds with Vasyl Vyshyvany and the Austro-Hungarian Ukrainian Legion?

Unlike Skoropadsky, the Austrian Archduke Wilhelm, referred to in Ukraine as Vasyl Vyshyvany, had a romantic enthusiasm for the "people" (*Volk*), which he greatly idealized. This idealization matched his ideas of a "glorious" past and Cossack freedom. Unlike the military commanders and diplomats, he did not think that the main reason for Austria-Hungary's presence in Ukraine was "mainly because of grain and to prevent Germany from getting a foothold."[267] From the

264 *Golos Iuga*, no. 12, 4 July 1918; cf. ibid., 207.

265 Ibid.

266 For instance, the telephone operator P. Smilianenko was beaten with a stick when she was suspected of giving information to the Bolsheviks: "Donesennia Katerynoslavs'koho huberns'koho starosty heneral-maiora Chernykova departamentu Derzhavnoï varty pro diï avstro-uhors'kykh viis'kovykh vid 29.6.1918"; cf. ibid., 198ff.

267 TsDIA Lviv, fond 309, op. 1, spr. 1198, Memoiren Wilhelms von Habsburg, Oberst der USS.

beginning, he saw Austria-Hungary as having a twofold mission in Ukraine: the defense of Austro-Hungarian positions in competition with the Germans and the promotion of Ukrainian national ideas. Sooner or later, this would bring him into conflict with Skoropadsky and with the German command. He considered his most urgent tasks to be the Ukrainization of Zaporizhia[268] and the struggle against the Hetman's policy of Russification.[269] As commander of the Austro-Hungarian Ukrainian Legion stationed near Oleksandrivsk (present-day Zaporizhia), he wanted to get close to the local Ukrainian population.

Some political milieus in Ukraine also contributed to the growing dissatisfaction in Kyiv, Berlin, and Vienna with the pro-Ukrainian policies of the archduke. In May 1918, some socialist organizations in Odesa launched an initiative to prepare an uprising against Skoropadsky's government and a handover of power to Archduke Wilhelm. But this project of the Odesa socialists found no support at meetings of the central committees of the Ukrainian Social Democrats and Socialist Revolutionaries, Odesa socialists, or officers of the Kyiv Sich Riflemen.[270] Colonel Petro Bolbochan launched another initiative to proclaim Archduke Wilhelm hetman of all Ukraine. According to his calculations, this would be a counterweight to German and Austro-Hungarian influence in Ukraine, remove the "Russian-German" regime of Hetman Skoropadsky, bring about a unification of Galicia with Ukraine and, in general, weaken the influence of the Central Powers.[271] Thus it was not just the Ukrainian socialists who associated Skoropadsky with a course that was too pro-German and pro-Russian. Some conservative circles also wanted an end to the Hetman regime and saw the alternative in a so-called "Habsburg solution."

The methods employed by both occupying powers to procure food were generally nothing other than expropriation and repression. Archduke Wilhelm gave his description of the situation: "With the permission of the Hetman, German units are going all over Ukraine and using force to restore the property of the *pany*.[272] From now on,

268 Southeastern Ukraine, once home to the Zaporozhian Sich.

269 TsDIA Lviv, fond 358, op. 3, spr. 166, 21ff., Brief von Wilhelm von Habsburg an den Metropoliten Andrei Sheptytsky aus Oleksandrivsk vom 24.5.1918.

270 Iurii Tereshchenko and Tetiana Ostashko, *Ukraïns'kyi patriot z dynastiï Habsburgiv: naukovo-dokumental'ne vydannia* (Kyiv, 2008), 36.

271 Ibid., 37.

272 In the Slavic languages, *pan* (pl. *pany*) is a term for "landlord," "employer," or "head of a family" (Eds.).

what the muzhiks[273] have tilled and sown will belong to the *pany*. Of course, the muzhiks are rebelling. Accounts are settled in blood. The muzhiks are being hung and shot, and villages are being burned. And of course it sometimes happens that the peasants slaughter German units. In one village, for instance, they killed four thousand Germans.[274] Then comes a punitive expedition. Blood flows again, men are hanged, and everything disintegrates. Whole areas are destroyed...."[275]

Archduke Wilhelm's Ukrainian Legion easily found a common language with the peasants, as its commanders spoke Ukrainian well. In 1918, the peasants considered their private property more important than nationality or religion.[276] Wilhelm von Habsburg was aware of this and was more considerate in dealing with individual incidents, as shown by an account he gave in Baden in August 1918:[277] "We came to the village. The members of my legion went around and talked to the peasants. Peace and order came to the village. They greeted us with bread and salt and took care of us. And wherever the legion went in Ukraine, that is how it was. What was needed was tact, nothing but tact and understanding of the soul of the Ukrainian peasants, which was how my riflemen behaved. They came through agitated and 'rebellious' districts, and immediately everyone calmed down. They even thanked us for coming by and gave us food, for which they did not want money."

The peasants were extremely surprised to meet soldiers and even officers of a foreign army who spoke Ukrainian. But what surprised people most was the strength of their convictions and their national consciousness. When the Austro-Hungarians captured Kherson, Oleksandrivsk, and Nykopil, soldiers of the Ukrainian Legion were stationed in those cities and, in permanent contact with the local population, propagated Ukrainian national ideas.[278] The legionnaires organized a national theatre with daily shows in Ukrainian and held concerts in the city parks, where the Ukrainian intelligentsia used to meet. Wilhelm supported the establishment of a Ukrainian

---

273 Russian term for "serf" (Eds.).

274 This figure is highly doubtful, as there is no information about such a large massacre. This may have to do with an attack on German colonists. (Eds.).

275 Ia. Okunevs'kyi, "Rozmova z arkhykniazem Vil'hel'mom dnia 4. serpnia 1918 roku," *Dilo*, no. 100, 8 May 1931.

276 Timothy Snyder, *Czerwony książę* (Warsaw, 2010), 115.

277 Okunevs'kyi, "Rozmova z arkhykniazem Vil'hel'mom."

278 Vasyl' Vyshyvanyi, "Ukraïns'ki Sichovi Stril'tsi z vesny 1918 r. do povorotu v Avstriï," *Dilo*, no. 243, 1 November 1938, 2ff.

newspaper, *Sich*, in which two Galician riflemen were active, Myron Zaklynsky and Kmet.[279]

The commander of the Ukrainian Legion was taking a risky step in supporting the establishment of schools and educational institutions. On his own initiative, he appointed soldiers to carry out this task in a number of districts. Two of his officers, Mykola Saievych and Dmytro Vitovsky, were given this task in Podilia and Kherson. The Ukrainian intelligentsia was impressed by these educational initiatives. They hoped that this cultural life of the Ukrainian population in southern Ukraine would be seen as a model and would attract other areas. Sofiia Tobilevych, the widow of the well-known Ukrainian dramatist Ivan Karpenko-Kary, wrote: "Led by officers and supported by experts in their fields—actors, singers, musicians—they introduced lectures for children and adults, organized films, concerts, theater productions, and festivals. This was a great cooperative cultural achievement that attracted the whole area."[280]

Throughout this period, Archduke Wilhelm managed not only to place his soldiers at the service of "Ukrainian national life" but also to ignore the commands of the Austro-Hungarian *Ostarmee*, which was insisting on more intensive counterinsurgency. Among the rural population, Wilhelm gained the reputation of a "red prince," but he was seen by the Austro-Hungarian High Command as a politically unreliable officer. The Hetman administration attempted, as quickly as possible, to wipe out any traces of this "Ukrainization" by the Ukrainian Legion.[281]

The Hetman administration also made sure that General Oleksandr Natiiv's Ukrainian division was transferred from Oleksandrivsk to Melitopil. This was to prevent any solidarity between the Ukrainian Legion and the Ukrainian Cossacks. During the short period in which both were stationed in the same city, they had grown very close. Together they had visited Khortytsia, Velykyi Luh, and other places important in the history of the Zaporozhian Cossacks. It was the view

279 Vasyl' Vyshyvanyi, "Ukraïns'ki Sichovi Stril'tsi z vesny 1918 r. do povorotu v Avstriï," *Dilo*, no. 244, 3 November 1938, 2ff.

280 Quoted in Tereshchenko and Ostashko, *Ukraïns'kyi patriot z dynastiï Habsburgiv,* 40.

281 In doing so, they did not refrain from petty measures, the sense of which is difficult to explain. When the Ukrainian Legion moved to Katerynoslav, the newspaper *Sich* in Oleksandrivsk was closed and the two Galicians arrested. It was only when their commander wrote a personal letter that they were released. A Russian newspaper then replaced the Ukrainian one. See Vasyl' Vyshyvanyi, "Ukraïns'ki Sichovi Stril'tsi z vesny 1918 r. do povorotu v Avstrii," *Dilo*, no. 245, 4 November 1938, 2ff.

of the *Ostarmee* command that such "fraternizing" was detrimental from the viewpoint of internal Austro-Hungarian relations and from that of Hetman Skoropadsky's authority.[282]

In spite of his aristocratic origins, Archduke Wilhelm was largely in agreement with the ideas of the left-wing Ukrainian parties on agrarian reform. It was his view that neither Field Marshal Eichhorn nor Skoropadsky would approve a moderate agrarian policy because they were themselves sympathetic to the estate owners. He did not support the return of the estate owners to their estates and opposed the executions of Ukrainian peasants. He was especially proud that "the Riflemen never hanged anyone, always did good, and were liked by everyone."[283] Of course, the activity of the Ukrainian Legion in southern Ukraine was just a small episode in the larger history of occupation policy. It can only serve as an indication of the variants and alternatives that existed to the policy of violent expropriation and punitive actions.

Conclusion

Although the Austro-Hungarian and German troops operated in Ukraine quite freely and without supervision, a certain formal distance had to be maintained in their relations with Ukrainian officials. The Ukrainian foreign ministry gathered and analyzed information about irregularities on the part of the soldiers of the Central Powers. These were then handed over to the diplomatic representatives of both states for further examination and decision. Dmytro Doroshenko recalled Austro-Hungarian occupation policy in Ukraine: "The Austrians put down the unrest in the villages in 1918 with great cruelty. On the pretext of 'fighting Bolshevism,' activists in the Ukrainian movement were arrested (for instance, in the Katerynoslav region) and dragged from one prison to another. Even when Kyiv heard about it, the foreign minister did not always succeed in getting the prisoners out of the clutches of the Austrian administration. The one glimmer of light in this Austrian occupation is the fact that there were compatriots of ours from Galicia and Bukovyna serving in the Habsburg army, sometimes in units of their own, as was the case with the Ukrainian Legion in Kherson and Katerynoslav. These compatriots were not numerous and served mostly in subordinate positions. But they did at least achieve

282 Tereshchenko and Ostashko, *Ukraïns'kyi patriot z dynastiï Habsburgiv,* 34ff.

283 Vasyl' Vyshyvanyi, "Ukraïns'ki Sichovi Stril'tsi z vesny 1918 r. do povorotu v Avstriï," *Dilo*, no. 246, 5 November 1938, 2ff.

something in compensation, for a time, for the negative consequences of the presence of the Austro-Hungarian army in Ukraine."[284]

Skoropadsky, too, expressed himself on the negative aspect of the presence of Austro-Hungarian troops. It was his view that theft was almost the norm in the Austro-Hungarian zone and that corruption and deceit had grown to an unprecedented extent.[285] Stepan Shukhevych remarked in his memoirs that among the staff of the troops behind the lines in Austria-Hungary there was a list of "profitable" posts for officers. One of the most attractive destinations was Ukraine: "Postings to Ukraine were the best, to the Albanian or Italian front the worst. Ukraine, because there one could steal, rob, order searches, in short, make a fortune."[286] Shukhevych was later appointed commander of military police in Odesa. He described Odesa as a good opportunity for Austro-Hungarian soldiers to enrich themselves because of the widespread corruption there: "You could really make quite a fortune. Rich, very rich merchants offered me beautiful and expensive gifts, but I refused them and left Odesa as poor as I was when I arrived there.... People I knew advised me repeatedly to take advantage of the opportunity and help myself, but I did not do it. I believed that there had to be one Ukrainian city ruled by law and order."[287] Shukhevych maintained that the military governor of Odesa, Eduard von Böltz, committed suicide at the end of the occupation because he feared that his financial misdemeanors would be discovered. He also maintained that the entire Austro-Hungarian civil staff in Odesa was involved in such activities.[288] From an economic point of view, Odesa was exceptionally attractive because the merchant fleet was stationed there.[289]

All in all, the presence of the Austro-Hungarian and German troops in Ukraine was characterized not only by an effort to support the establishment of a state administration and defend the country against Bolshevik Russia but also, in equal measure, by mass repressive measures against the Ukrainian peasantry.

---

284 Doroshenko, *Moï spomyny pro nedavnie-mynule*, 19–20.

285 Skoropads'kyi, *Spohady*, 184.

286 Stepan Shukhevych, *Moie zhyttia. Spohady* (London, 1991), 253.

287 Ibid., 255.

288 He claimed that the chief of the General Staff, Major Hemel, left Odesa with a fortune of 18 million *karbovantsi* and that the head of the political department, Police Councillor Harvasii, left with a similar amount (ibid., 256).

289 Skoropads'kyi, *Spohady*, 195.

4a. Russia's Ukrainian Policy before 1917

Alexei Miller

An important milestone in East European history was the Cossack uprising of 1648 led by Bohdan Khmelnytsky. The subsequent union between the Cossack Hetmanate and the Muscovite Tsarist Empire changed the relation of forces between Moscow and the Polish-Lithuanian Commonwealth and laid the foundation for a gradual westward expansion of the Russian Empire. In the course of the eighteenth and early nineteenth centuries, the Hetmanate and Sloboda Ukraine, which gradually acquired the name "Little Russia," were incorporated ever more closely into the Russian Empire. The administrative autonomy of the Hetmanate was continuously restricted and, under Catherine the Great, formally abolished. The last traces of this autonomy (the Little Russian Collegium) disappeared in the early decades of the nineteenth century.

The religious elite of the Hetmanate became prominent in the hierarchy of the Russian Orthodox Church already in the eighteenth century. The Cossack *starshyna* (officer caste) not only became a regional elite within the empire but was gradually incorporated into the Russian nobility. Its noble status was secured at the end of the eighteenth century and the beginning of the nineteenth, which is probably why its members offered no resistance to the abolition of regional autonomy.[1]

Representatives of the Kyivan clergy (Teofan Prokopovych/ Feofan Prokopovich) played a large role in the transformation of the Muscovite Tsardom into the Russian Empire, as well as in shaping Russian historical myth and a Russian image of national territory (Inokentii Gizel, author of the *Synopsis*).[2] Imperial policy turned the Cossack *starshyna* into part of the imperial nobility. With the opening of universities in Kharkiv (Kharkov) (1804) and Kyiv (Kiev) (1834), conditions were created at the beginning of the nineteenth century

---

1 Zenon E. Kohut, *Russian Centralism and Ukrainian Autonomy: Imperial Absorption of the Hetmanate, 1760s–1830s* (Cambridge, Mass., 1988); Zenon E. Kohut, "The Ukrainian Elite in the Eighteenth Century and Its Integration into the Russian Nobility," in *The Nobility in Russia and Eastern Europe,* ed. Ivo Banac and Paul Bushkovitch (New Haven, Conn., 1983), 65–97; *Zapadnye okrainy Rossiiskoi imperii*, ed. Mikhail Dolbilov and Alexei Miller (Moscow, 2006).

2 David Saunders, *The Ukrainian Impact on Russian Culture, 1750–1850* (Edmonton, 1985).

for the emergence of a local intelligentsia in whose ranks Ukrainian national ideas would ripen. The partition of Poland at the end of the eighteenth century eliminated the Dnipro (Dnieper) border, the existence of which for more than a century and a half had left deep marks on the development of the Ukrainian lands.[3] The subsequent movements of population, especially into New Russia,[4] annexed at the end of the eighteenth century, created in many respects the conditions for the emergence of our present-day conception of Ukrainian national territory.

Following the Polish uprising of 1830–31, the Southwestern Province became a theater of conflict between the Russian Empire and the Polish nobility (*szlachta*), each attempting to influence the process of identity formation of the numerically dominant Little Russian/ Ukrainian population. The Russian historical narrative had already, in the 1820s and 1830s, formulated the conception that they were part of the "Russian" population. The thesis that the Little Russians and Great Russians together belonged to the Russian nation was the ideological foundation of the policy that aimed to undermine Polish cultural influence in these lands.

In the 1840s and into the 1860s, the traditional Little Russian patriotism of the traditional elite was gradually giving way to the ideas of modern Ukrainian nationalism. The first instance of this was the narrow circle of the secret Brotherhood of SS. Cyril and Methodius, discovered by the authorities in 1847. It was followed in the 1860s by the milieu of the Kyiv Hromada (Community) and the editors of the St. Petersburg *Osnova* (Foundation, 1861–62). Most Russian officials and members of the Russian public perceived emerging Ukrainian nationalism as a threat not only to the territorial integrity of the empire but also to the construction of a Russian nation.[5] This occurred against the background of the Polish uprising of 1863–64 and the abolition of serfdom in 1861, all of which added a social dimension to

---

3 From an administrative viewpoint, the border remained in place throughout the nineteenth century. The territories on the Right Bank constituted the Kyiv gubernia, while in the mid-nineteenth century a form of administration was established on the Left Bank that was characteristic of the Great Russian gubernias. For a long time, there were no *zemstvo* administrations on the Right Bank. They were first introduced in 1911. To a large extent, this had to do with the dominant status of Polish estate owners, something entirely lacking on the Left Bank.

4 This included the territories north of the Black Sea, which, up to that point, had belonged to the Ottoman Empire and fell to Russia after the Russo-Ottoman war of 1768–74.

5 Cf. P. A. Zaionchkovskii, *Kirillo-Mefodievskoe obshchestvo (1846–1847)* (Moscow, 1959); Alexei Miller, *The Ukrainian Question: The Russian Empire and Nationalism in the Nineteenth Century* (New York and Budapest, 2003).

the problem. In 1847–48, the Russian government considered general restrictions unnecessary and limited itself to exiling the few members of the Brotherhood. It was only in the late 1850s and early 1860s that such measures began to be enforced. In 1859, as a defense against Polish influence, the use of the Latin alphabet ("Polish letters") was forbidden for the Russian language, including the "Little Russian and White Russian dialects." This decree also reflected a growing concern about the possible influence of Vienna on the Little Russians. The argument for the ban was that Vienna had attempted to introduce the Latin alphabet among the Galician Ruthenians.[6] In July 1863, half a year after the beginning of the Polish uprising, the minister of internal affairs, Petr Valuev, issued a circular forbidding the publication of books for the common people in the Ukrainian language, especially primary school books and Holy Scripture.[7] The officials thus opened the door to the use of administrative methods as a way of combating the emancipation of the Ukrainian language, in other words, to a policy of assimilation by means of prohibiting the Ukrainian language in education. In the short term, these measures were very effective. Support for the Ukrainian movement declined until the 1870s.

When the governor of the Kyiv gubernia from 1873 to 1875, Aleksandr M. Dondukov-Korsakov, found himself confronted by a new wave of the Ukrainian movement, he attempted to "tame" it rather than repress it. He offered Ukrainian activists certain possibilities for legal activity in the Russian Imperial Geographical Society and in the newspaper *Kievskii telegraf* (Kyiv Telegraph). This policy was initiated without the support of St. Petersburg, which made it possible for opponents of the Ukrainian activists in Kyiv, who thought of themselves as Little Russians, to persuade the bureaucracy in St. Petersburg in 1875 of the need to intervene. A commission was established to deal with the Ukrainian question. After complex internal wrangling in the upper levels of the tsarist bureaucracy, the so-called Ukase of Ems was issued, a series of instructions to different officials, signed by the tsar, on combating the Ukrainian movement.[8] Among other measures, the prohibition of Ukrainian books issued in 1863 was strengthened and extended to the theater. As in 1863, there was no unanimity among the

6 For a detailed discussion, see Alexei Miller, *The Romanov Empire and Nationalism: Essays in the Methodology of Historical Research* (New York and Budapest, 2008), 67–92.

7 For the text of the instruction, see A. E. Miller, *Ukrainskii vopros v politike vlastei i russkom obshchestvennom mnenii* (St. Petersburg, 2000).

8 On the text of the ukase, see Miller, *Ukrainskii vopros v politike vlastei.*

top levels of the bureaucracy about the adequacy of these measures. The opponents of the Ukrainian movement among the Little Russians in Kyiv once again played an important role.[9] In 1880 the governor of the Kyiv gubernia, Mikhail Chertkov, the governor of the Kharkiv gubernia, Dondukov-Korsakov, and Senator Aleksandr A. Polovtsov attempted to fundamentally moderate aspects of the Ukase of Ems, since it had proved to be counterproductive. Unlike in 1863, there was no decline in the activities of the Ukrainian movement. Instead, it had spread into Galicia, which was ruled by the Habsburgs. In the early 1880s, the Austro-Hungarian authorities and the Polish elite in Galicia had taken repressive action against the Russophile elements and started to promote pro-Ukrainian sentiment among the Ruthenian population of Eastern Galicia. The assassination of Alexander II put an end to attempts to revise the Ukase of Ems. The new commission on the Ukrainian question, which was supposed to draft a new policy, now met in completely different circumstances, under a new leadership, and made very few slightly moderating changes to the harshest prohibitions of 1876.

In the 1860s and 1870s, Russian discourse on the Ukrainian problem was consolidated. In this discourse, "Ukrainophilism" or "Little Russian separatism" stood for Ukrainian nationalism. In the 1870s, officials persisted in speaking of a Little Russian "dialect," foiling any plans for the creation of a Ukrainian "literary language" that could have replaced Russian as the language of education and high culture. Officials also continued to refer to "Little Russians," seen as a branch of the Russian nation, and considered "Ukrainian" an invention of anti-Russian forces. The unity of Little Russia, White Russia, and Great Russia was seen as the backbone of imperial strength and unity, analogous to the consolidation of the British, French, and German nations within their respective empires. This nationalist discourse was shared and actively promoted by those who saw themselves as Little Russians. The front line in the bitter struggle over the concepts "Little Russian/Ukrainian," "Little Russia/Ukraine," and "language/dialect" ran not between Great Russians and Ukrainians but between Great Russians and Little Russians on the one side and Ukrainians on the other. This struggle reflected the conflict between the different identity strategies chosen by various groups of educated and politically active people in Ukraine/Little Russia.[10]

---

9 For more detail, see Miller, *The Ukrainian Question*.

10 For more detail, see A. Kotenko, O. Martyniuk, and A. Miller, "Maloros," in A. Miller, D.

Socioeconomic Developments in the Late Nineteenth and Early Twentieth Centuries

In the second half of the nineteenth century and the beginning of the twentieth century, Russia experienced a period of intensive social and economic transformation. This had profound consequences for the development of the identity of different groups in Ukraine and for the attitude of political forces to the Ukrainian question. Migratory movements played an important role in all phases of development of the Russian Empire. They had a major influence on the processes of assimilation, shaping both the space of the empire and ideas about national territories. New Russia was among the main destinations for urban and rural migration in the nineteenth century. In the period between 1782 and 1858, around 1.5 million people, including serfs, migrated to this region. Between 1870 and 1896, the number of migrants remained high, 1.45 million. The end result of these migratory movements was that, at the end of the nineteenth century, Little Russians/Ukrainians made up about half the population of New Russia, while Great Russians constituted about 20 percent. It was only at the beginning of the twentieth century, when Siberia became the main destination for peasant migration, that the number of migrants to New Russia sank considerably (333,000 between 1897 and 1915).[11] As a result of this intensive migration, New Russia was claimed by Ukrainian nationalists as part of Ukrainian territory.

The abolition of serfdom opened up potentially great migration opportunities for the Ukrainian peasants, who suffered from an acute shortage of land. Until the 1890s, the government had reservations about peasant migration from the Southwestern Province because it feared a weakening of the Russian element vis-à-vis the "Polish threat." In 1879, there was even a secret instruction to the governors of the Kyiv and Vilnius gubernias to prevent peasant migration.[12] A report from Senator Polovtsov concerning a revision of the Chernihiv (Chernigov) gubernia in 1880 speaks of the "relatively strong urge of the peasants to migrate" and measures to "reduce the harmful effects" of this situation.[13] It was not until 1881 that the government issued "Provisional Regulations for Migration of Peasants on Free Land." This document, however,

Zdvizhkov, and I. Shirle, *Osnovnye obshchestvenno-politicheskie poniatiia v Rossii 18–nachala 20 v.* (Moscow, 2011).

11 See B. N. Mironov, *Sotsial'naia istoriia Rossii*, vol. 1 (St. Petersburg, 1999), 22–25.

12 National Library of Russia, Manuscript Department, fond 600, d. 1333, 28ff.

13 Daniel Beauvois, *Walka o ziemię 1863–1914. Pogranicze* (Sejny, 1996), 281; S. M. Sambuk, *Politika tsarizma v Belorussii vo vtoroi polovine XIX v.* (Minsk, 1980), 154.

was not published, and the peasantry was not informed for fear of provoking mass migration.[14] Mass migration of Little Russian peasants from Ukraine developed at the end of the nineteenth century and the beginning of the twentieth century. Before 1858, there were practically no Ukrainians/Little Russians in the Steppe province, but at the end of the nineteenth century there were already about 100,000. By 1917, as a result of Prime Minister Petr Stolypin's resettlement program, there were 800,000.[15] There was a similar development in the regions beyond the Urals. Before 1858 there were also practically no Little Russians in Western Siberia, but there were 137,000 at the time of the census of 1897. In Eastern Siberia there were 25,000 Ukrainians and, in the Far East, 61,000. By 1917, the number of Ukrainians in Western Siberia was 375,000, with 427,000 in Eastern Siberia and 427,000 in the Far East. In the Volga region in 1897 there were more than 545,000 Ukrainians. Altogether 2.5 million Ukrainians, that is, about 10 percent of the entire Ukrainian/Little Russian population, were living in areas that were territorially detached from Ukrainian gubernias.[16] In 1917, the number of Ukrainians living in gubernias bordering present-day Ukraine, in Tambov, Kursk, Voronezh, and Orel, was 2 million, with another 2 million living in the regions of Kuban, Tver, and Stavropol.[17] In regions with mixed populations of Great and Little Russians, the assimilation of Little Russians accelerated. In the census of 1926, at the height of the *korenizatsiia* (indigenization), when claiming non-Russian origins might well have proved advantageous, half the Little Russians in the Far East gave Russian as their mother tongue.[18] According to reliable estimates of Soviet demographers in the 1980s, 1.5 million Little Russians had "become Russian" in the second half of the nineteenth century.[19]

---

14 P. A. Zaionchkovskii, *Krizis samoderzhaviia na rubezhe 1870–1880 godov* (Moscow, 1964), 425.

15 Steven G. Marks, "Conquering the Great East: Kulomzin, Peasant Resettlement, and the Creation of Modern Siberia," in *Rediscovering Russia in Asia: Siberia and the Russian Far East*, ed. Stephen Kotkin and David Wolff (New York and London, 1995), 23–39.

16 S. I. Bruk and V. M. Kabuzan, "Chislennost' i rasselenie ukrainskogo ètnosa v XVIII–nachale XX v.," *Sovetskaia ètnografiia*, 1981, no. 5, table 3, 20–22.

17 Ibid., table 4, 23.

18 Andreas Kappeler, "Chochly und Kleinrussen: Die ukrainische ländliche und städtische Diaspora in Russland vor 1917," *Jahrbücher für Geschichte Osteuropas* 45, no. 1 (1997): 58; A. A. Novoselova, "Sibirskie khokhly: k voprosu ob ètnicheskoi prinadlezhnosti," *Ètnografiia Altaia i sopredel'nykh territorii* (Barnaul), no. 5 (2003): 27–28; A. A. Novoselova, "Ukraintsy v Srednem Priirtysh'e: identifikatsiia i samoidentifikatsiia v kontse 19–nachale 20 v.," in *Ukraina-Zapadnaia Sibir': dialog kul'tur i narodov* (Tiumen, 2004), 51–62; A. A. Novoselova, "Potomki belorusskikh pereselentsev v derevniakh Srednego i Nizhnego techeniia reki Tary," in *Ètnokul'turnye vzaimodeistviia v Sibiri (17–20 vv.)* (Novosibirsk, 2003), 267.

19 Bruk and Kabuzan, "Chislennost' i rasselenie," 26, 30.

From the 1860s, Russia saw rapid urbanization and industrialization. In 1860, Kyiv had 55,000 residents (just 10,000 more than in 1840), Kharkiv had 50,000, and Odesa (Odessa) 112,000. By 1874 the population of Kyiv had grown to 127,000. By 1881 the population of Kharkiv had risen to 128,000, and that of Odesa to 220,000. In 1860 Lviv (Lemberg, Lwów), with 60,000 residents, was the second-largest city after Odesa on the territory of present-day Ukraine. At the beginning of the 1880s, when the population of Lviv had grown to 70,000, it was also behind Kyiv and Kharkiv.[20] The growing cities and industrial areas became melting pots. At the time of the census in 1897, in the sixteen cities with more than 50,000 residents in the part of Ukraine that was in the Russian Empire, it was only in Poltava that more than half the population gave Little Russian as their mother tongue, even though more than 80 percent of the urban population of Ukraine, according to the same census, came from the gubernia in which their city was located.[21] This percentage increases when we take into account those who came from neighboring Ukrainian gubernias.

There was increased migration at the end of the nineteenth century as a result of industrial development. One of the main destinations was the Donbas, where coal mining started at the end of the 1890s. At the time of the census of 1897, when the industrial development of this region was just beginning, the population was 1,136,000, of whom 62.5 percent (710,000) were Ukrainian/Little Russian and 24.2 percent were Great Russian. This was similar to the process of Anglicization of South Wales in the nineteenth century.

The rail network in Ukraine increased threefold between 1865 and 1875 and grew at a rapid pace after that. In a memorandum to Alexander II written in 1864, Baron Pavel P. Korf clearly stated the consequences of this: "The Little Russian people today see the tsar as their bond with Russia and religion as their affinity with Russia; this bond and affinity will become stronger and inseparable.... The route to this is the railway.... It is not just goods that travel by rail but also books, ideas, customs and attitudes.... Great Russian and Little Russian capital, Great Russian and Little Russian ideas, attitudes and customs will blend, and these two already close peoples will become very much alike. Then just let the Ukrainophiles preach to the people

20 Patricia Herlihy, "Ukrainian Cities in the Nineteenth Century," in *Rethinking Ukrainian History*, ed. Ivan L. Rudnytsky (Edmonton, 1981), 136–37.

21 Peter Woroby, "The Role of the City in Ukrainian History," in *Rethinking Ukrainian History*, 208.

about Ukraine, about their struggles for independence and their glorious Hetmanate, even if they do it with the fiery verses of their Shevchenko."[22] The idea that social and economic developments would promote assimilation was widely shared by Russian and Ukrainian politicians. Of course, different conclusions were drawn from this. Many Russian politicians and officials thought that there was no need for political or administrative measures to promote the assimilation of the Little Russians; that things should be "left to take their natural course." This partly explains why so little attention was paid to the development of elementary schools in the Ukrainian gubernias. In the second half of the nineteenth century, there was little progress in the development of elementary schools in the whole empire. There was practically no increase in state expenditure for peasant schools between 1862 and 1895. Only 11.3 percent of the cost of elementary schools was covered by the state budget. The peasants themselves contributed three times that amount, and the *zemstvo* administration bore 43.4 percent of the costs. In the Southwestern Province, where there were no zemstvos before 1911, the situation was much worse. In gubernias without zemstvos, the school budget was one-third less.[23] It was not until the reign of Nicholas II that state expenditure for elementary schooling was substantially increased. By the outbreak of the First World War, Russia was about to introduce compulsory education. In this situation, the representatives of the Ukrainian movement found it necessary, as long as the assimilation process had not yet gone too far, to intensify their activities to whatever extent possible.[24]

Ukrainian and Russian Nationalism after the Revolution of 1905

The Revolution of 1905 brought about fundamental changes both in the political system of the Russian Empire and in the sphere of local politics. With political organizations no longer prohibited, legally

22 RGIA, fond 733, op. 193 (1863), d. 86, 20. Mikhail Katkov, describing in 1865 what he considered the most important measures for the Russification of the Kyiv gubernia, listed as number one the creation of a rail link between the Volga and the Dnipro. See M. N. Katkov, *Sobranie peredovykh statei "Moskovskikh vedomostei" 1865 goda* (Moscow, 1897), 757.

23 Cf. Ben Eklof, *Russian Peasant Schools: Officialdom, Village Culture and Popular Pedagogy, 1861–1914* (Berkeley, 1986), 89, 94.

24 Statements by Yevhen Chykalenko, one of the key figures in the Ukrainian movement at the beginning of the twentieth century, are typical: "Every city and every large area in Ukraine has been frightfully Russified": Ievhen Chykalenko, *Shchodennyk*, vol. 1, *1907–1917* (Kyiv, 2004), 281–82; "What you can do now with a few thousand, you will not be able to do then with millions when the people have become Russian": Ievhen Chykalenko and Petro Stebnyts'kyi, *Lystuvannia, 1901–1922 roky* (Kyiv, 2008), 72.

competing political forces emerged at both local and state level in elections to the city dumas and the State Duma, the newly created imperial parliament. In Kyiv, this political battle was reflected in the pages of Russian and Ukrainian newspapers, since the abolition of censorship in Ukraine also meant the abolition of restrictions on the use of the Ukrainian language in the press.

In the years 1906–8 the Ukrainian movement was on the upswing. In 1906 practically every city had its Ukrainian newspaper. By 1908, only one of those daily papers remained, *Rada* (Council) in Kyiv.[25] One of the reasons for this was administrative pressure from officials who imposed penalties for offenses against press law. But finances were the main reason for the loss of the Ukrainian provincial press. Even the Kyiv *Rada*, over many years, was unable to find more than two thousand subscribers and was only able to survive thanks to generous help from Yevhen Chykalenko and the existence of a single rich sponsor, Vasyl Symyrenko, who covered the annual deficit. Chykalenko described the situation in 1909 in these words: "The average urban resident who speaks the peasant Ukrainian language to a greater or lesser degree would not subscribe to our paper because he understands the Russian papers better and, what's more, those papers give him more news and news that is more up-to-date."[26]

The Society of Ukrainian Progressives (*Tovarystvo ukraïns'kykh postupovtsiv*, TUP),[27] founded in 1908, became a coordinating center for Ukrainian cultural and political organizations. Among the organizations linked to the TUP were the *hromady* (communities), semilegal groups of intelligentsia founded in the 1860s in a number of cities, and the cultural organization *Prosvita* (Enlightenment), which opened branches in a number of gubernias and cities immediately after the revolution. *Prosvita*'s influence was not equally strong everywhere. While it had the support of an extensive network of organizations in the Kyiv, Poltava, and Chernihiv gubernias, it had hardly any influence in other areas (Volhynia, Odesa, Kherson, Donbas).[28]

25 Steven Guthier, "Ukrainian Cities during the Revolution and the Interwar Era," in *Rethinking Ukrainian History*, 159.

26 Chykalenko, *Shchodennyk*, 1: 47–48.

27 Outside the direct influence of the TUP there was a small number of groupings of more radical nationalists such as Dmytro Dontsov and Mykola Mikhnovsky, who openly called for the overthrow of the Russian Empire and the creation of an ethnic Ukrainian state.

28 Heorhii Kas'ianov, *Ukraïns'ka intelihentsiia na rubezi XIX–XX stolit'. Sotsial'no-politychnyi portret* (Kyiv, 1993), 49. There is a clear record of publishing activity on the part of Ukrainian activists: by 1914 they had brought out 100,000 calendars, 200,000 copies of Shevchenko's *Kobzar*, and 10,000 copies of Hrushevsky's *Illustrated History of Ukraine*. Chykalenko's agricultural brochures were also widely distributed.

In 1908, the TUP initiated a bill signed by thirty-seven members of the State Duma to introduce the Ukrainian language in schools. The Kyiv Club of Russian Nationalists (KCRN),[29] founded that same year by Anatolii Savenko and Dmitrii Pikhno under the patronage of Prime Minister Stolypin, agitated against the draft with the result that it was not even placed on the agenda of the Duma.[30] Ukraine, especially Kyiv, thus became a battleground between two nationalisms deeply rooted there. As a consequence of a campaign initiated by the KCRN, local branches of *Prosvita* in the big cities were closed by the administration in 1910. In that same year, the KCRN celebrated its victory in elections to the Kyiv city duma, where it commanded a decisive majority.[31] It played a leading role among the Russian nationalists who formed the All-Russian National Union in 1911. At the start of the First World War, the KCRN, which at that time had around three thousand signed-up members, changed its name to Progressive Club of Russian Nationalists and joined the Progressive Bloc.

The most important journalistic opponent of *Rada* was *Kievlianin* (The Kyivan), which was close to the KCRN and continued the anti-Ukrainian line it had promoted since the 1870s. What was peculiar about the situation in Kyiv was that the Ukrainian activists and the Little Russian anti-Ukrainians were both directing their propaganda toward the same group, whose members identified themselves as *Malorossy* (Little Russians) or *Khokhly*. They had no fixed identity or political consciousness, and both sides wanted to turn them into nationalists, the one Ukrainian, the other Russian. In other words, the battle for the hearts and minds of individuals had begun and was added to the typical nineteenth-century conflict over abstract concepts such as *Maloross* or Ukrainian.

It corresponded to the logic of this struggle that both camps, whose supporters came from the same milieu and often knew one another personally, attempted to portray the other side in the darkest colors. The KCRN, in the discourse of *Rada*, was made up of Black Hundreds, arch-

---

29 The founders and members of the club thought of themselves as Little Russians. At the beginning of the First World War, the club was the most influential Russian nationalist organization in Kyiv, if not in the whole of Russia. The history of the club has not been adequately researched, which has to do with the fact that the club was one of the first targets of the Bolsheviks after they came to power in Kyiv (seventy members were shot), and the archive was confiscated by the Cheka.

30 Ricarda Vulpius, "Ukrainskii iazyk i shkol'noe obuchenie v pozdneimperskii period," *Ab Imperio*, 2005, no. 2 http://abimperio.net/.

31 For its election program, see *Sbornik kluba russkikh natsionalistov* (Kyiv, 1910), 27–30.

reactionaries, and traitors to their own nation.[32] In KCRN discourse, the circle around *Rada* and the TUP were *Mazepintsy*,[33] renegades, separatists, Russophobes, and agents of foreign powers, primarily Poland, but also Austria-Hungary and the German Empire.[34] While *Rada* considered the anti-Ukrainian Little Russians to be thoroughly reactionary, which was far from being the case, *Kievlianin* equally incorrectly described the Ukrainian nationalists as cosmopolitans, socialists, and unprincipled revolutionaries.[35]

The situation was different, however, when both sides spoke about the unpoliticized Little Russians. For the Ukrainians, these were victims of Russification, "unconscious Ukrainians" who had to be saved for the Ukrainian nation.[36] The Ukrainian discourse shared the Western view of the Russians as a half-wild Asiatic people incapable of living a European style of life. Politically, the eastern type of Great Russian was seen as incapable of democratically restructuring the state and recognizing the rights of minorities. This applied, moreover, not just to the advocates of monarchic order but also to the ally of the Ukrainian nationalists, the Constitutional Democratic (Cadet) Party.

---

32 Emotionally loaded terms for the anti-Ukrainian Little Russians abound in Chykalenko's journals: "hostile pseudo-countrymen" (93, 306), "traitors" (142), "corrupted by Moscow" (340), "our converts who now call themselves Russian nationalists" (256) (Chykalenko, *Shchodennyk*, vol. 1).

33 A reference to Hetman Ivan Mazepa (1639–1709) and a derogatory term for a "disloyal" Ukrainian.

34 There are numerous examples in the collected writings of anti-Ukrainian journalists: *Ukrainskii separatizm v Rossii* (Moscow, 1998); *Ukrainskaia bolezn' russkoi natsii* (Moscow, 2004). Savenko made the following assessment of the German orientation of the Ukrainian camp: "The alliance of Ukrainomanes with the Germans is nothing new. The German tendency of the *Mazepintsy* started when relations between Russia and Germany cooled. And when two armed coalitions confronted each other in Europe, the Dual Alliance and the Triple Alliance, then the Ukrainomanes finally attached themselves to militaristic Germanness.... The whole plan of the Ukrainophiles, the creation of an independent Ukraine, rests on the external defeat of Russia. In the same way, Mazepa placed his hopes in Sweden and Charles XII" (A. Savenko, "Zametki," *Kievlianin*, no. 38, 7 February 1909).

35 "To have a clear idea about the *Mazepintsy*, one should not forget for a minute the dual character of this movement. On the one hand, they play with quasi-national feelings, inasmuch as they present themselves as passionate nationalists of the Ukrainian nation recently invented in Austria. On the other hand, these gentlemen are demagogues of the most sinister kind in the pure *Haidamaky* manner. When not afraid to say so, many of them, socialists and cosmopolitans, flout every nation, the Ukrainian included.... For this reason, they are prepared to subject themselves to the Austrians, the Germans, even to the devil himself. Since their true slogan is 'Have-nots of the world, unite,' these have-nots belong to the revolutionary socialist parties and form one of their offshoots" ("Mazepinskaia opasnost'," *Kievlianin*, no. 60, 1 March 1914).

36 See, e.g., Chykalenko's letter of 16 April 1906 to Stebnytsky, in which he writes that among the deputies to the State Duma "there were very few conscious Ukrainians, but of course many of Ukrainian origin" (Chykalenko and Stebnyts'kyi, *Lystuvannia*, 44).

Yevhen Chykalenko, the leader of the TUP, wrote in his journal of Pavel Miliukov, the leader of the Cadets: "Twist it how you will, in the soul of every *Katsap*,[37] even the most progressive of them, there sits a centralist."[38] The economic position of Russian Ukraine was described as colonial.[39] The aspiration of many Little Russians to be closer to the Great Russians and their culture was dismissed as an error resulting from the traumas caused by enforced Russification. It was the credo of Chykalenko and the other Ukrainian nationalists that "all the Ruthenians, Little Russians, and *Khokhly* on the territory from the San to the Don should become nationally conscious Ukrainians."[40]

For the Russian nationalists who thought of themselves as *Malorossy*, the name *Maloross* had a "proud sound." They competed with the Ukrainian nationalists for the cultural inheritance of Little Russia, claiming for themselves many key figures from the Ukrainian pantheon, including Shevchenko, and declaring them to be Little Russian.[41] The KCRN saw itself as the true voice of the Little Russians: "I myself am a pure-blooded *Maloross* and love my country passionately, its wonderful nature, its customs, language, and legends, its history, just as I love the *Khokhly* with their laziness and their good-heartedness. But with my whole strength I hate the Ukrainophiles, this traitorous and vile movement." This was written a number of times by the leader of the club in the pages of *Kievlianin*.[42]

From a certain time, the KCRN claimed a leadership role for itself among the Russian nationalists in the whole state. This claim was based, among other things, on its electoral successes: "While the Great Russian gubernias returned a significant number of revolutionaries even to the third State Duma, Little Russia sent thoroughly Russian nationalists to the Tauride Palace. And while Great Russian Moscow

---

37 A derogatory Ukrainian term for Russians.

38 Chykalenko, *Shchodennyk*, 320.

39 Stebnyts'kyi, "Ukraïna v ekonomitsi Rosiï," in *Vybrani tvory* (Kyiv, 2009), 280.

40 Chykalenko, *Shchodennyk*, vol. 1 (Kyiv, 2004), 281–82.

41 Shevchenko's status would decline from "genius" to "talented poet" in the discourse of the KCRN, and his symbolic role as "father of the nation" was played down. Cf. *Kievlianin*, no. 116, 27 April 1908.

42 A. I. Savenko, "Zametki," *Kievlianin*, no. 134, 15 May 1908. This formula, created by Nikolai Rigelman and Sylvestr Hohotsky in the 1870s, became a kind of mantra in anti-Ukrainian Little Russian journalism. As Professor T. Lokot formulated it: "As a son of the Little Russian branch of the Russian family, I love everything Little Russian: the living Little Russian language (not the Ukrainian in which there is so much that is artificial and non-Little Russian), the Little Russian nature and, most important of all, the Little Russian people." See T. Lokot', "Kak byt' s ukrainstvom," *Golos Moskvy*, no. 277, 2 December 1911.

and St. Petersburg served as the bulwark of revolution, Kyiv, the center of Little Russia, became the center of the whole Russian patriotic movement."[43]

Compared with the first half of the nineteenth century, the discourse concerning the Little Russians had now definitely changed. If the previous concern had been to "rediscover" the "Russian character" of the Little Russians, which had been suppressed and displaced through Polish influences, there was now hardly any mention of Polish influence at the beginning of the twentieth century, and the Russian character of the Little Russians was taken for granted (or imagined) as naturally given. Although this Russian character had to be "protected" from the "poisonous influence" of Ukrainian propaganda, the Little Russian variety of the Russian character was claimed to be even more "solid" than the Great Russian variety, which succumbed all too easily to the temptations of revolutionary ideas and the deceptive imaginings of minority milieus from the periphery of the empire.

The rise in the electoral strength of right-wing Russian nationalists,[44] especially the KCRN, forced the Cadets to search for allies against the right among the supporters of the Ukrainian movement in the Southwestern Province. This cooperation was primarily tactical, since both sides had very different ideas about the "Ukrainian question" and problems of autonomy and federalism in the empire.[45] However, driven by the logic of party competition, the Cadets took on certain demands from the Ukrainian camp and intervened in the State Duma on behalf of the oppressed Ukrainians. The KCRN, on the other hand, whenever the government took action against the

---

43 A. I. Savenko, "Zametki. Po povodu 100-letiia so dnia rozhdeniia Gogolia," *Kievlianin*, no. 320, 16 November 1908.

44 The political right in Russia was organizationally very divided. The largest organizations were the All-Russian National Union, the Union of the Russian People, the Union of the Archangel Michael, and the Black Hundred groups. Their programs were characterized by xenophobia, monarchism, and frequently by hostility to constitutionalism. The Union of 17 October represented the center right. It supported the constitutional reforms of the October Manifesto but differed from the Cadets on the issue of concessions to demands for autonomy from the nationalists on the imperial periphery. To date there has been only one monograph on the right-wing movements: Daniil Kotsiubinskii, *Russkii natsionalizm v nachale stoletiia: rozhdenie i gibel' ideologii Vserossiiskogo natsional'nogo soiuza* (Moscow, 2001). The Kyiv Club of Russian Nationalists brought together a broad spectrum extending from the center right to the extremist supporters of the Black Hundreds.

45 While the Ukrainians insisted on national autonomy as a first step and really wanted to achieve that status within a federation, the Cadets not only rejected federalism in principle for Russia but also rejected national autonomy. What the Cadets preferred was territorial autonomy, whereby territorial units would be smaller and their borders would not be determined by national or ethnic criteria.

Ukrainian movement, called persistently for the suppression of the Ukrainian movement. It was against this background that both the KCRN and the TUP sought to influence public opinion in both capital cities regarding the Little Russians and the Ukrainian question.

Right-wing representatives from the Southwestern Province liked to allow peasant deputies to speak in the Duma as if they were speaking on behalf of the whole Little Russian peasantry. Hryhorii A. Andriichuk, a deputy from the Podilia gubernia, declared: "We reject all Ukrainophile propaganda, as we have never considered ourselves non-Russian. With whatever insidiousness the self-ingratiating Mr. Miliukov and his consorts may attempt to sow discord between us and the Russians, they will not succeed. We Little Russians are just as Russian as the Great Russians."[46]

The most effective propaganda coup of the anti-Ukrainian Little Russians in Kyiv was a book published in 1912 by the Kyiv censor Sergei N. Shchegolev under the title *The Ukrainian Movement as the Modern Stage of South Russian Separatism*. Four editions of the book were published before the revolution, and Shchegolev, following the first, more detailed edition, published a shorter version, better suited for propaganda purposes. It contained a wealth of material (in this respect, the book still remains the most detailed account of the Ukrainian movement at the time) and attempted to demonstrate, with numerous quotations, the separatist nature of the Ukrainian movement.

Petr Struve had broken with his fellow Cadets over the Ukrainian question, rejecting even a tactical alliance with the Ukrainian movement.[47] But in the case of Struve, as in that of Shchegolev, we find in that same year a tendency to legalize the concept "Ukrainian" and reinterpret it, inasmuch as it was used as a synonym for "Little Russian": "I am deeply convinced that a Little Russian or Ukrainian culture, as a local provincial culture, exists alongside the all-Russian culture and the all-Russian language."[48]

46 *Gosudarstvennaia Duma, Tretii sozyv. Stenograficheskie otchety. 1909*, vol. 3 (St. Petersburg, 1910), col. 3081. "We are Russians, and no one has the right to call us anything else," said the peasant deputy Matvii Andriichuk from the Volhynia gubernia a year later. He was almost the namesake of his colleague from Podilia: see *Gosudarstvennaia Duma, Tretii sozyv. Stenograficheskie otchety. Sessiia chetvertaia*, vol. 1 (St. Petersburg, 1910), col. 1280.

47 But Struve criticized the "reactionaries" who "shout about 'Mazepa treachery' and paint a frightening picture of an Austro-Polish-Ukrainian war against Russia to separate Ukraine from Russia." See P. B. Struve, "Obshcherusskaia kul'tura i ukrainskii partikuliarizm. Otvet Ukraintsu," *Russkaia mysl'*, 1912, no. 1: 85.

48 P. B. Struve, 'Obshcherusskaia kultura i ukrainskii partikuliarizm,' 66.

The Ukrainian camp very quickly concluded that it had to come up with an answer to Shchegolev in order to neutralize the propagandistic effect of his book in the imperial capitals.[49] Petro Stebnytsky and Oleksandr Lototsky, both influential figures in Ukrainian circles in St. Petersburg, put together a thick brochure that was published anonymously in St. Petersburg in 1914 under the title *The Ukrainian Question*. This text, directed at liberal readers in the capital, is interesting inasmuch as it consciously sought to adapt not only the ideological content but also the conceptual system to the reader. The terms "Little Russia," *Khokhol*, and *Katsap* are used without any of the negative connotations typical of the internal Ukrainian discourse. "Little Russia" and "Little Russian" are used repeatedly where, in the internal discourse, "Ukrainian" would most likely have been used.[50] The authors attempt to demonstrate that assimilation in Ukraine had been only superficially successful and that the low level of literacy was a consequence of the fact that classes were held in what, for the people, was a foreign (Russian) language. They called for a halt to police persecution of the Ukrainian movement, since it was not questioning the territorial integrity of the empire but only struggling for autonomy. The concepts "Little Russia" and "Ukraine" were thereby not only being raised for discussion and reflection in the hostile political camp but were also being used to analyze and manipulate the conceptual system of their opponents.

The attitudes of various political forces to the Ukrainian question were most clearly expressed during a debate in the State Duma in February 1914, when deputies questioned the actions of the police against Ukrainian celebrations on the occasion of the centenary of the birth of Taras Shevchenko. The fact that the question had been signed by some dozens of deputies from different parties indicated that a relatively broad coalition had been formed in the Duma that was prepared to support certain demands of the Ukrainians. Miliukov, the main speaker for the Cadets, called on the government to seek an agreement with the moderate Ukrainian leaders who were prepared to accept autonomy within Russia in order not to play into the hands of the more radical Ukrainian nationalists such as Dmytro Dontsov, who were strongly anti-Russian. Savenko was Miliukov's main opponent

49 Chykalenko and Stebnytsky discussed who should reply to Shchegolev that "Ukrainianism is not the result of some intrigue but rather, like the rebirth of any nation, has grown organically" (Chykalenko and Stebnyts'kyi, *Lystuvannia*, 284).

50 Stebnyts'kyi, *Vybrani tvory*, 290–308. "Little Russia" and "Ukraine" are often used as synonyms, separated by a comma (ibid., 313).

from the right and argued that the "moderate" view of Mykhailo Hrushevsky and other Ukrainian representatives was nothing but a tactic and that concessions would inevitably lead to an escalation of Ukrainian demands. Savenko demanded that "the police and the interior minister not be hindered in their work."[51] Some years later, in the emigration, Miliukov once against accused the Russian "nationalist intelligentsia,"' who, in alliance with the state authorities after 1863, had gradually damaged relations with all the various peoples of the empire, including the Ukrainians.[52] What one can say now is that, in the situation at the time, on the eve of the First World War, both speakers made comprehensible arguments. Miliukov was correct in pointing out that the policy of the right depended essentially on administrative measures. Savenko argued that the Ukrainians would not be satisfied with the concessions that Miliukov was willing to grant them. Miliukov himself was very well aware of this. By insisting in talks with his Ukrainian allies that, given the current relation of forces, they had to concentrate on practical measures, he was evading discussion of such contradictions. He attempted to persuade his Ukrainian partners that questions on which agreement could not be reached at that time would be resolved without difficulty after the overthrow of the autocracy. His expectation that the monarchy would collapse turned out to be perfectly accurate, as was his assessment that this would fundamentally change the nature of the Ukrainian question. What he did not foresee, however, was that the monarchy, and with it the empire, would collapse in such a manner that there would be no place in Russia either for his opponents, Savenko and his KCRN colleagues, or for his own partners, Chykalenko and his TUP colleagues, or for himself.

The First World War

On the eve of the First World War, the imperial authorities and the majority of the right and centrist forces represented in the Duma had no clear policy toward Ukraine. They did not want to exacerbate the tensions with the Ukrainians but, on the other hand, they had no idea how to reach an agreement with them. The great mass of the

51 *Gosudarstvennaia Duma, IV sozyv. Sessiia II. Stenograficheskie otchety. Chast' II. Zasedaniie 40.* 19 February 1914 (St. Petersburg, 1914), cols. 901–15, 927–33.

52 P. N. Miliukov, *Natsional'nyi vopros. Proiskhozhdenie natsional'nosti i natsional'nye voprosy v Rossii* (Prague, 1925), 154.

population on the territory of present-day Ukraine was remote from politics and had no pronounced national consciousness.[53] In Russia, Ukraine was seen as a threatened part of the imperial periphery and, at the same time, as a threatened part of national territory. In Ukraine/Little Russia, the struggle between the Ukrainian national movement and Russian nationalism intensified, with the latter finding support among the anti-Ukrainian Little Russians. In light of a certain thaw in Russian relations with Poland, especially with Roman Dmowski's National Democratic Party, Polish intrigue was no longer seen as playing the main role. This now shifted to German and Austrian machinations. Galicia, which had become a bulwark of the Ukrainian movement at the beginning of the twentieth century, was seen as playing a key role. At the same time, there were also strong Russophile circles in Galicia that were close to the anti-Ukrainian Little Russians in the Russian part of Ukraine. In Vienna, Galicia was similarly seen as a threatened borderland, as portrayed so vividly by Joseph Roth in his *Radetzky March*.

The approaching war inevitably mobilized nationalists throughout the Russian Empire, especially in the western periphery. The irredentists made Russian nationalist plans for the "liberation of Russian land from the Austro-Polish and German yoke." When Struve, in his famous article of 1914, "Great Russia and Holy Rus'," formulated Russia's tasks in the war, the top of the list was "to unify and reunite all parts of the Russian nation," in other words, to annex "Russian Galicia." Using the language of organic unity typical in nationalist discourse, he employed the metaphor of healing the national body, arguing that the annexation of Galicia was necessary for the "inner healing of Russia," since "the Little Russian branch, being part of Austria, had created and nourished the hateful so-called 'Ukrainian' question."[54]

The nationalists on the periphery, including the Ukrainians, were attempting feverishly to assess what might be the outcome of the war

---

53 The only Ukrainian daily newspaper, *Rada*, with a more or less constant subscriber base of two thousand between 1908 and 1911, was only able to increase the number of its subscribers to three thousand before the war. The right-wing Russian nationalist organizations had tens of thousands of members, for instance, in Volhynia. The membership of Black Hundred organizations exceeded one hundred thousand. These numbers, however, can be deceptive. Peasant membership was often purely formal and reflected the monarchism and anti-Semitism of these organizations rather than conscious support for Russian nationalism.

54 *Russkaia mysl'*, 1914, no. 12: 176–80.

and thought that the long-hoped-for changes would now be possible.[55] The situation was radically heightened by the outbreak of war. Most of the peasants became armed soldiers, and millions of people, especially in the western borderlands, were forced out of their normal sphere of life and their traditional locations. The ethnic factor became immensely more important in politics and in mass consciousness.[56] The daily horrors and harshness of war dispensed with conventional restraints at both the personal and the social level. In this context, it is also important that the neighboring imperial powers, Russia, Germany, and Austria-Hungary, had abandoned conventional limitations that they had followed for many decades in their mutual relations. For a long time, the macrosystem of continental empires in Eastern Europe had rested on the assumption that they would not attempt to destroy one another and depended on one another to manage the legacy of the Polish partitions. In the course of the war, however, which soon assumed the character of an all-out struggle for the very survival of empires, Vienna, Berlin, and St. Petersburg began actively to play the ethnic card to harm their enemies. They incited separatism in the competing powers while instigating repression against disloyal or suspect ethnic groups among their own subjects.[57] It can be said that the explosive spread of nationalism in the western periphery of the Romanov Empire resulted in general from the hardships of "total war" and in particular from the new competitive policies of the imperial powers.

At the beginning of the war, Russian policy as regards the Ukrainian question was essentially limited to repression of Ukrainian activists. Ukrainian newspapers were closed down, and Hrushevsky, the leader of the movement, was exiled to Simbirsk. As early as the autumn of 1914, the Russian army occupied all of eastern and part of western Galicia.[58] In their policy toward the Galician Ruthenians,

---

55 For the Poles, the First World War meant reunification and independence for Poland. For the Ukrainians, the war also strengthened the idea of unifying all of what they considered to be Ukrainian territory. The Armenians hoped to gain eastern Anatolia with the help of the Entente, and the Jews and Baltic Germans hoped for a German victory. All nationalists in the Russian Empire hoped that the autocracy would be replaced by a democratic system and that centralization would give way to autonomy or federalism. Some Muslims had the idea of a pan-Muslim or pan-Turkic union.

56 Mark von Hagen, "The Great War and the Mobilization of Ethnicity," in *Post-Soviet Political Order: Conflict and State Building,* ed. Barnett R. Rubin and Jack Snyder (London, 1998), 34–57.

57 See especially Eric Lohr, *Nationalizing the Russian Empire: The Campaign against Enemy Aliens during World War I* (Cambridge, Mass., 2003).

58 On occupation policy, see the book by Aleksandra Bakhturina, which, though questionable in its analysis, is rich in factual detail: *Politika Rossiiskoi imperii v Vostochnoi Galitsii v gody Pervoi Mirovoi voiny* (Moscow, 2000). See also Mark von Hagen, *War in a European Borderland:*

there was a complete lack of coordination among military and civilian officials and the representatives of the Orthodox hierarchy. They each undermined the policies being followed by other branches of the administration. The lack of clear political directives played a key role. In general, officials tended to regard the local inhabitants as Russians and saw the Greek Catholic Church and Ukrainian identity as something external, superficial, imposed by Vienna, the Vatican, and the Poles, but without any support among the population and therefore as something that could be got rid of easily once Russian power had been established. Ideas of this kind led to repression of the Ukrainian language and the Greek Catholic Church. Ukrainian newspapers and printing presses were closed down. Prominent representatives of the Greek Catholic Church were arrested, including the metropolitan, Andrei (Roman Maria Aleksander) Sheptytsky. This provoked anti-Russian sentiment among the local Ukrainian population. Defeats in the summer of 1915 forced the Russian army to withdraw from Galicia. More than a hundred thousand Russophile Galicians, who feared repression by Austrian officials and forced conscription into the Austro-Hungarian army, also fled with the Russians. The occupying Central Powers supported the Ukrainian nationalists and suppressed Russian nationalists in the occupied territories.[59] Under these changed circumstances, Russia now had to struggle to win the loyalty and sympathy of the Ukrainians, while Germany, which had a free hand in the Ukrainian question since there were no Ukrainians in the German Empire, now joined the list of players in the Ukrainian question alongside Poland, Vienna, and the Vatican.

Shortly before the second planned occupation of Galicia in 1916, the Russian agent Vsevolod P. Svatkovsky, who was active in Bern and had some influence on Russian policy in Ukraine, made an analysis of the experience of the first occupation. He considered it a serious

---

Occupations and Occupation Plans in Galicia and Ukraine, 1914–1918 (Seattle and London, 2007); Miller, *The Romanov Empire*, chap. 7.

59 Cf. Vejas Gabriel Liulevicius, *War Land on the Eastern Front: Culture, National Identity, and German Occupation in World War I* (Cambridge, 2000); Frank Grelka, *Die ukrainische Nationalbewegung unter deutscher Besatzungsherrschaft 1918 und 1941/42* (Wiesbaden, 2005). Compared to the earlier policy of the Russian Empire, quite revolutionary measures were taken, especially in relation to the Ukrainian language. Following an order from Marshal Hindenburg, the language of the local inhabitants (Polish, Lithuanian, and Belarusian) was to be respected in *Ober Ost*, while Russian was to be prohibited in the press, education, and administration. The hierarchy of languages in the Russian Empire was turned on its head. Of course, this had no immediate effect on the spread of particular languages, but it did have important symbolic consequences. For the first time, knowledge of the languages of the periphery became a real advantage. A similar policy was followed in Ukraine.

mistake that "in 1914–15, relying on the support of Russophile political circles in Galicia and of the nonpolitical majority of the Russo-Galician population, we not only completely neglected the Ukrainians and Ukrainianism but let them know, in the clearest possible manner, what our feelings and intentions were."[60] "The almost complete disappearance of Ukrainian separatism at the beginning was interpreted as proof of the weakness of Ukrainianism and the strength of the Russophile elements in the region, which, however, was not the true cause of this phenomenon. We had not noticed the chief factor in the political life of the Russian population in this region, namely its Polonophobia. For this population, Russian occupation had put an end to Polish rule. Hostility among Ukrainian circles in Galicia to Russia and to the 'Muscovites' existed more in theory, while their hostility to the Poles was a traditional phenomenon replete with practical political and economic implications. This hostility was the strongest characteristic of the whole Russian population of the region, our own as well as that of the Ukrainian camp."[61] Svatkovsky criticized Bishop Yevlogii and other persecutors of the Greek Catholics, whose repressive policies had turned the Ukrainians against Russia.[62]

Russian foreign agents paid close attention to changes in Vienna's and Berlin's Ukrainian policy. They reported not only on the repressive measures against Russophile Ruthenians at the beginning of the war, including the creation of internment camps at Thalerhof and Theresienstadt, where tens of thousands were detained and thousands died, but also on their concessions to the Ukrainians. For the first time since the 1870s, a non-Polish governor was appointed, General Hermann Kolar, who ordered his officials to respect the Ukrainian language.[63] The Austrian heir to the throne, Karl, then made a journey to Galicia during which he greeted the Ukrainians in their own language. Ukrainians were now frequently promoted to officer rank in the Austro-Hungarian army. Svatkovsky was also of the opinion that Hungary had its own Ukrainian policy, the goal of which was to bring all the Ukrainian territories within the Habsburg Monarchy under its rule in a kind of autonomy based on the Croatian

---

60 AVPRI, fond 135, op. 474, d. 27, 4.

61 Ibid.

62 Ibid., 4–6.

63 On Vienna's policy toward the Ukrainians in Galicia and Bukovyna, see Serhii Popyk, *Ukraïntsi v Avstriï 1914–1918. Avstriis'ka polityka v ukraïns'komu pytanni periodu Velykoï viiny* (Kyiv and Chernivtsi, 1999); *Ereignisse in der Ukraine, 1914–1922: deren Bedeutung und historische Hintergründe*, ed. Theophil Hornykiewycz, 4 vols. (Philadelphia, 1966–69). See also chapter 1b in the present volume.

model. This could then serve as a strong bastion against Russia.[64]

St. Petersburg was particularly concerned about reports of prisoner-of-war camps erected by the Germans and Austrians where Russian soldiers of Ukrainian origin were separated from the rest and received preferential treatment.[65] There is a special file in the archives of the Special Political Department of the Foreign Ministry[66] with statements from soldiers who had escaped from the prisoner-of-war camps, as well as a report from a chargé d'affaires in Bern, Mikhail M. Bibikov, who had succeeded in visiting two of those camps in Rastatt and Salzwedel. Bibikov estimated that about four hundred thousand men were being held there. Provisions were "much better than in the Russian camps." The soldiers knew that their privileged treatment was due to the fact that they were Ukrainians. They were being given classes in reading and writing in the usual Galician phonetic orthography. They also had lessons in Ukrainian history and literature. There were even Ukrainian newspapers. According to Bibikov's report, there were around forty thousand men who were particularly receptive to this propaganda and were being trained as members of a future Ukrainian army, engaging in maneuvers in special Ukrainian uniforms. "This propaganda," wrote Bibikov, "has a solid foundation. The results achieved are very satisfactory."[67]

The Special Political Department of the Foreign Ministry, originally created to influence the Slavs in Austria-Hungary, soon made the Ukrainian question one of its priorities. In addition to monitoring the policy of hostile powers, it worked on proposals for changing Russian policy. St. Petersburg now began seriously to discuss possible measures to secure the goodwill of the Ukrainians. In the summer of 1915, Mykhailo Tyshkevych, an estate owner from the Kyiv gubernia who saw himself as Ukrainian, socially conservative and loyal to the empire and its rulers, sent a declaration of loyalty by telegram to the tsar. Nicholas II replied, on 24 August 1915, in a telegram signed by Court Minister Vladimir B. Frederiks: "Sa Majesté m'a donné l'ordre de vous remercier ainsi que le groupe d'Ukrainiens réunis en Suisse pour les sentiments exprimés dans votre télégramme."[68] The revolutionary

64 AVPRI, fond 135, op. 474, d. 27, 8.

65 Ibid., 44–61.

66 Ibid., 26.

67 Ibid., 6ff. See also chapters 1b and 3b in the present volume.

68 Translation: "His Majesty has given me the task of expressing his thanks to you and to the group of Ukrainians in Switzerland for the sentiments expressed in your telegram" (AVPRI, fond 135, op. 474, d. 27, 12).

significance of this telegram for official discourse consists in the fact that the word "Ukrainian" is used in an official document instead of the previously obligatory "Little Russian," in what sounds like a direct quotation from the ruler himself. At the end of 1915, Hrushevsky was permitted to move from faraway Simbirsk to the university city of Kazan. The possibility of opening two Ukrainian secondary schools was discussed, and there were plans for the successor to the throne, accompanied by his orderly, the Little Russian Derevenko, to visit Galicia when the province was occupied again. Recommendations were made on how to handle the Greek Catholic Church, stressing the need to refrain from repressive measures of any kind. Lists were made of Ukrainian politicians, including politicians from Galicia, who could be attracted to the Russian side. Recommendations for achieving this stressed the overriding importance of the national question. It was therefore recommended that contact be established with individuals who would be willing to accept autonomy within Russia, and that such contacts should include even Ukrainian socialists of *Borot'ba* (Struggle), who, although they were "socialists," were also "altogether decent people."[69] Svatkovsky's opinion was that these concessions could be kept within a tight framework, since the unification of all Ukrainians in one state was so important to Ukrainian leaders that they would be willing to make extensive compromises with the Russian government, given that Russia alone was capable of uniting all the Ukrainian lands.[70]

Svatkovsky clearly thought it important to prepare the ground for an agreement on the Ukrainian question with the Allied powers, especially the United States. In 1916 he sent his agent Tsetlinsky to the USA to make contact with, among others, Ukrainian emigrants living there.[71] It is difficult to assess what further practical steps might have been taken in this revision of Ukrainian policy, as the monarchy was overthrown in February 1917.

The First World War and the Russian Revolution significantly changed the balance of forces in Ukraine. Ukrainian organizations were stronger, often thanks to the support of the warring powers. Armed Ukrainian units had been created, not just in the Austro-Hungarian army (the Ukrainian Legion) but also, following a command from General Lavr Kornilov in the summer of 1917, in the Russian

69 Ibid., 48–55.

70 AVPRI, fond 135, op. 474, d. 32, 3.

71 AVPRI, fond 135, op. 474, d. 27, 60–61.

army. At the same time, anti-Ukrainian forces had been significantly weakened. In Galicia this had to do with the exodus of Russophile Ruthenians in 1915 and the repression of Russophiles by Austria-Hungary. In Russian Ukraine, many Russian nationalists either left the areas occupied by the Central Powers in 1915 and 1917–18 or became targets of the occupying powers. In 1916–17 the Bolsheviks in Ukraine sounded the death knell for the Russian nationalists, whom they regarded as the main enemy. Members of the KCRN (more than seventy people) captured by the Bolsheviks when they took Kyiv were shot.

Disputes between the supporters of a Little Russian or Ukrainian orientation continued during the interwar period in the emigration and in Galicia, which now belonged to Poland. In Soviet Ukraine, *korenizatsiia* (indigenization) represented a radical break with the Ukrainian policy of the Russian Empire and of the Russian nationalists.[72] The concept of the all-Russian nation, which was supposed to embrace Great, Little and White Russians, was rejected, and the very notion of *Maloross* was forbidden. The Ukrainian nation was recognized by the Soviet authorities, taking territorial shape in the form of the Ukrainian Soviet Socialist Republic, which conducted an intensive policy of Ukrainization during the 1920s.

72 Cf. Miller, *The Romanov Empire*, chap. 7 and Conclusion.

4b. The Ukrainian Policy of Bolshevik Russia, 1917–1922

Bogdan Musial

On 17 March 1917, two days after the abdication of the tsar, the Central Rada was formed in Kyiv and immediately called for Ukrainian autonomy and the transformation of the tsarist empire into a federation of free nations. Very soon, all parties and social organizations in Ukraine supported this demand. Very few were thinking of independence at that time. Against this background, the Rada sent a memorandum to the Provisional Government in May 1917 demanding far-reaching Ukrainian autonomy, even to the point of creating Ukrainian armed forces.[1]

At the beginning of June 1917, the Provisional Government rejected these demands, whereupon the Rada not only did not concede but radicalized its position. It now claimed for itself the right to represent the Ukrainian people and, on 16 June, established the General Secretariat as the future government. On 2 July, a delegation from the Provisional Government arrived in Kyiv to negotiate with the Rada. Both sides wanted a compromise, and the delegation signed a document recognizing the autonomy of Ukraine.[2]

In the weeks and months that followed, the Rada adopted a number of measures, made decisions, and issued demands on the Provisional Government that went far beyond autonomy. The result was increasingly sharp conflicts with the Provisional Government. On 18 July 1917, the Rada declared the General Secretariat to be the supreme ruling body in Ukraine and, in September, openly demanded the right of self-determination for Ukraine. On 2 November, the Third All-Ukrainian Military Congress was held in Kyiv, attended by some three thousand delegates representing about three million Ukrainian soldiers in the Russian army. The All-Ukrainian Constituent Assembly

---

1 M. V. Sokolova, "Velikoderzhavnost' protiv natsionalizma: Vremennoe pravitel'stvo i Ukrainskaia tsentral'naia rada (fevral'–oktiabr' 1917)," accessed 1 November 2010, http://www.hist.msu.ru/Labs/UkrBel/sokolova.htm; Oleh Pidhainy, *The Ukrainian-Polish Problem in the Dissolution of the Russian Empire, 1914–1917* (Toronto and New York, 1962), 44–62.

2 M. V. Sokolova, *Istoriia Rossii. XX vek: 1894–1939* (Moscow, 2009), 443–45. The recognition of Ukrainian autonomy created a crisis in the Provisional Government, as a result of which the governing coalition fell apart. See Orlando Figes, *A People's Tragedy: Russian Revolution 1891–1924* (London, 1996), 420.

was announced while the congress was in session, paving the way for Ukrainian independence.[3]

Events unfolded very rapidly in Ukraine following the October putsch of 7 November 1917[4] in St. Petersburg and the Bolshevik seizure of power. The Rada rejected the Bolshevik claim to rule in Ukraine. The Bolshevik attempt to take power in Kyiv by force failed. Bolshevik forces were disarmed and driven from the city. The Rada also had to assert itself against the claim to power by representatives of the Provisional Government in Kyiv and the general staff of the Kyiv military district. On 11 and 12 November, forces loyal to the Rada fought against Russian forces in Kyiv and won. The pro-Russian troops then left the city, and the Rada assumed power.[5] Some days later, on 20 November, the Rada proclaimed the Ukrainian People's Republic. In its Third Universal, the Rada claimed full legislative and administrative powers for itself and for the General Secretariat as the government of the new republic. In its proclamation, it rejected the Bolsheviks' claim to power but declared, at the same time, that the new republic wanted to establish a federation, the nature of which was not clearly defined, with the other nations of the old Russia on the basis of equality.[6] The proclamation of 20 November did not therefore signify a final break with Russia.[7]

The measures taken by the new Ukrainian government in the military sphere were very important. The troops on the southwestern and Romanian front were renamed the "Ukrainian front" and placed under the command of the Rada government. This involved units from Brest-Litovsk all the way to Romania. Symon Petliura, a journalist, took over the important post of minister of war in the Ukrainian government with the task of creating a Ukrainian army out of these units. He was only partly successful in this task, as most of the Ukrainian soldiers had left their units and gone home.[8]

---

3 Sokolova, "Velikoderzhavnost' protiv natsionalizma"; Pidhainy, *The Ukrainian-Polish Problem*, 63–79.

4 25 October according to the Julian calendar.

5 Pidhainy, *The Ukrainian-Polish Problem*, 82–85.

6 D. V. Iarosh, "Universaly Ukraïns'koï Tsentral'noï rady – Konstytutsiini akty ukraïns'koï derzhavnosti 1917–1988 rr.: ïkh zminy ta istorychne znachennia," *Universitets'ki naukovi zapysky*, 2006, nos. 3–4: 41; Pidhainy, *The Ukrainian-Polish Problem*, 85–88.

7 Ibid.

8 Viktor Savchenko, *Dvenadtsat' voin za Ukrainu* (Kharkiv, 2006), chap. 1, accessed 6 November 2010, http://militera.lib.ru/h/savchenko_va/index.html; Pidhainy, *The Ukrainian-Polish Problem*, 96.

The Bolshevik Right of Self-Determination— "An Instrument in the Struggle for Socialism"

With regard to domestic policy, the most important watchwords and goals of the Ukrainian People's Republic nominally differed very little from those of the Bolsheviks, with the exception of centralization and basic rights. In addition to this, on 15 November 1917, five days before the proclamation of the Ukrainian People's Republic, the Bolsheviks issued their Declaration on the Rights of the Peoples of Russia. This declaration, signed by Lenin, Stalin, and Bukharin, promised freedom of self-determination to all the nationalities of Russia, including the right of secession and the creation of independent states.[9]

Nevertheless, the Bolsheviks rejected the Rada's proclamation of the Ukrainian People's Republic because what they really wanted, from the beginning, was a centralized "socialist" state over which they could rule. Stalin, in a conversation at the beginning of April 1918 with one of the journalists on the Bolshevik paper *Pravda*, explained Bolshevik goals with regard to the future shape of the Russian political system: "In Russia...the forced unity of tsarism will give way to a voluntary federalism, so that this federalism, in the course of time, may give way to an equally voluntary and fraternal unity of the working masses of all Russia's nations and ethnic groups. Federalism in Russia will be a transitional stage to a future socialist unity."[10]

According to Stalin, the central administrative ruling body of the Russian Federative Republic, including not only Ukraine but also Poland and all other peripheral regions of the old tsarist empire, was the Council of People's Commissars, in other words, the Bolshevik leadership.[11] The Council of People's Commissars (*Sovet Narodnykh Komissarov*, hereafter CPC) was established under Lenin's leadership on the day following the October putsch. Stalin was the people's commissar responsible for nationality policy.

The right to self-determination, like all other rights, was interpreted by the Bolsheviks in their own way ("dialectically"). They used it to legitimize and assert their own claim to power ("socialist unitarism"). Stalin declared this openly on 15 January 1918: "The principle of self-determination must become an instrument in the

---

9 *Istoriia Sovetskoi Konstitutsii. Sbornik dokumentov 1917–1957* (Moscow, 1957), 19ff.

10 Stalin's interview with a *Pravda* journalist on the organization of the Russian Federative Republic, published in *Pravda*, nos. 62–63, 3–4 April 1918.

11 Ibid.

struggle for socialism and subordinate to the principles of socialism."[12] From the outset, for ideological reasons, the Bolsheviks did not accept the formation of national states on the periphery of the old tsarist empire, regardless of their political orientation, and they used all possible means to counter such attempts. The case of Ukraine is exemplary, especially as the country was not just ideologically and politically but also economically important to the Bolsheviks. What was at stake was food (Ukraine had been the granary of the tsarist empire), energy (coal), and the steel industry of the Donets Basin. It comes as no surprise, therefore, that after the putsch and their initially failed attempt in Kyiv, the Bolsheviks kept up their efforts to conquer Ukraine. They attempted an uprising at the beginning of December 1918. Troops loyal to them attempted once again to use force to take power in Kyiv and other cities. These attempts were rebuffed by Ukrainian troops.[13]

A few days later, on 17 December, the Bolshevik regime issued its Manifesto to the Ukrainian People: "...we, the Council of People's Commissars, recognize the Ukrainian People's Republic and its right to secede from Russia or enter into a treaty with the Russian Republic on federal or similar relations between them. We, the Council of People's Commissars, recognize at once, unconditionally and without reservations, everything that pertains to the Ukrainian people's national rights and national independence."[14] At the same time, Lenin's manifesto was an ultimatum to the Rada, demanding that it submit itself militarily to the Bolshevik regime in order to join with the Bolsheviks in the struggle against counterrevolution. Further, Lenin demanded that the Rada cease attempts to disarm Bolshevik forces in Ukraine and that Ukrainian forces, which should join with the Bolsheviks to fight anti-Bolshevik insurgents in southern Ukraine, place themselves under Bolshevik command. The ultimatum also stated that, if no satisfactory reply were received within forty-eight hours, the CPC would declare war on Ukraine.[15]

On the same day that Lenin issued his ultimatum, the All-Ukrainian Congress of Soldiers', Peasants', and Workers' Deputies

12 Stalin's speech to the Third All-Russian Congress of Soviets of Workers', Soldiers', and Peasants' Deputies, held from 10 to 18 January 1918, in Stalin, *Works*, vol. 4, available at: http://www.marxists.org/reference/archive/stalin/works/1918/01/15.htm.

13 Savchenko, *Dvenadtsat' voin za Ukrainu.*

14 "Manifesto to the Ukrainian People with an Ultimatum to the Ukrainian Rada," 16 December 1917, in Lenin, *Collected Works*, vol. 26 (Moscow, 1964), 361–63.

15 Ibid.

began in Kyiv. The congress had been initiated by the Ukrainian Bolsheviks, who hoped that they could take power by "legal" means. The Rada government supported the calling of the congress, which began on 17 December. The Bolsheviks, however, found themselves in a minority. The great majority of delegates supported the Rada, which rejected Lenin's ultimatum and declared itself neutral in the Russian civil war. Most of the Bolshevik delegates then left the congress and went to Kharkiv.[16] The Ukrainian People's Republic was now at war with Bolshevik Russia. When the ultimatum of 17 December expired, the CPC declared war on the Ukrainian People's Republic (18 December). On the same day, the CPC appointed Volodymyr Antonov-Ovsiienko commander in chief of Bolshevik forces in the war against the Ukrainian People's Republic and against anti-Bolshevik forces in southern Ukraine.[17] In Kharkiv, the Bolsheviks created pseudo-Ukrainian ruling structures as a way of legitimizing externally their claim to power in Ukraine. The Bolshevik delegates from the All-Ukrainian Congress, who had left Kyiv on 18 December and gone to Kharkiv, proclaimed the Ukrainian Soviet Socialist Republic there on 22 December 1917.[18] Three days later, the Bolsheviks formed a Central Executive Committee and transferred to it all power in Ukraine. On 26 December, in a telegram to the CPC, the Executive Committee declared, in the name of "the Ukrainian people," that it opposed war with Russia, and concluded with these words: "In the name of the young Soviet power in Ukraine, we send our greetings to the consolidating all-Russian Soviet power."[19]

On 29 December 1917, the CPC welcomed the formation of the "Ukrainian Soviet Socialist Republic" and assured its "brother republic" of its full support "in the struggle for peace."[20] This created the "international" basis for the legitimation of its claim to power in Ukraine. On 1 January 1918, Lenin named Sergo Ordzhonikidze, a close confidant of Stalin, as special commissar for Ukraine. His task was to unite and lead the activities of Soviet organizations in Ukraine

16 Pidhainy, *The Ukrainian-Polish Problem*, 96–99. Pidhainy writes of more than 2,500 delegates, of whom only 60 were Bolsheviks. See also Savchenko, *Dvenadtsat' voin za Ukrainu*. According to Savchenko, there were 1,575 peasant and soldier delegates and 125 Bolshevik delegates.

17 Savchenko, *Dvenadtsat' voin za Ukrainu*.

18 Pidhainy, *The Ukrainian-Polish Problem*, 96–99.

19 Telegram from the All-Ukrainian Central Executive Committee to the CPC, 26 December 1917, in *Dokumenty po istorii grazhdanskoi voiny v SSSR*, ed. I. Mints and E. Gorodetskii, vol. 1 (Moscow, 1940), 54ff.

20 Declaration of the CPC, 29 December 1917, ibid., 57ff.

in all fields (such as military, provisions, and banking).[21] From mid-December, Bolshevik units were concentrated in Kharkiv and the surrounding area, and it was from here that they were to conquer Ukraine. Those troops of the Black Sea Fleet who had sided with the Bolsheviks operated in southern Ukraine. By the beginning of January 1918, they had taken a number of towns on the Black Sea coast.

The Rada attempted to organize resistance but had inadequate troops to counter the Bolshevik offensive. In the days and weeks that followed, the Bolsheviks captured eastern Ukraine and made advances in the south. In January 1918 the Red troops captured many towns in the east and south and advanced on Kyiv. Ukrainian forces were disintegrating. On the night of 29 January, the Bolsheviks in Kyiv organized an uprising with the participation of workers from city factories. Street battles followed, lasting a number of days, until troops loyal to the Rada managed to suppress the uprising on 4 February. Nevertheless, the hours of the Rada government seemed numbered in those days, as it was only in Kyiv and the surrounding area that they were able to hold out. Four days later, on 8 February, Bolshevik troops took Kyiv, and the Rada fled to Zhytomyr. By February, the whole of eastern and central Ukraine was in Bolshevik hands.[22]

The Central Powers Drive the Bolsheviks out of Ukraine

Support from the Central Powers meant that the Bolshevik occupation of Ukraine did not spell the end of the first Ukrainian nation-state. German troops began an offensive along the whole eastern front on 18 February 1918 and advanced 250 km in five days. They met with no resistance, as the Russian army had actually disintegrated. The Germans invaded Ukraine, followed ten days later by Austro-Hungarian troops.[23] Confronted with the German advance, the Bolsheviks reluctantly accepted the severe peace conditions set down by the Central Powers. On 3 March 1918, both parties signed a peace treaty in Brest-Litovsk. In this treaty, Bolshevik Russia gave up Poland, Courland, Latvia, Lithuania, Estonia, Finland, and Ukraine. "As a European power, Russia reverted economically and territorially to the

---

21 Lenin's nomination of Sergo Ordzhonikidze as special commissar for Ukraine, 1 January 1918, in *Leninskii sbornik*, vol. 25 (Moscow, 1945), 11.

22 For more detail, see Iaroslav Tynchenko, *Persha ukraïns'ko-bil'shovyts'ka viina, hruden' 1917–berezen' 1918* (Kyiv and Lviv, 1996); Savchenko, *Dvenadtsat' voin za Ukrainu*, 493.

23 For more detail, see Savchenko, *Dvenadtsat' voin za Ukrainu,* chap. 3.

position of Muscovy in the seventeenth century."[24] Russia lost one-third of its prewar population, four-fifths of its coal and iron reserves, and one-third of its grain.[25]

For Russia, the most painful loss was Ukraine because of its grain-growing areas and heavy industry (coal, iron ore, and steel). Karl Radek, one of the leading Bolsheviks, lamented the economic consequences of the Brest treaty: "The Brest peace treaty separated from Russia the industrial regions of Poland, the Baltic, and the Donets Basin, as well as the most fertile regions of Ukraine. It reduced the productive capacity of the Russian economy and hampered the task of healing the wounds of war...which can only be brought about by means of socialist organized production."[26]

The provisions of the Brest-Litovsk peace treaty were a humiliating defeat with serious consequences for the Bolshevik regime, if it were to last. Stalin spoke of a partition that the Central Powers had put in place between "socialist Russia and the revolutionary West."[27] Added to this were the catastrophic economic consequences of its territorial losses.

Not surprisingly, the Bolshevik regime never accepted its territorial losses. This was particularly true with respect to Ukraine. The Communist Party (Bolshevik) of Ukraine or CP(B)U was formed in April 1918. At its first party congress, in July 1918, it decided to affiliate itself with the Russian Communist Party (Bolshevik) as a regional organization. One of the initiators of the decision, the Russian German Emmanuil Kviring, declared that "the independence of Ukraine had no economic foundation" and that a prolonged separation of Ukraine from Russia would only be possible with foreign support. Mykola Skrypnyk, another delegate at the party congress, declared: "The independence [of Ukraine] serves as a cover for the counterrevolutionary struggle against Soviet power."[28]

In November 1918, one year after the October putsch, Central and Eastern Europe were again in the midst of upheavals that would turn the political map of the region on its head. In the autumn of 1918, the

---

24 Figes, *A People's Tragedy*, 548.

25 Sokolova, *Istoriia Rossii,* 501. See chapter 3a in the present volume.

26 RGASPI, fond 5, op. 1, d. 3068, The economic consequences of the Brest-Litovsk peace treaty. Points of a speech by Karl Radek, no date (1918), 166ff.

27 Stalin's article "Partition," *Zhizn' natsional'nostei*, no. 2, 17 November 1918.

28 Quoted from Elena Borisenok, "Vliianie pol'skogo faktora na politiku bol'shevikov po natsional'nomu voprosu. Bol'sheviki i ukrainskii vopros v 1917–1923 godakh," in *Revoliutsionnaia Rossiia 1917 goda i pol'skii vopros: novye istochniki, novye vzgliady,* ed. M. Volos and A. Orekhov (Moscow, 2009), 180ff.

German front was facing collapse, and the German government was forced to ask for a truce with the Western powers. This was signed on 11 November 1918 in Compiègne and amounted to a capitulation. Article 11 of the truce agreement provided for an immediate withdrawal of all German troops in the East, including from former Russian territories such as Ukraine, back to the German borders of 1914. Article 15 annulled the Brest-Litovsk treaty.[29] In the previous week, on 3–4 November, Austria-Hungary had signed a truce agreement with the Entente also agreeing to withdraw its troops immediately from the occupied territories and demobilize its army.[30] The Danube Monarchy collapsed shortly afterward.

A power vacuum existed in Central and Eastern Europe in the autumn of 1918, leading to the creation of a number of new states. A completely new situation also developed in Ukraine following the withdrawal of the Central Powers. Hetman Skoropadsky fled to Berlin in December 1918. The Directory took power in Kyiv, led by Symon Petliura and Volodymyr Vynnychenko, and revived the Ukrainian People's Republic. The Bolshevik regime once again renewed its claim to power in Ukraine, as in the other territories evacuated by the Central Powers. But the Bolsheviks always took care to ensure that their expansion had the appearance of granting the right to self-determination. On 29 November 1918, Lenin sent a telegram to Jukums Vācietis, commander in chief of the Red Army, with the following instructions: "As our troops advance westward and into Ukraine, provisional provincial governments should be created with the task of establishing soviets in the area. This has the good side that it prevents the chauvinists in Ukraine, Lithuania, Latvia, and Estonia from portraying our advance as an occupation and creates a favorable climate for the further advance of our troops."[31]

Two weeks previously, on 17 November, Lenin and Stalin had established the Ukrainian Revolutionary Council, which was to lead the struggle in Ukraine. Three days later, on 20 November, the Bolsheviks ("with the participation and direct support of Stalin") established the Provisional Workers' and Peasants' Government of

29 "Waffenstillstandsbedingungen der Alliierten, Compiègne, 11. November 1918": http://www.dhm.de/lemo/html/dokumente/waffenstillstand/index.html.

30 An English version of the truce agreement of 3–4 November 1918 at http://www.forost.ungarisches-institut.de/pdf/19181103-1.pdf.

31 Telegram from Lenin to the Supreme Commander, 29 November 1918, *Leninskii sbornik*, vol. 34 (Moscow, 1945), 53ff. According to the reference note (ibid., 54), it was Stalin who wrote the telegram (apart from the final sentence, not given here).

Ukraine.[32] On 29 November 1918, this government, led by Khristian Rakovsky, proclaimed the restoration of Soviet power in Ukraine. A few weeks later, the Bolsheviks began their offensive against the Ukrainian People's Republic.[33] At the end of 1918 Bolshevik troops, portrayed externally as "Soviet Ukrainian insurgents," began their attack on independent Ukraine. They occupied Kharkiv on 3 January and continued their advance. Ukrainian national units were disintegrating. Soldiers deserted, formed themselves into bands, robbed, plundered, and murdered. Whole units went over to the Bolsheviks. Ukraine sank into chaos, and the government of the young republic was unable to control the situation. The Reds advanced deep into eastern and northern Ukraine. They occupied Kyiv on 6 February and established their "Ukrainian" Soviet authorities, such as the "Ukrainian" Council of Commissars under Rakovsky. In the weeks that followed, the Bolsheviks captured central Ukraine and introduced an economic and political regime similar to that in other areas but much more radical: war communism in the countryside (requisitioning of food), the creation of committees of "poor peasants" to disrupt village life, and *sovkhozy* (state farms) to replace the estates.[34]

In April 1919 the Bolshevik regime decided to dispense with the appearance of an "independent" Soviet Ukraine. On 23 April 1919, the Politburo of the Central Committee of the Russian Communist Party asked the Central Committee of the Communist Party of Ukraine to work out how, and in what form, the "unification" of Ukraine with Russia could be achieved. At the same time, the Politburo sent Adolf Joffe to Ukraine to strengthen the "centralist-oriented elements" there.[35] Some weeks later, on 2 June 1919, the Politburo dissolved the "independent" Soviet Ukrainian armed forces, i.e., the Ukrainian Front, and placed its troops of the southern front (previously the 2nd Ukrainian Army) and of the 12th Army under the command of the Red Army. The Politburo also divided Ukraine into military districts.[36]

---

32 *Dokumenty po istorii grazhdanskoi voiny*, 433, n. 1.

33 Manifesto of the Provisional Workers' and Peasants' Government of Ukraine, 29 November 1918, in *Dokumenty vneshnei politiki SSSR, 17 noiabria 1917 g.–31 dekabria 1918 g.*, vol. 1 (Moscow, 1957), 582–86. On 30 November 1918 the commander of the Red Army's 10th Army, Kliment Voroshilov, had given his troops the order to "liberate" Ukraine: Order of Voroshilov to the troops of the 10th Army, 30 November 1918, in *Dokumenty po istorii grazhdanskoi voiny*, 433ff. The Bolshevik leaders, however, put off the offensive and concentrated their troops on the Ukrainian border, where there were still German troops.

34 Sokolova, *Istoriia Rossii*, 653.

35 RGASPI, fond 17, op. 3, d. 3, Minutes of session of RCP(B) Politburo, 23.4.1919, point II, 2.

36 RGASPI, fond 17, op. 3, d. 11, Minutes of session of Politburo, Central Committee of the RCP(B),

In August, the Politburo ordered the unification of the Ukrainian Special Commission to Combat Counterrevolution, Speculation, and Sabotage (VChK) with the Soviet Russian VChK.[37]

By April 1919, remnants of the Ukrainian national units under Petliura remained only in the western parts of Ukraine, in Volhynia and Galicia, where they were also fighting against Polish troops. In the summer of 1919, events took a turn. On 1 September 1919, after months of negotiations, the Ukrainian national government arranged a truce with Poland and a Polish-Ukrainian demarcation line.[38] The truce with Poland enabled Petliura to unite all the remaining Ukrainian national forces against the Bolsheviks, who were meanwhile confronting, for the second time, the collapse of their Ukrainian front and their rule in Ukraine. On 11 August 1919, Trotsky complained: "There are difficulties in Soviet Ukraine. The enemy is pressing us from all sides.... The black August of the previous year [in Russia] is being repeated in Ukraine.... The young Ukrainian Red Army...is withdrawing. The enemies are gloating."[39] The Bolsheviks in Ukraine at this time were being confronted by a White offensive and peasant uprisings that they themselves had provoked by their ruthless occupation policy.

Soviet rule had only been nominal in Ukraine in the first months of 1918. The Bolsheviks did not really have the time to establish their own power structures or to take the kind of measures that were typical for them, such as the ruthless requisitioning of food, mass terror, and the struggle against the church and against the urban and village elites. What they had promised was work for the workers and land for the peasants. The peasants remembered those slogans.[40] But the situation was completely different when the Bolsheviks occupied Ukraine for the second time in 1919. The peasants waited in vain for the land they had been promised as the Bolsheviks turned the estates into collective farms or large state farms. War communism raged in the countryside and in the towns, with its forced requisitioning

2.6.1919, point I, appendix 1, 1, 5. On 30 November 1918, the "interim government of the Ukrainian Workers' and Peasants' Government" established the Soviet Ukrainian Army, which was integrated on 4 January 1919 into the just established Ukrainian Front. See *Bol'shevistskoe rukovodstvo. Perepiska, 1912–1927* (Moscow, 1997), 77.

37 RGASPI, fond 17, op. 3, d. 21, Minutes of session of Politburo, Central Committee of the RCP(B), 16.8.1919, point 3b, 1.

38 Both sides had already agreed to a truce on 1 June 1919, but the Western Ukrainian forces did not abide by it. See Robert Potocki, *Idea restytucji Ukraińskiej Republiki Ludowej (1920–1939)* (Lublin, 1999), 44–49.

39 RGASPI, fond 325, op. 1, d. 48, Appeal by Trotsky, 12.8.1919, 1ff.

40 Savchenko, *Dvenadtsat' voin za Ukrainu*, chap. 12.

of food, plundering, political murder, and the mass terror of the VChK. Thousands of rural and urban residents lost their lives. This provoked widespread armed resistance, and local uprisings took place throughout Bolshevik-occupied Ukraine. In some cases, armies were formed by thousands of insurgents. Among the largest of them were the armies of Nykyfor Hryhoriiv in central Ukraine and Nestor Makhno in eastern Ukraine.[41]

Otaman Hryhoriiv had already organized a partisan unit during the period of German-Austro-Hungarian rule in Ukraine and supported Petliura afterward. He had about six thousand men at the end of 1918. In February 1919, however, he went over to the Soviet side. His unit was integrated as an independent brigade of the Soviet Ukrainian Division. On 7 May 1919, however, he mutinied and organized an anti-Bolshevik uprising in the rear of the Red Army, which was then fighting against Denikin's army. At this time, he was in command of more than 20,000 insurgents with access to 50 cannons, 700 machine guns, and 6 tanks. Their slogans were "Ukraine for the Ukrainians," "Power to the Ukrainian people's soviets without communists," and "Free trade in grain." The uprising engulfed the southern regions of Ukraine (Cherkasy, Uman, Kremenchuk, Katerynoslav, Mykolaiv, and other towns). In June, Hryhoriiv joined forces with another Ukrainian partisan leader, Nestor Makhno. But conflicts soon arose between them and, on 27 July, Makhno murdered Hryhoriiv.[42]

In eastern Ukraine in 1918, the anarchist Makhno had organized armed resistance to the occupation. Following the withdrawal of those armies, Makhno fought with the Bolsheviks against Petliura. In February 1919 he broke with the Bolsheviks. In the territories under his control, especially in the region of Katerynoslav, he created an anarchist peasant republic, centered in Huliaipole, in which Bolshevik power structures were not permitted, nor were such measures as the requisitioning of grain. At the end of May 1919, the Bolsheviks declared him an outlaw and took up arms against him and his formations. Denikin's offensive, however, forced them once again to form an alliance with Makhno. Makhno's army then made a decisive contribution to the Bolshevik victory over Denikin's forces.[43] The

---

41 Ibid.

42 For more detail, see Viktor Savchenko, *Avantiuristy grazhdanskoi voiny: istoricheskoe rassledovanie* (Kharkiv, 2000), http://militera.lib.ru/bio/savchenko/index.html.

43 Nestor Makhno, *Krest'ianskoe dvizhenie na Ukraine 1918–1921. Dokumenty i materialy* (Moscow, 2006), 5–27 and, among others, documents 107, 112, 115, 129, and 137.

Bolsheviks, however, had no intention of sticking to their agreement. At the beginning of January 1920, with Denikin's army defeated, Red Army troops began to encircle Makhno's forces. The Bolsheviks ordered Makhno and his troops to fight the Poles, but Makhno refused. The Bolsheviks then treacherously attacked Makhno's army, which numbered about twenty thousand men at the time.[44] A bitter and, for the Bolsheviks, pointless battle broke out in eastern Ukraine. On 26 June 1920, Feliks Dzerzhinsky reported desperately to Lenin: "I've had no luck with Makhno. We could deal with him quickly if we had a cavalry. But that's something I do not have."[45]

In the spring of 1919, hundreds of rebel groups and units were formed in Ukraine, making it impossible for the Bolsheviks to establish and maintain their rule. On 11 June 1919 Nikolai Podvoisky, a Bolshevik official sent to Ukraine, sent a memorandum to Lenin on the critical situation in Ukraine in which he wrote: "Kyiv was cut off for two months by counterrevolutionary bands.... In the spring [of 1919], the whole of petty-bourgeois Ukraine...became a counterrevolutionary camp."[46] The uprisings crippled the Ukrainian economy: food and other provisions, industrial production, transport, the production and delivery of wood and coal. Ukraine sank into economic chaos and political anarchy. Podvoisky complained in his memorandum that the country had become ungovernable. Two months would be needed to prepare the Red Army for these new circumstances and muster an army of thirty thousand men that would fight on the "internal front."[47] Two months later, the situation had not improved from the Bolshevik point of view. On 6 August 1919, prompted by a telegram from Trotsky, the Politburo of the Russian Communist Party debated this issue. Trotsky demanded that the regions around Kyiv, Odesa, Mykolaiv, and Kherson be cleared of the "banditry" that held sway in Ukraine and was preventing the recruitment and organization of an army there. The Politburo decided to send five hundred members of the Department for Special Tasks and from other reliable organizations, such as the VChK, to Ukraine.[48]

---

44 Trotsky to Stalin, 9 January 1920, in *Bol'shevistskoe rukovodstvo. Perepiska*, 113ff.; Stalin to Trotsky, 9 January 1920, ibid., 114ff.; Decision of the All-Ukrainian Revolutionary Committee of 9 January 1920, in Makhno, *Krest'ianskoe dvizhenie,* 301, doc. 193.

45 Dzerzhinsky to Lenin, 26 June 1920, in *F. Ė. Dzerzhinskii, Predsedatel' VChK-OGPU 1917–1926. Dokumenty* (Moscow, 2007), 192.

46 RGASPI, fond 17, op. 109, d. 43, 16–19, Memorandum to Lenin, 10 June 1919 (copy), 16.

47 Ibid.

48 RGASPI, fond 17, op. 3, d. 19, Minutes of Politburo session, 6 August 1919, 1.

In addition to the uprisings in Ukraine, the Bolsheviks were confronted, from May 1919, by a major offensive of Denikin's forces in southern Russia. His units advanced toward Moscow in the summer of 1919, with troops flanking westward into Ukraine. They soon drove the demoralized Bolshevik troops out of Ukraine, occupying the Donets Basin, eastern and southern Ukraine, and taking Kyiv on 31 August. On the day before, Ukrainian national troops had entered Kyiv. At this time, they were fighting with the Whites against the Bolsheviks and had already liberated large parts of central Ukraine.[49] But conflict soon emerged between the nationalist forces under Petliura and the Whites, who, like the Bolsheviks, rejected independence for Ukraine. The situation intensified and, on 11 September, Petliura declared war on Denikin's Volunteer Army and even asked Lenin for assistance. At the end of September, nationalist and Bolshevik forces ceased fighting each other. In October they became allies against the Whites, and the Bolsheviks promised to deliver weapons and munitions to the nationalist forces.[50]

On 11 October, the Politburo decided: "A political and military-technical agreement with Petliura is desirable. This agreement should be made public in order to compromise Petliura with the Entente.... All discussions are to be conducted as negotiations with the bourgeoisie of an oppressed nation that is opposed to Great Russian monarchism and imperialism."[51] On 11 September, the Politburo had decided to dissolve the whole Bolshevik governmental apparatus in Ukraine, leaving only a "nominal" Ukrainian government.[52]

On 20 October, Denikin's advancing Volunteer Army suffered a heavy defeat as it approached Orel, and again two days later at Voronezh. Other defeats followed, and the Whites began to retreat. In November and December 1919, the Bolsheviks again occupied almost the whole of central and eastern Ukraine and captured Kyiv at the beginning of December. By the end of December, the Whites held only the Crimea and Odesa. Petliura, of no more use to the Bolsheviks, fled with his units to Poland.[53]

---

49 Sokolova, *Istoriia Rossii*, 621–24, 654; Savchenko, *Dvenadtsat' voin za Ukrainu*, chap. 6.

50 Ibid.

51 RGASPI, fond 17, op. 3, d. 29, Minutes of Politburo session, 11 October 1919, 3.

52 RGASPI, fond 17, op. 3, d. 26, Minutes of Politburo session, 11 September 1919, Point 13, 1.

53 Sokolova, *Istoriia Rossii*, 654, 704–7; Savchenko, *Dvenadtsat' voin za Ukrainu*, chap. 6.

The "Unification" of Ukraine and Soviet Russia and the War with Poland

The Bolsheviks now began, during their third advance into Ukraine, to establish ruling bodies and complete the formal "unification" of Ukraine and Soviet Russia. On 20 and 21 November 1919, the Politburo debated its policy toward Ukraine and decided to proceed with the "careful preparation for the unification" of Ukraine and Soviet Russia that had been arranged on 2 June 1919. The Politburo also ordered the formation of an All-Ukrainian Revolutionary Committee that would take over from the "Ukrainian government" and govern until the convocation of the Ukrainian Congress of Soviets, which would decide on unification. The Politburo also decided to promote the Ukrainian language and culture and to liquidate the large landed estates and distribute the land among the poor peasants. The creation of state farms was to take place only in exceptional circumstances, and collectivization was to proceed without force.[54]

In the meantime, on 2 December 1919, Petliura signed an agreement in the name of the Ukrainian People's Republic with the Polish government that recognized the independence of Ukraine. Poland committed itself to support the Ukrainian People's Republic. In return, Petliura ceded to Poland the territories of Eastern Galicia and Volhynia, which were already occupied by the Poles.[55] This agreement prompted the Bolshevik regime, which was preparing an offensive against Poland,[56] to modify its Ukrainian policy.[57] On 9 February 1920 Georgii Chicherin, the people's commissar for foreign affairs, wrote to the Politburo of the Russian Communist Party and to Lenin personally that, according to Western media reports, Poland would demand the independence of Ukraine from Soviet Russia. Chicherin also assumed that Poland would attempt to achieve this by force of arms. He wrote: "Either we give up Ukraine or the Poles, following a war for Ukraine, will march on Moscow. Or we attempt to localize the war by means of an immediate separation of a Red

---

54 RGASPI, fond 17, op. 3, d. 41–42, Minutes of Politburo session, 20 and 21 October 1919; Resolution of the Central Committee of the Russian Communist Party on Soviet power in Ukraine: RGASPI, fond 17, op. 3, d. 42, 3–5.

55 Michał Klimecki, "Wojna czy pokój. Polsko-ukraińskie negocjacje 1918–1921," in *Polska i Ukraina. Sojusz 1920 roku i jego następstwa,* ed. Zbigniew Karpus, Waldemar Rezmer, and Emilina Wiszko (Toruń, 1997), 66–69.

56 Cf. Bogdan Musial, *Kampfplatz Deutschland. Stalins Kriegspläne gegen den Westen* (Berlin, 2008), 32–38.

57 In January 1920 the Politburo again discussed the Ukrainian question, the construction of a state apparatus, the forms of "unification" with Russia, and power relations in Ukraine. The aim was to complete the "unification" of Ukraine and Russia. See RGASPI, fond 17, op. 3, d. 54–55, Minutes of Politburo session, 13, 17–18, and 20 January 1920.

independent Ukraine. To avoid a Polish attack, we should reintroduce the independence of the Ukrainian Soviet Republic and postpone federation to a future date.... The working masses in the West see the struggle for Ukrainian independence as the authentic struggle of a nation against its oppressor."[58] Four days later, Chicherin confirmed his view of the situation and pointed out that anti-Bolshevik forces in Ukraine would support the Poles and Petliura. It was therefore essential to formally separate Red Ukraine from Soviet Russia.[59]

The Politburo then halted the formal incorporation ("unification") of Ukraine and Bolshevik Russia, especially as, on 25 April 1920, Polish units began an offensive against the Red Army in Ukraine as a way of preempting a Soviet attack. The strategic goal of "Operation Kyiv" was to drive Bolshevik forces out of central Ukraine beyond the Dnipro, thereby allowing the government of the Ukrainian People's Republic to exercise power and establish Ukrainian units that would take up the struggle against Soviet forces without the help of Polish troops. An anti-Bolshevik state was to be created that would then be a Polish ally.[60]

Bolshevik troops in Ukraine were not just fighting Polish units but were also being confronted with uprisings behind their lines. According to a VChK situation report for the period 15–30 April 1920, "Ukraine is now experiencing the next wave of uprisings."[61] Both central and eastern Ukraine were affected. Soldiers of the First Galician Brigade, consisting of Ukrainian Galicians, murdered the commissar and turned their weapons on the Bolsheviks. The Bolshevik leadership, as a result, had the remaining Eastern Galician units within the Red Army disarmed and their officers and soldiers interned. Hundreds of them lost their lives. Numerous "bands" attacked the retreating soldiers of the Red Army. Insurgent peasants killed communists as well as officers and soldiers of the Red Army.[62]

---

58 RGASPI, fond 17, op. 84, d. 93, Chicherin, People's Commissar for Foreign Affairs, to the Politburo of the Russian Communist Party, copy to Lenin, 10.

59 RGASPI, fond 17, op. 84, d. 93, Telegram from Chicherin to Trotsky and Rakovsky, copy to Stalin, 12.

60 See Musial, *Kampfplatz Deutschland*, 39–42.

61 RGASPI, fond 17, op. 84, d. 93, Report on the situation in Ukraine according to reports from special units of the southwestern front for the period 15–30 April and 2 June 1920, 48ff.

62 RGASPI, fond 17, op. 109, d. 84, Telegram from Rakovsky and Berzin, 28 April 1920, 14; RGASPI, fond 17, op. 109, d. 84, Report from Muraviev to Lenin, Dzerzhinsky, and others on the retreat of the Red Army from Ukraine, 17 May 1920, 18–24. On 27 April, Rakovsky reported that the Bolsheviks had shot about two hundred "Galicians." In Odesa, they had imprisoned another 1,500 "Galicians." Rakovsky spoke against the shooting of prisoners and recommended that they be sent to the North for political reeducation: RGASPI, fond 17, op. 109, d. 236, Telegram from Rakovsky to the Revolutionary War Council of the 14th Army, 27 April 1920, 5.

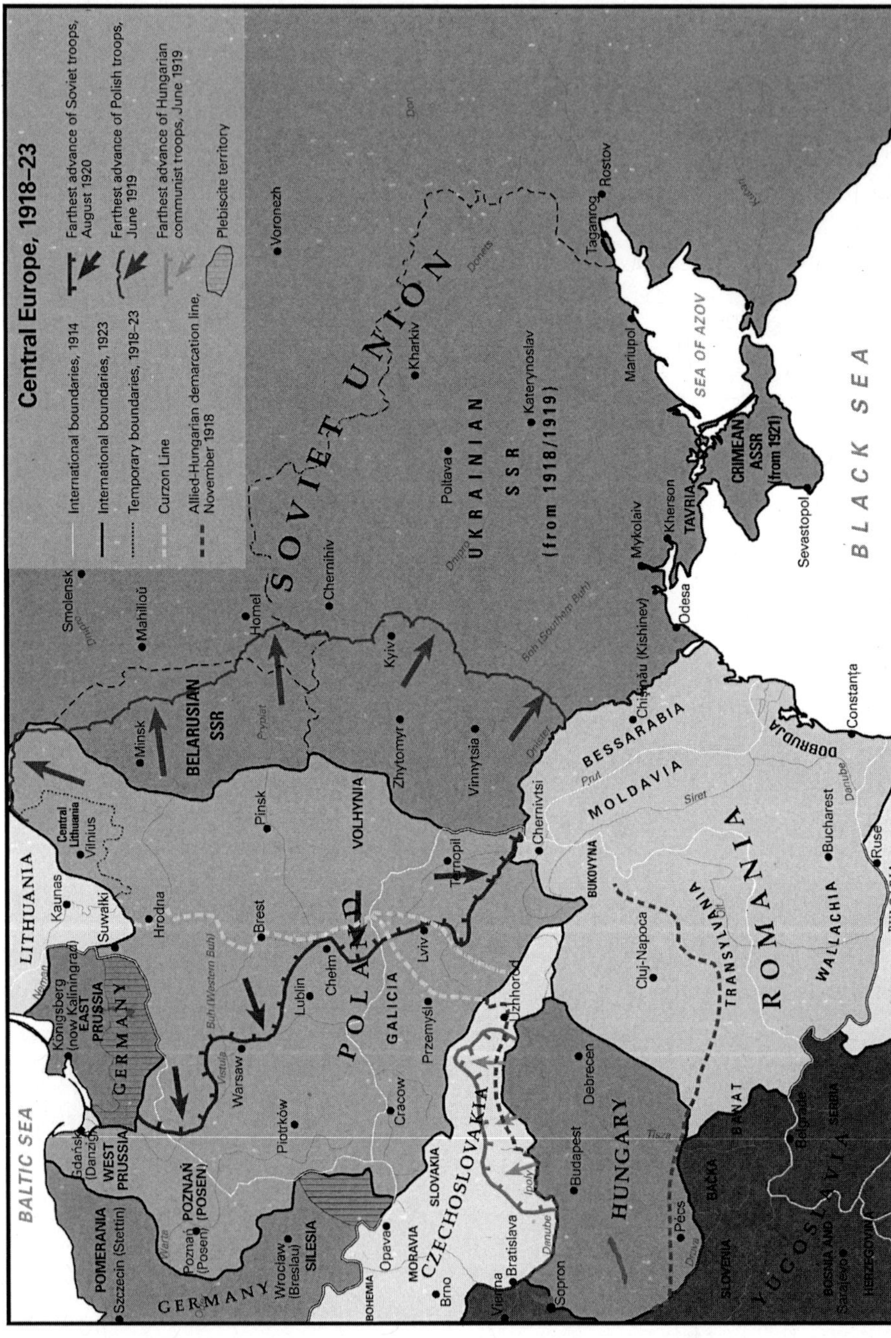

Map 7: Central Europe, 1918–23 (Magocsi, *Historical Atlas of East Central Europe*, 126)

The result was that Polish troops marched into Kyiv on 7 May and even moved eastward beyond the Dnipro. But they did not pursue the demoralized troops of the Red Army any farther. Piłsudski's plan was to establish a strategic line along the Dnipro and then, as rapidly as possible, to station Polish troops in the Belarusian sector to stem the advance of concentrating Soviet forces. But Petliura did not manage to raise forces strong enough to match the Red Army, although he had support in the country, as Stalin himself had to admit. On 11 June 1920, Stalin sent a telegram to Trotsky: "In the regions of western Ukraine, in the Kyiv region and, to some extent, in Poltava, Petliura has raised a serious force that can beat our Soviet forces. Village teachers, medical assistants, agronomists, and cooperative leaders support Petliura. They are organizing the middle and wealthy farmers against the revolution and the *katsap*....[63] The only thing the peasants know about Soviet power is that it has many troops and takes away their grain."[64] In the second half of May, however, the Bolsheviks regained the initiative and forced Polish troops out of Ukraine. By the end of June, Polish forces were more or less back to where they had been on 25 April, and the Red Army was preparing for a decisive offensive that commenced at the beginning of July.[65]

While Red Army units occupied central and western Ukraine and advanced westward, a partisan war against the Bolsheviks was raging in the Ukrainian hinterland. The Bolsheviks ruled the towns, but in the countryside it was the insurgents who were in charge. On 25 June 1920, Dzerzhinsky telegraphed from Kharkiv: "The whole counterrevolution is happening here in the [Ukrainian] countryside."[66] Jan Rutman reported, on 26 May 1920, on the work of the War Tribunals in Ukraine and stated that resistance was more widespread among the Ukrainian population than it was in Russia. Young and old men, women and children were taking part in the resistance. According to Rutman, they were fighting with firearms, pitchforks, and flails.[67] Dzerzhinsky, whom the Politburo had sent to Ukraine in April 1920 to fight "banditry," i.e., anti-Bolshevik uprisings,

63 Derogatory Ukrainian term for Russians.

64 RGASPI, fond 17, op. 109, d. 84, Telegram from Stalin to Trotsky, 11 June 1920, 36.

65 Musial, *Kampfplatz Deutschland*, 42–45.

66 RGASPI, fond 76, op. 3, d. 70, Telegram from Dzerzhinsky to Koris and Ksenofontov, 25 June 1920, 15.

67 RGASPI, fond 17, op. 109, d. 84, Report from Jan Rutman on the work of the War Tribunals on the southwestern front, 22 May 1920, 26ff.

reported on 22 May: "Tackling banditry here will not be so easy in the short term."[68] He was right.

The situation long remained critical for the Bolsheviks in Ukraine, and the country was practically ungovernable in 1920. On 15 October 1920, Lenin complained: "...we cannot get grain from Ukraine because warfare is raging there."[69] At the end of October 1920, according to the estimates of Soviet officials, there were about forty thousand armed "bandits" in Ukraine fighting against communist power.[70] The Bolsheviks did not have adequate forces at the time to break the armed anti-Bolshevik resistance and suppress the uprisings.

In the summer and early autumn of 1920, the main forces of the Red Army were deployed on the Polish front and against the forces of the ex-tsarist officer General Petr Wrangel. The Bolshevik westward offensive on the Polish front collapsed on 15 August outside Warsaw, and the triumphant advance turned into a desperate retreat in the second half of August. Confronted with a Polish counteroffensive and, at the same time, with uprisings behind their own lines, the Bolsheviks asked for a truce with the Polish government, which was arranged on 12 October. Peace negotiations were begun in Riga and concluded on 18 March 1921. The peace treaty established the Polish-Soviet border, and the Polish side withdrew all claims east of the new border and in Soviet Ukraine.[71]

In April 1920, Wrangel raised the Russian Army in the Crimea out of the remnants of Denikin's Volunteer Army and continued the fight against the Bolsheviks. In June 1920, Wrangel's forces began an offensive from the Crimea into southern Ukraine and had achieved remarkable success by September. It was against this background that Nestor Makhno, who had been fighting with his insurgent forces against the Bolsheviks since January 1920, changed sides again and, on 2 October 1920, formed an alliance with the Bolsheviks for the third time in order to fight Wrangel.[72]

---

68 RGASPI, fond 17, op. 3, d. 71–72, Minutes of Politburo session, 20 and 26 April 1920; RGASPI, fond 76, op. 3, d. 70, Dzerzhinsky to Ksenofontov, 22 May 1920, 6.

69 "Concluding Remarks at the Conference of Chairmen of Uyezd, Volost and Village Executive Committees of Moscow Gubernia, 15 October 1920," in Lenin, *Collected Works*, vol. 31 (Moscow, 1966), 336.

70 Telex from Frunze to Lenin, 7 February 1921, on the breakthrough in the struggle against Ukrainian banditry, in Makhno, *Krest'ianskoe dvizhenie na Ukraine 1918–1921,* 585ff.

71 See Musial, *Kampfplatz Deutschland*, 42–56.

72 Sokolova, *Istoriia Rossii*, 707–14; "Military and Political Agreement between the Government of the USSR and the Makhno Army, 2 October 1920," in Makhno, *Krest'ianskoe dvizhenie na Ukraine,* 485ff., doc. 269.

Following the implementation of the truce with Poland on 18 October 1920, Red Army troops under Mikhail Frunze, joined by Makhno's army, began an offensive against Wrangel that forced his troops to withdraw to the Crimea. In this desperate situation, Wrangel evacuated his troops with the help of the British fleet. The last ship with evacuees arrived in Istanbul on 16 November 1920.[73]

The "Pacification" of Ukraine and the Establishment of Communist Rule

In November 1920, the Bolsheviks finally achieved a definitive victory in the Russian civil war. They were now able to deploy all their forces for the suppression of peasant uprisings, including in Ukraine, which was now being defended only by peasant insurgents. Once the Bolsheviks were able to deploy all their forces systematically, these insurgents, in the medium and long term, were fighting losing battles.

On 2 November 1920, Trotsky wrote a memorandum on Ukraine that he sent to Lenin, Stalin, and other leading Bolsheviks. In his introduction, he wrote: "Soviet power has maintained itself in Ukraine up to now (and has done so very poorly) thanks especially to the authority of Moscow and to the Great Russian communists and the Russian Red Army.... The existing regime cannot be considered normal. Economically, Ukraine is an anarchy that is being covered by Moscow's bureaucratic centralism." Trotsky also pointed out that, even after the victory over Wrangel and Petliura, Ukraine remained the most vulnerable part of the republic. Without the Donets Basin, neither the Ukrainian nor the whole Russian economy could be rebuilt.[74]

On 26 November 1920, Trotsky informed Lenin that Ukraine was gradually building up enough troops and that the battle against the insurgents was now on the agenda: "In this way, it is completely possible to aim for an imminent breakthrough."[75] Four days later, the Revolutionary War Council met under Trotsky and discussed the tasks of military officials in Ukraine. The main task was the liquidation of Ukrainian "banditry" because "the elimination of bandits from Ukraine and the permanent security of the Soviet regime are a life-and-death issue for Soviet Ukraine and an issue of extraordinary importance for

73 Sokolova, *Istoriia Rossii*, 707–14.

74 RGASPI, fond 17, op. 109, d. 43, Trotsky's memorandum on Ukraine to Lenin, Stalin and others, 2 November 1920, 65–67.

75 RGASPI, fond 17, op. 109, d. 43, Telegram from Trotsky to Lenin and others, 26 November 1920, 75.

the whole Soviet Federation and its international situation."[76]

The War Council decided to unite all Soviet forces in Ukraine under the command of Mikhail Frunze. The southern front was given the task of defending the Donets Basin against Makhno "bands,"[77] as the Bolsheviks had broken their agreement with Makhno following the victory over Wrangel. On 24 November 1920, Frunze instructed his forces to destroy the *Makhnovshchyna* immediately. Two days later, Frunze declared Makhno and his army to be enemies of the Soviet Republic and of the revolution, ordering his troops to make a surprise attack and defeat them. The Makhno forces suffered heavy losses but were not wiped out. They renewed their fight against the Bolsheviks and caused them considerable losses. In the spring of 1921, however, Makhno's forces suffered heavy defeats and disintegrated into smaller groups that were gradually wiped out or disbanded. On 28 August 1921, Makhno and the remnants of his army crossed the border to Romania and ended their struggle against the Bolsheviks.[78]

The Makhno Army was certainly not the only major "band" in Ukraine, but it was the biggest. In order to liquidate these "bands," the Commission for the Liquidation of Banditry in Ukraine, led by Mikhail Frunze, was established in December 1920. Other members of the commission included Feliks Dzerzhinsky, Sergei Kamenev, and Khristian Rakovsky. In this struggle against "banditry," the Bolsheviks deployed internal security units, field troops of the Red Army, troops of the VChK and various other armed units, altogether a force of some hundreds of thousands, while the insurgent forces were estimated in May 1921 to number between forty and fifty thousand men. Nonetheless, in the winter of 1920–21 the situation for the Bolsheviks in Ukraine was so difficult that they had to employ partisan methods against the insurgents.[79]

---

76 RGASPI, fond 17, op. 109, d. 87, Protocol no. 134, session of the Revolutionary War Council of the Republic, 1 December 1920, 11f.

77 Ibid.

78 Frunze's order to his troops on the southern front, 24 November 1920, in Makhno, *Krest'ianskoe dvizhenie na Ukraine,* 532–34; Frunze's order to his troops on the southern front, 26 November 1920, ibid., 535; Savchenko, *Dvenadtsat' voin za Ukrainu*, chap. 12.

79 RGASPI, fond 76, op. 3, d. 70, Protocol no. 1, session of the Commission for the Liquidation of Banditry in Ukraine, 29 December 1920, 32; Regulation concerning command of all armed forces in Ukraine and representatives of the Revolutionary Military Soviet of the Republic (RVSR) in Ukraine, 29 December 1920, ibid., 33; Coded telegram to troop commanders in Ukraine, Comrades Frunze, von Sklaiansky, S. Kamenev, Lebedev, Dzerzhinsky, 4 January 1921, ibid., 36; RGASPI, fond 17, op. 109, d. 128, Report of the RVSR on the situation of the Red Army, 23 August 1921, 12–13^{v} (with data on Red Army deployments); Savchenko, *Dvenadtsat' voin za Ukrainu*, chap. 12 (data on the strength of Russian forces and of insurgents).

At the same time, the Bolsheviks were developing uniform guidelines for the combat of banditry in Ukraine that were signed on 8 December 1920 by Rakovsky, Frunze, and Molotov. The guidelines contained the following provisions: The population was to be disarmed. If weapons were not surrendered, hostages were to be taken and shot. Anyone who did not voluntarily surrender a weapon was to be shot. The population was to be considered liable for all attacks on transport lines and bridges. Hostages were to be taken from villages along the railway lines and telegraph lines up to a distance of fifteen versts.[80] In areas and localities particularly "infested by bands," the population was also to be considered liable for all anti-Bolshevik attacks; in such cases, hostages were also to be taken. Fines were also possible, as well as the burning or destruction of the houses of "bandits." Hostages were always to be taken from the better-off strata of the population. Thus the guidelines.[81]

These measures were nothing new in Ukraine. The Bolsheviks had been using such methods to fight against Ukrainian insurgents since 1919. In May 1919, Trotsky had ordered the disarming of the Ukrainian population. June 1919 was the deadline for weapons to be surrendered and, from 1 July, the non-surrender of weapons was to be punished ruthlessly.[82] On 30 June 1919, Rakovsky and Joffe informed Trotsky and Lenin about the critical situation in Ukraine and the many uprisings, which were to be combated by means of a general mobilization of men between the ages of 18 and 40, as well as by means of hostages and fines.[83]

With time, the Bolsheviks radicalized their "methods of combating banditry" in Ukraine and elsewhere. On 22 May 1920 Robert Eideman, commander of troops in the rear of the southwestern front in Ukraine, ordered the collection of weapons in the villages. If a village refused to surrender its weapons, it was to be surrounded, and hostages were to be taken from the village population and shot. If this was not enough, the village was to be bombarded by cannon. In villages known to support the Makhno movement, hostages were to be taken and shot if the village did not distance itself from the Makhno movement. Villages

80 A Russian unit of distance: 1 *versta* is 1.066 km.

81 Brief guidelines for the combat of banditry in Ukraine, 8 December 1920, approved by Rakovsky, Frunze, and Molotov, published in Makhno, *Krest'ianskoe dvizhenie na Ukraine,* 555–57.

82 RGASPI, fond 17, op. 109, d. 12, Telegram from Trotsky to Rakovsky and others, 28 May 1919, 19.

83 RGASPI, fond 17, op. 109, d. 43, Telegram from Rakovsky, Joffe, and others to Lenin, Trotsky and others, 30 June 1919, 23ff.

along the railway line were to be made responsible and considered liable for the security of the section of line assigned to them.[84]

On 22 May 1920, Jan Rutman also reported on the situation in Ukraine and on the work of the Bolshevik War Tribunals there. He reported widespread resistance and recommended the following method to "pacify" the Ukrainian villages: the number of kulaks in each village was to be established, and then one in five or one in ten, depending on the situation, was to be shot and their property confiscated.[85] Of course, these orders and recommendations were not just theoretical but were carried out in practice by the Soviet communists. They laid waste whole areas, burned villages, and tortured residents. In May 1921, for instance, the Bolsheviks "pacified" villages around Izium and Lyman (southeast of Kharkiv) as follows: "We called together an assembly, picked out five kulaks or suspected persons, and killed them with swords. Such measures intimidated the peasants and led them to reveal the bandits."[86]

On 7 February 1921, Frunze reported to Lenin on significant successes in the combat of "Ukrainian banditry." As a result, the number of bandits at the end of October 1920 (40,000) had gone down to 6,500. In spite of this success, Frunze was not especially confident: "Banditry has declined. That's a fact. But we can expect it to increase again in the spring."[87] Although Frunze's prognosis was correct, the Bolsheviks succeeded in defeating the major bands in Ukraine by the summer of 1921, as they did in other areas of the former tsarist empire under their rule.[88]

On 1 September 1921, there were still 2,500 "bandits" in Soviet Ukraine who, according to data from the Intelligence Directorate of the Red Army, were organized in groups and were fighting against communist rule. In the following weeks and months, according to Soviet estimates, there were 3,300 "bandits" and 58 "bands" on 15

---

84 RGASPI, fond 17, op. 109, d. 236, Telegram from the chief of the rear sector of the Southwestern Front, Eideman, to Zatonsky, 22 May 1920, 20.

85 RGASPI, fond 17, op. 109, d. 84, Report from Jan Rutman on the work of the War Tribunals of the Southwestern Front, 22 May 1920, 26ff.

86 Extract from newsletter no. 116 of the Secret Intelligence Section of the CPC of the USSR on the Makhno movement in Ukraine, 2 July 1921, in Makhno, *Krest'ianskoe dvizhenie na Ukraine,* 647.

87 Telex from Frunze to Lenin, 7.2.1921, on the breakthrough in the battle against Ukrainian banditry, in Makhno, *Krest'ianskoe dvizhenie na Ukraine 1918–1921*, 585ff.

88 Cf. Musial, *Kampfplatz Deutschland*, 77–85; Sokolova, *Istoriia Rosii*, 732–42.

October, growing to 6,752 by 1 November.[89] After that, the number of "bandits" and "bands" diminished, and the general "band situation" in Ukraine and elsewhere gradually improved. By the end of 1921, the Bolsheviks had withstood the worst and were now combating relatively few insurgents in Ukraine.[90] On 27 December 1921, Trotsky declared at the Ninth Congress of Soviets: "Banditry as a broad social phenomenon, as armed units of broader kulak masses and of parts of the middle peasant masses, is a thing of the past."[91]

It took unprecedented mass terror, costing the lives of many thousands of people, to break the resistance of the peasantry in Ukraine and elsewhere to Bolshevik rule. The total number of victims of Red revolutionary terror is estimated today to have been 2.31 million, hundreds of thousands of whom were Ukrainians. The best-known mass crimes committed by the Bolsheviks in Ukraine were: shootings in Kyiv in February 1918 (2,000 victims) and from February to August 1919 (3,000 victims), in Kharkiv from March to June 1919 (3,000 victims), in Odesa from April to September 1919 (2,200 victims), in Poltava from April to July 1919 (2,000 victims), in the Crimea from December 1920 to July 1921 (between 50,000 and 76,000 victims), as well as shootings of hostages in November 1921 (5,000 victims). The number of victims of Bolshevik terror in the countryside is unknown but was certainly in the tens of thousands.[92] Added to this were the victims of famine. In 1921–22 alone, according to estimates made at the time, more than 26 million people were suffering from hunger as a result of Bolshevik plundering. The regions especially affected were southern Ukraine, the Crimea, the Volga region, and the regions around the Kama River and the central course of the Don. The number of those who died from malnourishment in 1921 to 1922 is estimated to have been five if not six million.[93]

---

89 RGASPI, fond 17, op. 87, d. 332, Situation report no. 5 of the Main Intelligence Directorate of the General Staff of the Red Army on the activities of Russian White Guards abroad and on the internal front, 1 September 1921, 22ff.; RGASPI, fond 17, op. 87, d. 332, Situation report no. 7 of the Main Intelligence Directorate of the General Staff of the Red Army on the activities of Russian White Guards abroad and on the internal front,1 October 1921, 75; RGASPI, fond 17, op. 87, d. 332, Situation report no. 8 of the Main Intelligence Directorate of the General Staff of the Red Army on the activities of Russian White Guards abroad and on the internal front, 1 November 1921, 100–102.

90 Musial, *Kampfplatz Deutschland*, 83–85.

91 RGASPI, fond 325, op. 1, d. 72, Trotsky's speech to the Ninth Congress of Soviets, 27 December 1921, 33.

92 Sokolova, *Istoriia Rossii*, 550–51, 763–65.

93 I. B. Orlov, "NEP v regional'nom rakurse: ot usrednennykh otsenok k mnogoobraziiu," in

All this brought the armed resistance in Ukraine and other Bolshevik-ruled territories to an end, allowing the Bolshevik regime to stabilize and secure its rule. The gradual rebuilding of the Ukrainian and the whole Soviet economy began in the spring of 1921 with the New Economic Policy (NEP). Tax-in-kind replaced requisitioning, in other words, the peasants had to deliver part of their produce as tax to the government. They could dispose of the rest independently on the free market.[94] The NEP stimulated the development of the rural economy, small businesses, crafts, trade, and light industry in general, all of which enabled the supply of industrial goods to the villages.[95] This contributed to peace in the countryside. It was, after all, the forced requisitioning of food (war communism) that had frequently led to the peasant uprisings in the first place.

The Formation of the Union of Soviet Socialist Republics and the Ukrainian Question

In the summer of 1922, the Bolsheviks gave a new political form to the territories ruled by them. In August 1922 the Central Committee of the Russian Communist Party established a commission, chaired by Stalin, which was given the task of dealing with the mutual relations between Bolshevik Russia, Ukraine, Belarus, and the Caucasian Federation and making appropriate recommendations on how these should be regulated.[96] Until then, the individual republics had been formally independent and had their own governments. This was, of course, only a fictitious independence. In reality, it was Lenin and his comrades in the Politburo who ruled the individual republics.[97]

On the nationality question, Stalin worked closely with Dmytro Manuilsky, who consulted him on 4 September 1922 about the political system of Bolshevik states. Manuilsky thought that the republican system should be replaced by a system of autonomy, for which he argued as follows: "The experience of the past year has shown that

---

NEP: Ėkonomicheskie, politicheskie i sotsiokul'turnye aspekty, ed. A. S. Seniavskii, V. B. Zhiromskaia, and S. V. Zhuravlev (Moscow, 2006), 33–54; Nicolas Werth, "Ein Staat gegen sein Volk. Gewalt, Unterdrückung und Terror in der Sowjetunion," in *Das Schwarzbuch des Kommunismus. Unterdrückung, Verbrechen und Terror,* ed. Stéphane Courtois et al. (Munich and Zurich, 2004), 51–295; Sokolova, *Istoriia Rossii*, 763–65.

94 On 30 March 1921, the Politburo decided to end food requisitioning in Ukraine and introduce the free market: RGASPI, fond 17, op. 3, d. 144, Minutes of Politburo session, 30 March 1921, 3, 6–8.

95 Musial, *Kampfplatz Deutschland*, 68–76; Sokolova, *Istoriia Rossii*, 766–69, 776–80.

96 M. V. Aleksandrov, *Vneshnepoliticheskaia doktrina Stalina* (Canberra, 1997), 18ff.

97 This is clear from the Politburo minutes. See RGASPI, fond 17, op. 3.

the existing system in the periphery, especially in Ukraine, leads to numerous conflicts between central and regional authorities. This situation cannot continue." He went on: "The formation of independent republics on the periphery, with their own TsIKs [Central Executive Committees] and *Sovnarkomy* [Councils of People's Commissars], corresponded to a certain stage of our revolution that we could call the 'national' stage.... This was a necessary concession to the nationalist elements.... Without doubt, the introduction of autonomy where the regime had been 'independent' will influence the tempo of the transition that we call 'change by stages.' On the periphery of our republic, especially in Ukraine, the national element will delay this 'change by stages.' The introduction of autonomy will hold back the Ukrainian transition for a certain time, but it will not produce any national movement in opposition to this course because there is no basis for it among the Ukrainian intelligentsia. The Ukrainian peasant has no interest in 'national' questions and will no longer participate in political bands."[98]

This argument convinced Stalin, and at its session of 23–24 September 1922 the commission ratified Stalin's plan for the "autonomization" of the peripheral Soviet republics, in other words, their integration into the Russian Soviet Republic as autonomous formations.[99] The day before, Stalin had explained his plan to Lenin: "The existing disorder and total chaos are creating conflicts, complaints, and irritations and are crippling economic activity in the whole of Russia.... If we do not...now replace the formal (fictitious) independence with formal (and real) autonomy, it will be much more difficult in another year to defend the actual unity of the Soviet republics."[100]

Lenin was not convinced, however, and insisted on the formation of a union of "equal" Soviet republics and maintaining the appearance of independence of the peripheral republics. He was thinking of the future world revolution and the formation of a "Union of Soviet Republics of Europe and Asia." Lenin prevailed and, on 6 October 1922, the plenum of the Central Committee of the Russian Communist Party changed Stalin's plan. On 30 December 1922, the First Congress

98 RGASPI, fond 558, op. 11, d. 763, Manuilsky to Stalin, 4 September 1922, 1–3, in *TsK RKP(b) – VKP(b) i natsional'nyi vopros,* ed. L. S. Gatagova, L. P. Kosheleva, and L. A. Rogovaia, vol. 1, *1918–1933 gg.* (Moscow, 2005), 76ff.

99 Aleksandrov, *Vneshnepoliticheskaia doktrina Stalina*, 18ff.

100 Stalin to Lenin, 22 September 1922, in *TsK RKP(b) – VKP(b) i natsional'nyi vopros*, 78ff.

of Soviets approved Lenin's proposal for the formation of the Union of Soviet Socialist Republics (USSR). The USSR now existed as a political formation and continued until 1991.[101]

But nothing changed in the relations between the peripheral republics and Moscow. For the next sixty-nine years, the Ukrainian Soviet Republic existed with the appearance of independence, but de facto it was one of the provinces of the communist empire ruled from Moscow. By the same token, the formation of the USSR did not end the terror in Ukraine. It actually reached its high point in the 1930s, during the Stalin era. The consequences of communist rule were catastrophic for Ukraine and Ukrainians in every respect. It will take generations before the economic, social, and moral aberrations of the period of communist rule can be overcome in Ukraine.

101 Aleksandrov, *Vneshnepoliticheskaia doktrina Stalina*, 18ff.

4c-e. Limits to Power: Ukraine in the Strategies of the Allied Powers, 1917–1924[1]

Hannes Leidinger and Wolfram Dornik

Alliances, Strategies, Zones of Influence

The United States of America was critical of the way that the Habsburg Monarchy and the Ottoman Empire handled the nationalities question. It was less critical of the Romanov Empire in that regard. The US assessment was that Russia should not be broken up into individual regions and national units but, like the United States, should proceed to a multi-ethnic democratic society united by Russian culture. Washington was very pleased when the February Revolution of 1917 swept away the regime of Nicholas II. The American president, Woodrow Wilson, hoped that Russia, like the USA after it was liberated from colonial tutelage, would develop into a prosperous, economically buoyant democracy and thus a trading partner for the USA and an equal counterpart on the Eurasian continent. With their very rapid diplomatic recognition, on 19 March 1917, the Americans wanted to stabilize the Provisional Government under Georgii Lvov and keep it as an active player on the Eastern Front.[2]

France's reaction to the fall of the tsar was more hesitant. It was only after recognition of the new Russian government by Britain and Italy, France's allies in the war against the German- and Austro-Hungarian-dominated Central Powers, that France followed suit. The new government's willingness to continue the war, as part of an alliance that was now strengthened, since April, by the entry of the USA, led to the final disintegration of the Romanov army. The crisis of the Russian state intensified under Lvov's successor, Aleksandr Kerensky.[3] Following Entente military defeats and mutinies among French forces, and in the climate of an increasing willingness to make

---

1 This chapter is a shorter version of the separate chapters 4c (Hannes Leidinger), 4d and 4e (Wolfram Dornik) in the German edition of this book.

2 Clarence A. Manning, "The Ukrainians and the United States in World War I," *Ukrainian Quarterly* 12, no. 4 (1957): 351–54; Constantine Warvariv, "America and the Ukrainian National Cause, 1917–1920," in *The Ukraine, 1917–1921: A Study in Revolution,* ed. Taras Hunczak (Cambridge, Mass., 1977), 356ff.

3 AAÉ, AAC/AP, CPC, Guerre 1914–1918, Russie, vol. 649, Paléologue, no. 487 and vol. 648, Jusserand, no. 169. We would like to thank Jacques Benkemoun and Elizabeth Blaickner for assistance with archival research in London and Paris.

peace, strategists of the *Grande Nation* were thinking of a compromise with its enemies, whereby the territorial integrity of the old tsarist empire was up for discussion. A memorandum of October 1917 allowed the Habsburg Monarchy to have a protectorate in the form of a Polish-Ukrainian federation. Germany would have the upper hand in the Baltics and in Belarus in return for Alsace-Lorraine.[4]

But Berlin did not agree and, at the same time, Entente circles failed to bring Austria-Hungary over to their side by means of a separate deal.[5] Thus the planned agreement existed only on paper. The October Revolution was seen by the Western powers as an opportunity to insist on existing agreements, war aims, and alliance commitments. Talks between the Soviet government, the Council of People's Commissars (*Sovnarkom*, CPC), and the Hohenzollern and Habsburg Empires about a truce and peace were initially met by the Entente with little more than protest notes. What followed then was a double strategy. France's representatives, based in Iaşi in the south, the ambassador, Auguste de Saint-Aulaire,[6] and the head of the military mission, Henri M. Berthelot, would support the Cossacks and the Ukrainian nationalists against the Bolsheviks. In the area dominated by the Soviets, Henri Albert Niessel, the head of the military mission, and Joseph Noulens, the French ambassador, would maintain contact with the representatives of the Bolsheviks. Saint-Aulaire and especially Berthelot paid special attention to keeping Romania in the war and preventing Germany from appropriating the economic resources of Ukraine.[7]

Ukraine's highest political authority, the Central Rada, had already spoken to Noulens about financial assistance and had offered

---

4 SHD/AAT, série N, 1872–1919, 16N 3021, 3. Bureau A, "Note au sujet de l'attitude qu'il convient d'adopter à l'égard de la Russie." French government members and diplomats had a more reserved attitude toward the movement for Ukrainian autonomy or independence until the second half of 1917. They saw the nationalist movement as a threat to their Great Russian ally. They also frequently thought that the growing tendency toward independence was a result of manipulation by the Central Powers. Cf. Gustave Cvengroš, *La République Démocratique Ukrainienne – La République Française (1917–1922)* (Lviv, 1995), 13ff., 25.

5 Helmut Rumpler, "Kaiser Karl, die Friedensprojekte und das deutsch-österreichische Bündnis," in *Karl I. (IV.), der Erste Weltkrieg und das Ende der Donaumonarchie*, ed. Andreas Gottsmann (Vienna, 2007), 15–18; Wilfried Fest, *Peace or Partition: The Habsburg Monarchy and British Policy* (London, 1978), 202–4; V. H. Rothwell, *British War Aims and Peace Diplomacy 1914–1918* (Oxford, 1971), 79–87, 98–102; David Stevenson, *The First World War and International Politics* (Oxford and New York, 1991), 191ff.

6 For his view of the situation, see Auguste de Saint-Aulaire, *Confession d'un vieux diplomate* (Paris, 1953).

7 SHD/AAT, série N, 1872–1919, 7N 921, dossier 1, Clemenceau à Niessel, no. 13529 BS/3.

Georges Tabouis, the leader of the French military mission in Kyiv, cooperation with the Entente. Some representatives of the *Grande Nation* argued for very rapid negotiations in order not to offend "Francophile elements."[8] Paris led this effort, with the agreement of the Allied Supreme Council, and gave full authority to Tabouis, at the end of December, to represent France in a "de facto" independent Ukraine.[9] In the weeks that followed, there was a joint effort with British representatives to deliver major economic assistance to the young state while, on 17 January 1918, Saint-Aulaire informed a Rada delegation in Iaşi that France was prepared to formally recognize Ukrainian statehood and establish regular relations with Kyiv.[10]

The US, however, remained cautious. In a note from acting Secretary of State Frank Polk to the French ambassador in Washington, on 11 January 1918, Polk stressed that the US was "carefully observing" the situation in Ukraine but had come to no firm conclusion on the recognition of separatist movements in Russia. Auguste de Saint-Aulaire therefore insisted that the Rada adopt a pro-Entente position, something that some observers had begun to doubt in the meantime. Tabouis, who was carrying "in his pocket,"[11] so to speak, the confirmation

---

8 Ibid., 4N 40, dossier 3, Berthelot, nos. 30–35; AAÉ, AAC/AP, CPC, Guerre 1914–1918, Russie/Ukraine, vol. 694, Noulens, no. 1830.

9 On French recognition of Ukraine, correspondence with the USA, and similar steps by Great Britain at the beginning of 1918, see Cvengroš, *La République Démocratique Ukrainienne*, 21, 27, 34ff. Many scholars consider that Ukraine allowed itself to become an "example" of French nationality policy on the territory of the former tsarist empire. See especially Ghislain de Castelbajac, Sébastien de Gasquet, and Georges-Henri Soutou, *Recherches sur la France et le problème des nationalités pendant la Première Guerre mondiale (Pologne-Lithuanie-Ukraine)* (Paris, 1995), 127.

10 AAÉ, AAC/AP, CPC, Guerre 1914–1918, Russie/Ukraine, vol. 695, Clemenceau à Berthelot, no. 13625 BS/3.

11 Earlier literature on this subject pointed out that Tabouis did not have the authority to recognize Ukrainian sovereignty. It was emphasized that Ukraine only proclaimed its separation from Russia in the course of 1918. But developments in the winter of 1917–18 suggest that France was extremely flexible in relation to separatist tendencies in the old Romanov Empire. The attitude of the French foreign minister, Stephen Pichon, for instance, in connection with the recognition of Finland, an attitude supported by other individuals around Clemenceau, suggests a double tactic. Repeatedly stressed fears that national independence could only serve the interests of the Central Powers led Pichon to regard Finnish independence as a mere transitional stage in the creation of a Russian federation. But the foreign minister also stressed that the Allies had to stand by the Scandinavians in their struggle for independence in order to create a counterweight to German influence in the region. However, if no unity could be achieved among the "nations" of the former tsarist empire, then Entente support for an independent Finland would be a sensible strategy to counter Berlin's plans for hegemony. Cf. George A. Brinkley, "Allied Policy and French Intervention in the Ukraine, 1917–1920," in *The Ukraine, 1917–1921*, 325; Louis Clerc, "De la province russe à l'État scandinave. Évaluation du regard diplomatique français sur la Finlande (1900–1920)," in *Frontières du communisme. Mythologies et réalités de la division*

of official recognition, was instructed by Henri Berthelot not to take any hasty steps. There were numerous reports that, confronted with the Bolshevik threat, Kyiv could expect more from German weapons than from French economic assistance.[12] Ukraine then signed a peace treaty with the Central Powers on 9 February 1918. Russia followed on 3 March with the Treaty of Brest-Litovsk. Romania signed a few months later, making an agreement with Berlin and Vienna. In all cases, the agreements gave the stamp of approval to Wilhelmine and Habsburg dominance in the region.

Even during the occupation by the Central Powers, however, Great Britain did not completely withdraw from Ukraine. Lieutenant Colonel Joseph W. Boyle was sent on a secret mission to Ukraine by the British military attaché in Romania, Brigadier General C. Robert Ballard. Boyle was given a great deal of money (1 million Romanian lei and 1.1 million British pounds) and used it to create groups, consisting mostly of Bolsheviks, who instigated strikes and carried out sabotage of infrastructure in Odesa, Kharkiv, and Kyiv. According to Boyle, it was these groups that carried out the big explosions at weapons stores in Odesa and strikes in Kyiv in June and October. Even though the reports containing this information were written after 1919, his résumé reads like an extract from a spy novel: "First, it helped to detain a large force of the enemy in the Ukraine to deal with the unrest and guard the bridges and depots; up till the end of September, there were no less than 20 German divisions and 10 Austrian divisions there. Second, it disabled the Black Sea Fleet to a large extent. Third, it prevented the enemy from collecting as much supplies as they might have done had the railways been working well. In fact, the results were far greater than those of the mission of Sir J. Norton Griffiths, were less expensive, and were carried out in circumstances of greater danger."[13] Even though Ukraine was not in the British zone of influence following the division of Russian territory, activities of the British secret service promoted unrest in the country and impeded its economic exploitation by the Central Powers.

---

de l'Europe de la révolution d'Octobre au mur de Berlin, ed. Sophie Coeuré and Sabine Dullin (Paris, 2007), 68–71.

12 AAÉ, AAC/AP, CPC, Guerre 1914–1918, Russie/Ukraine, vol. 695, Saint-Aulaire, nos. 102–20; SHD/AAT, série N, 1872–1919, 4N 40, dossier 3, Berthelot, no. 1648.

13 Norton Griffiths was the British agent who, before the Central Powers' occupation of Romania, sabotaged the oil fields and put them out of action for a few months. See Michael Occleshaw, *Dances in Seep Shadows: Britain's Clandestine War in Russia, 1917–1920* (London, 2006), 105–7 (Eds.).

The suspicions of Austro-Hungarian intelligence officials that Entente officials were involved in the strikes and uprisings were not simply a figment of their imagination. However, during the remaining period until the end of the First World War, London did not again seriously consider supporting the Ukrainian independence movement.

Meanwhile, neither the British government under David Lloyd George nor the French government, led after November 1917 by Georges Benjamin Clemenceau, had any reason to break completely with Soviet Russia. It made sense to continue their relationship with the Communist Party leadership under Vladimir Lenin because relations between the new Kremlin leaders and the Wilhelmine Empire remained tense. There were conflicts on the demarcation line. Berlin's contacts with the Russian oppositionists and the propaganda campaigns of the people's commissars also poisoned the climate between the two.[14] Under those circumstances, England concentrated increasingly on the Bolsheviks. London's agent, Sir Robert Bruce Lockhart, followed them to Moscow, their new capital. At the beginning of May 1918, the Foreign Office instructed him to give cautious signals to the people's commissars that possible diplomatic recognition was imminent. The Allies were considering plans for intervention in Russia with the agreement of the Bolsheviks. There would be no interference in Russia's internal affairs; they would only revive the Eastern Front against the Central Powers.[15]

If the proponents of an understanding between Lenin's CPC and the Entente were not able to win the day, this was because of the dithering of the Allies' representatives over the different options, namely, whether to support the pro- or anti-Bolshevik forces on the territory of the old tsarist empire. The attitude of the Paris Foreign Office on the Quai d'Orsay also had a major influence on developments. Joseph Noulens, whose subordinate was Niessel's successor as leader of the military mission, Jean Guillaume Lavergne, himself a supporter of such an understanding, was given additional powers. Noulens had considerable freedom of action and became a key figure in working out anti-Soviet strategies, a development that would have been unthinkable without Clemenceau's agreement in principle.[16]

14 Iurii Fel'shtinskii, *Krushenie mirovoi revoliutsii*, vol. 1, *Brestskii mir. Oktiabr' 1917–Noiabr' 1918* (London, 1991), 350; ÖStA, AOK/Op.Abt., Ev. Grp.–R 1918: 12. Nachricht v. 16.6.1918; RGASPI, f. 17, op. 86, d. 112.

15 Bruce Lockhart, *Memoirs of a British Agent, Being an Account of the Author's Early Life in Many Lands and of His Official Mission to Moscow in 1918* (London and New York, 1932), 270ff.

16 SHD/AAT, série N, 1872–1919, 16N 3066, Noulens, no. 89 et Pichon à Clemenceau, no. 1567.

This increasingly unequivocal opposition to the Kremlin leadership led to direct intervention in Russia by France and its allies.[17] When it became clear that financial assistance alone to Lenin's weak opponents was not enough to achieve the single-minded goal of overthrowing the October regime, their attention turned especially to an intervention by Japanese troops. Tokyo, part of the anti-German Entente from the end of August 1914 and pursuing a determined policy of hegemony in East Asia, did not want to risk a conflict with the United States, which it regarded as a competing power in the Pacific region and, at the same time, an ally in the war.[18]

Under these circumstances, much depended on the attitude of the United States and Woodrow Wilson. To win the USA over to a limited action on the territory of the former tsarist empire, the Czechoslovak Legion was brought into play. The *druzhiny*, consisting of deserters and prisoners of war, were seen at the end of 1917 as independent units under French command. Their contribution to Allied intervention on the territory of the collapsed Romanov Empire should not be underestimated. However, the engagement of the Western powers remained limited. Their goals were unclear, shortsighted, and contradictory.[19] At one time it was a matter of securing Entente war supplies in Russia, on another occasion it was a matter of evacuating or supporting the Czechoslovak Legion, and at yet another time the goal was support for the Russian opponents of the October regime. There were always good reasons for entertaining doubts about their strength and their prospects of success, as well as for the need to weaken Germany by means of an "active Russian policy" and "maintenance of the Eastern Front."

Even without measures of this kind, it was clear that the anti-German alliance, especially after the arrival of US troops on the Western Front, was (materially) superior. The Central Powers were completely burned out and, to make matters worse for them, were deeply entangled in a civil war in Ukraine and in an intensive struggle to prevent the spread of revolutionary ideas.[20]

---

17 Sophie Coeuré, "Endiguer le bolchevisme? La 'Double frontière' dans le répertoire de l'anticommunisme (1917–1941)," in *Frontières du communisme*, 44.

18 SHD/AAT, série N, 1872–1919, 4N 63, dossier 3, Jusserand, no. 669.

19 See Hannes Leidinger and Verena Moritz, *Gefangenschaft, Revolution, Heimkehr. Die Bedeutung der Kriegsgefangenenproblematik für die Geschichte des Kommunismus in Mittel- und Osteuropa 1917–1920* (Vienna, Cologne, and Weimar, 2003), especially 277, 378–80, and 408ff.

20 John Grigg, *Lloyd George: War Leader 1916–1918* (London, 2002), 562.

The leadership of the British Empire, in particular, was slow to recognize this. Reports from the Foreign Office continued to focus on the desperate attempts to revise the Brest-Litovsk peace settlement and restore the Eastern Front. Discussions continued into the autumn of 1917 about an intervention of US troops in the western periphery of the former tsarist empire. This proposal came from the foreign-policy adviser of the US president, Edward M. House. Woodrow Wilson, however, was skeptical about the idea. This may have had to do with the fact that the British prime minister, Lloyd George, also favored an intervention by US troops on the Eastern Front, and Wilson feared that this would mean exclusion of the US from postwar plans in Western Europe.[21]

In London, at the beginning of 1919, the War Office summarized the events and decisions of 1918: "The political destiny of Russia was of no immediate concern to the Allies except in so far as it might, in the event of an inconclusive peace, assist in the continuity and enhancement of German military power."[22] The Ukrainian independence movement was also seen from this perspective. In the course of the peace negotiations between the Central Powers and the October regime, the US ambassador, David R. Francis, still in St. Petersburg, noted: "The language of the Ukrainian delegates agrees with the information received from the Allied agents at Kiev showing that the Entente can at present expect no effective help from the Ukraine. All that we can ask of her is to gain time to allow the Allied powers to act for the improvement of the general situation on this front. We again expressed the opinion that the only means of attaining this and consequently of deciding the attitude of the Ukraine in a manner conformable with the interests of our cause is to send to Russia an international [force] under the conditions we have indicated. It is well to note that this impression is shared by the Rumanian Government which has also had interviews with the delegates of the Ukrainian government."[23] Once the Ukrainian delegation had been admitted to the Brest-Litovsk talks, the US ambassador in St. Petersburg (later Moscow) recommended the simultaneous recognition of Finland, Ukraine, Siberia, the Don Cossacks, and the Soviet government because he saw the admission of the Ukrainians to the negotiations as a move on the

---

21 David M. Esposito, *The Legacy of Woodrow Wilson: American War Aims in World War I* (Westport, Conn., and London, 1996), 83–101, 110ff., 117–27.

22 TNA, FO 608/177, Short History of Events in Russia from November 1917–February 1919, 14.3.1919, 1.

23 NARA, US DoS, Papers relating to the foreign relations of the U.S., 1918. Russia, vol. 2, Washington, D.C. 1918, 660-63.

part of the Bolsheviks away from the all-Russian claim to power. The response of the British Foreign Office was unmistakably negative: "To encourage Ukrainian independence is to assist Germany's aims and also to endanger the future peace of Europe."[24]

What was increasingly coming to light in all this was the colonial and imperial interest of all the great powers in the territory of the former tsarist empire. The English and the French, just like Germany and its allies, were seeking their "place in the sun." A competition over zones of influence had begun within the different alliances. In December 1917, the West European powers agreed that France would prevail in Ukraine, Bessarabia, and the Crimea, while England would take the Caucasus, Georgia, Armenia, and Kurdistan. Debate remained about the Don region, and the British Foreign Office later wanted a revision of the previous agreements.[25] London had been in conflict with the plans of Clemenceau's government for some months because it saw them as questioning the agreements already reached. The proposal that Allied troops under French command should support Anton Denikin's Volunteer Army in the North Caucasus was seen by England as a violation of its sphere of interest.[26] From the viewpoint of the British Empire, there was reason to believe that the *Grande Nation,* after a "Siberian phase,"[27] would concentrate on the southern regions of the collapsed empire. Pierre Maurice Janin, the commander of Allied, mostly Czechoslovak, units in Siberia, informed his British partners that he would regard a new front east of Odesa, in the Crimea and at Rostov on the Don, as sensible. From there, according to Janin, Kyiv could be "secured" with Allied troops from the Balkans and from Palestine.[28]

These developments were then affected by the capitulation of the Central Powers, the reassignment of zones of influence, and the increasingly clear intention to "destroy Bolshevism" or at least to "contain" it. The commander of Allied forces in Thessaloniki, General Louis François Franchet d'Esperey, was asked by Clemenceau to develop plans with his Allied partners for a "bastion of resistance" in "southern Russia and Odesa" against Lenin's Soviet regime.[29]

---

24 TNA, FO 371/3349, No. 197.905, The Russian Situation, 11.1918.

25 TNA, FO 608/206, 331, 337.

26 TNA, FO 371/3342, 62.

27 Brinkley, "Allied Policy and French Intervention in the Ukraine," 327.

28 TNA, FO 371/3342, 59.

29 Gérard Unger, *Aristide Briand* (Paris, 2005), 391; see also Kurt Fischer, *Deutsche Truppen und Entente-Intervention in Südrußland 1918/19* (Boppard am Rhein, 1973), 43; Brinkley, "Allied Policy and French Intervention in the Ukraine," 331.

The involvement of Henri Berthelot indicated a reactivation of the forces that had been preparing anti-Soviet actions immediately after the October Revolution in Iaşi and Kyiv. In addition to France's local military mission, the others involved were France's ambassador to Romania, Gustave de Saint-Aulaire, and a member of the Tabouis mission, Émile Henno, who, as "consul," became the unauthorized representative of the Entente in Ukraine. These proponents of an active interventionist policy strongly supported the Whites under Anton Denikin, to whom Franchet d'Esperey had sent about thirty thousand weapons in November 1918.[30] The Allies were united around Denikin and, at the same time, were making preparations for the purchase of grain in southern Russia and its transport through Odesa. An Anglo-French commission led by the onetime British consul in Odesa, Sir John Picton Bagge, was established for this purpose.[31] He traveled to Odesa at the end of November. Britain, in the background, attempted to support the Ukrainians with deliveries of weapons, just enough for them to maintain the fight against the Bolsheviks but not offend the Whites. Britain's deliveries of weapons to the Ukrainians were stopped only when the French and Italians intervened in the British military missions. Those weapons would have been used against Poland, which was not in the interests of either France or Italy, as they planned for Poland to become a buffer state between Germany and Russia.[32]

Unlike just about a year before, in December 1917 and January 1918, the French were now supporting not the Ukrainian national movement but the emerging Polish state and the "White generals" of the old Romanov Empire. The Entente planned further deliveries of assistance to Denikin's army and sent Greek and French troops, although the designated commander of Allied forces in Ukraine, Philippe Henri d'Anselme, warned against active intervention in the region. D'Anselme indicated the war-weariness of the soldiers. Added to this was opposition in France. Journalists and parliamentarians in

---

30 SHD/AAT, série N, 1872–1919, 20N 225, Franchet d'Esperey, no. 5797/3 and no. 12564/2ch, 16N 3147, Franchet d'Esperey, no. 5955/3 and 16N 3172, Berthelot, no 83/3 and 139/3; AAÉ, AAC/AP, Z-Europe, URSS, Action des Alliés dans le sud de la Russie, vol. 226, Pichon à Saint-Aulaire, no. 42.

31 TNA, FO 371/3342, No. 184.858, Cereal Commission to the Black Sea, 7.11.1918; TNA, FO 371/3342, No. 190.940, Mr. Bagge, 18.11.1918; TNA, FO 371/3342, No. 191.958, Mr. Bagge's mission to Odessa, 20.11.1918; TNA, FO 371/3342, No. 192.650, Grain from Russia, 21.11.1918; TNA, FO 371/3342, No. 196.022, Wheat situation in South Russia, 27.11.1918.

32 TNA, FO 608/71/24, Polish oppression of Ukrainians, 24.1.1919, 394–96.

Paris were opposing the "anti-Soviet campaign." The left in particular proclaimed its solidarity with the Kremlin leadership, while the members of Clemenceau's government showed themselves to be ill-informed. The situation in southern Russia was confusing. The Central Powers' puppet regime under Pavlo Skoropadsky, which had tried in vain to shift to a pro-Entente course, had been overthrown by the Ukrainian nationalist Directory under Volodymyr Vynnychenko and Symon Petliura.[33] The British and French regarded the new power as a *quantité négligeable* that was "half Bolshevik" in any case, given its social and political program.[34] Émile Henno accordingly rejected the Petliura government, thus losing a potential partner that was soon having to defend itself against Moscow.[35]

"A Wretched Adventure"

When the first inadequately armed and poorly motivated French expeditionary forces, under the command of General Albert Borius, arrived in Odesa on 17 and 18 December, they were met by anything but a welcoming population. Henno had been in the city for a couple of weeks. Caught up in skirmishes with Directory troops, and with Henno's involvement, they installed a military governor in the city who was subordinate to Borius and had previously been part of the entourage of the Siberian "supreme ruler," Aleksandr Kolchak.[36]

Gradually, the Entente troops managed to secure their positions and expand their occupation zone. They departed from their original line by negotiating a truce with the Ukrainians and adopting a cooperative attitude toward the Directory's war minister, General Oleksandr Hrekov. Since French representatives soon came to regard the Whites as increasingly unreliable and weak allies, and Henno had

---

33 Andreas Kappeler, *Kleine Geschichte der Ukraine*, 2d ed. (Munich, 2000), 173.

34 TNA, FO 608/206, 349–55 and 608/207, 444. The reports that Pichon received about this had overestimated the strength of Skoropadsky's government and underestimated the chances of the Directory. See Brinkley, "Allied Policy and French Intervention in the Ukraine," 335.

35 AAÉ, AAC/AP, Z–Europe, URSS, Action des Alliés dans le sud de la Russie, vol. 225, Saint-Aulaire, no. 857; Jean Xydias, *L'intervention française en Russie, 1918–1919* (Paris, 1927), 123ff., 126ff. In the second half of November 1918, on Henno's initiative, there was a meeting in Iaşi between delegates of various anti-Bolshevik forces on the territory of the former tsarist empire. The Ukrainians were not formally represented. There were two delegates, however, who represented Skoropadsky's standpoint indirectly. The meeting was dominated by conservative groups. Henno expressed his contempt for the "chauvinist," "separatist," and "socialist" Directory under Vynnychenko and Petliura. See Brinkley, "Allied Policy and French Intervention in the Ukraine," 332, 337.

36 *Odessaer Zeitung*, no. 239, 21 December 1918, 1; cf. SHD/AAT, série N, 1872–1919, 16N 3188, Rapport Garchery.

lost influence, nothing now stood in the way of continuing the course they had begun. Henri Berthelot and Philippe d'Anselme encouraged further negotiations with Hrekov.[37]

Hrekov was speaking for a government that found itself in a hopeless situation vis-à-vis the Bolsheviks. Forced onto the defensive by the Reds and compelled to give up Kyiv, the Directory's representatives agreed to the extensive demands made by d'Anselme's chief of staff, Henri Freydenberg. The compromise had the appearance of a partial Ukrainian surrender. Under French pressure until the end of February 1919, and in spite of resistance and caveats,[38] they tolerated not only being placed under the military command of French generals but also foreign control of the country's railways and finance. They also agreed to a restructuring of the government and the resignation of Vynnychenko, whom d'Anselme regarded as an incorrigible left-wing extremist.[39]

French officers, in the manner of colonial masters, aimed to establish a protectorate without addressing the formal recognition of the Directory and independent Ukraine. Freydenberg's goal was rather to work toward a union of the territory with a greater Russia,[40] although this still did not satisfy Denikin's supporters. As resolute opponents of separatist currents, they saw the negotiations with Petliura's representatives as an affront and had the backing of British officials in this. The Foreign Office in London was deluged with reports and dossiers that decried the inabilities as well as the unlikeableness of the French and, not without hints from the Whites, emphasized Freydenberg's Jewish origins.[41]

The extent of annoyance at the actions of the *Grande Nation* can be seen in the reaction of the USA. Washington was outraged that the French were speaking in the name of the whole Entente when negotiating with the Ukrainians, in spite of the fact that the

---

37 SHD/AAT, série N, 1872–1919, 20N 729, Berthelot à Franchet d'Esperey, no. 240/3.

38 Cf. Cvengroš, *La République Démocratique Ukrainienne,* 58ff.; A. D. Margolin, *From a Political Diary: The Ukraine and America, 1905–1945* (New York, 1946), 37; A. D. Margolin, *Ukraina i politika antanty* (Berlin, 1921).

39 Brinkley, "Allied Policy and French Intervention in the Ukraine," 339; cf. SHD/AAT, série N, 1872–1919, 16N 3149, Rapport Freydenberg et d'Anselme. Freydenberg's plan in the "French zone of southern Russia" was to separate the areas held by the Russian Whites from those of the Ukrainian nationalist supporters of the Directory. Cf. Brinkley, "Allied Policy and French Intervention in the Ukraine," 338.

40 SHD/AAT, série N, 1872–1919, 20N 763, d'Anselme, "Rapport d'ensemble." For an account of the French position of 4 April 1919, see Brinkley, "Allied Policy and French Intervention in the Ukraine," 342.

41 TNA, FO 608/206, 111, 185ff., 331–37, 343, 379ff. On Freydenberg's Jewish origins, see FO 608/206, 245.

Directory under Petliura was waging a war on two fronts, in Eastern Galicia against Poland and in the north against the advancing Red Army. Robert Lansing, the leader of the American delegation in Paris, reported in a letter to the US State Department that Ukrainian representatives in Paris had passed him documents revealing details of the negotiations between the French and the Ukrainians in Kyiv in January and February 1919. These revealed the extensive demands that French emissaries had made on Petliura.[42] Reports of this kind caused the US to distance itself increasingly from its war allies.[43] In all this, a not unimportant role was played by the French-backed government in Warsaw. The Americans paid careful attention to the Ukrainian-Polish battles in Eastern Galicia between November 1918 and June 1919. The Council of Four at the Paris Peace Conference (Thomas Woodrow Wilson, David Lloyd George, Vittorio Orlando, and Georges Clemenceau) even decided in March 1919 to invite Polish and Ukrainian delegations to Paris to negotiate a peace treaty. From early 1919, the brutal behavior of Polish troops toward the civilian population and prisoners of war had caused outrage in the USA and strengthened the wish for a rapid peace agreement.[44] Such negotiations actually took place between 2 April and 13 May but were broken off without result.[45]

In the meantime, conflicts, rivalries, and skirmishes broke out among the opponents of the Bolsheviks as they discovered their own mutual hostilities. Local populations distanced themselves from the foreign intervention and from the interim regimes. Village insurgencies and regional insurrectionary armies that cooperated more or less closely with the advancing Red Army were getting greater support.

Under these circumstances, the French soon lost the military outposts of their "south Russian" occupation zone. Following the loss of Kherson, Greek detachments were ordered back from Mykolaiv. In March 1919, Entente units were forced to retreat to Odesa. About

---

42 NARA, US DoS, Records of the American Commission to Negotiate Peace, RG 256, M 820, Roll 486, No. 860e.00/43, Negotiations between the French Government and the Ukrainians, 7.4.1919.

43 NARA, US DoS, Records of the American Commission to Negotiate Peace, RG 256, M 820, Roll 486, No. 860e.00/57, French political efforts in the Ukraine, 11.4.1919.

44 NARA, US DoS, Commission for Negotiation of an Armistice between Poland and the Ukraine, RG 256, M 820, Roll 169, No. 181.21401/10, Minutes and Report; NARA, US DoS, Commission for Negotiation of an Armistice between Poland and the Ukraine, RG 256, M 820, Roll 169, No. 181.21402/1, Memorandum; NARA, US DoS, Commission for Negotiation of an Armistice between Poland and the Ukraine, RG 256, M 820, Roll 198, No. 183.9 Ukraine/2–19.

45 Jerzy Borzęcki, *The Soviet-Polish Peace of 1921 and the Creation of Interwar Europe* (New Haven and London, 2008).

eight hundred thousand residents of the city found themselves in an increasingly deplorable situation. They suffered from shortages of supplies, enormous price rises, a poorly functioning infrastructure, and problems of public safety. Marauding bands were a constant threat. There were attacks even in broad daylight, and numerous cases of robbery and murder. To make matters worse, there were disputes between the Russian Whites, the Ukrainians, and the Allied troops. The city divided into different zones. While the dealers and members of the old tsarist elite kept up the "glamorous, fashionable" life of the declining era, putting off the imminent apocalypse of the "old world" with their ghostly, graceful "dance on the volcano" in hotels, restaurants, and nightclubs, people in the workers' quarters were preparing for strikes and uprisings.[46]

Given the advance of Soviet troops, the only possibility left to d'Anselme was to contain social protest. But it was no longer possible to maintain order. The growing chaos was accompanied by plundering, White units opened fire, Entente units mutinied and were out of control. At the beginning of April, however, in spite of all the inadequacies and reports of doom, d'Anselme managed to evacuate his troops.[47]

Clemenceau issued a directive on this matter on 27 March, but it did not refer to the Crimea, where the Allies, under Colonel Eugène Gervais Trousson, were grappling with similar problems. As in Odesa, the Red forces offered an unobstructed withdrawal of foreign intervention forces. The truce that was arranged held only to a limited extent, and certain actions prompted Trousson, with the support of the commander of the French Black Sea Fleet, Admiral Jean François Amet, to maintain the front. From the outset, however, the soldiers and sailors were clearly reluctant, which showed that it was time to withdraw. On Amet's ships, many soldiers refused to obey. The restoration of discipline failed to satisfy the commanders. If peace was to prevail once and for all, declared Amet, this "unpopular" campaign against the Soviet Republic had to end.[48]

46 BAR, E 2300, 1000/7/6, 282. Moskau; M. S. Margulies, *God interventsii*, vol. 1 (Berlin, 1923), 217ff., 192, 200, 260.

47 Michael Jabara Carley, *Revolution and Intervention: The French Government and the Russian Civil War 1917–1919* (Kingston and Montreal, 1983), 171; Brinkley, "Allied Policy and French Intervention in the Ukraine," 341ff.

48 E. Moulis and E. Bergonier, *La Guerre entre les Alliés et la Russie (1918–1920)* (Paris, 1937), 175–81.

Philippe Franchet d'Esperey then authorized the end of the "south Russian adventure," which had been so powerfully attacked in the parliament in Paris. The parliamentarians' critical remarks, which influenced the soldiers, appeared in the newspapers. One article in *Liberté*, for instance, asked the French public whether there had ever been anything so "wretched" as "our policy in Ukraine." In the opinion of one parliamentarian, Henry Franklin-Bouillon, if the intervention there had been a good one, the French would have acted differently and at least have been able to help Petliura.[49]

Interests and Resources

The French foreign minister, Stephen Pichon, defended the actions of his prime minister, Clemenceau, and France's actions in defending its interests. This included measures taken against the Bolsheviks. It is not surprising, therefore, that the decision-makers in Paris opposed Woodrow Wilson and Lloyd George, who wanted to bring all the warring parties in the former tsarist empire, including Lenin's supporters, to the negotiating table. The planned negotiations on Prince Island near Istanbul, the so-called "Prinkipo policy," were sabotaged not least by the French prime minister and the Quai d'Orsay.[50]

Ukrainian press offices in Paris and London were attempting to influence public opinion and win support for Ukrainian independence and for Petliura.[51] In March, the press offices in Switzerland and London created a stir. It was claimed, in one press report, that the Entente had reached an agreement with Ukraine to the effect that Eastern Galicia would belong completely to Ukraine. This report created quite a stir in Warsaw, even though it soon became clear that it was an invention designed to disturb relations between Poland and the Entente. In a note of 11 March 1919, Edward Hallett Carr, later famous as a historian but engaged in 1917–18 in the Russian section of the British War Office, admitted that the treatment of Ukraine at the Paris Peace Conference had been "unfair." The peace conditions had corresponded neither to ethnographic circumstances nor to military

49 Vasyl Markus, *L'Ukraine Soviétique dans les relations internationales 1918–1923. Étude historique et juridique* (Paris, 1959), 188. Like many other deputies and dignitaries, Franklin-Bouillon had spoken out for the recognition of Finland: Clerc, "De la province russe à l'État scandinave," 68. There is an unfavorable account of Franklin-Bouillon in Georges-Henri Soutou, "La France et les Marches de l'Est 1914–1919," *Revue historique* 260 (1978), 386.

50 AAÉ, AAC/AP, E-Asie, Sibérie, vol. 7, Pichon à Martel, no. 66.

51 TNA, PRO 30/69/1800, Alexander Shoulguin, *The Problems of the Ukraine. The Ethnic Question. The National Culture. The Economic Life. The Will of the People* (London, 1919).

strength.[52] The treatment of Eastern Galicia in Paris demonstrated the low regard in which the Ukrainian question was held. The victorious powers were agreed that it would have to be dealt with as the leftover of a defeated enemy. But when Poland annexed western Ukraine, this was not at all what the Allied powers had in mind. For years, Eastern Galicia remained a bone of contention between Poland and the Allies, who thought that it should be administered by a representative of the great powers, Russia, or Czechoslovakia. But Poland would not give up the territory it had conquered and incorporated into its own state. The fait accompli was recognized by the Allies in 1923.[53]

Great Britain did not support Ukraine's independence at the Paris talks. Britain continued to set its sights on a united Russia under anti-Bolshevik leadership. This is clear from a comment of Lloyd George: "I only saw a Ukrainian once. It is the last Ukrainian I have seen, and I am not sure that I want to see any more."[54] The Ukrainians had obviously neglected to lobby for their demands in London.

But there were also other reasons why conditions were unfavorable for the creation of pro-Ukrainian sentiment. Although associations of Ukrainian exiles in the United States had the support of senators and members of the House of Representatives,[55] any corresponding assistance was ineffective. The Ukrainians themselves remained disunited, but what was much more important was the position of the president. In his Fourteen Points of early 1918, Woodrow Wilson did not have in mind a general "right of national self-determination." On the contrary, he had challenged the "Russian sister nations" that were struggling for independence to demonstrate "their intelligent and unselfish sympathy" for "Russia."[56] Dossiers later circulated in Washington about strengthening the Ukrainian national movement, but even here it was no more than a long-term plan for a Russian federation.[57]

---

52 TNA, FO 608/71/24, Polish oppression of Ukrainians, 24 January 1919, 397–99.

53 Margaret MacMillan, *Paris 1919: Six Months That Changed the World* (New York, 2003), 226.

54 Quoted ibid., 226.

55 Manning, "The Ukrainians and the United States in World War I," 351–54; Warvariv, "America and the Ukrainian National Cause," 356ff.

56 Erez Manuela, *The Wilsonian Moment: Self-Determination and the International Origins of Anticolonial Nationalism* (Oxford and New York, 2007), 40ff.; Klaus Schwabe, "Woodrow Wilson und das europäische Mächtesystem in Versailles: Friedensorganisation und nationale Selbstbestimmung," in *Nation und Europa. Studien zum internationalen Staatensystem im 19. und 20. Jahrhundert,* ed. Gabriel Clemens (Stuttgart, 2001), 89–98.

57 Warvariv, "America and the Ukrainian National Cause," 369–72.

The US delegation went to the Paris Peace Conference with a number of recommendations concerning independence for the previously Austro-Hungarian territories of Czechoslovakia and Hungary, as well as for Poland and Ukraine. But these documents did not shift Wilson's opinion. He stood by his position of restoring the borders of the Russian Empire. Only Poland would achieve independence.[58] Robert Lansing, in negotiations with the Ukrainian delegation on 30 June 1919, stressed "that the U.S. was not in favor of independence for the Ukrainians but that it was in favor of a single Russia, in which the various portions should have a certain degree of autonomy."[59] Within the Department of State, the most influential people continued to defend the view that the Ukrainian national movement was a creation of Austrian or German propaganda,[60] promoted especially during the war by the archbishop of Lviv, Metropolitan Andrei Sheptytsky.[61] Any premature recognition of the "peripheral nations" of Russia would prejudice a rational solution to the Russian question and would threaten any reunification of Russian territory.[62] This became a firm position in the months that followed.

The failure to grant Ukraine diplomatic recognition did not prevent the USA from developing careful economic contacts. In October 1919, liquidation stock from the USA to the value of 8.5 million dollars arrived in Ukraine and had probably already been paid for in cash or through the sale of food, alcohol, and private cars. The delivery of military vehicles was halted following French protests.[63] Frank Polk, obviously disturbed by this trade, wrote to the French prime

58 Ibid., 372–80.

59 NARA, US DoS, Records of the American Commission to Negotiate Peace, RG 256, M 820, Roll 488, Doc.–No. 860e.01/7, Mr. Lansing stated to the Ukrainian Delegation that the U.S. was not in favor of independence for the Ukrainians, 30.6.1919.

60 It cannot be absolutely confirmed that Baily was the source of this note, but the context of the documents suggests that this is highly likely: Harvard Libraries, Government Documents, Records of the DoS relating to Internal Affairs of the Ukraine (NARA microfilm publications), Film S 1040/M 1286, Roll 2, No. 860e.01/17, Division of Near Eastern Affairs (Russia). See also the order from the Department of State to the US ambassador in London to treat the Ukrainian national movement not as a product of ethnic or economic realities but as the result of Austrian and German propaganda: ibid., no. 18. DoS to Embassy London, 8.11.1919.

61 On Sheptytsky's role, see documents in *Ereignisse in der Ukraine 1914–1922. Deren Bedeutung und historische Hintergründe*, ed. Theophil Hornykiewicz, vol. 2 (Philadelphia, 1967), 408–53.

62 Harvard Libraries, Government Documents, Records of the DoS relating to Internal Affairs of the Ukraine (NARA microfilm publications), Film S 1040/M 1286, Roll 2, No. 27, Division of Russian Affairs, 3.2.1920.

63 NARA, US DoS, Records of the American Commission to Negotiate Peace, RG 256, M 820, Roll 488, No. 860e.51/4, US Liquidation Commission. War Department, 20.10.1919.

minister, Georges Clemenceau, clarifying the exact circumstances of the deliveries and offering greater detail about the goods delivered and where they were being stored.[64]

France's influence and resources were inadequate to begin a "campaign of the powers victorious in World War I against communism." The most decisive proponents of intervention were gathered in London around the British war minister, Winston Churchill. In 1919, London gradually gave up cooperating with France over Russia. Lord George N. Curzon had already expressed the view in June that Ukraine was in Denikin's zone of influence and was therefore an area of British interest. When Britain informed France in July that it would be supporting Denikin's forces in their operations in Ukraine and the Crimea, there was little France could do but accept it. The French insisted, however, that at least their direct interests should be protected.[65] Thus Ukraine returned once again, after a year and a half, to the center of British interests. The English military now observed events in Ukraine with greater attention. On 1 September 1919, the War Office instructed the leaders of British missions in Warsaw and Bucharest to cooperate as closely as possible in order to forge the Poles, the Ukrainians and eventually Denikin into a "continuous anti-Bolshevik front."[66]

In view of the conflicts, controversies, and divergence of interests between Symon Petliura's troops, Galician formations, Józef Piłsudski's Polish units, and Denikin's White Volunteer Army, with its Great Russian rejection of Ukrainian nationalism, Britain's plans proved to be mere wishful thinking. The weak and disunited Ukrainian forces were ground between the two fronts of their stronger opponents in the West and East, especially between Warsaw and Moscow.

But for the Whites as well, having received English support for much longer, things were also going badly. The defeat at Warsaw finally halted the advance of the Soviet army. The final attempt of Denikin's successor, Petr Wrangel, to attack the "commissars" and "soviets" from the Crimea had also failed. The de facto recognition of Wrangel by the French government under Alexandre Millerand was little more than a gesture of sympathy for the Whites. Paris now finally settled on a

---

64 The delivery consisted of clothing, blankets, medical provisions and medicines, 75 Cadillac cars, and 100 Harley-Davidson motorcycles. Cf. NARA, US DoS, Records of the American Commission to Negotiate Peace, RG 256, M 820, Roll 488, No. 8, Polk to Clemenceau, 4.12.1919.

65 Brinkley, "Allied Policy and French Intervention in the Ukraine," 343.

66 TNA, WO 158/752, Denikin's Relations with Romania, Ukraine and Separatists.

long-term alternative defensive plan, one that had been on offer for some time and was defended by the British, namely a *cordon sanitaire* of allied Central European states.

Lenin's supporters had, in the meantime, secured Moscow's hegemony in the western regions of the old Romanov Empire. They began by installing what was basically a Russian regime, then loosened the reins, but by the early 1920s they had made it clear that Soviet Ukraine, with its capital in Kharkiv, would have no independent foreign policy.[67] In the run-up to the formation of the USSR, decisions were made in Moscow and in the ministries of the Western powers. Great Britain took the first step when, in February 1920, it signed a treaty with the commissars on the exchange of prisoners of war, which then became a model for similar treaties with numerous other Western and Central European states and, in the long term, furnished the basis for conventional bilateral relations.

The New Economic Policy provided the framework for (re)entry into "business with Russia." In economic matters there was, not for the first time, a divergence of goals between Britain and France. The *Grande Nation*, which had suffered extensive losses between 1914 and 1918, was not as willing to make compromises as was the British prime minister, David Lloyd George. It was taken for granted by Clemenceau and his successors that "Germany had to pay." Something similar applied to Russia, which had incurred large debts to France until the end of Romanov rule. Financially stronger, England was the second major creditor in this part of the world, with 22.6 percent of foreign investments. But France, with 32.6 percent (13 billion gold francs), was by far the largest. The greater part of it (11.5 billion) was in securities guaranteed until 1917 by the Petrograd government under Tsar Nicholas II. Only a relatively small portion, 1.7 billion, was invested in enterprise, with great differences in the various regions of the empire. French capital was mainly invested in heavy industry and in mining, especially in Ukraine and the Donets Basin, where its financial participation was between 50 and almost 100 percent.[68]

Shortly after the overthrow of Nicholas, French industrialists began to fear the negative effects of the revolutionary upheaval. Inventories of loss were established when open conflicts emerged with

67 Hannes Leidinger, "Also sprach Sinowjew," in Barry McLoughlin, Hannes Leidinger, and Verena Moritz, *Kommunismus in Österreich 1918–1938* (Innsbruck, Vienna, and Bozen, 2009), 203ff.

68 René Girault, *Emprunts russes et investissements français en Russie, 1887–1917* (Paris, 1973).

the Council of People's Commissars following the nationalizations that occurred after Lenin had seized power.[69] After failed protests and interventions, the French government took over the Russian obligations and repaid the private investors at a reduced rate.[70]

Rivalries concerning commercial advantage, zones of influence, and strategic alliances led to the German-Soviet Treaty of Rapallo (1922). This treaty represented substantial damage to France's postwar policy.[71] The public was shocked. In the months that followed, its state leaders limped along behind international events that demonstrated the achievements of Soviet diplomacy and the end of the isolation of the October regime. Numerous countries signed trade agreements with Moscow and, in time, publicly recognized the young USSR.[72] London took this step at the beginning of February 1924. At the end of October that same year, Paris decided to establish regular relations with the Soviet Union.[73]

Contextualization and Assessment

Russia underwent a process of disintegration following the collapse of the Romanov Empire, a process that was then reinforced by the October Revolution and caused the West European powers to make significant changes to their East European strategies. The willingness of Britain and France to support an independent Ukraine represented a seesaw policy on the part of the Entente states, which made use of separatist movements while maintaining contact with the Soviet regime.

This brief period of just a couple of months, which began with the creation of the Soviet Republic in Petrograd and Moscow and ended with the dominance of the Central Powers in the western peripheral regions of the former tsarist empire in the spring of 1918, revealed the divergent interests of the anti-German allies.

---

69 Carley, *Revolution and Intervention*, 89–104, 123–41.

70 Ibid., 124.

71 Wolfgang Eichwede, "Der Eintritt Sowjetrusslands in die internationale Politik, 1921–1927," in *Osteuropa-Handbuch. Band Sowjetunion. Teil: Außenpolitik I*, ed. Dietrich Geyer (Cologne and Vienna, 1972), 150–212.

72 Ibid., 163, 179.

73 V. A. Dunaevskii and V. V. Gusev, "Russko-frantsuzskie i sovetsko-frantsuzskie otnosheniia v osveshchenii sovetskoi istoriografii (1917–1967)," in *Frantsuzskii Ezhegodnik 1967* (Moscow, 1968), 329–42; cf. Eichwede, "Der Eintritt Sowjetrusslands in die internationale Politik," 179ff.; Iu. V. Borisov, *Sovetsko-frantsuzskie otnosheniia (1924–1945gg.)* (Moscow, 1964); Maxime Mourin, *Les relations franco-soviétiques (1917–1967)* (Paris, 1967); Anne Hogenhuis-Seliverstoff, *Les relations franco-soviétiques, 1917–1924* (Paris, 1981).

Apart from their common focus on the Western Front and on strategies to relieve that front by means of measures in the East, the real goals of both the *Grande Nation* and the British Empire had to do with the establishment of zones of influence on the territory of the former tsarist empire. They also made different assessments with regard to reaching an understanding with the Bolsheviks. The complex tactics of the Entente states were also a result of the fact that this intervention in Russia was a historical precedent. The two-track approach was one of the consequences of this. On the English side, for instance, there was David Lloyd George's willingness to compromise with the Kremlin leadership and Winston Churchill's anti-communist crusade.

The Rada could not hope for support from London. Kyiv's break with the Bolsheviks following the October putsch was still regarded in a positive light, but its alliance with the Central Powers meant that Britain now saw Ukraine as a puppet of Berlin. This impression was further strengthened under the Hetmanate. The situation improved briefly in 1919 when Petliura formed an alliance with Poland. His rapid overthrow and the Bolshevik seizure of power meant that, from Britain's point of view, Ukraine was again at last part of Russia.

France, on the other hand, lacked the necessary political and economic strength for ambitious projects. Having run up against the limits of its own ability to influence events, France simply had to accept the stabilization of Soviet power and its establishment in Ukraine. Having weakened the position of Petliura's fragile government by the Quai d'Orsay's support for the territorial claims of Warsaw and Bucharest, Paris now had to accept Moscow's hegemony in Kyiv and Kharkiv.

Given the balance of forces, the French military had demanded that Petliura's Directory submit to Entente control and give up any claims to sovereignty. The direct intervention of 1918–19 was not motivated by recognition of an independent Ukraine but rather, in part, by imperialist colonialist goals. The fact that France had been the largest foreign investor in the tsarist empire and that the Russian Revolution had given it good reason to fear for its investments, not least in Ukraine, was another important factor here. The results of French strategy in this area were also less than had been expected. Here, as in the Treaty of Versailles, the maneuvers of the center-right governments of Clemenceau and his successors on the issue of compensation suffered a diplomatic setback. The Treaty of Rapallo, the coming together of Moscow and Berlin, was a clear demonstration of France's defeat and of the failure of its security policy. As a result,

France had even less of the authority and economic power that would have enabled her to be a significant negotiating and trading partner of the USSR or to continue to structure or even maintain the "Versailles settlement" in Central and Eastern Europe. The *cordon sanitaire* and the Little Entente had to give way to expansionist fascism and national socialism, and then to the Hitler-Stalin pact. The conflicts of the 1930s, the Second World War, and a bloody decolonization signposted the declining significance of a great power. The signs of its decline had been there for a long time but, in that moment of European restructuring between 1917 and 1924, they had not been clearly perceived.

Great Britain's predominance following the USA's withdrawal from Europe was also deceptive. The economy of the island kingdom had been massively weakened, and its state was highly indebted. London was forced to sell its international holdings, profiting both the USA and Japan. At the same time, independence movements and demands for compensation for damages suffered in the war were becoming stronger in the colonies, the dominions, and in Ireland. Under such pressures, Lloyd George had to retreat to the French position: under the banner of "make Germany pay," Berlin was now confronted with demands for reparations. In August 1919, the "ten-year rule" was adopted, promising no war in the next ten years. This reduction in defense spending begun in 1919 was also the beginning of Britain's decline as a world power.[74]

The United States was England's successor as global player. In spite of its political weight and corresponding economic and political power, it held back in the short and medium term from making a decisive entry into international politics. In a hesitant manner and with few forces, it began to engage itself in the territories of the former Romanov Empire. What Washington wished for in principle was a united Russian territory with strong regional autonomy under a stable, democratic, anti-Bolshevik, pro-Western government.[75] The Americans were particularly reticent, however, in the western peripheral areas of the old empire. After the withdrawal of the Central Powers, the USA considered the position of the Directory under Symon

---

74 Patrick O. Cohrs, *The Unfinished Peace after World War I: America, Britain and the Stabilisation of Europe 1919–1932* (Cambridge, 2008), 38ff.; Graham D. Goodlad, *British Foreign and Imperial Policy, 1865–1919* (London and New York, 2000), 98–100.

75 The Wilson administration may have been influenced by academics such as Ernest Denis: NARA, US DoS, Records of the American Commission to Negotiate Peace, RG 256, M 1107, Roll 46, No. 992, Report on Ernest Denis.

Petliura too insecure and unstable. They expressed their repeated concern that Petliura would rely on Germany and thus could create a new German puppet state.[76]

With regard to the various conflicting Central, East-Central, and East European states at the peace negotiations in Paris, Wilson played the role of a moderate mediator. Previous Russian territories, with the exception of Poland, the Baltic region, and Finland, would be handed over to Bolshevik influence. The USA had thereby unwittingly helped to stabilize the Soviet Union, its future deadly enemy in the Cold War.

76 This was emphasized in particular by the US ambassador to Great Britain, John W. Davis: Harvard Libraries, Government Documents, Records of the DoS relating to Internal Affairs of the Ukraine (NARA microfilm publications), Film S 1040/M 1286, Roll 2, No. 860e.01/7, Davis to Secretary of State, 31.1.1919.

4f. Poland's Ukrainian Policy, 1918–1922

Bogdan Musial

Before 1914 there had been neither a Polish nor a Ukrainian state. Polish territories were divided between Germany, Austria, and Russia, Ukrainian territories between Austria and Russia. But it was the Russian Empire that ruled over most of Polish and Ukrainian territory. Against such a background, the need for cooperation between the supporters of Polish and Ukrainian independence was obvious, which is why the Polish *irredenta* before 1914 dreamt of a joint Polish-Ukrainian march on Kyiv.[1]

The reality, however, proved much more complicated. Before Poland achieved its independence on 11 November 1918, Poland and Ukraine had even been at war with each other. On that day, the Polish Governing Council named Józef Piłsudski as *Naczelnik* (head of state with full powers) of the reestablished Polish state and assigned him the task of creating the first independent Polish government. Piłsudski thus became dictator and, at the same time, founding father of the new Poland. Until 1922 and then between 1926 and 1935, he influenced the history of the Polish state, including its policy toward Ukraine and toward Communist Russia, the Soviet Union.

Piłsudski was already quite familiar with Russia, the conditions there, Great Russian nationalism, and even the Bolsheviks.[2] When the First World War broke out, he saw the chance of realizing the dream of an independent Poland and a weakened Russia. He was convinced that the Russian Empire, Poland's greatest enemy, would be defeated by the Central Powers. He therefore organized Polish fighting units (legions) that entered the war on the side of the Central Powers against Russia. The military defeats suffered by Russian forces

---

1 Włodzimierz Suleja, "Piłsudski i Petlura," in *Polska i Ukraina. Sojusz 1920 roku i jego następstwa,* ed. Zbigniew Karpus, Waldemar Rezmer, and Emilina Wiszko (Toruń, 1997), 113–29.

2 Piłsudski was born in 1867 on Russian-ruled territory near Vilnius and grew up there. At an early age, he became involved in the struggle for Polish independence and against the tsarist empire, spending many years in Siberian exile as a result. He was repeatedly arrested and eventually had to flee (1901) to Galicia (southern Poland), then part of Austrian territory. He was one of the founders and leaders of the Polish Socialist Party (1892). From 1908, he began to form Polish rifle units in Galicia that would fight, in the future war that he saw coming, on the side of Austria-Hungary against the Russian Empire. Cf. Włodzimierz Suleja, *Józef Piłsudski* (Wrocław, 1995).

and the February Revolution of 1917 would contribute, in his view, to the weakening and eventual defeat of the Russian Empire.[3]

The events of 1917 seemed to open the way not only to Polish independence but also to the autonomy of many other nations of the empire, an idea that Piłsudski had been promoting for twenty years.[4] Initially, however, Poland remained an object of German power politics, a powerless observer of the turbulent developments in Central and Eastern Europe, the Bolshevik October putsch, the Russian civil war that followed, and the occupation of Ukraine by the Central Powers. Piłsudski himself was arrested by the German authorities in July 1917 because he had refused to subordinate himself and his legions to the Central Powers. Imprisoned in the fortress at Magdeburg, he was not released until November 1918. When Poland achieved its independence, the Russian Empire had already collapsed. A number of nations of the old empire had already declared their independence: Finland (November 1917), Lithuania and Turkmenistan (December 1917), Ukraine (January 1918), Estonia (February 1918), Belarus (March 1918), Georgia, Armenia, and Azerbaijan (May 1918), and Latvia (November 1918). In Russia itself, a bloody civil war was raging, as well as both Red and White terror.

Piłsudski saw Kyiv as the key to the Russian question. He regarded Ukraine, with its economic potential (grain, coal, iron ore and steel production) and its large population (around 30 million), as a natural ally of Poland against Russia. At this time (November 1918), the Ukrainian People's Republic (*Ukraïns'ka Narodna Respublika*, UNR) was fighting for its very existence against the Red Army. The Bolsheviks, with Lenin at their head, rejected Ukrainian independence and intended to occupy and sovietize it. The Bolsheviks had similar plans for other states that had emerged from the ruins of the tsarist empire, including Poland. The attempt, in November 1918, to take power in Poland through the councils collapsed in confrontation with the rapidly created structures of the reemergent Polish state. The Bolsheviks then began to militarily occupy territories claimed by Poland and to sovietize them. The result was the Polish-Soviet War, which did not end until October 1920.[5]

---

3 Andrzej Nowak, *Polska i trzy Rosje. Studium polityki wschodniej Józefa Piłsudskiego (do kwietnia 1920 roku)* (Cracow, 2001), 28.

4 Ibid., 30.

5 Ibid., 89–97.

Two weeks after he came to power, Piłsudski sent a special mission to Kyiv to discuss the possibilities of military cooperation with the Ukrainian People's Republic. In January 1919, delegates from Kyiv arrived in Warsaw to discuss disputed issues.[6] At the end of 1918, however, a Polish-Ukrainian military alliance was out of the question for Poland, since it had no army that could have come to the assistance of the hard-pressed UNR. In November 1918, Polish forces amounted to some 6,000 men, although their numbers grew rapidly. By January 1919, the Polish army had around 110,000 volunteer soldiers and officers.[7] Polish forces were not capable of engaging in serious military operations until the spring of 1919. Paradoxically, it was in a war against Ukraine over Eastern Galicia that the new Polish army fought its first battles. Polish-Ukrainian negotiations were therefore broken off in January 1919.

The Conflict in Eastern Galicia

Eastern Galicia was part of Austrian territory and had a complex ethnic structure. Its total population of 4.9 million was made up of 3.1 million Ukrainians, 1.1 million Poles, 620,000 Jews, and a few other small national groups. The Ukrainians dominated the countryside, while the cities were populated mostly by Poles and Jews. Austria-Hungary's relatively tolerant policy toward national minorities meant that Jewish and Ukrainian parties and organizations were able to exist and carry on activity alongside Polish ones. Ukrainian parties and organizations defended Ukrainian autonomy and promoted Ukrainian national consciousness. Although the Ukrainian intelligentsia had developed relatively quickly, the majority of the numerically large peasantry cared little for Ukrainian national issues. The Poles and the Jews dominated administration, education, culture, and economy. Lviv, the most influential city in Eastern Galicia, was considered by the Poles to be one of the most important Polish cities, along with Cracow and Warsaw.[8]

The Central Powers, Germany in particular, supported Ukrainian nationalism in order to play it off against Russia. In the peace treaty

6 Suleja, "Piłsudski i Petlura," 116; Michał Klimecki, "Wojna czy pokój. Polsko-ukraińskie negocjacje 1918–1921," in *Polska i Ukraina*, 43–79, 47ff.

7 Robert Potocki, *Idea restytucji Ukraińskiej Republiki Ludowej (1920–1939)* (Lublin, 1999), 83.

8 Cf. Piotr Eberhardt, *Przemiany narodowościowe na Ukrainie XX wieku* (Warsaw, 1994), 37–66; Torsten Wehrhahn, *Die Westukrainische Volksrepublik: Zu den polnisch-ukrainischen Beziehungen und dem Problem der ukrainischen Staatlichkeit in den Jahren 1918 bis 1923* (Berlin, 2004), 29–40; Timothy Snyder, *The Reconstruction of Nations: Poland, Ukraine, Lithuania, Belarus, 1569–1999* (New Haven and London, 2003), 122–37.

with Ukraine signed at Brest-Litovsk, the Central Powers promised territories to Ukraine that included the Kholm region, which had a majority Polish population. The initially secret plan to make Eastern Galicia and Bukovyna into a crownland of the Habsburg Monarchy (the Crownland Protocol) proved to be a time bomb. The Poles, who insisted on the indivisibility of Galicia, regarded these decisions as unjust and anti-Polish. The Polish-Ukrainian conflict was thus preprogrammed.[9]

When the Austro-Hungarian Monarchy collapsed in the autumn of 1918, Polish politicians in Galicia prepared themselves for the establishment of an independent Poland that would include Lviv and Eastern Galicia. Western Ukrainian politicians and activists, however, beat them to it and, on the night of 1 November, brought off a coup. With the help of Ukrainian national units, they occupied Lviv and other Eastern Galician towns and proclaimed the Western Ukrainian People's Republic as an independent Ukrainian state. The Polish residents of Lviv, taken by surprise, organized a defense in which even schoolchildren participated and, in a few days, drove Ukrainian forces out of most sections of the city.[10] In the other Eastern Galician towns, the Ukrainians had greater success, except for Peremyshl (Przemyśl), where the Poles won the upper hand. Polish forces soon made advances in other towns in the western part of Eastern Galicia. Poland failed in its attempts to resolve the conflict by means of arbitration. The Polish-Ukrainian War was already under way before Poland declared its independence.

On 22 November 1918, Polish troops succeeded in driving Ukrainian forces out of Lviv. But the city was under siege and under fire from Ukrainian units until April 1919. Immediately after the expulsion of the Ukrainians, there were anti-Jewish pogroms in which at least 73 people died. The Poles accused the Jews of having supported the Ukrainians in the conflict. A particular issue was the behavior of the Jewish militia armed by the Ukrainians.[11]

In the Polish-Ukrainian War, the Poles gradually won the upper hand. The Western Ukrainian leadership did not manage to mobilize most of the Ukrainian peasantry for its forces. The peasants were more interested in their own economic existence. Western Ukrainian activists therefore made use of social slogans, promising the Ukrainian peasantry a distribution of land. They used pressure and did not

9 Wehrhahn, *Die Westukrainische Volksrepublik*, 67–101.

10 Ibid. 102–34. See also chapter 2b in the present volume.

11 Ibid., 127–56.

hesitate to resort to force in order to mobilize the Western Ukrainian peasantry for their forces.[12]

The Entente states attempted to mediate in the Polish-Ukrainian conflict so as to bring it to an end as quickly as possible. In their view, the priority was the struggle against an aggressive and criminal Bolshevism. The Polish-Ukrainian War was preventing a united front of Polish and Ukrainian forces against the Red Army. In February 1919, a military commission under the French general Joseph Berthélemy negotiated a truce and a demarcation line that would give Lviv and the oil region to the south around Boryslav to Poland. Around 70 per cent of the territory of Eastern Galicia, according to this proposal, would remain part of Western Ukraine.[13]

The commission also concluded that the Western Ukrainian People's Republic was not a viable state, since the Eastern Galician independence movement was based on a very small stratum of intelligentsia. To win over the peasants, who had no interest in Ukrainian national issues, Western Ukrainian activists and politicians had promised them not only a distribution of land but also the houses and castles of Lviv. The Western Ukrainian leaders now had no control over the peasant unrest they had themselves provoked.[14]

The Polish side reluctantly accepted the conditions set by the commission, but the Ukrainian side rejected them and ended the truce. On 10 March, Western Ukrainian forces began a new offensive that collapsed after ten days at Lviv. This was a turning point in the Polish-Ukrainian War; from now on it was the Polish side that took the initiative. On the night of 14–15 April, Polish troops began a successful offensive with the result that, from the end of April, Lviv was no longer subjected to Ukrainian artillery fire. Polish troops continued their offensive in May and captured other Eastern Galician towns including, on 27 May, Stanyslaviv (present-day Ivano-Frankivsk), the seat of the Ukrainian authorities. By the end of May, Western Ukrainian forces and officials were holding on to only a few eastern areas, a fraction of the territory to which they had laid claim.[15]

Under pressure from the Entente, Poland ended its offensive in late May. Truce negotiations were renewed with representatives from Kyiv. But the Western Ukrainian side did not observe the truce and

---

12 Ibid., 176–84; Klimecki, "Wojna czy pokój," 53.

13 Wehrhahn, *Die Westukrainische Volksrepublik*, 184–96; Klimecki, "Wojna czy pokój," 48–57.

14 Klimecki, "Wojna czy pokój," 53.

15 Wehrhahn, *Die Westukrainische Volksrepublik*, 208–18.

launched a surprise offensive on 7 June, recapturing some areas. Poland was able to lay the blame for the continuing conflict on the Western Ukrainians. The Entente powers had sent a commission to Lviv to investigate numerous complaints about crimes against the population carried out by the Poles but also by the Ukrainians. The commission found no evidence of Polish crimes but plenty concerning Ukrainian ones. It also reported on the population's enthusiastic reception of the Polish troops as liberators "who restored law and order in territories previously laid waste by Ukrainian bands."[16]

The commission recommended that the whole of Eastern Galicia be occupied by Polish troops. On 25 June 1919, the Council of Foreign Ministers in Paris permitted the Polish government to renew its offensive in Eastern Galicia in order to occupy it completely. The Haller Army, armed in France, would be sent to Poland and deployed in the struggle against the communists. Eastern Galicia should be given autonomy within the Polish state, and the final decision on its status would depend on a referendum.[17]

On 2 July, led by Piłsudski, the Polish army began its decisive offensive against Western Ukrainian troops and forced them out of Eastern Galicia. Between then and 18 July, Western Ukrainian forces (around 20,000 men) crossed the Zbruch River and entered the territory of the Ukrainian People's Republic, controlled by Eastern Ukrainian troops.[18]

The Polish-Western Ukrainian War, from November 1918 to July 1919, cost the lives of about 25,000 soldiers, 10,000 Polish and 15,000 Ukrainian. It is difficult to estimate the number of losses among the civilian population, but it was probably less than the number of soldiers lost. Atrocities committed against civilians and prisoners of war were not carried out on a large scale.[19] Nonetheless, this war poisoned relations between Poland and Ukraine. For Poland, the problems of Eastern Galicia did not end with the defeat of the Western Ukrainians but went on for decades to play a major role in Poland's internal and external affairs. It was Stalin who resolved the problem in his own way during the Second World War. Eastern Galicia was

---

16 Ibid., 226.

17 Cf. ibid.; Kay Lundgren-Nielsen, *The Polish Problem at the Paris Peace Conference: A Study of Policies of the Great Powers and the Poles* (Odense, 1979), 385–87, 395.

18 Michał Klimecki, *Polsko-ukraińska wojna o Lwów i Galicję Wschodnią* (Warsaw, 2000), 257ff.; Wehrhahn, *Die Westukrainische Volksrepublik*, 223–34.

19 Michał Klimecki, "Ojczyzna dwóch narodów. Polsko-ukraińska wojna o Galicję Wschodnią (1918–1919)," *Biuletyn Instytutu Pamięci Narodowej*, 2010, no. 7–8: 14.

incorporated into the Soviet Union and forcibly sovietized. The Poles living there lost their homeland forever, and the Ukrainians lost their freedom for decades.

The Ukrainian People's Republic and Poland

The Ukrainian People's Republic declared its independence in January 1918. It included the territories of Eastern and Central Ukraine that had previously belonged to the tsarist empire. Its population in 1914 was around 31 million, of whom 23.3 million were Ukrainians (75 percent). In Eastern Galicia there were 3.1 million people who belonged to the Ukrainian nation.[20]

From the beginning, the main enemy of the Ukrainian People's Republic was the Bolshevik regime, although Denikin's Volunteer Army had also rejected Ukrainian independence. Russian nationalists regarded Ukraine as an integral part of Great Russia. Poland was also threatened by the Bolsheviks, but the danger was not so acute as it was for Ukraine. Poland also had problems with Denikin and his generals: they did not question Poland's independence, but they did question the territories claimed by Poland.[21]

Piłsudski understood quite well the importance of the Ukrainian question for Poland and was prepared to make compromises in Eastern Galicia. But he insisted as a minimum that the city of Lviv and the oil region around Boryslav should belong to Poland.[22] The first Polish-Ukrainian negotiations collapsed because of the conflict in Eastern Galicia. Then came the Polish-Ukrainian battles in Volhynia, beginning in January 1918.[23] Volhynia, in northwestern Ukraine north of Eastern Galicia, was a Russian-ruled area whose population was two-thirds Ukrainian. Poland claimed western Volhynia, while Eastern Ukraine claimed the Kholm region bordering on Volhynia.

The fighting in Volhynia lasted until June 1919, at which time the Eastern Ukrainian forces were having to fight on two fronts, in the east against the Red Army and in the west against Polish troops. In spite of this, the Ukrainian People's Republic never officially declared war on Poland because Symon Petliura, the military commander and, from

---

20 Eberhardt, *Przemiany narodowościowe na Ukrainie*, 57–59.

21 For a more detailed discussion, see Nowak, *Polska i trzy Rosje*, 104–33.

22 Suleja, *Józef Piłsudski*, 198ff.; Klimecki, "Wojna czy pokój," 47.

23 Zbigniew Karpus, "Ukraiński sojusznik Polski w wojnie 1920 roku," *Biuletyn Instytutu Pamięci Narodowej*, 2010, nos. 7–8: 16–33; Viktor Savchenko, *Dvenadtsat' voin za Ukrainu* (Kharkiv, 2006), chap. 8, accessed 6 January 2011, http://militera.lib.ru/h/savchenko_va/index.html. Savchenko writes that there had already been armed conflict in Volhynia in November 1918.

February 1919, the head of government, wanted to reach an agreement with Poland. In February 1919, he attempted in vain to persuade his Western Ukrainian allies to reach a compromise with Poland.[24]

The troops of the Red Army had taken Kyiv in February and later occupied other territories of the Ukrainian People's Republic. In April and May 1919, the Ukrainian units under Petliura held only the eastern areas of Volhynia and Eastern Galicia. The situation was critical, so Petliura decided to resume negotiations with Poland. Petliura had already signaled his willingness to renew negotiations in April. The talks began on 20 May in Lublin and resulted in a truce on 24 May 1919. The UNR relinquished its claims to Eastern Galicia and recognized Polish claims in Volhynia as far as the river Styr. This represented a capitulation to Polish demands but was not surprising, given the difficult situation in which the UNR found itself as it fought for its very survival. In return, Poland recognized the Ukrainian state and committed itself to rendering military assistance to Ukraine in the fight against the Bolsheviks. In addition, the UNR had to restore expropriated Polish properties (mostly estates) to their owners or pay compensation.[25]

The agreement, however, was not ratified, as the new political leadership of the UNR rejected its conditions. The negotiations continued in Lviv until 16 June 1919, when the Central and Eastern Ukrainian side agreed with the Poles on a truce and on a demarcation line based on the fronts of 1 June. Under pressure from the Western Ukrainians, however, this agreement was similarly not recognized because it represented a loss of most of the territories that they claimed. There was also some hope, at that time, that the offensive of the Western Ukrainian forces would be successful. On the Volhynian front, however, both sides maintained the truce.[26]

The end of the Western Ukrainian People's Republic and the extremely difficult situation of the UNR prompted the leadership to resume the negotiations with Poland that had been broken off in June. On 19 July, a UNR delegation arrived in Dęblin. It apologized for breaking the agreement of 16 June and declared that Ukraine wanted peaceful relations with Poland and a joint struggle against Soviet Russia. The delegation also proposed a "civilized" arrangement with regard to Eastern Galicia. Piłsudski supported, as he had done

24 Potocki, *Idea restytucji*, 44–49; Savchenko, *Dvenadtsat' voin,* chap. 8.

25 Cf. Potocki, *Idea restytucji*, 43ff.

26 Ibid., 44ff.; Karpus, "Ukraiński sojusznik," 16.

previously, the idea of Polish-Ukrainian cooperation, and truce negotiations began on 10 August, concluding on 1 September 1919. A demarcation line was established along the Zbruch River, and a neutral zone to the east of it. If Red troops entered this zone, they would be met by Polish forces. Both sides also agreed to the release of prisoners of war.[27]

The agreement took into account all of Poland's demands without Poland committing itself to offer military or political assistance to Ukraine. Nevertheless, this agreement represented a turning point in relations between Poland and Eastern Ukraine. With the Polish-Ukrainian conflict settled in Poland's favor, Piłsudski defended an independent Ukraine under Petliura's leadership.[28] From Poland's point of view, an independent Ukraine that did not question Poland's territorial claims in Eastern Galicia and Volhynia would be a strategic ally against the communists and the Great Russian nationalists.

The military value of this new ally was very small, since the UNR was then facing collapse. The Red Army and Denikin's Volunteer Army were fighting on territory claimed by the UNR over which of them would rule Ukraine. Denikin's army entered Kyiv on 1 September and occupied other Ukrainian territories as its main forces advanced toward Moscow. The situation of Petliura and his troops in September 1919 was so dramatic that he even asked Lenin for assistance in fighting Denikin's forces, against which he had declared war on 11 September. When Denikin's forces were defeated at Orel, they began to retreat. In November and December, the troops of the Red Army occupied almost all of Ukraine, and the remnants of the Eastern Ukrainian forces fled to Poland.

It was at this time that a new policy toward Ukraine crystallized in Poland, making it a guarantor of Ukrainian statehood. In October 1919, Poland began secret truce negotiations with the Moscow regime. One of the most important conditions insisted on by Piłsudski was a "cessation of attacks on Petliura."[29] This would have implied Moscow's recognition of an independent Ukraine, to which Lenin and his comrades would not agree. On 14 November, the Politburo discussed the Polish conditions for a truce and considered them acceptable,

---

27 Potocki, *Idea restytucji*, 45–49.

28 Ibid.

29 For a detailed account of the secret negotiations, see Nowak, *Polska i trzy Rosje*, 378–97; quotation on 387. The negotiations had to remain secret because the Entente powers, on which Poland depended, rejected all negotiations with the Bolsheviks at that time.

except for the cessation of the military conflict with Petliura. This was rejected by the Politburo, pointing out that "independent negotiations are being carried out with Petliura, which is why we cannot let our relations with him be made dependent on a third party."[30]

The condition with respect to Petliura was one of three points on which Piłsudski wanted to test the genuineness of Soviet Russian avowals that they wished to establish a truce and then peace.[31] In response to their rejection on the Petliura issue, Piłsudski informed the Soviet Russian side that "he would enter into no negotiations on the Petliura issue. He declared that, from the viewpoint of Polish interests, he could not allow Petliura to be defeated. He would therefore defend Petliura by force if he were attacked."[32] This was a declaration of war with regard to the Ukrainian question. Although the Polish-Soviet war had been going on since the spring of 1919, it was relatively quiet on the front after September. Of course, the open threat from Piłsudski could not hold back the Bolsheviks from occupying Ukraine. In December 1919 they took Kyiv and, by the end of the year, they had occupied most of Central and Eastern Ukraine. Piłsudski then broke off negotiations with the Russian communists and prepared for war with the Red Army.[33]

Polish reconnaissance had reported, as early as the summer of 1919, that the aim of the Russian communists was the invasion of Poland. This assessment was confirmed by further reconnaissance reports on Soviet Russian preparations for war against Poland. When the Bolsheviks finally settled the civil war in their favor, they began preparations for a major offensive on the Polish front. From January 1920, the Red Army concentrated its forces in the area around Smolensk, from where the main attack would be launched in the direction of Warsaw and farther toward the German border (the true goal).[34]

From the very beginning, the Polish military leadership had detailed knowledge of Soviet Russian preparations for their attack. In the summer of 1919, Polish cryptologists had succeeded in cracking the Soviet secret codes. From then on, Polish radio reconnaissance

30 RGASPI, fond 17, op. 3, d. 38, Minutes of Politburo session, 14.11. 1919, Point 4, 2.

31 The two other points were the cessation of Bolshevik agitation among Polish forces and a ten-kilometer neutral zone east of the Polish-Bolshevik front line, which was seen as a demarcation line. Cf. Nowak, *Polska i trzy Rosje*, 386ff.

32 Quoted in Nowak, *Polska i trzy Rosje*, 394.

33 Ibid., 396ff.

34 Ibid.; Bogdan Musial, *Kampfplatz Deutschland. Stalins Kriegspläne gegen den Westen* (Berlin, 2008), 32–40.

easily decoded thousands of coded telegrams from individual units of the Red Army. The Polish military leadership was therefore very well informed about the state of the Red Army, the course of battles on the civil war front, as well as the position and concentration of troops in preparation for the coming operations.[35]

At the beginning of December 1919, Petliura and the remnants of his forces (about 8,000 men) crossed the Polish front line. Around 2,000 Ukrainian soldiers remained on Red Army-occupied Ukrainian territory to continue the struggle as partisans. Polish officials disarmed the Ukrainian soldiers and officers and interned them. In January 1920, the Polish war ministry ordered that the Ukrainian soldiers and officers be treated not as internees or prisoners of war but as "military volunteers of foreign nationality."[36]

This decision was linked to the negotiations between Poland and Ukraine concerning an alliance, which had been under way since November 1919. On 2 December 1919, representatives of the Eastern Ukrainian government handed a declaration to the Polish side confirming that it recognized the existing Polish-Ukrainian demarcation line as the border, with Eastern Galicia and parts of Volhynia on the Polish side.[37] These concessions were welcomed on the Polish side, since the Supreme Council of the Peace Conference in Paris had decided, on 21 November 1919, that Poland's mandate in Eastern Galicia was a temporary one (25 years). The status of Eastern Galicia would then be decided by a referendum.[38]

In return, the Ukrainian side expected the recognition of the UNR as an independent state, material assistance for the Ukrainian army, and the release of Ukrainian internees and prisoners of war. In addition, Polish territory would be a transit zone for military hardware and the soldiers of the Ukrainian army.[39]

The alliance with Poland was seen by the UNR as the last chance to rescue Ukrainian statehood. In this predicament, Ukraine was ready to accept all of Poland's territorial demands, since the existence of the

---

35 Musial, *Kampfplatz Deutschland*, 39ff.

36 Karpus, "Ukraiński sojusznik," 17.

37 Klimecki, "Wojna czy pokój," 66ff. The declaration also said that a land reform, which would affect Polish estate owners in Ukraine, would be carried out only when a law had been passed by a democratically elected parliament. Until then, the rights of Polish estate owners would continue to be respected by regulations of both governments (ibid.).

38 Caroline Milow, *Die ukrainische Frage 1917–1923 im Spannungsfeld der europäischen Diplomatie* (Wiesbaden, 2002), 350–55; Werhahn, *Die Westukrainische Volksrepublik*, 248.

39 Klimecki, "Wojna czy pokój," 66ff.

Ukrainian state was at risk. Eastern Galician Ukrainian activists and politicians, who still saw Poland as Ukraine's main enemy, rejected these concessions. They left the Ukrainian diplomatic mission and published their protest on 2 December.[40] This led to a final break between the Western Ukrainian and UNR leaders but, at the same time, it facilitated the Polish-Ukrainian agreement. The negotiations led to a close military and political alliance. In February 1920, Ukrainian national units were being formed on Polish territory. By 25 April 1920, two Ukrainian divisions were ready for deployment—the 2nd Rifle Division, with almost 4,000 men, and the 6th Rifle Division, with more than 2,100 men. They were made up of Ukrainian volunteers (mostly onetime internees and prisoners).[41]

From the turn of the year 1919–20, Ukraine played a key role in Piłsudski's political and strategic considerations with regard to Soviet Russia. The separation of Ukraine from Russia, regardless of whether it was Red or White, would represent a permanent weakening of Russia because of Ukraine's economic significance. Without grain, coal, iron, or steel from Ukraine, Soviet Russia would be less of a threat to Poland and its neighbors. Piłsudski hoped that a Polish-Ukrainian alliance, with Poland playing the dominant role, would keep the aggressive Bolshevik regime in check, since he knew that Moscow did not want peaceful coexistence. Western Ukrainian activists and politicians were not the only opponents of Piłsudski's alliance plans. They also met with some opposition in Poland itself, especially from the National Democrats.[42]

In reality, Piłsudski had little room for maneuver in the spring of 1920. He and his military leaders knew about Bolshevik preparations for a great final offensive against Poland and realized that this was not just a question of borders but of the very existence of the Polish state, reestablished after 120 years. The Entente powers, especially Britain, had in the meantime come to terms with the Bolshevik regime and were seeking a settlement with Lenin. They turned down an offensive war against Moscow because they underestimated the ideological expansionism and criminal energy of the communists.[43] Against this background, Piłsudski's attempt to restore Ukrainian statehood and

40 Ibid., 67ff.; Potocki, *Idea restytucji*, 49–51.

41 Karpus, "Ukraiński sojusznik," 18–21.

42 For more detail, see Nowak, *Polska i trzy Rosje*, 559–83.

43 Ibid., 426–29; Richard H. Ullman, *Anglo-Soviet Relations, 1917–1921*, vol. 2 (Princeton, 1968), 317–32.

forge a Polish-Ukrainian alliance appeared to be the only possible solution. He thought it would be irresponsible and extremely dangerous to wait for the Bolsheviks to begin their offensive at a time favorable to them[44] and therefore decided to take the bull by the horns.

In his preparations for the final conflict with Lenin, Piłsudski sought an understanding with Russian anti-Bolshevik forces prepared to cooperate with Poland. He talked principally with Boris Savinkov, a onetime revolutionary and Russian politician who was arguing strongly for a Polish-Russian alliance against the Bolsheviks.[45] Unlike the Polish-Ukrainian alliance, the Polish-Russian negotiations came to nothing.

On 21 April 1920, representatives of the Polish government and the UNR signed a treaty of alliance. The treaty acknowledged Ukraine's right to independence and recognized the Directory as its government. Ukraine ceded Eastern Galicia, as well as parts of Volhynia and Podilia. The issue of land reform was left to a future Ukrainian constituent assembly. Until such a time, the rights of Polish estate owners would be regulated by special agreements. Minorities in Ukraine would have equal rights.

An integral part of the treaty was the agreement on a Polish-Ukrainian military alliance and the subordination of Ukrainian forces to Polish overall command. But the treaty also provided for Ukrainian command of their own forces once progress in the operation and operating conditions permitted. The Ukrainian government had the right to establish a governing administration in liberated Ukrainian territories. The costs of arming Ukrainian forces and of provisions for Polish and Ukrainian troops fighting in Ukraine would be borne by the Ukrainian government.[46]

Polish historians agree that the granting of rights to Polish estate owners whose land had already been distributed among the peasantry in 1918 was a political error. This made it easier for the Bolsheviks

44 Klimecki, "Wojna czy pokój," 71.

45 For more detail, see Nowak, *Polska i trzy Rosje*, 458–501. On 27 March 1920, Savinkov wrote to Piłsudski and challenged him to act, since only action could change the unfavorable political climate of weakness in the face of the Bolshevik threat in the West. If Piłsudski were to advance with his troops as far as Smolensk, that would make it clear to Russian nationalist circles in the emigration and to anti-Bolshevik forces in Russia that an alliance with Poland was essential to success (ibid., 480ff.).

46 Klimecki, "Wojna czy pokój," 71–73; Potocki, *Idea restytucji*, 57–63.

to promote anti-Polish propaganda.[47] Although the territorial concessions to Poland were extremely painful for Ukraine, Petliura and the UNR government had little choice. On 15 March 1920, Petliura wrote to Isaak Mazepa, the head of the Directory: "Poland aims to liberate us—for a price, of course: five districts of Volhynia.... In any case, without this or some other agreement with Poland, we would not be able to restore our statehood."[48]

"Operation Kyiv": The Attempt to Restore Ukrainian Statehood

On 17 April 1920, a few days before the signing of the Polish-Ukrainian alliance treaty, Piłsudski ordered his troops to attack the Soviet forces concentrated in Ukraine[49] although his Polish forces were significantly weaker than the Red Army in numbers and equipment, especially as the Poles had no reserves. Poland would certainly not be able to sustain a long war.

On 25 April 1920, Polish forces on the southern Ukrainian front made a surprise attack on the Red Army. The strategic goal of "Operation Kyiv" was to drive Russian forces out of central Ukraine across the Dnipro and help the UNR government recover power and establish more Ukrainian units that would then help the Polish troops in their struggle with Soviet Russia. An attack in the north, where the Red Army was concentrating its forces for the offensive against Poland, was to follow at a later time.[50]

On 7 May, Polish troops entered Kyiv and crossed the Dnipro east of the city. The front line ran from Chornobyl (north of Kyiv) along the Dnipro to Trypilia (south of Kyiv), and from there west of the Dnipro in a southwesterly direction as far as Volodarka (east of Bila Tserkva). Polish troops stopped there and did not pursue the defeated and demoralized units of the Red Army. They did not plan to occupy the whole of Ukraine: Polish forces were insufficient to accomplish that.[51]

The previously established Ukrainian units fought alongside the Poles. There were also numerous Ukrainian partisans and insurgents who attacked the retreating Red Army and Bolshevik activists and

---

47 Potocki, *Idea restytucji*, 58.

48 Quoted in Potocki, *Idea restytucji*, 55.

49 Klimecki, "Wojna czy pokój," 71.

50 Musial, *Kampfplatz Deutschland*, 39–42.

51 Ibid.; for more detail, see Norman Davies, *White Eagle, Red Star: The Polish-Soviet War 1919–1920 and the "Miracle on the Vistula"* (London, 2003), 105–29.

officials. On 26 April, Piłsudski addressed the Ukrainian people and assured them that Polish troops would remain on their soil only as long as it took for the legal Ukrainian government to resume power and the Ukrainian army to be in a position to defend the homeland from attack. The Directory also announced that the Polish troops had entered Ukraine as allies to fight their common enemy.[52]

The entry of Polish troops, however, was met with no great enthusiasm on the part of the Ukrainian peasants, who were rather restrained in their reaction. The leaders of the UNR also failed to mobilize large sectors of the population. Polish reports indicate that they were disappointed by the reaction and were in agreement about the cause: there was widespread resistance to the Bolsheviks, but the partisans and insurgent groups were really local militias. They were not part of a movement that could be regarded as nationalist, even though they had fought under the banner of independence and anti-Bolshevism. The real goals of this movement were to drive out or destroy the Bolsheviks and to prevent the requisitioning of food and grain, as well as the mobilization of men.[53] What was really decisive, however, in preventing the Ukrainian leadership from establishing stable structures of power was the lack of time. The Polish occupation of Ukraine west of the Dnipro was of short duration.[54]

The Soviet political and military leaders did not lose their nerve following the surprise attack of the Polish army. They accelerated the movement of troops to Belarus (the western front) in order to proceed with the offensive. The Red Army began its offensive on 14 May but was soon halted by Polish units. The Red troops were more successful on the Ukrainian section of the Polish-Soviet front. They forced Polish units out of Kyiv in June. By the end of June, Polish troops, with their Ukrainian allies, were almost back to their starting position of 25 April.[55]

The Red Army began its main attack on the western front on 4 July and was successful this time. Soviet troops also renewed their offensive on the southwestern front (the Ukrainian section) and were likewise successful. By mid-August, they had occupied large parts of Eastern Galicia and Volhynia and had reached Lviv, while their troops on the western front had reached Warsaw. Poland seemed destined

---

52 Potocki, *Idea restytucji*, 66–84.

53 Ibid.

54 Ibid., 84–100.

55 Musial, *Kampfplatz Deutschland*, 42–56.

to final defeat. But Polish units began a successful counteroffensive on 16 August, and the triumphant westward advance of the Red Army turned into a panicky retreat within a few days. Troops on the southwestern front operating in the Ukrainian section also had to retreat with heavy losses.[56]

By the beginning of October, Polish troops had occupied Maladzechna, Pinsk, and Lida (in present-day western Belarus), driven Soviet troops out of Eastern Galicia and large parts of Volhynia, and crossed the Zbruch. Ukrainian units had taken part in the fighting.[57]

Polish forces halted their offensive on 18 October, since both parties had agreed to a truce and a demarcation line in Riga on 12 October. Peace negotiations were then begun in Riga and ended on 18 March 1921. The peace treaty regulated the border between Poland and Soviet Russia.[58] Both sides had already committed themselves in the truce agreement to support "no foreign military operations against the other party to the treaty." This meant that the Poles had to renounce their military alliance of April 1920 with the UNR, which was then done. The Polish authorities ordered that all non-Polish units vacate their territory by 2 November 1920. Ukrainian units then left all areas that fell to Poland in the truce agreement and moved to areas that had been occupied by Poland a short time previously. There Ukrainian units intended to continue their fight against the Red Army.[59]

At the beginning of November, Ukrainian forces numbered about 40,000 men, of whom around 10,500 were battle-ready soldiers and officers. After a short and hopeless battle, the remnants of UNR troops and officials crossed the Zbruch again on 21 November. Around 20,000 of them were disarmed and interned by the Polish authorities. These included soldiers and officers, but also officials and women and children. There were about 15,500 citizens of the UNR interned on Polish territory in February 1921. Symon Petliura, along with government and central officials, was in Tarnów, while soldiers and officers were in a number of internment camps.[60] During the months and years that followed, their numbers gradually declined. They found work in Poland, traveled to other countries, or returned to Bolshevik, later Soviet, Ukraine. By the end of 1923, their numbers had gone down to about 3,100. On

---

56 Ibid.

57 Ibid.

58 Ibid.

59 Karpus, "Ukraiński sojusznik," 25 f.

60 Ibid., 26–33; Potocki, *Idea restytucji*, 107ff., 146–58, 183–88.

31 September 1924, the last of the Ukrainian internment camps was closed.[61] Petliura had to leave Poland at the end of 1923 and emigrated to Paris, where he was assassinated in May 1926.[62]

Thus ended the unequal Polish-Ukrainian alliance of April 1920. Thus ended also, for the next seventy years, the idea of an independent Ukraine. Polish domestic and foreign policy, however, continued to be influenced by the Ukrainian question until 1939. The Soviet regime exploited the Eastern Galician-Ukrainian *irredenta* against Poland and claimed Eastern Galicia under the pretext of uniting the Ukrainian nation in a single state. This was the goal that Stalin achieved in the autumn of 1939, with German assistance (the Hitler-Stalin Pact).

---

61 Karpus, "Ukraiński sojusznik," 26–33; Potocki, *Idea restytucji*, 183–88.

62 Waldemar Rezmer, "Symon Petlura (22 V 1879–25 V 1926). Szkic biograficzny," in *Polska i Ukraina*, 151–61; Emilian Wiszka, "Symon Petliura v Pol'shchi i Frantsiï (1920–1926)," in *Polska i Ukraina*, 163–75; Suleja, "Piłsudski i Petlura," 113–29.

Looking Ahead: A Comparison of the Occupation Regimes of 1918 and 1941–1944

Peter Lieb, Wolfram Dornik, and Georgiy Kasianov

Any comparison of the occupation regimes of 1918 and 1941–44 has to be made with care.[1] Basically, in making a comparison, we are not making an equation. Rather, we use this comparison and the demonstration of parallels and divergences in order to highlight long-term developments on the one hand and discontinuities on the other. In what follows, ten basic ideas will be presented.

1) First of all, the occupation of Ukraine was, in both cases, a military act. In the First World War, as in the Second, the invaders advanced very rapidly eastward, once by railroad and once with tank units leading the way, although in 1941 most of the army advanced on foot. Was the "railway campaign" of 1918 a precursor of the *Blitzkrieg* of the Second World War? As has been shown in a number of works, the concept of *Blitzkrieg* in 1939–40 was not a strategic but rather an operational or mainly tactical concept.[2] This reflected German military doctrine as it was developed at the end of the First World War and especially in the interwar period. Some of the key elements of this military doctrine were: the use of combined arms; the tactical deployment of the *Luftwaffe* to support ground forces; the delegation of responsibility to subordinate units; and the use of modern means of communication such as radio. What was decisive was the concentrated penetration of tank units on a relatively small section of the front, followed by a rapid independent advance deep into enemy territory. The

1 For general comparisons of the First and Second World War, see *Erster Weltkrieg – Zweiter Weltkrieg. Ein Vergleich. Krieg, Kriegserlebnis, Kriegserfahrung in Deutschland,* ed. Bruno Thoß and Hans-Erich Volkmann (Paderborn, Munich, Vienna, and Zurich, 2002). For the Eastern Front, see Rüdiger Bergien, "Vorspiel des 'Vernichtungskrieges'? Die Ostfront des Ersten Weltkriegs und das Kontinuitätsproblem," in *Die vergessene Front. Der Osten 1914/15. Ereignis, Wirkung, Nachwirkung,* ed. G. P. Groß (Paderborn, 2006), 383–408.

2 The fundamental work here is Karl-Heinz Frieser, *Blitzkrieg-Legende. Der Westfeldzug 1940* (Munich, 1995).

goal was to encircle the enemy, thereby inflicting more of a psychological than a physical defeat.[3]

There were some obvious differences between the Ukrainian campaign of 1918 and the early successes of the German army (*Wehrmacht*) in the Second World War. In 1918, for instance, fighter aircraft were not technically advanced enough to provide close air support. Planes were used in Ukraine, but only for identifying the enemy: since most Bolsheviks wore civilian clothes, this had only very moderate success.[4] As the army depended largely on the railway lines, its advance route was predetermined. Moreover, Bolshevik units were militarily on a par. General Kosch expressed this insight very well when, comparing the Ukrainian campaign to the great battles on the Western Front, he spoke of "clutter" (*Kleinkramm*).[5] Although there were these differences between 1918 and 1939–40, there were also a number of basic similarities. The following were the most obvious: the concentration of force on focal points, independent decision-making by subordinate officers in tactical matters, and rapid pursuit to allow the enemy no reaction time.[6]

2) The whole of Ukrainian territory was affected in both world wars, but the state structure of Ukraine was clearly different in 1941 from what it had been in 1918. What the Central Powers confronted, in the final year of the First World War and the second year of the Russian Revolution, was a chaotic country in which all social boundaries and systems of order were in question. The *Wehrmacht*, on the other hand, entered a country that had been "disciplined" by excessive violence for two decades. The brutal

3 After 1945, this doctrine was further developed by the Israeli Defense Force and, from the 1980s, by the US Army. In modern US doctrine this is known as "maneuver warfare" or sometimes "shock and awe." See Harlan K. Ullman and James P. Wade, *Shock and Awe: Achieving Rapid Dominance* (Washington, D.C., 1996); Robert R. Leonhard, *The Art of Maneuver: Maneuver Warfare Theory and Airland Battle* (Novato, Calif., 1991).

4 The Bavarian Cavalry Regiment made the following assessment of its battles in the Crimea: "It was our experience on operations that air reconnaissance of Bolshevik units was a complete failure.... The pilot cannot determine whether he is observing an advancing Bolshevik unit or a perfectly normal wagon transport of rural inhabitants." See BayHStA-KA, Kav.Div., Bd. 18. Kaiserl. Deutsches Gouvernement Sewastopol, Abt. Ia, Nr. 120, Bericht über die Tätigkeit der B.K.D. von Bierislawa bis zur Besetzung von Feodossija, 13.5.1918.

5 BA-MA, N 754/10, Brief Koschs an seine Frau v. 26.3.1918.

6 For more detailed discussions of geopolitics and military operations on the Eastern Front in both wars, see Hew Strachan, "Die Ostfront. Geopolitik, Geographie und Operationen," in *Die vergessene Front,* 11–26.

"persecution of the kulaks," collectivization, the annihilation of the political intelligentsia, and the knowingly accepted consequences of the catastrophic famine (*Holodomor*)[7] directed against the Ukrainian peasantry in the early 1930s had stabilized Soviet power.[8] In 1941, the Germans broke up Ukrainian territory, dividing it between Romania, the "District of Galicia" as part of the *Generalgouvernement*, the area of operations under German military administration, and the large civilian-administered *Reichskommissariat Ukraine*. At the local level, they made use of the existing administration. Many Ukrainians hoped initially in 1941, as they had in 1918, that with the help of the German occupiers they would be liberated from Moscow, and they therefore supported the new regime.[9] Disillusionment set in very rapidly in 1918, leading to uprisings between June and July that then gave way to resignation after these rebellions had been put down. It was similar in 1941. Initially the population greeted the *Wehrmacht* as liberators. There were also quite a few Ukrainians who participated in the persecution of the Jewish population. As part of the auxiliary police or the *Schutzmannschaften*, they supported the genocide. In response to the brutal German regime, the repression, and the breaking up of national territory, a partisan movement began in 1941–42 but was very violently suppressed. It was only toward the end of the occupation that the occupiers began to concentrate on integrating anti-Soviet nationalist elements in the hope of creating a broader base for the fight against the Red Army.

---

7 Cf. Barbara Falk, *Sowjetische Städte in der Hungersnot 1932/33. Staatliche Ernährungspolitik und städtisches Alltagsleben* (Cologne, Weimar, and Vienna, 2005); Otto Wenzel, "Holodomor. Stalins Genozid in der Ukraine 1932–1933 in Berichten der Deutschen Botschaft Moskau und des Generalkonsulats Charkow," *Zeitschrift des Forschungsverbundes SED-Staat, Schwerpunkt: Grenzüberschreitungen* 28 (2010): 5–24.

8 The number of victims of this policy is still disputed today. *The Black Book of Communism* gives the number of 6 million deaths from famine in 1932–33, about two-thirds of them in Ukraine, the rest in Kazakhstan, the North Caucasus, and the Black Sea region: Stéphane Courtois et al., *The Black Book of Communism: Crimes, Terror, Repression* (Cambridge, Mass., 1999). To this must be added the 2 million peasants who, in the years of collectivization, had their possessions robbed and were deported to Siberia and Central Asia. Of these, 30,000 were shot by the GPU: Jörg Baberowski, *Der rote Terror. Die Geschichte des Stalinismus* (Munich, 2003), 126. In the ethnic and national purges of 1936–38, more than 1.5 million people were imprisoned and more than 760,000 murdered (Baberowski, *Der rote Terror*, 200).

9 See Frank Grelka, *Die ukrainische Nationalbewegung unter deutscher Besatzungsherrschaft 1918 und 1941/42* (Wiesbaden, 2005).

3) In both cases, Ukraine was also occupied by allied armies under German leadership. In 1918 it was essentially two armies, the German and the Austro-Hungarian, that entered the country, supported by what were ultimately symbolic naval units from Turkey and Bulgaria. In 1941, the German army was accompanied by Hungarian, Italian, and especially Romanian units. The latter arrived in much larger numbers than the Bulgarians and Turks had been twenty-three years earlier, although qualitatively their influence was very small compared to that of the German military. One important difference had to do with the organization of troops during the invasion and occupation. In 1918 there was no overall command for the allied troops. The occupation administrations in the different zones were quite separate. It was only in the area of economic policy that the Germans led from May 1918, but even here there was a certain level of Austro-Hungarian participation. Between 1941 and 1945, the area was administered exclusively by the Germans. Only a small "morsel" was given to the Romanians as a reward for their participation in the campaign. It consisted of Bukovyna, Bessarabia, the Trans-Dnister region, and the area between the Dnister and the Boh (Southern Bug), with Odesa as its economic and political center.[10]

4) Another factor that should be noted in this comparison is the racist element. In 1918, the "perception of the Slavs among the Central Powers" was shaped by a "discourse about hygiene"[11] in relation to what the occupiers saw as mostly poor and decrepit villages and settlements. It was believed that, in the East, they were dealing with less "developed" people, and that the best way to achieve anything with them was by being harsh. But this does not necessarily mean that the Germans at that time felt themselves to be culturally superior to the people or held them in contempt. In their private reports, soldiers of the Central Powers frequently wrote of their admiration for the splendid Ukrainian cities. Unlike in 1941,[12] anti-Slavism was not a dominant element, and there was certainly none of the hatred expressed in World War II. An important factor then was the fact

---

10 Ekkehard Völkl, *Transnistrien und Odessa (1941–1944)* (Regensburg, 1996).

11 Peter Hoeres, "Die Slawen. Perzeptionen des Kriegsgegners bei den Mittelmächten. Selbst- und Feindbild," in *Die vergessene Front*, 199.

12 Cf. *Das Russlandbild im Dritten Reich*, ed. Hans-Erich Volkmann (Cologne and Vienna, 1994).

that the army and political landscape of their Austro-Hungarian ally was shaped in part by Slavic peoples, although they were disadvantaged and underrepresented, both domestically and in the army, when compared with their Hungarian- and German-speaking counterparts.[13]

In the Holocaust, of course, the anti-Semitic component was much more serious than the anti-Slavic one. From the beginning of the occupation in 1941, the annihilation of the Jewish population was carried out by the SS, the police, the local auxiliary police, some units of the Wehrmacht, and the local population.[14] But what was the situation in 1918? Groener's personal diary and German military documents are full of anti-Semitic expressions that are rhetorically similar to those of 1941–42. One of the orders from Army Group Eichhorn-Kiew, for instance, describes the Jews as "the principal rabble-rousers."[15] This attitude was widespread among the troops. For instance, in the judgment of the Bavarian Cavalry Division: "The Jews are the main rabble-rousers in the country. If we don't put a stop to them, we'll never have peace in this country."[16] For the XXXXI Reserve Corps, "the Jews...in spite of their appealing mask" were "our fiercest enemy."[17] Surprisingly, the commander of the 15th Bavarian Reserve Infantry Brigade, Major General Franz Samhaber, also blew the anti-Semitic trumpet—this despite the fact that his wife was Jewish:[18] "The mass of Jews are against the new government and against the German troops. They are against any government, since anarchy allows them to exploit the people's lack of culture and the general

13 The German cultural imperialism that Liulevicius found in the *Ober Ost* area is very difficult to identify in Ukraine. See Vejas Gabriel Liulevicius, *War Land on the Eastern Front: Culture, National Identity, and German Occupation in World War I* (Cambridge, 2000). See also Dennis E. Showalter, "'The East gives nothing back': The Great War and the German Army in Russia," *Journal of the Historical Society*, 2002, no. 2: 69–87.

14 Dieter Pohl, "Schauplatz Ukraine. Der Massenmord an den Juden im Militärverwaltungsgebiet und im Reichskommissariat 1941–1943," in Christian Hartmann et al., *Der deutsche Krieg im Osten 1941–1944. Facetten einer Grenzüberschreitung* (Munich, 2009), 155–96.

15 BayHStA-KA, Kav.Div., Bd. 21. Heeresgruppe Eichhorn, Abt. Ia, Nr. 1094/18 v. 23.5.1918.

16 BayHStA-KA, Kav.Div., Bd. 18. Bezirk Wolhynien West. Bay.Kav.Div., Abt. Ia, Nr. 272 W v. 16.6.1918.

17 BA-MA, PH 6–II/16. XXXXI. Reservekorps. Generalkommando, Abt. Ia, Nr. 12130, Bericht über die innere Lage, 31.10.1918.

18 BayHStA-KA, OP 47604, Nationalsozialistische Deutsche Arbeiterpartei, Gauleitung Sachsen, Rassenpol. Amt/Hauptstelle VI Dr. We./Ha. 40a/44, 27.4.1944. In this note of 1944, the Saxon *Gauleiter* asked for Samhaber's birth and death dates, since his wife was "fully Jewish."

disorder for their own purposes."[19] In fact, many Jewish merchants did very well out of the black market during the occupation period.[20]

Among the Austro-Hungarian documents, one also finds numerous anti-Semitic expressions and the claim that there were links between the Jewish population and Bolshevism. To demonstrate the split between widespread middle-class attitudes and left-wing ideology within the Jewish population, a report from the 4th Army described the poor Jewish population of Odesa as "thoroughly Bolshevik, Menshevik (Socialist Revolutionary)" and as a "very insecure element," while "the rich" were anti-Ukrainian and inclined toward the bourgeoisie.[21] In the daily reports to the command of the *Ostarmee* from the corps and divisions, Jews were repeatedly described as agitators or troublemakers close to the Bolsheviks.[22] The anti-Semitic tone occurred frequently, especially in Fleischmann's reports on the situation in Ukraine.[23] In mid-April, however, the representative of the Austro-Hungarian Foreign Ministry at AOK, Trauttmansdorf, made a request to the Operations Department that the troops intervene when local inhabitants carried out acts of violence against Jews. The Executive Committee of Austrian Zionists had made representations to the Foreign Ministry, based on reports from Copenhagen, about Jewish pogroms in Turkestan and Ukraine. The handwritten comment on this document, most probably from Arz, says: "For the time being, nothing to be done."[24] One can only speculate whether the writer was anti-Semitic.

We need to be cautious about seeing all these quotations as unambiguously anti-Semitic solely on the basis of our knowledge of the later Holocaust.[25] Rhetoric and reality were two different worlds in Ukraine in 1918. There were no anti-Semitic measures

19 BayHStA-KA, 15.Res.Inf.Brig., Bd. 7. K.Bayr.15.Res.Inf.Brigade, Nr. 2604, Bericht über die allgemeine Lage, 25.5.1918.

20 Henry Abramson, *A Prayer for the Government: Ukrainians and Jews in Revolutionary Times 1917–1920* (Cambridge, Mass., 1999), 100.

21 ÖStA, KA, AOK, OpAbt, Kt. 468, Nr. 1355, Bericht des 4. Armeekommandos (no date).

22 ÖStA, KA, NFA, 2. Armee, Op. AK, Kt. 308, 1918 Situations- und Tagesmeldungen, Nr. 8475/8.

23 ÖStA, KA, AOK, OpAbt., Kt. 469, Nr. 1481, Berichte über die politische Lage in der Ukraine Mitte April, 15.4.1918.

24 ÖStA, KA, AOK, OpAbt, Kt. 468, Nr. 1441, Judenpogrome in Turkestan und in der Ukraine, 15.4.1918.

25 Cf. Showalter, "'The East gives nothing back,'" 86, n. 26.

on the part of the occupiers. There are even reports of German and Austro-Hungarian units protecting Jews from attack.[26] Neither in the months before nor especially in the months that followed was the number of anti-Jewish pogroms as low as during the period of occupation by the Central Powers.[27] This is an unmistakable sign that the Central Powers protected the Jews as part of maintaining order in the country. They also wanted to avail themselves of the know-how of the Jewish traders and did not want to make themselves vulnerable to attack from their own Jewish populations or those of the Entente.[28] Another interesting fact is this: hardly any German regimental history from the immediate postwar period refers to the later typical Nazi "Jewish Bolshevik" bogeyman.[29]

5) This does not mean that the war in 1918, unlike 1941, had no ideological component. On the contrary, anti-Bolshevism was widespread in the armies of the Central Powers. At first they treated the Bolsheviks as prisoners of war, but, week by week, their attitude to their enemies became much more extreme. After a few weeks, captured Bolsheviks were generally shot without further ado. It is interesting that this happened only in Ukraine, not in the Baltics or other Russian regions.[30] With regard to the number of prisoners shot, the massacre at Taganrog in June 1918 eclipsed similar events from the Second World War. The fact that the German government and the Supreme Army Command (OHL) nonetheless continued to stand by the Brest-Litovsk peace treaty with Moscow demonstrates the contradictory character

26 Cf. BayHStA-KA, 15. Res.Inf.Brig., Bd. 7. Ldw.-Inft.-Regt. 327, Tgb. Nr. 4799 II, Bericht über das nach Tarastscha entsandte Kommando, 13.4.1918; Mark von Hagen, *War in a European Borderland: Occupations and Occupation Plans in Galicia and Ukraine, 1914–1918* (Seattle and London, 2007), 93.

27 Abramson, *A Prayer for the Government*, 79. According to Abramson, there were 1,289 officially registered pogroms against Jews in Ukraine between September 1917 and the end of 1921. But there were only 46 in the year 1918 until November, and an unknown number of these took place in January and February.

28 Grelka, on the other hand, argues for a stronger continuity of anti-Semitism: Grelka, *Die ukrainische Nationalbewegung*, 455–58.

29 So far, it is only the history of the Bavarian 6 Chevauleger Regiment that makes one mention of the "rabble-rousing Jew." See Otto Freiherrr von Waldenfels, *Geschichte des kgl. Bayer. 6. Chevaulegers-Regiments "Kreß" im Kriege 1914–1919* (Bayreuth, 1921), 115.

30 BayHStA-KA, 2. L.D., Bd. 20. Generalkommando VI. A.K., Abt. Ib, Nr. 850, Besondere Anordnungen Nr. 3, 16.3.1918; BayHStA-KA, 2. L.D., Bd. 22. 2. Bayr. Landwehr-Division, Abt. Ib, Nr. 3777, Spruch Nr. 871 an L.I.R. 2, 8.6.1918.

of Germany's eastern policy in 1918. In the case of Operation Barbarossa, even before the beginning of the campaign, the *Wehrmacht* had issued a number of orders that violated international law, especially the so-called "commissar order."[31] This decision to engage in warfare without limits had been made even before the war began and not, as was the case in 1918, only during the operation itself.[32] Nonetheless, the elimination of the Bolsheviks does represent a continuity between both wars and, in that sense, the "commissar order" of 1941 was not a novel breach.

6) There was a discontinuity, however, in the use of violence against civilian populations in combating insurgency. In 1918 the Germans did indeed use drastic measures to restore order. Armed insurgents who were captured were immediately shot; peasant homes and, in some cases, whole villages were burned down in acts of reprisal. There was no difference, in this respect, between the Germans and the Austro-Hungarians. The Germans were actually in the forefront in taking moderate measures, a policy that their Austro-Hungarian ally, after some initial hesitation, began to follow. Civilian populations were to be protected, and hostage-taking was forbidden. In 1918, the Germans also ascribed great value to the correct use of the court martial in dealing with criminal actions. The present study thus raises strong doubts concerning the thesis of the continuity of an alleged "German way of war."[33] One of the central orders from the commander of the *Wehrmacht* in Ukraine in 1942, General Karl

---

31 Felix Römer, *Der Kommissarbefehl. Wehrmacht und NS-Verbrechen an der Ostfront 1941/42* (Paderborn, 2008).

32 This does not rule out the fact that there were phases in Operation Barbarossa when the war remained more or less conventional, as Christian Hartmann has convincingly shown in his *Wehrmacht im Ostkrieg. Front und militärisches Hinterland* (Munich, 2009).

33 This thesis was first presented by John Horn and Alan Kramer in their book *German Atrocities 1914: A History of Denial* (New Haven and London, 2001). In more recent publications, however, Kramer distances himself explicitly from this thesis: Alan Kramer, *Dynamic of Destruction: Culture and Mass Killing in the First World War (*Oxford and New York, 2007). The thesis is now most strongly defended by Isabel V. Hull, *Absolute Destruction: Military Culture and the Practices of War in Imperial Germany* (Ithaca and London, 2005); Michael Geyer, "War and Terror: Some Timely Observations on the German Way of Waging War," in *War and Terror in Historical and Contemporary Perspective,* ed. Michael Geyer (Chicago, 2003), 47–69, accessed on 4 March 2011, http://www.aicgs.org/documents/warandterror.pdf. Geyer regards the conflict on the Eastern Front of 1914–18 as a "war of destruction": Michael Geyer, "Gewalt und Gewalterfahrung im 20. Jahrhundert – Der Erste Weltkrieg," in *Der Tod als Maschinist. Der industrialisierte Krieg 1914–1918,* ed. Rolf Spilker and Bernd Ulrich (Bramsche, 1998), 240–57. For a critical view, see Bergien, "Vorspiel des 'Vernichtungskrieges'?"

Kitzinger, on combating partisans is exemplary for the contrast with 1918. The "fundamental principle" was that "if there is any doubt about the choice of appropriate measures, the more severe one is the right one."[34] The notorious "military jurisdiction order" (*Kriegsgerichtsbarkeitserlass*) had de facto eliminated military justice as protection for the civilian population even before the military campaign began.[35]

7) One clear difference from the occupation strategy of the Second World War was that in 1918 the Central Powers never went so far as to put the nourishment of the Ukrainian population in hazard or deliberately to use hunger as a strategy for discipline or annihilation.[36] Quite the contrary. The "Ukrainian Food Council," in which both Ukrainians and the occupying powers were represented, invariably directed the distribution of food to those Ukrainian cities needing provisions. The guidelines for agrarian policy in the Second World War published by Erich Koch, the Reich's Commissioner for Ukraine in 1941–44, were the exact opposite of that practice: "Ukraine has to deliver what Germany needs. This task has to be carried out without considering the loss of life.... With regard to this task, the nutritional needs of the civilian population are completely irrelevant."[37]

---

34 IfZ-Archiv, MA-487, Wehrmachtbefehlshaber Ukraine, Abt. Ia, Nr. 4921 (3073)/42 geh., Richtlinien für die Befriedung der Ukraine, 28 June 1942.

35 See Hartmann, *Wehrmacht im Ostkrieg*, 702–6; Felix Römer, "'Im alten Deutschland wäre solcher Befehl nicht möglich gewesen.' Rezeption, Adaption und Umsetzung des Kriegsgerichtsbarkeitserlasses im Ostheer 1941/42," *Vierteljahrshefte für Zeitgeschichte* 56 (2008): 53–99.

36 The "hunger plan thesis" defended by Christian Gerlach and Alex J. Kay has not remained unchallenged, as none of the key documents that support it have been found at all levels of the hierarchy. See Christian Gerlach, *Kalkulierte Morde. Die deutsche Wirtschafts- und Vernichtungspolitik in Weißrußland 1941 bis 1944* (Hamburg, 1999); Alex J. Kay, *Exploitation, Resettlement, Mass Murder and Economic Planning for German Occupation Policy in the Soviet Union 1940–1941* (New York and Oxford, 2006). For general arguments against the thesis, see Klaus Jochen Arnold and Gert C. Lübbers, "The Meeting of the Staatssekretäre on 2 May 1941 and the Wehrmacht: A Document up for Discussion," *Journal of Contemporary History* 42 (2007): 613–26. On the treatment of Soviet prisoners of war, see Christian Hartmann, "Massensterben oder Massenvernichtung? Sowjetische Kriegsgefangene im Unternehmen 'Barbarossa,'" *Vierteljahrshefte für Zeitgeschichte* 49 (2001): 97–158; Reinhard Otto, Rolf Keller, and Jens Nagel, "Sowjetische Kriegsgefangene in deutschem Gewahrsam 1941–1945," *Vierteljahrshefte für Zeitgeschichte* 56 (2008): 557–602. Johannes Hürter's concept of "hunger calculation," on the other hand, has been widely accepted: Johannes Hürter, "Die Wehrmacht vor Leningrad 1941/42," *Vierteljahrshefte für Zeitgeschichte* 49 (2001): 377–440. See also Rolf-Dieter Müller's similar but very early contribution in *Das Deutsche Reich und der Zweite Weltkrieg*, ed. Militärgeschichtliches Forschungsamt, vol. 4 (Stuttgart, 1983).

37 Quoted in Götz Aly, *Hitlers Volksstaat* (Frankfurt am Main, 2005), 200.

8) With reference to the Austro-Hungarian military, the thesis has been discussed in recent years that its conservatism before and during the First World War caused it to fear any rise of nationalism both in its own ranks and in the occupied territories, such as Serbia ("the nation in arms").[38] This basic attitude, rooted in the traditions of the nineteenth century and upheld in the spirit of the supranational army, would not only protect the state and the monarchy but would make them equidistant with regard to the civilian population. This prevented the Austro-Hungarian army from using hunger as a weapon or using excessive violence against the civilian population in Ukraine in 1918. The army attempted to position itself as a guarantor for the protection of the civilian population against the entanglements of radicalized or nationalist (liberal) politicians; in the Ukrainian case, revolutionary and/or Bolshevik politicians. It was precisely this anti-modernist attitude of the military that most differentiated it from the occupation about a quarter of a century later. The officers of the First World War had their origins in the peaceful world of the European *fin de siècle,* while the *Wehrmacht* officers of the Second World War had been socialized in an environment of violence and political extremes. The First World War and the postwar turmoil were formative experiences for the generals. It was followed by the interwar period with the Paris peace settlements, the world economic crisis, and the radicalized domestic political discourses.[39]

This was the world in which the young *Wehrmacht* officers grew up. The blurring of the boundaries of violence between the military and civilians first became clearly apparent in the First World War, but its scope was relatively limited.[40] The experience of revolution, economic crisis, Bolshevism and fascism, whether at home or in Eastern Europe, whether supported or opposed, and the accompanying dissolution of social ties meant that the officers of Nazi Germany in the Second World War no longer so clearly

38 Gumz has elaborated this with reference to the example of the Serbian general governorate: Jonathan E. Gumz, *The Resurrection and Collapse of Empire in Habsburg Serbia, 1914–1918* (New York, 2009), 235–48.

39 Cf. Johannes Hürter, "Kriegserfahrung als Schlüsselerlebnis? Der Erste Weltkrieg in der Biographie von Wehrmachtsgeneralen," in *Erster Weltkrieg – Zweiter Weltkrieg,* 759–71; Johannes Hürter, *Hitlers Heerführer. Die deutschen Oberbefehlshaber im Krieg gegen die Sowjetunion 1941/42* (Munich, 2007).

40 Kramer, *Dynamic of Destruction.*

respected those boundaries as their fathers and grandfathers had done in the First World War. The most radical officers of the First World War later formed the core of the Nazi movement. They drew their own conclusions from the allegedly lenient attitude toward the occupied nations of the East. In the second occupation, the whip and the knout (a racist "land consolidation") would play the dominant role and thus lead to victory.

9) In both cases, Ukraine was seen as a central source of economic supplies. In both wars, Ukraine would compensate for losses at home caused by lost or reduced transport routes and suppliers.[41] In both cases, Ukraine was the door to Central Asia and therefore had special strategic significance. The difference, however, between 1918 and 1941–44 was that in the First World War, in spite of the world-power fantasies of army leaders and German annexationists, there was no definitive planning.[42] In the Second World War, however, the National Socialists had clear plans: Ukraine had a key part to play in Hitler's eastern policy.[43]

10) Finally and perhaps most importantly, the political circumstances in both cases were different. In 1918, the Central Powers marched into Ukraine as official protectors, even though both the German Empire and Austria-Hungary soon became de facto occupying powers. Nevertheless, the Ukrainian government, whether the Rada or the Hetman, was a political entity that had to be taken into account in the concrete structuring of the occupation. It had a certain foundation in international law that neither the Germans nor the Austro-Hungarians nor the Ukrainians questioned throughout the occupation, although, toward the

---

41 For general economic comparisons, see Rolf-Dieter Müller, "Totaler Krieg und Wirtschaftsordnung: Ausnahmezustand oder Chance eines grundlegenden Wandels? Deutsche Experimente in zwei Weltkriegen," in *Erster Weltkrieg – Zweiter Weltkrieg,* 43–55.

42 Michael Epkenhans has quite rightly pointed out that, in 1918, the top military leaders attempted, "by establishing a functional link between the negative developments in the West and the great new successes in the East, to ward off the consequences of the approaching catastrophe and thereby evade the 'dilemma of truth'— military defeat and the destruction of the traditional domestic order." See Epkenhans, "Die Politik der militärischen Führung 1918: 'Kontinuität der Illusionen und das Dilemma der Wahrheit,'" in *Kriegsende 1918: Ereignis, Wirkung, Nachwirkung,* ed. Jörg Duppler and Gerhard P. Groβ (Munich, 1999), 222.

43 White émigrés from Russia contributed to this. See Michael Kellogg, *The Russian Roots of Nazism: White Émigrés and the Making of National Socialism 1917–1945* (New York and Cambridge, 2005).

end of the summer of 1918, Austria-Hungary was becoming increasingly critical of the Brest-Litovsk treaty. Moreover, the Central Powers recognized the existence of an allied state on the territory they occupied, albeit a state heavily dependent on them. That international law was frequently overtaxed in 1918 or simply ignored when necessary has certain parallels with occupied Western (but not Eastern) Europe in the Second World War.[44] Not least because they feared putting even more resources into the administration of this state, in 1918 the Central Powers allowed Ukraine a certain degree of sovereignty and self-organization. It was difficult, in any case, to build concrete structures of occupation in such a short period, especially as the Central Powers had not developed a concrete Ukrainian policy in the preceding months and years.

The armed invasion of 1941, on the other hand, was seen right from the beginning as a war of conquest. Although the Ukrainian national movement had a certain amount of influence on the political activity of the German occupiers in this latter case as well, it was the National Socialist world view that was the cornerstone of the whole occupation policy.[45] This is demonstrated by the fact that, from 1941 to 1944, Ukraine was not administered by the military but by the civilian Reich Commissariat (*Reichskommissariat*) for Ukraine. During the three years of National Socialist occupation, it was possible to construct an entire regime for exploitation, terror, and annihilation. The ideological, political, and moral foundation was the racist doctrine of National Socialism and its concept of conquering "living space" (*Lebensraum*). The occupied territories were not seen as objects for the application of international law or interstate relations but rather, with their populations, as objects of extreme colonial exploitation and ideological warfare. These factors make it extremely difficult to compare the occupation regimes of the First and Second World Wars, whether with regard to treatment of the civilian population, the organization of the occupation, the system of resource exploitation, or the carrying out of reprisals.

---

44 Cf. Peter Lieb, *Konventioneller Krieg oder NS-Weltanschauungskrieg? Kriegführung und Partisanenbekämpfung in Frankreich 1943/44* (Munich, 2007).

45 Wendy Lower, *Nazi Empire-Building and the Holocaust in Ukraine* (Chapel Hill, N.C., 2005).

In this context, more analysis is needed on the extent to which the experience of the occupation in 1918 served as preparation for the occupation of 1941. The continuity of personnel seems to have been slight, but this also requires more intensive research. Initial studies suggest that very few of the later generals had personal experience of Ukraine in 1918. For instance, the later army commander General Hans von Salmuth had been a staff officer in Army Group Eichhorn-Kiew in June 1918, later in the staff of *Ober Ost*.[46] The case of officers of the Bavarian Cavalry Division who later became generals is informative here, too. All four of them who had served in this division at the beginning of 1918 had been transferred out of it before the later invasion of Ukraine.[47] A prominent exception, although he had very little influence on the Reich's eastern policy, was the Austro-Hungarian officer Eduard von Böhm-Ermolli. He became a citizen of the Reich with the annexation of the Sudetenland in 1938 and, in October 1940, at the age of 84, received the honorary rank of general field marshal. He was made honorary chief of the 28th Infantry Regiment before he died in December 1941.[48] But there was someone else who did think it necessary to draw some lessons from the 1918 occupation. This was Adolf Hitler himself, who regarded the Ukrainian policy at the time of the First World War as too moderate and as a mistake that he would not repeat.[49]

46 In 1948 a US military court in Nuremberg sentenced Salmuth to twenty years in prison for crimes committed in the course of Operation Barbarossa. He was free again in 1953. See Jörg Friedrich, *Das Gesetz des Krieges. Das deutsche Heer in Rußland 1941–1945. Der Prozeß gegen das Oberkommando der Wehrmacht* (Munich and Zurich, 1993).

47 Gustav Harteneck (1892–1984) was the only one to remain in the East until June 1918 as an ordnance officer in the Kyiv command. Eberhard Rodt (1895–1979) and Rudolf Freiherr von Waldenfels (1895–1969) joined infantry regiments in the West, and Gustav Freiherr von Perfall (1883–1969) became aide-de-camp to the king of Bavaria. Although he was a regimental commander in 1932, Perfall did not make a career in the *Wehrmacht*. He was promoted to lieutenant general but remained in the unprestigious post of inspector in the Wehrersatz-Inspektion in Nuremberg until dismissed from the army in 1943. Whether his monarchist attitude had a negative influence on his career in the *Wehrmacht* is uncertain but seems likely. See the personnel documents in BayHA-KA, OP 61495 (Harteneck), OP 27835 (Rodt), OP 61659 (Waldenfels), OP 61590 (Perfall).

48 Böhm-Ermolli was given a state funeral attended by Field Marshal Wilhelm Keitel. There is no detailed biography of Böhm-Ermolli, but there is an academic thesis: Richard Zahora, "Generalfeldmarschall Freiherr Eduard von Böhm-Ermolli," phil. DA (Vienna, 2005).

49 On the occasion of a visit from Rosenberg, Hitler pointed out the murder of "the greatest friend of the Ukrainians in the last war," Field Marshal Eichhorn. See Grelka, *Die ukrainische Nationalbewegung*, 443, n. 30.

Concluding Observations

Wolfram Dornik

We have attempted, in the present volume, to offer a more detailed examination of a period of Ukrainian and East European history in a transnational context and have been able thereby to demonstrate the complexity of Ukrainian state- and nation-building between 1917 and 1922. Since we began our endeavors on this topic, two questions have stood at the center of our discussion but have not been adequately dealt with in this work; hence they will now be examined more closely. First, what were the effects of the occupation of Ukraine by the Central Powers in 1918 on the states involved? Second, why did Ukraine fail to achieve independence?

***

In general, the occupation of Ukraine by the Central Powers must be judged to have been a fiasco for all those involved. The invasion of German and Austro-Hungarian troops brought Ukraine independence for a short time, but it was unable to free itself from the grip of its new allies. Berlin and Vienna had too great an interest in the strategic situation and the economic resources of the country. Long-term plans for the postwar period were already being made in 1918, especially within the German economy.

The initial situation seemed very favorable to the Central Powers. At Brest-Litovsk they saw the opportunity to make use of the Rada, which was desperately looking for international support, and they very quickly signed a peace treaty with it. Initially, the Ukrainian people had a basically positive attitude to the invading troops, hoping with their help to put an end to the revolutionary chaos, murder, dispossession, plundering, and lawlessness. During their advance, however, and during the period of uprisings in the early summer, the occupation troops began a harsh crackdown on Bolshevik insurgents in which it was difficult to distinguish insurgents clearly from civilians. Requisitioning of food by military means also did little to increase popular sympathy for the occupying troops. Although they made a renewed attempt to win the hearts and minds of the Ukrainian people with a change of strategy in May–June, with military tribunals and greater involvement of the Ukrainian authorities in fighting insurgency and collecting provisions, as well as more considerate treatment of the civil population, there was already too much scorched earth. Moreover, the economy could not be revived in spite of the apparent political stability. The Bolsheviks were able to use this quite cleverly in 1918 to mobilize people behind their own propaganda, something they managed to do again in 1919 after regaining control. The corruption and arbitrariness that prevailed in the Austro-Hungarian zone deepened reservations about the occupying troops. But it was especially their support for the large estate owners, seen by the mass of peasants as a counterrevolutionary act, as well as the installation of the Hetmanate without broad popular support, that destroyed the trust of the Ukrainians in "foreign assistance." What certainly spelled the death sentence for the Ukrainian ambitions of the Central Powers was their failure to offer more rapid and more impressive support for the construction of a stable state. Neither the Rada nor the Hetmanate managed to base themselves on a reliable administration or on a functioning instrument of public order, whether police, militia, or military, that could have dealt with internal Ukrainian conflicts. On the contrary, every attempt on the part of Kyiv to emancipate itself was eyed with mistrust in Berlin and Vienna, fearing that any military enhancement of the state could be, at some point, a problem for their own troops. In the countryside, therefore, armed confrontations continued between the large estate owners, seeking restoration of their property, and the mostly poor peasants and rural laborers. In the cities, the liberal bourgeoisie joined with the aristocratic elite that had fled from Moscow and St. Petersburg to confront the young workers' movement. There were also ethnic conflicts. The spiral of violence was halted briefly by the Central Powers in the summer of 1918 but flared up again, with undiminished relentlessness, following their withdrawal.

In general, the question can be asked whether the Central Powers were well advised when they overthrew the Rada. Even though their political leaders were inept in state-building and were unable to eliminate the chaos, the Rada did represent the broadest possible sector of the population. The installation of Skoropadsky, on the other hand, represented a significant step backward and a very narrow political focus. Even though the Hetmanate and the German occupying power attempted an even-handed policy, the symbolism of a large estate owner brought to power by German bayonets was disastrous both internally and internationally.

Contrary to widespread opinion today, the German troops, after their first few months in Ukraine in 1918, had a cooperative approach to combating insurgency. There were also some promising beginnings in economic cooperation. But whether preference should be given to a policy of exploitation remained unclear to the very end. These beginnings, however, had no long-term success. The number of uprisings declined in the summer but resumed as soon as the occupying troops and their Hetman regime were driven out of the country in October and November. The Ukrainian people's reception of the occupation troops in 1918 is a subject that still needs to be researched. It has been overshadowed by Soviet historiography and archival policy after 1918 and by the excesses of the years 1941–44. It is clear, however, that the popularity of the Central Powers declined in the course of their presence in Ukraine.

These circumstances affected not only the construction of a stable state but also Ukraine's economic production. The present study has demonstrated that one can hardly speak of economic exploitation of Ukraine by the Central Powers in 1918. Exports from Ukraine failed to meet Berlin's and Vienna's expectations or match what had been promised in Brest-Litovsk. The delivery of provisions, which began very slowly in March–April, was no more than a drop of cold water on a hot stone for the Austro-Hungarian population, although it received the greater share of deliveries at the beginning of the occupation. Only occasionally did deliveries reach the famine-stricken cities, especially Vienna. There was no noticeable general improvement in the supply of provisions. Problems of distribution and corruption within the Habsburg Monarchy were also partly to blame. Even the summer harvest brought no improvement, and the strike in July–August actually made matters worse. It was only with the addition of cattle, eggs, vegetables, military booty, and other goods that the deliveries could even begin to approach the million tons originally agreed upon. Exports were diminished much less than had originally been assumed by the consumption of the hundreds of thousands of foreign soldiers stationed in the country. Austria-Hungary and Germany had to assist Ukraine with deliveries of coal and oil products, in addition to the agreed textiles and agricultural machinery, and Berlin had to grant extensive credits. Financially, the occupation was a disaster for both countries.

A relatively well-functioning system of procurement was established between March and May 1918, but it was unable to get off the ground because of corruption, the growing unrest in the country, peasant dissatisfaction with the agreed fixed prices, and the long-term economic orientation toward Russia. The fiscal effects of the revolution were not adequately addressed either by the Ukrainian leaders or by the occupying powers. This would have been the key to making it attractive for the peasants to deliver their grain. The supply and distribution of exchange goods demanded by both traders and the rural population was inadequate. The Central Powers' buyers were bound by the fixed prices arranged with the Ukrainian government, but there was no confidence in either the currency or the price levels offered. This economic, social, and political cocktail led to the complete fiasco of the Central Powers' Ukrainian experiment.

For the Ukrainians themselves, the occupation did not bring the hoped-for outcome. The troops of the Central Powers brought about a short pause in the class struggle and in the civil war, but this did not lead to a sustainable stabilization of either the society or the state. In those parts of the country not adequately controlled by the occupying troops, unrest and chaos continued, though at a reduced level. The pragmatic connection with the Central Powers displayed at Brest-Litovsk was also, from the viewpoint of the Entente, hardly advantageous for Ukraine's long-term status in the international state system.

Contrary to the widespread image created by interwar Soviet propaganda and historiography of "brutal exploitation" of Ukraine by Wilhelmine and Habsburg troops, the real catastrophe was caused by the collectivization of that period. This reached its peak in the famine of 1932–33, which caused the deaths of millions of people in the largely agricultural southwestern regions of the Soviet Union (*Holodomor*). The local famines and shortages of 1918 were mostly limited to the towns and were the result of the postrevolutionary collapse of trade and infrastructure. They were also exacerbated by the accompanying problems of communication between producers and consumers. The procurement system created jointly by the Central Powers and the Hetmanate, especially the Ukrainian Food Council, actually did help to compensate and made possible a more rapid reaction to supply problems in the country.

Although the occupation was hardly a phase of amicable peace, it was nonetheless relatively peaceful compared with the previous revolutionary year between February 1917 and February 1918 and with the period after November 1918. When viewed from the present, the events of 1918 appear in a somewhat milder light as compared with the brutal Ukrainization/Sovietization, collectivization, the famine of 1932–33, the Stalinist purges, Nazi Germany's military campaign of destruction against the Soviet Union, and the Soviet reconquest of Ukraine, including the extension of its territory into Eastern Galicia and northern Bukovyna. Between 1941 and 1944, the tragic high points in this history of violence on Ukrainian territory in the first half of the twentieth century included the murder of Ukrainian Jews in the Holocaust, the conscious or willingly accepted murder of the Ukrainian population by famine, the impressment of more than a million young Ukrainian men and especially young Ukrainian women into forced labor, the murder of millions of Soviet prisoners of war, among them hundreds of thousands of Ukrainians, the division of society in the battle for Ukrainian territory, the destruction on three fronts during the conquest, partisan warfare, and the withdrawal of Nazi Germany.

***

We turn now to the second question posed in this concluding assessment: why Ukraine was unable to sustain, in the long term, the independence it had achieved in 1917–18. One important factor, already mentioned in the introduction, was that Ukrainian independence was not supported by any of the central players in the international community. From December 1917–January 1918, the Central Powers saw the opportunity of weakening Russia by means of Ukrainian independence, but this attitude was not without reservations. For the German Empire, an independent Ukraine would simply be an intermediate step on the road to a federal anti-Bolshevik Russia, which would be a German ally in the East and a German area of influence. Very few believed, as Field Marshal Eichhorn did, in the future of an independent Ukraine. Austria-Hungary was skeptical to the very end because it feared the claims of its own Ukrainian minority, which opposed Polish administration and the Polish national movement in Galicia. A Ukraine under the protection of Vienna was seen as a possibility, but the Austrians were realistic enough to know that it was not very likely. Their real fear was that Kyiv would come under the influence of Russia or Germany, and this would put strategic pressure on the Danube Monarchy.

The interests of the other two states among the Central Powers could not be adequately examined in the present study. Turkey, on account of the Crimean Tatars, obviously had an interest in the strategically important peninsula in the Black Sea but lacked the power to support its claim at that time. German interests in the Crimea were too important. Moreover, Istanbul was too concerned with threats in its own core territory and with domestic unrest. Bulgaria had never shown any interest in Ukraine and simply wished to develop economic relations. Bulgaria, however, had strong territorial interests in Romania, which were a central issue in the peace negotiations in Bucharest, and these interests drew Sofia away from a more active involvement with the Ukrainian question. With the Entente offensive on the Thessaloniki front in September, Bulgaria was concerned with the defense of its own core territory.

In the short term, there is no doubt that the alliance of the Ukrainian Central Rada with the Central Powers was a liberating stroke. With the assistance of the German military's iron fist, the Rada was able to return to Kyiv. In the medium term, however, the Rada politicians had backed the wrong horse. Austria-Hungary was cautious and more interested in Odesa, while Germany soon became dissatisfied with the Rada's activity and replaced it with the Hetman. Skoropadsky tried desperately to demonstrate his independence but did not succeed. His seizure of power tied him too closely to Berlin, a relationship that was further strengthened by his visit there in September 1918. When the Central Powers finally collapsed in November, he could no longer rely on trust at home or support from the Entente. He was rapidly replaced by the Directory and had to flee with the German troops to Berlin.

Although the Entente did not have a unitary policy on Ukraine, the central states belonging to it—the USA, Great Britain, and France—all shared a certain skepticism with regard to that country. Russia, of course, completely rejected an independent Ukraine. France made the most determined attempt to pursue its interest in Ukraine, but Paris had neither the military means nor the political power to sustain it. France had been too greatly weakened by the long war on its own territory, and its population was too war-weary. Battered by the "time of troubles," the Russian Empire, now apparently rising again under the "red banner," was too chaotic. Great Britain had a central strategic interest in Ukraine since it was the gateway to Central Asia and, were Germany to achieve dominance there, it would become a threat to British colonies in southern Asia. However, London concentrated on supporting Denikin and left Ukraine to French influence. It was only when this strategy failed that Britain turned its attention to Kyiv. But Britain was already too involved with the Whites in the Great Russian fairway to be able to offer support to separatist movements. In addition, London was cautious about the

Ukrainian national movement because of its links with Vienna and Berlin during the previous months and years.

The United States had the least interest in an independent Ukraine. Throughout the revolutionary period, Wilson stuck to his idea of a united democratic Russia that, like the USA in North America, would hold almost an entire content together as a multinational state. After a short democratic phase in 1917, however, this state came increasingly under the control of Bolshevik revolutionaries in the course of 1918. Wilson's idea was endangered, and the USA made one final but unsuccessful intervention. American foreign policy had hesitated too long to support the right forces and now saw itself confronted by a hostile regime. In all these considerations, Ukraine played only a very subordinate role.

From the perspective of St. Petersburg and Moscow, the Ukrainian question was absolutely clear. Regardless of whether it was ruled by a monarchy or a communist regime, Ukraine was economically, strategically, and politically too central to be allowed independence. The generals of the White opposition shared this view. The Bolsheviks understood better how to deal with the situation in the discourse of the period. They gathered the national movements together for their own purposes under the banner of "national self-determination" and "democracy" and gave them a formal pseudo-autonomy. The national movements were even played off against one another as a way of keeping them in check. That this strategy could not work in the long term has been demonstrated by the collapse of the Soviet Union, delayed until 1991, and the continuing conflicts over independence and borders.

At the international level, Ukraine had few potential allies with little influence. One of these was Poland, which was fighting for its own independence. But these potential allies found themselves in a conflict over territory that had been growing for decades. That conflict had long been limited to the intellectual circles of the national movements. But the creation of an apparently independent Polish state under the protection of the Central Powers from 1916 and the manipulation of Ukraine (and the Baltic states) in the struggle against Bolshevik Russia from 1917–18 gave the conflict real political significance. Following the collapse of the Central Powers and the creation of a genuinely independent Polish state in November 1918, the Ukrainian-Polish conflict became a bloody battle over Eastern Galicia and the Kholm region. The states of the Caucasus, themselves struggling for independence, were not practical partners. They were very weak, involved with internal conflicts, and caught in the fronts between the Russian-oriented White restorationist movement; the interests of the great powers; Turkey, which was struggling for its own survival; and the equally Great Russian-oriented Red revolutionaries.

There was another internal Ukrainian reason why Ukraine was unable to achieve independence. During this whole period, there was no internal consensus concerning the partners with whom and the orientation with which Ukraine could realize its independence. Indeed, the very notion of Ukrainian independence was in question. The Ukrainian national idea hardly existed among the largely illiterate peasant population. They spoke Ukrainian but did not concern themselves with the orientation of the state, who should lead it or, which came to the same thing, what it meant to be "Ukrainian." The urban elite of the Ukrainian national movement was divided over an orientation on Europe or on Russia. These different orientations were irreconcilable, and there were further divisions within each group. The European group, in particular, was divided over whether to orient itself on Warsaw, Berlin, Paris, London, or Vienna. There was no consensus over a middle way that could be both European and Russian. This is still a disputed question in Ukraine, and orientations change depending on who is in power. It remains to be hoped that, after the bloody twentieth century and more than two decades of actual independence, the Ukrainians will find an answer to the question, *Quo vadis Ukraine*?

Sources

Austria

Heeresgeschichtliches Museum (Army History Museum), Vienna
Plennyarchiv, Brief Harald Halls an Joachim Givens v. 26.1.1932
Bildarchiv, Bestand: Nordostfront

ÖNB Austrian National Library (Österreichische Nationalbibliothek), Vienna
Bildarchiv, Bestand: Kriegsalben (Erster Weltkrieg)

ÖStA, Austrian State Archives (Österreichisches Staatsarchiv), Vienna
Allgemeines Verwaltungsarchiv (AVA)
Nachlass: Böhm-Ermolli, B 1466.
Nachlass: Krauß, B 60.
Nachlass: Spannocchi, B 760.
Nachlass: Böltz, B 760.
Haus-, Hof- und Staatsarchiv (HHStA)
Ministerium des Äußern, Politisches Archiv I
Kt. 500, 523, 836, 902f., 1041f., 1056, 1076, 1081, 1092a.
Liasse Krieg 56/32 b.
Liasse Krieg 3f/Rußland 1918, Kt. 836.
Liasse Krieg 58, Ukraine, Kt. 1042.
Liasse XLVII, Krieg 1914–1918, Kt. 523.
Nachlass Czernin, Kt. 1092a.
Ministerium des Äußern, Politisches Archiv I
Kt. 152–154.
Kriegsarchiv (KA)
KA, AdT, 145. IBrig, Kt. 1378f.
KA, AdT, FABrig 59, Kt. 4131.
KA, AdT, FAR 59, Kt. 832.
KA, AdT, FJB 13, Kt. 754.
KA, AdT, UR 3, Kt. 800.
KA, AdT, UR 13, Kt. 801.
KA, FA, AOK, Evidenzbüro 1918, Nachrichtenabteilung, Kt. 3669, 3670, 3673, 3674, 3675, 3671, 3672.
KA, FA, AOK, OpAbt, Kt. 465-476.
KA, FA, AOK, OpAbt, Ev. Grp.-R 1918.
KA, FA, AOK, Ukraine Akten, Kt. 2.609-2.637.
KA, FA, NFA, AOK, KPQ, Kommandobefehle, Kt. 22.
KA, FA, NFA, HHK AK/AGKdo, 2. Armee, OpAK, Kt. 308f.
KA, FA, NFA, HHK AK/AGKdo, 2. Armee, QuAbt, Kt. 692, 693, 694, 695, 696, 697, 710, 723.

KA, FA, NFA, HHK AK/AGKdo, 4. Armee, Kt. 484f.
KA, FA, NFA, HHK AK/AGKdo, 7. Armee, Kt. 289.
KA, FA, NFA, HHK AK/KorpsKdo, 12. Korps, Kt. 1661–1663.
KA, FA, NFA, Kmdo. Odessa (Gouv.), Kt. 3870.
KA, FA, NFA, Sonstiges, Ukrainische Formationen, Kt. 1952.
KA,Nachlass Raabl-Werner, B 141/4, II. Teil.

Czech Republic

National Archives of the Czech Republic, Prague
F. Ukrainisches Museum, Kt. 44.

France

AAC/AP Archives of the Central Administration/Political Affairs (Archives de l'administration centrale/Affaires politiques 1914–1944), Paris
Correspondance politique et commerciale, 1896–1918, Guerre 1914–1918, Russie, vol. 648f., 694f.
Z-Europe, URSS, Action des Alliés dans le nord de la Russie, vol. 217, 225, 226.
Z-Europe, URSS, Bessarabie, vol. 620.
E-Asie, Sibérie, vol. 7.

AAÉ Foreign Affairs Archives (Archives des Affaires étrangères), Paris

SHD/AAT Historical Defense/Armed Forces Archives (Service Historique de la Défense/Archives de l'armée de terre), Paris
Série N, 1872–1919, 4N 40, 4N 63, 7N 810, 7N 921, 8N 15–16, 16N 3021, 16N 3023, 16N 3025, 16N 3064, 16N 3066, 16N 3147, 16N 3172, 16N 3181, 16N 3188, 16N 3191, 17N 622, 20N 225, 20N 729, 20N 763.

Germany

BA-MA Federal Archives/Military Archives (Bundesarchiv-Militärarchiv), Freiburg
N 46/171f.
N 754/10.
N 776/45.
PH 1/55.
PH 5-I/3, 5, 7.
PH 6-I/89.
RH 61/810, 847, 2315.
RM 41/62.

BArch Federal Archives (Bundesarchiv), Berlin-Lichterfelde
R 3101 (Reichswirtschaftsamt)/1096f., 1136f., 1164, 1166, 1168–70, 1180, 1190, 1194, 1220, 1303f., 1314, 1316, 1318, 1341.

BayHA Bavarian Central State Archives (Bayerisches Hauptstaatsarchiv), Munich
Bayerisches Hausarchiv, Geheimes Staatsarchiv
Nachlass Leopold von Bayern.
Kriegsarchiv
1. Kav.Brig., Bd. 7, 11–13.
15. Res.Inf.Brig., Bd. 1, 7, 30.
509 Quellenverzeichnis.
2. S.R.R., Bd. 6f.
29. InfReg., Bd. 2f.
4. Chevauleger Regiment, Bd. 1, 11.
4. Kav.Brig., Bd. 4.
5. Chevauleger Regiment., Bd. 1, 4.
Etappenkommandantur 54., Bd. 22.
Kav.Div., Bd. 18–22, 28, 51.
Landsturm Regiment 1., Bd. 4.
Ministerium Krieg, 1779, 1824.
OP 61495 (Harteneck), OP 27835 (Rodt), OP 61659 (Waldenfels), OP 61590 (Perfall), OP 47604 (Samhaber).

HStA Central State Archives (Hauptstaatsarchiv), Stuttgart
KTB des Stabes Korps Knoerzer.
7. Landwehrdividion, M 46/5e, 15f., 20f.
52. Landwehrinfanteriedivision, M 62/2. 52.
Kriegstagebücher von Infanterie Formationen, M 411/394, 395.
Kriegstagebücher von Feldartillerie- und Fußartillerieformationen, M 413/1214.
Nachlass Knoerzer, M 660/131.

Institut für Zeitgeschichte-Archiv (Institute for Contemporary History Archive), Munich
MA-487, Wehrmachtbefehlshaber Ukraine.

Great Britain

TNA The National Archives, London
FO 371/3012, 3018f., 390, 3283, 3342, 3347, 3349.
FO 373/3/16.
FO 379/3332.
FO 608/177, 71/24.
FO 608/201.

FO 608/206.
FO 608/207.
FO 608/247.
FO 608/331.
FO 608/337.
GFM 6/35f., 52, 99, 107.
KV 2/661.
PRO 30/69/1800.
T 1/12128.
WO 158/752.
WO 32 5697.
WO 33 967.

Hungary

War Archives, Budapest
F. II.220, Kt. 1, Magyar királyi 155. honvéd gyaloghadosztály.

Russian Federation

AVPRI Foreign Policy Archive of the Russian Empire (Arkhiv vneshnei politiki Rossiiskoi Imperii), Moscow
F. 135, op. 474.

GARF State Archive of the Russian Federation (Gosudarstvennyi arkhiv Rossiiskoi Federatsii), Moscow
F. 130, op. 2, 3.
F. 398, op. 2.
F. 439, op. 1.
F. 1236, op. 1.
F. 1791, op. 2.
F. 2313, op. 3.
F. 2314, op. 9.
F. 3348, op. 1
F. 5972, op. 1, 3.
F. 6817, op. 1.
F. 7506, op. 1.
F. r-393, op. 3.

RGASPI Russian State Archive for Social and Political History (Rossiiskii gosudarstvennyi arkhiv sotsial'no-politicheskoi istorii), Moscow
F. 2, op. 1.
F. 5, op. 1.

F. 17, op. 1, 3, 84, 87, 109.
F. 17, op. 86, d. 112.
F. 19, op. 1.
F. 76, op. 3.
F. 325, op. 1.
F. 558, op. 11.

RGIA Russian State Historical Archive (Rossiiskii gosudarstvennyi istoricheskii arkhiv), St. Petersburg
F. 733, op. 193 (1863).

Russian National Library, Manuscript Department, Moscow
F. 600, d. 1333.

Switzerland

BAR Federal Archives (Bundesarchiv), Bern
Eidgenössisches Politisches Departement
E 2001 A, Kt. 877, 931.
E 2001 B, Abteilung für Auswärtiges 1918–20 (Nr. 1000/1501, 1502), Kt. 13, Kt. 18.
E 2200.234, Schweizerische Vertretung Kiew, Nr. 1000/375.
E 2300, Politische und militärische Berichte der Auslandsvertretungen 1848–1965 (Nr. 1000/716),
Kt. 282,
Eidgenössisches Volkswirtschaftsdepartement
E 7800, Generalsekretariat 1907–1955 (Nr. 1000/1961), Kt. 185.

Ukraine

TsDAVO Central State Archive of Supreme Bodies of Power and Government of Ukraine (Tsentral'nyi derzhavnyi arkhiv vyshchykh orhaniv vlady ta upravlinnia Ukraïny), Kyiv
F. 2, op. 1.
F. 2311, op. 1.
F. 1118, op. 1.

TsDIA Central State Historical Archive (Tsentral'nyi derzhavnyi istorychnyi arkhiv), Lviv
F. 146, op. 7, spr. 4529.
F. 309, op. 2, spr. 109.
F. 358, op. 3, spr. 166, 1198.
F. 746, op. 1, spr. 6, 5.

United States

Harvard Libraries, Cambridge, Massachusetts
Government Documents, Records of the DoS relating to Internal Affairs of the Ukraine (NARA microfilm publications), Film S 1040/M 1286, 2 Rolls, Nr. 860e.00, Political Affairs, Nr. 4, Letter of the US Mission in Berne, 21.11.1918.

NARA National Archives and Records Administration, College Park, MD
US DoS, Records relating to Internal Affairs Russia and Soviet Union 1910–1929, War Series 6, RG 59, Russia, IV
US DoS, Records of the American Commission to Negotiate Peace, RG 256
M 820, Roll 198, 486, 488.
M 1107, Roll 13, 35, 46.
Commission for Negotiation of an Armistice between Poland and the Ukraine, RG 256,
M 820/Roll 169.

Newspapers from various archives

Basler Nachrichten, 27. March 1918
Buduchnist', 15.12.1899
Christlich-soziale Arbeiter-Zeitung, no. 8, 23.2.1918
Dilo, 6.1.1923, 14.5.1918, 1.11.1928, 8.8.1924, 8.5.1931, 1.11.1938, 3.11.1938, 4.11.1938, 5.11.1938
Golos Moskvy, no. 277, 2.12.1911
Kievlianin, no. 116 (27.4.1908), no. 134 (15.5.1908), no. 320 (16.11.1908), no. 38 (7.2.1909), no. 60 (1.3.1914)
Nasha platforma, no. 1, Vienna, 5.10.1914
Nova Rada, 25. 3.1917, 2.3.1917
Pravda, nos. 62–63, 3.–4.4.1918
Republyka, 1.4.1919
Russkaia mysl', 1912, no. 1; 1914, no. 12
Ukraïns'ke slovo, 20.1.1917, 15.2.1918, 20.2.1918
Washington Post, 18.2.1918

Internet sources

Armistice convention with Austria-Hungary. Protocol of Conditions of the Armistice between the Allied and Associated Powers and Austria-Hungary (Signed at Villa Giusti, November 3, 1918), http://www.forost.ungarisches-institut.de/pdf/19181103-1.pdf 4.3.2011.

Historisches Lexikon der Schweiz (HLS), http://www.hls-dhs-dss.ch/ 4.3.2011.

List of diplomatic missions of Austria-Hungary http://www.enotes.com/topic/List_of_diplomatic_missions_of_Austria-Hungary#cite_note-9 4.3.2011.

Memoirs of Alexander Isvolsky. Garden City, NY, and Toronto 1921, V–XV: http://www.archive.org/stream/recollectionsofa008591mbp 4.3.2011.

President Woodrow Wilson's 14 Points (1918), http://www.ourdocuments.gov/doc.php?flash=true&doc=62 4.3.2011.

The Supreme War Council, http://www.firstworldwar.com/atoz/versaillescouncil.htm 4.3.2011.

US DoS, Papers Relating to the Foreign Relations of the United States, 1918. Russia. vol. 2. Washington, DC 1918, http://digicoll.library.wisc.edu/cgi-bin/FRUS/FRUS-idx?id=FRUS.FRUS1918Russiav02 4.3.2011, 649–651.

US DoS, Papers Relating to the Foreign Relations of the United States, 1918. Supplement 1.

Waffenstillstandsbedingungen der Alliierten, Compiègne, 11. November 1918, http://www.dhm.de/lemo/html/dokumente/waffenstillstand/index.htm l 4.3.2011.

The World War (1918), http://digicoll.library.wisc.edu/cgi-bin/FRUS/FRUS-idx?id=FRUS.FRUS1918Supp01v0 1 4.3.2011, 465f., 496.

Published sources

Bonch-Bruevich, V. D. *Na boevykh postakh fevral'skoi i oktiabr'skoi revoliutsii* (Moscow, 1930).

Busemann, Melchior, ed. *Der Friedensvertrag mit Rußland vom 3. März 1918, das deutsch-russische Wirtschaftsabkommen nebst dem Vertragszolltarif und der deutsch-russische Zusatzvertrag* (Berlin, 1918).

Cherikover, I. E. *Antisemitizm i pogromy na Ukraine 1917–1918 gg.* (Berlin, 1923).

Czernin, Ottokar. *Im Weltkriege* (Berlin and Vienna, 1919).

Davies, Norman. *White Eagle, Red Star: The Polish-Soviet War 1919–1920 and the "Miracle on the Vistula"* (London, 2003).

Denikin, A. I. *Ocherki russkoi smuty*, vol. 4 (Paris, 1925).

Die deutsche Okkupation der Ukraine. Geheimdokumente (Strasbourg, 1937).

Dokumenty o razgrome germanskikh okkupantov na Ukraine v 1918 godu (Moscow, 1942).

Doroshenko, Dmytro. *Moï spomyny pro nedavnie-mynule* (Lviv, 1923).

Dragoni, Alfred von. "Die Kämpfe um Nikolajew und Cherson im Frühjahr 1918," Österreichische Wehrzeitung, 1928, no. 18: 2–3.

Frauenholz, Eugen. *Das K.B. 2. Kürassier- und Schwere Reiter-Regiment* (Munich, 1921).

Fritsche, Max. *Das königlich sächsische Landwehr-Infanterie-Regiment Nr. 106* (Dresden, 1925).

Fromm, Oberst. *Das Württembergische Landwehr-Infanterie-Regiment Nr. 126 im Weltkrieg 1914–1918* (Stuttgart, 1921).

Gebsattel, Ludwig Freiherr von. *Das K.B. 1. Ulanen-Regiment "Kaiser Wilhelm II. König von Preußen." Nach Kriegsakten, Kriegstagebüchern und Mitteilungen ehemaliger Angehöriger des Regiments* (Augsburg, 1924).

Geschichte des Bürgerkriegs in der UdSSR, vol. 1, *Die Vorbereitung der Oktoberrevolution* (Offenbach, 1999).

Gorki, Maxim. "Vom russischen Bauern," in Alexander W. Tschajanow, *Reise ins Land der bäuerlichen Utopie* (Frankfurt am Main, 1984), 89–110.

Gosudarstvennaia Duma, Tretii sozyv. Stenograficheskie otchety. 1909. Chast' 3 (St. Petersburg, 1910).

Gosudarstvennaia Duma, Tretii sozyv. Stenograficheskiie otchety. Sessiia chetvertaia. Chast' 1 (St. Petersburg, 1910).

Gosudarstvennaia Duma, IV sozyv. Sessiia II. Stenograficheskiie otchety. Chast' II. Zasedanie 40. 19 February 1914 (St. Petersburg, 1914).

Grazhdanskaia voina na Ukraine 1918–1920. Sbornik dokumentov i materialov v trekh tomakh, chetyrekh knigakh, vol. 1, bk. 1 (Kyiv, 1967).

Groener, Wilhelm. *Lebenserinnerungen. Jugend, Generalstab, Weltkrieg* (Osnabrück, 1972).

__________. *Der Weltkrieg und seine Probleme. Rückschau und Ausblick* (Berlin, 1920).

Hof- und Staats-Handbuch der österreichisch-ungarischen Monarchie für das Jahr 1918, vol. 44 (Vienna, 1918).

Hruschewsky, Michael. *Die ukrainische Frage in historischer Entwicklung* (Vienna, 1915).

Janin, Pierre Maurice. *Ma mission en Sibérie* (Paris, 1933).

John, Volkwart. *Brest-Litowsk. Verhandlungen und Friedensverträge im Osten 1917 bis 1918* (Stuttgart, 1937).

Das K.B. Reserve-Jäger-Bataillon Nr. 1, ed. Hans Muggenthaler, Hugo Ritter von Pflügel, and Martin Scheuring (Munich, 1935).

Katkov, M. N. *Sobranie peredovykh statei "Moskovskikh vedomostei" 1865 goda* (Moscow, 1897).

Kerchnawe, Hugo et al. *Die Militärverwaltung in den von den österreichisch-ungarischen Truppen besetzten Gebieten* (Vienna, 1928).

Khrystiuk, Pavlo. *Zamitky i materiialy do istoriï ukraïns'koï revoliutsiï 1917–1920 rr.*, vol. 2 (Vienna, 1921).

__________. *Zamitky i materiialy do istoriï ukraïns'koï revoliutsiï 1917–1920 rr.*, vol 3 (New York, 1969).

Konstytutsiini akty Ukraïny, 1917–1920. Nevidomi konstitutsiï Ukraïny (Kyiv, 1992).

Krauß, Alfred. *Die Ursachen unserer Niederlage. Erinnerungen und Urteile aus dem Weltkrieg* (Vienna, 1923).

Larin, Iurii. *Evrei i antisemitizm v SSSR* (Moscow and Leningrad, 1929).

Levyts'kyi, Ievhen. *Lysty z Nimechchyny* (Vienna, 1916).

__________. (Lewicky, Eugen). *Die Ukraine der Lebensnerv Rußlands* (Stuttgart and Berlin, 1915).

Levyts'kyi, Kost'. *Istoriia politychnoï dumky halyts'kykh ukraïntsiv. Na pidstavi spomyniv i dokumentiv* (Lviv, 1926).

Lockhart, R. H. Bruce. *Memoirs of a British Agent: Being an Account of the Author's Early Life in Many Lands and of His Official Mission to Moscow in 1918* (London and New York, 1932).

Lozyns'kyi, Mykhailo. *Halychyna v rr. 1918–1920* (Prague, 1922; repr. New York, 1970).

__________. *Ukraïns'ka revoliutsiia. Halychyna v rr. 1918–1920* (Vienna, 1922).

Ludendorff, Erich. *Meine Kriegserinnerungen 1914–1918* (Berlin, 1919).

Maleev, A. F. *Tridtsat' dnei evreiskogo pogroma v mestechke Krivoe Ozero* (Moscow, 1921).

Margolin, A. D. *From a Political Diary: The Ukraine and America, 1905–1945* (New York, 1946).

__________. *Ukraina i politika Antanty* (Berlin, 1921).

Margulies, M. S. *God interventsii*, vol. 1 (Berlin, 1923).

Miliukov, P. N. *Istoriia vtoroi russkoi revoliutsii* (Moscow, 2001).

__________. *Natsional'nyi vopros. Proiskhozhdenie natsional'nosti i natsional'nye voprosy v Rossii* (Prague, 1925).

Moulis, E., and E. Bergonier. *La Guerre entre les Alliés et la Russie (1918–1920)* (Paris, 1937).

Müller-Meinigen, Ernst. *Diplomatie und Weltkrieg. Ein Führer durch die Entstehung und Ausbreitung der Weltkrisis auf Grund der amtlichen Materialien*, vol. 2 (Berlin, 1917).

Naumann, Friedrich. *Mitteleuropa* (Berlin, 1915).

Niedermayer, Oskar Ritter von. *Meine Rückkehr aus Afghanistan* (Munich, 1918).

Noulens, Joseph. *Mon ambassade en Russie soviétique, 1917–1919*, 2 vols. (Paris, 1933).

Nowak, Karl Friedrich, ed. *Die Aufzeichnungen des Generalmajors Max Hoffmann*, vol. 1 (Berlin, 1929).

Omelianovych-Pavlenko, Mykhailo. *Spomyny* (Lviv, 1930).

Österreichisches Bundesministerium für Landesverteidigung – Kriegsarchiv, ed. Österreich-Ungarns letzter Krieg 1914–1918, vol. 1, *Das Kriegsjahr 1914* (Vienna, 1931).

Österreichisches Bundesministerium für Landesverteidigung – Kriegsarchiv, ed. Österreich-Ungarns letzter Krieg 1914–1918, vol. 7, *Das Kriegsjahr 1918* (Vienna, 1938).

Reichsarchiv, ed. *Der Weltkrieg, 1914–1918. Die Kriegführung im Sommer und Herbst 1918. Die Ereignisse außerhalb der Westfront bis November 1918*, vol. 13, *Die Kriegführung im Sommer und Herbst 1918 – Die Ereignisse außerhalb der Westfront bis November 1918* (Berlin, 1942).

Rohrbach, Paul. *Um des Teufels Handschrift. Zwei Menschenalter erlebter Weltgeschichte* (Hamburg, 1953).

__________. *Weltpolitisches Wanderbuch 1897–1915* (Königsstein im Taunus, 1916).

Romstedt, Max. *Das Kgl. Sächs. Landwehr-Infanterie-Regiment Nr. 133* (Dresden, 1924).

Seeger, Charles Louis. *Recollections of a Foreign Minister: Memoirs of Alexander Isvolsky* (Garden City and Toronto, 1921).

Shapoval, Mykyta. *Velyka revoliutsiia i ukraïns'ka vyzvol'na prohrama* (Prague, 1928).

Shekhtman, I. B. *Pogromy dobrovol'cheskoi armii na Ukraine* (Berlin, 1932).

Shreiber, S. K. "K protokolam pervogo vseukrainskogo soveshchaniia bol'shevikov," *Letopis' revoliutsii*, 1926, no. 5.

Sisson, Edgar G. *One Hundred Red Days: A Personal Chronicle of the Bolshevik Revolution. 25 November 1917–4 March 1918* (New Haven, 1931).

Skoropads'kyi, Pavlo. *Spohady. Kinets' 1917–hruden' 1918* (Kyiv and Philadelphia, 1995).

Sobotka, Felix. "Der Anteil Österreich-Ungarns an der Militärverwaltung in Rumänien 1917–1918," in *Die Militärverwaltung in den von den österreichisch-ungarischen Truppen besetzten Gebieten*, ed. Hugo Kerchnawe et al. (Vienna, 1928), 305–17.

Sokolov, K. N. *Pravlenie generala Denikina* (Sofia, 1921).

Sorokin, Pitirim. *Leaves from a Russian Diary* (New York, 1924).

Stalin, J. W. *Works*, vol. 4 (Moscow, 1953).

Trotsky, Leon (Leo Trotzki). *Die Geburt der Roten Armee* (Vienna, 1924).

__________. *History of the Russian Revolution*, 3 vols. (London, 1967).

__________. *My Life* (New York, 1960).

Ukraïns'ka RSR v period hromadians'koï viiny 1917–1920 rr., vol. 1 (Kyiv, 1967).

Velsen, Stefan von. "Ukraine. Die Ukraine und Wir. Ein Rückblick auf die deutsche Okkupation," *Preußische Jahrbücher*, no. 176 (1919): 260–66.

Vynnychenko, Volodymyr. *Vidrodzhennia natsiï*, 3 vols. (Kyiv and Vienna, 1920).

Waldenfels, Otto Freiherr von. *Geschichte des kgl. Bayer. 6. Chevaulegers-Regiments "Kreß" im Kriege 1914–1919* (Bayreuth, 1921).

Wilson, Woodrow. *President Wilson's Foreign Policy: Messages, Addresses, and Papers* (New York, 1918).

Wrangel, P. N. *The Memoirs of General Wrangel* (London, 1929).

Zatons'kyi, V. Z. "Iz spohadiv pro ukraïns'ku revoliutsiiu," *Litopys revoliutsiï*, 1929, nos. 5–6.

Zoloti vorota. Istoriia Sichovykh Stril'tsiv 1917–1919 (Lviv, 1937).

Zuckermann, S., ed. *Handelsstatistische Blätter*, 1918, no. 4.

Abbreviations

(French and German abbreviations in this list appear in archival and bibliographic references and are not translated into English)

AA Auswärtiges Amt
AAC/AP Archives de l'administration centrale/Affaires politiques, Paris
AAÉ Archives des Affaires étrangères, Paris
Abt(lg.). Abteilung
AdT Archiv der Truppenkörper
AGKdo Armee-Gruppen-Kommando
AK Armeekommando (österr.-ung.), Armeekorps (deut.)
Anm. Anmerkung
(k.u.k.) AOK (k.u.k.) Armeeoberkommando; bei den deutschen Truppen wird unter AOK ein den k.u.k. AK entsprechendes Kommando verstanden
AVPRI Arkhiv vneshnei politiki Rossiiskoi Imperii (Foreign Policy Archive of the Russian Empire), Moscow
BA-MA Bundesarchiv-Militärarchiv, Freiburg
BAR Bern Bundesarchiv, Bern
BArch Bundesarchiv, Berlin-Lichterfelde
Bay. Bayerisch
BayHA, Geh. StA Bayerisches Hausarchiv, Geheimes Staatsarchiv, Munich
BayHStA Bayerisches Hauptstaatsarchiv, Munich
Bd(e). Band/Bände oder Bund
betr./Betr. betreffend/Betreff
BIK Ludwig Boltzmann-Institut für Kriegsfolgen-Forschung
bzgl. bezüglich
bzw. beziehungsweise
Chev. Chevauleger
CP(B)U Communist Party (Bolshevik) of Ukraine
CPC Correspondance politique et commerciale
d. delo (dossier, file)
Div. Division
d.M. des Monats
Dok. Dokument
d.R. der Reserve
Ebd. Ebendort
ed. editor
EPD Eidgenössisches Politisches Departement
ErsBaon Ersatzbataillon
Et.K'drn Etappenkommandanturen
EVD Eidgenössisches Volkswirtschaftsdepartement
f. folgende
F. Fond (archival collection, fond)
FA Feldakten

FABrig Feldartilleriebrigade
Fas. Faszikel
FJB Feldjägerbataillon
Fn. Fußnote
FWF Fonds für Wissenschaft und Forschung
GARF Gosudarstvennyi arkhiv Rossiiskoi Federatsii (State Archive of the Russian Federation), Moscow
GenKmdo Generalkommando
GG Generalgouvernement
Gouv. Gouvernement
Habil. Habilitation
Hg. Herausgeber
HGM Heeresgeschichtliches Museum, Vienna
HHK Höhere Heereskommanden
HLS Historisches Lexikon der Schweiz
HStA Stuttgart Hauptstaatsarchiv, Stuttgart
IBrig Infanteriebrigade
ID Infanterie(truppen)division
IfZ Institut für Zeitgeschichte, Munich
Inf. Infanterie
inkl. inklusive
i.R. in Ruhe/im Ruhestand
Jg. Jahrgang
k. kaiserlich
Kav. Kavallerie
KD Kavallerie(truppen)division
Kdo Kommando
Kdt(en) Kommandant(en)
k.k. kaiserlich-königlich
KKRN Kievskii klub russkikh natsionalistov (Kyivan Club of Russian Nationalists)
Komsomol Communist Youth League
KorpsKdo Korps-Kommando
KPQ(u) Kriegspressequartier
Kt. Karton
KTB Kriegstagebuch
k.u. königlich-ungarisch
k.u.k. kaiserlich und königlich
(k.u.k.) MdÄ k.u.k. Ministerium des Äußern
Leg.Sekr Legations Sekretär
L.F.A.R. Landwehr Feldartillerieregiment
L.I.R. Landwehr Infanterieregiment
MG Maschinengewehr
MGG Militärgeneralgouvernement
milit. Militärisch
MilKmdo Militärkommando
muselman. Batls. muselmanisches Bataillon

NARA National Archives and Records Administration, College Park, MD, USA
NEP New Economic Policy
NFA Neue Feldakten
no. Numero
N.O.d.O.H.L. Nachrichtenoffizier der Obersten Heeresleitung
Nr. Nummer
Oblt. Oberleutnant
Obost/ObOst/Ob Ost Oberbefehlshaber Ost
OHL Oberste Heeresleitung
ÖNB Österreichische Nationalbibliothek
op. opis'/opys (archival inventory)
OpAbt Operations-Abteilung
ÖStA, AVA Österreichisches Staatsarchiv, Allgemeines Verwaltungsarchiv, Vienna
ÖStA, HHStA Österreichisches Staatsarchiv, Haus-, Hof- und Staatsarchiv, Vienna
ÖStA, KA Österreichisches Staatsarchiv, Kriegsarchiv, Vienna
östr.-ung. österreichisch-ungarisch
QuAbt Quartiermeisterabteilung
r./rr. rik/rokiv/roky year(s)
RCP(B) Russian Communist Party (Bolshevik)
Red. Redaktion
Res. Reserve
RG Record group
RGASPI Rossiiskii gosudarstvennyi arkhiv sotsial'no-politicheskoi istorii (Russian State Archive for Social and Political History), Moscow
RGIA Rossiiskii gosudarstvennyi istoricheskii arkhiv (Russian State Historical Archive), St. Petersburg
RKP(b) Rossiiskaia Kommunisticheskaia Partiia (bol'shevikov) Russian Communist Party (Bolshevik)
RSFSR Russian Soviet Federative Socialist Republic
S. Seite
SchR Schützenregiment
SFIO Section Française de l'Internationale Ouvrière
SHD/AAT Service Historique de la Défense/Archives de l'armée de terre, Paris
s.l. sine loco (no place of publication)
sovkhoz (state farm)
Sovnarkom Sovet Narodnykh Komissarov (Council of People's Commissars)
spr. sprava (dossier, file)
S.R.R. Schweres Reiter Regiment
SSSR Soiuz Sovetskikh Sotsialisticheskikh Respublik (Union of Soviet Socialist Republics)
Tgb. Tagebuch
TNA, FO The National Archives, Foreign Office, London
TNA, GFM The National Archives, German Foreign Ministry, London
TsDAVO Tsentral'nyi derzhavnyi arkhiv vyshchykh orhaniv vlady ta upravlinnia Ukraïny (Central State Archive of Supreme Bodies of Power and Government of Ukraine), Kyiv

TsDIA Tsentral'nyi derzhavnyi istorychnyi arkhiv (Central State Historical Archive), Lviv
TsK Tsentral'nyi Komitet (Central Committee)
TUP Tovarystvo ukraïns'kykh postupovtsiv (Society of Ukrainian Progressives)
u.a. und andere
Übers. Übersetzung
UdSSR Union der Sozialistischen Sowjetrepubliken (Union of Soviet Socialist Republics)
Ukrainian SSR Ukrainian Socialist Soviet Republic (Ukrainian Soviet Socialist Republic, 1937–91)
UNDP Ukrainian National Democratic Party
UNR Ukraïns'ka Narodna Respublika (Ukrainian People's Republic)
UPR Ukrainian Parliamentary Representation
UR Ulanen-Regiment
URSS L'Union des républiques socialistes soviétiques (Union of Soviet Socialist Republics)
(US) DoS (United States) Department of State
USPD Unabhängige Sozialdemokratische Partei Deutschlands
USSR Union of Soviet Socialist Republics
v./vv. vek/veka/veki century (centuries)
VChK Vserossiiskaia chrezvychainaia komissiia po bor'be s kontrrevoliutsiei, spekuliatsiei i sabotazhem (All-Russian Extraordinary Commission to Combat Counterrevolution, Speculation and Sabotage; Cheka)
Vgl. Vergleiche
VKP(b) Vsesoiuznaia Kommunisticheskaia Partiia (bol'shevikov) All-Union Communist Party (Bolshevik)
vol. volume
vyp. vypusk (issue)
WVB Waren-Verkehrs-Büro
z.B. zum Beispiel
ZUNR Zakhidno-Ukraïns'ka Narodna Respublika (Western Ukrainian People's Republic)
ZUR Zahal'na Ukraïns'ka Rada (General Ukrainian Council)

Ia Erster Generalstabsoffizier (Taktik und Operation)
Ib Zweiter Generalstabsoffizier (Versorgung)
Ic Dritter Generalstabsoffizier (Feindlagebild)
IIa Erster Adjutant (Offiziers-Personalangelegenheiten)
IIb Zweiter Adjutant (Unteroffiziers- und Mannschaftsangelegenheiten)
III Abteilung Gericht

Authors

Wolfram Dornik, Ph.D., born 1978 in Feldbach, Austria. Member, Ludwig Boltzmann Institute for Research on the Consequences of War (*Ludwig Boltzmann-Institut für Kriegsfolgen-Forschung*) in Graz since 2004. Research interests: First World War (occupation in Eastern Europe, Eastern Front, international relations); culture of memory in the Internet; Austrian history, 1914–55. wolfram.dornik@bik.ac.at

Georgiy Kasianov, Ph.D., born 1961 in Cheliabinsk, Russia. Head of the Department of Contemporary History and Politics at the Institute of Ukrainian History, National Academy of Sciences of Ukraine, since 2003. Research interests: Ukrainian history, nineteenth century to the present; history of ideas; post-communist politics of history. kasianov@irf.kiev.ua

Hannes Leidinger, Ph.D., born 1969 in Gmunden, Austria. Lecturer, Institute of History and Institute of Contemporary History, University of Vienna. Visiting professor, University of Vienna. Research interests: Austrian and Russian/Soviet history; film sources for Austrian history; Habsburg Monarchy; First World War; theories of history; historical sociology; research on capitalism, socialism, communism, and prisoners of war; military and espionage history. hannes.leidinger@univie.ac.at

Peter Lieb, Ph.D., born 1974 in Garmisch-Partenkirchen, Germany. Senior Lecturer, Department of War Studies at the Royal Military Academy, Sandhurst, UK, since 2005. Previously member of the Institute of Contemporary History (*Institut für Zeitgeschichte*) in Munich. Research interests: German army in the First and Second World Wars; war and violence; insurgency und counterinsurgency in the twentieth century; theories of war. peter_lieb@hotmail.com

Alexei Miller, Ph.D., born 1959 in Moscow. Senior Research Fellow, Institute of Scientific Information in the Social Sciences, Russian Academy of Sciences, Moscow. Professor, Central European University (Budapest), and Russian State University for the Humanities (Moscow). Currently Leverhulme Trust Professor at Manchester University. Research interests: empires and nationalism in Eastern and Central Europe; European political history. millera@ceu.hu

Bogdan Musial, Ph.D., born 1960 in Wielopole, Poland. Professor, Cardinal Stefan Wyszyński University in Warsaw. Research interests: twentieth-century history of Eastern and Central Europe, with emphasis on the Soviet Union, Poland, Belarus, and Germany, persecution of Jews, and Soviet partisan movements. b.musial@uksw.edu.pl

Vasyl Rasevych, Ph. D., born 1966 in Zadovzhe, Ukraine. Senior Research Fellow, Ivan Krypiakevych Institute of Ukrainian Studies, National Academy of Sciences of Ukraine, Lviv, since 2002. Research interests: Ukrainian history (Galicia, 1890–1921); Ukrainian memorial sites; politics of history. rasevych@gmail.com.

Index